Webster's New World™

Student Writing Handbook

Sharon Sorenson

Prentice Hall
Englewood Cliffs, New Jersey

Second Edition

ISBN 0-13-804857-6

1 2 3 4 5 6 7 8 9 10 97 96 95 94

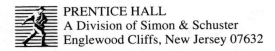

PRENTICE HALL
A Division of Simon & Schuster
Englewood Cliffs, New Jersey 07632

ACKNOWLEDGMENTS

Customarily, in the front pages of a book, an author lists of the people who have helped see the manuscript through to completion. In this case, the list is more than customary. The names here are those of truly special people. They offered advice, references, experience, and wisdom. But most of all they offered time—in every case, their most precious commodity. To all, I extend my sincere appreciation, not just for what they did but for who they are: dear, kind professionals who are also my friends, especially Valda Alsop, William Asbury, Rick Barter, Viola Blaser, Robert Edelman, Rosemary Ewing, James Gardner, Dr. Virginia Grabill, Mary Lou Heeger, Dr. Ed Jenkinson, Athalene Klein, Joyce Marlin, Ninalea McIntosh, Jona Monyhan, Rosemarie Norrick-Urash, Marcia Onnybecker, June Purcell, Ralph Rothert, John Russell, Jack Schriber, Sue Schriber, Dr. Ann Stuart, Edmund Sullivan, Virginia Thrasher, Sharon Tuggle, Dr. Laura Weaver, Susan Wolf, Jim Wootton, and many others who answered questions, offered opinions, made suggestions, and otherwise provided moral support.

Others agreed to allow their work to be included as models. A special thanks to those for their cooperation and willingness to help: Hillary Altekruse for her literary analysis, "Alone in a Crowded World: Emily Dickinson and Her Poems"; David Ciepley for his short story, "Spud"; Jo Ann McCulley for her literary analysis, "Chee and Old Man Fat: A Study in Contrast"; Karla Moore for her literary analysis, "Sylvia and the White Heron"; Jack B. Schriber for his poem, "Ode to a Tupperware Container"; Timothy L. Rife for his technical report, "Printed Circuits Versus Wire Wrapping"; Ann Commons Weil for her research paper, "Mother Goose: A Devoted Teacher"; and Jerome Welte for his laboratory report, "The Effects of Acid Rain on the Growth of Bulbous Plants."

Finally, a warm note of gratitude to Linda Bernbach, the editor who suggested the idea for this handbook, who has answered hours of long-distance questions, who has guided me through two previous projects, and whose exemplary professionalism should be a standard in the publishing industry. I hope she's awarded a hefty bonus when this book sells its first million copies!

CONTENTS

to Charlie . . .
      who has made all the difference.

Introduction

This book began with an ambitious goal: to meet the writing needs of all students. Acknowledging that "students" are not confined to a classroom, the idea was to develop a reference book that would assist readers in any situation, academic or personal. It would offer guidance for writing assignments across the curriculum, from accounting to zoology. And for personal reference, the book would help with resumes and letters as well as scholarship, college, and job applications. The book would include all kinds of writing, creative or technical, formal or informal. It would address all problems, no matter whether writers needed to study a model, find a quick definition and example in the Glossary, or follow an extended step-by-step explanation from the text. No matter whether students were writing, revising, or proofreading—or only preparing to write—no matter what, the book would meet all of the writers' needs.

It was, indeed, an ambitious goal.

Whether or not the book succeeds, only you, the reader, can ultimately judge. But having worked with students in both high school and college for nearly twenty-five years, I sincerely believe this book can guide you through every writing situation you will face. Others agree, including the many teachers and students I consulted about the various kinds of writing assignments, in and out of the classroom. Here's why we think the book works:

- The book is a reference work, a guide, a kind of "dictionary" of writing, not meant for cover-to-cover reading. You can pinpoint needed information with little reading.

- The alphabetical arrangement allows you to find quickly the sections which meet your specific needs. Cross-references refer you to related sections if you need additional help.

- The three parts of the book include:

  ○ a general discussion of how to plan, write, revise, and proofread,
  ○ a description of virtually every kind of writing, both academic and personal,
  ○ quick definitions and brief examples in the Glossary.

- The Writing section includes the ten common methods for developing any kind of writing. Bold type in the table of contents and page-edge borders within the text of Part II signify those ten special chapters and help you locate them quickly for frequent reference.

- Step-by-step instructions will help alleviate the fear of facing writing assignments. The instructions tell you what to do, how to do it, and how the finished product should look.

- The instructions include guidelines and checklists along the way to ease you through the task.

- Analyzing 58 kinds of writing, the book covers writing for long-term assignments, for all major content areas, test situations, and personal needs.

- The discussion of each kind of writing examines:

  - its characteristics,
  - the process for developing it, including prewriting, writing, revising, and proofreading,
  - sample papers to illustrate the characteristics and process,
  - analyses of the sample papers describing their important features.

- Models for each of six content areas aid writing across the curriculum:

  - English
  - Social Sciences
  - Science
  - Business
  - Vocational Education
  - Mathematics

- Wherever possible, models for a specific kind of writing deal with the same general topic for all five content areas. The result illustrates how to tailor writing for a specific audience.

- Parallel topics also further understanding. For instance, using the same novel as the subject to illustrate a book review, a literary analysis of a novel, a synopsis, and book reports for the five disciplines makes clear how one kind of writing *differs* from the others.

- The models are practical and readable, dealing with a wide variety of subjects of contemporary interest. Many have been written by high-school and college students. Teachers in the respective disciplines agreed to the models' success.

- The models include writing of all lengths, from single-paragraphs to full-length research papers.

- Models illustrating the process of revision emphasize the importance of revising for successful writing. Each model is followed by an analysis.

- Numerous illustrations, examples, notes, hints, and warnings help clarify solutions to common writing problems.

- Cross-references emphasize the relationships among the many facets of writing and help you understand terms or concepts which may otherwise hinder you.

- Frequent references to word processing, computer searches, and data banks—including a separate chapter on writing with a word processor—acknowledge the technical and electronic world in which you work.

As a result of its organization, many cross-references, and thorough treatment of each topic, this book should answer any need in any writing situation. I hope you agree. But more importantly, I hope that what you find in these pages will improve your writing—in school, on the job, and in your personal life. When that happens, this book will have met its goal.

Part I

A Process for Writing

To explain a process for writing is to tell you how to go about doing it. How to get ideas. How to put them together. How to get them on paper. How to polish them into a fine piece of writing. That is the general purpose of this book, and every writing chapter takes you through a step-by-step process for writing a particular product. This section, however, gives general background for what we call *process*, a term that refers to the four broad steps in writing anything: prewriting, writing, revising, and proofreading. We will present the general background in a step-by-step procedure, one you can follow easily. Later, in Part II, you will find that each specific writing chapter will follow a similar procedure, tailored for the particular writing product.

First we introduce the prewriting process—the kinds of things you do to get ready to write. Helpful hints to suggest how to think. How to plan. How to make choices. Next we show how prewriting work can allow you to write freely. We offer suggestions for writing. Then we help you with the real work in writing: showing how to polish your paper. Improve content. Improve structure. Improve emphasis. Improve continuity. Eliminate those bothersome mechanical errors. Finally, we talk about word processors and the implications of modern technology for the writing process.

Refer to this writing-process section regularly, no matter what you write. In fact, you will find frequent cross-references to this section throughout the book, suggesting that you use it to supplement the step-by-step processes found elsewhere. Together, they can see you through virtually any writing task you will face!

PREWRITING

Throughout Part II of this book you will find series of steps labeled *Prewriting*. The term generally refers to any kind of activity that helps you loosen up, think about your topic, analyze your audience, focus on purpose, or otherwise prepare to write. The prewriting steps vary with the kind of paper being discussed. Some papers are more complicated than others, and so some steps for getting ready to write are more complicated than others. For instance, one paper may require thorough primary or secondary research; but another may demand nothing more complicated than selecting and organizing appropriate details. In either case, the prewriting activities, when completed, will give you a product which can guide you in developing your paper. Usually, the product helps you focus your topic, narrows broad topics to more specific ones, and indicates the direction the paper itself will take. The product may be only a sentence and a list. Or it may be something as formal as a three-part thesis sentence and a fully developed outline. Whatever its form, the product will help you write your paper.

This section will look at five steps involved in two broad kinds of prewriting activities: gathering thoughts and information and planning the paper.

STEP 1. GATHERING THOUGHTS AND INFORMATION

What we write depends on what we think about. What we think about usually depends on what has happened to us, perhaps as a result of what we have read, what we have heard, what we have seen. The first part of prewriting demands that we focus on our thoughts, perhaps expanding them by seeking additional information. Probably a dozen or so different general activities help in gathering thoughts and information, but we will look at the following most common activities:

- reading (specific assignments, general background, and research)
- discussion (group and interview)
- personal reflection
- journal writing
- brainstorming
- list making
- daily experiences (what you see, hear, and do)

Reading: Specific Assignments

Reading is one way to prepare for writing. Perhaps you have a reading assignment to which you must respond. Perhaps you are summarizing the assignment, reacting to it, or in some other way showing that you have read and understood it. The assignment may also be a springboard from which you can make mental leaps to topics of related but special interest to you.

Reading: General Background

Frequently, however, the reading material is something other than a specific assignment. At one extreme, it may be general, almost casual reading which merely relates to classroom work and only indirectly applies to specific daily assignments. It may be in the form of periodical articles or books, perhaps by authors renowned in their fields.

Reading: Research

At the other extreme, reading may be so comprehensive as to be labeled *research*. It may require the use of the various periodical indexes, the card catalog, computerized data searches, or any other of the many guides to sources found in the library. In these prewriting situations, you are responsible not only for the additional reading, but also for finding the additional reading materials.

All of these reading activities—specific assignments, general background, and research—fall in the category of prewriting. The reading is helping you get ready to write.

Discussion: Group

Prewriting activities may also be oral and may include formal or infor-

mal discussion, in class or out. With classmates and friends familiar with the subject matter, you may discuss not only possible topics for your paper but also the possible content of your paper.

Discussion: Interview

Of course discussion can also come in the form of an interview. While the interview may be similar to an informal discussion, it differs in that you will have sought out the authority with whom you are speaking. His or her comments will likely become the basis for your paper. As a result, your paper is a kind of research paper although the source is primary rather than secondary and oral rather than printed. [*See* PRIMARY RESEARCH *and* SECONDARY RESEARCH *in the Glossary.*]

Personal Reflection

Prewriting activities may also be the result of personal reflection. If it is to result in writing, however, reflection usually needs direction. You can reflect on all manner of things, but without a general topic of concern or a specific assignment to address, reflection may be more akin to daydreaming than to prewriting and may never result in writing. Many writers use a variety of means for directing personal reflection, including journal writing, brainstorming, and list making.

Journal Writing

Serious writers frequently keep daily journals. They write about whatever attracts their attention, seems worthy of note, merits observation. Ironically, they find that the more they record, the more they observe. Thus, they argue, keeping a journal makes them more observant and helps them generate ideas about which to write. The idea of journal writing may suggest a goal of creative writing, such as short stories or poetry, but that is not necessarily the case. Journalists, copywriters, even students who must respond on a regular basis to written assignments find that keeping a journal helps them stay in shape, so to speak, to write the most vigorous papers.

Brainstorming

Brainstorming also helps focus personal reflection. Brainstorming involves offering ideas freely, without fear of criticism, allowing one idea to suggest another and another. You can brainstorm alone, but obviously the process is more effective in a group. As one idea generates another idea, you come up with new approaches to old ideas. The trick to brainstorming effectively is to allow the mind the freedom to make connections between ideas, no matter how strange the connections may seem at the time.

List Making

As a result of brainstorming, you may be able to generate lists which suggest composition topics and supporting ideas; however, lists can come as the result of other means as well. Generating lists helps you look critically at ideas and their relationships. You can create all kinds of lists:

- lists of main ideas
- lists of supporting details
- lists of examples
- lists of arguments
- lists of reasons

All are possible components of a composition. A list that is revised and arranged in logical order is, for all practical purposes, an outline. In many of the prewriting activities in Part II, you will find that generating lists is a primary way to pick out main ideas and then to find appropriate supporting ideas. As a prewriting activity, list making helps you collect your thoughts, plan and arrange them in logical order, and clarify the direction of your paper. The result is organized, unified writing. But more on that later. [*See Step 5 below.*]

Daily Experiences: What You See and Hear

Other kinds of prewriting activities occur almost as a coincidence of living. Sometimes you may be stimulated to write as a result of something you have seen: a film, an art exhibit, an accident, an animal in distress, a busy highway, a lonely farm pond, a thoughtful gesture, a construction site, a rare flower, a criminal act, a rude driver, a mime, a tornado, or a champion swimmer. For example, films frequently have a powerful message that may leave you sad, joyful, remorseful, even furious, a feeling that may be worthy of a description, a comparison-contrast, a classification, or a persuasion paper. Even television viewing may evoke similar kinds of reactions. You may react to news commentators and their methods of reporting the nightly news. You may react to a special report on a world crisis that evokes empathy and helps you write an opinion paper, or you may react to a variety show that stimulates your sense of humor and helps you write effective dialogue.

Daily Experiences: What You Do

Likewise, sometimes you may be stimulated to write as a result of something you have done: visiting a city dump, watching a track meet, sitting in the rain, falling out of a boat, suffering from loneliness, facing tragedy, enjoying success, completing a task, dieting, building a hang glider, catching a big fish, finding a lost wallet, helping a stranger, having an accident, being friends with someone special. For instance, sometimes hearing a particularly motivating speaker may help you sort through your own feelings enough to react in written form.

Summary

In brief, we are saying that day-to-day activities, if given attention, will effectively promote ideas for writing. Doing something as simple as taking an afternoon walk may suggest a dozen topics about which you can write. Children playing in the street invite danger by their behavior. You wonder why there is nowhere else to play. A driver coasts through a stop sign, neglecting the clear response that sign demands. His behavior makes you wonder about the causes for accidents in your neighborhood. The neighbor's dog comes bouncing out to wag his greeting. You wonder how dogs have become the domesticated man's-best-friend. So within your few minutes' walk, you discovered three possible topics to explore.

Prewriting activities result in ideas for compositions. The ideas may be in the form of a scratch outline or a list, and the scratch outline or list may become a formal, well-developed outline. In the process of refining that list or outline, however, you should complete four other prewriting activities: determining your purpose, analyzing your audience, formulating your topic or thesis sentence, and organizing your materials.

STEP 2. PLANNING THE PAPER: DETERMINING PURPOSE

Let's go back to that afternoon walk. You wondered why the children were playing in the street, why there was nowhere else to play. Assume you decide to write about that general topic. First, you must decide what you hope to accomplish as a result of your writing. Do you simply want to report information on the assumption that others may be interested? Do you hope to analyze the problem in effort to find an answer? Do you want to persuade local government to do something about the problem? Do you want to offer suggestions for alternate play areas? Do you want to warn the children about the dangers of playing in the street? In other words, you must decide why you are writing. What is your purpose? Put it in a sentence.

STEP 3.   PLANNING THE PAPER: ANALYZING THE AUDIENCE

Directly related to purpose is audience. Will you write to local government officials, to the children, to the newspaper editor, or to parents? Your audience determines dozens of details about your writing: vocabulary, sentence structure, formality, psychological appeals, organization, and approach. If you are writing about a technical subject to laymen, you must use laymen's vocabulary. If you are writing about a formal subject to an academic audience, your sentence structure should mirror the formality. If you are expressing an opinion to readers who will likely disagree, you will use different appeals and a different organization than you would with readers who will likely agree. You will tailor your writing about a political debate for an audience of politicians differently than you would tailor it for an audience of apathetic voters. Who is your audience? Name it. Analyzing audience is part of the prewriting process.

STEP 4.   PLANNING THE PAPER: WRITING THE TOPIC OR THESIS SENTENCE

At this point, you should be prepared to write a topic or thesis sentence. You know your purpose and you understand your audience, so what will you say to achieve your purpose with this particular audience? Write a sentence that states your topic, either for a paragraph or for a multi-paragraph paper. (A topic sentence states the topic of a paragraph, and a thesis sentence states each of the major topics in a multi-paragraph paper.) [*If you need additional help, see* PARAGRAPHS, KINDS: AS AN INDEPENDENT UNIT *in Part II for a detailed explanation of the development of a topic sentence. See* THEME *in Part II for a thorough explanation of the development of a thesis sentence.*]

STEP 5.   PLANNING THE PAPER: ORGANIZING THE MATERIAL

Finally, before you can write an effective paper, you must have some plan for presenting your main ideas. That plan is called *organization*. You may have a list developed from Step 1. If so, you are well on your way toward organizing your paper. Now you need to rearrange that list so that it becomes a plan for your paper. If necessary, you can transform that list into an outline. [*See* OUT-LINES, KINDS: FOR A PAPER *in Part II for a logical discussion of list making and formal outlining.*]

Generally, the organization will follow one of three plans: chronological order (as arranged in time), spatial order (as arranged in space), or some order of importance (as arranged by any measure of significance). The specific method of development [*as suggested in all the entries in Part II*] will also help determine organization.

Prewriting activities should result in two products: a topic or thesis sentence and a list or outline. Together, they will take you smoothly through the writing process.

While we have given a rather simplified explanation of prewriting activities, keep in mind that most writers do not go through a prewriting process, immediately begin writing, and never think back through prewriting activities again. Instead, because writers often move from prewriting to writing to prewriting again until they achieve their goal, the term we will use occasionally in this book is the *yo-yo approach*. Sometimes writing will not move as smoothly as you had hoped; you need additional preparation, additional thought, additional research, additional experience, additional reflection, additional discussion before your ideas form a unified, comprehensive piece of writing. If you will use the yo-yo approach as you work, the writing process will be less painful, and the prewriting activities will provide more inspiration for the writing process ahead.

WRITING

Once you have completed the five general steps in prewriting, the writing process should be fairly simple. Whether your prewriting activities resulted in a list, a scratch outline, or a formal outline, the process of writing the first draft is nothing more than the development of the prewriting-activity products. Probably the most important concept of writing is to have reached the point at which you are free to express your ideas without worrying about mechanical details, sentence structure and other formal writing techniques. Those details can be left as part of revising and proofreading.

So, with your prewriting activities behind you, you are ready to write. Follow these general steps to develop your rough draft.

STEP 1. GETTING SITUATED

Situate yourself in a comfortable spot free from distractions in whatever surroundings are most stimulating to your own creative process. For some writers, any kind of sound—music, voices, street noise—proves distracting. For other writers, background noise helps drown out other distractions. In any case, arrange to work in the situation most comfortable for you.

STEP 2. FOLLOWING THE PLAN

Follow the organization plan you developed during the prewriting process. Begin with the topic or thesis sentence and add the supporting details suggested in your list or outline.

STEP 3. USING THE YO-YO APPROACH

If the organization plan you developed during the writing process is not working well for your purpose, then, using the yo-yo approach, go back to the prewriting steps which dealt with organization and try a different plan. Implement the plan, using the thesis sentence and/or topic sentences as developed during the prewriting process. Add the supporting details in logical order as you rearrange them.

STEP 4. LETTING THOUGHTS FLOW

As you write, concentrate on allowing your thoughts to flow. Here's how:

- Do not struggle with words or spelling or punctuation or other mechanical details.

- Do not follow the urge to reread, restructure, and rewrite.

Rather, concentrate on getting your main ideas on paper, writing quickly, perhaps even informally.

STEP 5. FOLLOWING PARAGRAPHING TECHNIQUES

As your thoughts flow, make an effort to frame them into general paragraph structures. Even though you will polish structure during the revising process, the conscious concern over paragraph structure at this point may save some agony later.

[*If you are not familiar with the structure of a paragraph or a theme, study* PARAGRAPHS *and* THEME *in Part II before you attempt to write a paper. Check the Glossary for definitions and examples of terms with which you may be unfamiliar.*]

STEP 6. STICKING TO THE SUBJECT

Be sure you stick to your subject, thus maintaining unity. Avoid the temptation to wander off into interesting examples that do not support your topic or thesis sentence. Those examples will not help your purpose! As you think of them, use transitions to connect your ideas and to show relationships between and among ideas.

STEP 7. IGNORING (FOR THE MOMENT) TECHNICAL DETAILS

It should be obvious that what happens while you are writing is merely the result of using the products you developed in your prewriting work. All other kinds of technical work—the mechanics, grammar, usage, sentence structure, the fine points of parallelism, emphasis, and formal structure—can be left for the revising and proofreading processes.

STEP 8. WRITING THE ROUGH DRAFT IN ONE SITTING

Make every effort to complete the first draft in a single sitting in order to maintain a consistent tone and smooth continuity with less effort.

When you complete the first draft, you have passed a major hurdle. You have your thoughts on paper. You have developed the plan established in the prewriting activities. But this is the first draft—the rough draft, if you prefer. Rough drafts need polish. The polishing comes with revising and proofreading. So when you have the first draft finished, take a well-deserved break and come back ready to be objective about your work.

REVISING

You have finished the prewriting and writing steps, and now you are ready to revise.

During the process of revising, the really tough part of writing takes place. True, you have worked hard to write your paper; now you are merely making changes. The writing that occurs during revision, however, makes a mediocre paper a good paper. Revision adds variety, emphasis, coherence, transition, and detail. Revision eliminates wordiness, irrelevancies, and inconsistencies. Revision polishes, hones, and perfects. Thus, most professional writers agree that the real work comes in the revising.

So what happens in the process of revising? A writer looks at virtually everything involved in the process of writing: structure, organization, and emphasis. He thinks about ways to make his paper more interesting, either by content or by structure.

Let us look at the areas specifically. As you revise any paper, follow not only the suggestions for revision for that particular kind of paper as outlined in the respective sections of Part II, but make sure you consider each of these kinds of general revisions as well.

Cross-references are listed in most of the following steps. Thus, if you need additional information, you will know where to look.

So, let's go on to the Revising Steps.

STEP 1. CHECKING STRUCTURE: MULTI-PARAGRAPH PAPERS

If you have written a multi-paragraph paper, ask yourself the following questions to check its structure:

- Does the multi-paragraph paper begin with an introductory paragraph which includes an attention-getting device? [*See* THEME *in Part II and* ATTENTION-GETTER *in the Glossary.*]

- Does the paper include a thesis sentence? [*See* THEME *in Part II for a* thorough discussion of effective thesis sentences and their development.]

- Does the thesis sentence state or imply the content of each of the following body paragraphs?

- Does the thesis sentence establish the order of the body paragraphs?

- Have I maintained unity throughout the theme?

- Are there adequate transitional devices to connect the paragraphs? [*See* SAMPLE REVISION FOR TRANSITION *later in this section.*]

- Does the theme follow a logical order? Do the body paragraphs fol-

14

low a logical order? [*See* ORDER, IN PARAGRAPH DEVELOPMENT *in the Glossary.*]

• Does the conclusion reflect the thesis sentence and offer a summary, final statement, or final observation that relates to the thesis sentence?

As you examine the structure, also think specifically about development. Ask yourself these questions:

• Have I used the most logical and effective means of development? [*See* DEVELOPMENT, METHODS OF *in the Glossary.*]

• Are there additional methods of development that may add more specificity to my paper and help the reader better understand my point?

STEP 2.   CHECKING STRUCTURE: PARAGRAPHS

If you have written only a single paragraph, you must examine the paragraph structure as a single unit of composition. If you have written a theme, you must examine the theme structure in terms of individual paragraphs.

As you examine the structure of a paragraph, whether as a single unit of composition or as part of a larger composition, ask yourself the following kinds of questions:

• Does my paragraph include a topic sentence, either stated or implied? [*See the prewriting activities in* PARAGRAPHS *in Part II for a discussion of effective topic sentences.*]

• If the paragraph is part of a multiparagraph paper, does it begin with a transitional word, phrase, or sentence to tie it in with the previous paragraph? [*See* SAMPLE REVISION FOR TRANSITION *later in this section.*]

• Does my paragraph include sufficient specific details which support or explain the topic sentence? [*For an example, see* SAMPLE REVISION FOR SPECIFIC DETAIL *later in this section.*]

• Have I used the most appropriate means of developing that paragraph? [*Remember, you can use virtually any means of development as discussed in Part II or any combination of these methods. For a quick reference, see* DEVELOPMENT, METHODS OF *in the Glossary.*]

• Have I included specific rather than abstract details? [*See* ABSTRACT *and* SPECIFIC DETAIL *in the Glossary. Also see* SAMPLE REVISION FOR SPECIFIC DETAIL *later in this section.*]

• Have I maintained unity throughout my paragraph? That is, **have** I omitted any material that **does** not directly support the topic sentence? [*See* SAMPLE REVISION FOR UNITY *later in this section.*]

• Does my paragraph follow a logical method of organization? [*See* ORDER, IN PARAGRAPH DEVELOPMENT *in the Glossary.*]

• Have I included adequate transitional devices to connect the ideas within the paragraph? [*See* SAMPLE REVISION FOR TRANSITION *later in this section.*]

- Does my paragraph end with a clincher or concluding statement?

STEP 3. CHECKING STRUCTURE: SENTENCES

Finally, no matter whether you have written a multi-paragraph paper or a single paragraph, you will want to check the sentence structure. Ask yourself the following questions:

- Have I included a variety of sentence types? Simple sentences? Compound sentences? Complex sentences? Compound-complex sentences? [*See* SAMPLE REVISION FOR SENTENCE VARIETY *later in this section.*]
- Do my sentences begin in a variety of ways? For instance, do some sentences start with the subject while others start with an introductory phrase or introductory clause?
- Have I used a variety of modification structures?
- Do my sentences vary in length? A mere word count gives a quick answer. Because many writers tend to write sentences of similar length, varying the length usually requires a conscious effort.

Another means of adding strength to sentences is to choose specific details and use strong nouns and verbs. In an effort to check your work for strength, ask yourself these questions:

- Have I used specific words, the most precise words for the purpose? See *Webster's New World Thesaurus* for help with precise word

choice. [SEE ALSO REVISION FOR SPECIFIC DETAIL *later in this section.*]

- Have I used strong, specific nouns instead of weak, general ones? Have I talked about a fifteen-year-old star on the girls' cross-country team as opposed to a high-school athlete?
- Have I used strong, specific verbs as opposed to weak, general ones? Have I said, for instance, *The dog loped across the yard*, instead of *The dog walked across the yard*?
- Have I omitted excessive adjectives and adverbs that could be replaced with stronger nouns and verbs? For instance, instead of saying, *He walked slowly*, have I said, *He ambled*?
- Have I used active-voice as opposed to passive-voice verbs? [*See* ACTIVE VOICE *and* PASSIVE VOICE *in the Glossary.*] Of course, under certain circumstances, passive voice is preferable. Those special circumstances appear in the discussion of those respective kinds of writing in Part II.
- Have I, wherever possible, substituted strong action verbs for weak linking verbs? [*See* ACTION VERB *and* LINKING VERB *in the Glossary.*]
- Have I used appropriate vocabulary for the subject? Is the language too technical for my audience? Is it technical enough to be appropriate for the subject? Have I avoided colloquial and slang expressions? [*See* COLLOQUIAL EXPRESSION *and* SLANG *in the Glossary*]. Have I avoided other expressions too informal for the subject or the audience?

- Have I avoided trite expressions? [*See* TRITE *in the Glossary*.]
- Have I included figures of speech and imagery wherever appropriate to show maturity in writing and add reader interest? [*See* FIGURES OF SPEECH *and* IMAGERY *in the Glossary*.]

Finally, check your sentences for wordiness. The most powerful papers make significant points in few words. [*See* SAMPLE REVISION FOR WORDINESS *below, illustrating the process of eliminating wordiness*.] Think about every sentence, phrase, and word. Are you repeating yourself? Do you say *free gift*? What other kind of gift is there? Do you say *hot water heater*? There is no cold water heater. Do you refer to *Easter Sunday*? Is there an Easter Thursday? Be critical of your writing as you study every word. Eliminate excess.

STEP 4.   CHECKING EMPHASIS

In addition to structure and organization, you will want to look at your paper for proper emphasis. [*See* EMPHASIS, IN SENTENCES *in the Glossary for a quick reference, and see* SAMPLE REVISION FOR EMPHASIS *later in this section for an example*.] Emphasis begins at sentence level. If your sentences carry proper emphasis, usually your organization will maintain the same emphasis throughout the paper. So ask yourself the following questions about emphasis in regard to your sentences:

- Do I have the main ideas in the main clauses? [*See* CLAUSE, MAIN *in the Glossary*.]

- Do I have supporting ideas in subordinate clauses? [*See* CLAUSE, SUBORDINATE *in the Glossary*.]
- Have I put the most important ideas at the end of my sentences?
- Are the second most important ideas at the beginning of my sentences?
- Is the information in the middle of the sentences least important or worthy of the least emphasis?

Special emphasis is created by using particular structures. For instance, the use of a series establishes a rhythm. Parallel structures, especially, help the reader remember the items in the series. [*See* SERIES *and* PARALLEL STRUCTURE *in the Glossary*.] Other kinds of structural emphasis can occur, too. As a result, ask yourself the following questions:

- If I have used items in a series, are they structurally parallel?
- If I have listed several items in the course of several sentences, could I improve the listing by putting the items in a parallel series?
- Have I avoided dangling modifiers?
- Have I avoided ambiguous modification structures? [*See* AMBIGUITY *in the Glossary*.]

STEP 5.   CHECKING CONSISTENCY

The next thing you should check is consistency: consistent point of view and consistent verb tense. [*See* SHIFTS, CONFUSING *in the Glossary*.] If, for instance, you begin a formal essay with a third-person point of view, you must maintain it throughout. A short story, of course, allows certain options in shifts in point of view [*see* SHORT STORY *in Part II*], but expository writing allows no such shift. The questions you should ask about consistent point of view include the following:

- Have I used the point of view most appropriate for the purpose of my work? For instance, using a second-person point of view results in didactic writing, a style which may not endear you to your audience. A third-person point of view appears more formal, less personal. A first-person point of view is usually reserved for narratives or short stories, usually too informal for classroom work.

- Have I maintained a consistent point of view throughout the writing? Or, if I have switched points of view, have I done so with a purpose and within the framework of accuracy and acceptable style?

Next, check for consistent verb tense. For instance, if you began your paper in the present tense, then unless you are using a flashback, you must maintain the present tense throughout the paper.

A Note about the Samples: Now that you are familiar with the process of revision, study the following samples, which apply some of the more complicated steps above. The examples show changes in specific detail, unity, transition, sentence variety, and emphasis, then analyze the reasons for these changes. Note that the revisions read more smoothly, with greater clarity and emphasis.

—————— Sample Revision for Specific Detail ——————

The following passage [*an excerpt from the sample paper included in* THEME *in Part II*] illustrates the difference between a paragraph with and without specific detail.

Original Passage

In spring, the fishermen replace the hunters on Hovey Lake waters. They come to catch big stringers of fish in the early spring. Some are more successful than are others. They use all kinds of methods to try to catch fish. Only when the lake closes do the fishermen leave.

Revised to Add Specific Detail

In spring, the fishermen replace the hunters on Hovey Lake waters. Attracted by the spring crappie run, fishermen haul in hefty stringers of slabs and return to fish for bluegill. Evening campfires turn skillets full of fresh fillets into plates full of succulent morsels. Then sunrise sends the bass fishermen scurrying to secret waters, some to return with empty bags. One fisherman, however, boats three, one weighing in at eight pounds two ounces. Later in the day, a few trotlines yield spoonbill catfish, those prehistoric monsters weighing thirty pounds or more, as long as a man is tall. In later afternoon or early evening, a jug fisherman occasionally bags perch, catfish, or even a wily gar, long, slender, and sharp-toothed. Spring moves into summer, and summer moves into autumn. Only then, when the lake is closed for waterfowl migration, do the fishermen leave.

Analysis of the Sample Revision for Specific Detail

The original passage omits any reference to specifics. Note the following kinds of revisions:

- Specific kinds of fish are named in the revised passage. Rather than appearing in a list, however, the specific species' names are interwoven with additional details.
- Specific methods of fishing are named.
- Times of day and seasons are named.
- Specific word choice adds detail. Strong verbs like *haul, boats,* and *bags* as well as specific and colorful nouns like *stringers, slabs, succulent morsels,* and *monsters* enhance the details.
- Specific size descriptions add detail, including phrases such as *eight pounds two ounces* and *as long as a man is tall.*

——————————— Sample Revision for Unity ———————————

The following paragraph lacks unity. The writer fails to stick to his topic as indicated in his topic sentence. Instead, he allows his paragraph to hop from one idea to the next, as if he is reporting the wanderings of his own mind. Each sentence seems to remind him of a new topic! The revised paragraph, however, maintains unity. Every detail supports the topic sentence.

Original Passage

Nearly every community tries to combat the problems pigeons create. While pigeons are docile and provide enjoyment in the parks for those who like to feed them peanuts and popcorn, they also create a health hazard where they most frequently roost. Some experts try simply to change the roosting place. Of course, that only causes the health hazard to relocate. In fact, one year, officials used chicken wire to close off a favorite roosting place; so the pigeons began roosting in our garage. They created not only a health hazard but a financial burden as well. We had to have the car repainted as a result of the frequent stains on the hood. In spite of that, I really like pigeons. In fact, we used to raise pigeons when I was a child. Some of them are quite beautiful, not only because of their colors but also because of the ruffs around their necks or the long feathers along their legs. Of course, these are special breeds. Other special breeds are racing pigeons and those that fly in groups called kits, tumbling and diving to the spectators' delight.

Revised to Maintain Unity

Nearly every community tries to combat the problems pigeons create. While docile pigeons provide enjoyment for those who like to feed them peanuts and popcorn, they also create a health hazard where they most frequently roost. In addition, they deface buildings, monuments, and other public and private properties. To alleviate the problems, some communities erect wire barriers around the pigeons' favorite roosting places. Nearly invisible, the wire tends to be the least offensive relief measure. Other communities try various noise makers to scare the birds from their roosts. Sirens, clappers, gunshots, and mild explosions send the pigeons on their way. Of course, the noise disturbs human residents as well, so to some the solution seems more unpleasant than the problem. With either means of combating the problem, however, the pigeons simply move elsewhere. As a result, the problem does not go away; it merely relocates.

Analysis of the Sample Revision for Unity

The revised paragraph maintains unity throughout. Note how this happens:

- Every sentence directly supports the subject named in the topic sentence: combating problems pigeons create.

- Transitions establish the link between each sentence and the topic sentence, like *while, also, in addition, of course,* etc.

- Repetition of key words or their synonyms and pronouns which refer to those key words clearly indicate unity: *problem, solution, it, pigeons, they, their.*

- No sentence refers to extraneous details which detract from the topic of combating the problems the pigeons create.

—————————— Sample Revision for Transition ——————————

Transitions are words, phrases, clauses, and sentences which connect ideas. Transitions help the reader understand relationships like time, space, addition, emphasis, example, comparison-contrast, and cause-effect. For instance, *consequently* shows effect, *on the other hand* shows contrast, *eventually* shows time, and *in fact* shows emphasis.

Sometimes transitions appear as whole sentences. In that case, they connect major ideas between paragraphs in a full-length paper. [*See* THEME *in Part II for illustrations of transitional sentences.*]

Finally, transitions can be entire paragraphs. In a long paper, such as a research paper, a transitional paragraph connects ideas between major points. While a single major point may be supported by several paragraphs, a transitional paragraph helps the reader summarize the subtopics before moving to the next major point. In other words, the transitional paragraph summarizes what has come before and introduces what is still to come. [*See* RESEARCH PAPER *in Part II for an example.*]

The following paragraph omits almost all transitions. The revision which follows [*an excerpt from a sample paper in* OPINION *in Part II*] illustrates the frequency with which good writers use transitional devices to help their readers follow the logic and organization.

Original Passage

Candidates see the depressed economy as a major issue in the eighth district. Brolliette proposes tax incentives to lure big businesses into the area. The Republican incumbent voted for the huge tax incentive that brought two moderate-size businesses to the area. Citizens have been hit with major increases in their personal property tax bills. The businesses offered over 1,200 jobs. Almost all the jobs have gone to employees who accepted a transfer. One business' plant closed in the Southwest. Irate local citizens are footing the tax bill for jobs not open to them. Brolliette defends the position. Kinsingtonne warned City Council and County Council members that citizens would resent the increase. He fought for citizen protection before he announced his candidacy for office. He understands the working man's plight and the ramifications of big business on the little man's pocketbook.

Revised to Include Transitions

Each candidate sees the depressed economy as a major issue in the eighth district. Brolliette proposes tax incentives to lure big businesses in the area. The Republican incumbent, in fact, voted for the huge tax incentive that brought two moderate-size businesses to the area. Suddenly, however, area citizens have been hit with major increases in their personal property tax bills, some as much as double. Although the businesses have offered over 1,200 jobs, almost all have gone to employees who accepted a transfer as a result of one business' plant closing in the Southwest. So irate local citizens are footing the tax bill for jobs not open to them. Brolliette continues to defend the position. Kinsingtonne, on the other hand, warned City Council and County Council members that citizens would resent the increase. He fought for citizen protection even before he announced his candidacy for office. Apparently he understands the working man's plight and the ramifications of big business on the little man's pocketbook.

Analysis of the Sample Revision for Transition

The revision above includes single-word transitions and transitional phrases. The underlined transitions mark the revisions. Note that as a result of the added transitions, the paragraph now makes more sense.

————— Sample Revision for Sentence Variety —————

The sample paragraph below lacks sentence variety. Most sentences are about the same length and follow a similar structural pattern: subject/verb/modifiers.

The revised paragraph [*a sample paragraph from* CAUSE AND EFFECT *in Part II*] illustrates improved sentence variety. The structures include simple, compound, complex, and compound-complex sentences and the lengths vary from a few words to several lines.

Original Passage

Biologists have been studying the balance of nature at Isle Royale National Park. It is an unusual experiment. The park contains 210 square miles of wilderness. Scientists can study animal relationships there. The animals are not disturbed by man or other animals. Moose arrived on the island early this century. They probably came by swimming from the Canadian shore. The moose multiplied because they had no predators. They literally ate themselves out of house and home. They could not leave the island. They starved. They died in large numbers. A fire in 1936 nearly eliminated the browsing food moose eat. It was a disaster. The fire, in turn, opened large areas for new growth. The new growth was just the right diet for the huge animals. The herd grew. It outgrew its supply of food again. A severe winter in 1948-1949 caused an ice bridge to form. It bridged the Minnesota mainland to Isle Royale. A small pack of Eastern Timber wolves ventured across the ice. They found the island and the moose. Wolves are the only natural predators of moose. Scientists have watched the moose population grow and thrive. The moose population dwindles. The wolves die from lack of food. The moose population increases. The environment of the island is controlled. It includes a relatively small geographical area. Scientists can thus keep actual head counts. They can study the moose-wolf balance in detail. The balance of nature theory has proven itself accurate. What a lesson for man to learn! One scientific observer said, "The island's uniqueness lies in its complex yet simple system of natural processes. . . . In such a system a delicate balance is struck in which no one animal or organism is more important than another. And man's part? We must leave this balance to natural law, observing but not manipulating."

Revised to Include Sentence Variety

For the past fifty years biologists have been studying the balance of nature by means of a unique experiment conducted in the self-contained laboratory called Isle Royal National Park. The park, an island consisting of 210 square miles of wilderness, affords scientists the opportunity to observe animal relationships in an environment completely undisturbed by man. Sometime early in this century, moose arrived on the island, probably by swimming from the Canadian shore. Proliferating without predators, the moose herds by the early 1930's literally ate themselves out of house and home. Limited by the boundaries of the island, they starved, dying in large numbers. A disastrous fire in 1936 nearly eliminated the browsing food moose eat; but in turn, the fire opened large areas for new growth, just the right diet for the huge animals. So the herd grew. Again it outgrew its supply of food. Then, in 1948-1949, the severe winter caused an ice bridge to form from the Minnesota mainland to Isle Royale. By chance, a small pack of Eastern Timber wolves ventured across the ice, found the island, and found the moose. Wolves are the only natural predators of moose. In the course of the next several decades, scientists have watched the wolf population grow and thrive until the moose population dwindles. Then the wolves die from lack of food, and the moose population increases. As a result of the controlled environment of the island and the relatively small geographical area involved, scientists can keep actual head counts and study the moose-wolf balance in detail. The balance of nature theory has, in the decades of study there, proven itself accurate. What a lesson for man to learn! As one scientific observer said of the park, "The island's uniqueness lies in its complex yet simple system of natural processes.... In such a system a delicate balance is struck in which no one animal or organism is more important than another. And man's part? We must leave this balance to natural law, observing but not manipulating."

Analysis of the Sample Revision for Sentence Variety

The revision above includes sentences which vary both in length and in structure. Note these particulars:

- The sentences vary in length from four words to thirty words. Interestingly, the longest and shortest sentences appear next to one another. The result is a significant emphasis on the idea in the short sentence.

- The sentences vary in structure from simple sentences to compound-complex sentences. [*See entries in the Glossary to identify kinds of sentences:* SIMPLE, COMPOUND, COMPLEX, *and* COMPOUND-COMPLEX.]

- The sentences include a wide variety of modifiers: single-word modifiers, phrase modifiers, and clause modifiers.

- The sentences begin in a variety of ways: with prepositional phrases, with participial phrases, with subjects, with transitional words and phrases, with relative pronouns, with introductory clauses.

- The sentences include both exclamatory and interrogatory sentences, although typically most are declarative.

Sample Revision for Wordiness

Eliminating wordiness presents a challenge to some writers. The following two paragraphs [*taken from the first draft of the sample in* LETTERS, TO THE EDITOR *in Part II*] illustrate in the revision an effective elimination of wordiness.

Original Passage

Do we want continuing increased property taxes? Do we want to ignore drug-pushers and users? Do we want a "yes" man representing us in Congress? To answer "no" to these questions is to vote for Jerrald Kinsingtonne. Here's why.

When Republican incumbent Rodney Brolliette urged local authorities to provide tax incentives to lure businesses into our community, he ignored the cry from private citizens that they would pay with increased property taxes. Democratic candidate Jerrald Kinsingtonne spoke on their behalf, but no one in the Republican-controlled Council listened. Now, strapped with property tax bills double last year's rate, citizens know who they need to support. When Kinsingtonne pleaded their case, he wasn't a candidate. Now he is.

Revised to Eliminate Wordiness

Shall we increase property taxes? Ignore drug-pushers? Elect a "yes" man for Congress? To answer "no" is to vote for Jerrald Kinsingtonne. Here's why.

When Republican incumbent Rodney Brolliette fought for tax incentives to lure businesses here, he ignored Kinsingtonne's plea that private citizens would pay with increased property taxes. Now, strapped with tax bills double last year's rate, citizens know who they need to support.

Analysis of the Sample Revision for Wordiness

The revision above eliminates words, phrases, even whole sentences. As you compare the two passages, you will see that no ideas are omitted, but the revision gives the main idea greater emphasis. To reduce nearly 120 words to just over 60 words, the writer used phrases and clauses to combine ideas into single sentences. He used strong nouns and verbs to eliminate the need for modifiers. As a result of eliminating wordiness, the writer has secondarily improved his sentence variety.

Sample Revision for Emphasis

The following passage, an early draft of this chapter on revising, illustrates revision to achieve emphasis.

Original Passage

It is in the process of revising a paper that real writing takes place. That may sound strange because after all you wrote your paper and now you are merely making changes. Of course, that's true. The writing that takes place during the process of revision, however, is the writing that makes the difference between a paper and a good paper, between a good paper and a superior paper. Most professional writers will tell you the real work comes in the revising.

Revised to Add Emphasis

During the process of revising, the really tough part of writing takes place. True, you have worked hard to write your paper; now you are merely making changes. The writing that occurs during revision, however, makes a mediocre paper a good paper. Revision adds variety, emphasis, coherence, transition, and detail. Revision eliminates wordiness, irrelevancies, and inconsistencies. Revision polishes, hones, and perfects. Thus, most professional writers agree that the real work comes in the revising.

Analysis of the Sample Revision for Emphasis

The revision above illustrates a number of revision techniques, all of which enhance emphasis. Note the following particulars:

- Main ideas appear in the main clauses. For instance, in the original passage, the first sentence swallowed the main idea in a subordinate clause, *that real writing takes place*. In the revision, the main idea appears in the main clause, *the really tough part of writing takes place*.
- Subordinate ideas appear in subordinate positions. In the first sentence, for instance, the phrase *during the process of revising* appears as an introductory prepositional phrase which functions as an adverb. The modifier *merely* places a time limit on the main clause, further emphasizing *tough part*.

- The most important words, words which need emphasis, appear at the ends of sentences. Note the emphasis on *making changes, good paper,* and *revising.*
- Parallel series add emphasis to the concept of revising. Three parallel sentences begin with the word *revision.* Each sentence, however, emphasizes a different part of revision. The first says *revision adds;* the second says *revision eliminates;* the third says *revision polishes, hones,* and *perfects.* Note, too, that each sentence itself includes parallel structures: The first sentence includes a series of five nouns; the second, a series of three nouns; and the third, a series of three verbs.
- Further sentence strength is achieved by the elimination of linking verbs. In the original passage, all sentences but the last include a linking verb. The revision eliminates all linking verbs.
- Even though the second passage carries a stronger message, it is nearly the same length as the original passage.

Using these revision techniques should help you polish your own compositions. You will find additional suggestions for revising included in the sections in Part II which discuss specific kinds of writing. These suggestions will give you a good set of guidelines for thorough and effective revision, the really tough part of writing!

PROOFREADING

Once the paper has been revised so that the content and structure are as accurate and concise as you can make them, then you are ready to prepare the final draft. Whether you prepare the final draft by printing it on a word processor or by writing it out by hand, you will need to proofread it for accuracy. The following questions should help you do so.

Begin now where you stopped, with Revising Step 5. Use these questions in addition to those which are included in the proofreading sections for the specific paper you are writing.

STEP 1.   CHECKING FOR PUNCTUATION AND MECHANICS

Use the following questions to check for possible punctuation or mechanics problems:

- Have I punctuated my sentences accurately so I have avoided major sentence errors like fragments and run-ons? [*See references to each of the marks of punctuation in the Glossary.*]

- Have I included accurate punctuation so that the meaning of sentences is clear?

- If I used semicolons and colons, have I used them accurately?

- Have I used accurate capitalization?

- If documentation is required, have I documented accurately? [*See* RE-SEARCH PAPER *in Part II.*]

- Do superscript numbers for the end- or footnotes appear in the appropriate places, and is the documentation note complete and accurate, including its punctuation?

- Is the corresponding bibliography complete and accurate and punctuated correctly?

- Have I spelled all words correctly? Refer to *Webster's New World Dictionary* for preferred spellings.

STEP 2.   CHECKING FOR GRAMMAR AND USAGE

Use the following questions to help you spot possible grammar or usage problems:

- Do all of my subjects and verbs agree?

- Do nouns and pronouns agree both in number and gender?

- Have I used the correct verb forms, especially for irregular verbs?

- Have I used the objective case accurately where it is required?

- Do I maintain the use of the nominative case after a linking verb?

- Have I avoided using the adjective form when the adverb form is required?

These questions, answered positively, should allow you to proofread successfully and, therefore, produce an accurate final copy.

The many steps from prewriting to proofreading may suggest that writing must be a nearly insurmountable task. Not so! The more you write, the more these general guidelines will play in your mind. And the more that happens, the easier it will be to spot weaknesses on your own.

The chapters in Part II will provide specific step-by-step processes for writing a particular product. Applied to specific situations, the process will take on new emphasis. Your understanding of these general guidelines for prewriting, writing, revising, and proofreading will whisk you through those specific situations.

WRITING WITH A WORD PROCESSOR

The advent of the word processor has altered many students' approach to writing. In the past we had no choice but to write our first drafts in longhand. We littered the pages with cross outs, write overs, and such corrections as "see item 1 on page 4," or "insert A here." Even those of us who wrote our first drafts at the typewriter used scissors and tape to rearrange paragraphs, insert material, or delete sentences and paragraphs. Then we retyped. And retyped!

The word processor now allows us to develop a rough draft, make revisions as we go, and produce a neatly printed copy at any stage of the process.

USING THIS BOOK WITH YOUR WORD PROCESSOR

This book is organized to facilitate the use of a word processor. At the keyboard, you can easily follow the step-by-step methods for developing any particular kind of writing. For instance, although many writers may prefer to develop prewriting lists and outlines by hand, many pieces of software provide opportunities for expanding outlines and developing compositions from notes. Depending on the capabilities of the software you are using, you may choose to follow that pattern. Students who know the keyboard well and regularly use word processors will compose their first drafts at the keyboard. As you write a first draft, you will find that your writing proceeds much more quickly when you can free your thoughts and allow yourself to write almost as if you are speaking. For many, the word processor provides that speed and freedom. If you are a fast typist, you will certainly benefit from turning to the word processor immediately for the composing process.

Once the initial composition is drafted, the word processor provides options otherwise unavailable. For instance, you can save the work on a disk and recall it later. You can print it. Or both. Assume for the sake of this discussion that you choose to print a copy as well as to save it on a disk. Consider the options for revising. With a printed copy in hand, you may begin making revisions with pen or pencil. Maybe making revisions requires painstaking effort on your part. Maybe you need to read every sentence and think of every single punctuation rule that may apply before moving on to the next sentence. Quite possibly, too, viewing your writing on the computer screen is more difficult than viewing your writing on paper. This, of course, is determined by the quality of the monitor from which you are reading.

On the other hand, if the printed words on your monitor are easily read, you may choose to revise directly on the screen, typing in, erasing, adding, moving, exchanging words or letters—using the word-processing commands available to you—rather than doing the work first by hand and then transferring it to the computer. The writer who truly relies on the capabilities of word processing will revise at the keyboard. Too many writers, unfortunately, use the word processor only as a substitute typewriter, entering what they hope is a final draft, thus neglecting the word processor's real capabilities for the revision process.

EASING AND IMPROVING THE REVISION PROCESS

So you can revise on screen or off.

In either case, consider the impact the word processor has on the revision process. In the past if you had a paper revised, polished, recopied or typed, and ready to turn in, you had spent hours preparing the final product. Then, when you read it over that last time, you noticed one or more minor weaknesses you could eliminate—a weak verb, an awkward phrase, a wordy sentence. You could eliminate the weakness, but to do so meant recopying or retyping a whole page. The choice was easy: "It's too much trouble to redo the paper to correct that minor problem. Forget it. I'll leave it the way it is." With the

availability of a word processor, the choice changes: "Oh, I'm glad I caught that! I'll call up the file, make those quick changes, and print another copy. It'll take just a minute." This situation alone should indicate the impact the word processor has had on improving the quality of writing. Even professional writers admit that with a word processor they will make far more revisions than they did in the past. Educational research also seems to suggest that students who use word processors usually complete more effective revisions than those who do not.

The organization of this book will help you take advantage of the available technology and improve your revisions. Every section describing a particular kind of writing includes suggestions for revising. Following those step-by-step guidelines, you can use the word processor's capabilities to make quick work of the task. Here's how. First, you can make simple revisions like correcting misspelled words, deleting or inserting words or phrases with the easy-to-carry-out commands basic to word-processing software. Second, the word processor makes it easy to try some things you would never try otherwise. For instance, the revising guidelines may ask you to check for the most effective organization. By using the "move" command to move a sentence or a paragraph or two paragraphs to another location, you can test alternate patterns of organization and see if the work improves as a result. If not, you can simply move the material back to where it was. The only way you could have done this in the past was to write on just one side of your paper, cut the pages apart, tape them together in a different order, and then recut and retape to return them to the original order. The old cut-and-paste method was so cumbersome that the trial reorganization never occurred. By checking alternate organizational plans via the word processor, however, you may improve both the organization and readability of your composition.

Another advantage of the word processor is the printed copy itself. Many times readers are misled by the appearance of a paper. By always having a printed copy available, you can read your paper objectively at any stage of the prewriting/writing/revising/proofreading process. There are no arrows, sloppy handwriting, or uneven margins to distract you from the content. As a result, sometimes you spot errors in the printed form that you would not notice in a written copy. For instance, the omission of transitional devices may become apparent to you as you read neatly printed pages. Misspelled words become more obvious because they "look funny" in print. Consistently short or consistently long sentences tend to show up more readily, and monotonous word choices glare as you read printed copy. Perhaps it's psychological, but because you are reading a professional-looking copy, you are expecting—unconsciously, perhaps—to hear with your inner ear a smooth, professional-sounding prose. The expectation helps you target rough spots.

In brief, the word processor helps make writers more professional in their work. It allows them to be more critical without the interference of extraneous, distracting items, like arrows and tape and cross outs. The word processor makes them more conscious of the fact that writing is a skill which can be polished and perfected.

SOLVING THE PROBLEMS

Using a word processor, however, is not always a joyous experience. Certain problems develop as a result of the software's capabilities and limitations.

Documenting Sources

The most troublesome problems you will face using a word processor are in writing a technical or research paper, or any other paper that requires documentation or alternate spacing within a page. For instance, to set apart charts or, in some formats, a long quotation, writers customarily shift from double-space to single-space, sometimes indenting from both left and right margins. Some word-processing software does not permit the use of both single- and double-spacing within the same document. The solution seems to be to avoid anything that calls for an unusual format. Since that is neither practical nor desirable, what else can you do? Find alternate software or allow blank space on the page and enter the material by means of a standard typewriter, preferably one with similar type. Recently, many so-called "standard" formats have been altered to accommodate word-processing. Some style manuals, for example, no longer demand that long quotations be single-spaced or indented from the right. Most style manuals prefer endnotes or parenthetical notes to footnotes. And letters commonly follow a format easily set up on a word processor.

Underscoring Titles

But other problems remain. Some word-processing software does not give an underscoring command, and some printers will not accept it. Thus, underlining the titles of books, magazines, and other major works becomes impossible, either within the text or within a bibliography or endnote/footnote entry. The simple solution is to use black ink and a straight edge to underline those items by hand. Another solution may be to insert the pages in a typewriter and add the underscores. Most research papers also require the use of superscript numbers (numbers raised a half space above the standard line of print) for documentation. Many pieces of software do not have a command to print superscript, and again many printers will not accommodate the command. You can type the documentation numbers with a typewriter or enter them neatly by hand in black ink. As another alternative, you may be able to use parenthetical notes, which eliminate the necessity of superscript numbers. While we are talking about superscript numbers, we must acknowledge that the same situation

occurs with subscript numbers (numbers dropped a half space below the standard line of print). You will probably use subscript numbers most often for a math or science paper. Again, about the only way to have a subscript appear in print is to leave the space while developing the text on your word processor and then add the number later either by typewriter or by hand.

Including Charts and Other Illustrations

In addition, technical papers usually require charts, graphs, tables, figures, illustrations, etc. Most of these are not easily entered using typical word-processing software. On the other hand, graphics software will produce superb charts, graphs, and tables. Their professional appearance enhances your work. Of course, the software must be accompanied by a printer which will print graphics, and neither software nor hardware is cheap. The alternative is to leave ample blank space at the point at which the graphic will appear. Then make a paste-up for the graphic and add it to your final draft.

ENJOYING THE ADVANTAGES

Although we have looked at a few of the negative points, we must not overlook the positive ones. Word-processing offers real assets in complicated situations. Most software, for instance, offers an automatic centering command so that titles, lines of poetry, and so forth, appear perfectly with little effort on your part.

In addition, developing a table of contents is easy with the use of the word processor because numbers can be aligned, in some cases automatically and in some cases by tab sets, so they appear on the screen as they will appear on the printed copy. If your computer and monitor permit, you may be able to see the whole page as it will appear in print. You can control where pages will end, so that paragraphs do not break with only a few words on the following page or with only a single line on the previous page. The pages can be numbered automatically and consecutively throughout your paper, sometimes either at the top or the bottom, at the right margin or in the center. Page headings can often be inserted at a number of positions, either left, right, or center. Typing a title page also requires little effort with spacing and centering commands taking the real work out of the task.

Ultimately, the word processor improves writing and saves time. Consider, for example, the manuscript for this book. A professional typist, willing to type forty hours a week, suggested she would need eight or nine weeks to type a final draft of the roughly 1,600 pages. By contrast, after all revisions were entered into the computer, the printer—a relatively slow one—produced a final draft in less than three days. Imagine, if you will, the time and effort such a manuscript would require if each of its many drafts were typed on a typewriter. To put it simply, the word processor makes big projects smaller.

Admittedly, using a word processor creates a few minor problems, but for the most part, it really helps us in the writing process. Learning to take advantage of its capabilities may take some effort, but your effort pays off in improved writing. Not that the word processor magically solves writing problems (although some software comes close); but with the professional appearance of every draft and the time-saving convenience of the revising process, you may notice and correct the errors heretofore left marring final drafts. And the organization of this book will help you make the best use of the word processor.

PART II

TYPES OF WRITING

This section discusses over sixty specific kinds of writing, listed under forty general categories. They are arranged alphabetically for quick reference, and appropriate cross-references offer additional help.

The discussion for each type of writing follows a similar format:

- The *Overview* defines and explains the general purpose of the designated kind of writing.

- The *List of Characteristics* names the typical features found in the specific kind of writing.

- The *Process Section* takes you step-by-step through the method of preparing the particular kind of paper and includes:

  ○ *Prewriting Steps*, which help you find ideas, select good details, and organize your thoughts,
  ○ *Writing Steps*, which direct your thinking toward the development of a good paper,
  ○ *Revising Steps*, which show you how to check content and structure,
  ○ *Proofreading Steps*, which focus on mechanics, grammar, usage, and spelling.

- *Sample Papers* illustrate two kind of features:

  ○ the typical features of the individual kind of paper,
  ○ the appropriate emphasis for papers of this kind when developed for different curricular areas.

- *Analysis* of each model points out two kinds of qualities:

  ○ typical features of the certain kind of writing,
  ○ structural and stylistic techniques enhancing the work.

- *Cross-references* to other parts of the book offer frequent opportunities for additional clarification.

ADVERTISING

Advertising, a lucrative, multimedia business, probably provides writers more opportunities for employment than virtually any other kind of writing except, perhaps, journalism. People who write for advertising agencies or for themselves on a free-lance basis write what is commonly referred to as *copy*. Advertising copy is designed to sell a product, create an image, or generate good will or a good company name. Because its purpose differs so radically from that of other kinds of writing, advertising copy, often called simply *ad copy*, has unique characteristics.

Characteristics

Catching the reader's eye, the listener's ear, and the television viewer's attention demands copy that relies on psychological impact as well as on powerful writing techniques. In general, advertising copy

- uses concise, powerful structures,
- frequently employs fragments, even single words or short phrases written as if they were sentences,
- relies on imagery, sound, and word play,
- relies heavily on psychological appeals,
- may be limited in number of words by space allowed in the overall layout or by seconds allowed in the commercial [*see also* SCRIPTS, KINDS: RADIO *and* SCRIPTS, KINDS: TELEVISION *later in* Part II],
- frequently relies on titles, headings, captions, or words and phrases otherwise appearing in different sized print to attract attention to main ideas,
- studiously avoids any excessive verbal structures,
- may include paragraphs which act as thought groups but not paragraphs in the traditional expository sense.

Process

Use the following steps to develop advertising copy.

PREWRITING

STEP 1. STUDYING THE PRODUCT AND THE IMAGE

In order to determine the saleable features of a product or a company image, a copywriter must learn about the product or the company. This is done by interviewing the client, product users, by using the product oneself, by reading about the product, and by talking with the people involved with the product's design or production. Sometimes the client will have an idea that he or she wants to pursue—a particular sales approach, campaign, or manner in which the product or company image should be promoted. At other times, the sales campaign will be the product of the advertising agency, perhaps in direct cooperation with the copywriter. If the copywriter is responsible for creating the idea, then he or she must spend ample time discussing, planning, thinking, rethinking, and evaluating whatever plan he or she and other members of the agency can create.

The brainstorming that takes place in these kinds of sessions helps you as a writer to focus on basic concepts the client may find satisfactory. By the time you finish learning about a product and the image that the client hopes to create, you should have a list of general ideas. Your list may include sales features, product features, or the company's versatile attributes.

In general, you are looking for distinctive features or qualities in this product or company that are unmatched by competitors. Ask yourself the following questions:

- How is this product or company different from others of its kind?
- What does this product or company claim to have that other products or companies of a similar nature do not claim?
- What benefits does this product or company offer its customers?

Refine your list to include answers to these questions.

STEP 2. DEFINING THE AUDIENCE

No matter how much you know about the product or the company, if you do not clearly identify the audience, your copy will fail. If you are selling a product to a housewife with five children, you will use an approach very different from one used to sell that same product to an executive assistant at a large corporation. Both persons may be convinced to use the product and may find it the most satisfactory product on the market to meet their needs, but their needs differ. Therefore, the advertising campaign for each audience will differ.

So, identify the audience. Will the copy be used in a mass-marketing campaign across the media? Will it be a direct-mail flier? Will it appear in a catalog mailed to selected potential customers? Find out from the client what to expect.

Once you have identified the audience, begin to think about what will influence it. Is the audience most interested in economy? In quality? In reputation? In creativity? In long-term usefulness? In short-term adaptation? In product availability? In extravagance? In the importance of using the "right" name?

When you can answer these questions, you understand your audience.

WRITING AND REVISING

STEP 3. DEVELOPING THE COPY

Writing successful ad copy relies on writing and revising in a kind of yo-yo pattern in which it is hard to separate the writing from the revising. Most copywriters admit that they struggle with every word and sometimes throw out every word and start over. In fact the whole prewriting/writing/revising process assumes a single back-and-forth pattern to the extent that most professional copywriters cannot define the separate steps of the process. To them, the process is a single step.

Since writing and revising follow the yo-yo effect in ad copywriting, use the following questions to guide you through the process:

- Is my copy concise, omitting any words or phrases not absolutely essential?

- Does my copy rely on very short sentences, perhaps even fragments of only a word or two?

- Have I omitted all long sentences?

- Have I arranged longer copy in paragraph form, not as a paragraph in expository writing, but as a group of words expressing a single thought?

- Have I used especially powerful nouns and verbs?

- Have I used the most precise word in every instance? See *Webster's New World Thesaurus* to help with word choice.

- Have I used effective word play?

- Have I relied on writing techniques which attract attention by creating imagery and sound: parallel structures, items in series, innuendo, figurative language, rhythm, or other similar devices? [*See* PARALLEL STRUCTURE, SERIES, IMAGERY, FIGURES OF SPEECH, *and* RHYTHM *in the Glossary.*]

- Have I created the most positive image possible for the product or the company without misrepresentation?

- Have I used the most effective psychological appeal to address the intended audience?

- If my copy is designed to fit a specific layout, will it, in fact, fit the space provided?

- Likewise, will the copy enhance the theme of the layout?

- If my copy is designed for a radio or television spot, can it be read—with expression—in the typical thirty-second or sixty-second time frame?

Make any revisions suggested by these questions. Remember, you should be able to answer an honest "yes" to each of them.

PROOFREADING

STEP 4. CHECKING THE FINAL PRODUCT

Once you have completed the yo-yo pattern of prewriting/writing/revising, check the copy for precision—in spelling, punctuation, and technicalities. While copywriters often break the traditional rules of grammar, mechanics, and usage, they do so with a purpose. They know that by breaking the rule, they can achieve a greater goal. Examine your work carefully for any violation of the rules. If you include such a violation, make sure it results in improved copy.

Strive for precise word choice. Consult *Webster's New World Thesaurus* for better synonyms or antonyms. Check spelling by consulting *Webster's New World Dictionary*.

Check punctuation to make sure it will not cause your reader to misread or misunderstand the copy. Because copywriters use punctuation more freely than do other professional writers, be certain that your use of punctuation helps the copy rather than clutters it with extraneous marks.

Finally, when you feel you have proofread accurately, make sure your copy reflects the format it ultimately will follow. If the copy is to be printed, emphasize its spacing and paragraphing and any other techniques which will help the typesetter arrange your copy in the most effective manner. If the copy is to appear as a radio or television spot, follow the special formats set out in SCRIPTS in Part II.

Sample Advertising Copy

A copywriter wrote the following as part of a corporate-image brochure. The brochure aims to sell the company's image rather than a specific product.

If you're working for your microcomputer, you're caught in the eternal trap.

Your microcomputer should work for you.

Do what you want done.

The way you want it done.

Without compromise.

With you in control.

That's the ultimate key to business microcomputer utilization.

The key to success.

MBI gives you that control.

Efficiently.

Quickly.

MBI. Masters working with masters.

Meeting your microcomputer business needs.

Talking success.

Analysis of the Sample Advertising Copy

The ad copy above sells a corporate image. The product is service. The audience is restricted to businesses which use microcomputers and need programs specifically designed to meet their needs. The ad copy includes these key ingredients:

- Short, punchy word groups, mostly fragments, hit hard the key ideas.
- The psychological appeal to business principles—efficiency, control, effectiveness, success—attract the intended audience.
- The arrangement of the copy makes it read quickly.
- The writing is tight, with no extraneous words or punctuation marks.
- Paragraphing follows thought groups, sometimes including only a word or two.

Following these general characteristics, you can begin developing ad copy. The best way to develop a thorough understanding of advertising, however, is to read printed ads and to watch and listen to commercials on television and radio. The experience will give you an understanding of the subtleties of the work.

ANALOGY

An analogy explains an idea by making a comparison. The analogy may explain how something works, how something looks, what something means. Usually, an analogy compares something hard to understand with something easy to understand. In short, an analogy serves to make the complex simple.

How does an analogy differ from a simple comparison? While the analogy explains the likenesses between two things, usually these two things do not belong to the same group. For instance, an analogy would not compare two kinds of apples. That is merely a comparison. [*See* COMPARISON and CONTRAST *in Part II.*] An analogy could, however, compare making long-term investments in the stock market with planting an apple orchard, showing how long each takes to develop into a profitable venture and how many dangers lurk along the way. Such an analogy compares something abstract or complicated (making long-term investments in the stock market) with something concrete or easy to understand (planting an apple orchard).

Characteristics

An analogy includes characteristics which set it apart from a simple comparison. A good analogy

- presents an extended comparison of two things in different classes,

- differs from a simple comparison which serves only to clarify relationships between or among items in the same class,

- compares the complicated with the simple, the unfamiliar with the familiar,

- functions to explain or clarify a complicated or unfamiliar item or idea,

- resembles a metaphor but is extended and serves to explain or to clarify,

- can add drama, humor, and/or interest to an explanation,

- shows imagination on the part of the writer,

- stimulates the readers' imagination and interest.

Process

The following steps will help you develop a successful analogy.

PREWRITING

STEP 1. CHOOSING A TOPIC

In order to select a suitable topic for an analogy, think of a comparison that will allow you to use a familiar, everyday concept to explain the more complicated concept. Start by naming the complicated concept you have been asked to explain. Then, by brainstorming, perhaps with a fellow student, think of situations or ideas in other, probably unrelated, fields that may make a suitable comparison. [*See* PREWRITING *in Part I for additional suggestions.*]

As you search for comparisons, remember that an analogy is simply an aid to explain or clarify. Consider it a word game that allows you to help your readers use their imaginations to deal with a difficult concept.

Example: You must explain how stalactites form. You imagine several possibilities for an analogy:

- Stalactites grow from a substance like molten lava.

- Stalactites form the way an ice-cream machine fills cones.

- Stalactites form the way icicles form.

- Water dripping from a cave ceiling is like sap dripping from a tree, both forming columns of hardened materials.

- Stalactites grow longer the same way a blue wasp's nest grows longer.

Write out several similar comparisons for your own topic. As you think of possible topics for an analogy, keep in mind two suggestions:

- Avoid choosing a comparison that breaks down after only a brief correlation. In order to choose an effective subject for your analogy, you need at least three points of comparison. As a result, you may have to try several possible topics. If you can find only one or two comparisons, you probably need a better topic for the analogy.

- At the other extreme, avoid searching for a comparison that will never break down. Remember, the comparison set out in an analogy will, by its very nature, eventually break down. The purpose of the analogy is to offer an explanation; it will not withstand critical, logical evaluation in an argument. (Thus, since the comparisons presented in an analogy will eventually break down, you leave yourself open for critical attack if you base an argument on an analogy.) On the other hand, using an analogy in any kind of composition, including an argumentative one, can clarify by explaining an abstract idea or complicated process. Simply recognize its limits.

On the basis of these two suggestions, evaluate the comparisons you developed. Select the one which seems most suitable.

STEP 2. PLANNING THE COMPARISONS

Make a parallel set of lists, one for each of the two items the analogy will compare. List every basis for comparison you can find. Use the following example to help you create your lists:

Formation of Stalactites	Formation of Icicles
from ceiling of cave	from eaves of house
residue	freezing
cause of "freezing"	cause of freezing
speed of drip	speed of drip

STEP 3. CHOOSING VOCABULARY

Look for words that will describe both items. Using a parallel vocabulary will effectively and subtly extend the comparison, creating a more imaginative and interesting analogy. Refer to *Webster's New World Thesaurus* for effective synonyms and antonyms.

For example, in the comparison above, some words common to both topics come to mind:

freezing	dripping	ceiling
droplets	icicles	formations
water	running	grow
growth	form	trickle

We can use the words to talk about the growth of both stalactites and icicles. Using a parallel vocabulary will enhance the analogy.

STEP 4. ORGANIZING AND CONSIDERING THE POSSIBLE PLANS

Arrange the comparisons in logical order. Probably you will choose one of the following:

If you are explaining how something works, organize the analogy in chronological order. Let the readers follow the process from beginning to end. [*See* CHRONOLOGICAL ORDER *in the Glossary.*]

On the other hand, if you are trying to explain an idea or define an abstract term, organize the analogy in order of importance, either from the most to the least obvious comparison or from the most to the least important. [*See* ORDERS OF IMPORTANCE *in the Glossary.*]

Using the list you developed in Step 2, arrange the points of comparison in the most suitable order for your subject and your purpose.

STEP 5. ORGANIZING AND PLANNING THE WHOLE

Whether the parts are organized chronologically or by order of importance, the entire analogy must take on either a part-by-part or whole-by-whole organization. The usual pattern is to explain the familiar or the easy-to-understand first, followed by the unfamiliar, complicated, difficult-to-understand. Consider each of the methods of organization:

Part-by-part organization requires the writer to explain a single point or part of the comparison, first for one topic of the analogy and then for the other topic. Next the writer explains the second point, or part, of the comparison for each topic of the analogy; and so on until he completes the analogy.

By contrast, **whole-by-whole organization** allows the writer to explain all points of one topic of the analogy and then all points of the other topic. The following diagram best illustrates the two patterns:

Part-by-part organization:

Point 1
  Topic A
  Topic B
Point 2
  Topic A
  Topic B
Point 3
  Topic A
  Topic B

Whole-by-whole organization:

Topic A
  Point 1
  Point 2
  Point 3
Topic B
  Point 1
  Point 2
  Point 3

Now, let's put part-by-part and whole-by-whole organization together with chronological order or one of the orders of importance discussed in Step 4.

First, consider part-by-part organization. If it is also organized chronologically, then Point 1 will come first in time. Both Topic A and Topic B will be included in Point 1. Following will be Point 2, the second item in time order, and so on.

Consider a chronological, part-by-part analogy to compare the stock-market index to a roller-coaster ride:

Point 1: January
  Topic A: roller-coaster ride
  Topic B: stock-market
    index
Point 2: June
  Topic A: roller-coaster ride
  Topic B: stock-market
    index
Point 3: December
  Topic A: roller-coaster ride
  Topic B: stock-market
    index

If the part-by-part analogy is organized by order of importance, Point 1 will represent the item of greatest importance.

Now consider the whole-by-whole organization. If the whole-by-whole analogy is also organized chronologically, then again Point 1, this time in Topic A, will be the first item to appear in time. Upon completion of Topic A, the pattern will repeat for Topic B.

A chronological whole-by-whole analogy comparing the stock-market index for the past twelve months to a roller-coaster ride might read:

Topic A: roller-coaster ride
  Point 1: beginning of
    ride—thrills
  Point 2: middle of ride—chills
  Point 3: end of ride—spills
Topic B: stock-market index
  Point 1: January—
    beginning of ride
  Point 2: June—middle of
    ride
  Point 3: December—end of
    ride

Similarly, if the analogy is organized by order of importance, Point 1 will still be the item of greatest importance. The pattern will repeat itself for Topic B.

With these options in mind, choose the organizational pattern that will best suit your topic and purpose. You should also consider which organizational pattern will have the greatest impact on your audience. Do not hesitate to try several patterns until you find the one that works best.

WRITING

STEP 6. IMPLEMENTING THE PLAN

With the preparation and planning carefully done, you are ready to prepare the first draft of your analogy. The following suggestions may help:

- Begin your composition with a topic sentence or thesis sentence that states the analogy. [*See the prewriting activities in* PARAGRAPHS, KINDS: AS AN INDEPENDENT UNIT *in Part II for a thorough discussion of topic sentences. See the prewriting activities in* THEME *in Part II for a thorough explanation of thesis sentences.*]

- Using the organizational plan selected in Step 5 above, develop the analogy, maintaining unity within each division of the paper. [*See* REVISING: SAMPLE REVISION FOR UNITY *in Part I.*]

- Use details and vocabulary that help readers follow subtle parts of the analogy as well as the more obvious stated parts. [*See* SPECIFIC DETAIL *in the Glossary for a quick reference, and see* REVISING: SAMPLE REVISION FOR SPECIFIC DETAIL *in Part I for explanations and examples.*]

- Aim for good sentence variety and adequate emphasis. [*See* REVISING: SAMPLE REVISION FOR SENTENCE VARIETY *and* REVISING: SAMPLE REVISION FOR EMPHASIS *in Part I for examples.*]

- Make sure the parallels are adequately developed and clarified by transitions so that readers follow a smooth development. [*See* REVISING: SAMPLE REVISION FOR TRANSITION *in Part I.*]

- Conclude with a summary or clincher that ties together the analogy. [*See* CONCLUSION *in the Glossary.*]

REVISING

STEP 7. CHECKING THE CONTENT

As you revise your first draft, ask yourself these questions to guide possible rewrites:

- Does my topic sentence (or thesis statement for a theme) clearly state the analogy?

- Does the topic sentence (or thesis statement) appear at or near the beginning of my paper?

- Does the organizational pattern follow throughout the analogy so readers are not confused?

- Are transitions sufficient to develop smooth parallels between the two topics being compared? [*See* REVISING: SAMPLE REVISION FOR TRANSITION *in Part I.*]

- Do the details provide sufficient comparison?

- Do all the details support the topic so that I have maintained unity throughout the paper? [*See* REVISING: SAMPLE REVISION FOR UNITY *in Part I.*]
- Is the vocabulary suitable for the analogy and for the audience?
- Have I used strong nouns and verbs and avoided flowery modifiers? Refer to *Webster's New World Thesaurus* for help with precise word choice.
- Are sentences varied in both length and structure and are they appropriate for both the subject and the audience?
- Have I used the appropriate tone and mood for the topic? [*See* TONE and MOOD *in the Glossary.*]

- Does the paper conclude effectively?

See also REVISING in Part I for additional suggestions for the general process.

PROOFREADING

STEP 8.   CHECKING THE DETAILS

When you have completed the revising process, prepare the final draft. Then, check it for punctuation, grammar, mechanics, and usage. Eliminate spelling errors by referring to *Webster's New World Dictionary*.

A Note about the Samples: The following samples illustrate part-by-part and whole-by-whole organization; chronological order and order of importance, and fully developed paragraphs and an analogy used to introduce a longer paper.

─────────────── **Sample for English** ───────────────

Students in an English class were asked to explain how people learn to write well and how they recognize when their writing is effective. One student decided that the abstract explanation of good writing is elusive, so he choose to develop his explanation by means of an analogy:

Writing, The Baker's Plan

Writing well is like baking well. Recipes for each abound; but the true professionals, the ones who make their living at their craft, rely on their experience and a kind of sixth sense to alter the recipes. The baker does more than mix flour, eggs, shortening, and leavening; he uses his senses—sight, taste, and touch— to get the proportions right. So the writer does more than mix nouns, verbs, modifiers, and punctuation marks; he uses his senses—sight, sound, and touch—to get the emphasis right. Each strives for the right consistency, the right texture, the right effect, perhaps with just a touch of the dramatic, a spice, an herb, a well-turned phrase. Each acknowledges that timing is all, timing the rising and baking, timing the sentence and the conclusion. In the end, each achieves the palatable product.

Analysis of the Sample for English

The paragraph above illustrates the use of an analogy to explain an abstract idea (*writing well*) in terms of a concrete, more familiar, idea (*baking well*). Note the following:

- The paragraph begins with a topic sentence that states the analogy.
- The part-by-part organization allows readers to follow the analogy in chronological arrangement from start to end.
- Each point about the baking reminds readers of a similar point in writing: *a touch of the dramatic, a spice, an herb, a turn of phrase.*
- The vocabulary suggests subtle comparisons and conjures elements shared by the two subjects: *consistency, texture, effect, the dramatic*—all words applicable either to baking or writing.
- The conclusion uses *palatable* denotatively in the sense of *taste*, and connotatively, in the sense of *acceptability*. The sense of taste, of course, becomes one not just of physical but also of judgmental, esthetic taste.

One can argue, of course, that extending the comparison much more will cause it to break down. Writing, after all, is more difficult than baking. Remember, however, that the analogy serves only to explain or clarify, not to define or defend. All analogies, carried too far, will ultimately break down. Such is their character.

Sample for Social Sciences

While studying a unit in economics, students concentrated on the law of supply and demand and its effect on the economy. As part of an assignment, they were asked to explain how the law works. One student decided, as a supplement to more specific examples, to include an analogy that would not only indicate her thorough understanding of the principle but also heighten excitement in what may otherwise be only an average paper. Here is the analogy she used:

Seesaw Economy

The effect on prices of the law of supply and demand is somewhat like the effect of two children on a seesaw. When one child is down and gives a strong push to go up, the other child must necessarily come down. With careful, light pushes and mutual attention to balance, however, the two children can stop the seesaw parallel to the ground. Only a slight movement on the part of either child will send the seesaw pivoting on its fulcrum, but the balance is possible. So it is with supply and demand. If demand is up and supply is down, the prices soar. A big push from supply, however, may soon send the supply end of the seesaw well above demand. Prices plummet. The market, the fulcrum, determines the rise and fall. Finally, when the perfect balance exists between supply and demand, then prices, too, level, a point which economists call equilibrium.

Analysis of the Sample for Social Sciences

This comparison of the law of supply and demand with children on a seesaw illustrates most of the principles of a good analogy. Think about the following points:

- The topic sentence establishes the analogy.
- The paragraph uses the whole-by-whole method of organization, from the most important comparison to the least. By first showing the children on the seesaw and allowing them to balance themselves, the writer prepares the reader to visualize the ups and downs of supply and demand.
- While shared vocabulary is somewhat limited in these two comparisons, the final use of the word *level* does draw strength from the earlier *parallel*. The common use of *push* for both topics of the comparison further enhances the analogy on a less obvious plane.
- Sentence variety and vocabulary suit subject, analogy, and audience.
- Transitions help the reader move smoothly from one topic to the other.
- Transitions like *when, however, so it is with*, and *finally* nudge the reader to follow the organizational plan.

True, the analogy will break down with further examination. The law of supply and demand includes more complicated principles than does a simple seesaw. For purposes of basic explanation, though, the analogy works. Remember, the writer planned the analogy only as an introduction to a longer assignment which will include specific details and further examples. Certainly the analogy functions well to introduce a complicated discussion of an abstract subject.

─────────────── **Sample for Science** ───────────────

After studying the creation of caves and the formations in them, students were asked to write a paragraph explaining how stalactites form. One student decided to explain the process by means of an analogy, comparing the formation of stalactites to that of icicles.

Icicles of Rock

Stalactites form in caves much the way icicles form from the eaves of houses. When sunshine melts the snow on the roof, water begins dripping. Because the air temperature is well below freezing, however, the droplets turn to ice. As additional droplets form and refreeze on their way to running the course of the preceding droplets, the icicle begins to form. During the warmest times of the day, the icicle lengthens: the droplets trickle faster and thus travel farther before they refreeze. During cooler times, the icicle grows larger at its base, the droplets running more slowly and freezing quickly. Each tiny droplet, however, adds to the size, either to the length or the circumference, of the growing icicle. So it is with stalactites, one of the carbonate speleothems. As rainwater seeps through the ground, the carbonic acid in the rainwater dissolves the limestone, forming calcium carbonate. Trickling into caves where no sandstone cap blocks their path, the droplets fall from the cave roof to the floor. As each droplet falls, a tiny deposit remains, "frozen" to the ceiling. What causes the "freezing?" The water loses carbon dioxide to the cave air, rendering the water less acidic. For this and other reasons, the water cannot retain as much calcium carbonate; therefore, some calcium carbonate precipitates, leaving minute deposits on what is to become a stalactite. The faster the drip, the longer the stalactite grows, becoming more conical. As a result, the deposits "freeze" into colorful stone-like icicles, forming one cubic inch of stalactite in about a hundred years.

Analysis of the Sample for Science

The analogy above permits the explanation of a relatively complicated process by means of an everyday phenomenon. The following specific principles make the analogy effective:

- The topic sentence announces the analogy.
- The organization is whole-by-whole, with the discussion of the familiar, the icicle, coming first, followed by the discussion of the more complex, the stalactite.
- Chronological order appears in both topics.
- The vocabulary allows the repetition of the words *trickle* and *freeze*, but the scientific section employs the use of quotation marks around *freeze* to emphasize its uncommon (in this case, unscientific) use.
- Other words enhance the subtle comparisons in the analogy: *eaves* and *roof* both suggest structures from which the formations hang; *air* affects both formations; and, since both topics relate to water, words common to a discussion of water aid the analogy.
- Transitions like *because, however, as, during, so it is, as a result, similar to,* and *like* combined with the repetition of key words organize and define relationships.
- The conclusion, which in this paragraph merely makes a final statement, functions as a clincher for the comparison.

Sample for Business

As part of a business class, students were asked to describe what makes a good manager. Because being a good manager requires many abstract qualities, one student decided to develop an analogy comparing a good manager with a good gardener.

The Gardner in the Office

A good manager is like a good gardener. Each begins by looking at the conditions under which he or she must work. Given a specific climate and specific working conditions, each must adjust. Within the given environment, however, both the manager and the gardener can choose the right commodities: the right personnel, the right plants. Because not all people and all plants react the same to the environment, however, a good manager as well as a good gardener will attend to the differences. Some people work well under pressure; others do not. Some plants produce well in partial shade; others do not. Nurturing people as well as plants can improve production. Even when harvest time comes, the gardener knows to expect a higher yield from a tomato plant than from a corn stalk; but knowing that, he planted more corn than he did tomatoes. Likewise, the manager knows to expect a different yield from people with different responsibilities; so she hires accordingly. Finally, when the crops are sold, the gardener does not measure each bean's worth; he considers the total garden's yield. So, the manager measures the department's worth. Granted, though, if the eggplant does not produce anything, the gardener will not replant it next year; and if a worker does not produce, the manager must consider eliminating that employee. If, on the other hand, the gardener feels he should have tended the eggplant more carefully, sprayed it for insects, watered it, or fertilized it, then he may consider replanting, hoping that with better care, the eggplant will be a better producer. Likewise, the good manager may realize she has not tended the worker as much as she might, talking with him about problems, offering suggestions for improved output, or altering the worker's responsibilities. She may give the worker another opportunity. So, managers, like gardeners, reap what they sow.

Analysis of the Sample for Business

By using an analogy to talk about good management, the writer discusses characteristics without belaboring the point. The creative approach adds interest to the subject. On the other hand, however, the analogy simplifies, perhaps oversimplifies, the concept of manager, a fact which may be offensive for some assignments. Since the purpose of an analogy, however, is to simplify in order to explain or clarify, a writer must accept the possibility of oversimplification.

Consider these additional points which make the analogy above a suitable one:

- The topic sentence clarifies the analogy.
- The part-by-part organization allows the writer to discuss each point in terms of both the manager and the gardener.
- The generally chronological order moves from planting to harvesting.
- The vocabulary allows the writer to further the analogy by discussing such mutual ideas as working conditions, attending, production, yields, reaping, and sowing.
- Transitions help the reader follow the development of the analogy, especially words like *both, each,* and *likewise,* as well as the repetition of the key words.
- The concluding sentence ties together the two subjects and uses an adage to complete the comparison.

——————— Sample for Vocational Education ———————

In a woodworking class, students were asked to explain how to select a piece of lumber. The following analogy, which functions as an introduction, allows the writer to make some important points about wood selection:

Choices

Choosing the right piece of wood for a project is like choosing a friend. Although a person may not choose the same friend for a fishing buddy that he does for a date at the homecoming dance, he usually has a reason for selecting the friend he does. For instance, a fisherman may prefer the companionship of another experienced fisherman, but fishing ability has nothing to do with dancing ability. So it is with selecting a piece of wood for a project. A piece of bird's eye maple may be desirable for a gunstock but impractical for a bookcase. The woodworker chooses lumber for its ability to hold weight, resist splitting or warping, finish well, and show good grain.

Analysis of the Sample for Vocational Education

The analogy above, which compares selecting wood to selecting friends, allows the writer to make a significant point: one selects different kinds of lumber for different projects. Think about the following characteristics as they appear in the model:

- The topic sentence establishes the analogy.
- Organized whole by whole, the analogy first discusses the familiar subject, friends, and then the less familiar subject, choosing the right lumber.
- The analogy serves as an introduction for a longer paper.

Sample for Mathematics

Math students were asked to compare learning mathematics to some other real-life situation. One student wrote the following:

Math as a Box of Tools

A thorough knowledge of mathematics is like a full box of mechanic's tools. If you have all the tools—like the knowledge of fractions, percentages, ratios, and algebraic operations—you are equipped to do any job that comes along, whether that job is determining the trajectory of the ball in a football game, gas mileage for an automobile, the power requirements for a piece of machinery, the interest earned on a bank account, the ratio of insecticide to water in a spray mix, or the cost of a long-term loan. The tools not only enable the user to cope with daily problems, they also appreciate in value with increased understanding and experience on the part of the mechanic.

Analysis of the Sample for Mathematics

The following characteristics appear in the analogy above:

- The first sentence states the analogy.
- The remainder of the paragraph gives examples to support the analogy, and the examples illustrate real-life situations.
- The final sentence suggests the present and increasing value of the mathematics "tools."
- This model paragraph represents an excellent journal or learning log entry. (*See* JOURNAL *later in Part II.*)

The above models and their analyses should help you develop an analogy suitable to whatever situation you confront. You may choose to use an analogy only as an introduction, only as a single point in a longer paper, or as a paper in itself. In any case, you will follow the same developmental process set out above.

ANALYSIS

An analysis paper examines or interprets. The writer may discuss the various parts of something to show their relationship to a whole, or he may discuss the results of something to show benefits, effects, or causes. Because *analysis* is such a broad term, this book examines several kinds of analyses. The list below will direct you to the specific section most helpful for your purpose.

You may be preparing an analysis which:

- examines the cause of a condition or situation,
- interprets the effects of a condition or situation,
- analyzes a problem,
- explains how a condition or situation came into existence.

[*If so, see* CAUSE AND EFFECT, *elsewhere in Part II.*]

You may be preparing an analysis which:

- interprets a piece of literature,
- evaluates the results of a literary technique or condition.

[*If so, see* LITERARY ANALYSES, *elsewhere in Part II.*]

You may be preparing an analysis which:

- analyzes how to do something,
- discusses how something was done,
- examines the meaning, implication, or reason for a condition or situation.

[*If so, see* PROCESS ANALYSIS *and* DESCRIPTION *elsewhere in Part II.*]

ANNOUNCEMENT

An announcement serves to let people know about significant events: meetings, policy changes, new information, forthcoming appearances. Company representatives make announcements to the media; political candidates make announcements to their constituents; teachers make announcements to their classes; organization presidents make announcements to their members; radio broadcasters make announcements to their listeners. Through announcements, we learn about everything from upcoming meetings to weather conditions, from promotions to layoffs, from war to peace. Announcements have a significant impact on most people's lives. As a result, it is mandatory that announcements be clear, complete, and accurate.

Characteristics

A good announcement should

- give all the pertinent details: who, what, why, when, where, and how,
- use clear, simple language,
- be complete but concise,
- offer an explanation for unusual or unexpected events.

Process

Use the following plan to prepare an announcement:

PREWRITING

STEP 1. GETTING THE BASIC INFORMATION

On separate lines, list the pertinent questions to be answered by the announcement: who? what? why? when? where? and how? Then, answer each of the questions in the simplest, most direct way you can.

STEP 2. ORGANIZING THE DETAILS

Ordinarily an announcement is so brief that organization is relatively unimportant. Sometimes, however, the length or content suggests a particular organization:

- If the announcement is lengthy, you can use the inverted pyramid organization, listing all the important ideas first (who, what, why, when, where, and how), adding explanatory notes later. [See INVERTED PYRAMID ORGANIZATION in the Glossary.]
- Sometimes, the explanation—the why—must precede the pertinent

items simply because the reader or listener has no reason to react unless he hears the explanation. For instance, an announcement to attend a meeting at a certain time and place will get little or no reaction if it fails to attract the attention of its intended audience. Sometimes, then, the *why?* and the *who?* must precede the other essential details.

Plan the organization of your announcement to meet the needs of the situation.

WRITING

STEP 3. DEVELOPING THE FIRST DRAFT

Combine all the information from the lists into good sentences. Group similar kinds of information together into sentences or put related ideas together into one sentence. Develop sentences which put main ideas in main clauses and thus emphasize your main ideas. [*See* REVISING: SAMPLE REVISION FOR EMPHASIS *in Part I.*]

REVISING

STEP 4. CHECKING CONTENT

Check for completeness. Ask yourself these questions:

- Have I included all the details from my list?
- Have I added explanations where necessary?
- Have I anticipated the reader's or listener's questions and answered them?

Revise so that you can answer "yes" to the above questions.

Then, read the completed announcement aloud to check for clarity. As you read, think about these possible problems:

- Are the sentences too long and rambling for clear reading or listening? Or have I written short, clear sentences?
- Do all of the sentences sound alike and create a monotonous reading? Or have I created variety in the sentence structure to emphasize main ideas?
- Are some details buried in a hodgepodge of words? Or have I used an uncluttered style so that readers or listeners will catch all the details?

Tighten your message until it is as concise as possible while still maintaining clarity. [*See* REVISING: SAMPLE REVISION FOR WORDINESS *in Part I.*]

Revise until you can honestly answer "yes" to the second question in each of the three items above.

As a final check, count the words in each sentence. Do you have sentences with more than fifteen or twenty words? If so, shorten them. Put the main ideas in the main clauses and the supporting ideas in subordinate clauses. [*See* REVISING: SAMPLE REVISION FOR EMPHASIS *in Part I.*]

Finally, have someone unfamiliar with the situation read the announcement and react to it. Is there anything missing that readers or listeners need to know? Ask the pertinent questions (who, what, why, when, where, and how) of your reader. Are the answers obvious?

Revise as necessary for clarity, completeness, and accuracy.

PROOFREADING

STEP 5. TAKING A CRITICAL LOOK

Double check your accuracy. Carefully note every detail and ask yourself basic questions:

- Are dates, both days of the week and days of the month, accurate?

- Are times accurate, indicating Central Standard Time, Eastern Time, Pacific Daylight Time, etc?

- Are places clearly identified, including street addresses or simple directions for finding a location?

- Are names included where necessary, and are these people identified by title as well?

- Are other details accurate?

———— Sample Announcement ————

The chairman of the board of a local company released the following announcement to the news media.

News Release

On June 10, Karson Manufacturing will break ground for a $6 million expansion. Lamont Karson, chairman of the board, announced the expansion will provide additional employment for 230 workers by late next year. The addition to their present location will allow the company to increase production of its current stamping operation. Increased sales and anticipated additional increases over the next year warrant the expansion, and current profits will help finance the addition. The information was made public at today's stockholders' meeting.

Analysis of the Sample Announcement

Here is a critical look at the sample announcement above:

- It answers the pertinent questions: who (*Lamont Karson, chairman of the board*), what (*announced a $6 million expansion of Karson Manufacturing*), why (*because of increased sales and anticipation of additional increases*), when (*breaking ground within six weeks and in operation late next year*), where (*at their present location*), and how (*by using current profits for expansion*).

- We have to assume spelling is accurate and titles are correct, and other matters appear to be accurate.
- The sentences are short, none more than twenty words. The main ideas appear in the main clauses.
- While there may be further questions, like what kinds of profits did the company show and how long has the expansion project been in the planning stages, the purpose of the announcement is fulfilled. Additional information may well appear in a news article, but the announcement is complete as it is. [*For comparison, see* NEWS ARTICLE *elsewhere in Part II which develops the topic of the sample announcement above into a full-length article.*] A comparison of the two samples will help you better understand how to maintain brevity in an announcement.

ARGUMENT

To present an argument is to persuade someone to agree with you. An argument gives reasons. [*If you are writing a paper that will simply express an opinion, see* OPINION *elsewhere in Part II. If the purpose of your paper is to persuade readers to follow a certain course of action see* PERSUASION *elsewhere in Part II.*]

AUTOBIOGRAPHY

By definition, an autobiography is the story of the writer's life. Unlike a biography, in which a writer researches and reports on someone else's life, the autobiography reveals what the writer chooses to tell about himself. An autobiography, however, unless it is book length, does not tell about the writer's life from birth to present; rather, it focuses on some significant event, object, or person that reveals something important about the writer. An autobiographical sketch may be as short as a paragraph or as long as a book. Whatever its length, however, it should read like a good piece of nonfiction, even a good short story, but certainly not like a list of events.

Characteristics

Most commonly, an autobiography includes a rather definite set of characteristics. An autobiography

- reveals an understanding of one or more personality traits of the writer,

- limits itself, unless of book length, to describing a particular event, object, or person that has influenced the writer,

- explains, perhaps indirectly, the effect or result of the influence [see CAUSE AND EFFECT in Part II],

- reads almost like fiction, certainly maintains interest and maybe even provokes,

- may follow the same characteristics as a narrative [see NARRATION in Part II],

- often includes many characteristics of good fiction: setting, plot, characters, flashback, figurative language, symbolism, etc. [see SHORT STORY in Part II and SETTING, PLOT, CHARACTERIZATION, FLASHBACK, FIGURES OF SPEECH, and SYMBOL in the Glossary],

- includes dialogue as necessary or as it enhances the telling of the story [see DIALOGUE in Part II],

- permits writer's style to offer additional subtle self-revelations.

Process

For the sake of explaining the writing process, we will assume here that you are developing a multi-paragraph autobiography. Use the following steps to plan and develop your paper.

PREWRITING

STEP 1. THINKING ABOUT THE SUBJECT

Jot down perhaps a dozen questions about yourself. The questions may refer to your reactions, your emotions, your behavior. Use questions which ask about particular situations:

- Why did I say angry things to my mother last evening?
- Why did I pass the test I thought I'd failed?
- Why do I hate snow?
- Why am I always afraid I'll be late for class, work, or appointments?

If you are developing the autobiography for a specific audience, you may want to gear your questions toward a particular subject area. For instance, if you are writing for a group of fellow youth-group members, you may list such questions as these:

- Why do I need the support of my peers when I make a decision?
- Why am I usually sitting on the fringes of the group, participating mentally but not physically?

STEP 2. NARROWING THE SUBJECT

Look at your list and choose one question which seems the most interesting to you. Do not concern yourself with whether or not the question is important to the world, only whether or not it is interesting enough that you want to explore the possible answers.

When you have selected the one question which seems most interesting to you, list a half dozen or so possible answers. Be open-minded and creative in your approach, ruling out no option. Consider objects, events, and people that may have influenced your answer.

Now select one answer that seems most accurate.

POSSIBLE PITFALL: The inexperienced writer almost invariably attempts to cover too much material in one simple autobiographical sketch.

To avoid that possible pitfall, make sure that you select only *one* of the questions about which to develop your autobiography. If, during the course of developing the sketch, you feel your question is too narrow, you may choose to broaden it. Before you do so, however, you should consider first whether or not you have included sufficient details in responding to the chosen question.

In any case, do not expand the concept by adding another question. That will merely confuse both the issue and the readers and ultimately destroy the organization.

STEP 3. CHOOSING THE ORGANIZATIONAL PLAN

The organization of an autobiography is usually either chronological or cause and effect. Of the two options explained below, select the organization most effective for your purpose.

Chronological

The chronological organization allows the writer to present an autobiography much the way he would present a narrative. [*See* NARRATION *in Part II.*] The paper begins at the beginning, telling the story in a straightforward manner. The writer takes the reader through a series of events directly toward the conclusion that offers some revelation about the writer's actions, behavior, or beliefs. A more sophisticated narrative may also include a flashback [*see* FLASHBACK *in the Glossary*], a technique which allows the author to skip back in time to offer insight on a current situation.

Cause and Effect

The cause-effect organization [*see* CAUSE AND EFFECT *later in Part II*] forces the writer to deal more specifically with events, situations, objects or people and how they affected reactions, behaviors, beliefs. In this case, the writer may use one of two approaches:

- In one approach, he may begin with the effect and show how it came to be. For instance, he may begin his autobiography by admitting that he always feels a kind of nagging terror when he drives across the two-mile-long suspension bridge near his home. Readers are left with the expectation that an explanation will follow.

The remainder of the autobiography will relate information about some event, situation, object, or person that explains the long-term nagging terror.

- In the second approach, the writer may reverse the process and choose to relate information about some event, situation, object, or person, allowing the reader to follow in suspense. The suspense comes from the expectation that what is being related will lead to some insight about the writer.

Choose the organization most effective for your purpose.

WRITING
STEP 4.   FOLLOWING THE PLAN

Develop your autobiographical sketch according to the plan you selected in Step 3 above. Include details that will allow readers to feel what you have felt, see what you have seen, think what you have thought. In other words, use good description to involve readers in your own experiences. [*See* DESCRIPTION *elsewhere in Part II and* REVISING: SAMPLE REVISION FOR SPECIFIC DETAIL *in Part I.*]

Use whatever techniques of good fiction seem appropriate for your sketch. [*See* SHORT STORY *in Part II.*]

REVISING
STEP 5.   IMPROVING THE CONTENT

When you have finished the first draft of your autobiographical sketch, read it for content. Ask yourself these questions to determine if certain parts may benefit from revision:

- Does my introduction grab the reader's attention in the same manner as a good short story?

- Does the introduction help the reader focus on the narrowed subject of the sketch, a particular event, object, or person that has influenced me?

- Does the sketch read almost like fiction, maintaining interest, even suspense, while offering nonfiction details?

- Will dialogue, or additional dialogue, make the sketch more readable, more real, more human?

- When the reader finishes the sketch, will he or she understand why or how the event, object, or person influenced me?

- Does the sketch conclude or merely quit? Does an effective clincher tie together the contents? [*See* CONCLUSION *in the Glossary.*]

- Have I used a personal style which offers additional insight for the reader?

- Have I varied my sentences, both by length and by structure? [*See* REVISING: SAMPLE REVISION FOR SENTENCE VARIETY *in Part I.*]

- Have I maintained effective emphasis? [*See* REVISING: SAMPLE REVISION FOR EMPHASIS *in Part I; see also* REVISING *in Part I for additional suggestions for general revision.*]

PROOFREADING

STEP 6. CHECKING THE DETAILS

Check for mechanics, grammar and usage. If you have used dialogue, be sure to double-check punctuation and paragraphing of the quotations. [*See* PARAGRAPHS, KINDS: IN DIALOGUE *in Part II.*]

Check word choice and spelling. See *Webster's New World Thesaurus* and *Webster's New World Dictionary.*

Sample Autobiography

Following the steps above, the writer has prepared the suggested list of questions, examined them and chosen the following question on which to base her autobiography: Why did I enjoy being alone in a crowd? Notice that the question itself never appears in the autobiography, but the answer is obvious by the end of the sketch.

Alone in a Crowd

Last year, just prior to our community's annual Fall Festival, the small weekly newspaper that I work for gave me what I thought was the ideal assignment. I was to spend as much time as possible during the week-long festivities capturing those so-called human interest photographs. My mind reeled. The Fall Festival! A whole week to select the choicest foods from the hundreds of booths! A whole week to see over 800,000 people who would flock to the festival! A whole week to see friends I hadn't seen since last year's festival! I'd stuff myself with all the fried, sugared, salted junk until I was miserable; and in the process, I'd catch up on all the gossip. And I'd get paid for doing it. What a life!

The first afternoon, camera in hand and camera bag slung across my left shoulder, I headed toward the kiddie rides. Children, joyous and uninhibited, always provide great human interest shots; these proved no different. The toddler in the pink sweat suit, terrified by the merry-go-round, didn't hesitate to scream her fears. A great picture, her grubby fist knuckling a tear-stained face. The pint-sized cowboy in boots and ten-gallon hat obviously found riding the bumper cars every bit as good as riding the range. Another great picture, her hat flopping over her eyes after a resounding bump from behind.

That's when Alan showed up. "Hey, look at you in the kiddie park! Fancy meeting you here. What's up?" Alan was chaperoning his kid sister for a few hours, looking for his own entertainment. Apparently I was it. But then, wasn't I looking forward to meeting old friends?

"Hi, Alan. Gosh, long time no see. What are you doing these days?" For some reason I didn't care how he answered, or if he answered. Frankly, I don't remember what he said. Fortunately, his sister was taking her turn in the bumper cars, so I managed to escape without his following me.

From the kiddie rides, I hit the first block of food booths. The smell intoxicated me. Bratwurst, fudge, elephant ears, kuchen, pizza, apple cider—anything to tempt the taste buds. Oh, but just look at the people queued up to buy whatever tidbit rewarded them at the end of the long line! Changing to a 105 mm lense to photograph them unaware, I stood back, watching. There! The woman with a string of caramel draped at least a foot from her lips to the caramel apple she was eating. Then that guy with the sauerkraut dangling from the corner of his mouth. And that kid taking his first bite from that wonderfully buttery cinnamon sugared elephant ear—elephant ear from ear to ear! What shots!

"Hey, Hotshot, what's with the camera bit when there's all this wonderful food?"

I turned to the voice I recognized, tempted to take Sherry's picture, too. Indeed, she would have made quite a picture, a cup of apple cider wedged in the crook of her left arm, a stacked ham sandwich, half eaten, in her left hand, and a bag of three French waffles swinging from her right hand.

"Hey, Hotshot, yourself," I responded, trying to sound casual. "Just on assignment, that's all. What's with the horde of food? You on a diet?" I tried to be funny, an effort to cover up my tension. Why was I frustrated? Sherry, of all people. One of my best friends. We should share a few jokes, revel in our mutual joy of finding each other at the festival, and head out to have a great evening together.

I couldn't wait to get away.

So that day melted into the following ones. By week's end, I had taken twelve rolls of film and cranked out some exciting candid shots. The editor's rare moment of praise added a satisfied glow to the week's work. Lurking in the shadows, though, was something less than a glow. It gnawed and irritated, like a stone in a shoe. I'd spent the week at the festival, seldom eating and rarely speaking to anyone. I had resented any intrusion—for that's the way I came to view it—on my privacy. I had detached myself from the crowd, watched the crowd as individuals, studied their expressions, their mannerisms, absorbed in and by the sensations. Alone in the crowd. And I had grown.

Analysis of the Sample Autobiography

The autobiography above attempts to answer why the writer enjoyed being alone in a crowd. Can you, in one sentence, explain why? If so, the autobiography succeeds. The following points help make it a satisfactory autobiography:

- The multiparagraph sketch follows a chronological organization.
- It bears many of the characteristics of a narrative. [*See* NARRATION *elsewhere in Part II.*]
- The informal style offers further insight into the author's personality.
- The dialogue included, appropriate for the informal style, sounds natural, not contrived.
- The paragraphing helps the reader follow change of speakers. [*See* PARAGRAPHS, KINDS: IN DIALOGUE *in Part II.*]
- Vocabulary and sentence structure suggest not only an informal style, but casual characters and a casual situation. Note that only informal writing will permit the use of incomplete sentences.
- The dialogue uses accurate punctuation, including commas setting off the interrupting phrases and quotation marks indicating exact words.
- Sentence fragments, usually inappropriate in nonfiction, serve a specific purpose here. [*See* FRAGMENT *in the Glossary.*] Their use, however, should not be misconstrued to mean that sentence fragments are appropriate for all autobiographies. Not so. Here, the fragments show further informality of style; but more importantly, the fragments suggest the author's staccato series of impressions. In other words, the fragments are used for stylistic purposes. Furthermore, their use makes the sketch read more like fiction, one characteristic sometimes apparent in an autobiography. By contrast, an autobiography written in a formal style will not include sentence fragments.
- Paragraph development [*see* PARAGRAPHS *later in Part II*] is typical of fiction, not of expository writing. The paragraphs lack topic sentences and carefully structured development. Instead, they follow the narrative form, a change in time or character determining a change of paragraph. Again, a more formal autobiography will take a more formal approach, including a formal paragraph structure.

In general, the autobiography above is successful. The writer answers the questions she asked of herself. We know that she learned something as a result of her experience; but more importantly, she learned what she must do in order to be a successful photographer, a skill she obviously cherishes. Granted, we don't know how old she is, where she was born, who her parents are, where she went to school, or where she lives. On the other hand, we have a general idea of her age; we know how she feels about people; we understand her mixed attitudes toward the Fall Festival; and we understand her new insight into her own professional responsibilities and what they require of her.

BIOGRAPHY

A biography is the story of a life. It may vary in length from a paragraph to a book. Most frequently, however, when students are asked to write a biography, the expected product ranges from a well-developed paragraph to a research paper. [*See* RESEARCH PAPER *later in Part II.*] We will examine here the short biographical sketch. Regardless of the length, the steps, organization, and pitfalls will be the same whether the writer must prepare a long or short account of a life.

Characteristics

Although a biography is the story of someone's life, unless the biography is book length, it cannot begin to recount all the details of a full lifetime. In addition, because the writer is describing someone else's life, he cannot write without research, either primary or secondary. [*See* PRIMARY RESEARCH *and* SECONDARY RESEARCH *in the Glossary.*] As a result, a carefully prepared biography should include

- an effective introduction which includes background information that places the subject in a specific setting,

- a focus on the subject which allows the writer to limit the lifetime material to a manageable subject [*see* FOCUS *in the Glossary*],

- an approach appropriate for the audience,

- details which support the specific focus, including effective anecdotes and quotations [*see* SPECIFIC DETAIL *in the Glossary*],

- evidence of research or knowledge of the subject,

- clear, logical organization,

- effective transitions to help readers follow the organization [*see* TRANSITION *in the Glossary*],

- consistent style, assuring the omission of plagiarism [*see* PLAGIARISM *in the Glossary*],

- interesting reading, not a list of facts and figures.

Process

Students who prepare biographies usually do so as part of a class assignment. If the subject is not assigned, the content area suggests the subject and emphasis. Use the following steps to plan and develop a biography, regardless of its length.

PREWRITING

Step 1. Doing the Secondary Research

Assuming you have identified the subject of the biography, complete the secondary research by consulting available sources:

- If the subject is included in a general encyclopedia entry, begin with that. Usually an encyclopedia will serve as a guide for further research.

- Check specialized encyclopedias and other reference books, particularly *Current Biographies.*

- After your preliminary search, consult the library's card catalog or computer-search facilities for further references. For instance, you may find the subject's autobiography; you may find books and articles by other biographers. [*See* Card Catalog *and* Computer Search *in the Glossary.*]

- Check the *Reader's Guide to Periodical Literature* for magazine articles that provide additional kinds of information, including bibliographies. [*See* Reader's Guide to Periodical Literature *in the Glossary.*]

- The vertical file may include some information. [*See* Vertical File *in the Glossary.*]

- Newspaper articles, less readily located, may also include interesting highlights. Research in other areas will suggest dates and newspapers most likely to yield any material.

- If you have access to special collections, usually housed in museums or in special-collections library rooms, examine the subject's personal effects: mementos, personal letters, and diaries or journals.

Too many students think they can read a single encyclopedia article and develop an adequate biography. Before you can write sensitively about another human being, however, you must understand him or her—the personality, the frustrations, the joys, the motives, the goals, the strengths, the weaknesses, the contributions, the failures. Seek out as many potential sources as you can.

The greater the variety of source material you have, the more complete, accurate, and interesting your biography will be.

Step 2. Doing the Primary Research

Complete whatever primary research you can. How much you do depends on several factors: the extent of the biography, the availability of secondary research, the availability of primary-research sources, and the time allotted for research.

Obviously, an extensive biography must rely on every possible source available and will require months—maybe even years—of thorough research. Most of you will not be delving that deeply to develop a biography. The availability of secondary research, then, may determine how much time you can devote to primary research. Consider these two situations:

Situation One

Even though your subject may have had books and articles written about him or her, you gain a different insight into your subject through primary research. Here's what to do:

- If your subject is still living, you should try to interview him or her at length. [*See* INTERVIEW *in the Glossary.*]

- Find people who know the subject, worked with or are related to him or her. Talk with these people to get a broader perspective of your subject.

- Talk with a recognized authority or scholar who has studied your subject extensively. Compare his or her comments with the results of your own research.

Situation Two

If the subject of your biography has received no journalistic coverage, all of your research will be primary:

- If he or she is still living, you must interview your subject.

- In addition, you must locate his or her friends, neighbors, and relatives.

- For the sake of perspective, you should interview your subject's enemies—or at least his or her opponents. They will most likely broaden your perspective.

STEP 3.   SELECTING A FOCUS

When you have completed your general research, select a focus for your biography. An especially lengthy research paper may successfully develop more than one focus, but probably not more than three.

In order to select a single focus, think about those aspects of the subject's life most directly related to the content of a course you are taking, especially if you are writing the biography as an assignment for that course. If, for instance, you are doing a biography on Benjamin Franklin for a social-science class, you will probably focus on his work as an ambassador. If you choose the same biographical subject for a science class, however, you will probably focus on his work as an inventor. For an English class, you will probably discuss his writing and his wit.

You may, on the other hand, select the single focus to show a broader understanding of your subject. For instance, while writing for a social-science class, you may acknowledge Franklin's expertise as an ambassador but dwell on his contributions to the shipping industry as a result of his work as an oceanographer who discovered the Gulf Stream.

STEP 4.   LISTING THE DETAILS

After you have selected a focus, make a list of the details which will illustrate it. The details may include the following:

- personality traits
- business experiences
- comments by critics
- self-evaluation
- educational background

- contributions to his or her field(s) of endeavor
- effects of those contributions
- any other details which introduce readers to your chosen focus on the subject's life

Write your own list now.

STEP 5. ORGANIZING THE DETAILS

Arrange the details in a logical order. For biographies, the order is almost always chronological. [*See* CHRONOLOGICAL ORDER *in the Glossary.*]

STEP 6. DEVELOPING THE SETTING

In order to help readers locate your subject in an historical time frame, jot down details about the period in which the subject lived. Note locations, dates, and historical events. For instance, was the subject struggling through college during World War I, or was he being schooled by a private tutor at home during the Golden Age of Greece? By weaving these details into the context of the biography, readers better understand your subject.

Prepare a brief list now of possible details to establish the setting for your subject's story.

WRITING

STEP 7. DEVELOPING THE INTRODUCTION

The introduction for a multi-paragraph biography does not rely on the time element. Rather, it follows a separate plan:

- The introduction sets the time and place and literally introduces the subject of the biography. Refer to the list you developed in Step 6 above. The reader will appreciate, however, a creative introduction, not just a list of names, dates, and places. The introduction may include, for instance, a quotation attributed to the subject, a perceptive comment from a critic, or merely the writer's reaction to the subject. [*See* INTRODUCTION *in the Glossary.*]

- The introduction should conclude with a thesis sentence. The thesis sentence narrows the subject of the biography and indicates the writer's focus. [*See* THESIS SENTENCE *in the Glossary for a quick reference, and see* THEME *later in Part II for a thorough explanation of effective thesis sentences.*]

In a paragraph-length sketch, the introduction may be only a sentence or two; but in a long paper, the introduction will be a full paragraph. [*See* THEME *later in Part II for a clear explanation and example of an introductory paragraph.*]

STEP 8. BUILDING THE BODY

Take note of three items as you develop the body paragraphs of the biography:

First, using the lists developed in Steps 4–6 as a result of your primary and secondary research, select details for the body paragraphs that support the topic sentence.

Some hints:

- Be selective; choose only the most telling details.

- Discuss them in chronological order, or establish cause-and-effect relationships as appropriate. [*See* CAUSE AND EFFECT *in Part II and in the Glossary.*]

- Use a variety of methods to develop the paper—examples, comparison and contrast, cause and effect, perhaps analogy and definition, as well as description [*see these methods of development discussed under their separate entries in Part II*]. Whichever method of development you choose, the development should be organized chronologically.

Second, as you develop the body paragraphs, remember that the details must be adequate to support the focus.

Some hints:

- Be reasonable. Two or three details will be insufficient to explain Benjamin Franklin's contributions as an ambassador.

- At the same time, however, be careful not to stray into a discussion of sidelights. They may be interesting; but if they do not support or explain the selected focus, they do not belong in the biographical sketch. [*See* UNITY *in the Glossary and* REVISING: SAMPLE REVISION FOR UNITY *in Part I.*]

Third, the sketch may be enhanced by anecdotes or quotations to add variety and interest.

Some hints:

- Anecdotes and quotations must support or explain the focus.

- To include them just to add a bit of human interest is to lose unity in the paper.

- Give credit to your sources for the anecdotes, quotations, and other information. A formal paper will require some kind of formal documentation (footnotes, endnotes, or parenthetical notes as well as a bibliography) for all information sources. An informal paper, however, may use a text reference and omit other formal means of documentation. [*See* RESEARCH PAPER *in Part II for additional information on documentation.*]

STEP 9. ADDING THE CONCLUSION

The biography should conclude with an emphasis on the focus established in the introduction. Obviously, a biography need not end with the subject's death. The subject may still be living! The reader will respond with greatest interest to a conclusion which dwells on the subject's significant contributions rather than on the bare facts of names, dates, and places.

REVISING

STEP 10. CHECKING THE CONTENTS

Reread your completed paper to look for possible weaknesses. [*See* REVISING *in Part I for a thorough explanation of revision techniques.*] In addition, ask yourself these questions to help you spot weaknesses peculiar to a biography:

- Have I researched thoroughly and carefully to avoid writing a biography which misrepresents the subject?

- Does my biography reflect the research accurately?

- Have I avoided personal bias so that I do not misrepresent the subject?

- Did I avoid too much name-date-place information?

- Have I included meaningful details to support the focus?

- Are names, dates, places and details accurate?

- Does the biography read well, or does it sound like a list of facts and figures?

- Does the reader get a good glimpse of the subject?

You should have answered "yes" to each of the questions above. If you cannot, use the questions to which you answered "no" as a guide for revising weaknesses in the biography.

PROOFREADING

STEP 11.   CHECKING FOR ACCURACY

When you have finished revising, check for final details. Use the *Webster's New World Dictionary* and *Webster's New World Thesaurus* to check spelling and word choice. Double-check sources for any inconsistencies in dates or details and for accuracy in documentation. Then read for grammar, mechanics, and usage errors.

A Note about the Samples: The following sample biographies all deal with the same man, John James Audubon. As you study the sketches, however, you will note that the focus changes in each. In other words, as the writers selected their respective focuses, they took into consideration the content area for which each was writing the paper. As a result, the focus parallels the subject matter: The paper for English class talks about Audubon as a writer; for social sciences, as a man of the frontier; for science, as an ornithologist; for business, as a businessman; for vocational education, as a man using his skills to earn a living.

—————— Sample for English ——————

The following biography, developed as a single paragraph, focuses on John James Audubon as a writer. Compare it with the others that follow to see how the emphasis changes to meet the needs of the content area.

Woodsman Audubon as a Writer

Most people worldwide recognize John James Audubon as an artist, the self-trained painter of birds who was the first to depict them life-sized and in motion. As an artist whose life spanned the years roughly between the American Constitutional Convention and the beginning of the Civil War, Audubon studied his subject more carefully than any other of his contemporary ornithologists. In addition to his painting, however, Audubon also wrote about the birds, their habits and their habitats. His constant struggle to write effectively endears him to the hearts of modern readers who lack his otherwise genius-like characteristics. For instance, in the Ornithological Biography, a five-volume text to accompany his paintings, Audubon wrote with telling insight about the subject to which he devoted the last half of his life. As Michael Harwood points out, Audubon, like many other struggling writers, called on information from his "old journals and memorandum books, which were written on the spot" (John James Audubon, quoted in Audubon Demythologized New York: National Audubon Society, n.d. 10). From the beginning, he indicated that the work would not be a scientific one; he had inadequate training for that. Little did he know, however, what an effort he would face in order to produce even an unscientific work. In fact, the final work which was published for the buying public probably bears little resemblance to the first several drafts. Because he included many stories of the wilderness, as one critic notes, while the books were a pioneering work, "they were flowery, rich with moralizing and anthropomorphizing. That reflected his time, in which educated men looked to nature for spiritual messages" (Harwood 10). Audubon wrote with the flair and flamboyance he learned as a child growing up in France, but he had the wisdom to hire William MacGillivray, a Scottish ornithologist, to edit his work and add anatomical descriptions. MacGillivray, like a good critic, regularly and repeatedly argued with and questioned Audubon, forcing him to write with greater accuracy; however, Audubon's lifelong habits of exaggerating and embellishing were difficult to break. As a result of his critics, though, including MacGillivray and other academic naturalists, Audubon finally forced himself to restrain his flowery style. His diaries nevertheless retain the embellished style. So even though he called himself "the American Woodsman" who liked simply to tramp in the woods and watch the birds, he wrote with a woodsman's style far from simple. Like other writers, he struggled to change to make his work acceptable to the buying public. As a result, genius artist that he was, Audubon's struggles as a writer give him a humanizing quality worth empathy.

Analysis of the Sample for English

The biographical sketch above focuses on Audubon's writing. The writer selected that focus, of course, because he was preparing the sketch for an English class assignment. Note these additional details:

- As suggested in the Steps above, Audubon's renown as an artist is acknowledged in the first two sentences, but the focus of this biographical sketch, his writing, is introduced in the third sentence.

- The fourth sentence suggests the writer's attitude toward Audubon's struggles.

- The details which follow are presented in logical order, from most important to least. Because the details relate to only two works, the *Ornithological Biography* and Audubon's diaries, there is little on which to base chronological organization. Instead, the writer emphasizes the larger work and concludes with a reference to the smaller work. The writer can emphasize Audubon's struggle to refine his style by pointing to the diaries.

- The use of quotations both from Audubon and from a critic add interest and further details supporting the focus of the biography. The full publication information in parenthetical notes credits the source, and the brevity of this paper suggests no need for more complicated documentation or a separate bibliography.

- Without mentioning specific dates or places, the writer lets readers know when and where Audubon lived.

- The conclusion ties together the significance of the focus chosen for this English class assignment.

———————— Sample for Social Sciences ————————

The following sample biographical paragraph focuses on John James Audubon as a frontiersman, a focus appropriate for the content area.

Audubon, the Frontiersman

Artist John James Audubon, recognized ornithologist, embodied what contemporary Americans refer to as the American frontiersman. Born two years before the Constitutional Convention, he died shortly before the Civil War. During those rugged developmental years, French immigrant Audubon left Pennsylvania, crossed the mountains, and made his way down the Ohio River to settle first at Louisville and then at Henderson, Kentucky, at that time the rugged, untamed edge of the frontier. When he brought his girl-next-door bride, Lucy, from Pennsylvania to a log cabin in Henderson, she grieved at leaving her family and fine comforts behind. Perhaps she had a right to grieve, for the trip across the mountains by a tumultuous stagecoach ride and, at times, on foot or on horseback, demanded far more of her than any other experience Lucy had ever had. Then, after a sojourn in Louisville, when they finally reached what would be their home, Audubon himself, in his journal, described Henderson as "one of the poorest spots in the Western Country." Although the life there was painful for Lucy, the rest of the world can be grateful for that "poor spot." As a result of his experiences there, Audubon began the work which finally brought him ongoing fame: painting birds. The wilderness rich with wildlife gained Audubon's nearly full-time attention, and he dedicated himself to a goal of painting every bird he encountered. The frontier offered species no one else had studied, and Audubon is credited with "discovering" a number of new birds. His travels along the frontier, up and down the Mississippi from Louisville to New Orleans, allowed him to see birds from north to south and to sight water birds, land birds and birds of prey. Treks up the Missouri River into a farther Western wilderness provided even more species for Audubon's brush. Reading Audubon's diaries recounting his ventures into the frontier offers modern Americans a glimpse of the time when the West (now the Midwest) was a different place—an environment alive with birds now extinct, an almost impenetrable wilderness without roads, where transportation was an exercise in torture, and where the waterways provided the easiest means of getting from one remote point of population to another. As a result, to understand Audubon's life is to gain an inside view of the frontier life.

Analysis of the Sample for Social Sciences

The Audubon biographical sketch developed for a social science class examines his life as a representative of the American frontier. Note these specifics:

- The first sentence states the focus.

- The remainder of the sketch, organized chronologically, gives details to support the idea of *frontiersman representative.*

- A quotation from Audubon's diary adds interest to the supporting details. Because the writer indicates the source of the quotation within the text, no further documentation is required in this informal paper.

- The conclusion draws the readers' attention again to the specific focus of the biography.

- When readers are finished, without having read lists of dates, names, and places, they know when and where Audubon lived and gain insight into how reading Audubon's diaries can teach them even more about the American frontier in the early nineteenth century.

While the biography ignores Audubon's contributions to science and his failure as a businessman, readers were told in the first sentence that the emphasis would be on the frontiersman idea. To include details supporting other ideas would cause the sketch to lose unity.

Sample for Science

The writer of the following John James Audubon biography focuses on Audubon's contributions as an ornithologist. The focus parallels appropriate subject matter for a science paper.

Artist Audubon as Ornithologist

Two hundred years after his birth, John James Audubon continues to gain world acclaim as a painter of birds. As an ornithologist, however, he made equally significant but less widely acclaimed contributions to the world of science. During Audubon's life, birds now extinct soared the skies in pest-like abundance. Audubon's diaries speak of hordes of annoying passenger pigeons killed in masses and left lying where they fell for the hogs to eat. He wrote of bald eagles and trumpeter swans readily sighted. He described marshes, woods, and skies thick with birds. More importantly, however, he wrote in detail about their habits and habitats. Unlike other ornithologists who studied dead specimens in a laboratory and whom Audubon called "closet naturalists," Audubon studied birds alive in their natural environments. While scientists and artists, including Audubon, commonly shot their specimens for close study, Audubon always studied the birds first alive, watching their behavior, even studying their migratory habits. He may well have been the first to band birds to see if the same individuals returned to the same habitat each spring. As a result, when Audubon wrote the <u>Ornithological Biography</u> to accompany his paintings, he noted, "No man living knows better than I do the habits of our birds . . . and with the assistance of my old journals and memorandum books, which were written on the spot, I can at least put down plain truths, which may be useful." The details in both his writing and in his painting illustrate superiority to anything produced by his contemporaries. He made the mistake, however, of including in the bird biography some tall tales about his life on the frontier. The inclusion affected his reputation as a reliable observer. As a result, his contributions to the field of ornithology were shrouded by criticism from his colleagues, much the result of what one critic calls "quirks in his personality and style." Critic Robert Cushman Murphy suggests the bird biographies "have become a half-forgotten treasure ... surely replete with information that compilers of later works have not yet used." The world has more to learn about Audubon the scientist.

Analysis of the Sample for Science

Audubon the scientist becomes the focus for this biography. Written for a science class, it includes these characteristics:

- The sketch points out first the differences between Audubon and his contemporary ornithologists. By clarifying Audubon's pioneering effort, the writer can then deal with the biography chronologically.

- The writer discusses Audubon's method of research, then his writing, followed by his unscientific annecdotes, concluding with his discredit in the scientific community.

- By ending the biographical sketch with a critic's words about the potential wealth of important information remaining in the many volumes, the writer places Audubon in a scientific niche which aids the readers' understanding.

- The writer enables readers to draw assumptions without being spoon-fed. For instance, readers know Audubon was born two hundred years ago and that he experienced a very different environment along the then-frontier from the one Midwesterners know today.

- Since the writer indicates the sources of his quotations within the text of his paper, he omits further documentation. In some classes, with some instructors, this kind of documentation will be sufficient. Follow your instructor's requirements. Hard scientific data needs more complete documentation. [*See* RESEARCH PAPER *in Part II.*]

Without being critical, the writer explains the times of which Audubon was a part, when passenger pigeons were slaughtered as pests, when gentlemen scientists did not favor field research, when the infant field of ornithology provided rich opportunities for study and discovery. The result is a biographical sketch that reveals more than just facts on the surface.

Sample for Business

For a business class, the writer of the following biography focuses on John James Audubon's experiences as a businessman and entrepreneur.

Giving Up Business for the Birds

John James Audubon gained well-deserved recognition as an
artist and ornithologist. As a frontiersman, he evoked the interest
of his European contemporaries fascinated with the wild America.
As a businessman, however, Audubon provided his biographers with
room for argument. Many critics claim he was too busy frittering
away the hours chasing birds in the woods to be a successful
businessman, but other critics say the struggling nation's forces
over which he had no control created his downfall. Whatever the
case, he landed in debtors' prison, leaving his penniless wife alone
with two children. Audubon's business problems began when he and
a fellow Frenchman set up an importing business in Louisville.
Shortly thereafter, as a result of the Napoleonic Wars and their
effect on American shipping, Congress passed the Embargo Act in
1807 and cut off overseas trade. Thus ended the import business
and the partnership. While his partner blamed Audubon's frequent
forays into the woods as the cause of failure, surely the embargo
affected an import business, too. Audubon returned to Henderson,
Kentucky, where he owned land, slaves, and a sturdy log cabin, and
there he became a shopkeeper. He took risks. As critic Michael
Harwood wrote, "That sort of thing was characteristic of the place
and time: Every man stood a chance to make a fortune if he simply
dared to try for it" (<u>Audubon Demythologized</u> New York: National
Audubon Society, n.d. 4). Audubon tried, but when the war with
England caused blockades to be set up at the ports of entry, he
failed again. After the war, Audubon built a steam mill in
Henderson, a gigantic affair with significant potential. The
community failed to grow the way Audubon had anticipated it
would, so the mill failed, too. Then the banks failed. Like many other
businessmen, Audubon was in debt, and the failing banks cost him
his business and personal property. He declared bankruptcy and
faced debtors' prison. As a result of his disastrous business affairs,

however, Audubon gave the world far more than he was ever paid. Only when Audubon had nothing else to turn to did he begin painting birds with a serious goal—to earn money. Like many other artists, he struggled financially for most of his life. Sadly, his story is one of business decisions affected both by divided attention and economic factors beyond his control and even beyond his understanding. In the end, however, he gave the world his art treasures, one collection of which sold recently for well over $1.5 million!

Analysis of the Sample for Business

The biographical sketch above focuses on Audubon as a businessman. Note these details:

- The first two sentences acknowledge his other, more famous, contributions; the third sentence establishes the focus of this sketch.

- In order to set the scene, the writer introduces the conflict among biographers who examine Audubon's businesses and then tells her readers the outcome: debtors' prison.

- The remainder of the biographical sketch, organized chronologically, details Audubon's business experiences and ultimate failure. By noting that the business failures caused Audubon to begin painting, the writer suggests the world can be grateful for them.

- Some indirect information shines through the direct retelling of the facts. For instance, by using a narrative approach [*see* NARRATION *in Part II*], telling a story of Audubon's business ventures, the writer lets the reader see the man in his time.

- Using parenthetical documentation permits the writer to credit her source for the quotation. The brevity of the paper suggests this simple documentation form, thus omitting the need for a bibliography. Use whatever documentation your instructor requires.

- By concluding with the positive contribution of the artist to the business of the contemporary art community ($1.5 million, at that!), the writer softens the characterization of Audubon as a failure. Simultaneously, she extends the business point of view in Audubon's biography from the nineteenth century to the twenty-first century.

The classic argument of whether man makes the times or the times make the man creeps through the sketch. The writer never suggests her own opinion of the cause of Audubon's business failures—whether they were the result of Audubon's divided attention, or the result of economic factors beyond his control or both—but a reader can surmise from the details which argument he or she chooses to believe. Certainly the sketch offers nearly equal supporting details for either argument.

Sample for Vocational Education

The following biography of John James Audubon focuses on his ability to use his skills to earn a living. The focus, appropriate for the vocational content area, shows a side of Audubon not included in the biographical samples above.

Audubon's Worldwide Fame

As an artist, John James Audubon earned worldwide fame for his daring new approach to painting birds. Although he began teaching himself to draw birds in his early manhood, not until mid life did he assume the serious goal of painting every specimen he could find. Roaming the American frontier during the early nineteenth century, he discovered a wealth of subject matter. Because he studied the birds alive in their natural surroundings, even though he painted the details from a dead specimen, he depicted the birds in a lifelike pose unmatched by that in the work of any of his contemporaries. Other artists used static side views, recalling a kind of bird-like imitation of Egyptian art. Critic Michael Harwood explains that to aid himself in depicting the lifelike poses, Audubon "devised a method of wiring up a freshly killed bird— giving the model an armature, as if it were a piece of sculpture— which permitted him to pose it as he recalled it in life." Audubon's real contribution to bird art, however, was his insistence that every bird, whether hummingbird or bald eagle, be painted life-sized. So his paintings took a huge format, referred to as the "elephant folio." Yet another characteristic developed as Audubon grew with his art. The background detail gave critics as much to study as did the birds. Often enhanced with other creatures and an abundance of plant life, the paintings attempted to put the full-sized lifelike birds in natural settings. When the paintings were finished, Audubon had 435 plates. Today, a single set of those prints, bound in the elephant folio, will bring about $1.5 million, not a bad price for an artist who spent most of his life in poverty.

Analysis of the Sample for Vocational Education

By focusing on Audubon as an artist, the biography designed for a vocational class deals with Audubon's claim to fame. In one way, however, this biographical sketch seems to violate the principle of chronological organization. While other factors rise to the readers' attention, the pattern does follow a time sequence. Note these details:

- The writer begins with an overview to explain why Audubon differed from his contemporaries. The entire sketch focuses on the distinctive differences.
- Readers follow Audubon from his youthful self-instruction to his mid life beginning of a serious career. The time sequence continues as further Audubon trademarks emerge.
- As the artist expands his career, readers see the developmental process, up to the estimated current value of his works. So while the biography focuses on the distinctive trademarks of Audubon's work, a necessary aspect of a vocational-education approach to the man, the chronological organization remains loosely in place.
- Selected details support the paper's focus adequately but without burden.
- Readers know who, what, why, when, and where without any list-like rendering of names, dates, and places.
- The expository approach allows the writer to present Audubon's characteristic style without departing from good organization and without relying on narrative. A story-telling approach here could weaken the writer's credibility in regard to an understanding of Audubon's art.
- The conclusion enhances the point of view and brings readers back to the present, better informed about the value of Audubon's work.
- Because the writer credits the source of quoted material within the text of the paper, further documentation is omitted. Some instructors will encourage simplified documentation in short papers such as this. Use whatever form of documentation your instructor requires. [*See* RESEARCH PAPER *in Part II for details about documentation forms.*]

These sample biographical sketches and their analyses should enable you to develop a biography limited by a suitable focus.

BOOK REPORT

A book report summarizes and offers a reaction to a book, either fiction or nonfiction. While it always includes certain details, a book report is usually tailored to its reader. Thus, a book report written for an English class will have very different content from one written for a social science or vocational class. As opposed to a book review [*see* REVIEW *later in Part II*], the book report strives only to report what the book includes, reflecting only briefly, perhaps indirectly, the reader's reaction to it. Emphasis usually falls on those aspects of the book directly related to the subject matter of the class for which the report is prepared. In fact, a book report is often used to prove that the writer has gained knowledge from outside reading in the subject area.

Characteristics

Book reports usually follow a rather simple format which will include

- the title of the book,

- the author's name,

- the characters, setting, and point of view in a work of fiction [*see* CHARACTERIZATION, SETTING, *and* POINT OF VIEW *in the Glossary*],

- a one-paragraph synopsis of the book [*see* SYNOPSIS *in Part II and in the Glossary*],

- the topic or theme of the book as it relates to the subject matter of the class for which the report is being written [*see* THEME *in the Glossary*],

- the writer's reaction to the book, particularly as related to anything he or she may have learned from reading it,

- direct quotations from the book to support general statements.

Process

Realistically, a book report cannot deal with every aspect of a book. Use the following steps to plan, organize, write, and revise a successfully focused book report.

PREWRITING

STEP 1. NARROWING THE TOPIC

Complete a careful reading of the book, making notes as you read. Notes may include important names, dates, incidents, and significant ideas, as well as a notation of the page numbers on which you find those incidents and ideas introduced. Take note of significant passages which may be useful for supporting detail in the book report.

When you've finished reading, sort through your notes for *subject-matter ideas*. A subject-matter idea is one directly related to the subject of the class for which you are preparing the report: English, social sciences, science, business, or vocational education. Put a check mark by the two or three most important subject-matter ideas. These will be the ideas on which your report will focus.

For example, after reading a work of fiction, *The Clan of the Cave Bear*, for a science class, a writer checked the two following subject-matter ideas as most important:

- biology of prehistoric plants and animals,
- fictionalized representation of the theory of evolution.

Note that the subject-matter ideas above relate directly to the science class for which the writer is preparing the book report. Selecting these subject-matter ideas determines the emphasis of the report.

STEP 2.   SELECTING DETAILS

Think about the book's two or three subject-matter ideas listed in Step 1 above. List three or four details that explain the book's contribution to that subject matter. Remember to direct your choices toward the content of the class for which you are preparing the report.

For instance, the writer can support the subject-matter ideas listed in Step 1 above with the following details:

- biology of prehistoric plants and animals:

  ○ life at edge of glacier
  ○ animals like woolly mammoth, cave bear, horses
  ○ medicinal and edible plants

- fictionalized representation of the theory of evolution:

  ○ Neanderthal people's characteristics
  ○ destiny of Neanderthal
  ○ Cro-Magnon's characteristics

Complete your own list of details. This list will serve as a scratch outline for the body of your book report. [*See* OUTLINES, KINDS: FOR A PAPER *in Part II.*]

STEP 3.   CHECKING THE AUTHOR

Check to see if the author has written other books, noting especially those of similar subject matter. (Note: The book itself will usually list the author's previous books, but you may need to check the card catalog.) If the author has written additional books, is this the most recent or one of the earlier books? Making note of earlier or later books by the same author will lend perspective to your report.

Second, check the author's background and make note of anything that particularly relates to this book's subject matter.

STEP 4.   ORGANIZING THE OVERALL PLAN

The book report usually reflects a simple pattern of organization. Use the following plan:

Introduction

The introduction includes the basic information: the book's title, author, and topic or theme. In a work of fiction, the introduction may also identify major characters and setting.

If the author has written other books of a similar nature, include that notation either here or in the concluding paragraph. Likewise, either here or in the conclusion, include a sentence or two about any pertinent details regarding the author's background.

Body Paragraphs

A book report usually includes three or four body paragraphs. The first body paragraph is a synopsis of the book, organized in the same order as the book itself. [*See* SYNOPSIS *in Part II for an example and explanation of the process for developing the summary.*]

The next two or three body paragraphs explain the two or three topics you listed in Steps 1 and 2 above. Develop a separate paragraph for each, using incidents, examples, and supporting quotations from the book. These paragraphs will probably be organized in order of importance. [*See* ORDERS OF IMPORTANCE *in the Glossary.*]

Conclusion

The final paragraph summarizes the book's contribution to the subject area and includes the reader's reaction to the book, particularly as it relates to the subject matter. This paragraph should be arranged so that the report's most important evaluative comment is the final one, a kind of concluding remark for the entire report.

WARNING: When writing book reports, inexperienced writers tend to summarize the book instead of writing a synopsis and then dealing specifically with the theme or topic as it relates to the subject matter of the class for which the report is being written. Remember that the bulk of your report should explain the two or three subject-matter ideas selected in Steps 1 and 2. The synopsis is only about one-fifth of an effective report.

WRITING

STEP 5. FOLLOWING THE PLAN

Write your report based on the organizational plan spelled out above. Pay attention, also, to the following general guidelines:

- Make the synopsis concise.

- Include sufficient supporting details from the book to develop your two or three subject-related paragraphs. [*See* REVISING: SAMPLE REVISION FOR SPECIFIC DETAIL *in Part I.*]

- Provide adequate transitions to help the reader move easily from sentence to sentence and idea to idea. [*See* REVISING: SAMPLE REVISION FOR TRANSITION *in Part I.*]

- Maintain unity within each paragraph and within the report as a whole. Omit irrelevant details. [*See* REVISING: SAMPLE REVISION FOR UNITY *in Part I.*]

- Use vocabulary and sentence structure appropriate for the subject and the audience.

- End with an effective clincher. [*See* THEME *in Part II for a discussion of effective conclusions.*]

REVISING

STEP 6.   CHECKING THE CONTENT

Once you have finished the first draft, check the content of your book report against the following guidelines:

- Does the first paragraph include the basic information: the book's title, author, and topic or theme?

- Does the first paragraph include a thesis sentence [*see* THESIS STATEMENT *in the Glossary and* THEME *in Part II*] and any pertinent information about the book's preparation or the author's background?

- Is the one-paragraph synopsis concise?

- Are the two or three subject-related ideas developed in separate paragraphs?

- Are the subject-related ideas supported by details and quotations from the book?

- Are all details relevant to your thesis? [*See* REVISING: SAMPLE REVISION FOR UNITY *in Part I.*]

- Are quotations from the book included to provide support and authenticity?

- Are the quotations accurately enclosed in quotation marks and accurately punctuated?

- Do transitions connect ideas within and between the paragraphs? [*See* REVISING: SAMPLE REVISION FOR TRANSITION *in Part I.*]

- Do word choice and sentence structure seem appropriate to the subject and the audience? [*See* REVISING: SAMPLE REVISION FOR EMPHASIS *in Part I.*]

- Are sentences varied, both in length and structure? [*See* REVISING: SAMPLE REVISION FOR SENTENCE VARIETY *in Part I.*]

- Does the organization emphasize the report's main ideas?

[*For additional general suggestions for revision, see* REVISING *in Part I. A combination of these suggestions with those above should provide guidelines for thorough revision.*]

PROOFREADING

STEP 7.   CHECKING THE DETAILS

When you have completed the revisions and prepared your final draft, check for accurate spelling and good word choice. Consult your *Webster's New World Dictionary* and *Webster's New World Thesaurus* for help. Using the Glossary of this book, check also the grammar, mechanics, usage, and punctuation for accuracy. Make any final corrections necessary.

A Note about the Samples: Following are book reports, all of the same novel, developed for five subject areas. Recognize that some books are far more appropriate for certain classes than are others. In fact, your teacher or instructor may assign a specific book or give you a reading list from which you must choose a book. The approach taken here should not be misconstrued to mean that any book is appropriate for any class or subject area. After you have read the five reports, however, you should be better prepared to write effective reports. [*See also* REVIEW, *elsewhere in Part II, to compare a book report with a book review, and see* LITERARY ANALYSES, THE SAMPLE FOR A NOVEL, *also in Part II, to compare a book report with a literary analysis of a novel. The same novel serves as the subject of the book report, the book review, and the literary analysis.*]

Sample for English

Students in an English class were asked to read and report on books set in a time period other than the present. Students were also asked to relate themes in the book to subject matter discussed in class. The writer whose book report appears below tailored the report to meet that assignment.

Language and Logic Cave Woman Style

The second book of a trilogy, The Valley of the Horses fictionalizes the beginning of civilization in the Asian area north of the Beran Sea. Like Jean M. Auel's other two books, The Clan of the Cave Bear and The Mammoth Hunters, this one gets its foundation from archaeological research supporting the evolution of man. In this unusual historical novel, the reader follows Ayla, a child of the Others, who has been reared by the Clan of the Cave Bear and then ejected from the Clan when she violates customs she can neither understand nor accept. In exile in the valley of the horses, she survives five years alone until she meets Jondalar, a man of the Others. They face a major obstacle: they cannot communicate. Ayla has no verbal language, and Jondalar cannot understand the nuances of her gestures and facial expressions.

Ayla faces a lonely struggle for survival after her death curse by the Clan. To solve basic survival problems, she must use logic: alone, how can she kill, butcher and process an animal large enough to feed her through the severe winter; alone, how can she provide clothing, cooking utensils, sleeping skins, and shelter for protection; alone, how can she protect herself from the dangers around her? Her training as a medicine woman and her knowledge of hunting coupled with the large brain characteristic of the Others allow her to succeed. Also as a result of her background, she saves Jondalar's life after a lion mauls him and kills his traveling-companion brother. Jondalar is the first of the Others that Ayla has seen. After Ayla's medicinal powers help Jondalar regain his health, the two of them suffer from their inability to understand each other's customs. Jondalar finally teaches her to speak, however, and they establish a strong bond, sharing their creative ideas to reach solutions for both the physical and mental problems they face as a team.

Among the many concepts about the development of civilization that Auel weaves into her novels to stimulate the reader's imagination and curiosity, one of the most intriguing is the development of language. Without writing a history of the development of language, Auel forces the reader to deal with the transition from nonverbal to verbal to written communication. The Clan, characterized as Neanderthals, used only grunts, facial expressions, and gestures to communicate. As Jondalar notes in one encounter, he was "aware, peripherally, that the young flathead (Clan member) and the female were waving their hands and making gutteral sounds." He adds that he "had an impression they were communicating." By contrast, the Others use almost entirely a spoken language. In fact, when Ayla tries to explain to Jondalar how she guides her horse, she can only say, "Whinney just knows where I want to go." The horse senses her muscular nudges and reactions and knows where Ayla wants to go, a phenomenon Jondalar has difficulty understanding. Written language, however, is unknown to either of them. While Jondalar explains sculpture to Ayla, neither of them draws representations as a preliminary written language. On the other hand, Ayla does make marks on sticks to keep track of the days and months. Interestingly enough, though, she cannot count the many marks she has made; Jondalar calculates her lonely stay at over five years.

Another intriguing idea presented in The Valley of the Horses to stimulate the reader's imagination about the development of civilization deals with the importance of logic for survival. Much of the development of the various civilizations was aided by the people's ability to reason and solve problems. The Clan people, described by Auel to resemble the forerunners of Homo sapiens, had memories but could not learn anything new. They could not reason. They did whatever they did because it was all they knew. Necessarily, then, Ayla was feared. As a woman, she learned on her own to hunt, something no Clan woman could or would think of trying to do. Because the Others had a larger brain, they could learn new things, adapt to their surroundings, and, yes, verbalize. In one instance, when Ayla discovers by accident that striking together two pieces of flint can produce fire, the author says of the accident: "That was the serendipity. Ayla supplied the recognition and the other necessary elements: she understood the process of making fire, she needed fire, and she wasn't afraid to try something new." The implication, of course, is that Others succeeded and thrived; the Clan died.

Auel suggests other topics for thought about man's development: how Ayla first learns to start a fire with flint, how she learns to use a horse to help her, how she learns to communicate in a kind of extrasensory way with animals, how Jondalar learns to construct a craft to move on water. All are woven into the plot as naturally as any other event in an historical novel. The difference between this and more typical historical novels is merely setting; but the research—biological, geographical, geological, zoological, anthropological, sociological, and archaeological—exhibited by the author makes for astounding, thought-provoking reading. As the second book of the series, however, <u>The Valley of the Horses</u> undoubtedly evokes the greatest comment on the development of languages and the importance of the ability to reason in the development of civilizations. That Auel could do all of that and still maintain suspense and drama in a complicated plot significantly credits her creative ability.

Analysis of the Sample for English

As you study the sample book report above, consider the following items:

- The introductory paragraph includes the necessary information: title, author, characters, setting, and theme. We learn, too, that the author has written three books in the series; the other two are named but not discussed. (Ultimately, six novels will complete the Earth People series.)
- The second paragraph presents a synopsis of the 550-page book in one paragraph. Probably the most difficult part of the book report to write, the synopsis must do what it does here: give only a sketch of what happens.
- In the third and fourth paragraphs, the writer narrows the discussion to topics most appropriate for an English class, language and logic. While obviously the writer could say much more about the book, its theme, its plot, or its development, he must somehow limit the report. By choosing two significant, subject-related topics for a brief discussion, the writer makes good use of the book-report format.
- The fifth paragraph suggests additional points of interest which further develop the theme, indicates the breadth of the research, and concludes with a reference to the points made in paragraphs 3 and 4, emphasizing the creativity evident in this unusual historical novel.
- Distinctive terms are included to merge style with the content area, words like *fictionalize, historical novel, nonverbal* and *verbal communication,* as well as other references to a novel's structure.
- Direct quotations from the book, accurately set apart with quotation marks, support the general statements and lend authenticity to the report.
- Other characteristics of effective theme development are evident throughout the paper.

Without a doubt, the above book report could have taken several approaches for an English class. For example, the writer could have chosen two to four main ideas about plot, particularly how Ayla manages to survive alone. The report could have dealt with character, discussing the emotional problems Ayla faced both alone and with Jondalar. The report could have concentrated on setting, describing by way of comparison the two cultures represented by Jondalar and Ayla. The options are many. On the other hand, a book report need not be critical writing [*see* LITERARY ANALYSES *in Part II*], nor need it be a review [*see* REVIEW *later in Part II*]. Remember, a book report merely tells what the book is about and relates it to the subject area.

Sample for Social Sciences

In a sociology class, students were asked to read and report on books, either fiction or nonfiction, that examine cultural habits, particularly as those habits can create prejudices. The writer whose report appears below met that assignment.

Prehistoric Prejudice

The second book of a trilogy, The Valley of the Horses is an historical novel which fictionalizes the beginning civilization in the Asian area north of the Beran Sea, an area in which many anthropologists locate the beginnings of civilization. Like Jean M. Auel's other two books, The Cave of the Clan Bear and The Mammoth Hunters, this one gets its foundation from archaeological research supporting the evolution of man. The reader follows Ayla, a child of the Others who has been reared by the Clan of the Cave Bear, as she meets Jondalar, a man of the Others. The Clan characterizes the end of the Neanderthal people, and the Others characterizes the beginning of the Cro-Magnon people. Set 25,000 years ago near the end of the Ice Age, the book clarifies the differences between the two peoples.

Ayla faces a lonely struggle for survival after her death curse by the Clan. To solve basic survival problems, she must use logic: alone, how can she kill, butcher and process an animal large enough to feed her through the severe winter; alone, how can she provide clothing, cooking utensils, sleeping skins, and shelter for protection; alone, how can she protect herself from the dangers around her? Her training as a medicine woman and her knowledge of hunting coupled with the large brain characteristic of the Others allow her to succeed. Also as a result of her background, she saves Jondalar's life after a lion mauls him and kills his traveling-companion brother. Jondalar is the first of the Others that Ayla has seen. After Ayla's medicinal powers help Jondalar regain his health, the two of them suffer from their inability to understand each other's customs. Jondalar finally teaches her to speak, however, and they establish a strong bond, sharing their creative ideas to reach solutions for both the physical and mental problems they face as a team.

It is the couple's inability to understand each other's customs that creates the conflict in the last half of the book. Jondalar, one of the Others who look down on the Clan as animals, is outraged when he finds that Ayla, obviously also one of the Others, has lived with the Clan and has even had a child by one of them. His outrage stems from his background. As a youth, he had shared in whispered conversations and rude jokes about the Flathead females, as the Others referred to the Clan women. "You know the one about the old man who was so blind, he caught a flathead female and thought it was a woman..." Flatheads were to be feared and territory was to be protected from them. As one stocky leader suggested, "Maybe we should get up a flathead hunting party and clean the vermin out." Jondalar knew that Flatheads could walk upright but only with a bowlegged, slightly bent shuffle. They had only crude spears, fashioned from sharpened sticks. They merely wrapped skins around them, neither cut nor stitched to fit. Quite simply, he saw them as "half-animal, half-human abominations!"

His outrage at learning about her relationship to the Clan leaves Ayla confused and frustrated. Tall and blond, quite different from the short, stocky, dark, hairy Clan people, Ayla grew up believing she was ugly. Different was ugly. So she accepts the Clan—both the people and their ways—as normal. She has seen no other humans until Jondalar. Because she understands the Clan's humanness, their sensitivity, their customs, and their interpretation of the spirit world, she cannot understand Jondalar's reaction. It is only after several highly emotional scenes and obvious innocence on her part that Ayla is gradually able to give Jondalar enough insight into the Clan world that he begins to see his error. He struggles with reason. "Could Ayla be that? Could she be defiled? Unclean? Filth? Evil? Honest, straightforward Ayla? With her Gift of healing? So wise, and fearless, and gentle, and beautiful." Ultimately, when he acknowledges that animals don't recognize a spiritual world, Jondalar is able to accept the fact that maybe—only maybe—Clan people are human.

The obvious parallel of these two representatives of opposing cultures with contemporary society leads the reader to wonder whether civilization has made much progress in the area of human relations and willingness to accept and understand other cultures. Indeed, Auel has dealt with a delicate subject in such a distant context that some readers may find the parallel invalid. With other themes readily a part of the trilogy, a reader may well choose to discuss them instead. The obvious intent of the plot of <u>The Valley of the Horses</u>, however, surely must be to help the readers see what Jondalar sees: without thorough understanding and insight, without walking in the other fellow's moccasins, so to speak, one cannot understand his ways. Too often, what is different is ugly; what is different is wrong. It is called prejudice.

Analysis of the Sample for Social Sciences

The following specific analytical comments emphasize the difference between a book report for an English class and one of the same book for a social sciences class:

- The first two paragraphs in the social sciences book report are very similar to those in the book report for English. The differences are subtle: a reference to the area *where archaeologists believe civilization began*, and the omission of such phrases as *unusual historical novel*. Certainly the plot, summarized in paragraph 2, will be the same for any subject area.

- The obvious differences come, then, in paragraphs 3 and 4. The writer approaches this complicated novel via the sociology strand. By dealing specifically with the understanding the two characters must gain from each other about their respective cultures, the writer tailors her report to the social science subject area. The paragraphs merely summarize those specific areas of conflict; they do not evaluate or respond critically. [*For a comparison, see* LITERARY ANALYSES *and* REVIEW *later in Part II.*]

- The conclusion further enhances the social science emphasis. By concluding with a reference to paragraphs 3 and 4 and acknowledging the presence of other themes, the writer first broadens the scope and then zeros in on her main idea, ending with an application of the theme to contemporary society.

- Note that direct quotations, punctuated accurately, help support the general ideas.

- Effective transitions help readers move smoothly within as well as between paragraphs.

Note that the social science book report follows the same organization and structure as did the English book report. The difference comes from the choice of subject matter for discussion. As always, the subject matter must relate to the content area of the course for which the report is being prepared.

──────────── **Sample for Science** ────────────

As part of a biology class, students were asked to select a book from a list of works of fiction and report on the use of scientific knowledge as it helps develop either the plot or the background of the book. One student, whose book report appears below, selected *The Valley of the Horses*. Note how the writer meets the assignment.

When Science in Fiction Is Not Science Fiction

The second book of a triology, <u>The Valley of the Horses</u> fictionalizes the beginning of civilization in the Asian area north of the Beran Sea. Like Jean M. Auel's other two books, <u>The Clan of the Cave Bear</u> and <u>The Mammoth Hunters</u>, this one gets its foundation from the archaeological research supporting the evolution of man. The reader follows Ayla, a child of the Others who has been reared by the Clan of the Cave Bear only to be ejected from the Clan when she violates customs she cannot understand or accept. In exile in

the valley of the horses, she survives five years alone until she
meets Jondalar, a man of the Others.

Ayla faces a lonely struggle for survival after her death curse
by the Clan. To solve basic survival problems, she must use logic:
alone, how can she kill, butcher and process an animal large
enough to feed her through the severe winter; alone, how can she
provide clothing, cooking utensils, sleeping skins, and shelter for
protection; alone, how can she protect herself from the dangers
around her? Her training as a medicine woman and her knowledge
of hunting coupled with the large brain characteristic of the Others
allow her to succeed. Also as a result of her background, she saves
Jondalar's life after a lion mauls him and kills his traveling-
companion brother. Jondalar is the first of the Others that Ayla has
seen. After Ayla's medicinal powers help Jondalar regain his health,
the two of them suffer from their inability to understand each
other's customs. Jondalar finally teaches her to speak, however, and
they are able to establish a strong bond, sharing their creative ideas
to find solutions for both the physical and mental problems they
face as a team.

The obviously well-researched novel brings to life a number of
scientific aspects of the prehistoric world. For instance, the reader
gains an understanding of life at the edge of a glacier. How
interesting to learn that because of the severe cold and resulting air
turbulence above the glacier, lands adjoining the ice field are dry
and nearly barren. The glacier feeds the rivers with its spring melt,
and readers see the rampage and the ravages. Plants and animals
native to the prehistoric setting, many of which are now extinct,
also come to life for the reader. "Many of the animals were huge—
bison and cattle half again as large as their later counterparts;
giant deer with eleven-foot racks; woolly mammoth and woolly
rhinoceros." The relative size of the woolly mammoth startles the
reader when he sees a human standing above the mammoth's eye.
Likewise, the reader learns about plants and their uses. "Her

collection of beargrass, cattail leaves and stalks, reeds, willow switches, roots of trees, would be made into baskets, tightly woven or of looser weave in intricate patterns, for cooking, eating, storage containers, winnowing trays, serving trays, mats for sitting upon, serving or drying food." Thus the biological and botanical details of the Ice Age make a formidable impact on the reader.

In addition to the biology and botany of the prehistoric world, Auel includes significant references to the theory of evolution. The reader meets Clan people who, although they can walk upright, walk bowlegged and slightly bent. They are short, stocky, dark, and hairy, their foreheads sloping backward from their eyebrows, all characteristic of scientific evidence distinguishing the Neanderthal man. Their short necks and lack of a chin make Ayla, born of the Others, appear to them to be deformed. She is tall, with long, straight legs, blond hair, and blue eyes that water, characteristic of scientific evidence distinguishing the Cro-Magnon man. She assumes she is ugly. Because her arms are long and straight, however, she can use a sling more effectively than any of the men of the Clan, a fact that ultimately costs her a place in the society. When Ayla violates a taboo and invades the secret ritual meeting of the men, the medicine man, called the Mogul, claims that tradition indicates such violation will be the end of the Clan. The prediction is Auel's way of dealing with the death of one branch of the human tree.

While the book is fiction, the scientific principles encompassed in the plot, setting, and characters make much of prehistoric theory and archaeological evidence real to the mind's eye. Then, to pick up the newspaper and read of another discovery of an ancient skeleton somewhere in Asia makes the parallels more obvious and the reading of both more interesting. Quite simply, the scientific reality woven into the historical novel makes the nonfiction aspects more readable and more memorable.

Analysis of the Sample for Science

The biology book report must, obviously, focus on scientific issues and concerns. As a result, paragraphs 1 and 2 are quite similar to those same paragraphs in the English and social sciences reports. Note these differences:

- Paragraph 3 points out the specific insights a reader gains from Auel's descriptions of prehistoric situations related to glaciation, particularly the geology and plants and animals.

- Paragraph 4 points out the insights related to and supported by archaeological research on evolution.

- The concluding paragraph emphasizes the value of the book, not as a scientific document but as a realization of theories and concepts. By concluding that *The scientific reality woven into the historical novel makes the nonfiction aspects more readable and more memorable*, the author points out both the value and the weakness of the book in the field of science.

- Direct quotations enhance the report, not only for support but to illustrate the thoroughness of the research.

- Effective transitions move readers through the report.

- Other characteristics of a good theme are evident throughout the report. [*See* Theme *later in Part II.*]

——— Sample for Business ———

In a general business class, students were asked to read and report on a work of fiction or nonfiction which deals with a business principle. Although *The Valley of the Horses* did not appear on the suggested reading list, the instructor approved a student's request to use it for her report. Below you will see how the student met the assignment.

The Early World of Barter

The second book of a trilogy, <u>The Valley of the Horses</u> fictionalizes the beginning of civilization in the Asian area north of the Beran Sea. Like Jean M. Auel's other two books, <u>The Clan of the Cave Bear</u> and <u>The Mammoth Hunters</u>, this one gets its foundation from archaeological research supporting the evolution of man. The reader follows Ayla, a child of the Others who has been reared by the Clan of the Cave Bear, to her meeting with Jondalar, a man of the Others.

Ayla faces a lonely struggle for survival after her death curse by the Clan. To solve basic survival problems, she must use logic: alone, how can she kill, butcher and process an animal large enough to feed her through the severe winter; alone, how can she provide clothing, cooking utensils, sleeping skins, and shelter for protection; alone, how can she protect herself from the dangers around her? Her training as a medicine woman and her knowledge of hunting coupled with the large brain characteristic of the Others allow her to succeed. Also as a result of her background, she saves Jondalar's life after a lion mauls him and kills his traveling-companion brother. Jondalar is the first of the Others that Ayla has seen. After Ayla's medicinal powers help Jondalar regain his health, the two of them suffer from their inability to understand each other's customs. Jondalar finally teaches her to speak, however, and they establish a strong bond, sharing their creative ideas to find solutions for both the physical and mental problems they face as a team.

The novel provides insight into one of business' most basic principles: barter. The Clan people, by whom Ayla was reared, do not barter. While the division of labor is clear within the Clan and as long as enough members exist in a Clan they can survive, they depend only on their immediate surroundings for resources. As a result, when resources dwindle, the Clan people move; they do not seek alternative resources or alternative sources. On the other hand, Jondalar's people maintain trade with other tribes, not only for natural resources but also for skills. For example, Jondalar as a young man lives with another tribe to learn from the most respected craftsman the techniques of making flint tools. In another example, he trades two extra fine pieces of flint from a faraway area for the promise of hospitality on his return visit. When his host exclaims, "I was going to visit . . . next year to get some flint from the Lanzadonii mine. There is no better stone," Jondalar responds, "I have some Lanzadonii flint with me. . . . I'd be happy to give it to you if you'd like it." Concerned over the value of the flint, Jondalar's host counters with, "I'd be happy to take it, but I'd want to give you something in return. I don't mind getting the better side of a good trade, but I wouldn't want to cheat you." And so the trade is completed.

The most complicated form of barter evidenced in The Valley of the Horses, however, is a trade system developed by two tribes so closely dependent upon one another that intermarriages can occur only in pairs. "Maybe we need to find him a river woman so he can become a Ramudoi. It's only fair. . . ." The Ramudoi is a hunting tribe which lives in wooden shelters; the other is a boat-building tribe. Because each can offer to the other skills and services as well as resources like fish and game, the two tribes have intertwined so thoroughly that relationships are too complicated for the visiting Jondalar to understand. During his visit there, however, they teach him their refined boat-building skills. He learns that the principle of building their boats "was to enclose a pocket of air within a wooden shell. It was a significant innovation." He repays their instruction with labor and new tools, the only resource he has to offer at the time. As they say of him, "It's not the boats, it's the tools we use to make them. Jondalar, you'll always be a toolmaker at heart."

Even though the book is fiction, Auel's assumptions about the beginning of civilizations are obviously couched in careful research. Although "business" as a term seems hardly appropriate to the prehistoric cultures, the concepts were beginning to develop. To examine with Auel how barter affected the ultimate existence of a tribe clarifies the reader's understanding of the importance of the division of labor enriched by barter.

Analysis of the Sample for Business

Like the previous sample book reports, this one is tailored for the specific subject area. Following the organizational plan set forth in the beginning of this section, the book report above includes these characteristics:

- In the introductory paragraph, the reader finds all the pertinent information.
- Paragraph 2 contains a synopsis of the plot.
- Paragraphs 3 and 4, like those in the earlier reports, tailor the report to the content area and, in this case, deal with a discussion of barter, a basic business principle.
- The conclusion, echoing the content of the previous two paragraphs, attempts to place the book's treatment of the subject in perspective.
- Direct quotations add supportive detail.
- Transitions function well, moving readers through the report.

Sample for Vocational Education

As part of an introductory vocational class, students were asked to investigate the discovery or invention of a work-saving device. The student whose book report appears below met the assignment by reading a work of fiction.

Learning by Necessity

The second book of a trilogy, <u>The Valley of the Horses</u> fictionalizes the beginning of civilization in the Asian area north of the Beran Sea. Like Jean M. Auel's other two books, <u>The Clan of the Cave Bear</u> and <u>The Mammoth Hunters</u>, this one gets its foundation from the archaeological research supporting the evolution of man. The reader follows Ayla, a child of the Others who has been reared by the Clan of the Cave Bear, to her meeting with Jondalar, a man of the Others.

Ayla faces a lonely struggle for survival after her death curse by the Clan. To solve basic survival problems, she must use logic: alone, how can she kill, butcher and process an animal large enough to feed her through the severe winter; alone, how can she provide clothing, cooking utensils, sleeping skins, and shelter for protection; alone, how can she protect herself from the dangers around her? Her training as a medicine woman and her knowledge of hunting coupled with the large brain characteristic of the Others allow her to succeed. Also as a result of her background, she saves Jondalar's life after a lion mauls him and kills his traveling-companion brother. Jondalar is the first of the Others that Ayla has seen. After Ayla's medicinal powers help Jondalar regain his health, the two of them suffer from their inability to understand each other's customs. Jondalar finally teaches her to speak, however, and they establish a strong bond, sharing their creative ideas to reach solutions for both the physical and mental problems they face as a team.

It is Ayla's struggle to survive alone that gives the reader the greatest insight into how new work-saving techniques may have come into being. First, as Ayla faces the problem of killing, butchering and processing a large animal, she stumbles into a long-term situation which eventually eases her workload. With the aid of a pit trap, she kills a horse. Only after the slaughter is complete does she realize the mare has a colt. Because her instinct as a medicine woman is to care for living beings, she takes the colt back to her cave, raises it, and, in the course of time, learns to ride it and rely upon its speed to hunt from it. "The ride was a thrill she could hardly contain. The very idea of going along with a horse when it galloped filled Ayla with a sense of wonder. She had never dreamed such a thing was possible. No one had." Later, after another big kill, Ayla is faced with the problem of getting a deer carcass back to her cave, a distance of several miles. She discovers quite by accident how to use two poles, harnessed to the horse, to function like a sled. In short, her experiences exhibited one principle: "Only in the animal called human did survival depend on more than strength and fitness. Already puny compared with their carnivorous competitors, mankind depended on cooperation and compassion to survive."

In addition to her rather remarkable discovery of using animals to help with her work, she also discovered new kinds of tools. By accident, she learned that two pieces of flint, struck together, would produce a spark. By experiment, she learned that attaching flint tools to a wooden handle improved their usefulness.

By necessity, she experimented with plants to find the right combination to help a lion cub and later Jondalar regain their health. Finally, by watching Jondalar and studying his clothing, she learned to use bone needles to stitch hides, thus creating more form-fitting garments.

Auel presents a fascinating story for even the most casual reader. Furthermore, however, she includes thought-provoking details about the development of tools and other discoveries that reduced work. In fact, Ayla seems to embody the maxim "Necessity is the mother of invention." The details seem almost afterthoughts to the plot development, but in fact they generate some of the best reading. Certainly the reader can appreciate from this prehistoric perspective the phenomenal assistance man now has to ease his labors.

Analysis of the Sample for Vocational Education

Tailored for the vocational education content area, the book report above follows the general outline given earlier in this section:

- Paragraph 1 gives the pertinent introductory information.
- Paragraph 2 gives the synopsis of the book.
- In paragraphs 3 and 4 the writer directs his attention to the subject matter of vocational education, that of seeking assistance in a job too big for the laborer and that of seeking improved tools to complete a job. Each paragraph develops one idea.
- The paragraphs include support from direct quotations from the book.
- Finally, the conclusion indicates that while *necessity is the mother of invention*, the book adds a certain perspective to the advantages of modern labor aids. In brief, the book report emphasizes the content appropriate for the class for which it was written.

After studying the sample book reports and analyses above and by following the process set out at the beginning of this chapter, you should be able to develop a satisfactory report for any content area.

CAUSE AND EFFECT

The cause-effect paper analyzes a situation from one of two directions. It may examine the cause or causes of a situation. In that case, it answers questions like "What caused these rock formations?" "How did the incumbent lose the election?" "Why did the City Council reject the petition for rezoning?" "What makes a lathe work?" The result is known, but the paper explains what brought it about. The analysis reveals the cause, the why, the how.

On the other hand, the cause-effect paper may examine the effect or effects of a situation. In that case it answers questions like "What will happen if PCBs are spilled into the river above the city's water intake?" "How do FCC regulations affect what the television viewer sees?" "What happens if I overdraw my checking account?" "How will safety glasses protect me during certain industrial processes?" In these cases, the cause is known; the paper explains the result, the effect.

The cause-effect relationship demands careful development in a composition, but that development is often the basis for further kinds of development. For instance, if you know the cause of a problem, then the solution may be to eliminate the cause. Thus, you can develop a problem-solution paper by first examining the cause-effect relationship. Or if you know the effects of several actions, then you can classify the actions according to the effects and develop a classification paper. Or if you know the cause of a specific historical event, then you can write an accurate definition of the event. Likewise, in order to write a process-analysis paper, you must acknowledge both causes and effects. Dealing with a cause-effect relationship, therefore, often helps a writer develop papers by others methods as well.

Characteristics

Usually a cause-effect paper, either a paragraph or longer, will include the following characteristics:

- an analysis of the cause or causes of a specific effect,

- an analysis of the effect or effects of a specific cause, or, in a really complicated paper,

- an analysis of both the cause(s) and the effect(s) of a specific situation, and, in any case,

- evidence of clear, logical relationships.

In addition to clearly established cause-effect relationships, a cause-effect paper also

- begins with a good introduction,

- includes a clear topic or thesis sentence [*see* TOPIC SENTENCE *and* THESIS SENTENCE *in the Glossary*],
- shows clear organization,
- uses effective transitional devices [*see* TRANSITIONS *in the Glossary*],
- develops clear supporting details [*see* SPECIFIC DETAIL *in the Glossary*],
- maintains unity [*see* UNITY *in the Glossary*],
- demonstrates effective sentence variety,
- builds effective emphasis,
- uses vocabulary appropriate for the subject and the audience,
- concludes logically.

Process

The following steps will help you plan and develop a cause-effect paper, either a short, paragraph-length analysis or a full-length paper. [*Refer also to* PARAGRAPHS *in Part II for a careful analysis of paragraph structure and to* THEME *in Part II for additional information about writing a full-length paper.*]

PREWRITING

STEP 1. FINDING A TOPIC

If you must select your own topic, do so by brainstorming to list situations appropriate for the paper. [*See also* PREWRITING *in Part I for additional suggestions for topic sources.*] Try these steps:

- As you brainstorm, think of topics you have studied recently. Without thinking about order or logic,

jot down ten or fifteen topics as quickly as they occur to you. In an economics class, for instance, the list of topics may include these items:

  - monopolies
  - oligopolies
  - perfect competition
  - capitalism
  - production
  - supply and demand
  - inflation
  - socialism
  - communism
  - distribution equilibrium point

- Now that you have topics, the cause-effect situations will be evident. For instance:

  - How does a monopoly form? (causes)
  - What happens to the price of products produced by a monopoly? (effects)
  - What factors are involved in production? (causes)
  - When production is slowed, what happens to the economy? (effects)
  - What brings about inflation? (causes)
  - How does inflation affect the stock market? (effects)
  - What happens to production during periods of high inflation? (effects)

Any of these topics are suitable for a cause-effect analysis.

After you have brainstormed to generate a list of topics, pick one which interests you and formulate a question similar to those above. The purpose of your paper will be to answer that question.

STEP 2.   DECIDING ON CAUSE OR EFFECT

When you have a topic, either assigned or selected by the process above, decide whether your analysis will examine causes or effects. If you are not sure, try restating the question so that you use the word *cause* or *effect*. For instance, the question above, "When production slows, what happens to the economy?" can be reworded to ask "When production slows, what are the *effects* on the economy?" The rewording clarifies that you will be writing about effects. On the other hand, the question "How do monopolies form?" can be reworded to ask "What *causes* monopolies?" Then you understand that you will be analyzing causes and explaining how monopolies come into being.

STEP 3.   SELECTING THE MAIN IDEAS

With your topic stated as a question, jot down as many answers as you can. To answer a complicated or technical question, you may need to do research, but we will assume here that you already know the answers. [*For a thorough discussion of the process of developing a research paper, see* RESEARCH PAPER *later in Part II.*] The word "answers" takes a plural form under the assumption that your chosen topic will not have a simple, single cause or effect. If it does, it probably does not merit an analysis.

Use the following example to help you develop a list of answers. Assume that a writer is developing a

paper to explain why various groups of people have come to a remote island, called Isle Royale, in Lake Superior. That writer's list of answers may look like this:

- to study the wolf population
- to study the moose population
- to harvest the lumber
- to explore
- to sightsee
- to fish commercially
- to hike
- to mine copper

List answers to your own question now.

STEP 4.   NARROWING THE TOPIC

When you have listed all the answers you can think of, decide which three or four are most important. Set them aside before going on to Step 5.

For instance, the writer working with the list above chose to narrow his topic to deal only with early groups of people who came to Isle Royale. As a result, he limited his answers to these three:

- to mine copper
- to harvest lumber
- to fish commercially

STEP 5.   ADDING SUPPORTING DETAILS

Using the list of answers as topics, add three or four supporting details to each item. The supporting details may be examples, illustrations, definitions, analogies, comparisons, contrasts, or other explanations. Use the following sample list as a guide for developing your own:

- To mine copper
  - prehistoric people
  - first settlers
  - last miners
- To fish commercially
  - early success
  - declining success
  - present success
- To harvest lumber
  - in the 1890s
  - in the 1920s

This list is, in fact, a scratch outline. [*If you need a more formal outline, see* OUTLINES *elsewhere in Part II. The explanation there will help you convert the scratch outline into a formal outline.*]

STEP 6.   ORGANIZING THE DETAILS

You must choose a pattern of organization appropriate for your subject. For instance:

- A paper analyzing the economic results of slowed production may take a chronological approach (What happens first? What happens next?) or an order of importance approach (What is the most important effect? The next most important? The least important?).
- An analysis of the impact of World War II on an industry may take an order of importance approach (either from most important to least or least important to most).
- A descriptive analysis of the effects of a tornado may take a spatial approach, following the path

of destruction (e.g. from southwest to northeast).

Select the organizational plan that will best suit your subject: chronological order, spatial order, or one of the orders of importance. [*See the entry for each in the Glossary.*]

STEP 7.   CHECKING THE LOGIC

The following flaws in thinking can occur in the development of a cause-effect paper:

- a cause-effect relationship based only on a time relationship,
- a cause-effect relationship based upon coincidence,
- a cause-effect relationship simplified by citing only the immediate causes when more remote causes are equally important.

To deal with these potential logic problems, try these three suggestions:

Suggestion 1

Sometimes Situation B appears to be caused by Situation A simply because A happened before B. But merely because an earthquake occurred immediately after a heated argument does not mean that the argument caused the earthquake! Be sure the cause-effect relationship you analyze depends on more than a time relationship.

Suggestion 2

Sometimes an analysis breaks down because the writer finds what seems to be more than a time relationship but in fact is merely coincidence. A court of law would label such analyses as circumstantial. For instance, if a monkey plays with a camera long enough, it may manage to take a decent picture. The picture, however, is not proof that the monkey has learned how to take pictures. It is only coincidence. Do not include what may be coincidence as primary evidence of causes or effects.

Suggestion 3

Certainly any analysis must cope with recent and more remote causes and effects. The length of your paper determines how far back or forward you can take your analysis. The real problem, however, occurs when the writer looks at remote causes or distant effects *instead of* recent ones. While indeed a serious automobile accident was ultimately caused by the invention of the automobile, such a remote cause is ridiculous in light of the immediate cause: the driver ran a stop sign. Be sure your analysis deals with recent causes and effects, delving into the remote past or distant future only as logic and space allow.

WRITING

STEP 8. FOLLOWING THE PLAN

As you develop your cause and effect paper, follow the organization established in the Steps above. [*Refer to* THEME *if you are writing a full-length paper, and refer to* PARAGRAPH (*both in Part II*) *if you are writing a shorter paper. Both sections will help you develop effective structure.*]

REVISING

STEP 9. CHECKING THE CONTENT

Use the following questions to determine where your paper may need revision:

- Have I clearly established the cause-effect relationship by using transitional devices?

- Have I avoided logical fallacies?

- Does the paper begin with an effective introduction? Does it give something of the background and include a thesis or topic sentence? [*See* THESIS SENTENCE *or* TOPIC SENTENCE *in the Glossary.*]

- Is the paper well-structured? [*See* REVISING: CHECKING STRUCTURE *in Part I.*]

- Have I maintained unity by omitting unrelated ideas? [*See* REVISING: SAMPLE REVISION FOR UNITY *in Part I.*]

- Does each body paragraph include a topic sentence? Does it relate directly to the thesis statement? [*See* THEME *in Part II for a complete explanation.*]

- Is my conclusion effective? [*See* CONCLUSION *in the Glossary.*]

- Have I used good sentence structure and achieved effective sentence variety? [*See* REVISING: SAMPLE REVISION FOR SENTENCE VARIETY *in Part I.*]

- Do my sentences generate appropriate emphasis? [*See* REVISING: SAMPLE REVISION FOR EMPHASIS *in Part I.*]

If you cannot honestly answer "yes" to each of these questions, you have discovered areas in need of revision.

[*In addition, see* REVISING *in Part I for general information, including a more detailed list of questions for guiding your revision.*]

PROOFREADING

STEP 10.   CHECKING FOR DETAILS

Read your paper for accurate mechanics, usage, and grammar.

Check for accurate spelling and word choice. See *Webster's New World Thesaurus* and *Webster's New World Dictionary* for reference.

A Note about the Samples: The following cause-and-effect papers all deal with a single subject: Isle Royale National Park. By using one topic, we can illustrate how to select specific topics to relate to specific content areas.

You will note that some samples deal with causes, some with effects, and some with both.

As you study, you will discover the papers vary from a single paragraph to a full-length, five-paragraph theme. You may want to compare several to see how structure affects content.

Sample for English

Students in an English class were asked to analyze a specific vacation spot. In other words, the question they were to answer is as follows: What causes some people to choose _____ as a vacation spot? The following cause-and-effect paragraph is one student's analysis.

Choosing a Vacation Spot

Some people choose vacation spots because their friends went there last year or because the advertisements make the place look luxurious. Others choose spots that meet their special interests. For instance, some people prefer a vacation spot away from tourists or bustling crowds. The only crowds they want to see are crowds of wildlife—flora and fauna. They do not demand luxurious accommodations but enjoy a quiet view of the water. Sunrises and sunsets fascinate them more than neon lights and glittering marquees. A lone wolf or loon call drifting over the steady slap of waves on the rocks lulls them to sleep far more readily than rumbling trucks on a nearby interstate. They do not mind the inconvenience of a five-hour boat trip to reach a place where these phenomena greet them, for they appreciate the fact that no tourist can come jouncing in in an automobile, adding noise and air pollution to a virtually pristine environment. Most important, however, they welcome the absence of outside stress: no radios, no television, no roads, no vehicles, no contact with the outside world for as long as they choose to stay. These people choose to vacation at Isle Royale National Park.

Analysis of the Sample for English

The cause-and-effect paper exhibits many typical characteristics:

- The writer enumerates the causes for visiting Isle Royale National Park.
- The organization permits the writer ample opportunity to build to the topic sentence, here the last sentence of the paragraph.
- Organized by order of importance, from least important to most important, the writer begins with the second most important reason for choosing the park as a vacation spot: few people. Next he lists the least important reason, the comfortable but not luxurious accommodations; and finally he concludes with the most important cause, the absence of stress from the outside world. While some writers may arrange the materials differently, this writer suggests personal preferences by the order of his arrangement.
- Although the writer does not begin by saying, *These issues caused us to choose Isle Royale National Park for our vacation spot*, the readers recognize by the end of the paper that these have been the guiding issues for the analysis.
- Being subtle, the writer lists issues and then indicates that the chosen vacation spot fulfilled the preference.
- The conclusion, without elaborating, tells the reader what to expect at Isle Royale.
- The cause-effect logic follows smoothly.
- The varied sentence structure provides easy reading.
- Specific details create clear mental pictures.
- Grammar, mechanics, and usage are accurate.

In general, then, the paragraph generates an effective causal analysis.

---------------- **Sample for Social Sciences** ----------------

The following five-paragraph cause-and-effect paper analyzes what caused various early groups of people to come to what is now Isle Royale National Park.

The Riches of Isle Royale

Isolated in the far reaches of Lake Superior, Isle Royale has lured people to its mysterious shores for centuries. Over the past four thousand years, only three natural resources have merited man's battle with the isolation and climate; and in every case, the battle was at worst sporadic and at best relatively short-lived.

The lumber industry fought the shortest-lived battle. During only two periods did the lumber industry attack the island, first in the 1890s and again in the early 1930s. In each case, a natural disaster halted operations. In the earlier period, a flood which caused the log barrier to break scattered the entire year's harvest into Lake Superior; and during the second period, a fire burned nearly a quarter of the island, leaving the lumber company's assets in ashes. Fortunately, at least for the island's ecology, its isolation and thin soil, which will not support tall stands of trees, discouraged the lumber industry from doing further damage to the ecosystem.

The second natural resource that caused man to come to Isle Royale was the abundance of fish. Commercial fishing began before 1800 and continues today, albeit in a considerably reduced manner. Early on, nearly every protected cove had a fish house or fisherman's cottage, although most fishermen and their families occupied the island only seasonally. Now, plagued by a decline of fish and increase in expense, commercial fishing only suggests what once was. Primarily an individual enterprise, commercial fishing in the area enjoys the protective coves and inlets abundant in the archipelago. While catches of the prized whitefish have declined for unknown reasons, the fishermen also face man-made disruptions of the area's fishing. Sea lampreys and smelt, both introduced by man or as a result of man's interference, have significantly affected the fish population. The remaining fishermen, mostly park service employees, attempt to maintain the vocation as part of the island life.

The primary attraction to Isle Royale, however, has been its potential for precious copper. Prehistoric Indians, like most others who came after them, explored the island during the short summer season, leaving the whipping subzero winds to batter only the trees and rocks. Although experts do not know exactly when or why Indians first crossed the water to Isle Royale, carbon dating indicates they were there by 2000 B.C. In their search for copper, they used the beach cobbles to hammer away the rock and expose the copper veins. Prized for spear points, implements and decorative ornaments, the copper attracted Indians to the island for over 1,000 years. Their occupation sites indicate their peak activity period from 800 to 1600 declined until by the 1840s the Indian culture in the entire Lake Superior area diminished. When white miners came in the 1840s, only two Indian camps remained. Copper mining activity, still only sporadic after the Indians left, resulted in only small quantities of the precious metal. As the largest operation, the Minong Mine employed nearly 150 miners during the late 1800s. They and their families established the largest white man's settlement on Isle Royale. When that mine went out of business, it left behind piles of "poor rock," some yawning pits, and little else. Nothing remains of the town.

Now people come to Isle Royale for only one natural resource: wilderness. Protected by the National Park System, the island is as close to primeval North woods as any other land in the United States. That may be a more precious commodity than the natural resources any copper, fish, or lumber industry has sought.

Analysis of the Sample for Social Sciences

While the sample causal analysis for English was paragraph length, the analysis above is a typical five-paragraph paper. [*See* THEME *in Part II.*] Note these specifics:

- The first paragraph sets out the cause-and-effect relationships to be examined: What caused people to come to Isle Royale?
- Secondarily, almost coincidentally, the paper also looks at causes for the people's leaving.
- The introduction includes the thesis sentence, the final sentence in the first paragraph.
- The introduction establishes the order in which the body paragraphs will be developed.
- Each paragraph examines one cause for their coming: lumbering, fishing, and mining.
- Each paragraph includes ample supporting details to develop the main ideas.
- The paragraphs are obviously arranged by order of importance, from least important to most important.
- Effective transitions help readers follow the organization and recognize the order of importance.
- The intent of the analysis is to describe why people have come to the island over the centuries. Following logically, however, are other cause-effect relationships.

Note that in dealing with the lumber industry, the writer suggests other causal relationships: the effect of the shallow soil on tree growth, the effect of floods on lumbering, and the effect of fires on Isle Royale. Again, in discussing the fishing industry, the writer suggests other possible topics for further analysis: causes for the decline of whitefish, effects of the sea lamprey on the fish populations, and the effects of smelt on fish populations. Then, in the discussion of the mining industry, certain questions remain unanswered, questions which a cause-and-effect paper could answer: effects of the copper-mining industry on the ecological system of the island, causes for the industry's collapse, and effects of the industry's collapse on the island's future. Finally, by examining indirectly the island's inability to provide an economic base for permanent habitation, the writer comments on the causes for people leaving the island's isolation and inclement weather. The fact that these questions are answered only cursorily or ignored completely does not suggest that the writer has failed in her analysis; she has written what she set out to write. On the other hand, these additional analyses, either addressed or implied, merely suggest the complicated relationships in otherwise apparently simple analyses. Be prepared to find such open-ended situations when you try to analyze a complicated subject.

If you have supported your stated subject adequately, you have no cause for alarm. To develop other suggested causal relationships would be to destroy the unity of your paper.

Sample for Science

The following cause-and-effect paragraph, still dealing with the general subject of Isle Royale, illustrates a topic appropriate for a science class. While a number of subjects suitable for a scientific cause-and-effect paper appeared in the discussion above for the social science paper, the following subject emphasizes the effects rather than the causes.

The Significance of Balance-of-Nature Studies
at Isle Royale National Park

For the past fifty years biologists have been studying the balance of nature by means of a unique experiment conducted in the self-contained laboratory called Isle Royale National Park. The park, an island consisting of 210 square miles of wilderness, affords scientists the opportunity to observe animal relationships in an environment completely undisturbed by man. Sometime early in this century, moose arrived on the island, probably by swimming from the Canadian shore. By the early 1930's, proliferating without predators, the moose herds literally ate themselves out of house and home. Limited by the boundaries of the island, they starved, dying in large numbers. Then a disastrous fire in 1936 nearly eliminated the browsing food moose eat; but in turn, the fire opened large areas for new growth, just the right diet for the huge animals. So the herd grew. Again it outgrew its supply of food. Then, in 1948-1949, the severe winter caused an ice bridge to form from the Minnesota mainland to Isle Royale. By chance, a small pack of Eastern timber wolves ventured across the ice, found the island and found the moose. Wolves are the only natural predators of moose. In the course of the next several decades, scientists have watched the wolf population grow and thrive until the moose population dwindles. Then the wolves die from lack of food, and the moose population increases. As a result of the controlled environment of the island and the relatively small geographical area involved, scientists can keep actual head counts and study the moose-wolf balance in detail. The balance-of-nature theory has, in the decades of study there, proven itself accurate. What a lesson for people to learn! As one scientific observer said of the park, "The island's uniqueness lies in its complex yet simple system of natural processes. . . . In such a system a delicate balance is struck in which no one animal or organism is more important than another. And man's part? We must leave this balance to natural law, observing but not manipulating."

Analysis of the Sample for Science

In a single paragraph, the causal analysis explores the effect on the moose population when wolves moved onto the island, a dynamic cycle usually expressed by biologists in terms of *natural balance*. The writer deals effectively with the explanation. Note these specifics:

- In order to succeed with her explanation, the writer had to deal with both causes and effects. For instance, she explained what caused the moose population to expand and decline and then repeat the cycle before the wolf population was introduced. Already the natural balance existed. She had at least to suggest what caused the wolves to arrive on the island and what caused them to thrive and then decline and thrive again. In the process of examining causes, the writer tied together sufficient information to indicate the effects of wolves on the moose population, and vice versa.

- The chronological organization flows smoothly, allowing readers to follow the rise and fall of populations.

- The logical relationships avoid the potential pitfalls. The frequent repetition of the rise-and-fall pattern over the past decades emphasizes the evidence.

- Sentence structure, varied but appropriately technical for its scientific nature, offers clarity and good detail.

- No extraneous material destroys unity.

In short, the paper offers a sound analysis suitable for a science class.

———————————— **Sample for Business** ————————————

The following cause-and-effect analysis was prepared for a business class. The assignment was to examine the causes for a particular business' failure.

The Failure of the Copper-Mining Industry on Isle Royale

The copper-mining industry on Isle Royale may have been doomed to failure even before it began. With a number of natural obstacles facing a mining operation on an isolated island, expenses soared. Situated in the northwestern part of Lake Superior, Isle Royale lies fifteen miles from Minnesota and nearly seventy miles from Michigan's Upper Peninsula. Any industry located there must necessarily deal with both the frigid, unyielding winters and the isolation. The mining industry was, of course, no exception. Three interrelated causes probably joined forces to destroy the industry.

First of all, miners and their families living on the island faced total dependency on water transportation for every need. While some game and an abundance of fish provided food, few men could be spared from the mine to hunt or fish. The severe climate and short growing season all but eliminated any other potential food supplies on the island. As a result, any needs—clothing, supplies, parts, livestock, fuel, or staples—depended on the boats' timely and safe arrival. During the long winter months, ice blocked boats from entering the harbors or even nearing the island. As a result, miners may have gone months at a time without parts or tool replacements necessary for their work. They and their families no doubt faced a grim life, choosing to leave as soon as possible.

Second, water transportation also provided product export. Without boats, the copper ore merely accumulated at the mine site. The waters around the island chain, notoriously treacherous and frequently stormy, often claimed the boats before they reached their destinations. Such maritime accidents no doubt took their toll on the mining operation.

Third, added to the serious problems of isolation, the island mines faced the same problem as other mines of the period: declining prices. Many mines could increase production and thereby offset the price decline. On Isle Royale, however, copper quantities appeared to be insufficient to make increased production practical. Furthermore, the mines at Isle Royale had to deal with the added expenses unnecessary at other mine sites. No doubt few alternatives remained but abandonment.

So, as a result of the expensive dependency on dangerous and sometimes unreliable shipping combined with the decline of copper prices, Isle Royal bears only ghostly reminders of a once-busy industry.

Analysis of the Sample for Business

The causal analysis theme above [*see* THEME *later in Part II*] speculates on three reasons for the failure of the copper-mining industry on Isle Royale. The following details suggest how the writer succeeds:

- The theme's organization relies on order of importance, but at the same time the cause developed in each paragraph is part of the overall cause: the island's isolation.

- While the writer is careful to use qualifying words like *no doubt, probably,* and *may,* the causal analysis flows logically.

- Varied sentence structure, good emphasis, and accurate grammar, mechanics, and usage combine to create a good theme.

- Since the writer follows the tight organization established in the introduction and presents each of three interrelated causes, the theme also maintains unity.

- The writer develops good structure throughout his paper. [*See* REVISING: CHECKING STRUCTURE *in Part I.*]

- Specific details enhance the paper and give readers a clear understanding of the writer's intent.

- Effective transitions help the paper flow smoothly.

─────────── **Sample for Vocational Education** ───────────

The following sample paper shows the effects of isolation on the skills required of Isle Royale maintenance personnel.

Working on Isle Royale

Isle Royale National Park, located in Lake Superior, is the most isolated of all the national parks. Its location results in peculiar problems, especially for maintenance personnel. A supply boat makes the run to the island once a week, weather permitting, but the only other contact the staff has with the mainland is via two-way radio. As a result, Isle Royale workers must be prepared to meet any emergencies and have on hand whatever parts, tools, and equipment they may need. The island generates its own electricity, so maintenance personnel must be able to solve any electrical problems or else the entire community is in the dark. Furthermore, the island maintains its own water supply. So maintenance people must understand the workings of the supply, purification, and pumping systems. And what comes in must go out. Maintenance personnel are also responsible for the garbage disposal and waste-water treatment systems. Complicated by the island's location, the maintenance problems at Isle Royale reach limits unknown to most park-maintenance workers.

Analysis of the Sample for Vocational Education

The effects described in the paragraph above result from the single cause established in the opening sentence. Note these additional details:

- The writer has presented the effects from most obvious to least obvious.

- Sufficient detail allows the reader to acknowledge the complications inherent in even minor repairs.

- Because the writer deals only with the effects of isolation on the skills required by maintenance staff, he maintains unity.

—————————— **Sample for Mathematics** ——————————

Math students were to respond to the following problem: In order to increase the water storage capacity from 5,000 to 10,000 gallons, workers on Isle Royale built a new cylindrical tank the same height but twice the diameter of the old one. When filled, the new tank held much more than 10,000 gallons. What caused the problem?

Water Storage Problem

The volume of a cylinder is calculated by multiplying the area of the base by the height. Since the new tank was the same height as the old one, the only change occurred in the area of the base. In this case, the diameter was doubled, which at first glance may appear to double the area. In fact, however, doubling the diameter quadruples the area of the base. Here's why. Since the area of a circle is calculated by using the formula πr^2, the area varies as the square of the radius. When the diameter doubles, the radius also doubles. When the doubled radius is squared, the area increases by four since $\pi(2r)^2 = 4\pi r^2$. When this new area is used to figure the volume of the cylinder, whose height remains the same, the volume quadruples. Thus the new tank holds 20,000, not 10,000 gallons.

Analysis of the Sample for Mathematics

The paragraph above explains the cause for a given effect and illustrates a problem solving technique.

- The first sentence states the principle in the problem and prepares readers to follow the logic behind the solution.
- The formulas are accompanied by explanations which clarify the cause of the tank's too-large capacity.
- The final sentence presents the logical conclusion.

By using these samples, you should be able to develop a satisfactory cause or effect paper. Be sure to clarify your purpose and organization in the topic or thesis sentence and then maintain unity with supporting details.

CHARACTER SKETCH

A character sketch, sometimes called a *characterization* or *profile*, focuses on one or two dominant aspects of a real or imaginary person. The sketch reveals a character trait or traits which the writer believes readers will find informative or at least interesting. Frequently used by both magazines and newspapers, character sketches attract attention (and encourage sales) because most people like to read about other people, not their stereotypical characteristics, but the unusual ones. Sometimes, too, teachers ask for a characterization of a real or fictional person you have been studying: a major historical figure, an inventor or scientist, a leader of some cause, the protagonist or antagonist in a novel, short story, or drama. In addition, fiction writers sometimes write sketches of their major characters for a planned short story or novel. The sketches help develop consistent characters.

Characteristics

A character sketch usually includes the following kinds of information:

- a character who is in some way unusual,

- a single focus on the character,

- details about the character which help the reader understand the focus,

- character actions which help the reader understand the focus,

- character conversations which help the reader understand the focus,

- direct or indirect descriptions of the character.

Process

The following planning and writing steps will help you complete a satisfactory character sketch.

PREWRITING
STEP 1. SELECTING A SUBJECT

Sometimes the subject of a character sketch is assigned; other times the writer selects the subject. If you select the subject, begin by brainstorming and creating a list of names. [*See also* PREWRITING *in Part I for additional suggestions for sources of topics.*] You may head your list with titles like these:

- People at Work
- People at My Family Reunion
- People Who Live on My Block
- People in My Sorority/Fraternity

- People in My Club
- People on My Athletic Team

When you have a list of a dozen or so people, think about each person individually. Ask yourself questions like these:

- What is his or her most unusual characteristic?
- How is this person's view of life different from that of most other people?
- How is the person different from most others like him or her?
- What would someone who meets him or her for the first time be most likely to notice—or least likely to notice?

These questions and others like them will give you a basis for choosing a subject for your character sketch.

STEP 2. DETERMINING THE FOCUS

Now that you have selected a person about whom you can write, list all the possibile characteristics you can think of that make this person interesting or unusual.

You may have a list something like this:

- called "world's oldest hippie"
- considers self a medical healer
- invents "contraptions"
- built own house
- eats strange herbs and plants
- makes violins
- raises own food—garden, goats, bees

- usually looks dirty

From your list, select one idea on which to build a character sketch. Put that idea in a sentence. Note that the idea may include more than one item from your list. For instance, "considers self a medical healer" may include eating the strange herbs and plants and raising his own food. All three may, in fact, define "world's oldest hippie." The following example illustrates a single focus:

> My neighbor, whom we call "the world's oldest hippie," considers himself a healer, using strange herbs and plants, all of which he raises himself.

In a single sentence, write the one idea on which you think you can build your character sketch.

STEP 3. SHOWING YOUR READER

The most important part of writing an effective character sketch is showing, not telling, something about your subject. Ask yourself at every sentence, "Am I telling, or am I showing?" If you write *Richard loved children*, then the reader must simply take your word for it. Instead, *show* that Richard loved children. Write something like this:

> Richard always met the neighborhood children at the bus stop. Even at 72 he was spry enough to bat balls, throw frisbees, and play a short game of basketball. But when he met us at the bus, he always had some new trick to show us—a

wooden top that would spin for minutes without toppling, a wooden doll-like creature that would climb a pair of ropes, a wooden man that turned flips. Always wooden. Carved and sanded and assembled in his cluttered little shop. He gave them away to whoever seemed to show the greatest fascination with the trick of the day.

Not once does the writer say that Richard loved the children, but readers know.

Select one situation in which you can best show your chosen character to readers.

STEP 4. CHOOSING A MEANS OF CHARACTERIZING

You can show, rather than tell about a character by using one or a combination of means. Consider any or all of these options:

Description

To help the reader see and know the character, describe any significant features about him or her or the surroundings of the sketch. Indirect description can be more effective than direct description. And remember, even in the course of describing, to show rather than tell. [*See* DESCRIPTION *in Part II.*]

Weak, telling   He was sloppy.

Better, showing   He dragged his sleeve through the spaghetti sauce.

Action

Rather than tell readers about the character, show the character in action. By watching people's behavior, we can learn about them.

Weak, telling   She was glad to see me.

Better, showing   When she saw me, she ran, arms open, to give me that wonderful bear-hug hello.

Conversation

Let your character talk. Use the same kinds of words and sentence structure in the dialogue as the character really uses. You will, of course, enclose the dialogue or monologue in quotation marks. [*See* DIALOGUE *and* PARAGRAPHS, KINDS: IN DIALOGUE *in Part II.*]

Weak, telling   Jeremy seemed nervous.

Better, showing   "No. I'm okay. Don't bother." Jeremy's tight voice left me unconvinced. "It's just. . . . Well, no, I'm okay. Really." He studied his fingernails.

Often these three means—description, action, and conversation—are combined in a narrative style resembling an excerpt from a short story. [*See* NARRATION *in Part II. For fictional character sketches, see* SHORT STORY *later in Part II.*]

STEP 5. DETERMINING THE POINT OF VIEW

Next, you must decide from which point of view to present your character sketch. [*See* POINT OF VIEW *in the Glossary.*] Whether you are writing fiction or nonfiction will, in part, help determine point of view. In a nonfiction sketch, a first-person point of view permits you to describe the character by being a part of the description. You become the "I." A third-person point of view allows you to stay outside the description. The reader sees the character more objectively. Of course, your observations determine how you handle the character sketch, but the third-person point of view maintains a distance many nonfiction writers prefer.

In a fiction sketch, a first-person point of view does not usually mean that the "I" is the writer. The "I" is probably a fictional narrator, whose observations of and experiences with the character will affect the reader's interpretation. Likewise, the third-person point of view may be omniscient, representing far more than a writer-observer knows in a nonfiction situation. [*See* SHORT STORY, STEP 5: PREWRITING—SELECTING POINT OF VIEW, *in Part II.*]

Select the point of view which will best enable you to present the character to your reader.

WRITING
STEP 6. PUTTING IT ALL TOGETHER

In Step 3, as you made your initial plans, you selected a particularly telling situation, conversation, or description by which to introduce the character.

Now, as you write, follow whatever means of organization best suits your purpose. [*See* ORDER, IN PARAGRAPH DEVELOPMENT *in the Glossary.*] A character sketch can assume virtually any organization. Certainly one of the orders of importance could function well. Often a sketch will read almost like a piece of fiction, so time order may be appropriate. Because of its similarity to fiction, the sketch may also include flashbacks, especially if you want to develop the sketch stylistically. [*See* FLASHBACK *in the Glossary and other details about fiction in* SHORT STORY *in Part II.*] For this kind of writing, you may choose any organizational pattern or combination of patterns which best suit the situation.

Write the sketch now, including description, dialogue, and action, showing rather than telling.

REVISING
STEP 7. CHECKING FOR CONTENT

When you have completed your first draft, consider the following questions as you reread to spot possible weaknesses:

• Does my character become real to the reader?

- Have I made him or her sound special rather than stereotypical?
- Have I maintained a single focus rather than rambling about all kinds of interesting details? [*See* REVISING: SAMPLE REVISION FOR UNITY *in Part I.*]
- Do all details—descriptions, actions, conversations—support the single focus?
- Are details logically organized?
- Does the reader hear and see the character?
- Does the dialogue accurately reflect the character? [*See* DIALOGUE *in Part II.*]
- Since actions speak louder than words, does the reader see the character in action?
- Have I been subtle with details rather than blunt and bold? [*See* REVISING: SAMPLE REVISION FOR SPECIFIC DETAIL *in Part I.*]
- Do I show rather than tell what the character is like?

- Do I maintain good emphasis, putting main ideas in main clauses? [*See* REVISING: SAMPLE REVISION FOR EMPHASIS *in Part I.*]

Any questions to which you cannot answer an honest "yes" may suggest areas which need revision.
[*See also the guideline questions for general revision in* REVISING *in Part I.*]

PROOFREADING

STEP 8. CHECKING THE DETAILS

As you proofread, check punctuation, especially in conversations. [*See* DIALOGUE *in Part II.*] Correct any grammar, mechanics, or usage problems you find. Check the Glossary for quick definitions, examples, and further cross-references. Finally, check *Webster's New World Dictionary* and *Webster's New World Thesaurus* for spelling and vocabulary choice.

--------------- **Sample Character Sketch** ---------------

The following character sketch exhibits most of the characteristics listed above. As you read, watch for "showing" words and phrases.

Mr. Biddleman: He Is What He Eats

"Come into the kitchen with me. I'm eating just now." A hint of British accent added a musical quality to his old-man voice. "Let me get you some tea."

A fine old bone-china plate sat on the painted wooden table piled high with books and junk mail. Whatever was on the plate—unrecognizable by local standards—smelled like a wild combination of garlic and sage.

"Shove the books over; I've your tea here." He placed on the table a cup and saucer that matched the plate. On another saucer were two brownish cookies or thin cakes. "I must say it's so great to see you, my boy. What brings you around to my humble abode?" A glance around the room emphasized humble but not poor. Books tumbled over one another on every sitting place but one, the ladder-back rocker in the corner by the window.

"Just visiting. What are you reading lately?"

"Most recently I've been reading up a bit on the ancient herbal medicines. You know the Incas. . . ."

Listening to the details of his past day's reading helped put the room in perspective. The plants on the windowsill, the aroma from the oven, the cookie-cakes on the table, the food in his plate, the trays of dried leaves on the refrigerator, the strings of dried flowers and pods hanging from the ceiling light, the bags of dried grains in the corner, and the fresh vegetable cuttings in the sink wove their way into his recounting of his latest reading.

"It's all in what you eat, you know. Eat up." The cookie-cake things seemed to grow uglier by the minute. He wiped his plate clean with some kind of dark brown bread, stuffed the hunk in his mouth, and wiped the dribble from his chin. "Eat up, my boy, eat up!"

Only when the door slapped shut on squeaky hinges after his final goodbye did the overwhelming sensory bombardment drift away with the air. Ah, fresh air.

Analysis of the Sample Character Sketch

The character analysis above achieves a description of a peculiar neighbor without *telling* the reader that he is peculiar. Note how:

- The writer shows the eccentricities by allowing readers to see a series of seemingly incongruous characteristics:

  ○ The man uses fine bone china but eats in clutter on an old painted table.
  ○ His speech and the abundance of books *tumbling on every sitting place* suggest an educated man with an eccentric lifestyle.

- Readers see the kitchen, full of herbs living, drying, and dried, and make the connection with the old man's reading.
- Although readers do not know for sure, they suspect the old man may have only recently become fascinated by the effect of certain herbs on one's physical and/or mental being.
- The visitor, obviously unprepared for the experience, finds the situation a bit more than he can bear.
- The writer *shows* that the visitor is eager to leave, *shows* that the old man's conversation causes the boy's mind to wander, *shows* that the cookie-cakes are unappetizing. A good characterization, you will recall, shows; it does not tell.

- The methods of development obviously include all three mentioned above: description, action, and conversation:
  - The readers witness the descriptions, see the room, the clutter, the details. They see books, a ladder-back rocker, foods, china, painted table, refrigerator, sink, etc. All aid in characterizing the eccentric old man.
  - The readers see the old man in action, not just what he's doing during the visit but what he's been doing prior to the visit.
  - The readers hear his voice, his words, his accent.
  - The writer chooses a third-person point of view. Notice, however, that readers see the old man from the boy's point of view.
  - The mechanics of writing this particular characterization call for accurate use of quotation marks and accurate paragraphing to indicate change of speaker. Inaccuracies here will confuse the reader and cause the characterization to fail. [*See* PARAGRAPHS, KINDS: IN DIALOGUE *in Part II.*]

With the process, suggestions, model, and analysis above, you should have a good idea now how to develop a successful character sketch of your own.

CLASSIFICATION

A classification paper serves one purpose: to clarify relationships. By examining the parts and their relationships, readers may better understand the whole.

To develop a classification paper, a writer divides his subject into logical groups. In an English class, for instance, he or she may group authors by the period in which they wrote or group poems by their theme. In a social science class, the writer may group leaders according to the causes they represented or group eighteenth-century immigrants according to the geographical areas in which they settled. In a science class, where scientific method relies heavily on classification, the writer may group animals according to their habitat or group plants according to their reproductive means.

In addition to developing a paper whose sole purpose is to classify, a writer can often enhance a general assignment by using classification. For instance, a paper which examines the economic opportunities in a geographical area may use classification, perhaps classifying economic opportunities into two kinds: investment opportunities and employment opportunities. Such development by classification helps the writer present a well-organized discussion of the topic and also helps readers grasp the overall topic and see how it relates to specific details. Only when readers can see the parts in relationship to the whole will they really understand the subject. Using classification helps achieve that end.

Characteristics

A paper developed by classification usually exhibits most, if not all, of the following characteristics:

- a clear statement of the subject,

- an identification of the means by which the subject will be divided into smaller groups,

- a statement of the number of smaller groups the writer will address,

- an explanation of each of the smaller groups which identifies the groups and distinguishes between or among them,

- clear transitions which help readers identify and follow the explanation of each of the divisions,

- a clear organization which limits the discussion of a single division to a single paragraph or single section of the paper,

- logical order appropriate for the subject,

- a conclusion which restates or draws attention to the subject, means of division, and number of groups in the classification.

Process

The following steps will help you plan, organize, develop, and revise your classification paper.

PREWRITING

STEP 1.   CHOOSING A TOPIC

If you must select your own topic, begin by brainstorming, possibly with a fellow student, listing topics you have studied recently. [*See also* PREWRITING *in Part I for additional suggestions for other sources of topics.*] Try completing the following statement:

Recently, we have studied different kinds of _____ .

Whatever words fit in the blank may be suitable topics for your classification paper. You may have completed the statement above with words like these:

business letters	computer keyboards
lettering styles	watercolor methods
advertising	
poetry	pest control
production means	points of view
	recession
taxes	leavening agents

These topics may suggest others as you brainstorm your own class situation.

STEP 2.   CHOOSING A MEANS OF DIVISION

Once you have selected a topic or had one assigned, you are ready to think through the possible divisions. First, decide the means by which you will divide the subject. Consider these examples:

- business letters divided according to purpose
- computer keyboards divided according to ease of use
- lettering styles divided according to upper case and lower case
- watercolor methods according to wetness of brush
- advertising according to media
- pest control according to application method

Choose the means that best suits your subject.

STEP 3.   NAMING THE DIVISIONS

When you have decided on the means by which you will divide the subject, jot down the two, three, or four divisions you have determined. For instance, examine the topics and their divisions below:

- poetry divided by rhyme scheme: haiku, sonnet, and villanelle
- point of view divided by person: first-person, second-person, third-person
- production means divided by automation: piecework, assembly line, robotics
- recession divided by degree: creeping, galloping, and runaway
- taxes divided by application: property, income, inheritance
- leavenings divided by ingredients: yeast, baking soda, baking powder

POSSIBLE PITFALL: Be sure your divisions are logical. Sometimes divisions overlap. For instance, look at the following illogical example:

> schools divided by grades: elementary, middle, junior high, and senior high

Because middle school, which often includes grades six through eight, overlaps junior high school, which usually includes grades seven through nine, the divisions are illogical. Instead, divide schools into these logical classifications:

> schools divided by grades: elementary, middle, and high school, or

> schools divided by grades: elementary, junior high, and senior high

STEP 4. WRITING THE TOPIC OR THESIS SENTENCE

Now that you have divided your subject, you are ready to write the topic or thesis sentence. [*See* TOPIC SENTENCE *and* THESIS SENTENCE *in the Glossary.*] This sentence should list the subject, the means, and the number. Look at the following sample thesis sentence:

> When applying pesticides, one must understand the differences among the four formulations: liquids, dusts, wettable powders, and emulsions.

Subject:	pesticides
Means:	formulations
Number:	four

Write your own topic or thesis sentence now and check for subject, means, and number.

STEP 5. LISTING DETAILS

With your topic or thesis sentence in front of you, develop a list for each of the items you will classify. In the lists, name the specific details you will discuss for each.

> Three general kinds of advertising bombard the unsuspecting consumer: print, television, and radio.

Subject:	advertising
Means:	medium
Number:	three

print	television	radio
magazines	moving image	sound effects
print size	sound effects	good voice
copy	visual	copy
visual	copy	timing
photographs	timing	anyplace
readable	auditory	auditory

STEP 6. ORGANIZING AND THINKING ABOUT THE PARTS

Using the lists you prepared in Step 5 above, organize the details. Look for similar categories in each of the lists that will help you group ideas. In the example above, for instance, two lists included "auditory" and two included "visual." The column headed "television" included both terms. Study the reorganized lists below to see how other terms have been grouped and reorganized. Note also that some items from the original list have disappeared from the reorganized list.

print	television	radio
visual	visual and auditory	auditory
copy	copy	copy
availability	availability	availability

Now the lists are parallel. [*See* PARALLEL STRUCTURE *in the Glossary.*] They include the same number of items, and the items appear in the same order on each list. The reorganization suggests logical divisions for the discussion of each of the topics.

Reorganize your lists to show logical divisions and parallel structure.

STEP 7. ORGANIZING AND THINKING ABOUT THE WHOLE

A classification paper must reflect logical organization which the reader can follow. For instance, if advertising is classified according to medium (print, television, or radio), which of the media will you discuss first? Why? The answer will determine your choice of organization. [*See* PREWRITING *and* REVISING: CHECKING FOR ORGANIZATION *in Part I.*]

Consider these possibilities:

First, you may organize the kinds of advertising by some order of importance. [*See* ORDERS OF IMPORTANCE *in the Glossary.*]

- from most to least expensive
- from smallest to largest audience
- from most to least effective
- from most to least cost-efficient
- from most to least creative

An equally appropriate option is the reverse of any of these orders of importance.

Likewise, you may choose to organize advertising media from the oldest to the newest, thus relying on chronological order. [*See* CHRONOLOGICAL ORDER *in the Glossary.*]

So, which do you use? That depends on the purpose of your paper. If you want to present an historical perspective, the chronological approach will do quite well. If you are trying to convince a client that he should spend the money for a multimedia advertising campaign which your advertising firm will develop, then you will most likely use one of the orders of importance.

No matter how you organize the overall classification paper, however, keep the following suggestions in mind for each of the subtopics:

- Show your organization in the topic or thesis sentence by listing the topics in the order in which you will discuss them. For example:

   Advertising uses different techniques in each of the three media: radio, print, and television.

- The thesis sentence implies the writer will discuss radio advertising first, then print advertising, and finally television advertising.

- Discuss each of the parallel subtopic details (listed in Step 5 above) in the same order for each topic. For radio, for instance, discuss visual/auditory details first, then copy details, and finally availability details. Repeat the same order for print and then for television advertising.

WRITING

STEP 8. FOLLOWING THE PLAN

With the preparation and planning behind you, you are ready to prepare the first draft of your classification paper:

- Begin your classification with the topic sentence (for a paragraph) or introductory paragraph and thesis sentence (for a theme).

- Develop each of the topics in the order in which they appear in the topic or thesis sentence.

- Follow the organizational plan you chose in Step 7 above.

- Be sure to include sufficient details so that the reader can identify each item separately and, when finished, see the relationship of each to the whole.

- Use a vocabulary and sentence structure appropriate to your audience.

- Use effective transitions to make the paper flow smoothly. [*See* TRANSITIONS *in the Glossary.*]

- End with a conclusion that effectively ties together the ideas in your paper. [*See* CONCLUSION *in the Glossary.*]

REVISING

STEP 9. CHECKING THE CONTENT

As you reread your classification paper, ask yourself the following questions to determine what revisions may be necessary:

- Does my topic or thesis sentence clearly state the subject, the means of classification, and the number of items into which the subject is classified?
- Are the divisions logical?
- Does the topic or thesis sentence appear at or near the beginning of the paper?
- Are the details sufficient for clarity? [*See* REVISING: SAMPLE REVISION FOR SPECIFIC DETAIL *in Part I.*]
- Have I maintained unity throughout the paper? [*See* REVISING: SAMPLE REVISION FOR UNITY *in Part I.*]
- Did I organize the paper effectively, probably according to some order of importance? [*See* REVISING: CHECKING FOR ORGANIZATION *in Part I.*]
- Have I included effective transitions to help readers move smoothly from one sentence to the next, from one paragraph to the next? [*See* REVISING: SAMPLE REVISION FOR TRANSITION *in Part I.*]
- Do my transitions help show the relationships between the subtopics and the general subject of my classification?
- Are my words and sentences appropriate for my audience?
- Have I used strong nouns and verbs and avoided flowery modifi-

ers? [*See* REVISING: SAMPLE REVISION FOR WORDINESS *in Part I.*]

- Are the sentences varied both in structure and in length? [*See* REVISING: SAMPLE REVISION FOR SENTENCE VARIETY *in Part I.*]

- Do my sentences and paragraphs create the appropriate emphasis for my subject? [*See* REVISING: SAMPLE REVISION FOR EMPHASIS *in Part I.*]

- Is the tone appropriate? [*See* TONE *in the Glossary.*]

- Does the paper conclude effectively?

[*For general guidelines for revision, see* REVISING *in Part I. Use the questions and suggestions there to polish your paper further.*]

PROOFREADING

STEP 10. CHECKING THE DETAILS

When you have completed the revising process in Step 9 above, prepare your final draft. Then, check it for punctuation, grammar, mechanics, and usage.

See *Webster's New World Thesaurus* to check for accurate word choice, and see *Webster's New World Dictionary* to check for accurate spelling.

A Note about the Samples: With the planning, organization, writing, and revising information in mind, study the following model classification papers and their analyses. Each paper deals with some aspect of the general topic of Mammoth Cave National Park. Note that specific topics are tailored for specific content areas. In addition, note that the five sample classification papers include single-paragraph papers as well as three-, four-, and six-paragraph themes. The samples also illustrate both order of importance and chronological order. By comparing the five samples, you should gain a broad understanding of the classification method of development.

—————— Sample for English ——————

Students in an English class were asked to classify some aspect of a hobby or activity they enjoyed. One student classified basketball games by back-alley, intramural, and interscholastic competition; another classified recreational reading by best-seller novels, classical literature, and periodicals. Yet another student classified hiking trails both by location and by difficulty. This double classification shows clear organization, as seen below.

Hiking at Mammoth Cave National Park

While the average tourist goes to Mammoth Cave National Park to walk through part of the cave, the avid hiker discovers two very different kinds of hiking in the park: below ground and above ground. Even in those two locations, he can find anything from easy ambling to rugged adventure.

Below ground, in the cave system, the trails range from wide, gentle paved paths softly illuminated with indirect lighting to muddy crawl holes dimly lit by hand-carried kerosene lanterns. The easy trails, sometimes only a half-mile long, require little effort along their paved meanderings. The moderate trails, usually a mile or more long, include steps with handrails and sometimes short but steep hills. The rugged trails, however, usually several miles long, require climbing and endurance along hundreds of steps or ladders, over steep sometimes slippery hills, and through narrow passages that bang elbows. The really tough trails, called "adventure trails" in the park literature, may take most of the day to traverse and include long stretches of crawl spaces unsuitable for anyone with even a tinge of claustrophobia. Scrambling over boulders and across muddy streams with only the dim helmet lights and smokey lanterns to show the way, hikers come above ground at the end muddy, perhaps a bit ragged, but glowing with excitement for having shared the cave's secrets.

Above ground, the hikers can select again from easy, broad trails to rugged endurance tests. The easy trails meander for a mile or so through hardwood and cedar forests and along cliffs that drop a sheer hundred feet or more to Green River. With little effort, hikers can enjoy the flora and fauna. A moderate trail, perhaps a mile or so long, may include some hills, but scenery across the nearly mountainous vistas make the mild effort worth the exertion. The rugged trails, long and steep, demand dirty-knee climbing, bottom-dirty sliding, and body-tiring huffing and puffing. Hikers snake up limestone cliffs and struggle over house-sized boulders. They trudge along sandy river banks and climb steep forested hills. They explore sinkholes and intriguing little caves scattered throughout the park. They finish the trail tired but enriched by the variety of experiences. So above ground or below, the land which boasts the longest known cave in the world offers two very different kinds of hiking, either kind with as little or as much challenge as the hiker prefers.

Analysis of the Sample for English

The model paper above includes the general characteristics of a classification paper:

- It includes a clear statement of the general topic (hiking at Mammoth Cave National Park) and indicates the number (two) and the means (by location, below and above ground) of the classification.

- To aid the reader in following the organization, the writer includes a second sentence to explain that both kinds of hiking, below and above ground, include another classification: from easy to rugged. Thus, the organization of the entire paper is explained in the introduction.

- Each of the two subgroups is discussed in its own paragraph, below-ground hiking in the second paragraph and above-ground hiking in the third.

- The organization, by order of importance from more well-known (below ground) to less well-known (above ground), is whole-by-whole. [*See* WHOLE-BY-WHOLE ORGANIZATION *in the Glossary.*] The four kinds of trails below ground are discussed in the second paragraph, and the three kinds of trails above ground are described in the third paragraph, in each case from the easiest to the most difficult (another kind of order of importance).

- Images like *house-sized boulders, dirty-knee climbing, crawl spaces unsuitable for anyone with even a tinge of claustrophobia* help the reader see the different kinds of trails. [*See* REVISING: SAMPLE REVISION FOR SPECIFIC DETAIL *in Part I.*]

- Since no extraneous details appear, the paper maintains unity. [*See* REVISING: SAMPLE REVISION FOR UNITY *in Part I.*]

- Transitions appear throughout to help the reader follow the organization. Words like *below ground, above ground, easy, moderate,* and *rugged* are repeated to provide transition from one idea to the next. Other transitions include words like *however, at the end,* and *again.*

- The sentences flow smoothly and use a direct, simple vocabulary which suits the subject.

- The conclusion reiterates the introduction and adds a spark of interest about *the longest known cave in the world*.

Sample for Social Sciences

The following six-paragraph theme, developed by classification, meets an assignment for an anthropology unit in a history class. Using the same general topic of Mammoth Cave National Park, the specific narrowed topic now reflects social science content. After reading the model, study the analysis.

The People and the Cave

Mammoth Cave, the longest cave in the world, has one unusual finger of history outside its geological and environmental history, and that is the history of its people. In general, the people fall into four historical groups: the prehistoric Indians, the early Kentucky settlers, the tourists, and the serious explorers.

Over 4,000 years ago, prehistoric Indians made use of the cave's shelter during winter. The constant fifty-four degree temperature in the dry cave preserved their remains so well that archaeologists have learned not only about their implements and clothing but also about their agricultural and mining habits. For some unknown reason, however, the Indians left the cave about the time of the birth of Christ, and the cave system remained uninhabited and undisturbed until nearly 1800.

Legends describe the discovery of the cave in 1797 by an early Kentucky hunter named Houchin who was chasing a bear. His discovery led early settlers to the cave's riches, for unlike the prehistoric Indians who used the cave primarily for shelter, the settlers sought the minerals. Not until the War of 1812, though, did this group of people receive much notice. At that time, the enterprising settlers mined a seemingly endless supply of nitrate for the production of gunpowder, an operation conducted with the aid of slaves.

By the 1830s, the ownership of the cave changed, and that brought the next group of people, the tourists. The new owner brought three black slaves to the cave, and because of their significant exploration, discoveries, and charming personalities, they popularized the cave. Tourism grew. Then another new owner, with money for promotional activities, added a posh hotel which attracted wealthy visitors, some of them famous, who found it *the* vacation place. Over the decades, tourists continued to swarm to Mammoth Cave, first by stagecoach, then by train, and now by automobile and every imaginable recreational vehicle. They come to see the cave's magnificent formations, its multiple levels, its hugeness. They want ease of walking and electric lighting, a well-informed tour guide, and a sense of the spectacular. Certainly, they get it all.

In the midst of the early stages of tourism, another group of people, the serious explorers, came, first out of curiosity and then out of serious scientific research. Today, the explorers remain. In 1972, a major discovery referred to as the Big Connection placed the Mammoth Cave system on the charts as the longest cave in the world. Discoveries continue. As recently as 1983 another cave system was found to connect with Mammoth Cave, and authorities believe there is the potential for at least another five hundred miles of passages to be discovered. Explorers, curiosities whetted by the suspicions of additional undiscovered, unexplored passages, regularly undertake expeditions to be the first to walk through unchartered territory, perhaps the final frontier on this earth.

Obviously, then, the cave system will continue to attract people, both tourists and explorers, for years to come.

Analysis of the Sample for Social Sciences

The classification theme above varies considerably from the example for English. Note these particular features:

- The thesis statement includes the topic (*people at Mammoth Cave*), the means (*historical groups*) and number (*four*).

- Each of the four groups is discussed in a separate paragraph, and the paragraphs appear in the same order in which the groups are listed in the thesis statement.

- Organization follows a chronological pattern, using the whole-by-whole method. [*See* WHOLE-BY-WHOLE ORGANIZATION *in the Glossary.*]

- The details for each group include two kinds of information: when they came to the cave and why they came. Note that the details are thus somewhat different from those in the English sample. The historical significance takes a prominent place in a paper for a history class.

- The writer maintains unity by omitting details that may be interesting but are not relevant to one of the four groups.

- Transitions both between and within paragraphs enable the reader to move smoothly through the composition. Note the repetition of such words as *Indians, settlers, tourists,* and *explorers* to carry out the organizational plan. Other transitions include words like *first, however, until, unlike, though, then,* and *while*, and phrases that show time progression like *over 4,000 years ago, by the 1930's, in 1972,* and *as recently as 1983.* All are effective transitions.

- Sentences vary in length from quite short to fairly long and vary in structure from simple to compound-complex.

- Vocabulary appropriate to the subject and audience includes specific images. [*See* REVISING: SAMPLE REVISION FOR SPECIFIC DETAIL *in Part I and* DESCRIPTION *in Part II.*]

- The paper concludes with a single sentence, carrying the last two groups, the tourists and the explorers, into the future.

The classification theme for social science achieves its purpose. If it has a fault, it may attempt to cover too much in too short a space, but perhaps the assignment offered little alternative.

Sample for Science

The nature of scientific study suggests the importance of classification in a science class. Scientists regularly sort, show relationships, and classify. The following paper illustrates classification development suitable for a science class.

Animals in Mammoth Cave

In Mammoth Cave, biologists have identified nearly 150 animal species, but only about 30 can be considered common. These cave-dwelling animals fall into two groups: Part-time cave dwellers, called trogloxenes, who move freely from inside to outside, and permanent cave dwellers, which include both troglophiles and troglobites.

The trogloxenes depend less on sight than do other animals and thus can find their way in and out of the cave in the dark. They rely on the cool, constant temperatures and the high humidity for protection either in winter or summer. These animals, all of which feed outside the cave, include raccoons, pack rats, cave crickets, and bats. Animals like raccoons spend only brief periods in the cave for protection. Pack rats and cave crickets spend part of every day in the cave and reproduce there, both of them using chemical trails to find their way to and from their shelters. The most generally recognized cave animals, the bats, use the cave primarily for hibernation, depending on the cold air drafts from outside to slow their metabolism so that their fat reserves will last through the winter.

Of greater interest to scientists, however, are the permanent cave dwellers, those animals which can survive in the dark environment where lack of plant life severely limits the food chain. Troglophiles can live outside the cave, but the environment outside the cave must be similar to that inside. For instance, they can survive under rocks and undercut banks or under the tree litter in the forest. Over the centuries, however, certain troglophiles have evolved so that those which remained inside caves became a separate species, the troglobites. They have evolved for survival, so they can detect minute food sources and use little energy for survival. For instance, they have lost seeing eyes and any coloration. Because of the constant temperature and humidity in the changes. The evolutionary process has given them large sensory structures which can detect water movement or air movement, a sense which helps protect them from predators and obstacles and helps them locate prey. As a final evolutionary quirk, their reproduction depends on the added food supply brought as a result of seasonal flooding. Since length of daylight cannot trigger an annual biological calendar, the troglobites must be ready to reproduce quickly. As a result of these evolutionary changes, they are literally confined to the cave. The permanent cave dwellers include beetles, spiders, millipedes, mites, springtails, bristletails, fish, crayfish, shrimp, isopods, amphipods, and flatworms.

The animals at Mammoth Cave provide obvious examples for scientific study. Some animals use the cave as only a part of their environment while others depend entirely upon the cave for their survival. Evolutionary changes within the full-time cave residents provide curious examples for scientific investigation.

Analysis of the Sample for Science

The whole system of scientific identification is based on classification, and the sample above indicates the appropriateness of the classification method of development for a science paper. The following comments point to the general success of the approach:

- The topic sentence indicates that the classification of cave animals will be divided according to their dependency on the cave (*means*) and divided into two groups (*number*).
- Each of the two body paragraphs describes one of the groups.
- Details for each group separate one from the other, clearly establishing that one group is really a cave visitor while the other depends on the cave for survival.
- Within the second group, two subdivisions are identified, further evidence that classification is of particular benefit to the scientific paper.
- The writer maintains unity in each body paragraph and throughout the entire paper.
- Transitions help the reader move from sentence to sentence and from paragraph to paragraph. Specific transitions include the repetition of words like *animals, cave dwellers*, and the pronouns which refer to them like *they, these*, and *those*. Other transitions include words and phrases like *thus, however,*

greater interest, but, inside, outside, for instance, over the centuries, so, as a result, and *while.*

- The use of technical terms is appropriate to the scientific subject matter and the audience.
- Numbers appear in Arabic rather than word form, a typical treatment in a scientific paper. Some formal papers may include both words and numerals to eliminate any possible misreading.
- The sentences vary both in length and structure.
- As a conclusion, the final paragraph restates the main idea and indicates its importance to the subject matter.

The paper above meets the general requirements for a good classification paper. Its suitability for the science class is obvious.

Sample for Business

The classification paper will often appear in business circles. For instance, while introducing new products, a report may discuss the kinds of sales approaches necessary for different kinds of clients. Likewise, a company executive may prepare a report enumerating the kinds of money-saving techniques he plans to implement during the next year.

The following classification paper, using the same general Mammoth Cave topic as above, directs its attention to business principles. The writer develops the subject in a single paragraph, so note how this single-paragraph classification paper differs from the longer sample papers above.

Business Opportunities around Mammoth Cave

While Mammoth Cave National Park is a business within itself, controlled and operated by the National Park Service, the area surrounding the park offers a multitude of business opportunities. Four general categories of opportunities meet the needs of tourists. First, tourists have basic needs, one of which is lodging. Only a limited variety of hotel and motel accommodations, from luxurious to economical, exists in the immediately adjoining areas, and so potential business opportunities exist in that field. Because many tourists arrive with their own accommodations in the form of tents or recreational vehicles, however, other lodging needs offer alternate business opportunities. For these people, campgrounds with and without hook-ups come at a premium during peak seasons. Second, whether they come as hotel/motel guests or as campers, tourists need food. Restaurants, from gourmet to fast-food, now far from readily available, may offer potential business. For those tourists who prefer to cook their own, packaged goods and fresh fruits and vegetables are simply unavailable nearby. Third, because of the atypical climate in the cave—a constant cool, damp 54 degrees—many tourists come without appropriate wearing apparel. Nowhere in the immediate vicinity can one buy a sweater or sweatshirt, jeans or long socks for comfort in the cave. Fourth, in spite of the opportunities available in the park, tourists who stay more than a couple of days will seek other recreational opportunities. A canoe livery could enhance water sports on the Green River. For those less inclined toward the rugged exercise necessary for extensive enjoyment of the park, a miniature golf or par-three golf course could offer a viable alternative. Even a few tennis courts, theaters, or small theme park may offer alternate business opportunities. In short, for the entrepreneur, opportunities exist. Further market research and investment analysis will determine which has the greatest potential.

Analysis of the Sample for Business

The sample classification paper above, a single paragraph, follows the general characteristics set out in the beginning of this section. Study the following analysis:

- The first sentence discusses the general idea of the paper, but the second sentence, the topic sentence, establishes that the paper will deal with four classes of business opportunities based on tourist needs (*means*).
- The four classes are emphasized with numeric transitions, *first, second, third,* and *fourth.*
- Organization moves from the most obvious tourist need to the least.
- Transitions, including the numeric ones, help the reader move smoothly through the paragraph.
- Specific nouns name specific business ventures.
- The writer maintains unity throughout.

- Vocabulary and sentence structure, appropriate for the subject, aim at a business-oriented audience.

- The conclusion acknowledges the writer's cursory examination of the subject and admits need for far more careful analysis prior to investment.

Sample for Vocational Education

The following model classification paragraph deals with a single subject, introduced in the social science model above, the use of Mammoth Cave for the production of gunpowder. The writer develops the topic in a single paragraph.

Saltpeter Operation in Mammoth Cave

Used for making gunpowder during the War of 1812, the saltpeter operation at Mammoth Cave required, in addition to the cave's supply of nitrate, two kinds of natural resources available in the hills of Kentucky: wood for construction and wood for burning. The wood for building the square vats and for making pipes required long, straight grain. Tulip poplar trees, abundant in the surrounding hills and ravines, met the requirement. Constructing the vats required little special skill, but forming the wood pipes required special tools and patience. Workers used hand augers to bore out the centers of the typically straight poplar logs. Then they tapered the end of one log and reamed out the end of the next log, thus permitting the two logs to slip together. The system of log pipes carried water from the nearby Green River into the cave for production of the saltpeter. The second kind of wood, however, served an entirely different purpose in the saltpeter operation. In fact, the wood was not used as wood; it was used as ash. It provided potassium. So, by burning hickory and oak, both rich in potassium, the workers produced an ash that, when the nitrate solution trickled through it, caused the calcium nitrate to become potassium nitrate, or saltpeter. Thus, the natural resources above the cave allowed the useful conversion of a mineral inside the cave.

Analysis of the Sample for Vocational Education

The paragraph follows the prescribed general characteristics. Furthermore, it includes a suggestion of process [*see* PROCESS ANALYSIS *in Part II*], and includes some characteristics of a cause and effect paper [*see* CAUSE AND EFFECT *in Part II*]. Note the following classification characteristics:

- The topic sentence tells the reader the general topic (*natural resources*), the means (*above ground*), and the number (*two*).
- The organizational pattern uses chronological organization (*from construction to operation*) in the whole-by-whole pattern (*wood for construction* in the first part of the paragraph and *wood for burning* in the second part).
- The details indicate the reason for the selection of the particular woods (*straight grain, high potassium content*).
- The writer maintains unity by omitting irrelevant details.
- Transitions allow the reader to move smoothly from one sentence to the next. Especially notable is the transition from the first idea (*wood for construction*) to the second (*wood for burning*). Note that the transition is really two complete sentences.
- Sentence structure, vocabulary, and tone are all appropriate to the audience, although some of the scientific names are not household words. Certainly, however, the reader can understand the general idea even if he or she does not understand the chemical process.
- The conclusion ties together the two parts of the classification and shows the relationship to the whole.

The explanation of characteristics and process along with the sample papers and their analyses should give you a solid background for preparing your own classification paper. Checking the cross-references will also further your understanding.

CLASSIFIED AD

A classified advertisement, commonly called a *classified ad*, appears in a newspaper or magazine for the purpose of selling goods or services or recruiting employees. Since the cost of these ads varies according to the number of words, the ad writer aims for brevity. Unlike other kinds of writing we have examined, the classified ad frequently does not include complete sentences, uses abbreviations, and follows an unusual organization.

Characteristics

A classified advertisement usually includes

- a word or phrase to give a concise name to the goods or services offered for sale or sought,
- words or phrases to present a concise description of special features of the goods or services, especially those features which set this product or position apart from similar ones,
- the price of the goods or services,
- the phone number or address to which interested persons should make inquiries.

Process

The following steps will help you plan and compose a classified advertisement.

PREWRITING

STEP 1. SELECTING THE NAME

In most cases, the name of the goods or services will be evident. For instance, if you are selling a used sofa, the name is obvious: *sofa*. If you are seeking someone to fill the position of *night clerk*, the name is obvious: night clerk. In some cases, however, the writer must determine a name.

For example, assume you are selling a set of plans to build a patio. The plans include not only a blueprint but step-by-step instructions, progressive diagrams, and a list of materials, tools, and equipment needed for the job. You need a concise name for the product. You may choose *complete patio plans*.

Write the concise name for your product or position.

STEP 2. CHOOSING DESCRIPTIVE WORDS

In order to distinguish your product or position from others similar to it, you need something we refer to as *sales features*. In the example above, the sales features include the blueprint, the step-by-step instructions, the diagrams, and the list of materials, tools, and equipment.

These are the specific items that will help sell your product or position.

Write a list of descriptive words that will help sell your product.

STEP 3. ADDING OTHER DETAILS

Make a separate list of the additional necessary details. These include a phone number or address. You may choose to include a price. You may include other specifics such as, but not limited to, the following:

- time of day phone number is in service (Example: *between 8* AM *and 5* PM),

- response time needed (Example: *allow three weeks for delivery*),

- method of selection (Example: *applications accepted*).

STEP 4. CONSIDERING THE READER

Most people read classified ads quickly, noting only the first few words. Thus, the words for the entire ad must be arranged in order of importance. Use this general method:

- First give the product or position name.

- Next give descriptive sales features.

- Finally add details.

WRITING

STEP 5. INCLUDING THE ESSENTIALS

When you write the classified ad following the steps above, omit any words not absolutely necessary. [*See* REVISING: SAMPLE REVISION FOR WORDINESS *in Part I for an example of eliminating unnecessary words.*] Remember, too, the ad need not include complete sentences: phrases, even single words, are acceptable as sentences in a classified ad. Abbreviations are appropriate.

REVISING

STEP 6. CHECKING FOR CONCISENESS

When you have finished the ad, use the following guide to revise it:

- Cross out any words not absolutely necessary. If the magazine or newspaper for which you are preparing the ad includes a base rate for up to a specific number of words, you may wish to limit your ad to that number.
- Omit articles and prepositions. [*See* ARTICLES *and* PREPOSITION *in the Glossary.*]
- Check to see that all essential information is included.
- Make sure that you have begun with the most important words and followed them with the less important words and phrases.
- Check for possible abbreviations or shortened word forms. The following examples may help you:

  Use *phone* instead of *telephone*.

Use *call* instead of *phone*.

Use *in person* instead of *personally*.

Use *SASE* instead of *self-addressed stamped envelope*.

Use *after 5:00* instead of *call after 5:00*.

Use *applications accepted* instead of *applications being accepted*.

Use *negotiable* instead of *price is negotiable*.

PROOFREADING

Step 7.   Checking for Accuracy

Be absolutely certain to check the following details for accuracy. An inaccurate ad wastes your money!

- Is the phone number, including the area code, accurate?

- Is the address, including zip code, accurate?

- Is the essential information included? Is it accurate?

- Is the punctuation accurate to separate words and phrases in place of sentences?

- Does the ad include sufficient information to eliminate needless calls or unnecessary correspondence?

- Is the ad as concise as it can be?

——————— Sample Classified Ads ———————

The following classified advertisements follow the characteristics suggested above. After you have studied the ads, compare your thoughts with the analyses below.

Part-time assistant, retail clothing. Hours flexible; some benefits. Apply in person. 240 Main.

Antique dining table, six chairs, cherry, needlepoint seats. $1,200 delivered in area. 763-1432.

Complete patio plans, instructions, diagrams, materials list. SASE, $4.50. PLANS, 410 E. Ridgewood, Oakfield, GA 56842.

Analyses of the Sample Classified Ads

The following analyses refer to the sample classified ads above. Compare the samples with your own:

- All three ads begin with the name of the goods, product, or position. In the first ad, the position named is *part-time assistant*. In the second ad, the goods named are *antique dining table, six chairs.* In the third ad, the product named is *complete patio plans.*

- The descriptive words follow. In Ad 1, the descriptive words include *retail clothing* and *hours flexible; some benefits.* In Ad 2, the descriptive words are *cherry* and *needlepoint seats.* Ad 3 includes a series of sales features: *instructions, diagrams, materials list.*

- The added information varies with the purpose of the ad. Consider these specifics:

  ○ In Ad 1, the only added information indicates the applicant should apply in person at the given address. No wages are listed, perhaps because the position offers minimum wage or because the wage is negotiable. No city is listed in the address since the ad appears in a local newspaper.

  ○ In Ad 2, the added information names the price, indicating that it includes delivery *in area* and gives a phone number, thus suggesting that further information is available by phone. No area code is included.

  ○ Ad 3 includes several bits of added information. *SASE* is a common abbreviation meaning to send a *self-addressed stamped envelope,* in this case along with $4.50, to the listed address. The address is complete, including zip code.

- None of the ads includes a complete sentence.

- All of the ads use punctuation to separate words and phrases describing or giving added information:

  ○ Commas separate words of equal modification.
  ○ Semicolons separate larger thought units.
  ○ Periods separate sections.

- Abbreviations are included as appropriate.

These analyses should help you evaluate your own classified ad and, perhaps, help you save money when you place it in a newspaper or magazine.

COMPARISON AND CONTRAST

A comparison-contrast paper allows the writer to show similarities in otherwise unlike subjects and differences in otherwise similar subjects. Usually, a writer does not analyze similarities in subjects already recognized as similar or differences in subjects recognized as different.

For specific kinds of assignments, the comparison-contrast paper is essential. In fact, some assignments may specifically ask that you compare or contrast certain ideas: Compare the attitudes of the North and the South immediately prior to the Civil War. Compare the poetry of Walt Whitman with that of Carl Sandburg. Contrast two methods of accounting and indicate which is the better method for specific purposes. Sometimes an essay test will include questions which require a comparison-contrast answer: Contrast the economic principles of socialism with that of capitalism. Compare and contrast two Shakespearian sonnets that describe or seem to refer to the Dark Lady. Contrast the suitability of enriched flour with that of self-rising flour for baking bread. [*See also* ESSAY-QUESTION RESPONSES *in Part II for further discussion of writing answers to test questions.*]

In the process of developing a comparison-contrast paper, the writer will inevitably rely on a number of other methods of development as well, including analogy, definition, description, cause and effect, narration, or process. [*See entries for each in Part II.*]

Following are the characteristics and steps in the process for developing a comparison-contrast paper.

Characteristics

A paper developed by means of comparison or contrast usually includes the following characteristics:

- a subject suitable for comparison or contrast so that a comparison shows similarities of generally unlike subjects and a contrast shows differences of generally similar subjects,

- a topic or thesis sentence which establishes the general comparison or contrast [*see* TOPIC SENTENCE *and* THESIS SENTENCE *in the Glossary for quick reference, and see* PARAGRAPHS *and* THEME *in Part II for discussion and examples*],

- an organization clearly developed either whole-by-whole or part-by-part or likenesses-differences [*see entries for each in the Glossary and detailed explanation in Step 3 below*],

- details which clarify the similarities or differences,
- precise transitions which help the reader single out the differences or similarities [*see* TRANSITION *in the Glossary*],
- unity within individual paragraphs and, in the case of a theme, within the entire paper [*see* UNITY *in the Glossary*],
- a conclusion which reiterates the purpose of the paper, to show comparisons or to show contrasts, or, in rare occasions, to show both [*see* CONCLUSION *in the Glossary*].

Process

The following steps will help you plan, organize, develop, revise, and proofread your comparison-contrast paper.

PREWRITING

STEP 1. SELECTING SUITABLE SUBJECTS

Subjects suitable for a comparison-contrast paper must meet two of these three qualifications:

- The two subjects to be compared must be generally different so that the writer can establish similarities:

  Potatoes and onions, while obviously different, show similarities as root crops: planting procedure, harvesting, storing.

- The two subjects to be contrasted must be generally similar so that the writer can establish their differences:

  Catalpa and white-pine lumber, both soft woods, differ in weathering qualities, rot resistance, and usefulness indoors and out.

- The comparison or contrast must be of significance to the reader:

  The differences between dogs and cats as pets are so obvious that readers will not waste time reading about them.

In many cases, the subject will be assigned, such as in an essay test. [*See also* ESSAY-QUESTION RESPONSES, KINDS: TEST QUESTIONS *elsewhere in Part II.*] In other cases, you may have to select the subject yourself. In order to select a suitable comparison-contrast subject, think of content-related topics you have recently studied:

two economic theories

two contemporary poets

two mathmatics principles

two similar chemical compounds

two Impressionistic artists

two political figures in the same office

two political figures running for the same office

two thematically similar stories

two kinds of hardwood lumber

two kinds of lathes

two recipes for whole-wheat bread

two approaches to disciplining children

[*See also* PREWRITING *in Part I for additional suggestions for sources of topics.*]

Make a list of potential subjects. Think through each of them in terms of similarities and differences. Select one which seems to offer the greatest potential for a paper.

STEP 2.   CHOOSING DETAILS

After you have selected a suitable subject, decide whether you can most effectively show similarities or differences. As you think through the subject, remember that a third alternative may be to show both similarities and differences. Although the organization becomes more complicated when you show both, this third alternative may be the best in some situations.

After you have reached a decision, jot down three or four major similarities or differences or both. Your list may look like this:

Topic: Methods of Disciplining
            Children
Approach: Differences
Details: Nonverbal message
            Verbal message
            Reward/reinforcement

STEP 3.   ORGANIZING THE WHOLE

The comparison-contrast paper may be organized according to one of three patterns: whole-by-whole, part-by-part, or likenesses-differences. Which organization you use

depends entirely on which works best for the subject. In some cases, one method may be as effective as another. Following are brief summaries of each of the three methods:

Whole-by-Whole Pattern

Using the whole-by-whole pattern of organization, the writer explains all of one subtopic before she discusses the second. For instance, in the list in Step 2 above, the writer discusses one method of discipline in terms of nonverbal messages, verbal messages, and reward/reinforcement. Then, she discusses the second. The general outline looks like this:

First method of discipline:
    Nonverbal messages
    Verbal messages
    Reward/reinforcement
Second method of discipline:
    Nonverbal messages
    Verbal messages
    Reward/reinforcement

[*For sample papers developed by the whole-by-whole pattern, see the* SAMPLE FOR SOCIAL SCIENCES *and the* SAMPLE FOR SCIENCE *below.*]

Part-by-Part Pattern

Using the part-by-part pattern of organization, the writer explains the main point of both subtopics before introducing another point. For instance, using the same example as above, the writer discusses nonverbal messages in both the first method of discipline and then the second method of discipline. Then, the writer discusses verbal messages and finally, reward/reinforcement. The general outline looks like this:

Nonverbal messages:
  First method of discipline
  Second method of discipline
Verbal messages:
  First method of discipline
  Second method of discipline
Reward/reinforcement:
  First method of discipline
  Second method of discipline

[*For sample papers developed by the part-by-part pattern, see the* SAMPLE FOR ENGLISH *and the* SAMPLE FOR VOCATIONAL EDUCATION *below.*]

Likenesses-Differences Pattern

Using the likenesses-differences pattern of organization, the writer deals with *both* comparisons and contrasts. In this pattern, the writer discusses in one paragraph all the similarities of the two methods of discipline and in another paragraph all the differences. The general outline may look like this:

Similarities
Nonverbal messages:
  First method of discipline
  Second method of discipline
Verbal messages:
  First method of discipline
  Second method of discipline
Reward/reinforcement:
  First method of discipline
  Second method of discipline
Differences
Nonverbal messages:
  First method of discipline

Second method of discipline
Verbal messages:
  First method of discipline
  Second method of discipline
Reward/reinforcement:
  First method of discipline
  Second method of discipline

Or, the general outline may look like this:

Similarities
First method of discipline:
  Nonverbal messages
  Verbal messages
  Reward/reinforcement
Second method of discipline:
  Nonverbal messages
  Verbal messages
  Reward/reinforcement
Differences
First method of discipline:
  Nonverbal messages
  Verbal messages
  Reward/reinforcement
Second method of discipline:
  Nonverbal messages
  Verbal messages
  Reward/reinforcement

[*For a sample paper developed by the likenesses-differences pattern, see the* SAMPLE FOR BUSINESS *below.*]

How items are organized within the specific patterns will determine the emphasis. [*See* EMPHASIS *in the Glossary.*]

STEP 4. ORGANIZING THE PARTS

No matter which of the organizational patterns the writer follows, he must still determine which details he will discuss first and last. Think about the set of subjects and details we have worked with above. The writer must decide whether nonverbal messages are more important than verbal messages and whether reward/reinforcement is most or least important. The internal organization, then, may be one of the orders of importance. [*See* ORDERS OF IMPORTANCE *in the Glossary.*]

Whichever order you choose, keep these guidelines in mind:

- The topic you discuss last will have the most impact on your reader.

- The topic you discuss first will have the next greatest impact on your reader.

- The details in the middle attract less attention and sometimes are nearly buried, a situation that may or may not be beneficial to your subject.

- These general guidelines apply both to the overall organization of the broad topics and to the internal organization of the details.

[*See the* SAMPLE FOR SCIENCE *and the* SAMPLE FOR BUSINESS *below for examples of orders of importance.*]

Chronological organization or spatial organization may also be appropriate for the internal organization of comparison-contrast papers. [*See both entries in the Glossary. Note also the spatial organization in the* SAMPLE FOR ENGLISH *and the* SAMPLE FOR SOCIAL SCIENCES *and the chronological order in the* SAMPLE FOR VOCATIONAL EDUCATION BELOW.]

Choose the internal organization which best suits your subject and enables you to achieve the greatest emphasis.

STEP 5. DEVELOPING THE TOPIC OR THESIS SENTENCE

When you have completed the organizational plan and decided on the order that will achieve the greatest emphasis, you are ready to develop the topic sentence, or, in the preparation of a theme, the thesis sentence. [*See* TOPIC SENTENCE *and* THESIS SENTENCE *in the Glossary, and see* PARAGRAPHS *and* THEME *in Part II.*] The topic or thesis sentence should indicate not only the general subject and whether the paper will deal with comparisons or contrasts, but also the organization. For example:

Two methods of disciplining children show vast differences between the verbal and nonverbal messages as well as the reinforcement techniques.

The topic sentence above indicates the subject (*two methods of disciplining children*), establishes a purpose of contrast (*vast differences*), and indicates the order (the discussion of *verbal and nonverbal messages* will be followed by a discussion of *reinforcement techniques*). The implication of the topic *reinforcement techniques* appearing last is that it illustrates the greatest differences between the two methods of discipline and, perhaps, offers the best means for determining which method to choose.

WRITING

STEP 6.   DEVELOPING THE FIRST DRAFT

Following the organization plan selected in Steps 4 and 5 above, develop the first draft of your comparison-contrast paper. Be sure to use techniques of good writing:

- If you are developing a paragraph, begin with the topic sentence. [*See* PARAGRAPHS *in Part II.*]

- If you are developing a theme, begin with a suitable introductory paragraph which concludes with the thesis sentence. [*See* THEME *in Part II.*]

- Follow the organizational plan. If it does not work, go back to Steps 4 and 5, alter the plan, and begin again.

- Add sufficient details to clarify the differences and/or similarities.

- End with a concluding statement or concluding paragraph that restates or summarizes your topic.

REVISING

STEP 7.   CHECKING THE CONTENT

As you reread your comparison-contrast paper, ask yourself the following questions to pinpoint possibly necessary revisions:

- Does my topic or thesis sentence clearly state my subject and the organization of my paper?

- Do I follow the organization established in my topic or thesis statement?

- Is the organizational pattern the most effective for my subject and purpose? [*See* REVISING: CHECKING ORGANIZATION *in Part I.*]

- Does the order best emphasize the most important points? [*See* REVISING: SAMPLE REVISION FOR EMPHASIS *in Part I.*]

- Does the paragraph structure follow my organizational plan? [*See* REVISING: CHECKING STRUCTURE *in Part I.*]

- Are there sufficient details to support the topics? [*See* REVISING: SAMPLE REVISION FOR SPECIFIC DETAIL *in Part I.*]

- Have I maintained unity by omitting unrelated details from the paper? [*See* REVISING: SAMPLE REVISION FOR UNITY *in Part I.*]

- Are transitions precise and adequate to clarify and emphasize the comparisons or contrasts to readers? [*See* REVISING: SAMPLE REVISION FOR TRANSITION *in Part I.*]

- Are the words and sentences appropriate to the subject and the audience?

- Have I used strong nouns and verbs and avoided flowery modifiers? [*See* REVISING: SAMPLE REVISION FOR WORDINESS *in Part I.*]

- Is the sentence structure varied? [*See* REVISING: SAMPLE REVISION FOR SENTENCE VARIETY *in Part I.*]

- Is the tone appropriate for the subject? [*See* TONE *in the Glossary.*]

- Does the conclusion end the paper effectively? [*See* CONCLUSION *in the Glossary.*]

[*See also* REVISING *in Part I for additional general guidelines for the process of revising.*]

PROOFREADING

STEP 8. CHECKING THE DETAILS

When you have completed the revisions suggested by your analysis in Step 7 above, proofread your paper for accuracy. Check punctuation, grammar, mechanics, and usage. Refer to the Glossary to help you proofread accurately. You will find rules, examples, definitions, and explanations there to help you. Check *Webster's New World Dictionary* and *Webster's New World Thesaurus* to correct spelling and improve word choice.

A Note about the Samples: You will find the following samples and their accompanying analyses helpful in crystalizing your understanding of how to develop a comparison-contrast paper. The samples, which include both single-paragraph papers and a five-paragraph theme, all deal with the general topic of clothing. Note, however, that specific topics relate directly to the content areas. After studying these models and their analyses, you should be prepared to write an effective comparison-contrast paper.

─────────────── **Sample for English** ───────────────

The following single-paragraph paper was developed for a drama class. The assignment asked students to prepare an introductory paragraph to accompany illustrations of period costumes.

His and Hers Clothing

Over the centuries, as men's clothing has changed, so has women's. When men wore hats for dress, so did women. While men's hats were generally the sterotypical black top hats, women's were plumed, flowered, veiled, broad brimmed, and bright. When men wore celluloid stand-up collars, women wore high-necked dresses. Even though the men's collars were all alike, women's were decorated with lace, buttons, and jewelry. When men wore gloves, so did the women, not for warmth but as part of the coordinated whole. When men wore high-topped, high-buttoned shoes, women wore the same with a high heel added. Although most shoes were

black, the women's sported pointed toes and stitched or cut
patterns. So, while the dress of men and women has made
simultaneous changes, the women's fancier details added femininity.

Analysis of the Sample for English

The comparison-contrast paragraph above illustrates some of the characteristics we have discussed:

- The topic sentence, the first in the paragraph, establishes the subject and the comparison.
- The general organization is part-by-part since the writer talks first about men's hats and then women's, next about men's collars and then women's. (A whole-by-whole organization would have required the writer to talk about men's apparel and, when he finished that, to talk about women's apparel.)
- The specific order is spatial—from head (*hat*) to foot (*shoes*).
- As the writer compares the simultaneous changes, he also points out some specific differences, always showing the women's apparel as fancier, more decorative.
- The transitions clarify the change, especially with words like *when* and *while*. Other transitions emphasize the more decorative women's apparel, words like *even though* and *although*.
- The sentence structure maintains the balance of the comparison. Equal numbers of sentences apply to each subtopic in the paragraph.
- The conclusion ties together the comparison and sets out the contrast.

Sample for Social Sciences

As part of a unit on the American Revolution, students wrote papers about some human aspect of the war: personal problems soldiers faced, business difficulties those at home faced, or bitter disagreements among family members. The assignment required that papers deal with something different from typical textbook subjects. One student wrote the following single-paragraph paper comparing the clothing worn by American and British soldiers.

Clothing the Soldiers

During the American Revolution, the American and British
soldiers wore different kinds of uniforms. Most American soldiers,
straight from their homes and fields, wore what they had: hand-

stitched jackets, homespun shirts, leather suspenders, drop-front pants, and homemade shoes. Their hats were as varied as the hat makers. They made do with their lack of similar dress, understanding that rank had its privileges, but making no effort to document it with stripes or stars or bars. They presented a motley group. Unwittingly, however, they wore what, by comparison, was nearly camouflage. On the other hand, the British soldiers were attired in the smart English uniform: red coats, white pants, knee-high black boots, and cocky hats. Their commanders' uniforms marked their prestige. In the fighting field, however, which was home to the American farmers and hunters, the British found their white pants dirty, their boots muddy, and hats knocked askew. What is more, the red and white gleamed like a beacon in any forest or meadow, making amazingly easy-to-spot targets. In fact, the two white belts that crossed their chests made perfect targets. One could debate whether the war was won or lost because of the soldier's clothing.

Analysis of the Sample for Social Sciences

The social sciences sample provides an interesting comparison with the sample for English in several respects. Study the two and note the following:

- The topic sentence, the first sentence in the paragraph, clarifies the subject and the purpose.
- The general organization is whole by whole. First the reader learns about the American soldiers' dress and then about the British soldiers'.
- The order is generally from top to bottom. The reference to the headgear returns the reader to the top.
- Transitions move the reader in an orderly fashion from one topic to the next, an entire sentence providing the transition from the American soldier to the British.
- The order remains constant throughout the paragraph. The topic sentence mentions first the American soldier's clothing, and indeed that is discussed first in the paragraph. And, since jackets are mentioned first for the American soldier, they are likewise mentioned first for the British soldier. Even later, the order remains as the writer refers to *red and white* as opposed to *white and red*.

- Sentences vary both in length and structure.
- Active voice adds emphasis. [*See* ACTIVE VOICE *in the Glossary.*]
- The conclusion emphasizes the differences and leads to speculation.

─────────────── **Sample for Science** ───────────────

As part of a laboratory experiment, students tested the flammability of various substances. Each student reported on a part of the experiment. The student whose paper appears below compared the flame resistance of three fabrics common in clothing.

A Comparison of Flame Resistance among Fabrics

In the process of determining flame resistance among three common fabrics, the experimenter carefully measured two controlled variables: the time the fabric was exposed to flame and the distance of the fabric from the flame. As a result, all test measurements were consistent. Under these controls, three fabrics were tested: polyester, cotton, and wool. Results indicated that the least flame-resistant fabric was polyester. Within thirty seconds' exposure to the flame, the polyester sputtered, melted, then extinguished itself, leaving a blackened, charred sample. The second least flame-resistant fabric was cotton. It scorched badly when exposed to flame, but it did not burn unless held in the flame for a minimum of forty-five seconds. The most flame-resistant fabric was wool. It would not burn unless held steadily in the flame for more than one minute. The results of this test suggest that those people who plan to be near open flame, such as a campfire, would be safest wearing wool.

Analysis of the Sample for Science

Because the science paper is typically very different from an English or social sciences paper, the model above merits attention, especially in terms of the following specifics:

- The topic sentence, which appears first, indicates the basis of the comparison—a laboratory test. Because of the nature of a science paper, it must account for the testing process, even if only briefly as in this paragraph.
- The general organization follows the whole-by-whole pattern, giving all details for one fabric before moving to the next.
- The internal pattern of organization follows an order of importance, from the least flame-resistant fabric to the most.
- Each comparison includes a one- or two-sentence summary of test results as a basis for comparison.
- Vocabulary and sentence structure are appropriate to the subject and the audience.
- Transitions move the reader smoothly through the organization, especially with words like *least, next, more,* and *most.*
- The report maintains the third-person point of view by referring, appropriately, to *this experimenter.*
- The conclusion clarifies the comparison by extending the meaning of the test results to daily living.

Sample for Business

As part of an Advertising unit, students in a business class were asked to compare and contrast advertising campaigns from two or more competitive companies. One student compared and contrasted three mail-order clothing companies. Her four-paragraph paper appears below.

A Comparison of Leading Clothing Catalogs

Mail-order catalogs generate big business in the clothing industry. As a result of the direct-to-the-door competition, the catalogs have become subjects of intense study in terms of advertising techniques. Three such catalogs, apparently equally successful in their respective marketing campaigns, embody significant similarities while at the same time illustrate astounding differences.

Each of the three catalogs uses only full-color photographs. No black and white photographs or line drawings appear in any of them. The paper quality, nearly equal in all three, suggests a "slick" advertisement. All catalogs feature high-fashion items, sportswear, lingerie, and limited footwear. In every case, the item descriptions carry typical advertisers' buzz words, obviously selected to give the product the best image without obvious misrepresentation. Finally, all three include some kind of general guarantee of "satisfaction or your money back," a toll-free number for information or ordering, and an order blank which accommodates charge customers.

On the other hand, each catalog embodies astounding differences. One is size. The catalogs vary from standard 8 1/2″ x 11″ to a mid-size 5″ x 7″ to a half size 4″ x 5 1/2″. While the smallest catalog includes eight more pages than the largest, the total number of items listed is just over half that of the largest catalog. Second, the photographic backgrounds for the models range from shabby to sleek. The mid-sized catalog uses nondescript backgrounds, including wood-paneled walls which reflect glare from lights, windows with poorly hung drapes, and painted walls which, under the intense camera light, show imperfections as shadowy effects. At the other extreme, the smallest catalog uses all career-oriented backgrounds, with models standing beside or in front of executive desks, wooden filing cabinets, computer systems, airline ticket counters, or other CEO-related settings. The models carry briefcases, gold pens, computer disks, legal pads, and calculators. Finally, the models' facial expressions and body positions vary considerably. The largest catalog uses models whose expressions are cold, impersonal, distant, maybe even arrogant. The mid-sized catalog's models seem untrained, most assuming an amateur grin, eyes on camera, body pose less than advantageous either for the model or for the clothing. The models in the smallest catalog, however, assume relaxed expressions and poses, almost too relaxed for the business atmosphere in which they are photographed.

In short, then, the mail-order clothing business has reached massive proportions, so much so that catalogs compete in sensitive, subtle ways for the home buyer's business. One who understands the psychology of advertising can sort through the various messages the three catalogs send to their customers.

Analysis of the Sample for Business

The theme-length comparison-contrast business paper above illustrates several options we have not yet seen. Note the following specifics:

- The opening paragraph sets the scene and concludes with the thesis sentence. The reader is prepared to read about both similarities and differences in the three catalogs.

- The general organization of the comparison-contrast theme follows the likenesses-differences pattern. All similarities are set out in the first body paragraph while all differences appear in the second.

- The specific order within the general pattern follows an order of importance. Both body paragraphs move from the most obvious to the least obvious.

- Abundant transitions help the reader move from the broad category of likenesses to the broad category of differences. The transitions also help the reader sort through the differences among the three catalogs. (For actual class purposes, you probably should cite the catalogs by name, providing a clearer reference for the reader.)

- Vocabulary and sentence structure are appropriate to the subject and the audience.

- The paper maintains unity throughout, each paragraph dealing only with details supporting its topic sentence.

- Specific details allow the reader to see both likenesses and differences, including details about color, background, clothing types, model's attitudes, and general descriptions.

- The conclusion, set out in a separate paragraph as theme organization would have it, returns the reader's attention to the popularity and business impact of the subject. At the same time, the conclusion admits that the *astounding differences* require a skilled analyst to determine the total message.

Sample for Vocational Education

In a clothing class, students wrote papers to compare or contrast two sewing techniques. The single-paragraph paper below compares two kinds of seams.

The Differences between Two Common Clothing Seams

Two common seams appear in both men's and women's clothing: the plain seam and the flat-felled seam. The two kinds of seams require different sewing methods and result in different appearances and different strengths. The plain seam requires the seamstress merely to place two pieces of fabric right sides together and run a single row of stitches 5/8" from the raw edges. The flat-felled seam, on the other hand, requires the seamstress to place the pieces of fabric this time wrong sides together and stitch a plain seam. At this point, however, she is far from finished. Next, she must press open the seam allowances and trim one seam allowance to 1/8". After turning under the raw edge of the remaining seam allowance, she presses it over the trimmed edge. Finally, she top stitches the pressed seam to the garment close to the folded edge. When these two kinds of seams are finished, they present very different appearances. The plain seam shows only a single line where the fabric joins, but no stitching shows. The two raw edges are hidden inside the garment. On the other hand, the flat-felled seam shows two rows of stitching on the right side of the fabric and no raw seam edges appear inside or out. It adds a classic detail which enhances sportswear. Finally, the seams can be compared by their strength. A plain seam with its single row of stitching is necessarily weaker than two rows of stitching. The added width of fabric between the two rows of stitching on the flat-felled seam further enforces the seam strength. And the flat-felled seam cures fraying edges, another strengthening feature. In short, the plain seam, because it is easy to sew, is more frequently used; but the flat-felled seam, although it requires greater sewing skill, adds strength and classic detail to the garment.

Analysis of the Sample for Vocational Education

The comparison-contrast paragraph above effectively contrasts two kinds of seams. Think about the following specifics as you evaluate the model yourself:

- The topic sentence names the subject and the three major differences.
- The part-by-part organization permits the writer to discuss the sewing method, the appearance, and the strength of each kind of seam.
- The chronological order allows the reader to follow the organization from sewing to finished product.

- In every case, to follow the pattern of organization, the writer discusses first the plain seam and then the flat-felled seam.
- Transitions move the reader from step to step and from detail to detail.
- Vocabulary and sentence structure fit the subject and the audience.
- The conclusion makes a final statement in support of the flat-felled seam.

Sample for Mathematics

A clothing designer wanted a pattern spaced on a length of fabric in geometric sequence. Math students compared arithmetic and geometric sequences. The following is one response:

Arithmetic and Geometric Sequences

An arithmetic sequence has numbers arranged so that each number in the list has the same difference between it and the one before. For instance, an arithmetic sequence can be 1, 4, 7, 10, 13, and the difference between any number and the previous number is three. Another arithmetic sequence can be 2, 6, 10, 14, 18, and the difference between any two adjoining numbers is four. On the other hand, a geometric sequence has numbers arranged so that each number in the list is multiplied by a constant value to get the next number in the list. For instance, a geometric sequence can be 3, 6, 12, 24, 48, where the constant multiple is two. Another geometric sequence can be 4, 16, 64, 256, 1024, where the constant multiple is four.

Analysis of the Sample for Mathematics

In comparing arithmetic and geometric sequences, the writer used the following techniques:

- The first part of the paragraph explains arithmetic sequence and gives two examples.
- The comparison is introduced by *on the other hand*.
- The second part of the paragraph explains geometric sequence and gives two more examples, thus showing readers the difference between the two kinds of sequences.

After studying the models and their analyses, you should be able to follow the process and develop a comparison-contrast paper that will be quite acceptable for any purpose you plan.

DEFINITION

A definition paper is particularly useful in dealing with abstract terms like *democracy, love, hope,* and *ethics.* In some cases, when a special term requires a definition, the dictionary definition will suffice. In other cases, however, a whole paragraph or even a full-length theme may be necessary. For instance, a single-sentence definition of *artificial intelligence* may be adequate for the lay person, but the scientific community involved in the research may provide a several-page definition. Or, a test question may ask you to define a term. One question may require as an answer a three-page definition of capitalism, while another may require a single-sentence definition of economics. Be sure you understand to what extent the instructor expects you to define. [*See also* ESSAY-QUESTION RESPONSE, KINDS: TEST QUESTIONS *in Part II.*]

What we are saying is that the scope of the definition depends on the purpose, and the purpose generally depends on the audience.

Characteristics

In general, regardless of length, a definition

- identifies the term to be defined,
- identifies the class to which the term belongs,
- identifies the difference between this term and all others in the class. For example:

  A card catalog (term to be defined) is an index (class to which the term belongs) of all the books in a given library (difference between card catalog and all other indexes).

- uses terminology suitable for the audience, reducing technical terms to lay terms for the lay audience,

- sometimes uses the negative to identify what the term is not,
- may include examples by way of explanation,
- may include process analysis [*see* PROCESS ANALYSIS *in Part II*],
- may include cause and effect [*see* CAUSE AND EFFECT *in Part II*],
- may include comparison, especially to show the unfamiliar in terms of the familiar [*see* COMPARISON AND CONTRAST *and* ANALOGY *in Part II*],
- may include description [*see* DESCRIPTION *in Part II*].

Process

The following process will help you plan, organize, write, and revise a definition. You will need to use the same process whether you write a single sentence or a full-length theme; here we will use a middle ground, the paragraph, by way of example.

PREWRITING

STEP 1.   PUTTING THE TERM IN ITS CLASS

When you define a term, either within the context of another paper or as a paper in itself, you must first put the term in its class. In other words, to what larger group does this term belong? Consider the examples below:

Term	Class
conifer	tree
capitalism	economic philosophy
hypothalamus	part of the brain
gross income	income
acrylic	paint

Now, for the term you must define, list the class to which it belongs.

STEP 2.   DECIDING THE DIFFERENCE

After you have named the class to which the term belongs, you must decide how this term is different from all others in its class. Study the following examples:

Term	Class	Difference
conifer	tree	stays green year round
capitalism	economic philosophy	encourages free enterprise
hypothalamus	part of the brain	controls metabolism
gross income	income	before expenses are deducted
acrylic	paint	works like oil but dries quicker

Now write a sentence in which you put the term in its class and show the difference between it and other members of its class. For example:

A conifer is a tree which stays green year around.

This sentence may become the topic or thesis sentence for your paragraph or theme. [*See* TOPIC SENTENCE *and* THESIS SENTENCE *in the Glossary for quick reference, and see* PARAGRAPHS *and* THEME *in Part II for a complete discussion of paragraph and theme structure.*]

STEP 3.   CHOOSING EXPLANATORY DETAILS

If your definition requires more than a single sentence, then you will need to determine which details will best complete the definition. Think about the following possibilities:

Analogy or Comparison

You may define *the law of supply and demand* by comparing the price fluctuations with the behavior of children on a seesaw. [*See* ANALOGY *and* COMPARISON AND CONTRAST *in Part II.*]

Process or Structural Analysis

A *kiln* can be defined by structural analysis, describing how it is constructed, and by process analysis, describing how it is used. [*See* PROCESS ANALYSIS *in Part II.*]

Cause or Effect

To define *mulch* as *any organic matter which smothers unwanted vegetation and, as it deteriorates, enriches the soil* is to define by effect. The definition explains how the mulch affects what it covers.

Description, Details, Examples

You can best define *technical report* by describing its contents and appearance and by offering an example of a typical technical report.

Negation

By establishing what is not, you can define what is. To say that a *fireplace* is *not an efficient means of heating* is to define by negation.

Combination of Methods

Photosynthesis can be defined by explaining the process (process analysis), by showing the effects of the process (cause or effect), and by describing the effect when the process breaks down (description, example, cause or effect, and negation).

Choose the most appropriate means of defining the term and list as many details as you can using that means.

STEP 4. ORGANIZING THE DETAILS

Next, arrange the details in some logical order. You may choose chronological order, spatial order, or some order of importance [*see entries for each in the Glossary*] according to the demands of your subject.

WRITING

STEP 5. MAKING THE DEFINITION CLEAR

As you write your first draft, think of your audience:

- Will they understand the terminology?
- Will they be able to follow the organization?
- Do transitions help them see relationships among the subtopics?
- Are the details sufficient to explain the term?

REVISING

STEP 6. CHECKING THE CONTENT

As you reread your definition, ask yourself these questions to check for areas for possible revision:

- Does the topic sentence put the term into its class and then show the differences between it and all other members of its class?

- If the term is abstract, does the definition include specific details and examples to help the reader understand the abstraction? [*See* REVISING: SAMPLE REVISION FOR SPECIFIC DETAIL *in Part I.*]

- If the term is technical, does the definition reduce the term to layman's language or provide specific examples the layman will understand?

- If the term names a process, does the reader learn about the process?

- If the term names a situation, does the reader learn about the situation, its causes and effects, as appropriate?

- If possible, does the reader see the unfamiliar in terms of the familiar, perhaps by means of a comparison, a contrast, or an analogy?

- Can the reader follow a clear organization with the help of effective transitions? [*See* REVISING: SAMPLE REVISION FOR TRANSITION *in Part I.*]

- Does the conclusion satisfy the reader with all he or she should know about the term? [*See* CONCLUSION *in the Glossary.*]

[*In addition, see* REVISING *in Part I for general guidelines for improving structure and polishing style.*]

PROOFREADING

STEP 7. CHECKING THE DETAILS

When you have completed the revising process in Step 6 above, you are ready to prepare your final draft. Then check your work for grammar, mechanics, usage, and punctuation. Consult *Webster's New World Dictionary* and *Webster's New World Thesaurus* to check spelling and to improve word choice.

A Note about the Samples: The following single- and two-paragraph definitions illustrate definition by description, example, effect, process analysis, structural analysis, negation, comparison, and combinations of methods. Study the samples and the analyses which follow.

Sample for English

The following definition, developed for a drama unit in a literature class, uses a combination of methods, including comparison, description, example, and effect.

The Proscenium Arch

Originated in 1618 in Parma, Italy, at the Farnese Theater by an architect name Aleotti, the proscenium arch gave the audience a new kind of theater experience. The proscenium arch is a style of stage construction that frames the performing area as if with a picture frame. Its development has been labeled as the beginning of the modern stage; and as such, the frame-like structure, for the first time, literally separated the audience from the actors. The separation physically and psychologically enhanced the impact of the performance. Until this time, many performances occurred on platforms, some of them makeshift affairs set up in the town square. The typical platform, even in a fine theater, simply sat in front of an ornamented facade. With the development of the proscenium arch which placed the action behind the "picture frame," the architect permitted the visual expansion of the stage. Using the arched structure, Italian set designers experimented with linear perspective and soon added movable sets to change scenery, thus, giving the audience the illusion of expansive settings. Indeed, stages sometimes are as much as one hundred feet deep and need little illusion. Still, the proscenium-arch theater opened new vistas to the set designers, the actors and actresses, and the audience.

Analysis of the Sample for English

The single-paragraph definition above illustrates a number of the principles discussed in the writing process:

- The topic sentence, the second in the paragraph, names the term to be defined (*proscenium arch*), puts it in its class (*style of stage construction*), and identifies the difference between this and others in its class (*"frames" the stage*).

- Clearly intended as introductory remarks, the definition uses such technical terms as *facade, set designers, movable scenery,* and *linear perspective.* The terms, however, probably have some meaning for the audience.

- Enhancing the definition, a comparison with earlier stage construction helps the reader recognize the significance of the proscenium-arch development.

- An explanation of the effects (in a cause-effect relationship) also clarifies the impact of the arch design.

- The *frame* analogy, allows the reader to compare the unfamiliar term with the familiar.

- The conclusion makes a final statement about stage construction and summarizes its impact.

—————————— **Sample for Social Sciences** ——————————

The following two-paragraph paper explains a kind of tax. Prepared to meet an assignment in an economics class, the definition relies primarily on process analysis and comparison.

Value-Added Tax

Value-added tax is a kind of corporate tax that taxes each step of production only for the proportionate value it has in the final product. It is an alternate means of taxing industrial processes and, according to some political analysts, encourages business and additional employment. Consider, for instance, the aluminum industry. Under present corporate tax laws, the ore is mined, sold to the smelters and taxed. Then the ore is smelted, sold to the aluminum companies, and taxed. Next the aluminum is cut into sheets, sold to can producers, and taxed. Then the sheets are formed into cans, sold to beverage companies, and taxed. Finally, the cans are filled with fruit juice, sold to consumers, and taxed.

Value-added tax eliminates the standard tax at each step and taxes only the amount of value that step adds to the final product, in this case, the canned drinks. For instance, if a piece of ore is worth $1.00, and the smelted aluminum from that ore is worth $3.00, the smelter pays tax on the $2.00 value added. If the piece of aluminum now valued at $3.00 forms aluminum cans worth $5.00, the can maker pays the tax not on the $5.00, but on the $2.00 value added. Finally, the $5.00 worth of cans, filled with beverage, are now worth $15.00, so the beverage company pays tax on the $10.00 added value. The consumer pays no tax except, of course, indirectly in increased prices.

Analysis of the Sample for Social Sciences

The definition above follows many of the process suggestions:

- The thesis sentence, the first sentence in the paragraph, identifies the term (*value-added tax*), the class (*a kind of corporate tax*), and the difference between it and others in its class (*taxes each step of production only on the value added toward the final product*).

- The remainder of the first paragraph uses the aluminum industry by way of example to describe the present taxing method.
- The second paragraph illustrates the differences in the value-added taxing method.
- The comparison-contrast development follows the whole-by-whole approach. [*See* COMPARISON AND CONTRAST *in Part II, and see* WHOLE-BY-WHOLE ORGANIZATION *in the Glossary.*]
- Parallel construction enhances the organization and provides smooth transition for the reader. [*See* PARALLEL STRUCTURE *in the Glossary.*]

Sample for Science

The following paragraph is one student's response to an essay question on a chemistry test. Students were asked to define *quantum numbers*. Further instructions indicated the definition should be no more than a well-developed paragraph. [*See also* ESSAY-QUESTION RESPONSES, KINDS: TEST QUESTIONS *in Part II.*]

Quantum Numbers

Quantum numbers are numerical descriptions which, when taken together, describe a given electron in a given atom. There are four quantum numbers for every electron. The first, called the principal quantum number, describes the energy level of the electron. The second, called the orbital quantum number, describes the shape of the orbit in which the electron moves. The third, called the magnetic quantum number, describes the electron's orientation in space. The fourth, called the spin, describes the clockwise or counterclockwise spin of the electron around its own axis. Together, the four numbers describe an electron, and no two electrons in an atom can have the same four quantum numbers.

Analysis of the Sample for Science

The definition of quantum numbers in the paragraph above is obviously aimed at an audience with some understanding of electrons and their function, and most beginning chemistry students have that understanding. As a result, the definition uses some technical terms that to a student who has never had

- The topic sentence identifies the term to be defined (*quantum numbers*), the class (*numerical description*) and the difference between it and others in its class (*describe an electron*).
- The definition separates the term into its four parts, and by analyzing each of the parts, defines the whole.
- The organization follows an order of importance. [*See* ORDERS OF IMPORTANCE *in the Glossary.*]
- Transitions effectively separate the four kinds of quantum numbers and help show the distinctions among them. [*See* TRANSITIONS *in the Glossary.*]

───────── **Sample for Business** ─────────

The following paragraph defines *net profit* by using negation and process analysis. The student reponse is in answer to a test question in a business principles class.

Net Profit

When a business must determine success or failure, it looks at net profit. Net profit is the money made after all expenses are deducted. It is not a measure of sales or income. That is gross profit, or how much money actually came into the business. Beginning with gross profit, the business deducts salaries and wages, cost of employee benefits, cost of raw materials, cost of manufacturing or production, cost of maintenance and depreciation, and all other business expenses, either direct or indirect, for the year. When all expenses are deducted from the gross profit, what is left is net profit. That is the traditional "bottom line."

Analysis of the Sample for Business

The sample definition follows the general guidelines for the process:

- The topic sentence includes the term to be defined (*net profit*), the class (*money*), and the difference between it and others in its class (*what is left after expenses are paid*).
- The term is negated, that is, explained in terms of what it is not.
- The remainder of the paragraph lists some of the major deductions from gross profit to show that what is left is net profit.
- The simple, straight-forward organization, from what is not to what is, makes the definition easy to understand.

———————— **Sample for Mathematics** ————————

Students in math class were asked to define *scientific notation*. The following is one student's response.

Scientific Notation

When writing extremely large or small numbers, you may sometimes have so many digits that you cannot read them or even pronounce whatever words it may take to say them. (What comes after trillions?) To more easily write those very large or small numbers, mathematicians use a method called scientific notation. To write a number in scientific notation, you move the decimal point from its present location one place to the right of the first digit that is not a zero. In other words, you write the number so that it has a value between 1 and 10, rounding off as necessary. Then you multiply the number by 10 raised to the power equal to the number of places that the decimal point was moved. If you move the decimal point from the right to the left, the exponent is positive. For example, 9,238,648,500 written in scientific notation is 9.24×10^9. On the other hand, if you move the decimal point from the left to the right, the exponent is negative. For example, .00000092 written in scientific notation is 9.2×10^{-7}. So scientific notation makes numbers shorter and easier to read and mathematical operations easier to complete.

Analysis of the Sample for Mathematics

As a definition, the paragraph above uses several special techniques:

- The topic (third) sentence identifies the term (scientific notation), the class (method) and the difference between it and others in its class (for writing very large or small numbers).
- The explanation of the process for writing scientific notation (*see also* PROCESS ANALYSIS *elsewhere in Part II*) helps readers further understand the definition.
- The examples clarify scientific notation, including both positive and negative exponents.

DESCRIPTION

Certain situations require papers that are completely descriptive. You may be asked to describe a setting or a microscopic specimen. In addition, almost all papers require some description. For instance, how could a writer talk about the process by which something is made without describing the steps in the process? Cause-effect, comparison-contrast, definition, narration, literary analysis, analogy—almost anything you write may include description. [*See separate entries for each kind of writing in Part II.*]

Good description relies on the five senses. The reader should see, hear, taste, smell, and feel. [*See* IMAGERY *in the Glossary.*] At the same time, however, good description is synonymous with clarity. It conveys information accurately. Consider the following possible topics for a descriptive paper:

Describe the Battle of Bull Run.

Describe the capabilities of an electronic typewriter.

Describe your experience as a student leader.

Describe William Faulkner's symbolism in *Light in August*.

Describe your favorite pet.

Describe capitalism.

Describe a memorable scene.

As you can guess from the examples above, description in a literary sense differs considerably from that in a practical sense. Literary description emphasizes imagery and figures of speech [*see* IMAGERY *and* FIGURES OF SPEECH *in the Glossary*], while practical description emphasizes clear information. In this chapter we will compare both sorts of description. The sample descriptive papers further illustrate the differences between the two.

For the purposes of this section, we will assume that you must develop an entire paper using description. As you use description to develop parts of other papers, you will employ the same techniques but perhaps in abbreviated form.

Characteristics

A descriptive paper serves only to describe. Usually, however, the paper includes the following general characteristics:

- a subject worthy of description,
- an emphasis, either direct or indirect, on the five senses,
- use of figures of speech, especially to enrich the description and spark reader interest [*see* FIGURES OF SPEECH *in the Glossary*],

174

- a topic or thesis sentence which names the subject to be described and establishes the attitude toward the subject [*see* TONE *in the Glossary*],
- one of three patterns of organization: chronological, spatial, or an order of importance,
- a single, consistent tone and mood [*see* MOOD *in the Glossary*],
- details which support the tone and mood,
- unity within the paragraphs and the paper as a whole,
- vocabulary which clarifies,
- varied sentence structure, which enhances the general attitude and adds appropriate emphasis,
- an effective conclusion.

Process

In order to plan, organize, write, revise, and proofread your description, use the following process.

PREWRITING

STEP 1. CHOOSING A TOPIC

Ordinarily almost any topic can lend itself to description. Think about the subjects you have studied most recently in the various content areas:

cooking utensils	globes, maps
machines	writing techniques
audio-visual equipment	art supplies
	wiring harnesses

keyboard position	
rough-cut lumber	chemical reactions
radio-script writing	camera functions

As you think about the subjects, choose one that fits the purpose. [*See also* PREWRITING *in Part I for additional suggestions for sources of topics.*]

STEP 2. NARROWING THE TOPIC

The subjects listed above are too broad for a single descriptive paper. In order to narrow the topic, list subtopics for each general topic. Use the following example as a pattern:

General subject:
　globes, maps
Subtopics:
　outline maps
　regional maps
　resource maps
　topographical maps
　political maps
　world maps

As you list the divisions of your subject, you will find a topic narrowed enough for a descriptive paper. In the list above, for instance, you may choose *topographical maps* for a descriptive paragraph.

Select the narrowed topic before you go on to Step 3.

STEP 3. DETERMINING THE PURPOSE

Next, think about what you hope to accomplish with your description. Who will read it? What purpose do you hope to achieve by it? (If the topic has been assigned, the purpose is probably stated or implied in the assignment.)

Stop now and determine the purpose. State your purpose in a single sentence. For example:

The description of a topographical map will explain the purpose of its lines and symbols, especially as they are helpful to hikers.

The statement of purpose will help you select relevant details.

STEP 4.   SELECTING THE DETAILS

After you have narrowed the topic and determined your purpose, you must select appropriate details for your description. Assume, for instance, that you have chosen to develop a description of a topographical map. You may list the following details:

contour lines

elevation indicated

ridges, valleys

increasing vs. decreasing elevation

good for hikers, backpackers

help plan routes

Now, select details that specifically support your purpose. In the example above, for instance, the details about hikers, exploration, and planning routes are only of secondary importance to the purpose of the paper. Revised to meet the purpose

of the paper, the list now looks like this:

- indicates rate of incline
  - increasing elevation
  - decreasing elevation
- indicates ridges
- indicates valleys

STEP 5.   ORGANIZING THE DETAILS

Now you are ready to arrange the details in some kind of order. If the subject is set in time, you will probably prefer to use chronological order, perhaps including a flashback. [*See* CHRONOLOGICAL ORDER *and* FLASHBACK *in the Glossary.*] For a different kind of subject, you may select an order of importance. [*See* ORDERS OF IMPORTANCE *in the Glossary.*] Or, for a description of a setting or scene, you may choose to use spatial order. [*See* SPATIAL ORDER *in the Glossary.*]

The example above can probably best be organized by an order of importance, describing first the most obvious characteristics of the topographical map (*the snake-like lines*) and then describing the less obvious characteristics (*degree of incline or decline*).

Select the method that seems most logical for your subject and number the details in that order.

STEP 6.   DEVELOPING THE TOPIC OR THESIS SENTENCE

Finally, you are ready to write a topic or thesis sentence. [*See* TOPIC SENTENCE *and* THESIS SENTENCE *in the Glossary for quick reference, and see*

PARAGRAPHS *and* THEME *in Part II for complete details and examples.*]

Refer to the statement of purpose developed in Step 3 above. Keep the same idea in your topic or thesis sentence. If you are writing a paragraph, your topic sentence should include these specifics:

• stated subject to be described

• attitude toward subject

Examine the following topic sentence and then develop one for your own descriptive paper.

The topographical map may look like a child's inept efforts to follow the lines, but a closer look shows three purposes for the squiggly dividing marks.

WRITING

STEP 7. FOLLOWING THE PLAN

To prepare your first draft, begin with the topic or thesis sentence and develop supporting details in the order you selected in Step 4 above. As you write, try to include techniques that will enhance your description:

• Use colorful language, specific nouns and vigorous verbs, especially those that create images of the senses.

• Where appropriate, make a conscious effort to include figures of speech, allowing subtle comparisons to spark the reader's imagination.

• Include adequate supporting details to clarify the subject being described. [See SPECIFIC DETAIL *in the Glossary.*]

• Conclude with a clincher that adds a final bit of descriptive imagery.

REVISING

STEP 8. IMPROVING THE CONTENT

When you have completed the first draft, you are ready to check for possible revisions. Almost every paper can be improved, so look at your description using the following questions to suggest possible improvements:

• Does my topic or thesis sentence clearly state my subject and identify the attitude of my description? [See PARAGRAPHS *and* THEME *in Part II for examples and detailed explanation.*]

• Do I follow a specific organizational plan? [See ORDER, IN PARAGRAPH DEVELOPMENT *in the Glossary.*]

• Is the organizational plan effective, or would a different one be better?

• Does the paper maintain a consistent tone throughout? [See TONE *in the Glossary.*]

• Are there adequate details to clarify the subject being described?

[*See* REVISING: SAMPLE REVISION FOR SPECIFIC DETAIL *in Part I.*]

• Do the details stimulate the reader's five senses, or at least most of them?

• Where appropriate, do figures of speech enhance the description?

• Does the vocabulary suit the subject, attitude and audience?

• Does the sentence structure add emphasis or variety? [*See* REVISING: SAMPLE REVISION FOR SENTENCE VARIETY *in Part I.*]

• Does the paper maintain unity? [*See* REVISING: SAMPLE REVISION FOR UNITY *in Part I.*]

• Are transitions adequate to move the reader smoothly from sentence to sentence and from paragraph to paragraph? [*See* TRANSITION *in the Glossary and* REVISING: SAMPLE REVISION FOR TRANSITION *in Part I.*]

• Does the paper avoid flowery modifiers, using instead strong nouns and verbs? [*See* REVISING: SAMPLE REVISION FOR WORDINESS *in Part I.*]

• Does the conclusion end the paper effectively? [*See* CONCLUSION *in the Glossary.*]

[*For additional, more general guidelines, see* REVISING *in Part I.*]

PROOFREADING

STEP 9.   CHECKING THE DETAILS

When you have completed whatever revisions the questions in Step 8 suggested, proofread your paper for accuracy. Check punctuation, grammar, mechanics, and usage. Refer to the Glossary for help with specific punctuation, grammar, mechanics, and usage problems. The rules, examples, definitions, and explanations there will help solve those problems. Use *Webster's New World Dictionary* and *Webster's New World Thesaurus* to check spelling and to improve word choice.

A Note about the Samples: Now that you are familiar with descriptive papers, examine the following samples and their accompanying analyses to study the application of the process described above. Each describes some feature of cedar, as a tree or as lumber, appropriate for the content area. As a result, you will be able to see how descriptions vary according to their purpose. What is suitable in a literary description, for instance, will not be suitable in a scientific description.

After studying the samples and their analyses, you should be able to develop an appropriate description for whatever purpose you have.

Sample for English

Students in an English class studied descriptive-writing techniques and then wrote single-paragraph descriptions of a memorable scene. As you would expect, the assignment emphasized description in the literary sense. One student, whose paragraph appears below, described a cedar tree growing along the edge of a cliff.

The Stately Cedar

A gnarled cedar clutches the limestone cliff. Its trunk twisted and bent, the stalwart has bowed and sighed in decades of mock worship to the wind, never budging from its king-of-the-mountain perch. In the searing sun, its incense drifts across the wind-clean rock, and the feathery dark blue-green foliage casts only thin shadows on the gray-white floor. Forever stirring breezes across the cliff top trade mindless whispers with the Ancient One. It stands as the Maker's champion of endurance.

Analysis of the Sample for English

The paragraph above includes all the characteristics of a good literary description. Note the following specifics:

- The topic sentence, which is also the conclusion in this paragraph, names the topic (*champion*, which the reader understands now to be the cedar tree) and indicates the attitude (*endurance*).
- Images to affect four of the five senses appear throughout the paragraph:
    Sight: gnarled, twisted, bent, bowed, king-of-the-mountain perch, searing sun, feathery dark blue-green, thin shadows, gray-white floor
    Sound: sighing, stirring breezes, whispers
    Touch: gnarled, clutches, limestone, twisted, searing sun, wind-clean, feathery, stirring breezes
    Smell: incense
- Figures of speech add subtle interest to the description:
    Personification: clutches, twisted and bent, bowed and sighed in worship, never budging, king-of-the-mountain perch, breezes trade whispers, Ancient One, champion
    Allusion: stalwart, king-of-the-mountain perch, Ancient One, champion
    Alliteration: clutches the cliff, bent and bowed, searing sun . . . incense

Onomatopoeia: sighed, searing, whispers

Metaphor: stalwart, wind-clean rock, gray-white floor, mindless whispers, champion

- Organized chronologically, from distant past to today, the description also moves from physically distant to close.
- The transitions, primarily repetition of words and phrases and their respective pronouns, connect the sentences smoothly. [*See* TRANSITION *in the Glossary.*]
- Use of active voice and action verbs throughout makes the description more powerful. [*See* ACTIVE VOICE *and* ACTION VERB *in the Glossary.*]
- Sentence structure varies from simple to complex, including complex series.
- The conclusion, which is also the topic sentence, ties together the details in the paragraph, all of which illustrate endurance in spite of obstacles.

Sample for Social Sciences

Students in a United States history class were asked to describe typical furnishings in an American home in the late 1800s. After visiting a living museum, one student prepared the following description of a hope chest. Appropriately for a social sciences class, the description also incorporates a cultural statement. By describing the contents of a bride's hope chest—often made of cedar—the writer is able to describe prized home furnishings. Note, too, that as a result of the writer's approach, the description takes on a narrative quality. [*See* NARRATION *in Part II.*]

The Cedar Chest: A Cultural Statement

As she propped open the hinged lid carved with the traditional hearts and doves, the sweet aromatic cedar scent wafted up, filling the room like incense with a home-at-last comfort. Inside the cedar chest lay the material realities of the bride's dream for a happy home. In the far left corner, a Trail to Dublin quilt lay folded, its tiny stitching attesting to the work of family quilting bees, its red and white now dimmed in the candlelight. Crowded against it as if for protection, a pair of pewter candlesticks, still free from wax, waited like sentinels to grace the bride's table. An Aladdin oil lamp, its chimney wrapped in tissue, squatted against the quilt but closer to the front, away from the pewter. The lamp's shining nickel bowl distorted the reflection of the embroidered table runner, folded carefully on top of the knotted comforter to the right. In the far right corner, the precious family heirlooms lay linen-wrapped, awaiting the new bride's home: a hand-carved springerle board, the family Bible, an ivory comb and brush set, and a floral picture made of hair. She closed the lid to the chest and traced with her finger the date carved on the front: 1892.

Analysis of the Sample for Social Sciences

The paragraph above illustrates description in a combined literary and practical sense. Although it includes fewer figures of speech than did the sample for English, it includes enough imagery and figurative language to make what could be a lackluster paper into an interesting one. Consider the following characteristics:

- The topic sentence appears as the second sentence in the paragraph: *Inside the cedar chest lay the material realities of the bride's dream for a happy home.* It states the subject (*material reality*, i.e., contents of cedar chest) and the attitude (*dream for a happy home*).
- Images affect most of the five senses. The absence of the other two senses, taste and sound, seems reasonable in light of the topic. Note these images:

     Sight: carved, traditional hearts and doves, Trail to Dublin quilt, tiny stitching, red and white dimmed, candlelight, pewter, free from wax, Aladdin oil lamp, wrapped in tissue, stood against the quilt, closer to front, shining nickel, distorted reflection, embroidered, knotted comforter, linen-wrapped, hand-carved springerle board, Bible, ivory comb and brush set, floral picture made of hair, date on front read 1892

     Smell: aromatic cedar scent

     Touch: propped, carved, crowded against it, tissue, shining lamp bowl, knotted comforter, traced date

- Although this paragraph includes fewer figures of speech than did the model for English, it does include images that help the reader see more than the specific details:

     Simile: like sentinels, like incense

     Personification: attesting to, crowded, squatted, lay, awaiting

     Alliteration: sweet cedar scent, happy home, pair of pewter, reflection of runner, lay linen-wrapped

- Details are sufficient to clarify the subject.
- Active voice and action verbs add emphasis. [*See* ACTIVE VOICE *and* ACTION VERB *in the Glossary.*]

- Organization follows a spatial order, from left to right. [*See* SPATIAL ORDER *in the Glossary.*]
- Transitions help the reader follow the order, from the opening of the lid, from left to right inside the chest, and then to the outside front. [*See* REVIS-ING: SAMPLE REVISION FOR TRANSITION *in Part I.*]
- Sentence structure varies from simple to complex. [*See* SENTENCE STRUCTURE *in the Glossary.*]
- Since a single attitude prevails, it helps maintain unity throughout the paragraph. [*See* UNITY IN THE GLOSSARY.]
- The conclusion helps the reader focus on the reference in the title to *cultural statement.*

Sample for Science

In a botany unit, biology students were to give a scientific description of a species of tree. They were to include growing conditions and ecological relationships as well as physical descriptions of shape, size, leaves, trunk, fruit, and root system. The following paragraph is one student's response to the assignment. It is obviously practical but also includes a few literary devices that underscore the writer's skill.

Red Cedar, The Stalwart Tree

The red cedar, <u>Juniperus virginiana</u>, sometimes called red juniper or simply cedar, grows in dry, rocky areas from Nova Scotia and Ontario south to Florida and west to the Dakotas, Nebraska, and Oklahoma. While it prefers hills, it does not grow at high altitudes and will grow as well along lakes and streams. Usually no more than forty feet tall with a trunk no more than twenty inches in diameter, it generally takes a rather conical shape unless quite aged. Mature trees spread wider and become round-topped or, in inhospitable climates, even distorted, particularly when exposed to harsh winds as on a cliff or shore line. The red cedar's ridged or lobed trunk, often buttressed at the base, has a light reddish-brown bark that hangs in shreddy strips, fringed at the edges. The four-sided twigs, green from the covering of minute leaves, support dark green or reddish-brown leaves 2 mm or less long, scalelike, opposite in pairs. The leaves, which stay on for several years, closely overlap and are generally oppressed, rounded, glandular. Crushed, they emit an aromatic odor, and the oil from these leaves is used as perfume. The fruit, about the size of a small pea, fleshy, dark blue, tasting sweetish with a resinous flavor, provides food for songbirds, turkey, grouse, quail, fox, and opossum. The tree's worst enemy is fire, and even a small fire will damage its root system which lies close to the soil surface. Although few insects bother the red cedar, it is the bridging host for apple rust. As a result, orchard growers make up the minority which strives to rid their area of these tough, stalwart, and often picturesque trees.

Analysis of the Sample for Science

The descriptive paragraph prepared for a science class includes notable differences from other descriptive paragraphs. Note the following peculiarities:

- Scientific description requires a distinctive terminology. As a result, such terms as *Juniperus virginiana, ridged, lobed, buttressed, opposite in pairs, oppressed, glandular,* and *bridging host* may not be completely familiar to lay readers but are appropriate for the scientific description.

- In spite of the scientific emphasis, words which appeal to the senses do appear:

  Sight: conical, wider, round-topped, distorted, ridged, lobed, buttressed, reddish-brown, shreddy, fringed, four-sided, green, 2 mm long, scalelike, pairs, overlap, rounded, glandular, dark blue

  Smell: aromatic odor, perfume

  Taste: sweetish with resinous flavor

  Touch: shreddy strips, fringed, fleshy

- Figures of speech are limited, but some words suggest comparison: *conical, buttressed, shreddy, scalelike, fleshy,* and *about the size of a small pea*. Scientific descriptions rely on precise, often technical, wording and seldom include specific use of figures of speech.

- Details support the areas of useful scientific description: habitat, overall appearance, bark, twigs, leaves, berries, and enemies.

- The organization is in order of importance, from general to specific, from overall to minute. [*See* ORDERS OF IMPORTANCE *in the Glossary.*]

- The single attitude, that of objective viewer, helps maintain unity.

- Sentence structure and vocabulary meet the needs of the subject and the audience, including technical terms and some rather compact, complicated sentences.

- The clincher sentence, which offers a final statement, takes the reader back to the general.

Sample for Business

As part of a unit on determining value in investments, business students were asked to describe some factor that affects the value of a property in a highly practical sense. The student whose paragraph appears below chose to describe the use of cedar as a building material and its effect on the value of the building. Note that in spite of its practicality, the description does include imagery and a certain amount of figurative language.

Building for Value: Use Cedar

When deciding to invest in buildings, one must, of course, consider their durability. If construction materials include wood, the wary investor rightfully throws up his guard. Cedar, however, allows him to drop his guard, at least a little. As a construction material, cedar has been tested to be 80% as strong as white oak; its fine grain resists warping or shrinkage. More importantly, it resists rotting; so exposure to weather, soil, and water will not result in rapid decay. Cedar fence posts, for instance, often stand longer than the men who set them. The wood also weathers to a soft patina, so cedar shingles look warm and natural on rustic structures. Cedar channel-lap siding with its knots accenting the weathered patina will add a rustic look as well. Inside, rough-cut, unstained aromatic cedar panels give the room a reddish-cream warmth. Inside closets, the planed cedar scares away moths and silverfish, providing protection to woolens without offensive mothballs or insect sprays. Inside or out, cedar adds strength, beauty, endurance, and, therefore, value to a structure.

Analysis of the Sample for Business

By describing the characteristics rather than just the appearance of cedar, the above sample offers yet another use of description. Note, however, that the descriptive approach is nearly the same. Think about the specifics listed in the analysis below:

- The topic sentence, the third in the paragraph, specifies the subject and clarifies the attitude: *Cedar, however, allows him to drop his guard, at least a little.*
- The description includes images which affect the senses:

  Sight: fine grain, soft patina, warm and natural on rustic structures, knots, weathered patina, rough-cut, unstained panels, reddish-cream, planed

  Smell: aromatic cedar, offensive mothballs or insect sprays

  Touch: fine grain, rough-cut, unstained panels, warmth, planed

- This paragraph, unlike the other examples, describes characteristics, like weather resistance, protection against insects, and durability. These kinds of descriptions do not rely heavily on sensory images or figures of speech. Subtle comparisons can, however, help the reader understand a point:

  Allusion: throws up his guard, drop his guard

  Comparison: 80% as strong as white oak, cedar fence posts stand longer than the men who set them

  Personification: posts stand, cedar scares away and provides protection

- Active voice and mostly action verbs create effective emphasis. [*See* ACTIVE VOICE *and* ACTION VERB *in the Glossary.*]
- The organization, arranged in spatial order, moves from outside to inside, to inside closets. [*See* SPATIAL ORDER *in the Glossary.*]
- Transitions help the reader follow the organization. [*See* REVISING: SAMPLE REVISION FOR TRANSITION *in Part I.*]
- Sentence structure varies from simple to complex. [*See* REVISING: SAMPLE REVISION FOR SENTENCE VARIETY *in Part I.*]
- The single attitude throughout the paragraph helps maintain unity. [*See* REVISING: SAMPLE REVISION FOR UNITY *in Part I.*]
- The conclusion, which refers to the organization, *inside or out*, ties together the main points: strength, beauty, endurance, and value.

Sample for Vocational Education

In a woodworking class, students were asked to describe the qualities of one kind of wood in the construction of furniture. The following paragraph is one student's practical description.

The Charm of Finished Cedar

Any piece of cedar—in furniture, a chest, or a tiny jewelry box—takes on an unmatched appearance. No other wood, stained or unstained, can equal the creamy-red color unique to red cedar. Coloration ranges from a deep purplish rose-red to a cream with only a hint of pink. Over the largest surface, however, red-ochre dominates. The light, close, straight grain revealed in an edge-grained cut contrasts dramatically with the sweeping V's and gentle flares of a flat-grained cut. The grain pattern, its color heightened by satin varnish, plays like dancing flames in the mind's eye. While the wood is not especially hard and will therefore mar easily, and while it does tend to splinter and have little or no bending strength, it is exceedingly easy to work and is among the most warp-resistant woods known. Having once been used for skiffs and other light boats, it is still used for trim and finish in luxury canoes, motor boats and yachts. With its primary use in making lead pencils, red cedar touches literally everyone's life. Specialty cedar articles, however, are still guaranteed to make a treasured gift.

Analysis of the Sample for Vocational Education

As a descriptive paragraph, the sample above deals with content effectively. Consider the specifics:

- The topic sentence names the subject (*cedar*) and the attitude (*unmatched*).
- Arranged in an order of importance, the details move from overall color to predominant color, to specific markings. [*See* ORDERS OF IMPORTANCE *in the Glossary.*] The details support the attitude.
- The sensory images are primarily sight: *creamy-red, deep purplish rose-red, cream with hint of pink, red-ochre, close and straight grain, grain's sweeping V's, gentle flares, heightened by satin varnish.*
- One figure of speech, a simile, adds to the reader's interest: *plays like dancing flames in the mind's eye.*
- The sentences are mostly simple, but they include compound parts. As a result, sentence length varies considerably.
- The conclusion reiterates the topic sentence and applies the understanding to *treasured gift.*

──────── Sample for Mathematics ────────

One student created a cedar jewelry box but wanted to add an elliptical piece to decorate the top. In order to cut the piece, he first had to mathematically describe the ellipse so that it would fit on the ten-inch by sixteen-inch rectangular lid. The following is his description.

Creating an Ellipse

In order to create an ellipse that would just fit the 10″ × 16″ lid, I started a graph by drawing intersecting axes X and Y:

From the center of the lid, the distance to the right edge was 8″ and the distance to the top was 5″. Then I used the mathematical formula for an ellipse to plot points on the graph:

$$\frac{x^2}{a^2} + \frac{y^2}{b^2} = 1, \text{ where } a = 8 \text{ and } b = 5$$

By solving the equation for Y in terms of X and substituting values for X, I created the following table, which, when plotted on a graph, creates a description of a perfect ellipse.

x	8	6	4	2	0	−2	−4	−6	−8
y	0	±3.31	±4.33	±4.84	±5	±4.84	±4.33	±3.31	0

Analysis of the Sample for Mathematics

A mathematical description varies considerably from most other kinds of descriptions. In this sample, the student explains the process (*see also* PROCESS ANALYSIS *later in Part II*) for generating a mathematical description of an ellipse. Note that the description is in the form of a formula solved.

These samples and their analyses, along with the explanation of process, should prepare you to write effective descriptions suitable for any purpose.

DIALOGUE

Dialogue is conversation. Narratives, character sketches, autobiographical sketches, biographies, and short stories all depend on dialogue to stir the readers' imagination and promote their understanding of character. And drama exists entirely on the basis of dialogue. Listening to someone's spoken words gives us a glimpse into part of his or her personality—in fact, an important aspect of personality. Politicians, for instance, win or lose elections based on their spoken word. Teachers and pastors make their points via the spoken word. Marriages thrive or disintegrate with the spoken word. So writers use dialogue to make characters, either real or imaginary, live for the reader.

Characteristics

Writing successful dialogue demands special attention to the techniques. In general, dialogue

- shows the speaker's exact words by enclosing them in quotation marks,
- includes spelling clues to indicate dialect or speech patterns,
- produces natural-sounding conversation, usually using short sentences and contractions,
- may include sentence fragments to illustrate a speaker's exact words or to enhance style [see FRAGMENTS in the Glossary],
- uses phrases like *he yelled* or *she snarled* to allow the reader to "hear" the words in the context of the situation,
- relies heavily on accurate punctuation, including commas, end marks, and apostrophes as well as quotation marks,

- shows a change in speaker by a change in paragraphing [*See* PARAGRAPHS, KINDS: IN DIALOGUE *in Part II*],
- includes description, not just of voice and expression but also of mannerisms and other nonverbal means of communication.

Process

Use the following prewriting, writing, revising, and proofreading steps to produce successful dialogue.

PREWRITING

STEP 1. LISTENING TO THE CHARACTER

If you are writing about a real person, you have a responsibility to quote accurately. Using a tape recorder will certainly help, but if that is not possible, use the following guidelines. Make notes as you listen:

- What is the person's usual vocabulary? Does word choice suggest education or lack of it? Are certain words or phrases often repeated, like *actually, generally speaking,* or *well, I declare*?

- Are the sentences short and choppy or moderately long? Does the person answer *Yep* instead of *Yes, I think so*?

- What tone of voice does the speaker use? Does he or she shout, whisper, rasp, hiss, or whine? How would you describe the voice?

- Does the character occasionally use poor grammar?

- Does the person drop word endings, saying *walkin'* for *walking* or *talk* for *talked*?

- Does pronunciation reflect a dialect, words like *cain't* or *musta* for *can't* or *must have*?

If the character is not real, then you must listen in your mind. Ask yourself the same questions as suggested above, and then make sure the speech pattern is consistent with the character. For instance, a well-educated character is not likely to use poor grammar, but an uneducated character may not use poor grammar either. He may have learned by listening. If, then, you show evidence of his having learned other things by listening, it may be out of character for him to use poor grammar. So let your character talk with others and listen with your mind's ear. Perhaps you can mimic the talk, record it, and then write it from the recording. [*See* PREWRITING *in Part I for additional suggestions.*]

STEP 2. WATCHING THE CHARACTER

Dialogue also includes description of mannerisms and other nonverbal means of communication. As a result, as you listen, you must also watch. Make notes as you ask yourself questions like these:

- How does the character stand or sit? Does he or she slouch, lean on a cane, prop chin in hands? How else can you describe posture?

- What does the character do with his or her hands? Does he jab the air with a pipe-filled fist; does she unceasingly rub her thumbs together, or spin her wedding band?

- How can you describe the person's eyes? Are they clear or cloudy, sparkling or dull? Do they pierce the listener or wander off into an undefined distance?

- What visual evidence is there of facial reaction to comments? A frown, a fading dimple, a grin, a cocked head, a dropped jaw?

- What visual evidence is there of other physical reaction to comments? A shifting of position, a crossed leg, folded arms, leaning forward?

Again, if your character is imaginary, you should think through these same kinds of questions, watching your character in your mind's eye. Maintain a description appropriate for—and consistent with—his or her personality.

WRITING

STEP 3.   RECORDING THE CONVERSATION

Regardless of the context in which the dialogue appears, the writing process is the same:

- Write the exact words of the speaker, including spellings that will help the reader hear the pronunciation of the words.

- Use sentence fragments as appropriate or necessary to enhance characterization or maintain style.

- Unless you are writing a script, enclose the speaker's words in quotation marks. [*See* SCRIPTS *elsewhere in Part II.*]

- Add descriptions that will help the reader hear the tone of voice or vocal inflections.

- Add descriptions that will help the reader see the speaker's nonverbal reactions.

- Start a new paragraph each time a new character speaks.

REVISING

STEP 4.   CHECKING THE CONTENT

Read the dialogue aloud, perhaps with a friend or friends who will read other characters' parts. Listen carefully to the dialogue, asking yourself these questions:

- Does the conversation sound natural? Have I avoided a stilted, awkward, uncharacteristic speech pattern?

- Does the conversation fit the character? Are his words and sentences appropriate for his age, sex, education, environment, occupation, and emotional attitude?

- Will the reader be bored with too much irrelevant conversation, or is every part essential to furthering the plot or the characterization?

- Is the dialogue snappy, to the point, avoiding lengthy speeches or lengthy sentences?

Make whatever changes you can to improve the natural conversation flow and still achieve your purpose, whether that purpose is to further the plot in a drama script or to enhance a character sketch, autobiography, or narrative.

PROOFREADING

STEP 5.   CHECKING THE TECHNIQUES

Certain techniques peculiar to writing dialogue require attention beyond the usual checks for grammar, mechanics, and usage:

- Check paragraphing. You may include description relating to the character or the situation in the same paragraph, but you must begin a new paragraph when another character begins speaking. [*See* PARAGRAPHS, KINDS: IN DIALOGUE *in Part II. See also* SCRIPTS *in Part II for writing dialogue for plays, television, or radio.*]

- Check quotation marks. Have you enclosed the speaker's words, but not his thoughts, in quotation marks? If the speaker's words run more than one paragraph, have you started each new paragraph with quotation marks but ended only the last paragraph with them?

- Are commas, question marks, and exclamation marks used in correct relationship with the quotation marks?

- Are apostrophes used to show omission of letters or dropped endings?

- Are spellings appropriate for the dialogue, words in some cases spelled to indicate pronunciation?

- Do capital letters begin not only your sentences but the sentences of the speakers?

- Are any grammar or usage errors within the dialogue intentional, designed to characterize the speaker?

- Are narrative and descriptive sections free from grammar or usage errors?

If you use the process above and proofread carefully, you should be able to develop a satisfactory dialogue.

Sample Dialogue

The following sample dialogue is appropriate for fiction or for character sketches, autobiographical sketches, narratives, or biographies. [*If you are developing dialogue in script form, see* SCRIPTS *in Part II for more appropriate examples.*]

Watching

Clarence leaned into the oars, looking at but not seeing the pink polish on Irene's bare toes. The wind tore at the boat's direction, aiming it to the east of the inlet.

"Don't you think we'll be gettin' there afore long?" An edge of fear slipped into her words, belying her masked smile.

"Aye, we'll be there soon." A long silence bore down between them, lengthened by the distant rumble, the screech of oarlocks, and the seemingly interminable rhythm of dip-splash, dip-splash, dip-splash. "Yep, we'll be there soon."

She studied his face, his eyes averted, and wondered if he was lying. The western sky roiled. He watched her pink-painted toes grip her sandals. No use looking up. He knew too well the creases between her eyebrows and the worry lines on her forehead, even the weak smile that usually accompanied her worry lines.

"We have some water left," she said, "in the thermos here. Don't you want a drink? You're working so hard." He knew she was trying to be helpful, supportive, in spite of her fears. But he couldn't dare stop rowing, the wind as it was.

"Not just yet. But have some yourself," he added.

She loosened the top, tipped up the thermos, took two swallows and wiped the dribble from her chin. She wasn't thirsty, and the water had no taste. "It's still cold. Sure you don't want some?" He shook his head; she closed the thermos.

The sky, like some smothering blanket, hung above them, threatening. She looked over her shoulder, allowing the bluster to wrap her hair across her face. "We're almost there!"

He heard the relief in her voice. "Yep, we'll make it now." She heard the "now" and knew.

Analysis of the Sample Dialogue

The dialogue above, while it relates only a minor incident, includes examples that illustrate what dialogue can do:

- The actual words in the conversation are minimal.
- The dropped endings and word choices help the reader "hear" the conversation, the voices, the inflections, and the dialect.
- Sentence fragments aid in developing a natural-sounding conversation.
- The facial expressions, the nonverbal mannerisms, and the characters' thoughts tell more than the words. The reader can infer all kinds of details: the couple know each other well; he knows what her face looks like without looking; he sees her toes give away her fears; each recognizes the underlying unspoken messages behind the other's words; she suspects when he's lying; she recognizes the *now* as an affirmation of his effort to comfort her earlier.
- The paragraphing allows the reader to follow the speakers without *he said* or *she said* after every quotation.
- Description and narration, developed in the paragraph structures, show the meanings behind the words—the fears, suggestions, and the mindless comments.
- Good description, that which shows rather than tells [*see* DESCRIPTION *in Part II*], helps the reader see, hear, feel, and taste the details.
- Accurate punctuation and capitalization help the reader follow the dialogue.

Using the process, model and analysis above, develop dialogue that follows these suggestions. You should have a satisfactory product.

DIRECTIONS

You may be asked to write directions that will explain how to do something or how to reach a destination. [*In either case, see* PROCESS ANALYSIS, *later in Part II.*]

EDITORIAL

An editorial expresses an opinion. As part of the editorial page of a newspaper or magazine, the editorial differs significantly from news or feature articles. [*See* FEATURE ARTICLE *and* NEWS ARTICLE *elsewhere in Part II.*] Concise and direct, it takes a position on a controversial issue, offers evidence and reasons to support the position, anticipates counter arguments and frequently calls for specific action. Editorials usually receive a more prominent placement in the newspaper or magazine than do the opinions expressed by the general public in letters to the editor. [*See* LETTERS, KINDS: EDITORIAL *later in Part II.*] In fact, editorials frequently sway voters to decide issues, force public officials to change positions, cause injustices to be righted, and influence labor and management to settle differences. Sometimes, of course, editorials take unpopular positions and raise the ire of readers; but fortunately, the right of freedom of the press permits reader response. [*Because the editorial expresses an opinion, often seeks to persuade, and can include the same content as a letter to the editor, see the following sections of Part II in order to develop your own editorial*: OPINION, PERSUASION, *and* LETTERS, KINDS: EDITORIAL.]

ESSAY

The term *essay* refers to any short piece of writing that analyzes or interprets something in a personal way. Much of a writing that you do to complete class assignments is essay writing. Your instructor may ask that you write an essay describing the effects of radiation on the human body. Your task is to show effects. [*The section called* CAUSE AND EFFECT *in this book will best meet your needs.*]

Since so much of what you write is likely to be in essay form, this book discusses nearly a dozen kinds of essays. See the specific section that most accurately describes the kind of essay you must write. Clue words from the assignment will help you select the most helpful reference section. For instance, if your essay must *show the relationships*, you will classify or possibly compare or contrast. If your essay must *describe*, you will use description. If you must *convince readers to follow a prescribed course of action*, you will use persuasion. If you must *explain why you feel as you do*, you will use opinion. The following types of essays are described in Part II:

Analogy	Literary Analyses
Cause and Effect	Narration
Classification	Opinion
Comparison and Contrast	Persuasion
Definition	Process Analysis
Description	Research Paper
Essay-Question Responses	Review

[*If you need more general help with developing a basic paragraph or theme, see* PARAGRAPHS *and* THEME, *both in Part II, for a thorough explanation of structure and sample papers for comparison.*]

ESSAY-QUESTION RESPONSES

Students must frequently prepare essay responses. Teachers ask students to answer essay-test questions; scholarship and college admission application forms require essay responses; and contests are won or lost on the basis of essays. A science test may require the student to "explain the process of photosynthesis." A scholarship or college admission application form may ask applicants to "explain how a book you have read recently affected your attitude toward man's relationship to the environment." Contest sponsors will award a $1,000 prize to the contestant preparing the best 100-word answer to "What makes you most proud to be an American?"

Being able to write good essay responses, then, can be—quite literally—a valuable asset.

Characteristics

Any essay response includes some basic characteristics. Keep in mind, however, that various kinds of responses (as discussed below) will require different emphases. In general, an essay response

- is directed toward a specific audience,

- maintains a tight focus on the question or topic,

- relies on transitional devices to clarify the focus,

- uses formal but not unnatural structure, vocabulary, and style,

- shows command of the subject matter,

- follows a clear plan of organization,

- includes specific examples to support the topic or thesis statement,

- shows, rather than tells.

We will examine four kinds of essay-question responses. The characteristics above apply to all four, but below you will find additional characteristics peculiar to the specific responses.

COLLEGE-ADMISSIONS APPLICATION ESSAYS

Purpose

While test scores, letters of recommendation, grades, and lists of activities [*see* SHORT ANSWERS, KINDS: LISTS *in Part II*] all influence college-admission personnel, virtually every college or university requires as part of its admission application form at least one essay. Some require several. In every case, the admission personnel look for two qualities: content and evidence of writing ability.

They want to see how you handle challenging topics, how—or if—you can think, and how well you can use the language.

Note two implications of what you've just read:

1. You should remember the audience. You are writing for the admission people. They read thousands of essays, many dull and poorly written. Make yours lively, personal, and polished, and you will have attracted their attention.

2. You should write honestly. The student who writes to sound impressive, using five-syllable words and circuitous sentences, attracts attention, but it's the wrong kind. Do not write *It is uppermost in my mind to walk the hallowed halls of Some University and share great thoughts with the world's greatest minds.* Instead, say what you really mean: *I have been interested in Some University since the day I read about Dr. Important and learned that he and his student-research teams have contributed to the world's understanding of black holes.*

In short, the college admission essay response should

- keep in mind its readers, and
- talk to them honestly and specifically.

Types of College Admission Application Essays

The types of college admission application essays vary, but most will fall into these general categories:

- essays about yourself, your interests, or your activities
- essays explaining why you want to attend that college or university
- essays responding to a thought-provoking statement, a book, or a contemporary problem

The first kind of essay response seeks a better understanding of you as an individual. The topics may have wording similar to the following:

- What are your career preferences?
- Tell us anything about yourself, your activities, your interests, or your goals that will help us know you as a person.

- If you were to describe yourself in terms of a fictional character, who would it be? Explain your answer.

Sometimes the topic is broad enough to allow the student to choose his own avenue of response:

> In reading and evaluating your application, we hope to gain as complete a picture of you as possible, but our knowledge of you is necessarily limited to the information provided us. Why not, then, use this opportunity to tell us about anything you think we should know....
> (*Brown University*)

Whether the required response permits broad interpretation (as in the topic immediately above) or merits a more specific approach (as in choosing a fictional character to explain yourself), the essay demands specific details. Only through showing, not telling, can the admission people learn about you. Obviously the toughest part is deciding which details to include. The approach is much like that for the autobiographical sketch [*see* AUTOBIOGRAPHY *in Part II*]. Use the same process and the same means of limiting your subject. For instance, since you should write about some aspect of your life that shows readers who you are, you may choose to focus on how your work backstage gave you an appreciation for the importance of behind-the-scenes work in any job. Perhaps as a result of four years of baby-sitting with the same three children, you have learned how familiarity affects discipline. Or perhaps your ex-

periences when your best friend moved away helped you realize that real friendships must be cultivated; they don't just happen.

No matter your subject, your responsibility is to show who you are and give insight to your personality, interests, or aspirations. Choose details that will permit you to do so. [*Again, see* AUTOBIOGRAPHY *in Part II for process and an example.*] Above all, remember that readers are looking for evidence of your ability to think and write.

The second kind of essay response is the college admission application essay which requires you to explain why you want to attend that particular university. Beyond seeking evidence of your ability to write and show an effective command of the language, this essay probes your understanding of the school to which you are applying. The questions are usually direct:

- Why do you think our school is appropriate for you?

- How did you become interested in our school?

- Why do you think our school can best meet your career preferences?

- Why do you believe our school can best fulfill your academic interests?

Obviously, your answers must be specific and reflect an accurate understanding of what the school is all about. For instance, does the school offer a degree in your area of interest? Are there reasons beyond academics that attract you to the school?

What does this school offer that other schools do not?

In order to respond effectively to these kinds of essay questions, you should

- Study the catalogs, brochures, courses of studies, any other printed information available regarding the school, its curriculum, and its activities.

- Talk to students currently enrolled and ask about the courses, instructors, and school in general. Ask about extracurricular activities, campus life, and areas of special interest to you. Recent alumni may also provide good insight.

- Visit the campus, if possible, before you develop your essay or report for an interview. References to your visit will help you include specific details.

With your homework behind you, you can get on with the essay. Avoid the general kinds of responses: *Blank University will provide the best education for me because it has fine courses in the area in which I hope to major.* Instead, aim for details, for showing, not telling: *Blank University attracted my attention as soon as I saw the cyclotron and talked with two of the professors doing independent research with it.* [*See also* SHORT ANSWERS: BRIEF RESPONSES *in Part II for a sample short answer to a similar question.*]

The third kind of essay response is the college admission application essay which looks for personal reaction to thought-provoking topics and probably allows you to tell more about yourself—albeit indirectly—

than the topics which ask for specific responses. The questions may read something like these:

> Compose a letter to your U.S. Congressional Representative in which you express your opinion on a public policy issue of current importance. In your letter you should include a brief factual description of the issue, your views on the issue, and the reasons why you believe as you do. Remember that the influence your letter will carry depends on the clarity of your views and the soundness of your argument. (*Earlham College*)

> What book or author has particularly impressed you? Please explain the significance of your choice. We encourage you to incorporate plot elements only as necessary to support your thesis. (*DePauw University*)

> Imagine the year is 1881. You may expect to live for another thirty-five years. What person would you most want to know well during that time? For what reasons? (*Swarthmore College*)

Topics like these require essay responses similar to those already developed. The first, for instance, asking for a persuasive letter, will follow the process and models in the PERSUASION section later in Part II. The second is a type of literary analysis and will follow the format and process set out in the LITERARY ANALYSES section, also in Part II. The third, a what-if fictional situation, should focus on "reasons," and so the essay may be an opinion or cause and effect. See OPINION and CAUSE AND EFFECT in Part II.

No matter the topic or your approach to it, keep in mind that the purpose of any written response on an application form is twofold:

- to help the admission people get to know you as a person,

- to help them better understand your academic abilities, especially your writing ability.

Process

No matter which kind of essay you write, you will follow the same general process of prewriting, writing, revising, and proofreading. The guidelines below should be helpful.

PREWRITING

STEP 1. THINKING ABOUT THE TOPIC

As you narrow your focus, make lists and ask yourself questions. The following questions will help you think of suitable topics and suggest other appropriate questions:

- What activities have I participated in during the last four years? Which have brought me the greatest satisfaction? Why? Have I grown as a result of those activities? How?

- In what community projects have I participated? How have they affected me or my interest in civic pride and responsibility? Did I learn to understand or appreciate government or social conditions? Did I have my eyes opened to some alarming or exciting facility or situation?

- Which academic classes maintained my interest? Why? How has that affected my aspirations? What additional research have I done beyond the confines of the classroom to further my interest or explore the possibilities of the class subject?

- What goal was the most difficult for me to attain? How did I overcome that difficulty? Did I gain some insight about myself or my surroundings as a result?

- Who has most influenced my life? A real person or a fictional one? How has he or she influenced me and how have I changed as a result? Is the change good?

- Where have I traveled? What did I see or do there that most impressed me? Why was I impressed? Did the experience affect my attitude toward someone or something?

- What happens at home that most affects me? How? Does that help me grow, help me become more self-disciplined?

- What have I read that has affected the way I think or what I do? What effect has it had? What part of the reading caused me to react as I did?

Once you have these lists and responses in front of you, you will be well on your way toward developing a specific focus for your essay.

STEP 2.   DEVELOPING A FOCUS

After you have considered options like those above—as well as any others you may think of—talk with friends, teachers, counselors, or alumni about possible responses. Sometimes their reactions to possible topics will help you gain objectivity in your planned response.

With their suggestions in mind, select the specific approach you will use. Write *in a single sentence* what your essay response will accomplish. Consider these examples:

Do not say:
My response will explain why I want to attend Blank University.
Write instead:
Blank University includes three world-renowned musicians among its faculty, and they can help me pursue my goal as a master of wind instruments.

Do not say:
I read a book recently that has influenced my ideas about mid-life career changes.
Write instead:
The biography of John James Audubon helped me understand that mid-life career changes, while sometimes financially painful, often bring deep personal satisfaction.

The sentence you have written will serve as a topic sentence for your essay response.

STEP 3.   CHOOSING DETAILS

With your topic sentence in front of you, list the specific details which will help you explain your idea. Remember that details will help your essay stand out among the thousands that the admission people read.

WRITING

STEP 4.   GETTING THE IDEAS ON PAPER

As you write the first draft, forget about spelling and mechanics. Get the ideas down in support of the topic sentence. Do not be afraid to include ideas that seem not to fit. Maybe they belong somewhere else in the essay, or maybe they do not belong in it at all; but you can always take them out or move them during the revision process. For now, get them on paper so you do not lose them.

REVISING

STEP 5.   ADDING AND DELETING IDEAS

Once you have your ideas down, get away from the job for at least a day. Then reread the topic and your response to it. Ask yourself these questions:

- Do I respond specifically to the topic?

- Do my details support specific parts of the topic? [*See* REVISING: SAMPLE REVISION FOR SPECIFIC DETAIL *in Part I.*]

- Have I maintained unity? [*See* REVISING: SAMPLE REVISION FOR UNITY *in Part I.*]

- Is there an obvious order to my essay, or do I wander aimlessly as thoughts occur? [*See* ORDER, IN PARAGRAPH DEVELOPMENT *in the Glossary.*]

- Is the essay consistently lively, clear, and descriptive?

- Have I avoided the deadly trap of trying to sound sophisticated by using five-syllable words and circuitous sentences? [*See* REVISING: SAMPLE REVISION FOR WORDINESS *in Part I.*]

- Does the essay reflect my personality and my interests? Is it personal?

- Does it show thought? Have I avoided vague and empty sentences?

As you answer these questions, you will have a basis on which to make revisions. When you have completed a second draft, ask the same questions to determine the success of your revision. If you can, ask a peer to read your essay and respond to the same questions.

STEP 6. POLISHING THE WRITING

When you have revised so that the content clearly reflects your best ideas, you are ready to polish the essay. [*See* REVISING *in Part I for questions to guide your general revision.*] Use the questions below to guide revisions particularly important to the college admission application essay:

- Do I use transitions effectively to show relationships between and among ideas? [*See* REVISING: SAMPLE REVISION FOR TRANSITION *in Part I.*]

- Have I varied both the length and structure of my sentences? Do I show sophisticated writing techniques? [*See* REVISING: SAMPLE REVISION FOR SENTENCE VARIETY *in Part I.*]

- Does my sentence structure show effective emphasis? [*See* REVISING: SAMPLE REVISION FOR EMPHASIS *in Part I.*]

- Is my vocabulary appropriate for the subject and the audience?

- Have I chosen the most powerful or most effective words? [*See* CONCRETE, SPECIFIC DETAIL, CONNOTATION *and* DENOTATION *in the Glossary.*]

PROOFREADING

STEP 7. CHECKING THE DETAILS

The necessity of proofreading should be obvious. Your accuracy with spelling, mechanics, grammar, and usage will certainly reflect your command of the language. Consult your dictionary and thesaurus as well. Unless instructed otherwise, your final copy, submitted with your application, should be typed. If you use a word processor, use a printer with letter-quality type.

——— Sample College-Admission Application Essay ———

The essay below is a response to the following college admission application topic: *Discuss some issue of local or national concern and its importance to you.*

Last year our community destroyed part of its own heritage when the wrecking ball brought down the ornate Gothic structure that was once the railroad station. Such was the media's wording: the wrecking ball brought it down. In fact, we, the citizens of this community, brought it down. Mincing words to avoid blame falls short of accepting reality. Although city officials purportedly made an attempt to locate potential developers, many of us questioned their seriousness. Deadlines, extended twice, came and went with "not even a nibble" of interest. So now the old railroad station is gone. Its demolition testifies that historic preservation, only a fancy word for some local individuals with stately old homes, lacks meaning for the general citizenry. How sad. For instance, many contemporaries living in the fast lane lack the roots that give stability and sense of direction from the perspective of where they have been. In contrast, the picture in our family album shows Mother, aged twelve, standing in the crowd waiting at the railroad station for debarking passengers, steam puffing from beneath passenger-train cars. Grandma and Grandpa stand together, their suitcases piled against a post, waiting for Uncle Frederick's approaching surrey. That is "heritage." That is where I came from, my family, a picture that tells me more than names and places. Their life style spills out for me. But the station is gone. My children will never see what they should not have been denied. They will not walk through waiting rooms or hallways where their great-grandparents walked; they will not share the heritage. The sabotage hangs as a sin on this community's shoulders.

Analysis of the Sample

The essay response above achieves what we have discussed in the explanation and process analysis above. Note these specifics:

- The response to the topic takes a local approach and adds personal interest. The destruction of a railroad station has obviously affected the writer; so as a result, the essay gives her an opportunity to respond specifically to an issue that matters.

- Specific details abound. We see the structure of the station (*Gothic*), learn about the family (through the details in the photograph), and recognize the writer's reaction (*should not be denied, sin on community's shoulders*).

- The response allows a glimpse of the writer's personality. (Do you not have an idea now what the writer's interests are?)

- The writer uses a good variety of sentence structures and an effective vocabulary to demonstrate command of the language.

College-admission people who read these kinds of essays take note of the writers!

CONTEST ESSAYS

Purpose

Contests have sponsors. Sponsors have inherent interests. To win a contest, you must, within the framework of the contest rules, say what the sponsors want to hear, something in line with their interests. Such contest sponsors look for people with philosophies similar to their own.

Usually the topic blatantly suggests the sponsor's purpose or interest:

- In an essay of no more than one typewritten page, explain why you are proud to be an American. (*contest sponsored by the Veterans of Foreign Wars*)

- Define good citizenship in 100 words or less. (*contest sponsored by the Daughters of the American Revolution*)

- Develop an essay which explains how our community can best attract visitors. (*contest sponsored by the Chamber of Commerce*)

- In 100 words or less, share with our readers your most memorable holiday experience. (*contest sponsored by the local newspaper*)

If you plan to develop a contest essay, keep in mind the following suggestions:

- Stick to the topic.

- Be precise and concise.

- Cling to specifics, especially the dramatic or touching.

- Be certain to follow all rules exactly. If a word count is included, abide by it. You will be disqualified if you neglect the rules. (When counting words, you need not count the articles *a, an,* and *the.* Some contests, however, expect you to count every five spaces as a word.)

- Look for a unique approach. Something different will attract the attention of judges exhausted from reading hundreds of ho-hum entries.

Process

As you plan a contest-essay response, use whatever process is appropriate for the kind of essay required. For instance, if you must define good citizenship, see DEFINITION in Part II of this handbook for a detailed step-by-step process and for models and accompanying anaylses. If you must develop an essay expressing an opinion, follow the process spelled out and illustrated in the section in Part II labeled OPINION. You may also use DESCRIPTION, PERSUASION, CLASSIFICATION, or ANALOGY, all in Part II. To the processes outlined in these respective chapters, add the suggestions above for contest essays. The result should yield an effective—perhaps winning—essay response!

————— Sample Contest Essay —————

A local newspaper contest asked readers to explain in 100 words or less a memorable family experience. Since the contest announcement appeared in early summer, the topic implied family vacation or at least family summer activities. One reader prepared the following essay:

Family Reunion

Memorable family reunions signify family-favorite dishes at the carry-in dinner. Uncle Ned roasts a whole pig in his homemade cooker, and Grandma brings hot German potato salad, a recipe in which the first ingredient is twenty pounds of potatoes. Aunt Millie's corn salad earns the only rave reviews among the dozens of relishes and vegetable salads. Everyone, though, saves room for a wedge of Aunt Georgia's black-walnut angel-food cake, her own closely guarded recipe. That and a dollop of Uncle Pat's hand-churned ice cream add the final touches to a feast. I can taste it all now, even though it's been six years since both Grandma and Uncle Ned died.

Analysis of the Sample

The less than 100-word essay above seems appropriate for the contest on these points:

- It focuses on the contest topic but includes a bit of drama to heighten reader attention.
- By using present tense throughout, the writer maintains a feeling of "now" even though we learn in the final sentence that the memories are six years old.
- Details offer good images [*see* DESCRIPTION *elsewhere in Part II*].
- The essay follows the few rules required for the contest. (For the word count, hyphenated words and proper names were counted as single words and articles were not counted.)

SCHOLARSHIP APPLICATION ESSAYS

Purpose

While much of a scholarship application is devoted to grades, test scores, and letters of recommendation, and while part of the application requires mere lists or brief statements [*see* SHORT ANSWERS *elsewhere in Part II*], another part of many scholarship applications requires you to develop an essay response to some general topic. Topics range from the very broad (Why is a good education important?) to the highly personal (What peculiar family problems suggest need for financial assistance?).

Scholarship applications, like college admission applications, establish your identity, setting you apart from the hundreds or thousands of other applicants. As a result, your essay response should accomplish two purposes:

• Allow your reader to know you personally, to see you as an individual among the hundreds or thousands of other applicants.

• Prove that you are mentally alert, fluent, and personable.

Both goals can be met by a well-written, carefully developed essay response.

Process

In the case of a specific, personal question, your job is clearly defined. Answer to the point, with specific details, statistics, examples. Be straightforward, honest, candid. And be concise but complete. Follow the same process as for any paragraph or theme. [*Refer to appropriate sections in Part II of this handbook:* DESCRIPTION, DEFINITION, CAUSE AND EFFECT, PROCESS ANALYSIS, *etc.*]

In the case of a broad topic use the same process as outlined for College Admission Applications Essay responses above. Follow the same warnings, avoiding chronological listings or dryly recounting facts in dull thoughtless prose. Use specifics; be personable; keep it lively.

Sample Scholarship Application Essay and Analysis

Since the scholarship essay is very much like that of the College Admission Application essay, see the sample and analysis in that section above. [*For additional information about scholarship application answers, see* SHORT ANSWERS *later in Part II of this handbook.*]

TEST ESSAYS

Purpose

Requiring students to respond with essays allows an instructor to find out how well they really understand a subject. Students can write easily about what they understand. In test situations, however, you must plan carefully what you will say. Time limits demand that you structure your response to present your understanding in the best possible manner.

Types

Certain clue words identify the kind of response your teacher is seeking. The following list indicates appropriate responses.

ANALYZE   Show parts in relation to a whole. [*See* CAUSE AND EFFECT, PROCESS ANALYSIS, COMPARISON AND CONTRAST, DESCRIPTION, *and* LITERARY ANALYSES *elsewhere in Part II.*]

Example: Analyze the relationship between state and local governments.

Other clue words: show the process, explain the means by which, describe the effects, clarify the causes, criticize

COMPARE   Show the similarities of two or more things. [*See* COMPARISON AND CONTRAST *in Part II.*]

Example: Compare two of Shakespear's sonnets in terms of their references to the Dark Lady.

Other clue words: similarities, resemblances, liknesses, comparison, alike

CONTRAST   Show the differences between two or more things. [*See* COMPARISON AND CONTRAST *in Part II.*]

Example: Contrast direct current with alternating current.

Other clue words: differences, contrasting, differ, different

CRITICIZE   Discuss the strengths or merits of a given topic. [*See* LITERARY ANALYSES *in Part II.*]

Example: Write a critical analysis of the structure of the following sonnet.

Other clue words: point out the strengths and weaknesses, critical analysis, evaluate, analyze

DEFINE   Clarify the meaning of a given topic. [*See* DEFINITION *in Part II.*]

Example: Define metamorphosis as it applies to the German cockroach.

Other clue words: definition, explain the meaning, clarify

DESCRIBE Give details. [*See* DESCRIPTION *and* PROCESS ANALYSIS *in Part II.*]

Example: Describe the process of developing black-and-white film.

Other clue words: explain, show, description

DISCUSS Elaborate upon the specific details involved in a general idea. [*See* DESCRIPTION, PROCESS ANALYSIS, OPINION, COMPARISON AND CONTRAST, *and* CAUSE AND EFFECT *in Part II.*]

Example: Discuss the impact of tax reform on limited partnerships.

Other clue words: explain, discussion, talk about

DEMON-STRATE Show an aspect of something by giving details. [*See* PROCESS ANALYSIS *or* DESCRIPTION *in Part II.*]

Example: Demonstrate the importance of safety devices in a metal-working shop.

Other clue words: show, illustrate, explain, describe

EXPLAIN Give reasons for a thing being as it is. [*See* DESCRIPTION, PERSUASION, *and* OPINION *in Part II.*]

Example: Explain how a bill becomes law.

Other clue words: show, why, what, how

ILLUSTRATE Explain a main idea through use of specific examples. [*See* COMPARISON AND CONTRAST, DESCRIPTION, PROCESS ANALYSIS, OPINION, CAUSE AND EFFECT, *and* LITERARY ANALYSES *in Part II.*]

Example: Define *deus ex machina* and illustrate from at least six plays.

Other clue words: show, give illustrations, give examples, how

INTERPRET Indicate the meaning or significance of a given topic. [*See* LITERARY ANALYSES, DESCRIPTION, CAUSE AND EFFECT, COMPARISON AND CONTRAST, *and* PROCESS ANALYSIS *in Part II.*]

Example: Interpret Hamlet's soliloquy, "To Be or Not to Be."

Other clue words: analyze, interpretation, significance, meaning of, show influence of, analyze

PREDICT Indicate a logical outcome of an action or condition. [*See* CAUSE AND EFFECT *and* OPINION *in Part II.*]

Example: Predict the results of pH variables on soil in terms of vegetation growth potential.

Other clue words:	anticipate, prediction, if . . . then, what . . . if
SUMMA-RIZE	State concisely the main points of a topic. [*See* PRECIS, PARAPHRASE, *and* SYNOPSIS *in Part II.*]
Example:	Summarize the issues involved in the Populist Movement.
Other clue words:	state briefly, brief review, give the main points, discuss the main ideas
TRACE	Follow a series of events in chronological order. [*See* CAUSE AND EFFECT, DESCRIPTION, NARRATION, PROCESS ANALYSIS, *and* LITERARY ANALYSES *in Part II.*]
Example:	Trace the development of adding machines.
Other clue words:	follow, follow the development, outline

The essay-question clues above will help you know what your instructor expects in your answer. Use the clue words to shape your essay's content.

Process

Answering questions on an essay test requires more, however, than knowing what the teacher or instructor expects in your answer. Planning takes the driver's seat. Here's how:

PREWRITING

STEP 1. PLANNING YOUR TIME

When you get your test copy, first look through the test. Look for answers to these questions:

- What kinds of questions are there?
- How many questions are there?
- Do the directions say that I must answer all questions, or do I answer only some of them?
- How much time do I have for the entire test?

When you have answers to these questions, plan a schedule for yourself. If the test includes one section of twenty-five multiple-choice questions and another of two essay questions, you must allot sufficient time for each of the essay questions. Perhaps you have an hour in which to take the test. You may plan a schedule like this:

20 minutes	25 multiple-choice questions
40 minutes	2 essay questions

This allows slightly less than one minute per multiple-choice question and twenty minutes apiece for the essay questions.

Next, plan how to spend the twenty minutes allotted to each essay question. For example:

4 minutes	**planning**
13 minutes	**writing**
3 minutes	**checking, revising**
20 minutes	

STEP 2.   PLANNING THE CONTENT

During the four-minute planning period, follow these steps:

- Read the question carefully and look for the clue words that indicate what your teacher or instructor wants.

- Make a list or scratch outline of the main ideas. [See OUTLINES *elsewhere in Part II.*]

- Organize the list by numbering the items in the order in which you will include them in your essay response.

- Reread the question for accuracy and decide if you have included in your list everything required by the question.

- Anticipate the time you can spend on each item. If, for instance, you have four main items and thirteen minutes, you can spend three minutes on each item. Obviously, you must plan to be concise.

STEP 3.   ORGANIZING THE RESPONSE

You have already organized the main ideas in Step 2 above. Now you must organize each response. In general, follow this plan:

- Give an introductory statement, usually beginning with the same words as or words similar to those in the question.

- State your topic sentence if the answer requires only a single para-

graph. [See TOPIC SENTENCE *in the Glossary for quick reference, and see* PARAGRAPHS *in Part II for detailed explanation and examples.*]

- State your thesis statement if the answer requires a several-point response. [See THESIS SENTENCE *in the Glossary for quick reference, and see* THEME *in Part II for detailed explanation and examples.*]

- Present the main ideas and the specific support.

- Conclude the response, restating the general topic.

WRITING

STEP 4.   KEEPING TO THE POINT

As you write, follow your plan carefully. Remember, you have no time to be distracted or go off on tangents. Try to remember these guidelines:

- Keep to the point. Avoid padding with unrelated details or allowing stray ideas to get in your way.

- Follow the outline you planned in Steps 2 and 3.

- Be specific. Use dates, names, places, formulas, details—whatever concrete evidence best supports the topic.

- Watch the time so you do not overextend in one area and slight another. You'll lose valuable points for incomplete answers.

REVISING AND PROOFREADING

STEP 5. CHECKING YOUR RESPONSE

Because you have only three minutes planned for checking your response, you will do any quick revising and proofreading as a single step. Check for spelling; accurate names, dates, and details; omissions; repetitions; and grammar, usage, or mechanical errors. Your instructor understands that you do not have time to recopy, so make your corrections as neatly as possible.

——— Sample Test Essays and Analyses ———

Sample papers appear alphabetically by type of essay throughout Part II. To help you find the most appropriate example, refer to the section above titled, TYPES OF ESSAY QUESTIONS. References listed parenthetically refer to sections in Part II where sample essays and their respective analyses are included. Thus, if an essay-test requires a definition, you will find model essays in the section labeled DEFINITION.

FEATURE ARTICLE

The feature article gives information of human interest. The label *feature* covers a broad range of newspaper or magazine articles which include everything except straight news, editorials, or advertising. [*For comparison, see* NEWS ARTICLE, EDITORIAL, *and* ADVERTISING *elsewhere in Part II.*] Generally feature articles attempt to involve the reader emotionally.

Because of its human-interest approach, the feature article allows the writer considerable opportunity for creativity. While the subject of a feature may be related to a news item, the article will not follow the pyramid structure of a straight news piece. Rather, it is more likely to include conventions of fiction: plot, character, dialogue, and symbolism. [*See separate entries in the Glossary.*] A feature is a creative article that deals with real events, issues, and trends; but unlike straight news articles, it places emphasis on the people involved rather than on the facts of news.

Characteristics

A feature article generally

- evokes an emotional reaction: joy, sympathy, anger, frustration, contentment, or some other emotion,
- gives depth and meaning to complicated issues or news items, thus clarifying and interpreting events,
- follows the techniques of good creative writing [*see* SHORT STORY *elsewhere in Part II*],
- avoids the pyramid structure of a straight news story,
- follows an organization appropriate for the subject [*see* ORDER *in the Glossary*],
- uses an introduction (*lead*) that attracts readers,
- uses a tone and style appropriate to its subject,
- achieves success by being researched and brightly written.

Process

Use the following steps to develop a feature story.

PREWRITING

STEP 1.   FINDING THE STORY

If you are not assigned a subject, your search begins with finding the right topic. Your topic should be related to breaking news or current issues or trends. Seeing a good topic for a feature article in the midst of the so-called "hard" news depends on your curiosity. In short, your creativity determines how you will deal with a subject.

For instance, if the breaking news deals with tornado damage to the school, your feature story may result from an interview with the teacher who first spotted the twister approaching the building and sounded the alarm which prevented serious injury to people in the building. Or your feature story may result from a personal tour of the building, noting damage to the classrooms, reporting pencils jammed into concrete-block walls, and observing pine needles pinning pages to bulletin boards. Remember, feature articles usually evoke some kind of emotion. Finding the human interest aspect of hard news leads you to feature articles.

STEP 2. GATHERING THE INFORMATION

Whether the information comes from your own account, interviews with eyewitnesses, or printed sources, you must gather as much information as possible. Even though a feature article is not a straight news story, its facts must be accurate and its message valid.

STEP 3. DETERMINING THE TYPE OF FEATURE

Your purpose determines the type of feature you will write. Features are limited only by the writer/reporter's imagination; however, a few basic types are suggested by the general purpose.

The Human-Interest Feature

The most common of the feature articles, the human-interest feature does what it says: describes some unusual aspect of the life of an ordinary human being, an aspect which makes him or her interesting. Sometimes the story reports success in spite of great odds. Sometimes it recalls a tragic predicament. Sometimes it shares a continuing struggle supported only by hope and faith.

The Personality Feature

Often a human-interest feature takes on greater depth and turns into a personality feature. In many respects, the personality feature resembles a characterization. [*See* CHARACTERIZATION *earlier in Part II.*] The main character may be known or unknown but will have done something of interest to others. Maybe the person developed a product that has become an international retail item; learned to overcome shyness and became a political candidate; travels to school each day on roller skates. Usually the personality feature shows how a person gained recognition.

The How-To Feature

The how-to feature is not much more than a process analysis article [*see* PROCESS ANALYSIS *elsewhere in Part II*], but it usually takes a do-it-yourself approach.

The Past-Events Feature

Sometimes features focus on historical events or celebrations. Stemming usually from library research, such features provide human-interest history lessons. The story of a Japanese-American citizen's imprisonment in the United States during World War II helps readers see the complexity of human emotion during war. Published on December 7, the anniversery of Pearl Harbor, the story takes on added emotional impact.

The News Feature

A human-interest focus on breaking news results in a news feature, an article which adds personal involvement to what may otherwise be a distant, seemingly unimportant current event. An interview with the parents of a soldier wounded in an overseas battle brings personal emotion into the report of an event in which readers may have no other involvement.

Determine the kind of feature you plan to write.

STEP 4.   CHOOSING THE SINGLE FOCUS

When you have determined your purpose (and, thus, the kind of feature you plan to write), force yourself to write a single sentence that explains the specific focus the article will take. Although this sentence probably will not appear in the article, it will help you frame your thoughts. The sentence may look something like this:

Tara's mouse-like dolls began as whimsical gifts from her sewing room but have become

a million-dollar-a-year international business.

(The feature article, a human-interest piece, will explain how Tara achieved success.)

WRITING

STEP 5.   DETERMINING THE ORGANIZATION

Decide how you can best present the information in your feature. Will an order of importance be best? [*See* ORDERS OF IMPORTANCE *in the Glossary.*] Will a flashback [*see Glossary*] work better? Will chronological order be better? [*See* CHRONOLOGICAL ORDER *in the Glossary.*]

Choose the approach most effective for your purpose.

STEP 6.   DRAFTING THE LEAD

The lead, or introduction, must catch the reader's attention and make him or her want to read more. Use any attention-getting device [*see* ATTENTION-GETTER *in the Glossary*] suitable to your topic. Make sure, too, that the lead sets the tone for the article. [*See* TONE *in the Glossary.*]

STEP 7.   DRAFTING THE BODY

Following the organizational pattern you selected in Step 5 above, develop the body of the feature article. Keep in mind the creative nature of the feature, and realize that your best tool for writing is an inquisitive mind. Use techniques appropriate to short-story writing [*see* SHORT STORY *later in Part II*] and strive to achieve an easy style.

STEP 8. DRAFTING THE CONCLUSION

The conclusion of a feature article is much like the conclusion of a short story: it gives an air of finality and ties together any loose ends. It may also refer back to the lead. It usually does not, however, end with a summary or conclusion in the manner of a traditional expository composition.

STEP 9. PREPARING THE HEADLINE

Sometimes feature writers have the opportunity to develop their own headlines; in other cases someone else assumes this responsibility. If you develop your own, or if someone else accepts your suggestions, you should add a headline which attracts reader attention and pinpoints the focus of your article.

REVISING

STEP 10. CHECKING FOR GOOD WRITING TECHNIQUES

Since the feature article is more nearly creative writing than anything else, revise the piece according to these suggestions:

- Does the article reflect careful, complete research?

- Do I attract my reader's attention in the opening paragraph?

- Does the article maintain interest throughout?

- Did I follow a logical organization to achieve my purpose?

- Have I maintained unity? [*See* REVISING: SAMPLE REVISION FOR UNITY *in Part I.*]

- Have I varied sentence structure in keeping with the tone and purpose? [*See* REVISING: SAMPLE REVISION FOR SENTENCE VARIETY *in Part I.*]

- Are transitions sufficient to guarantee smooth reading? [*See* REVISING: SAMPLE REVISION FOR TRANSITION *in Part I.*]

- Does the word choice show freshness and originality?

- Have I eliminated wordiness? [*See* REVISING: SAMPLE REVISION FOR WORDINESS *in Part I.*]

- Do I use good story-writing techniques? [*See* SHORT STORY *in Part II.*]

PROOFREADING

STEP 11. CHECKING THE DETAILS

In the journalistic trade, writers refer to *copyreading* rather than *proofreading*. Copyreading occurs in the newspaper business when the writer completes his final copy. He reads to correct his own errors. On the other hand, proofreading takes place after the printed proof is ready. Then the writer reads for others' errors.

Whatever you call it—copyreading or proofreading—be sure to check your final copy carefully for grammar, mechanics, and usage errors. If the publication for which you are writing has its own style manual, check it for stylistic details. Eliminate spelling errors by referring to *Webster's New World Dictionary*.

After you have studied the characteristics and process for development of a feature article, study the sample feature article below to see how one student completed a feature article.

The analysis which follows examines the merits of the story. Together, they should help you develop your own effective feature article.

──────── Sample Feature Article ────────

Compare this feature news article with the sample in NEWS ARTICLE later in Part II to note the differences between a news article and a feature article.

Community Grows as Karson Grows

Together, the employer and the employees pay over a million dollars in state and local taxes each year. Together, they provide materials for about one-fourth of the automobiles produced in the United States. Together, they have showered stockholders with over a half-million dollars in dividends in the past five years. Together, they make up Karson Manufacturing, the area's largest employer.

Karson Manufacturing began as a garage operation when in 1932 the late Rodney Karson started machining parts for local businesses. As business expanded, he moved to the current location on Oak Road. But the site was hardly the same then as today. Photographs in the 1942 edition of the Daily News show the company as little more than a series of one-story brick buildings, obviously added as needed. Not until 1962 did the present facility begin to take shape. Additions in 1969 and 1978 resulted in the current facility.

George Hatman, Vice-President of Manufacturing, began with the company in 1938. "I still remember my interview with Mr. Rodney Karson. He wore a blue work shirt, sleeves rolled up, with black suspenders holding up his work pants. He looked like all the rest of the workers except for his hat. He wore this funny felt bowler with a red hat band. Usually he kept a pencil stuck in the hat band. Don't know why. Never saw him use it. But that's the way he showed up for the interview. Funny, but I'd worn my best suit. Thought I should try to impress him.

"We didn't talk long. Asked me a few questions about experience. I didn't have any but I was willing to work. So you know what he said? He said, 'Well, get yourself home, son, and put on some work clothes. Come back this afternoon and we'll see what you're made of.' That's what I did. And I'm still here."

Hatman believes that Karson's philosophy made the company what it is today. "He figured if you wanted to work, you were a good man to have on the team. And that's what we have here—a team. We all pull together, work together, make decisions together, show success together. It's a heck of a team to be on!"

And together, the Karson team today announced a six-million-dollar expansion. As a result, the local community as well as Karson will grow. Together.

Analysis of the Sample

As a feature article, the sample above includes the characteristics which make it a satisfactory representation. Note the following specific details:

- The sample generally falls into the "past-events" category, but it also includes a bit of a personality profile. Such an article would probably run the same day as the news story [*see sample in* NEWS ARTICLE] announcing the Karson expansion.
- The organization is roughly chronological, beginning with the present and then going back to the company's origins and moving forward.
- The introduction (or *lead*) catches the reader's attention, sets the tone for the article, and introduces the theme, *togetherness*.
- Paragraph structure follows short-story writing techniques.
- Dialogue creates most of the emotional impact of the piece. By using the speaker's words and sentence structure, the writer permits him to share personal experiences which shed light on the elder Karson's personality.
- The article maintains a single focus, showing how togetherness has helped the company grow.
- The conclusion makes a final statement without summarizing or restating.

Journal

A journal, sometimes called a learning log, records—or logs—what you have learned. Usually kept on a daily basis in a spiral notebook as informal personal writing, the journal may be a voluntary learning tool or a required part of a course in any curricular area. Generally a writer's journal holds responses to assignments, class discussion, or outside reading.

Characteristics

The characteristics of a journal vary from class to class, teacher to teacher, and student to student. Usually, however, journal entries

- are made on a regular basis, often daily, and are dated for identification,
- respond to a prompt, usually given by the teacher or found within the assigned reading,
- record what you have learned, or struggled to learn, in a given class,
- include summaries, responses, reactions, definitions, questions, or unsolved problems you have about assignments, discussions, or outside reading in any curricular area,
- may include entries that are sentences, lists, paragraphs, diagrams, illustrations, or charts,
- are considered informal writing, usually not evaluated as a piece of writing, and thus,
- generally ignore the formal processes of prewriting, writing, revising, and proofreading (when,

in fact, the journal may serve as a prewriting activity for certain future writing assignments—*see* PREWRITING *in Part I*).

Process

Because journals or learning logs are usually written as informal responses to learning situations, they lack the formal process of other written products. Instead, you will most likely be asked to respond to a prompt like one of the following:

In English class:
In what ways are Sylvia and the heron alike in the short story "The White Heron"? [*See* LITERARY ANALYSIS, *the "Sample Literary Analysis of a Short Story" for a sample response.*]

In social sciences class:

Colonial brides kept what they called a "hope chest." Based on your reading, what items do you think might be included? [*See* DESCRIPTION, *the "Sample for Social Sciences" for a sample response.*]

In science class:
If a farmer wants to quit using pesticides, what can he do to improve insect control? [*see the sample in* NOTES, FOR A CLASS.]

In math class:
What is the difference between an arithmetic sequence and a geometric sequence? [*See* COMPARISON AND CONTRAST, *the "Sample for Mathematics" for a sample response.*]

In business class:
Imagine that you own a photography studio. What kinds of advertising do you think you should use? [*See* PROCESS ANALYSIS, *the "Sample for Business" for a sample response.*]

In vocational education class:
Explain in one sentence the purpose of a bulkhead. [*See* SHORT ANSWERS, *the "Samples of Short Answer Definitions" for a sample response.*]

As the examples above illustrate, a journal entry may be a single sentence, a list, a paragraph, or several paragraphs. Unlike the samples above, however, the journal entry frequently is not polished writing. It often serves, on the other hand, to organize thoughts or to find (or form) ideas for later finished products.

LAB REPORT

A laboratory report, commonly called a *lab* report, details the procedures and findings of primary research in a laboratory situation. [*See* PRIMARY RESEARCH *in the Glossary.*] As such, it is a unique kind of technical report. [*See* TECHNICAL REPORT *elsewhere in Part II for comparison.*] While most lab work concerns some aspect of the science world, it is quite probable you may be asked to develop a lab report in a business or vocational class as well. In any case, the report requires attention to minute details of equipment, procedure, and analysis, all examined carefully by logical, critical detachment. Follow the procedures and general format suggested below.

Characteristics

A lab report generally

- summarizes the proceedings of a laboratory experiment,
- presents the summary in clearly defined and clearly labeled sections of the paper,
- includes adequate visual aids in the form of charts, graphs, diagrams, and/or tables,
- acknowledges sources used for background research,
- uses the technical language appropriate for the content area.

The real world of research—outside the confines of a classroom—relies heavily on accurate and comprehensive reports. Variations of the formal lab report are published in professional journals throughout the world. The importance of lab reports goes beyond content classes, having far-reaching implications in the career and scientific worlds.

Process

Obviously, before a writer prepares a lab report, he or she will have done extensive lab work. Less obviously, the writer will also have done a considerable amount of work prior to beginning the actual laboratory experiment. An outline of the process appears below.

PREWRITING

STEP 1. RAISING THE QUESTION

The first step in any general laboratory investigation is posing the question. Sometimes, even though you probably have a general idea of what you hope to accomplish, you may not have formed the specific question.

So, force yourself to put a question in writing. For example:

Does the color of a plastic-worm fishing lure help determine its effectiveness?

STEP 2. STATING THE PROBLEM

Once you have raised the question, you must logically determine what problem exists that prevents you from answering the question. This problem will be the crux of your laboratory investigation.

In the example above, for instance, we can state the problem as follows:

Are fish capable of color perception?

STEP 3. COLLECTING INFORMATION ON THE PROBLEM

Before laboratory work begins, you must be familiar with the available information about the problem. For instance, if you are trying to determine if fish are capable of color perception, you will probably want to collect information to answer the following questions:

- What do people say about color?
- How many colors are used in plastic fishing worms?
- What color plastic worms do professional fishermen use?
- Have some colors proven more successful than others?
- Has anyone else done any research on this subject?
- What does that research show or not show?

Background reading may be part of the classroom assignment or part of class discussion. On the other hand, you may need to do library research or even primary research to familiarize yourself with the problem, its complexities, its possible solutions, the potential results. The background reading is also necessary to generate certain parts of the formal lab report:

- You will summarize your research findings in the first part of the lab report, called the *Statement of Problem*. In fact, that brief section of your lab report is very much like a mini-research paper. [*See* RESEARCH PAPER *in Part II.*]

- The statement of problem, like a mini-research paper, also includes documentation. [*See* RESEARCH PAPER *for more precise information on the accurate form for parenthetical documentation, endnotes, or footnotes.*]

- You may choose to use direct quotations, paraphrases, or precis in the statement of problem. [*See* PARAPHRASE *and* PRECIS *in Part II. For accurate documentation of each, see* RESEARCH PAPER *in Part II.*]

- The final page of your lab report, titled *References*, will cite the books and periodicals consulted during your background reading.

After you have written the specific question you hope to answer and before you do any additional work, get the research materials you will need, prepare bibliography cards, and, as you read, complete note cards. [*See* NOTES, KINDS: FOR A PAPER *in Part II.*]

STEP 4. DEVELOPING THE HYPOTHESIS

The hypothesis is an educated guess based on the information currently available. For purposes of your laboratory investigation, it is a positive statement asserting what your experiment will prove—or disprove. The single sentence must indicate the specific anticipated outcome of the experiment, an outcome based at this point only on the preliminary research:

Hypothesis:

Fish can detect colors.

STEP 5. DETERMINING THE PROCEDURE

Next, logic and creativity will help you determine the procedure by which you can prove or disprove your hypothesis. The procedure may involve a single or multiple steps. In either case, it must be based on previous scientific knowledge and a logical application of fact. And in either case, the test must be valid. In other words, if repeated, the test must give the same results. A valid procedure may involve a control group and an experimental group, and it may require specific measurements of time or minutes of observation. The simplicity or complexity matters not. You only want to establish a means by which you can test the hypothesis—conclusively if possible.

Assume, for instance, that you want to prove whether or not fish can detect colors. Perhaps you use a series of colored lights and note whether the fish are attracted to a specific color. Perhaps you simultaneously dangle six or eight different colored plastic fishing worms and note how many fish nudge or nibble how many times at each color. Perhaps you change the arrangement of the colors to prove that the fish are attracted to color and not to placement. Perhaps you even have a control group and an experimental group, one well fed and the other hungry to determine whether fish react more readily to a color simply because they are hungry. And, of course, you may use all of these procedures!

In short, the procedure is based on the problem.

STEP 6. TABULATING THE DATA

In the process of conducting your laboratory investigation, you will collect and tabulate the data regarding the control and the experimental groups, noting responses and reactions, keeping accurate records of time, dates, chemicals, solutions, procedures, etc.

STEP 7. ANALYZING THE DATA

Any statistical work to be completed will be done at this point. Keep in mind, however, this warning: The cliche that liars can figure and figures can lie sometimes characterizes student scientists. As you analyze the data, be sure the analysis describes what actually happened, not what you hoped would happen.

STEP 8. REACHING A CONCLUSION

Based on the investigation and the tabulation and analysis of the resulting data, you will be able to reach a conclusion. The conclusion is based upon data interpretation, and it will prove, disprove, or prove with certain reservations the hypothesis.

WRITING

STEP 9. PREPARING THE INTRODUCTION

The lab report begins with an introduction which includes three specific sections: *statement of problem*, *purpose*, and *hypothesis*.

First, label the introduction by inserting the title, INTRODUCTION, centered, in all-capital letters. No exposition appears between the title and the statement of problem.

Statement of Problem

Label the subtopic, underlined, at the left margin. As you state the problem, you should review Step 2 above. A good statement will include examples of the problem, identify related research, and describe briefly its bearing on the problem. In most cases, documentation should be incorporated in the text in the following manner:

- Enclose in parentheses the author's last name, followed by the page reference on which the idea or quotation was found.
- If the author's name appears in the text proper, then enclose only the page reference in parentheses.

- If the book or article is unsigned, use only the title of the article in parentheses.

[*If your instructor prefers endnotes or footnotes to parenthetical documentation, see* RESEARCH PAPER *in Part II for sample formats.*]

Purpose

Again, at the left margin, label and underline the section title. In most cases, based on your work in Step 2 and Step 4 above, you should be able to state the purpose of your laboratory investigation in a single sentence.

Hypothesis

After you label this section of your paper, write the single-sentence hypothesis developed in Step 4 above.

STEP 10. DESCRIBING THE PROCEDURE

To describe the procedure, you are in essence writing a process-analysis paper. [*See* PROCESS ANALYSIS *later in Part II.*] Follow these specific suggestions:

- Label this section PROCEDURE, centered, in all-capital letters.
- Organize the material in chronological order.
- Include a description of materials and equipment used, but do not formulate a list. Incorporate the description in the general discussion of procedure.
- Use past tense and passive voice. [*See* PAST TENSE *and* PASSIVE VOICE *in the Glossary.*]

- Use metric measurements.
- Include graphics as necessary to explain procedure or illustrate methods or materials. Graphics may include tables, figures, or illustrations.
- All visual aids should be titled and clearly defined. [*See additional information about graphics in* TECHNICAL REPORT *in Part II.*]

STEP 11. STATING DATA ANALYSIS

As you did for the introduction and procedure sections, you will label this part of your paper DATA ANALYSIS, centered, in all-capital letters. Data analyses must be comprehensive. Use these guidelines:

- Use past tense and passive voice for stating results.
- Use whatever method best explains the results: a narrative, a summary, charts, graphs, illustrations, comparison and contrast statements, or cause and effect statements. Do not be repetitious; use the one best method. [*See also* TECHNICAL REPORT *in Part II for additional examples and explanations.*]
- Be thorough but concise. Avoid flowery words and verbose language.
- Organize this section by an order of importance. [*See* ORDERS OF IMPORTANCE in the Glossary.]

STEP 12. DEVELOPING THE CONCLUSION

The conclusion includes three specific parts: a summary of findings, possible causes for error, and a concluding statement. Place the label CONCLUSION, centered, in all-capital letters. Label each subtopic, underlined, at the left-hand margin.

Summary of Findings

The summary of findings should be a matter-of-fact statement reflecting the proof or disproof of the hypothesis. Usually a single statement will be sufficient. It is conceivable that the summary-of-findings statement will be ''No results were found.''

Possible Causes for Error

Because every researcher is subject to the critical eye of his fellows, the objective lab report will include a critical description of what may have caused variation in laboratory results. Scientific investigation demands critical controls, and acknowledgment of any variation lends credence to your lab report as well as to you as a researcher.

Discuss each possible cause in a separate paragraph. The paragraph may lack complete development as we think of it in a traditional, expository sense.

Concluding Statement

The final statement indicates whether the purpose of the experiment was accomplished and the hypothesis proved. A further statement may indicate the significance of the results.

STEP 13.   DEVELOPING THE APPENDIX

Sometimes statistical, narrative, or descriptive information is included in the appendix. Usually this information would be cumbersome in the text, and, while it adds strength or support to the results, it is not essential for reporting the laboratory process.

A reference should appear in the text to any materials included in the appendix, and all materials in the appendix must be titled and labeled descriptively. Materials should be grouped into separate appendices (i.e., Appendix A, Appendix B, etc.) if they support separate parts of the procedure or data results.

STEP 14.   PREPARING THE BIBLIOGRAPHY

The bibliography may be a list of works cited in the statement of the problem or, more commonly, a list of sources consulted. [*Use a form set out in the sample bibliography entries in* RESEARCH PAPER *later in Part II.*]

STEP 15.   ADDING THE FINAL TOUCHES

Finally, the report needs a table of contents, a table of graphics, and a title page. Use the sample paper which follows as a model by which to develop these pages. Be sure to check for accuracy of pagination.

REVISING

STEP 16.   CHECKING THE CONTENT

As you reread your report, check for the following problem areas:

- Are all sections clearly labeled?
- Does the table of contents accurately reflect the specific sections of the report?
- Is each section well-organized?
- Are the descriptions complete, clear, concise, and accurate?
- Are all graphics clearly labeled and titled?
- Are graphics incorporated into the text at appropriate places?
- Does the text refer the reader to the appropriate graphics?
- Are materials not essential to the content but relevant to the research included in the appendix?
- Does the table of figures and charts accurately reflect the graphics included in the report, even those in the appendix?

Finally, try to read your report as an objective outsider. What problems will a fellow researcher have reading your report? Will he raise objections about certain sections or certain statements? Will he find logical flaws? Revise to solve those problems.

[*Check writing techniques as suggested in* REVISING *in Part I. Use the questions there as a guide for further revision.*]

PROOFREADING

STEP 17.   CHECKING FOR ACCURACY

The lab report's accuracy depends on more than correct spelling, punctuation, grammar, and usage. While these aspects must be accurate, in addition the tabulations must also be accurate, the tables and figures correct, and the conclusions logical. Finally, as you proofread, also watch for typographical errors and formatting flaws.

—————————— **Sample Lab Report** ——————————

The following model lab report was developed according to the process explained above. Study it and the analysis which follows as you prepare your own report.

THE EFFECTS OF ACID RAIN ON
THE GROWTH OF BULBOUS PLANTS

Jerome Welte
Senior Science Seminar
March 21, 1988

TABLE OF CONTENTS

LIST OF TABLES AND FIGURES

INTRODUCTION

Statement of Problem

For many years, acid rain has raised major concerns among environmentalists and conservationists as well as among the general public. Scientists have contended that rain-made acid from various sources has been damaging trees, bridges, buildings, lakes, crops, and the world's most vital resource, its soil. In fact, acid rain has become a problem of such magnitude that the federal government has taken action. By creating the National Acid Precipitation Assessment Program, the government is starting to search for ways to halt this dangerous phenomenon.

Besides the damage to forests and lakes, a more serious and devastating result from acid rain is beginning to attract attention: the damage to common plants such as grasses, flowers, and crops. The extent of acid-rain damage to crops will likely prove to be comparable to the extent of ozone damage, or about 5% of the cash value (Peterson 7).

While acid-rain damage is subtle, it is nevertheless occurring, partially through a gradual but steady increase in soil acidity. According to Lance Evans, however, most damage to plants caused by acid is the result of foliar impact, not increased soil acidity. His discovery that broad-leaved plants seem to be the most sensitive to acid rain supports his theory (Schultz 57).

Unfortunately, the acidity of rain appears to continue to increase. Researchers now believe that the normal pH for rainfall is closer to 5.0 than to 5.6, the previously assumed value that reflected the amount of carbon dioxide dissolved in water ("Acid Rain Annual Report"). According to these statistics, then, since a pH below 5.6 is considered harmfully acidic, almost any precipitation is potentially dangerous (Schultz 56).

In the Northeast, average rainfall has now reached a 4.2 pH value. At first, according to Schultz, the 4.2 value was thought to be

ten times more acidic than normal (55). Recently, however, Chris
Bernabo, executive director of the National Acid Precipitation
Program, determined that the rainfall in the Northeast is only about
7 times more acidic than unpolluted rainfall ("Acid Rain Annual
Report").

Something desperately needs to be done to prevent future
destruction, but exactly what measures should be taken is still in
question.

Purpose

The purpose of this experiment is to determine if acid rain has
an effect on the growth and development of bulbous flowers through
the forcing and growing periods, and to determine if water of
varying pH values produces different effects on the growth of these
bulbs.

Hypothesis

Water acidity hinders the growth of bulbous flowers.

PROCEDURE

On November 11, twelve each of five kinds of bulbs were
planted in Baccto Potting Soil: Keizerkroon and Appeldoorn Elite
tulips, Dutch Master daffodils, grape hyacinths, and crocuses. They
were divided into three groups of four of each type of bulb, covered
with layers of newspaper (for insulation purposes), then placed in
an area in which the temperature ranged from -4°C to 5°C. This
procedure was designed to force the bulbs.

Periodically they were checked and watered with their
respective pH rain as needed. (See Table 1, Early Distribution of

Water by Frequency and Volume.) The amount of water was measured carefully using measuring spoons or cups to ensure accuracy.

TABLE 1   Early Distribution of
Water by Frequency and Volume

Date		Amount per Bulb
Nov.	23	30 ml
Dec.	1	15 ml
Dec.	15	15 ml

On January 7, after 57 days of simulated winter, all bulbs were brought into an area that had a temperature range from 13°C to 18°C. The layers of paper were not removed, thus slowing the beginning of bulb growth. This procedure was followed in order to make the transition from winter to spring conditions less drastic, a transition which otherwise may have had a limiting effect on the growth of the bulbs.

After four days in this environment, the bulbs were placed in a warmer area (18°C to 21°C), placed under artificial sunlight, and the paper removed.

Then, the bulbs were observed every day for growth and soil dryness. If needed, the bulbs were watered with a predetermined amount per bulb. (See Appendix A, Water Distribution by Frequency and Volume.) The plants were misted with water with a relative pH value to simulate light rain or dew.

After 30, 42, and 55 days from January 7, the bulb's leaf growth was measured. A meter stick was used to measure the leaf length from the bulb to the top of the longest stem. These measurements were recorded.

The simulated acid precipitation was produced by using distilled water in three separate containers in which concentrated sulfuric acid (H_2SO_4) was added to produce the desired pH value. No sulfuric acid was added to the pH 7 water. The solutions were mixed; then the pH reading was taken using a calibrated pH meter.

If the pH reading was too high or too low, the solution was either diluted or subjected to more acid to obtain the desired pH 4 or pH 5 value.

DATA ANALYSIS

The following graphs illustrate the growth patterns and comparisons of each type of bulb as measured after 30, 42, and 55 days of growth. All growth was measured and averages were calculated to arrive at a mean height of the growth in the three different pH-value sets. (The data supporting these graphs appear in Appendix B.)

Taking all bulbs into consideration, those watered with the pH 5 solution produced the greatest height and appeared most hearty on the dates measured. However, the daffodils showed a deviation from the norm and produced the greatest height and appeared most hearty when watered with a pH 7 solution.

FIGURE 1   Height of Keizerkroon Tulips

The Keizerkroon tulip bulbs showed patterned growth until near the time of flowering, when the bulbs watered with the pH 5 solution grew rapidly. Overall, the plants appeared healthy, but the pH 4 bulbs were noticeably stunted.

FIGURE 2   Height of Appeldoorn Elite Tulips

Every Appeldoorn Elite tulip bulb of this type seemed to be severely hindered in its growth. Overall, little difference was recorded until the pH 5 bulbs grew nearly an average of 7 1/2 centimeters in 13 days near the time of flowering. The bulbs watered with the pH 7 water were, on the average, stunted the most.

FIGURE 3   Height of Dutch Master Daffodils

The Dutch Master daffodil bulbs watered with the pH 7 solution clearly grew and matured faster than the other two sets. On the last measuring day, the pH 7 bulbs remained the tallest.

FIGURE 4   Height of Crocuses

Crocus bulbs exhibited steady growth patterns. On the final measuring date, the pH 4 bulbs were slightly taller than the pH 5 and pH 7 bulbs. The three sets grew steadily throughout the growing period.

FIGURE 5   Height of Hyacinths

The Hyacinths grew rapidly in the first 30 days. The pH 5 bulbs were the tallest and seemed most healthy, especially just before the blooms emerged. The pH 7 bulbs nearly stopped growth just before the flowering period.

CONCLUSION

Summary of Findings

This investigation indicates that acid rain interferes with proper plant growth.

Possible Sources of Error

Even though every bulb was planted with at least one inch of surrounding area between bulbs, some bulbs had slightly larger surrounding space. This situation may have caused accelerated growth but would vary the obtained data only slightly.

Slight differences were recorded in the production of the artificial acid rain. The pH 4 solution actually ranged from 3.85 to 4.1; the pH 5 solution ranged from 4.9 to 5.1; and the pH 7 solution ranged from 6.8 to 7.0.

The use of sulfuric acid in preparing the rain solutions could cause slight differences in the growth of the bulbs, but not in that of the ones watered with the pH 7 solution. The sulfuric acid may produce differences from natural rain because natural rain is lowered to a pH of 5.6 from natural carbon dioxide in the air instead of from the sulfuric acid. The acidity in natural rain is increased as a result of sulfur dioxide from man-made pollution.

Concluding Statement

The hypothesis was correct. The data showed that the growth of bulbous flowers is deterred by water's increased acidity.

Appendix A

TABLE A-1   Distribution of Water by Frequency and Volume

Date	Amount per Bulb
Jan. 7	60 ml
Jan. 11	15 ml
Jan. 17	25 ml
Jan. 21	15 ml
Jan. 23	20 ml
Jan. 26	15 ml
Feb. 2	15 ml
Feb. 4	60 ml
Feb. 6	15 ml
Feb. 9	60 ml
Feb. 11	60 ml
Feb. 14	60 ml
Feb. 20	60 ml
Feb. 24	60 ml

Appendix B

Tables of Periodic Height Measurements and Averages
of All Bulb Growth

TABLE B-1   Height of All Bulbs and Averages in Centimeters
after 30 Days

Type of Bulb	pH 7	pH 5	pH 4
Keizerkroon Tulips			
bulb 1	5.1	8.9	6.4
bulb 2	3.8	8.9	4.4
bulb 3	12.1	5.1	7
bulb 4	4.4	7.6	6.4
Averages	6.4	7.6	6.1
Appeldoorn Elite			
bulb 1	5.1	7	5.7
bulb 2	5.7	5.7	5.1
bulb 3	6.4	7	5.7
bulb 4	5.7	7	7
Averages	5.7	6.7	5.9
Daffodils			
bulb 1	20.3	6.4	7.6
bulb 2	5.7	5.7	5.1
bulb 3	26.7	15.2	7.6
bulb 4	27.9	17.8	15.9
Averages	20.2	11.3	9.1
Crocuses			
bulb 1	14	12.7	15.2
bulb 2	16.5	14	12.7
bulb 3	14.6	14	17.8
bulb 4	15.2	16.5	15.2
Averages	15.1	14.3	15.2
Hyacinths			
bulb 1	15.2	16.5	17.8
bulb 2	22.9	17.8	13.3
bulb 3	15.2	22.9	12.1
bulb 4	12.7	17.8	16.5
Averages	16.5	18.8	14.9

TABLE B-2   Height of All Bulbs and Averages in Centimeters
after 42 Days

Type of Bulb	pH 7	pH 5	pH 4
Keizerkroon Tulips			
bulb 1	22.9	5.7	8.9
bulb 2	5.1	11.4	5.1
bulb 3	5.7	9.5	8.9
bulb 4	6.4	10.2	8.3
Averages	10	9.2	7.8
Appeldoorn Elite			
bulb 1	7	8.3	7.6
bulb 2	8.3	7.6	7
bulb 3	7.6	8.9	7.6
bulb 4	7.6	7.6	8.9
Averages	7.6	8.1	7.8
Daffodils			
bulb 1	33.1	20.3	17.8
bulb 2	27.9	10.2	16.5
bulb 3	36.8	26.7	15.2
bulb 4	6.4	14	15.2
Averages	26.1	17.8	16.2
Crocuses			
bulb 1	24.1	19.1	24.1
bulb 2	20.3	20.3	21.6
bulb 3	22.9	21.6	20.3
bulb 4	22.9	21.6	22.9
Averages	22.6	20.7	22.2
Hyacinths			
bulb 1	27.3	25.4	22.9
bulb 2	22.9	24.1	16.5
bulb 3	22.2	25.4	24.1
bulb 4	19.1	22.9	17.8
Averages	22.9	24.5	20.3

TABLE B-3   Height of All Bulbs and Averages in Centimeters
after 55 Days

Type of Bulb	pH 7	pH 5	pH 4
Keizerkroon Tulips			
bulb 1	27.9	17.8	10.2
bulb 2	7.6	9.5	12.1
bulb 3	8.9	15.9	5.7
bulb 4	7	16.5	10.2
Averages	12.9	14.9	9.6
Appeldoorn Elite			
bulb 1	9.5	10.8	8.3
bulb 2	9.5	10.2	16.5
bulb 3	8.3	22.9	7.6
bulb 4	8.9	17.8	12.1
Averages	9.1	15.4	11.1
Daffodils			
bulb 1	35.6	28.6	21
bulb 2	31.8	24.1	17.8
bulb 3	5.1	14	18.4
bulb 4	27.9	17.8	17.8
Averages	25.1	21.1	18.8
Crocuses			
bulb 1	22.9	30.5	22.9
bulb 2	33	30.5	33
bulb 3	30.5	30.5	33
bulb 4	22.9	22.9	30.5
Averages	27.3	28.6	29.9
Hyacinths			
bulb 1	27.9	27.9	26.7
bulb 2	24.1	33	22.9
bulb 3	23.5	30.5	22.9
bulb 4	21	34.3	24.1
Averages	24.1	31.4	24.2

REFERENCES

Abelson, Philip H. "Acid Rain." Science 8 July 1983: 115.

"Acid Rain Annual Report." Science News 23 June 1984: 392.

Krug, Edward C. and Charles R. Fink. "Acid Rain on Acid Soil: A New Perspective." Science 5 August 1983: 520.

Marshall, Eliot. "Acid Rain: A Year Later." Science 15 July 1983: 392-393.

_____. "Acid Rain Researchers Issue Joint Report." Science 24 June 1983: 1359.

Peterson, Ivars. "New Reports Urge Action on Acid Rain." Science News 2 July 1983: 7.

Schultz, Warren Jr. "Is Acid Rain Eating Our Gardens?" Organic Gardening July 1984: 55-58.

Taylor, Ronald H. "The Plague That's Killing America's Trees." U.S. News & World Report 23 April 1984: 58-59.

Analysis of the Sample

The model above follows the process outlined in the explanation for developing a lab report. You will note certain specifics that will further help you develop your own report:

- The format, with sections clearly labeled, allows a reader to move quickly through sections of little interest.

- The table of contents and the list of tables and figures clarify the organization and permit the reader to find specific sections or graphics quickly.

- While technical terminology is kept to a minimum, appropriate vocabulary appears throughout. Some reports may require a higher frequency of technical vocabulary.

- All measurements are given in the metric system.

- All data reported appear in logical order, both on the graphs and in the appendixes. For instance, Figures 1–5 report statistics in centimeters. The reader can move logically from the bottom of the chart to top to see increased growth. Likewise the reader can move logically from left to right to follow the time span. [*See* TECHNICAL REPORT *later in Part II for additional information about developing logical and accurate graphs, charts, figures, tables, etc.*]

- The parenthetical documentation included within the text provides adequate but simple citation of reference materials. [*Compare this format with that in the models for* RESEARCH PAPER *later in Part II.*]

- The graphics, especially in the section titled *Data Results,* enhance or even replace text. Effective visual aids can provide significant support to all technical reports.

- The bibliography includes works consulted as well as works cited.

By using the steps outlined above, you should be able to prepare a lab report to meet the needs of virtually any situation.

LETTERS

By means of letters, we communicate with our friends, our enemies, our business associates, our government, even our computers. In addition, many people choose to express their opinions regularly in letters to newspaper and magazine editors.

We all must write business and social letters. It is probably safe to say that the most important writing we will do over the course of our lives is letter writing. Letter writers deal with everything from huge financial transactions to delicate personal emotions. While letters follow a format very different from any other kind of writing, learning the techniques generally offers few complications.

This section will discuss each of three kinds of letter writing, arranged in alphabetical order: the business letter, the editorial letter, and the social letter. In the general category of business letters, we will examine four kinds: a personal business letter, a request for information, a letter of complaint, and a letter to accompany a resume. Within these sections, you should be able to find examples similar to almost any kind of letter you will write.

BUSINESS LETTERS

Business letters deal with innumerable matters, but most fall into one of two groups: those which relate to our professional lives and those which relate to business matters in our personal lives. By discussing business letters in general and then showing specific variations, we hope to guide you through successful business-letter writing.

Writing letters requires nearly the same skills as writing exposition. While paragraphs in letters do not often follow the same paragraph structure we see in other kinds of writing, good writing skills are as important in business letter writing as they are anywhere. Without a clear, effective letter, the recipient will have no idea how to respond. That could cost you a job!

Characteristics

What should a good business letter include? First, it must *look* business-like. Immaculate appearance is essential. In order to maintain an excellent appearance, the business letter should

- appear on 8 1/2" × 11" plain white paper, preferably at least a twenty-pound bond,

- be typewritten or printed on a letter-quality printer, in either case using a good ribbon that produces crisp, dark print,
- be free of messy erasures or blobs of correction fluid,
- maintain ample margins with an even left margin and a right margin as even as possible and with top and bottom margins reasonably equal,
- use a heading on all pages beyond the first, a heading which includes the name of the addressee, the date, and the page number.

Second, in order for a business letter to look business-like, it must include the six parts of good busines-letter form:

1. heading, three lines made up of
   a. the writer's street address,
   b. the writer's city, state, and zip code,
   c. the date on which the letter is written,
2. the inside address, three or more lines made up of
   a. the recipient's name,
   b. the recipient's title or position, if known,
   c. the company name,
   d. the company's street address,
   e. and the company's city, state, and zip code,
3. a salutation, like *Dear Mr. Glatter, Dear Dr. Hansen,* or *Gentlemen,* followed by a colon.

Note: Use the name if you know it: *Dear Mr. Smith.* If you do not know a name but only a title, use *Dear Chairperson, Dear President, Dear Sec-* retary, *Dear Sir, Dear Madam,* or whatever is appropriate. If you know neither a name nor a title, use *Gentlemen, Ladies,* or *Ladies and Gentlemen.* The salutation should agree with the inside address.

4. the body of the business letter, arranged in paragraph form,
5. a closing, like *Yours truly* or *Sincerely yours* followed by a comma,

Note: Use the following closings for the following purposes:
   a. *Yours truly* (with or without *very*) when the salutation is the impersonal *Gentlemen* or *Dear Sir* and when the tone of the letter is cold and formal or when you are in doubt about what to use,
   b. *Sincerely* or *Cordially yours* (with or without *very*) when the addressee's name appears in the salutation and the tone of the letter is personal and friendly,
   c. *Respectfully yours.* (with or without *very*) when the letter is addressed to a person of high rank.
6. the writer's signature, written (not printed) in ink, followed by the typewritten name.

In addition, a business letter may include

- an attention line, used when a letter is addressed only to a company or to a department rather than to an individual,

Note: The attention line appears immediately after the inside address and before the salutation. It begins with the word *Attention* followed by the name of the specific department to which the letter should be forwarded, like *Attention: Sales Department*. *Never* use a person's name in the attention line. If you know the person's name, use it in the inside address and omit the attention line.

- a subject line, which appears immediately after the salutation,

The subject line begins with the word <u>Subject</u> followed by a colon and a few words or a phrase to state the subject of the letter. Use initial capital letters to name the subject.

- a writer's identification, which appears immediately below the typewritten signature and identifies the writer's title or position,

Note: The writer never signs his name with a title or position preceding or following his name.

- reference initials, which appear at the left margin below the typewritten signature line and identify the typist, like *kjs* for Kirsten Joo Seng,
- enclosure notation, which appears immediately below any reference initials and indicates something is enclosed with the letter,

Note: If you have more than one item enclosed, use one of three appropriate messages: <u>Enc.</u>, <u>2 Enclosures</u>, or <u>Enc. 2</u>.

- copy notations, which appear immediately after any enclosure notation and indicate who will receive copies of the letter, like *cc: Sales Department*,

- a postscript (PS), which appears immediately after any copy notations.

Note: A postscript is always the last item in a letter. It allows the writer to include something he forgot to mention in the body or sometimes to call attention to an important detail.

Third, the parts of the business letter should be arranged in one of three styles:

- block style, which begins every line in every part of the letter at the left margin,
- modified-block style, which uses no indentation and which begins all lines in the heading and closing at the center of the page (a style often referred to as *standard format*),
- modified-block style with indented paragraphs, which follows the same format as the modified-block style with the addition of an indentation for every paragraph.

[*Examples of each of these styles appear in the* SAMPLES AND ANALYSES *section later in this chapter.*]

In addition to appearance and form, the good business letter also maintains characteristic standards of writing. Those standards require that a business letter

- follow standard grammar, mechanics, and usage rules,
- follow standard spelling,
- maintain courtesy and diplomacy,
- display clear, precise writing,
- avoid highly complex, convoluted sentences,

- omit ambiguous words, phrases, or sentences,
- eliminate excess words, phrases, or sentences.

While the list of characteristics may seem unreasonably long, keep in mind that much of what makes business-letter writing different from other kinds of writing is form. As a result, you will find the rest of the information simple and quick to follow.

Process

Developing a business letter goes quickly after a few preliminary preparations. Follow these steps for best results.

PREWRITING

STEP 1. GATHERING THE NECESSARY INFORMATION

In order to work efficiently, you should gather all the necessary names, titles, addresses, records, or other papers you will need to develop the letter. Use current titles and addresses. A quick phone call can verify the information or provide updated information. Many times the business switchboard operator can give you the information you need. The importance of current, accurate information justifies even a long-distance call, especially for important matters.

STEP 2. PLANNING THE BODY OF THE LETTER

Since much of the business letter form requires only that you put accurate information in certain parts of a prescribed format, the only planning necessary is for the body of the letter.

First, write a single sentence that says what you want this letter to accomplish. Start with the phrase: "The purpose of this letter is to. . . ." Then complete the sentence. Develop a sentence similar to one of the following examples:

> The purpose of this letter is to direct the exchange of a sweater ordered from a mail-order company for the same sweater in a larger size.

> The purpose of this letter is to get information about the tourist attractions in and around Denver.

> The purpose of this letter is to apply for the position of sales manager in the company.

When you have clearly stated the purpose of your letter, begin making a list of the important ideas to be included. Be sure to include the following details and characteristics.

For a Personal Business Letter

- the account or other identification number, as applicable,
- the date of the transaction, contractual agreement, conversation, or other business contact,
- any necessary background information,
- a direct statement of what you want of the reader: a reply, an appointment, or, perhaps, no action.

For a Request for Information

- specific details about the information you are requesting: dates, places, and general-interest areas for tourist information; specific areas of inquiry for printed information,

- details about payment,

- directions for forwarding the requested information: to whom, where, by what means, at whose expense.

For a Letter of Complaint

- the order, identification, serial, catalog, or part number of the consumer item,

- the name of the consumer item,

- the date of purchase or of the agreement, contract, lease or other business dealing,

- a specific explanation of the problem,

- the name and/or title of any company representative with whom you have previously talked regarding the problem,

- a reference to any guarantee or warranty agreement,

- an explanation of what you want done to correct the problem,

- photo copies of any information which may aid the resolution of your complaint,

- an attitude of courtesy and tact, regardless of your frustration or anger.

For a Letter to Accompany a Resume

- an inside address and a salutation naming the specific person who makes personnel decisions,

- a polite reference to the company, its product line, its reputation, or, if you have met, a polite reference to the person addressed,

- a reference to the accompanying resume,

- emphasis on your areas of greatest strengths as a potential employee,

- an expression of willingness to learn new skills, travel, relocate, work irregular hours, begin with a part-time position, etc.

WRITING

STEP 3. DEVELOPING THE IDEAS INTO A LETTER

With the preliminary work completed, developing the body of the letter should go quickly. As you write, remember a few guidelines:

- Get to the point immediately.
- Provide any necessary details to clarify your point for the reader.
- Be concise.
- End with a courteous sentence.

REVISING

STEP 4. CHECKING THE CONTENT

Check the content of your letter for accuracy. Ask yourself the following questions as a guide for possible revision:

- Does the first sentence state the purpose of the letter?

- Are adequate details included in order that the addressee can understand my point and, if necessary, respond?

- Have I avoided excess verbiage and complicated sentences?

- Is my letter courteous, polite, business-like?

- Does the final sentence conclude the letter courteously without compromising my position?

Make any revision suggested by these questions, and follow the guidelines below as you type a final copy. Before you mail the letter, however, follow the proofreading suggestions below.

STEP 5. TYPING THE FINAL COPY

As you type the final copy of your letter, either on a typewriter or at the computer, ask yourself these questions in order to think about accuracy and appearance. Check additional details in the proofreading section below.

- Does the heading begin on line fifteen (2–1/2″ from the top of the page)?

- Is the heading accurate, including my full address and zip code as well as the date?

- Does the inside address begin four lines below the heading?

- If I am using printed letterhead, did I add the date and begin the inside address four to ten spaces below the date to adjust for appearance?

- Is the inside address accurate and complete, including a current title or position of the addressee?

- Does the salutation begin two spaces below the inside address?

- Are all words in the salutation capitalized accurately?

- Is the salutation appropriate for the occasion and followed by a colon?

- Does the body begin two spaces below the salutation and follow a consistent format?

- Is the body typed single-spaced with a double space between paragraphs?

- Are the left and right margins nearly equal, the left margin even and the right margin as nearly even as possible?

- If my letter runs onto a second page, have I avoided having only three or four lines on the second page?

- If I must divide a paragraph at the bottom of page one, have I included at least two lines of the paragraph on page one and included at least two lines on the top of page two?

- Does the second page begin one inch from the top with a heading that includes the name of the addressee, the page number, and the date?

- Have I started page two of the body of the letter three lines below the heading?

- Have I maintained the same side margins on the second page as on the first?

- Does the closing appear two lines below the body?

- Is only the first word of the closing capitalized?

- Is the closing appropriate and followed by a comma?

- Is my signature in blue or black ink, signed, not printed?

- Does the typewritten signature appear four lines below the closing in order to allow room for the written signature?

- Does my written signature omit any titles or references to position, like *Mr., Dr., Ms., Professor,* or *Manager?*

- Is the typewritten signature accurate, including any necessary designations of title or position?

- Are any other necessary notations included, like carbon copy lines, attention lines, subject lines, etc.?

- Is the format consistent, either in block form or in one of the two modified-block forms?

- Are the top and bottom margins nearly equal?

Make any necessary revisions based on the guiding questions above. If necessary, for the sake of an immaculate, business-like appearance, retype or reprint the letter.

PROOFREADING

STEP 6. CHECKING THE TECHNICAL DETAILS

Check grammar, mechanics, and usage. In addition, consider the following questions as you proofread:

- Have I punctuated the heading correctly, using a comma between the city and state but no punctuation between the state and zip code? Did I include a comma between the day of the month and the year? Did I omit punctuation at the ends of the lines?

- Have I punctuated the inside address correctly, using a comma to separate the name of the addressee from his title or position if both are listed on the same line? Did I punctuate the address correctly?

- Have I maintained accurate capitalization throughout?

- Do I use accurate terminology throughout the letter? Check *Webster's New World Thesaurus* for accurate synonyms.

- Is my spelling absolutely correct? In the case of alternate spellings, do I use the preferred spelling? See *Webster's New World Dictionary* as a final reference.

When you have typed a final copy, proofread it carefully, and sign it. The letter is ready to prepare for mailing.

PREPARING FOR MAILING

STEP 7.   THE FINAL STEP

In order to maintain an immaculate, business-like appearance, we need to discuss two last points: addressing the envelope and folding the letter.

Addressing the Envelope

Follow these steps:

- Use a plain white envelope, preferably letter-size.

- Put your return address, including your name, in the upper left corner of the envelope, using the same style as you used in the heading of the letter.

- Begin the mailing address on line fourteen of a letter-size envelope and on line twelve of a small envelope. Start at the vertical center of the envelope. The mailing address should appear exactly as it does in the inside address of the letter.

- Be sure to add sufficient postage.

Folding the Letter

If you are using a long envelope, fold your letter in thirds, folding the bottom third toward the top and then the top third down. Insert the letter in the envelope with the open end of the letter toward the top of the envelope. [See Figure 1.]

If you are using a short envelope, first fold your letter in half, bringing the bottom up to the top. Then fold that into thirds by bringing the left third toward the right and the right third over the left. Again, insert the letter in the envelope with the open end of the letter toward the top of the envelope. [See Figure 2.]

Finally, seal the envelope and check for sufficient postage.

Mailing the Letter

If you are mailing the letter first-class, you may drop it in any postal-service box. If, on the other hand, you are sending it as certified mail (which, if a return receipt is requested, provides a record of delivery) or as registered mail (which provides top security for valuable or hard-to-replace items), then you will need to mail it from a post office. If you are sending it as express mail (for guaranteed one-day delivery), you can, if you have in hand the necessary forms, mail it from an express mail box. Private carriers also deliver letters and parcels—some overnight, some within a day, some within two days. Of course, you must pay extra for the speedy service.

Study the following sample business letters and their analyses for further guidelines.

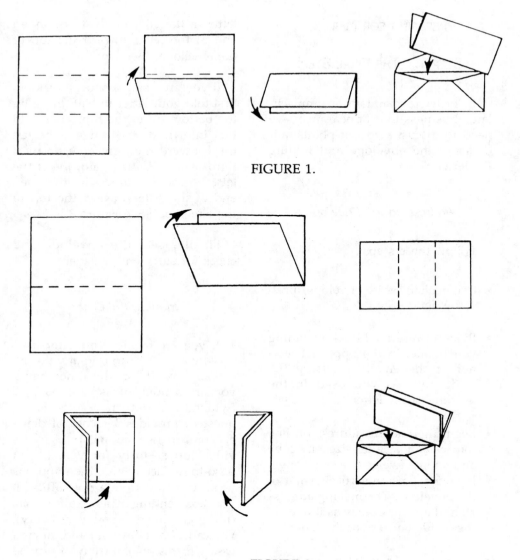

FIGURE 1.

FIGURE 2.

Sample Personal Business Letter

The following letter verifies in writing an important telephone conversation. The purpose in such a letter is to record a specific event. As telephone conversations are subject to your-word-against-theirs arguments, it is wise, in important matters, to verify them.

1234 Shortridge Road
Catharge, New Mexico 98765-4321
July 29, 1988

Mr. Wilbur Offenberg
Vice President of Accounts
Finner, Hopewell, and Finner Securities
7890 Jarrell Financial Center
Irontown, Washington 56789-0123

Dear Mr. Offenberg:

I am writing to confirm our telephone conversation this morning
regarding my account No. 567890 with Finner, Hopewill, and Finner
Securities. As you recall, I requested that $5,000 be moved from account No.
567890 into my joint account No. 123456.

In the course of our conversation, you agreed to make that transaction
immediately in order for me to take advantage of the improved interest rate
effective August 1. At the same time, I agreed to sign a withdrawal/deposit
slip and forward it to you in today's mail. You will find the slip enclosed,
registering the request for the $5,000 transfer of funds.

I appreciate your help in this matter. This kind of service makes it a
pleasure doing business with Finner, Hopewell, and Finner.

Respectfully yours,

F. Brody Kleindorf

F. Brody Kleindorf

Enc.

Analysis of the Sample Personal Business Letter

The personal business letter follows the standard format (modified-block
style). Note that the left margin is flush except for the heading, closing, and
signature. Compare this with the following two letters which illustrate the block
and the modified-block with indented paragraphs.

In addition, note these characteristics:

• The six parts of the letter are evident: heading, inside address, salutation,
body, closing, and signature.

- An enclosure notation shows that the withdrawal/deposit slip is enclosed.
- The heading and inside address follow the same style. Nothing is abbreviated. You may write out the name of the state or use the standard two-letter abbreviations. Follow the same form throughout the letter and on the envelope.
- The salutation is followed by a colon.
- The two body paragraphs discuss a single idea each. Each is concise.
- The final paragraph represents a good courtesy paragraph.
- The closing is appropriate and followed by a comma.

Sample Request for Information

The following letter requests information. Written in block style, the left margin is flush throughout the letter.

1803 State Highway 43 North
South Plaine, OH 48691-4968
November 18, 1988

Mr. Glenn K. Yonkers
Midwest Regional Tourism Division
1400 North Cross Street
Nashville, TN 48815-5188

Dear Mr. Yonkers:

Our family is planning a two-week trip through Kentucky and Tennessee during the summer of 1988. Please send a brochure or pamphlet listing the scenic attractions of eastern Tennessee and a highway map for the state. Because we are photography buffs and avid hikers, we are interested specifically in geographic scenery, not man-made attractions.

Please send the two items to me at the address above. I understand this is a service you provide for those planning vacations in the area.

We're looking forward to our visit to your part of the country.

Sincerely yours,

Gerald Kleimann

Gerald Kleimann

Analysis of the Sample Request for Information

The sample above follows the general characteristics of a good business letter. As a model of a block-style letter, note that the left margin is straight throughout, including the heading and the closing. Because it is much faster to type or set up on a word processor, the block-style letter has gained popularity with many business people.

In addition, note these particular features:

- The heading and inside address maintain the same style, each using the approved two-letter abbreviation for the state followed by the zip code.

- The salutation and closing are appropriately business-like.

- The body of the letter, brief and specific, covers the basic requirements for a letter of request.

- The courtesy sentence is neither too gushy nor too cold.

- The signature line is accurate.

Sample Letter of Complaint

The following letter maintains the modified-block style with indented paragraphs. Note, too, that it maintains courtesy in spite of the writer's obvious unhappiness.

4157 Southland Drive
Oxmoore, SC 61842-5073
January 23, 1988

Customer Relations Office
Kalaxton Manufacturing Company, Inc.
12700 Broadmore Way
New Richland, AL 38741-2763

Gentlemen:

Six weeks ago on December 15, I purchased a Kitchen Kit Appliance Aid, model A-4001-6, at the Trenton Store in Oxmoore. I have tried for several weeks now to understand the operator's manual, but so far I have been relatively unsuccessful. As a result, I don't know whether I am operating the Appliance Aid improperly or whether it is malfunctioning. When I try to cut French fries, for instance, I get grated rather than cut potatoes. Likewise, when I use the slaw cutter, what comes out looks more like mush than slaw.

I have talked with the retailer at Trenton who claims he knows nothing about the Appliance Aid's operation. Could you tell me, please, where I can find someone in the Oxmoore area who can demonstrate the Aid and who can also tell me whether my Aid is malfunctioning or whether I am, in fact, operating it improperly.

I am looking forward to your response.

Very truly yours,

Claudette McMooney

Claudette McMooney

Analysis of the Sample Letter of Complaint

The above letter appears in modified-block style with indented paragraphs. Although the form is not as popular as the previous two, certain businesses still prefer it.

Note these additional features:

- Because the writer did not have the name of a specific person at Kalaxton Manufacturing Company, she could write only to *Customer Relations*. Generally, this title will get your letter where it needs to go.
- The salutation is also appropriate.
- The two body paragraphs give the company representative sufficient information to know which appliance the writer has, its model number, its date and place of purchase, and the customer's problem.
- By asking for a specific response, the writer lets the addressee know exactly what she hopes to accomplish. She is not asking for a replacement or repairs; she is not asking for a refund.
- The final courtesy sentence appropriately expresses a business-like attitude.
- The closing and signature are accurate and appropriate.

———— Sample Letter to Accompany a Resume ————

The following letter, written in modified-block style, probably the most popular of the three styles, serves to introduce the writer to a potential employer. The accompanying resume [*See* RESUME *later in Part II*], lists the applicant's qualifications.

12806 South Pike Road
Mt. Simon, Lousiana 23306-1229
September 4, 1988

Ms. Krista McGallahan
Personnel Manager
Feagley Electronics Company
3456 Longway Drive
Judson, Virginia 43210-3210

Dear Ms. McGallahan:

Having worked with Feagley computers regularly in various computer centers for the past three years, I am looking forward to an opportunity to work with the company as a full-time employee.

Experienced in both software programming and alteration to meet customer needs and in tutoring clients, I am qualified as a software-hardware technician, able to alter software to make it compatible with most brands of hardware, including that developed by Feagley. As you can see from the accompanying resume, I also have an associate degree in business with a minor in computer education.

I am looking forward to an interview for a position with Feagley Electronics. I will call in a week for an appointment.

Sincerely yours,

Kevin L. McDermitt

Kevin L. McDermitt

Enc.

Analysis of the Sample Letter to Accompany a Resume

The above letter accompanies the resume sample found in RESUME, later in Part II. Compare both to better understand the relationship of the cover letter to the resume itself. In addition, note these features:

- Like any other business letter, the letter to accompany a resume must maintain an immaculate, business-like appearance and follow proper form.

- In addition, the letter is really another opportunity to sell yourself as a potential employee. Saying something nice about the company certainly will not spoil anything. Note the effect of this process in the first paragraph of the sample.

- Finally, do not repeat all the information included in the resume, but do point out the most impressive qualifications and put your best foot forward.

The characteristics, processes, models, and analyses above should enable you to develop satisfactory business letters.

EDITORIAL LETTERS

In a letter to the editor, you can express your opinion about relevant issues and expect to have a wide audience. While all letters to the editor express an opinion, some aim to convince; others aim only to inform. Some express appreciation or condolences; others merely question. Some hope to destroy apathy; others unwittingly create it. Generally, however, people write letters to the editor to voice their opinions on issues that to them, at least, merit the time and effort.

Most commonly, a letter to the editor of a local newspaper expresses an opinion about an issue of interest to that publication's readers, including local, state, national or international matters. Letters about moral and religious issues, local political battles, proposed changes in state tax levies, national legislative issues, personal-interest lobbies, local street repair, and even the neighbor's annoying dogs commonly fill the letters-to-the-editor pages.

A letter to the editor of a magazine will most likely react to an article which appeared in a recent issue, either expressing appreciation, taking issue with the author's position, or adding an interesting sidelight.

Characteristics

A letter to the editor includes some of the same characteristics as a business letter, but obviously its purpose demands other specific characteristics as well. In general, a good letter to the editor should

- be brief, including no more than 300 words in its body (where a word equals five spaces),

- address a timely subject,

- attract the reader's attention, thus increasing the chances of its being published,

- express clearly, probably in the first sentence, your opinion,

- provide details adequate to support your opinion,

- anticipate the reader's point of view and potential questions,

- indicate thorough knowledge of the subject,

- follow an organizational plan that best attracts reader attention,

- suggest, if possible, a solution to the problem or issue and offer as well a means of implementation,

- omit phrases like *I think, in my opinion, it seems to me* or *I, for one* since a letter to the editor is already recognized as your opinion,

- avoid name-calling, sweeping generalizations, and unfair accusations,

- maintain a courteous, polite tone,

- include your signature and typewritten name since newspapers and magazines rarely publish anonymous letters,

- include a phone number where you can be reached, preferably during the day, for verification,

- follow either a business-letter format or a less formal but more easily read format as described in Step 6 below.

While the organization of letters to the editor will vary as much as the writers themselves, good writing techniques will enhance any letter. Thus, using a comparison or contrast, cause-effect, analogy, description, definition—or any of the other methods of development—will improve the letter's effectiveness. [*See* COMPARISON AND CONTRAST, CAUSE AND EFFECT, ANALOGY, DESCRIPTION, DEFINITION, *and entries describing other methods of development in Part II.*]

Similarly, good sentence structure and accurate grammar, mechanics, and usage will likewise improve your letter's effectiveness. [*See* REVISING *in Part I.*]

Process

Writing a letter to the editor requires much the same process as developing an opinion paper. [*See* OPINION *later in Part II.*] In addition, because it may also try to convince the reader to agree with the opinion expressed, it follows a process similar to that for developing a persuasion paper. [*See* PERSUASION *later in Part II.*]

Using the following process, however, should help you develop a satisfactory letter.

PREWRITING

STEP 1. STATING YOUR OPINION

Before you attempt a letter to the editor, think about what you really want to say. Recognizing that a letter to the editor must be brief (no more than 300 words, preferably fewer), you should be able to put your main idea into a single sentence. If you cannot, then you may have the basis for more than one letter. Write your main idea now. Omit opening phrases like *this letter will serve to convince. . .* or *the purpose of this letter is to. . . .* Instead, state your opinion. Consider the following examples, and then write your own:

> The County Council should initiate action to merge city and county governments for the sake of economic stability.

> Local media have distorted the reasons for Fire Chief Daikerson's dismissal.

> The recent article entitled "Minding Your Own Business" omitted two potentially serious stumbling blocks for someone who is considering establishing his own business.

Compare your statement with the examples above. Does it follow a similar approach?

STEP 2. PLANNING THE SUPPORTING DETAILS

Planning the supporting details calls for two thought processes. First, with your statement of purpose in front of you, think about the examples, situations, illustrations, descriptions, comparisons, analogies, causes, or effects that will help you explain your point of view. Make a list of possibilities.

Next, think about the newspaper or magazine reader. What will attract the reader's attention? With what can the reader most easily identify? What message hits closest to home? Make a list of these ideas.

Finally, survey your two lists. How can they best fit together? If your audience identifies with the problem of unemployment, then what situation, illustration, or cause will best serve that identification?

Answering these questions will help you select supporting details.

Since the letter must be brief, select only those details which will most directly affect the reader. You may need no more than two or three details, certainly no more than four. (Remember the 300-word limit.)

STEP 3. ORGANIZING THE DETAILS

Choose a logical plan of organization. Here's how. First, see CHRONOLOGICAL ORDER, SPATIAL ORDER, and ORDERS OF IMPORTANCE in the Glossary so that you understand the general plans of organization.

Next, think about the many kinds of development available to you as a letter writer. [*See* DEVELOPMENT, METHODS OF *in the Glossary.*] Will your letter have a greater impact using one method of development over another? Will you offend the reader if you present certain ideas too early or late?

Third, think again about the audience analysis you completed in Step 2 above.

Now, using all that information, list the details in their most effective order. You may need to try several plans before you find a really effective one.

WRITING

STEP 4.   FOLLOWING THE PLAN

As you write, keep in mind the items listed in the Characteristics section above. Begin with some means of catching the reader's attention. Justify what you have to say.

Follow with a statement of your opinion and proceed with the supporting details as you organized them in Step 3 above. Remember to stick to the point and to avoid excess verbiage.

As part of the conclusion, suggest either a course of action, a solution to the problem, or a means by which to implement the solution.

REVISING

STEP 5.   POLISHING THE CONTENT

Getting your ideas on paper puts you over the hurdle. Now you can polish those ideas and put them in the best light for your reader. As you revise the content, ask yourself the following questions:

- Have I presented my opinion clearly? Will the reader understand exactly how I feel?

- Do I give enough examples, illustrations, situations, and other details? Will the details help the reader feel the same way? [*See* REVISING: SAMPLE REVISION FOR SPECIFIC DETAIL *in Part I.*]

- Would different details improve the explanation of my opinion?

- Have I been concise? Have I omitted repetitious or insignificant details? Have I avoided getting carried away by my emotions? [*See* REVISING: SAMPLE REVISION FOR WORDINESS *in Part I for ways to eliminate extra words.*]

- Are sentences polished, placing emphasis on the most important ideas? Are main ideas in the main clauses? [*See* REVISING: SAMPLE REVISION FOR SENTENCE VARIETY *in Part I.*]

- Have I used the techniques of emphasis? [*See* REVISING: SAMPLE REVISION FOR EMPHASIS *in Part I.*]

- Do transitions connect and show relationship among the ideas? Have I used the most effective transitions? [*See* REVISING: SAMPLE REVISION FOR TRANSITION *in Part I.*]

Revise as necessary so that you can answer "yes" to the questions above. [*See* REVISING *in Part I for additional, more general guidelines for polishing.*]

STEP 6.   TYPING THE FINAL DRAFT

Next, type a final copy of your letter. In order to prepare the inside address, find the editor's name on the editorial page. If you cannot find it, call the paper.

You may use a typical business-letter format [*see* BUSINESS LETTERS, *above*], or, as some editors prefer, you may type your letter on a single standard 8–1/2" × 11" sheet of paper, double spaced, maintaining standard margins. Although this format permits you to omit a formal heading and inside address, you should begin with the salutation *Dear Editor* to identify your purpose. In addition, your name and address must appear on the page, preferably at the end. Most papers will not print your address or phone number, but the editor must have this information for verification. Remember, too, that newspapers rarely print anonymous letters.

PROOFREADING

STEP 7. CHECKING THE MECHANICS

Before you mail your letter to the editor, check carefully for the mechanical details. [*Check Part I and the Glossary for explanations and examples of writing techniques*]. Finally, check the letter carefully for spelling and word choice. Check *Webster's New World Dictionary* for spelling accuracy. Then refer to *Webster's New World Thesaurus* for precise word choice.

If you used a business-letter format, ask yourself the following specific questions regarding the form of the letter:

- Have I included an accurate and complete heading, including today's date, properly punctuated?

- Have I included an accurate and complete inside address, including the editor's name and title, all properly punctuated?

- Did I use an appropriate salutation followed by a semicolon?

- Is the spacing accurate between the heading and the inside address, between the inside address and the salutation, and between the salutation and the body of the letter?

- Is the closing appropriate for a letter to the editor?

- Have I signed the letter?

- Have I included my daytime phone number?

- Is the spacing accurate between the body of the letter and the closing and between the closing and the signature?

- Have I followed a consistent style, either the block, the modified-block, or the modified-block style with indented paragraphs?

- Is my letter neat and businesslike?

If you used the less formal format, ask yourself these questions:

- Did I begin with the salutation *Dear Editor* to identify my purpose?

- Have I limited my letter to a single page?

- Did I maintain standard margins (2" at the top, 1–1/2" at the left, and 1" at the right and at the bottom)?

- Is my letter double-spaced, neat, and free from typing or printing errors?

- Does my name appear on the page, preferably at the bottom, along with my address and day-time phone number?

You should be able to answer "yes" to these questions.

When you are satisified the letter is the most effective you can write, fold it, and mail it in a properly addressed envelope. [*See Step 7 in* BUSINESS LETTERS, *above, for instructions.*]

Sample Editorial Letter

The following letter to the editor expresses the writer's opinion regarding an upcoming congressional election. Compare the letter below with the persuasive essay [*see* PERSUASION *later in Part II*] and the opinion essay [*see* OPINION *also later in Part II*], both of which deal with the same subject. By comparing the three, you can better recognize their similarities and differences.

3456 Georgetown Road
Salt River, Kansas 77068-6695
October 23, 1988

Mrs. Pauletta Henry, Editor
The Salt River Journal and Times
100 Second Street
Salt River, Kansas 77069-6851

Dear Editor:

Shall we increase property taxes? Ignore drug pushers? Elect a "yes" man to Congress? To answer "no" is to vote for Jerrald Kinsingtonne. Here's why.

When Republican incumbent Rodney Brolliette fought for tax incentives to lure businesses here, he ignored Kinsingtonne's warning that private citizens would pay with increased property taxes. Now, strapped with tax bills double last year's rate, citizens know whom to support.

Both candidates oppose illegal drug use. Brolliette proposes unannounced testing. Let's pretend for a minute. You go to work one morning and discover you must submit to a test. You had the flu two weeks ago; the doctor prescribed medicine. You took it. As directed. Now, you test positive. You're a drug user. Period. Kinsingtonne proposes instead a stiff crackdown on dealers: more arrests, stiffer penalities. Should you be harrassed for others' wrongdoings? Kinsingtonne doesn't think so either.

In the controversy over a proposed hazardous-waste incinerator here, Kinsingtonne took an early stand to fight the plan, even before a majority joined him. Finally, Brolliette announced "me too" opposition. Too little, too late. Kinsingtonne risks what he must for what is right. And he does it now.

So there's little question of how to vote next Tuesday. Think about a "yes" man in Congress. Think about harassment over drug testing. Think about your tax bill. See what I mean?

Yours truly,

Norman K. Blackwade

Norman K. Blackwade

Analysis of the Sample Editorial Letter

The sample above exhibits the characteristics of a good letter to the editor. Note particularly the following items:

- The letter consistently follows the modified-block style and exhibits good format—even margins; accurate spacing; and complete and accurate heading, inside address, salutation, body, closing, and signature.

- The body of the letter clearly presents the writer's opinion.

- The opening paragraph catches the reader's attention. Anyone is interested in his pocketbook, and taxes hit the pocketbook. Most people feel frustrated about excessive illegal drug use. And the idea of a yes-man does not please many. So the writer uses these three approaches to attract readers.

- The opening paragraph also states the writer's point of view.

- The following three paragraphs present details to support the writer's opinion, each paragraph providing illustrations and examples to explain one point.

- The paragraphs eliminate all wordiness. [*To see how to achieve brevity, see* REVISING: SAMPLE REVISION FOR WORDINESS *in Part I.*]

- By the final paragraph, the reader may agree with the writer, but the writer forces him or her to think once again about three major issues. The writer reverses the order so that he concludes with the issues closest to home—the tax bill.

Compare this letter with the SAMPLE FOR SOCIAL SCIENCES in PERSUASION in Part II, and with the sample paper in OPINION, in Part II. Note that the editorial letter blends many of the characteristics of the two. At the same time, however, note these differences:

- While the writer chose a relatively formal style for the persuasive and the opinion essays, he uses an informal style for the letter to the editor. Note the use of *you*, the frequent contractions, and the sentence fragments (like *Period.* and *Too little, too late.*)

- Note that the letter omits many of the supporting details used in the persuasive and opinion essays. It includes only the most important details. Brevity, remember, characterizes a letter to the editor.

- In addition, the arrangement of details varies from that in the two essays. The letter discusses taxes first, in case the reader fails to finish the letter. Most people put their pocketbooks before the environment and illegal-drug use. Tax bills hit home!

- The letter relies on personal reaction. In the third paragraph, for instance, the writer directs the reader's attention to his or her own situation if Brolliette's proposal were approved. By putting the reader in a specific situation, an uncomfortable situation at that, the writer better illustrates his point.

With these points in mind, you should be able to write an effective letter to an editor. When you finish, check your letter against the questions in the Revision and Proofreading sections and then compare it with the sample and its analysis above. Then mail it!

You should heed, however, one final warning. Since letters to the editor may appear in print as soon as a few days or as late as six weeks after you send it, you may choose to recall your letter if it no longer deals with current events. If such a situation occurs, you may simply call the editor and ask that the letter be destroyed. Let's hope your letter sees print before that time!

SOCIAL LETTERS

Social letters, sometimes called *friendly letters*, bear little resemblance to business or editorial letters. Most omit a heading and include only the date. Friendly letters do not include an inside address. The salutation usually addresses the reader by first name, and the closing suggests personal relationships. Social letters are rarely typed, although busy people who rely on word processors are likely to type them, insisting that a letter via a word processor is better than no letter at all!

Apart from format and style, the content of a social letter also bears little resemblance to business or editorial letters. In general, a social letter will serve one of the following purposes:

- to correspond with a friend or relative in lieu of a personal conversation,
- to thank someone for a gift, entertainment, or other kindness,
- to congratulate someone for an achievement,
- to offer condolences,
- to extend an invitation,
- to accept or decline an invitation.

The social letter, considerably less structured than most other forms of writing, usually follows the writer's whims. As a result, the social or personal letter is just that—personal.

Characteristics

Although the social letter is less structured than other letters, certain characteristics will usually be evident. Most social letters

- include a heading unless the receiver knows you so well that he does not need to be reminded of your return address,
- include a date, usually for later reference (sometimes friends keep personal letters for years!),
- use an appropriate, friendly salutation followed by a comma,
- follow an informal style, like written conversation, unless the subject of the letter, like an invitation to a rather formal affair or an expression of condolence, requires a somewhat more formal style,
- use an appropriate, friendly closing, followed by a comma,
- include a signature line but no typewritten name, even if the letter for some reason is typewritten or produced on a printer,
- follow the same style on the envelope as in the letter, either handwritten or typewritten.

Process

The process of writing a social letter follows a more relaxed approach than virtually any other piece of writing.

PREWRITING

STEP 1.   GETTING READY TO WRITE

If you are writing a friendly letter just to keep up-to-date with friends and family, you may want to jot down a list of items you want to be sure to mention. This will keep you from forgetting some detail you wanted to share.

If you are writing a thank-you note, a note of condolence, or an expression of congratulations, you probably have only brief comments and need nothing more than to try a couple of drafts until the note sounds just the way you want.

If you are writing an invitation, put the vital information in a list to make sure you do not omit any essential details: date, time, place, purpose, dress, and an R.S.V.P. if necessary. (*R.S.V.P.* is an abbreviation for the French *répondez s'il vous plaît*, which means *please respond*. Such a notation on invitations requires recipients to let you know whether or not they will attend, thus enabling you to make appropriate preparations.)

WRITING

STEP 2.   PUTTING YOUR THOUGHTS ON PAPER

With no more effort than we have suggested above, you will probably be ready to write. Since friendly letters usually reflect your personality, you should write from the heart. While some general organization will help your friends and family follow your thoughts, you need not depend on outlines or formal paragraph structure. Do use good grammar. Do write effective sentences. Do make your letter interesting. Do use accu-

rate spelling and mechanics. Do follow good usage. At the same time, however, aim for a conversational style, as if you were talking face to face with your reader.

REVISING AND PROOFREADING

STEP 3.   CHECKING THE LETTER

Before you mail a social letter, do what you would do with any piece of writing: check it over. Sometimes we omit words or word endings; sometimes we misspell words; sometimes a sentence does not sound the way we thought it would when we wrote it. Check for these kinds of problems. Sometimes the reader is offended by a written remark that you intended as humor. Sometimes the reader may misinterpret your intentions by the way you word a sentence. Try reading the letter aloud to yourself to catch any possible problems.

When you are satisfied with the letter, fold it, put it in a properly addressed envelope, and mail it! [*See Step 7 in* BUSINESS LETTERS, *above for instructions.*]

Sample Social Letter

The following social letter, an invitation to an outdoor cookout, illustrates one of several kinds of social letters.

1010 Meadowbrook Lane
St. Philips, MN 58761-3313
July 8, 1988

Dear Gretchen,

    Before these delightful summer evenings grow short, Bob and I are looking forward to an outdoor picnic with a group of our dearest friends— you, of course, among them! On Saturday, July 23, we hope you'll join us for an old-fashioned barbecue at our home, with appetizers at 5:00 and dinner at 6:30. Dress casually, since we'll be on the lawn. And maybe a sweater, in case the evening breeze grows cool.

    Please let us know we can expect you!

Love,
Linda

Analysis of the Sample Social Letter

The social letter above, in the form of an invitation, includes the essential details: time, date, place, purpose, dress, and a request for a response. Note that the style maintains a friendly, informal air, including a sentence fragment (*And maybe a sweater. . . .*). Note the heading but the absence of an inside address. The salutation greets the addressee by her first name. The closing expresses a personal relationship; and the signature, first name only, indicates a close friendship.

The information above on business, editorial, and social letters should help you not only to understand the differences among the letters but to develop satisfactorily your own letters for whatever purpose you may face.

LITERARY ANALYSES

Students are asked to write literary analyses most often in literature classes. The assignment may require a critical overview of the author, an analysis of specific literary elements; or a well-organized evaluation of a specific literary work, such as a novel, short story, drama, poem, or nonfiction article or essay. No matter its purpose, an effective analysis of any piece of literature must demonstrate thorough understanding of the literary work under discussion.

Writers face three kinds of analyses—of an author, literary elements, or specific works. Within those three, however, the options vary significantly. For instance, the writer may discuss a specific poem in terms of the author's characteristic use of literary devices, thus combining the three general kinds of analyses into a single specific analysis. Likewise, a writer may develop a thorough analysis of a short story merely by discussing its theme. As we work through the octopus-like literary analysis, then, we will examine the primary characteristics and some variations found in typical analyses. The examples included vary from single-paragraph analyses suitable for response on an essay test [*see also* ESSAY-QUESTION RESPONSES *in Part II*] to a longer paper suitable for a major assignment. To help you better understand the various kinds of analyses, most of the samples deal with Emily Dickinson and her work. Sample literary analyses for the short story and the novel by necessity deal with alternate authors. In addition, a full-length paper included in the literary elements section deals with recurring imagery in *Moby Dick*. The accompanying evaluation of each analysis helps put it in perspective with the other examples.

FOR AN AUTHOR

The analysis of an author presumes familiarity with an author's work; thus, it is probably the most demanding of all the types of literary analyses. While an author analysis may require formidable research, a student can write an intelligent paper by considerably narrowing the topic. For instance, by dealing with one or more short representative works, a writer can develop a logical, well-supported analysis illustrating an author's typical theme. Likewise, by treating an atypical work a writer can develop a logical, well-supported analysis showing how that work differs from the author's usual style or subject matter.

Following are the general characteristics for a literary analysis for an author.

Characteristics

While certain of the following characteristics are peculiar to an analysis for an author, others are more general characteristics and should be included in most any literary analysis. Compare them with other types of literary analyses discussed later. A good literary analysis of an author should

- show evidence of a broad understanding of an author's work, including style and general themes,

- include a topic or thesis sentence narrow enough to develop fully within the scope of the paper [*see* TOPIC SENTENCE *and* THESIS SENTENCE *in the Glossary for quick reference, and see* PARAGRAPHS *and* THEME *in Part II for detailed explanation and examples*],

- include details from specific works to support general statements in the topic or thesis sentence,

- enclose all direct quotations in quotation marks,

- paraphrase long passages when citing from the author's works [*see* PARAPHRASE *later in Part II*],

- show evidence of research, including documentation, particularly in a long or complicated paper [*see* RESEARCH PAPER *in Part II for information on footnoting and on bibliography entries*],

- follow a rather formal writing style, including the use of third-person point of view [*see* POINT OF VIEW *in the Glossary*],

- use the present tense to discuss the work but the past tense to discuss the background,

- conclude with a general statement about the author supported by the content of the paper [*see* CONCLUSION *in the Glossary*].

Process

Use the following process to develop a literary analysis of an author.

PREWRITING

STEP 1.   READING THE AUTHOR

In order to write an analysis, the primary—and forever ongoing—demand is for a careful reading and thorough understanding of the author's work. If you have not read all of it, then be certain that you have read at least all representative works. In many cases, more than one reading may be necessary.

STEP 2.   DOING NECESSARY RESEARCH

A lengthy paper may call for not only your own analysis but that of others. Be sure you understand what is expected of you. If research is part of the job, be thorough in your examination of others' evaluations. Your paper could, in fact, analyze contrasting reactions to the author.

[*If you must do research, see* RESEARCH PAPER *later in Part II for an explanation of the research process, particularly note-taking and documentation. In addition, see* PARAPHRASE, PRECIS, *and*

Notes, Kinds: For a Paper *later in Part II.*]

STEP 3. NARROWING THE SUBJECT

Writing a literary analysis of an author requires a thoughtful decision about narrowing the subject. You cannot say everything there is to say about any author in a short paper. So, you must decide which topics to include and which to omit from the discussion. Your purpose determines your decision. Clearly, if the purpose of the analysis is to discuss the author's favorite literary devices, the devices must be part of the analysis. Your purpose dictates as much. On the other hand, if you propose your own interpretation of the author's work which other writers have neither mentioned nor discussed, then you will limit your discussion to evidence supporting your unique position.

No matter the purpose, the analysis can deal with only as many aspects of the author as space permits. You have to decide how much evidence will be necessary to support each idea. As a result, any analysis must deal with only a limited subject, always leaving other ideas unstated and unexplored. Make no effort to include everything you know about an author. Resist the temptation to include unusual details just for the sake of interest.

Jot down now the main idea you want to develop in your paragraph or paper. Then, think through the main idea. Which three or four supporting ideas will explain, clarify, or illustrate your main idea? List those three or four ideas.

STEP 4. WRITING THE TOPIC OR THESIS SENTENCE

A carefully worded topic or thesis sentence must—absolutely must—clarify the direction and purpose of the paper. In Step 3 above you narrowed your subject, wrote a main idea, and listed three or four supporting ideas. Now, using this information, develop a topic or thesis sentence. [*See* TOPIC SENTENCE *in the Glossary for quick reference, or see* PARAGRAPHS *in Part II for a careful explanation and examples of the topic sentence. See* THESIS SENTENCE *in the Glossary for quick reference, or see* THEME *in Part II for a careful explanation and examples of the thesis sentence.*]

Compare your topic or thesis sentence with the examples below:

Topic sentences:
Neil Simon's light-hearted one-liners make his plays box-office successes.
(A series of examples from a half dozen successful plays will support the topic sentence.)

Alvin Toffler predicts a future worth fearing. (Examples from *Future Shock* and *The Third Wave* will show fearful futures.)

Thesis sentences:
Susan Howatch attracted contemporary readers with three books exhibiting her prowess as a Gothic novelist. (Each of the three body paragraphs will illustrate the Gothic characteristics of separate Howatch books:

Penmarric, Sins of the Fathers, and *The Rich Are Different.*)

Herman Wouk uses his understanding of the phenomenon of war to build exceedingly long, complex, and poignant novels. (Two supporting paragraphs will deal with the complexity and poignancy of *The Winds of War* and *War and Remembrance.*)

STEP 5.   CHOOSING A METHOD OF DEVELOPMENT

A literary analysis may be developed by a variety of methods, including comparison and contrast, cause and effect, and opinion. [*See separate entries for each in Part II.*] Parts of the paper may also include definition, description, and analogy. [*See also separate entries for each in Part II.*] Think about the possible ways by which you can develop your topic or thesis sentence.

For instance, if you plan to show how events in an author's life influenced her to write certain novels, then a cause and effect development may be the most useful. If you plan to explain your admiration for an author's style, then an opinion paper may best serve your purpose.

Select the method which seems best for your purpose.

STEP 6.   ORGANIZING THE PAPER

With the topic or thesis sentence in front of you, you should have little difficulty developing a plan for the paragraph or paper. Organize the list of details developed in Step 3

above. Use chronological order or some order of importance. [*See* CHRONOLOGICAL ORDER *and* ORDERS OF IMPORTANCE *in the Glossary.*]

If you are developing a longer paper, list two, three, or four supporting ideas under each of the main ideas. For all practical purposes, you have developed a scratch outline. [*See* OUTLINES *elsewhere in Part II.*] Your outline should give a miniature view of your completed paper.

WRITING

STEP 7.   FOLLOWING THE PLAN

The careful planning you have done in Steps 1–6 will pay off now with relative ease in writing. Begin with your introductory statement and topic or thesis sentence. Develop your ideas in accord with your outline, changing the outline as needed if the order seems faulty. As you write, try to include the following:

- specific supporting details from the work itself, either quoted word for word and enclosed in quotation marks [*see* QUOTATION MARKS *in the Glossary*] or paraphrased [*see* PARAPHRASE *in Part II*],

- transitions to bridge ideas and paragraphs [*see* TRANSITIONS *in the Glossary*].

In addition, as you write, be sure to avoid the following potential pitfalls:

- giving a mere summary of the plot rather than a discussion of your ideas,

- quoting the author's works without accurate use of quotation marks,

- using glittering generalities—words, phrases, or whole sentences—without the support of examples or details.

Finally, add a conclusion that effectively ties together your main ideas with a clincher (in a paragraph) or a concluding paragraph (in a longer paper). [*For additional help with conclusions, see* PARAGRAPHS *or* THEME *in Part II.*]

REVISING

STEP 8. POLISHING THE CONTENT

If you have followed the suggestions above, your first draft will be in reasonably good shape. Take time now to review the items in Step 7, checking to see that you have indeed heeded their advice.

When you feel satisfied, ask yourself the following questions to check for other areas of possible weakness:

- Have I used good sentence structure? [*See* SENTENCE STRUCTURE *in the Glossary.*]

- Does the structure emphasize main ideas? [*See* REVISING: SAMPLE REVISION FOR EMPHASIS *in Part I.*]

- Is the structure varied? [*See* REVISING: SAMPLE REVISION FOR SENTENCE VARIETY *in Part I.*]

- Have I maintained a consistent third-person point of view?

- Have I used the present tense to discuss the author's work and the past tense to describe the author's background?

- Have I used specific rather than general words and phrases? [*See* REVISING: SAMPLE REVISION FOR SPECIFIC DETAIL *in Part I.*]

- Have I avoided plagiarism by using quotation marks around words not my own? [*See* PLAGIARISM *in the Glossary.*]

- Have I eliminated any materials which do not support my main idea? [*See* REVISING: SAMPLE REVISION FOR UNITY *in Part I.*]

- Have I included adequate transitions to provide coherence between sentences and paragraphs? [*See* REVISING: SAMPLE REVISION FOR TRANSITION *in Part I.*]

Finally, see REVISING in Part I for further questions which will suggest additional areas for possible revision.

Revise the content of your first draft so that it reads smoothly and follows good writing style.

PROOFREADING

STEP 9. CHECKING THE MECHANICAL DETAILS

When you have the content molded into a solid, well-developed composition, make a final check for the mechanical details. Be particularly careful in checking quotations or references from outside sources. Check not only for accuracy in quotations and in their punctuation, but also for accuracy in documentation. [*See* RESEARCH PAPER *in Part II for additional information.*]

Then check for accurate spelling and word choice by referring to *Webster's New World Dictionary* and *Webster's New World Thesaurus*. Make a final accurate copy of your work.

─────── **Sample Literary Analysis for an Author** ───────

The following sample paper uses three representative poems to discuss the characteristic style of poet Emily Dickinson.

Alone in a Crowded World:

Emily Dickinson and Her Poems

Emily Dickinson lived a solitary life, maintaining little communication with people and the outside world. In fact, she preferred nature and the Deity over people and things of this earth, so the extensive travels to which her poems refer took place only in her mind. Three representative poems indicate how Dickinson related her lonely life in her work.

Her solitary life reflects a personal choice. "This is my letter to the World/ That never wrote to Me," Dickinson writes while expressing her resentment toward society. The only "person" who truly understands her, Dickinson says, is Mother Nature. Although Dickinson admits she cannot see the actual person, she nevertheless remains convinced that Mother Nature is real and sincerely cares for her children, Dickinson concluded. As a result, the poet sees little need to communicate with the less faithful outside world.

Perhaps because of her identification with Mother Nature, Dickinson also expresses a fondness for nature and the supernatural. She admits preferring to be alone with the birds and the trees in her garden to attending a gala event with hundreds of people. As part of her belief in the supernatural, however, she faces the reality of death and often wonders what follows. While she admits that she has never spoken with God, she believes she is assured of a place in Heaven. In "This World Is not Conclusion" she states, "A Species stands beyond-/ Invisible, as Music-/ But positive, as Sound." Throughout the poem, Miss Dickinson talks about the attempts man has made through the years to explain the metaphysical and how he has failed, so in this manner she affirms her belief in nature and the supernatural.

Because she maintained a solitary life, however, she used her imagination to explore the outside world. In the poem "I Never Saw a Moor," Dickinson embarks on a mental journey admitting that while she has never seen many places, she knows "how Heather looks/ And what a Billow be," referring to the moors and the seashores of England. Her solitary life, then, did not close her mind to the outside world, no matter how sadly it reflected itself to her. An avid reader, Dickinson no doubt traveled through her books as well as through her obviously active mind.

Poems such as these give us a clear picture of Emily Dickinson's beliefs, choices, and lifestyle. Dickinson, who preferred to see no adults other than her own family, expressed her characteristic attitudes in her poetry: her reciprocal love of Mother Nature, her corresponding belief in the supernatural, and her delight in mental voyages. While the people of her era described her as eccentric, unethical, even rebellious, she has proved to be one of the greatest poets of all time.

Analysis of the Sample Literary Analysis for an Author

The five-paragraph theme above illustrates one kind of literary analysis, that using representative works to discuss the author. The three poems, each addressed in a separate paragraph, serve to introduce the author. Note these specific characteristics:

- The first paragraph introduces the three ideas developed successively in the following paragraphs. The final sentence of the first paragraph functions as the thesis sentence. The reference to *three poems*, as yet unnamed, suggests the means by which the ideas of solitary life, respect for nature and the spiritual, and the mental travel will be developed.

- Quotations from the three poems, enclosed in quotation marks, support the writer's main ideas.

- The slash or diagonal mark (/) shows where lines of poetry end.

- References to other ideas in the poems, paraphrased rather than quoted, further support the main ideas.

- The organization of the body, in order of importance from most to least important, follows the order set out in the introduction.
- While the first paragraph, discussing Dickinson's life, is written in the past tense, paragraphs discussing her works are in the present tense. Since the works still exist but Dickinson does not, the change in tense is logical.
- Likewise, the fourth paragraph begins and ends in the past tense, discussing her life, while the middle uses the present tense, discussing her work as it continues to exist.
- The conclusion, like the introduction, uses past tense to reflect on Dickinson's life.
- Sentence variety, both in structure and length, credits the writer with good style.
- Transitions link sentences as well as paragraphs into a smoothly flowing composition.

In general, then, the five-paragraph literary analysis above serves as a reasonable example of an analysis of an author. Compare the paper with others in the section for a thorough overview of writing about literature.

FOR LITERARY ELEMENTS

An analysis for literary elements explores or evaluates a technical aspect of a literary work. Probably the most common approach to writing about literature, the analysis of a literary element thoroughly examines some literary device that helps weld together the mosaic of the entire work. Common elements include the following:

- characterization
- setting
- plot
- theme
- dialogue
- point of view
- rhythm
- rhyme

- imagery
- figures of speech
- symbol
- tone
- mood

While the analysis of literary elements can deal with a wide variety of subjects, a paper on any technical subject should include certain characteristics.

Characteristics

Below are two lists of characteristics. One shows elements included in virtually any analysis of literary elements. The other shows elements included in the specific topics. A combination of the lists will give a thorough description of the respective approaches to this kind of analysis.

First, any analysis of literary elements should

- show a thorough understanding of the work as it gains meaning from the literary element(s),
- include an introduction naming the work and its author,
- include a topic or thesis sentence specifically stating the literary element to be discussed and at least an implied approach by which that

discussion will be developed [*see* TOPIC SENTENCE *and* THESIS SENTENCE *in the Glossary for a quick reference, and see* PARAGRAPHS *and* THEME *in Part II for a detailed explanation and examples*],

- follow a clear plan,
- include specific details from the work, either quoted [*see* QUOTATION MARKS *in the Glossary*] or paraphrased [*see* PARAPHRASE *later in Part II*],
- show how the literary element enhances meaning,
- document any references to outside sources,
- interpret the literary work through the examination of the literary element(s),
- follow a rather formal writing style, including the use of the third-person point of view,

- use the present tense to discuss the work but the past tense to discuss the background,
- conclude with a reaction to the literary device as it expands the work's meaning.

Specific characteristics for compositions dealing with the various literary devices include the following:

For Character

- an analysis of what the character says, thinks, and does, pointing out any discrepancies,
- an analysis of what others say about the character,
- an analysis of any differences between what the reader observes of the character and what others say about him or her,
- an evaluation of any direct description by the author about the character,
- a statement of position as protagonist or antagonist [*see* PROTAGONIST *and* ANTAGONIST *in the Glossary.*]

For Setting

- an evaluation of the relationship of setting to the work's mood [*see* MOOD *in the Glossary*],
- an evaluation of the setting as it reflects the work's theme [*see* THEME *in the Glossary*],
- an evaluation of the setting's impact on the characters,
- an analysis of the impact the setting has on the conflict [*see* CONFLICT *in the Glossary*],

- an explanation of change in setting as it affects change in mood, characters, or conflict.

For Plot

- an analysis of the exposition, or beginning, of the story, drama, or novel,
- an evaluation of the rising action [*see* RISING ACTION *in the Glossary*],
- an analysis of the climax, or high point [*see* CLIMAX *in the Glossary*],
- an analysis of the falling action [*see* FALLING ACTION *in the Glossary*],
- examination of special techniques of plot, like foreshadowing and flashback [*see the Glossary entries for* FORESHADOWING *and* FLASHBACK].

For Theme

- a statement of the major idea or theme of the story, drama, or novel,
- an analysis of evidence supporting the theme.

For Dialogue

- a description of the dialogue's purpose,
- an analysis of its appropriateness, considering word choice, sentence length, and cadence,
- an analysis of its impact on characterization [*refer to the section of this list* FOR CHARACTER *above*],
- an analysis of its impact on the plot [*refer to the section of this list* FOR PLOT *above*].

For Point Of View

- a description of the point of view: first, second, or third person, including the third person omniscient [*see* POINT OF VIEW *in the Glossary*],

- an analysis of the impact of the point of view on theme, plot, conflict, or characterization.

For Rhythm

- a description of the rhythm's pattern [*see* RHYTHM *in the Glossary*],

- an analysis of the impact of any departure from the pattern,

- an evaluation of the impact of rhythm on word or thought groups.

- an evaluation of rhythm as one of the many sound devices available to a poet, including its interaction with the other devices to create an overall impact.

For Rhyme

- a description of the pattern, including internal rhyme if any [*see* RHYME *in the Glossary*],

- an analysis of the impact of any departure from the pattern,

- an evaluation of the impact of rhyme on word or thought groups,

- an evaluation of rhyme as one of the many sound devices available to a poet, including its interaction with the other devices to create an overall impact.

For Imagery

- an indication of the specific image or images being analyzed [*see* IMAGERY *in the Glossary*],

- an explanation of the development of the image or images throughout the work,

- an analysis of the importance of the image or images to the meaning or enjoyment of the work,

- an evaluation of the interrelationship between the image or images and other literary elements.

For Figures Of Speech

- an indication of the specific figure(s) of speech being analyzed [*see* FIGURES OF SPEECH *in the Glossary for a list and examples of the most common figures of speech*],

- an explanation of the use of the figure(s) of speech throughout the work,

- an analysis of the importance of the figure(s) of speech to the meaning or enjoyment of the work,

- an evaluation of the interrelationship between the figure(s) of speech and other literary elements.

For Symbolism

- a careful explanation of the development of the symbol [*see* SYMBOL *in the Glossary*],

- a symbolic interpretation of the work, including citations of specific instances throughout the work,

- an evaluation of the overall impact of the symbol on the work's theme or underlying message.

For Tone

- a description of tone as it appears throughout the work or within a specified section of the work [*see* TONE *in the Glossary*],
- an analysis of how the author achieved this tone,
- an explanation of the impact of the tone on the work's theme.

For Mood

- a description of mood as it appears throughout the work or within a specified section of the work [*see* MOOD *in the Glossary*],
- an analysis of how the author achieved this mood,
- an explanation of the impact of the mood on the work's theme.

Process

Use the following process to develop an analysis of a particular literary element within a work.

PREWRITING

STEP 1. READING FOR ANALYSIS

With any literary analysis, careful reading precedes any other activity. Once you decide which of the many elements you will discuss in a given work, whether as a result of an assignment or personal preference, reread the work searching for exam-

ples. Study the element's relationship to other parts of the work and its impact on the work.

As you reread, make notes. If you are using your own copy of the book, you may wish to pencil in notations of important words, phrases, passages. If you are using a copy not your own, take notes on note cards, separate sheets, or gummed note sheets that can later be removed from the page without marring the print. [*See* NOTES, KINDS: FOR A PAPER *in Part II.*]

STEP 2. NARROWING THE TOPIC

When your careful reading is finished, you are ready to narrow the focus of your paper. If, for instance, you want to write about the setting of a short story, you must decide what you will develop as your main idea. Will you discuss how it enhances the theme, how it puts hardships on the characters, how it suggests the mood? Or if you want to write about an important image in a poem, will you discuss how the author develops it, the effect it has on the poem's meaning, what it means?

Narrowing the topic to a specific focus comes most easily by looking for repeated ideas in your notes from Step 1 above. The focus must lend itself to thorough development within the limits of your paper and deal with some important aspect of the work.

Determine the direction your topic will take. Write a sentence or two stating the focus. For example:

Emily Dickinson's biographer said she domesticated the universe. Her images make the spiritual world as familiar as household items.

STEP 3.   PLANNING THE PAPER

Having determined the direction of your paper, make a list of examples from the work that will support that topic. Use the notes you developed in Step 1 above. Your list may look something like this:

Dickinson's domestic images:
"housewife" items
broom
dusting
sewing items—thread, ravelings, etc.
apron
scattered duds
sweeping

Then, with a list that includes the supporting details you plan to use, organize the items in some logical manner. The organization may show relationships, cause and effect, comparisons or contrasts, or opinion. [*See* CAUSE AND EFFECT, COMPARISON AND CONTRAST, *or* OPINION *in Part II.*] Or you may arrange the items by some order of importance or perhaps by the chronological order of the appearance in the literary work. [*See* CHRONOLOGICAL ORDER *and* ORDERS OF IMPORTANCE *in the Glossary.*]

When completed, the organized list may look something like this one:

Dickinson's Domestic Images:
  A. Housewife chores
    1. Sweeping
    2. Dusting
  B. Seamstress items
    1. Thread
    2. Ravelings
    3. Duds

The organization in the outline above follows the chronological organization of the poem from which the examples come. Note that some items from the original list have been reworded or even omitted. You may need to make similar changes in your own list. [*For further examples, see* OUTLINES, KINDS: FOR A PAPER *in Part II.*]

POSSIBLE PITFALL: Because the student's most frequent error in writing any kind of literary analysis is summarizing plots instead of analyzing, be absolutely certain you develop a plan similar to the one above. Then *follow it!* So doing will prevent your falling into the common trap.

STEP 4.   CHECKING OTHER SOURCES

If your assignment demands outside research, use the plan developed above to guide your reading. It is quite possible, however, that you need not do research other than that with the literary work itself. Follow your instructor's suggestions.

If you do outside research, take careful notes, making sure to include quotation marks around an author's exact words. When you transfer this material to your own paper, you must be able to document accurately in order to avoid plagiarism. [*See* RE-

SEARCH PAPER *in Part II for a complete discussion of note-taking, quotations, and documentation. See also* NOTES, KINDS: FOR A PAPER, PRECIS, *and* PARAPHRASE *in Part II for help with note-taking.*]

WRITING

STEP 5.   FOLLOWING THE PLAN

Write the first draft by following the plan you completed in Step 3 above. Begin with an introductory statement or an introductory paragraph, depending on whether you are writing a paragraph or a full-length paper. [*See* PARAGRAPHS *and* THEME *elsewhere in Part II.*] Include in the introductory segment the following specifics:

- title of the work,

- author's name,

- specific literary element to be discussed,

- perhaps an indication of that element's importance in the overall work.

Follow the introductory segment with your topic or thesis statement.

Develop the subtopics or the body paragraphs, following the plan established in Step 3 or revising the plan as necessary. Try to include the following kinds of details:

- sufficient examples to clarify your ideas,

- specific supporting details from the work, either quoted or paraphrased,

- transitions from one supporting idea to another and from one main idea to another,

- transitions that help your reader follow your organization and the relationships among your ideas. [*See* TRANSITIONS *in the Glossary.*]

Finally, add a conclusion that refers to your topic or thesis statement and makes some general statement about the literary element as it lends importance to the work.

REVISING

STEP 6.   IMPROVING THE CONTENT

As you read your first draft, you should be able to spot areas that can be strengthened. Try asking yourself the following questions:

- Is the introduction effective and complete?

- Is the plan clear?

- Are transitions adequate and effective? [*See* REVISING: SAMPLE REVISION FOR TRANSITION *in Part I.*]

- Have I developed paragraphs adequately with sufficient supporting details, including specific details from the work, either quoted or paraphrased? [*See* REVISING: SAMPLE REVISION FOR SPECIFIC DETAIL *in Part I.*]

- Have I avoided plagiarism by using quotation marks around words not my own and documenting accurately? [*See* PLAGIARISM *in the Glossary.*]

- Do the main ideas work together to say something about the literary element as it affects the entire work?

- Have I avoided retelling the story?

- Have I maintained a rather formal writing style, using the third-person point of view and accurate verb tense?

- Is the vocabulary, including appropriate literary terms, accurate?

- Are my sentences varied both in length and in structure? [*See* REVISING: SAMPLE REVISION FOR SENTENCE VARIETY *in Part I.*]

- Do my sentences carry the most effective emphasis for their respective subjects? Are the main ideas in the main clauses? [*See* REVISING: SAMPLE REVISION FOR EMPHASIS *in Part I.*]

- Does the conclusion refer to the topic or thesis sentence and at the same time make a general statement about the effect of the specific literary element on the work as a whole? [*See* CONCLUSION *in the Glossary.*]

Determine areas of weakness and make the necessary revisions. You may need to make several revisions before you have a paper which satisfies all the suggestions above.

[*In addition, see* REVISING *in Part I for further questions which will suggest other areas for possible revision.*]

PROOFREADING

STEP 7.   CHECKING DETAILS

As you read your final draft, check for details of grammar, mechanics, and usage. Consult the Glossary for explanations and examples that will help you solve writing problems.

Finally, check spelling and word choice. Consult *Webster's New World Dictionary* and *Webster's New World Thesaurus* for reference.

A Note about the Samples: Now that you know what an analysis of a literary element should include and what process you should follow in order to develop an effective analysis, study the three following examples and their respective analyses. The first sample traces the images in a Dickinson poem, the second analyzes the characters of a short story, and the third, a full-length paper, examines the development of a single symbol in a novel. By comparing these and other sample papers throughout this section, you will better understand the various kinds of analyses.

Sample Literary Analysis for an Image

The following single-paragraph analysis of an image in a poem illustrates the characteristics of an analysis of a literary element. Compare this example with a three-paragraph analysis of the same poem in the sample for literary works.

Mother Nature Domesticated

Emily Dickinson's poem "She Sweeps with Many-Colored Brooms" works well because of a predominant image. An extended metaphor, which is sustained throughout the poem, generates the domestic image. Because Emily Dickinson lived as a recluse and because she felt Mother Nature was her only real friend, many of her images domesticate Mother Nature in a manner that makes the spiritual familiar. In "She Sweeps" Dickinson uses common household images to describe Mother Nature creating a sunset. The apron-clad housewife sweeps but forgets to dust. A careless sweeper, she "leaves the shreds behind." She also leaves scattered duds and threads and ravelings from her sewing strewn across the eastern sky. The clouds, which she sees as flying aprons, stay until the "brooms fade softly into stars." By using the sweeping-dusting-sewing images, Dickinson makes the universal sunset the result of a careless housewife; thus, as biographer Van Wyck Brooks put it, she domesticates the universe.

Analysis of the Sample Literary Analysis for an Image

The single paragraph above includes the basic characteristics of an analysis of a literary element. Note these details:

- The introductory segment includes a topic sentence as the first sentence.
- Details both paraphrased and quoted from the poem support the main idea. Adequate details appear without retelling the poem's story or paraphrasing the entire work.
- Varied sentence structure enhances the formal style.
- The present tense appears accurately throughout the discussion of the work.
- Transitions effectively connect ideas.
- The paragraph follows clear organization.
- The conclusion refers not only to the topic sentence but to the importance of the image in Dickinson's style. [*See* FOR AN AUTHOR, *above*, to compare this comment with a literary analysis of Dickinson as an author.]

Be sure to compare this sample with the later sample on the same poem. [*See* FOR LITERARY WORKS, *below*.]

——————— **Sample Literary Analysis for Character** ———————

   The following analysis, also a single paragraph, contrasts two characters in a short story as the contrast affects theme. Thus, the paragraph follows the organization of a comparison-contrast paper [*see* COMPARISON AND CONTRAST *in Part II*] but follows the content plan for a literary analysis.

Chee and Old Man Fat: A Study in Contrast

   Juanita Patero and Siyowin Miller in "Chee's Daughter" depict the two main characters so that their contrasts emphasize the story's theme. Chee and his father-in-law, Old Man Fat, exhibit significant personality differences. For example, Chee works and lives on his farm, while Old Man Fat works in a small trading post near the highway. Chee is strong and hard-working; he enjoys being outdoors, working on his farm. On the other hand, Old Man Fat shows nothing but laziness. He stays inside the trading post and does as little work as possible. In addition, Chee depends only on himself and the land. To earn money, he sells the crops he grows on his farm. Old Man Fat, in contrast, depends on the trading post and on other people. He charges tourists to see his Navajo mother-in-law weaving and to see the inside of a "real" Navajo home. Perhaps, though, their personalities show the greatest differences in their general attitudes. Chee, the very caring and generous person, loves his farm with all his heart. He believes that "a man took care of his land and it in turn took care of him." In contrast, Old Man Fat, greedy and selfish, does not care about land or anyone else; he cares only about himself and making money. The difference between the two characters underlines the story's theme: Land, the most precious natural resource, will not forsake a man who shares the "feeling of wholeness and of oneness with the sun and earth and growing things." It is caring for land that allows Chee to finally regain his daughter from Old Man Fat, caring for land that, unlike people, does not cheat.

Analysis of the Sample Literary Analysis for Character

The single paragraph above illustrates an analysis of a literary element developed by means of contrast. These special effects bear noting:

- The introductory sentence includes the essential information.
- The topic sentence, here the second sentence of the paragraph, establishes the contrast to be developed.
- The organization flows smoothly with the use of the part-by-part plan. [*See* COMPARISON AND CONTRAST *for methods of organizing comparison and contrast papers, and see* PART-BY-PART ORGANIZATION *in the Glossary.*]
- Effective transitions move the reader smoothly through the paragraph and maintain clear parallel contrasts: *for example, while, on the other hand, in addition, by contrast, though,* etc.
- Details from the story provide adequate support for the three subtopics.
- The analysis avoids the common pitfall of retelling the story.
- The conclusion refers to the topic sentence and makes a statement to indicate the importance of the literary element on the work as a whole.

———————— Sample Literary Analysis for a Symbol ————————

The following full-length paper analyzes the use of a single symbol in a long novel. A complex paper discusses a complex text, and it illustrates both creativity and understanding of one element of a highly complex novel. Compare this paper with others in this section, not only in terms of development but also in terms of content and structure.

Melville, the Weaver

In the course of his novel <u>Moby Dick</u>, Herman Melville sets out three basic parts of a complex motif of weaving. By careful examination of each in the order in which they appear, one can see a beautifully structured motif emerging.

The first part of this motif appears in the chapter "The Mat-Maker":

> As I kept passing and repassing the filling or woof of
> marline between the long yarns of the warp, using my own
> hand for the shuttle, and as Queequeg, standing sideways,
> ever and anon slid his heavy oaken sword between the
> threads ... it seemed as if this were the Loom of Time, and I

myself were a shuttle. . . . The straight warp of necessity, not
to be swerved from its ultimate course; . . . free will still free
to ply her shuttle between given threads; and chance,
though restrained in its play within the right lines of
necessity, and sideways in its motions directed by free will,
though thus prescribed to by both, chance by turns rules
either, and has the last featuring blow at events.

Melville leaves no question in his reader's mind at this point.
Every symbol of the larger motif is spelled out: Necessity, the warp,
is being woven with free will, the woof. Though restrained by both
necessity and free will, chance, the force behind the shuttle, yields
the final result.

Now that Melville has introduced the motif, he becomes more
symbolic in "As Bower in the Arsacides":

... the industrious earth beneath was as a weaver's loom,
with a gorgeous carpet on it, whereof the ground-vine
tendrils formed the warp and woof, and the living flowers
the figures. . . . Through the lacings of the leaves, the great
sun seemed a flying shuttle weaving the unwearied
verdure. . . .

Now amid the green, life-restless loom of that Arsacidean
wood, the great, white, worshipped skeleton lay lounging—a
gigantic idler! Yet, as the ever-woven verdant warp and
woof intermixed and hummed around him, the mighty idler
seemed the sunning weaver; himself all woven over with
the vines. . . . Life enfolded Death; Death trellised Life; the
grim god wived with youthful Life, and begat him curly-
headed glories.

A paradox seems to emerge: Both the sun, traditionally a life
force, and the gigantic idler, an obvious death symbol, are named as
weavers—the gigantic idler a "sunning" weaver, at that! The last
line, however, resolves the apparent paradox: The grim god, here
obviously Death, and youthful Life are wedded. They have become
one and act together as the force behind the shuttle, that force
already recognized as chance. Man, therefore, has no control over
life or death. He cannot, within Melville's symbolism, use his free
will to weave the pattern of life as he wishes: He lacks "the last

featuring blow at events." Indeed, Ishmael did state, "It seemed as if I myself were a shuttle," but the word "seemed" offers the key. Even Job knows (VII, vi) that "My days are swifter than a weaver's shuttle." People cannot control their days.

Melville wants his readers to recognize that this search for the whale, this quest in the open sea, and, more figuratively, this lifetime quest for answers is in some way fated. In "Faustine," Charles Swinburne puts it this way: "For in the days we know not of/ Did fate begin/ Weaving the web of days that wove/ Your doom." Similarly, in Moby Dick's epic qualities creeps a constant awareness of foreboding, a repetition of premonitions, the divinity but at the same time the terror of whiteness: the bleached ship Albatross reminiscent of the becalmed, scorching, death-filled trip of Coleridge's "Rime of the Ancient Mariner," the symbolic third day of the chase, the third time down for the whale, the third time out for Fate's lieutenant. Fate is interwoven through the entire novel. All of this evidence of fate, this quest for answers, however, is a major part of life. Oedipus sought answers; but he knew he could not get them all, was warned that he should not. Santiago pushed too far and was almost unable to returned to society. So Ahab pushed too far. Because Ahab pushed too far does not mean, though, that Melville would prefer the stagnation of the lee shore. The full life comes only with that spark of divinity which causes man to search.

Carrying the motif to its final major part, Melville, in "The Gilder," shows the reader the real magnitude of this symbolic mat:

> But the mingled, mingling threads of life are woven by warp and woof: calms crossed by storms, a storm for every calm. There is no steady unretracing progress in this life; we do not advance through fixed gradations, and at last one pause.... Our souls are like orphans whose unwedded mothers die in bearing them: the secret of our paternity lies in their grave, and we must there to learn it.

The original woven mat of "The Mat-Maker" has, then, emerged finally as a symbol of man's life on the one hand and the pattern of all life on the other, both made up of storms and calms, of troubles and solutions, of evil and goodness. Melville would not have his reader forget that there is both evil and goodness, and he thus emphasizes that there is a calm for every storm. Shakespeare, in fact, in <u>All's Well that Ends Well</u> (IV, iii) emphasizes that same idea: "The web of our life is of a mingled yarn, good and ill together."

How the final motif emerges can be represented this way:

Part	Warp	Woof	Weaver
1	Necessity	Free Will	Chance
2	Vines	Vines	Sun/Life/Chance
2	Vines	Vines	Skeleton/Death/Chance
3	Storms	Calms	Chance

Thus, as Queequeg's wooden sword by chance packed tightly or loosely the woof of free will through the warp of necessity, so the sun, by chance, caused the vines to wrap themselves around the idler's skeletal ribs. Nevertheless, since death is part of life, i.e., since "Life enfolds Death," the mat of life cannot be completed until death occurs. As Thomas Gray puts it in his "Ode for Music," "Weave the warp and weave the woof,/ The winding-sheet of Edward's grave." Thus, even though death is equated to chance, it is a chance that will inevitably come—fate, if you will—and it is only when the mat is completely woven; only after necessity, free will, and chance have intermingled into one piece; only after death can one see the full pattern of life. Only then is the quest for life's answers finished. So Starbuck notes as his end is near that "Strangest problems of life seem clearing." His mat is ready to be bound.

Numerous other incidents within the novel carry out the motif as well. Perhaps one of the most obvious is the warp and woof of Ahab's charts, the lines representing longitude and latitude. Certainly Ahab exerts free will in plotting the course of his ship across such warp and woof. "The Chart" would seem to indicate that his calculations were quite scientific; but the element of chance, the fact that the White Whale may not be there, is never denied. So Ahab plots his life across his charts never knowing where death may chance to come. He knows, however, that his death has been predicted as coming only by means of hemp. How interesting to note that hemp, too, is woven. Indeed, Ahab is said to weave the rope's yarns around the pole of his specially-made harpoon. "This done, pole, iron, and rope—like the Three Fates—remained inseparable. . . ." Again, the element of chance, the famous three sisters, is paralleled with the weaving motif.

The three mates of the <u>Pequod</u> could, perhaps, suggest yet another weaving motif. Flask, who never questions, imagines, or thinks, could represent the limited and calculated variation of the warp. Starbuck, the one who "bucks the stars," who would oppose necessity and chance, obviously represents the woof of free will. Stuff, who professes the postulates of fatalism, represents chance. Together, they weave the mat of the voyage.

Melville's weaving motif stands, then, as a representation of a philosophy of man's life in particular and in intermingling, interacting, multifaceted life in abstract.

Analysis of the Sample Literary Analysis for a Symbol

The full-length paper above includes certain characteristics not otherwise addressed in this section. [*See* RESEARCH PAPER *for additional information about writing research papers.*] The following characteristics are unique to a longer paper:

- Long quotations, supporting the major points of the paper, are set in from both margins and typed single-spaced. Even though they are direct quotations, no quotation marks are used. The format replaces the punctuation. [*See* RESEARCH PAPER *in Part II for an alternate format more easily set up on computer.*]

- Documentation is omitted for quotations from the novel. Some instructors may ask that the numbers of the pages from which the quotations are taken appear parenthetically after the quoted passage. Follow your instructor's preference.

- Frequent references to other pieces of literature, although optional, enhance a literary paper, particularly for more advanced classes. References that indicate other authors' use of similar techniques broaden the reader's literary understanding.

- The parenthetical notes to show outside sources provide a quick, easy means for limited documentation.

- Using a chart to clarify major aspects of the symbol helps the reader visualize the writer's ideas. The chart, again an optional device, nevertheless provides a clever, if unconventional, way to summarize the paper's ideas to this point.

Other aspects of the paper are typical. The paragraph structure, supporting details, organizational plan, transitional devices, sentence structures, and formal style all follow the characteristics of a satisfactory literary analysis. While certainly *Moby Dick* provides ample materials for thousands of additional pages of analysis, the writer has dealt suitably with a single symbol and showed its effect on the novel.

FOR LITERARY WORKS

When asked to analyze an entire literary work, whether it be a long, complicated novel or a single-page poem, the writer must take a systematic approach. The analysis of a literary work differs from that of a literary element. The basic difference is that the analysis of a literary work will focus on several related ideas or elements, trace them throughout the work, and illustrate the impact of those ideas on the work as a whole.

Because literary analysis may take so many directions, however, we can best examine its possibilities by looking first at its general characteristics and the general process for writing it, and then at a series of examples.

The examples for drama, nonfiction, and poetry, like those above for author and for literary elements, focus on Emily Dickinson. By comparing these examples, you will better be able to see how various kinds of literary analyses take separate approaches, even when they deal with similar subjects. In addition, each example includes its own analysis. Together, the examples and analyses in this section and in the sections above combine to present a solid foundation on which to build your own analysis.

Characteristics

A literary analysis of a specific work will have characteristics similar to those of an analysis focusing on literary elements; however, certain additional details usually appear. In general, a literary analysis of a specific work

- shows evidence of a thorough understanding of the entire work as a representative of its genre,

- includes an introduction naming the work and its author, and, as necessary, naming the specific type within the genre, such as Elizabethan, contemporary, musical, or morality (types of drama); biography, article, essay, or journal (types of nonfiction); historical, science fiction, fantasy, or Russian (types of novels),

- analyzes a combination of literary elements as they relate to one another or as they work together to achieve an overall effect,

- includes a topic or thesis sentence specifically stating the approach the analysis will take and at least an implied means of organization [*see* TOPIC SENTENCE *and* THESIS SENTENCE *in the Glossary, and see* PARAGRAPHS *and* THEME *in Part II*],

- follows a clear organizational plan,

- includes specific details from the work, either quoted [*see* QUOTATION MARKS *in the Glossary*] or paraphrased [*see* PARAPHRASE *later in Part II*], which support the topic or thesis,

- includes, if necessary, background research,

- follows a rather formal writing style, including the use of a third-person point of view,

- uses the present tense to discuss the work but the past tense to discuss the background,

- concludes with a reaction to the work as a representative of its genre, but limits the reactions to only those topics discussed in the paper.

Process

Use the following process to develop a literary analysis discussing a literary work.

PREWRITING

STEP 1.   DETERMINING THE TOPIC

After you have read the entire work, you must determine the specific approach your paper will take. One of the most frequent mistakes students make in writing an analysis is venturing off the analysis to simply retell the plot. As a result, you must be particularly cautious to select a topic and develop it, using elements of the plot only as they support your topic, your ideas.

If you have not been assigned a specific topic, use these questions to help you select a general topic:

- Does the work rely on some unusual characteristic for its success? Are there shortcomings as a result of this atypical characteristic? Advantages?

- Does the work exhibit some particularly strong characteristic that elevates it as a model of its genre?

- Does the work exhibit some unique characteristic that sets it apart from its genre?

- Are certain literary elements particularly attractive to readers' interests (or to your interest in particular)?

- Do certain literary elements combine in an unusual manner to further enhance the work's theme or overall impact?

- Are underlying elements, less obvious to casual readers, helpful in furthering the work's impact?

- Will unraveling complicated symbols or images enhance the reader's enjoyment of the work?

- Do certain characteristics of the work attract your attention because of their relationship to other works?

Your reaction to these questions should help you find a general topic which interests you. Write down the general topic in a sentence or two. Then list phrases that suggest ideas from the work which support that topic.

General topic:
The play "The Belle of Amherst" uses only a single character to depict the biography of Emily Dickinson. By doing so, the dramatist can allow Emily to do what most characters in a play cannot.

Details:
    have conversations with
        those offstage
    share secrets with audience
    show her impishness

STEP 2.   READING FOR ANALYSIS

Now that you have selected a general topic, reread the work noting specific examples which support your idea. Either take notes on separate note cards or mark the pages with slips of color-coded paper (using different colors to mark supporting details for different topics). If you are using your own copy of the book, you may also choose to mark specific passages.

As you read, add to or delete items from your list of supporting topics. As you reread, thinking in terms of your general topic, you can add important details and delete less supportive details. Revise or expand your list as necessary.

STEP 3.   PLANNING THE PAPER

Using your general-topic sentence and list of words or phrases developed and revised in Steps 1 and 2 above, develop a topic or thesis sentence suitable for your paragraph or paper. Then arrange the revised and expanded list of details in a logical order. The order may show relationships, opinion, cause and effect, or comparison and contrast. [*See* OPINION, CAUSE AND EFFECT, *and* COMPARISON AND CONTRAST *in Part II.*] You may also use chronological order or some order of importance. [*See* CHRONOLOGICAL ORDER *and* ORDERS OF IMPORTANCE *in the Glossary.*]

Next, make some final judgments about the items listed. Are some so insignificant that you will have trouble developing them well? Are some too broad to develop in only a single paragraph? If so, what logical divisions can you see? Do you have too many subtopics to develop in a single paper? If so, can you choose the three or four most important or most telling in terms of your general topic? Change the list as necessary.

When you finish, you will have a scratch outline of your paper. If your assignment requires it, develop a formal outline from this informal list. [*See* OUTLINES, KINDS: FOR A PAPER, *later in Part II.*]

Revise your statement of purpose (as written in Step 1 above) so that you have a well-written topic or thesis sentence.

STEP 4.   DOING RESEARCH

If your assignment requires outside sources, use the statement of purpose to guide your reading. Take careful notes so that you can document accurately. Be certain to enclose any words not your own in quotation marks. Such precautions will help you avoid plagiarism in your final work. [*See* PLAGIARISM *in the Glossary. Also see* RESEARCH PAPER, NOTES, KINDS: FOR A PAPER; PRECIS; *and* PARAPHRASE *in Part II for additional help as needed.*]

WRITING
STEP 5.   FOLLOWING THE PLAN

Now you are ready to write the first draft of your analysis. Begin with an introductory statement or an introductory paragraph, depending on whether you are writing a paragraph or a full-length paper. [*See*

PARAGRAPH *and* THEME *elsewhere in Part II.*] Include in the introductory segment the following specifics:

- the title of the work,
- the author's name,
- specific kind of work within the genre [*see Characteristics, above*],
- and perhaps an indication of the work's importance within the literary world or within the author's career.

Next, include the topic or thesis sentence you developed in Step 3 above.

Develop the subtopics in your paragraph or the supporting body paragraphs in your full-length paper. As you do, try to include the following content:

- sufficient examples to clarify your ideas,
- supporting details taken from the work, either quoted or paraphrased,
- specific supporting detail, if necessary, from outside sources, either quoted or paraphrased and accurately documented,
- transitions that connect one supporting idea with another and one main idea with another,
- transitions that help readers follow your organization and see the relationships among your ideas [*see* TRANSITIONS *in the Glossary*].

Finally, add a conclusion that refers to your topic or thesis statement and makes some general statement about the work as it represents the genre. Limit the general statement, of course, to only those matters discussed in your paragraph or longer paper.

REVISING

STEP 6.   IMPROVING THE CONTENT

As you read your draft, ask yourself these questions to pinpoint any areas of possible weakness:

- Have I included the necessary information in the introduction?
- Does the introduction give the reader a reason for reading the analysis?
- Can the reader follow my plan or do I need to improve it?
- Are transitions adequate to show relationships among ideas? [*See* REVISING: SAMPLE REVISION FOR TRANSITION *in Part II.*]
- Have I developed paragraphs adequately with sufficient supporting details, including specific details from the work, either quoted or paraphrased? [*See* REVISING: SAMPLE REVISION FOR SPECIFIC DETAIL *in Part I.*]
- Have I avoided plagiarism?
- Do the main ideas work together to say something about the work as a whole?
- Have I avoided retelling the story, instead referring only to elements which support my main ideas?
- Have I maintained a rather formal writing style, using a third-person point of view and accurate verb tense?
- Is the vocabulary, including appropriate literary terms, accurate?

- Are my sentences varied both in length and in structure? [*See* REVISING: SAMPLE REVISION FOR SENTENCE VARIETY *in Part I.*]

- Do my sentences carry the most effective emphasis for their respective subjects? Are the main ideas in the main clauses? [*See* REVISING: SAMPLE REVISION FOR EMPHASIS *in Part I.*]

- Does the conclusion refer to the topic or thesis sentence and at the same time make a general statement about the work? [*See* CONCLUSION *in the Glossary.*]

As you answer the questions above and determine areas of weakness in your paper, make the necessary revisions. You may need to make several revisions before you have a paper which satisfies all the suggestions above.

[*In addition,* see REVISING *in Part I for questions that will guide other general revisions.*]

PROOFREADING

STEP 7.   CHECKING DETAILS

As you read your final draft, check for those details which can distract your reader: problems with grammar, mechanics, and usage. Consult the Glossary for explanations and examples that will help you solve writing problems.

Finally, check spelling and word choice. Consult *Webster's New World Dictionary* and *Webster's New World Thesaurus* for reference.

A Note about the Samples: Now that you know what an analysis of a literary work should include and how you go about writing it, study the following examples and their respective analyses for further understanding. You will find examples for a drama, a nonfiction piece, a novel, a poem, and a short story. They vary from single-paragraph, to three-paragraph, to five-paragraph papers.

———— Sample Literary Analysis of a Drama ————

A literary analysis of a drama frequently deals with such specific literary elements as character, dialogue, setting, plot, and theme. It never deals only with a single element; rather, it shows the relationships among those elements. It also frequently deals with the specific techniques of drama, like staging, props, costumes or lighting, discussing how they make the play effective—or not. The fact that meaning, form, techniques, and background interrelate to make a play work gives the writer ample choices for developing an analysis. Showing interrelationships, you will remember, helps distinguish between an analysis of a literary work and an analysis of a literary element.

The following sample analysis for a drama illustrates the writer's examination of a combination of elements which makes the unusual characteristics of this play particularly suitable for its theme.

When a Belle Is not a Belle

Because "The Belle of Amherst" by William Luce is a one-person dramatized biography, it bears little resemblance to most plays. On the other hand, because Luce uses only the single character, he is able to dramatize the solitary life of Emily Dickinson. As the only character in the play, Emily tells her own story in dialogue directed toward the audience with whom she shares "secrets;" by conversation with offstage characters, which allows the audience to glimpse her daily life with her family; and by examples of her impishness, which show the audience something other than the strange recluse she seemed to be.

The play opens with Emily talking directly to the audience about her fear of seeing so many people at one time. "I never see strangers and hardly know what I say," she explains. The reclusive poet of Amherst, Massachusetts, shares secrets with the audience which sees possible reasons for her apparently strange behavior. "Why should I socialize with village gossips?" she asks, adding that "I give them something to talk about. I dress in white all year round, even in winter." The audience must chuckle at her antics, especially when, later in the play, she adds, "I've never said this to anyone before, but I'll tell *you*. I do it on purpose. The white dress, the seclusion. It's all—deliberate." She even shares with the audience the recipe for her famous black cake, thus letting them in on yet another "secret."

In order for the audience to share Emily's point of view, they also see her on her home turf. Although they never glimpse other members of the household, they do learn about them during Emily's conversation with these offstage characters. For instance, the audience learns that her brother, Austin, has received eleven valentines. The audience witnesses a conversation with an unseen suitor, one whom she may choose to escort the Belle of Amherst. Likewise, her conversation with an unseen Mr. Higginson, the poet who she hopes will be her mentor, seems a fantasy, a reliving of those important moments in her life. So, while the conversations with characters offstage enhance the audience's understanding of Emily's life, they add to the strange aura of her life.

The strangeness, however, is tempered by her impishness. What else can one call her behavior? She must assume a sly smile when she says, "I'm told one woman in Amherst is imitating me now. Probably Clarissa Cartwright. Just what Amherst needs—another eccentric." She mimics the village gossips, poking fun at their poking fun at her. Of one of the gossips, she says, "To spare the expense of moving, I directed her to the cemetery." Even her own family is the butt of her impish comments. Of her sister Vinnie, Emily says, "She snores like a poker and shovel and pair of tongs." The humor tempers the strange.

In short, then, "The Belle of Amherst" describes a most unlikely belle. Only in her fantasies is the poet the society belle. Instead, in an unusual play that doubles as a biography and in a play that includes but a single character, Luce shows his audience a warm, humorous recluse who plays a game with an unknowing Amherst society. Only the audience is in on the secret. The insight makes the recluse more human.

Analysis of the Sample Literary Analysis of a Drama

The sample literary analysis of a drama illustrates most of the general characteristics and includes some specific details worth noting. Consider these features:

- The introduction names the play and the author and establishes its unique position among drama forms, that it is biographical and that it includes only a single character.
- The introduction leads to the thesis statement which lists the paper's three main ideas in the order in which they will be discussed, from the most to the least obvious.

- Supporting details are quoted directly from the play, enclosed in quotation marks, or paraphrased.
- The paper avoids retelling the plot.
- The three main ideas combine to describe the literary work as a whole and discuss its ability to succeed in spite of its peculiar approach and form.
- The paper relies heavily on, but does not deal only with, character. Because it mentions techniques of staging (dialogue directed at the audience and conversations with offstage characters) and Luce's unusual approach to the genre, the paper meets the more general qualifications of a literary analysis of a work.
- The language and structure are formal, and the verb tense is appropriately present in the discussion of the work.
- Sufficient references help readers understand ideas indirectly related to the paper. For instance, the title is explained without the writer ever saying, *The title refers to the fact that Emily Dickinson, who lived in Amherst, Massachusetts, hoped to be a belle of the ball but in actuality achieved that only in her fantasies.*
- Transitions help clarify the organization. Both words and phrases as well as entire sentences serve to join the paragraphs and the sentences within the paragraphs.
- An effective conclusion makes a reference to the thesis sentence without repeating it and reaches some general conclusions about the play.

—— Sample Literary Analysis of a Nonfiction Work ——

The nonfiction label applies to more than a half dozen kinds of writing, each of which follows its own technique and/or form: essays, biographies, autobiographies, speeches, letters, journals, and diaries. Even newspaper and magazine articles fall into the nonfiction genre. Frequently, then, a literary analysis of a nonfiction work will focus on author style—the characteristics of sentences and paragraphs and their effect.

The following sample analysis illustrates this very kind of analysis. The subject, like that in the literary analysis of a drama above, is the biography of Emily Dickinson. The writer focuses on the techniques of writing nonfiction.

Emily Dickinson: The Peculiar One

In his biography of Emily Dickinson, Van Wyck Brooks uses a vocabulary that enhances his obvious attitude toward Dickinson, that she is peculiar. His expressions suggest the mysterious. "She spoke from the shadows," he writes, and follows with "These letters were also peculiar," thereby suggesting that speaking from the shadows is peculiar. He includes a description of clipped and pasted letters used to address the envelopes and thus reinforces the attitude. Descriptions of her meeting Colonel Higginson, the poet who she hoped would be her mentor, include her "soft, breathless voice" toward a man certain "there was something abnormal about her." Other phrases Brooks uses include a description of Emily as a "hurrying whiteness," and a reference to her vanishing "like a ghost or an exhalation." The reader sees Emily "fluttering about the porch like a moth in the moonlight," a woman with a "microscopic eye" whose "imaginagion dwelt with mysteries and grandeurs." While Brooks no doubt reports on his research accurately, his vocabulary creates what is an apparently conscious effort to mystify rather than demystify Emily Dickinson to his readers.

Analysis of the Sample Literary Analysis of a Nonfiction Work

The single paragraph analyzing Brook's style is a typical example of a literary analysis of a piece of nonfiction. While nonfiction often includes characters, plot, setting, and many of the other literary elements, much of what makes nonfiction successful (since the author must rely on unalterable facts) is author style. The paragraph above includes these characteristics:

- The topic sentence, here the first, combines with other details to introduce the paragraph.

- The many details in the paragraph support the purpose announced in the topic sentence.

- By showing, through details both quoted and paraphrased, rather than telling, the writer allows the reader to draw his or her own conclusions.

- Varied transitional devices prevent tedium.

- A concluding sentence makes reference to the topic sentence without repeating it and also clarifies the writer's point about Brooks' biography.

- Sentence structure maintains a formal style and simultaneously shows variety both in structure and length.

- The present tense, maintained throughout, serves the analysis well.

———— Sample for Literary Analysis of a Novel ————

A literary analysis of a novel probably offers more options than any other kind of analysis. Some writers will react to a novel based on their own involvement with it, particularly if it has had some personal impact on them. Other writers will remain more objective and deal with literary elements and techniques, especially as they develop a theme or message. Still other writers will focus on the full meaning of the novel—the overt message as well as the underlying themes, symbols, and implications. They react to the author's broad comments about the world, its people, its societies, its cultures. Any of these approaches fit the general characteristics of a literary analysis of a novel. Be cautious, however, that you do not lapse into a literary review [*see* REVIEW *in Part II*] if the assignment is to prepare a literary analysis.

The following sample analysis permits you to compare a book report, a book review, and a literary analysis of a book. Because the same novel is the subject in all three sections [*see also* BOOK REPORT *and* REVIEW *in Part II*], you can see how writers approached the novel to meet the characteristics of each of the three kinds of writing. Studying the differences and similarities will further your understanding of a literary analysis.

Ancient Science Fiction

Transporting readers across 25,000 years to an alien civilization sounds like the topic of a good science-fiction novel. Tradition usually requires that science fiction move its readers ahead, not back; yet in Jean Auel's The Valley of the Horses prehistory becomes a subgenre of science fiction. Set in the convergence of Neanderthal and Cro-Magnon civilizations, Valley illustrates a nontraditional approach to science fiction. Auel's extensive scientific research for the series, referred to as the Earth Children series, generates the science-fiction quality. Readers learn about prehistoric biology, geology and human anatomy, all based on hard scientific data. Combined with Auel's fictionalized speculation of the society, its people, its culture, its spiritual beliefs, the novel allows readers to glimpse an alien world. Combined, the backward time leap to an alien society, the scientifically accurate environment, and the speculative, even hypothetical but still fictionalized aspects generate a solid argument to categorize Valley as science fiction.

Alien societies characterize many works of science fiction. Valley throws the reader back 25 millennia to a civilization as strange as any developed by Isaac Asimov. The Neanderthals are aliens, described as subhuman, animal-like creatures, dark, hairy, and chinless, with ridged eyebrows and flat heads. In spite of their subhuman characteristics, however, the clan members follow a highly ritualistic spiritual tradition, far more complicated and symbolic than that of the Cro-Magnon people. Auel also endows the Neanderthals with Memories, an expanded brain capacity that enables them to know everything their ancestors knew but that renders them incapable of learning anything new. As a result, to modern readers the alien society takes on an additional aura of mystery.

In spite of its hypothetical, speculative society, the novel, like others in the series, shows rich scientific detail. Auel traveled all over the world to study archeological sites, to talk with experts on wolves, to sleep in an ice cave, to learn to knap flint, to study glaciers. Her ongoing research gives the reader technical details about medicinal plants, poisonous plants, even birth-control plants; details about woolly mammoths, wild horses, cave lions, wolves, and hyenas; details about glacier flow, glacier melt, and glacier atmosphere. Her characters can discuss in detail the attributes of certain flint for certain tools. Through the characters, the reader also learns how to hunt certain game, find plants for food, store both to sustain life during the long, excruciating winters, and provide for other necessities of life: clothing, footwear, bedding, cooking and storage utensils, shelter, and fire. Every amenity must be found, caught, processed, drilled, woven, braided, cut, or somehow altered to suit the purpose. It is the science of prehistoric man: botany, biology, geology, anatomy, and archaeology.

Within the scientific research, however, Auel emphasizes that all three novels' events grow from her imagination. Valley represents Auel's fictionalized version of how people first learned all manner of skills: to ride a horse, to make fire with flint, to hunt animals too big and too fast to kill with sling or spears, to use animals to help carry a heavy load, to traverse wide rivers, to make boats, to improve shelters from simple caves to man-made structures, to make more sophisticated tools. Valley also represents Auel's fictionalized version of evolution, including the reason for the demise of the Neanderthals and the success of the Cro-Magnons. Auel's guess as to how tribes moved across Europe and Asia during the last Ice Age in the midst of the changing geography makes fascinating reading. Her speculation of their relationship with the spiritual world, their burial customs, their preparation for the afterlife, their use of hallucinogenics for contacting the spirits—all show Auel's imagination at play with sketchy facts. Her interpretation of anthropological evidence lays the foundation for the novel.

Indeed, The Valley of the Horses as well as other books in the Earth Children series may be the most unusual example of science fiction to appear on modern book shelves. Taking the reader to a fictionalized, alien civilization situated in a scientifically correct environment, Valley does what Auel says she likes in books: "I like stories that pick me up and put me down somewhere else. 'What if'—that's the great thing fiction writers work with." The "what if" in The Valley of the Horses results in a blend of science and fiction of a different vintage!

Analysis of the Sample Literary Analysis of a Novel

The literary analysis of a novel can include dozens of aspects. The sample above presents an argument for thinking of a novel as a special kind of science fiction. Thus, the analysis does several jobs at once: it presents an argument supported by details from the book; it presents an analysis of science-fiction characteristics as they appear in the book; and it includes the general characteristics for a literary analysis of a novel. Note the following details:

- The introduction includes the vital information and establishes the basis for the argument that the book is a special kind of science fiction.
- The thesis sentence points out, in the order to be discussed, the three main ideas the writer will develop in the three body paragraphs.
- Each paragraph is supported by details from the novel, all of which appear as paraphrases, even list-like series. Quotations are omitted for brevity.
- Transitions provide clear connections between ideas.
- Sentence structure maintains a rather formal writing style and simultaneously illustrates good variety. Complicated sentences, some of which include complicated series, contrast with short, simple sentences.
- The present tense appears appropriately in the discussion of the work.
- A concluding paragraph not only refers to the thesis sentence, but also states the author's attitude. The quotation by the author probably appeared on a jacket cover; thus the writer did not document its source.

Sample Literary Analysis of a Poem

To write a literary analysis of a poem, a writer must select a combination of elements which, peculiar to that poem, create some significant impact on the poem's meaning. An analysis of a poem may consider sound devices, structure, tone, mood, theme, imagery, figure of speech, symbol, point of view, setting, perhaps even character. [*See entries for each in the Glossary.*] It may offer comparisons, contrasts, description, cause and effect, and opinion. [*See entries for each in Part II.*] Unlike an analysis of a single literary element [*see* FOR LITERARY ELEMENTS, *above*], the analysis of a poem must deal with the overall effect of the work. Compare the following analysis with the earlier example [*in* FOR LITERARY ELEMENTS].

Mother Nature Domesticated

Emily Dickinson's poem "She Sweeps with Many-Colored Brooms" serves as a typical representative of Dickinson's style. The extended metaphor, sustained throughout the poem and emphasized by the absence of a clear rhyme pattern, enables her to achieve the compact multiple meanings for which she is recognized. Because Dickinson lived as a recluse and because she felt Mother Nature was her only real friend, much of her poetry domesticates Mother Nature in a manner that makes the spiritual familiar. In the poem

"She Sweeps with Many-Colored Brooms," Dickinson uses the common household words to describe Mother Nature's sunset. Mother Nature uses a broom, dusts, and wears an apron. She also leaves shreds, ravelings, and threads as she litters the eastern sky with duds. On the literal level, then, Mother Nature is, indeed, the housewife, emphasized by the line, "Oh, housewife in the evening west." The poem suggests the vivid colors—purple, amber, emerald—that Mother Nature has painted the sunset sky, colors Dickinson obviously enjoys until "brooms fade softly into stars—/ And then I come away."

The extended metaphor, however, suggests some underlying questions the reader must consider. Mother Nature shows herself less than a tidy housewife. She leaves shreds behind, does not dust the pond, and drops ravelings and thread, and litters. Even her brooms are spotted. That Dickinson refers to the untidy housewife may suggest irreverence, but it may also suggest a mature awareness that few mothers are perfect. In fact, the adoration for the sunset's loveliness more clearly illustrates a daughter's love than it does a lack of respect.

Probably, in fact, Dickinson admires the variations Mother Nature sweeps into the sunsets, variations like those in Dickinson's own poem. The rhyme is sprung to avoid a singsong effect, and the result emphasizes Dickinson's message. For instance, in verse one, "behind" almost rhymes with "pond" and in verse two, "thread" almost rhymes with "emerald," but in verse three "fly" fails completely as a rhyme with "away." Instead, as the reader listens for a near rhyme, thinking "fly," his thought, jolted by the absence, carries "fly" with "away." Dickinson, the recluse, relied on the spiritual world to take her away from the domestic, and watching the sunset made her own spirit soar until the stars emerged. Then she returned to this world, her garden, her home, her own room. As biographer Van Wyck Brooks said, Dickinson domesticated the universe.

Analysis of the Sample for a Poem

The three-paragraph composition above analyzes a single poem. Note some of the specific features in this paper:

- As a three-paragraph paper, the sample above illustrates a format unlike others we have examined in this section. The first paragraph is both an introduction and the development of the first point.

- The thesis statement, the second sentence in the first paragraph, suggests the three topics to be discussed.

- The paper follows an order of importance, beginning with the most important idea, the extended metaphor, and building other ideas on that.

- By looking at a combination of extended metaphor, potential problems with meaning (i.e., irreverence), and the impact of missing rhyme, the analysis deals adequately with the poem's total effect. In this manner, too, it sets itself apart from an analysis which deals with only a single literary element.

- Transitions help the reader see connections between ideas within and between paragraphs.

- Varied sentence structure enhances the quality of the paper. The main ideas appear in main clauses.

- The paper maintains a formal style, aided by the consistent use of a third-person point of view and accurate verb tense, the present to discuss the work and the past to discuss the background.

- The conclusion, the final part of the third paragraph, not only emphasizes the points in the paper but broadens its message by applying the techniques evident in this one poem to much of Dickinson's poetry.

—— Sample Literary Analysis of a Short Story ——

A short story analysis can take almost as many approaches as that for a novel. For instance, it can trace the development of a character and show the relationship between the development and the theme. Or it can show how point of view creates sympathy for a character. It can describe the setting and show its effect on mood and, in turn, show how mood affects theme. It can deal with structure, tone, style, and theme. It can express opinion or cause and effect. In the interest of providing yet another kind of literary paper, however, we will look at a sample which develops a comparison. The following literary analysis combines the organizational pattern of a comparison-contrast paper with the content of a literary analysis [see COMPARISON AND CONTRAST *in Part II*]. Compare this paper, too, with the short story analysis above which deals only with setting [*see* FOR LITERARY ELEMENTS *above*].

Sylvia and the White Heron: A Comparison

An interesting comparison in Sarah Orne Jewett's short story "The White Heron" enhances the reader's understanding of the author's message. The comparison between one of the main characters, a young girl named Sylvia, and the white heron allows the reader to better understand their similar personalities. For instance, both find comfort in the outdoors, especially the wilderness. Just as the white heron naturally inhabits the woods and water, Sylvia, although less naturally, spends nearly all of her time in the same setting. As the reader learns, "it seemed as if she never had been alive at all before she came to live at the farm." In addition, both characters are shy. For example, Sylvia has a difficult time relating to and getting along with other people. Likewise, the white heron, frightened, flies away if only an annoying pair of catbirds approaches. Perhaps, however, the most significant similarity between the two is that both of them keep secrets well. The white heron, ever silent, never attracts the attention of others, thus keeping its nesting site a mystery. Similarly, even though Sylvia sees the nest of the somewhat rare bird, she never reveals the secret, not even to a young man who offers a princely ten-dollar reward for the information. Thus, Sylvia and the white heron possess certain traits that cause the reader to think in terms of mirror images, each character enhancing the other. Seeing the characters in juxtaposition helps the reader react positively to Sylvia's behavior as she reflects the heron's natural behavior. Thus the reader comes to better appreciate Jewett's message: All living beings are children of nature, and all share a common bond. The preservation of that bond can have no selling price. For Sylvia to give away the heron's secret is to give away his life; and because Sylvia has become one with the heron, to give away his life is to give away her own.

Analysis of the Sample Literary Analysis of a Short Story

In a single paragraph, the analysis above develops a comparison that does more than merely analyze character. In this respect, the paragraph follows the characteristics of an analysis for a literary work. Note these specifics:

- The topic sentence specifies the purpose of the paragraph.
- The three supporting details, each in turn supported with examples from the short story, including one quotation, clarify the main idea.
- Effective transitions show relationships among the ideas throughout the paragraph.
- Arranged in order of importance, the ideas build from most obvious to least obvious, from least impact to greatest impact. The culmination of the comparison illustrates the strength of Sylvia's character.
- Varied sentence structure maintains an effective and rather formal style.
- A third-person point of view and a consistent present tense in the discussion of the work also aid in developing an effective formal style.
- The conclusion reemphasizes the introduction. In addition, it permits the writer to make a more general comment about the effect of the comparison.

The many explanations, examples, and analyses above should provide an ample foundation on which to build your own literary analysis. Regardless of topic, length, or kind of work you must analyze, you will surely find an example here to guide your work.

MEMORANDUM

A memorandum or memo (plural: *memoranda*) is a letter designed to be used within a department, or between the departments or branches of a business. Frequently, a printed form provides the format. In other cases, employees follow the approved format found below.

Characteristics

A memo

- follows a format which includes a heading with *To, From, Subject,* and *Date,*
- conveys a company-related message about anything from sales to the company bowling league,
- is written like a business letter, with the main idea in the first paragraph followed by necessary details and finally, if required, a request for action or response,
- is usually more informal than formal,
- records or requests an action (implying the sender keeps a copy),
- follows a standard format which calls for single-spaced, block paragraphs [*see* LETTERS, KINDS: BUSINESS *in Part II*], two spaces between paragraphs, and three between the heading and the body.

Process

Use the following steps to develop an accurate, business-like memorandum.

PREWRITING

STEP 1.   RECOGNIZING A NEED

Before you write a memo, know exactly why you are writing it. Consider some of these possible reasons:

- You are requesting action. Perhaps you want to confirm the dates for your vacation with your superior.
- You are confirming an action. If your supervisor asks you to file a report by the end of the month, a memo on the 25th noting that the report has been filed will show that you have followed through.
- You are summarizing the results of a committee meeting.
- You wish to announce a departmental meeting.

While we cannot begin to list every purpose of a memo, the ideas above will help you determine the specific purpose of your communique.

STEP 2.   PREPARING THE HEADING

By developing the heading first, you focus your attention on the audience and force yourself to name your subject in a few words. Answer these four questions:

- To whom, specifically, is the memo addressed?

- From whom is the memo coming? You? Your department?

- What is the subject of the memo? Put it in a few words.

- What is the complete date of the memo's distribution?

By answering these questions, you can complete the heading. Use one of these forms:

To:	Name
From:	Name
Subject:	Title
Date:	Date

(The names, title, and date begin two spaces to the right of the colons.)

To:	Name
From:	Name
Subject:	Title
Date:	Date

(The names, title, and date begin two spaces to the right of the longest line.)

Note that in one form the colons are aligned. In the other form, the headings align on the left margin. In both cases, the names, title and date are aligned. Companies often preprint memo forms, thus eliminating the need to set up either format.

STEP 3. PLANNING THE MESSAGE

Now you will need to organize your thoughts before you write. The message should appear in three parts. Use the following plan to make notes for your message:

- Paragraph 1 should include the main idea. What, in one or two sentences, do you need to convey? Are you announcing a new policy? Jot down the main points.

- Paragraph 2 gives details. If you are announcing a new policy, how will it affect the reader? If you are requesting suggestions, why do you need them? Why should the reader respond?

- Paragraph 3, if necessary, requests action or response. If the reader must complete some form, spell out what to do. If the reader is to put a suggestion in writing, say to whom to address the comments and by when.

WRITING

STEP 4. COMPLETING THE MEMO

When you have planned the details, follow the organization set out in Step 3 above and write the memo. Use clear language and simple sentences. Be direct and informal. Avoid stilted language and trite expressions.

REVISING

STEP 5. CHECKING CONTENT

As you reread your memo, ask yourself these questions:

- Is the heading clear, precise, dated accurately and completely?

- Will my reader understand the message?

- Are the details sufficient to support the main idea? Is the explanation adequate?

- Have I included deadlines, specific actions, names, and places as necessary?

- Are my sentences simple and clear?

- Have I used a conversational vocabulary, or have I resorted to buzz words and stilted language?

Use these questions to guide revision. When you believe the content is accurate and complete, type a copy and sign your initials beside your name in the heading.

PROOFREADING

STEP 6. CHECKING THE MECHANICS

When the final copy is typed, proofread it carefully. Make sure you have made no omissions or typing errors. Check the spelling. Read for grammar, usage, and mechanics precision.

Sample Memorandum

The following memo follows the process set out above and illustrates one reason for writing a memo.

V * I * P
VIDEO INSTRUCTIONAL PRODUCTS

To:	Mearl Evans, Sales Department Manager
From:	Sara Davidson *SD*
Subject:	New Product Proposal
Date:	November 8, 1988

CONFIDENTIAL

The New Products Committee hopes to present a proposed new product to the VIP Board of Directors at their December meeting. The first draft of the proposal outlines the product concept, potential sales, and cost estimates for a new industrial training film.

The new training film follows the design of earlier products used in industry on video cassette recorders. It will focus on the pest-control industry. Its primary purpose will be to train pest-control technicians to eradicate pests in residential and commercial properties while maintaining safety standards for both the PC technician and personnel working or living in the area. The product, an innovation in both pest control and in training, appears to have good market potential.

The committee looks forward to presenting the proposal to you and your staff prior to the December Board meeting. We think you will have valuable contributions to make to the overall plan and can suggest methods by which the proposal can best be presented to the Board. By next Friday, please suggest a time most appropriate for our discussion.

Analysis of the Sample Memorandum

The memorandum above serves the purpose of maintaining communication between departments and involving personnel at all levels in the development of a potential new product. Note these specifics about the memo itself:

- The company name and logo are preprinted at the top of the memo form as are the words *To, From, Subject,* and *Date.*
- The heading lists a title for the addressee but no title for the writer. The tendency is to be more formal with the addressee than with the writer.
- The heading concisely indicates the subject matter. Note the initial capitals.
- The complete date is essential for future reference.
- The *Confidential* notation emphasizes what employees already know: competition requires secrecy about the development of new products.
- The message follows the typical organization, with the main idea in paragraph 1, details in paragraph 2, and a request for action in paragraph 3.
- While the vocabulary uses business terminology (*cost estimates, pest-control technician, eradicate,* and *residential and commercial properties*), the language is not stilted or filled with buzz words.
- Sentence structure is simple and clear.
- The tone is polite and suggests professional courtesy, especially in seeking interdepartmental cooperation.

Good memos are really a matter of courtesy. People working together do a more effective job if they understand their respective roles. Communication goes a long way to maintain that relationship. Memos help serve that purpose.

MINUTES OF A MEETING

If you are elected secretary of a club or organization, your primary responsibility will be to take notes of what happens at any membership meeting. These notes are called *minutes*. They simply record the official business that occurs during a meeting. If the club or organization is relatively large, the meetings will be more formal than if the organization is small. The more formal the meeting, the more formal the minutes. Regardless of formality, however, certain characteristics will be evident in the minutes of any meeting.

Characteristics

The minutes of a meeting should include

- the date, time, and place of the meeting,
- the name of the person who calls the meeting to order,
- a list of those present, or, in a large group, the number of members present,
- a notation of handling of the minutes of the previous meeting,
- a notation of committee reports and actions,
- a list of unfinished business,
- a record of elections or appointments,
- an explanation of any business transacted, including any motions made (sometimes, but not necessarily, the name of the proposer and seconder of the motion) and any actions taken,
- a list of important dates and facts,
- an indication of the next meeting date, time, and place,
- the time of adjournment,
- your signature and typewritten name, along with the date (sometimes preceded by *respectfully submitted*, a phrase now considered outdated).

Process

The following steps will help you prepare accurate and complete minutes of a meeting.

PREWRITING

STEP 1. PLANNING FOR THE MEETING

Before the meeting, you should complete two preliminary steps:

- Study the agenda, if there is one. The agenda [*see* AGENDA *in the Glossary*] will serve as a skeleton outline for your minutes.
- Prepare a list of the items to include in your minutes. Use the list of characteristics above to develop your list, and allow enough room

to take notes. In some cases, a line will be ample, but for reports, unfinished business, and new business, you may wish to allow a full page.

STEP 2.   TAKING NOTES

Arrive early and seat yourself in the front of the room near the presiding officer.

Using your prepared list as a guide, take careful notes of everything that happens. Strive for accuracy, asking as necessary for a motion to be repeated or for the names of those who make and second motions.

To avoid inaccuracies, you may wish to read a motion aloud directly from your notes just prior to the president's asking for a second or just prior to the vote. This will give everyone, including you, a chance to agree on wording and to understand the motion.

WRITING

STEP 3.   PREPARING THE FIRST DRAFT

As soon after the meeting as possible, at least within the next day or two, write out the minutes in rough draft. Waiting too long after the meeting will add to the difficulty of maintaining accuracy:

- Your notes will get "cold," and you may have trouble remember-

ing what your abbreviations mean.

- You may have trouble reading your own handwriting. Notes written in haste sometimes become indecipherable after several days, simply because you cannot remember the general context in which they were taken.

- Your recollection of specific details will fade with time.

So, even though you may not have to read the minutes for a month, prepare them as soon as possible.

While the format for minutes is somewhat flexible, the organization is always the same: chronological. [*See* CHRONOLOGICAL ORDER *in the Glossary.*] Even if the order of business [*see* ORDER OF BUSINESS *in the Glossary*] varies from the agenda, you will record the minutes as the events actually occurred. Normal order of business is as follows:

- Meeting called to order

- Minutes read and unanimously approved, approved as corrected, or approved as submitted

- Reports presented by committees

- Unfinished business discussed

- Elections held

- New business presented

- Announcements made

- Next meeting date, time, and place established

• Meeting adjourned

Finally, when you have completed the minutes, you need to check for accuracy.

REVISING

STEP 4. CHECKING FOR ACCURACY

The most common errors in minutes result from one of two causes:

• inaccurate information,

• incomplete information.

For instance, you may misunderstand a motion and record it inaccurately. Or maybe you mistakenly write *not* for *now*, thus changing the meaning of a motion. On the other hand, you may simply neglect to include such important information as the names of those making and seconding motions, the voting results, and any inconclusive discussions which became unfinished business.

Ultimately, accurate minutes require complete notes taken throughout a meeting. Even if you take such detailed notes that you later decide some minor points of the discussion need not be included, you should have adequate details to prepare accurate, complete minutes.

Finally, when you have revised the minutes and made a neat final copy, preferably typed, sign your name and record the date.

PROOFREADING

STEP 5. CHECKING FOR DETAILS

When you have completed the final draft, read it for mechanical details: typographical errors, misspellings, inaccurate punctuation. These errors can cause the minutes to be misread and in extreme cases create the potential for legal action. Legal cases have been won or lost over the use of a comma. Your responsibility is not to be taken lightly.

Ultimate proofreading occurs as you read the minutes for approval. Whatever revisions the membership demands are made on the final copy and noted as revisions in the next meeting's minutes.

--- **Sample Minutes** ---

The minutes below and the analysis which follows illustrate the characteristics described above.

JUNIOR CIVITAN CLUB
Regular Monthly Meeting

The regular monthly meeting of the Junior Civitan Club was called to order on Tuesday, January 28, 1988, 3:00 PM in Room 29 at Central High School by President Staci Marlin. Twenty-seven members answered roll call. Three were absent.

The minutes of the December meeting were read and approved as corrected.

The treasurer reported a balance of $104.86 in the treasury.

The membership committee reported positive reaction to the membership drive held during the two weeks' period from January 6 through January 17. Eight new members will join the club at the February meeting. During discussion, it was suggested that the club plan an informal reception at the end of the next meeting to welcome the new members. The membership committee will consider the suggestion.

Little progress was reported by the apple-sale committee. The sale is scheduled for the third week of May, and the current emphasis is on scheduling workers to sell the apples at the afternoon and evening athletic events. Ron Richards, chairman, indicated he expected to have the schedule completed by the March meeting.

A slate of officers was presented by the nominating committee in preparation for the election of new officers during the March meeting. The nominees were Francis Wittington, President; Jerome Hudson, Vice-President; Gaila Schwartz, Treasurer. The current secretary has another year remaining in office.

In matters of unfinished business, President Marlin reported that the food donations collected by the club were well received at the local food bank during the Christmas season. The club donated nearly $400 worth of staples. In other unfinished business, Yolanda Wong requested that the club reach a decision about Civitan

Scholarship applicants since time is nearing for the application deadline. She made a motion, seconded by Joyce Kozlowski, that at the regular February meeting the club select by secret ballot a representative from the organization to apply for the $500 scholarship, representation to be based on club participation and club support. The motion passed.

No new business came before the membership. Members were reminded of the dates for the Junior Achievement exhibit next weekend, February 3 and 4, since Civitan members like to support fellow students' activities. In addition, Lanny Collins, student athletic director, suggested members watch for posters announcing dates for spring sports meetings.

The next regular meeting of the Central High School Civitan Club will be held February 25, 1988, at 3:00 PM in Room 29 at Central High School.

The meeting was adjourned at 4:15 PM.

Brandon Hartwell

Brandon Hartwell
January 31, 1988

Analysis of the Sample Minutes

The minutes above include all the vital information. For instance:

- We know by the heading the title of the meeting and that it was a regular meeting.
- The introductory statement, paragraph 1, includes the date, time and place of the meeting, the name of the presiding officer, and a report of attendance.
- Paragraph 2, a single sentence, indicates how the minutes of the previous meeting were handled.
- Then begins a series of three paragraphs about three reports. Paragraph 3 describes the report from the membership committee, including discussion from the membership. Since no motions were made, names of those commenting are not listed. Paragraph 4 describes the report from the apple-sale committee, and paragraph 5 describes the report from the nominating committee. Specific names are listed only where needed.

- Paragraph 7, dealing with unfinished business, summarizes the discussion, indicates a motion made, and, although unnecessarily, states by whom and by whom seconded. We know that the motion passed. The motion, obviously somewhat complicated, is worded to include all matters of importance: when the action is to be completed (*at the regular February meeting of the club*), how the selection is to be made (*by secret ballot*), what the selection means (*an opportunity to apply for a $500 scholarshsip*), and the basis of the selection (*club participation and club support*). Each of these items must be included in the minutes because of the impact on future action in the club.

- Although no new business was transacted, notation of that fact is necessary in paragraph 8 to avoid the possible misunderstanding that such business was simply omitted from the minutes.

- In paragraph 9 are the announcements and reminders to members. While not part of the club's actual business, these items are of general interest.

- Paragraph 10 specifies the date, time, and place of the next regular meeting.

- The final paragraph gives the time of adjournment.

- Finally, the secretary omits a complimentary close and instead merely adds his signature, and typed name. The date is not the date of the meeting, but the date on which he completed the final copy of the minutes.

If you follow the model above when you take minutes for your own club or organization, you will prepare good minutes.

NARRATION

In simple words, a narration (or *narrative*) tells a story. Sometimes narration is used as a means of development whereby a writer explains his purpose. Sometimes narration is only part of a paragraph or paper developed primarily by some other method. For example, narration often appears in character sketches, autobiographies, biographies, and short stories. [*See* CHARACTER SKETCH, AUTOBIOGRAPHY, BIOGRAPHY, *and* SHORT STORY *elsewhere in Part II.*] Other than an expository paper which uses narration as its total means of development, the short story probably relies most heavily on narration.

Narration involves the reader in what you are discussing. It can allow you to make a point without sounding didactic, being too blunt, or letting the reader know your message until the very end.

Characteristics

Whether it be the development of an entire paper or only a segment of a paper, narration has certain characteristics. A narration will

- tell a story,

- have a theme rather than a topic sentence [*see* THEME, *as it relates to short story, in the Glossary*],

- be written in the first person,

- tend to be factual,

- include description [*see* DESCRIPTION *in Part II*],

- include dialogue [*see* DIALOGUE, *elsewhere in Part II*],

- rely on sensory details for impact [*see* SPECIFIC DETAIL *and* IMAGERY *in the Glossary*],

- utilize the techniques of storytelling [*see* SHORT STORY *in Part II*],

- follow a chronological organization [*see* CHRONOLOGICAL ORDER *in the Glossary*].

Process

The process by which to develop narration is very similar to that of writing a description or short story. The following steps should help you develop a successful narration.

PREWRITING

STEP 1. PLANNING THE NARRATION

Topics for narrations are usually personal experiences that relate an event of interest to the reader; but in the course of telling about the event, the writer makes a point. Think about interesting situations or events in which you have been involved. Perhaps you witnessed an automobile accident, found a stray puppy, bought a new car, were interviewed for a job, met an unusual door-to-door salesperson, experienced a frightening carnival ride. Any of these can result in a narration. [*See* PREWRITING *in Part I for additional suggestions.*] The purpose of that narration may be to entertain, or it may also have a more serious message.

So now, write a sentence summarizing the point of the narration you plan to write.

STEP 2.   PLANNING THE DETAILS

Once you have selected a topic, planning the details becomes a simple matter of listing the events you want to include. As you will recall from the Characteristics section, above, narration is usually developed in chronological order. As you develop your list, then, arrange it in the order of occurrence. Keep in mind that narration can employ some of the characteristics of storytelling. It can include flashbacks [*see* FLASHBACK *in the Glossary*], foreshadowing [*see* FORESHADOWING *in the Glossary*], or other variations of chronological order to enhance the storytelling qualities.

Complete your list of events before you go on to Step 3.

WRITING

STEP 3.   FOLLOWING THE PLAN

Writing the narration is a matter of telling the story from beginning to end. As you write, include certain techniques to generate interest for the reader. Consider the following:

- Write good description. Show the reader what happened, don't tell. [*See* DESCRIPTION *in Part II.*]

- Dialogue helps the reader see the characters in lifelike situations. [*See* DIALOGUE *in Part II.*]

- Use specific details, especially those that provide sensory images. [*See* SPECIFIC DETAIL *and* IMAGERY *in the Glossary. Also see* REVISING: SAMPLE REVISION FOR SPECIFIC DETAIL *in Part I.*]

- Employ the techniques of short-story writing, particularly those of character development, setting, and plot. [*See* SHORT STORY *in Part II.*]

- Since a narration is not actually a short story, aim toward brevity and maintain a first-person point of view.

REVISING

STEP 4.   POLISHING THE CONTENT

A narration, like any other piece of expository writing, should include good writing techniques. In order to revise your narration, ask yourself the following questions and make any revisions necessary so that you can answer "yes" to these questions:

- Have I told a story from a consistent, probably first-person point of view?

- Does the story move smoothly in chronological order?

- Have I used the techniques of storytelling: sensory images, specific details, dialogue, and elements of characterization, setting, and plot? [*See also* REVISING: SAM-PLE REVISION FOR SPECIFIC DETAIL *in Part I.*]

- Have I used good paragraphing techniques, dividing paragraphs appropriately according to change in speaker or topic? [*See* PARAGRAPHS, KINDS: IN DIALOGUE and DIALOGUE *in Part II.*]

- Have I included main ideas in main clauses?

- Does my sentence structure emphasize ideas? [*See* EMPHASIS, IN SENTENCES *and* SENTENCE STRUCTURE *in the Glossary, and see* REVISING: SAMPLE REVISION FOR EMPHASIS *in Part II.*]

- Are my sentences varied in length and structure to prevent monotonous reading? [*See* REVISING: SAMPLE REVISION FOR SENTENCE VARIETY *in Part I.*]

- Have I maintained the reader's interest throughout?

- Does my narration reach a satisfactory conclusion?

- If my narration has a message, is it clear?

PROOFREADING

STEP 5. CHECKING THE MECHANICAL DETAILS

Proofreading should involve two steps. First, check for grammar, usage, and mechanics problems. [*See the Glossary for definitions, explanations, and examples.*] Check punctuation in dialogue with care.

Second, check for accurate spelling and word choice. See *Webster's New World Dictionary* for spelling and *Webster's New World Thesaurus* for accurate word choice. Remember that good strong nouns and verbs can take the place of weak, wordy adjectives and adverbs. Proper use of your thesaurus will strengthen your composition.

--- **Sample Narration** ---

The following narration exemplifies the characteristics and process set out above. Study it and the analysis which follows for a better understanding of the development of an expository narration.

The Chinese Birth Party

"The party at 6:00," Yim said. "You be there?" I had made a commitment. Now it was time. I had never before attended a Chinese party, and this was a special one for Yim and his family, a celebration of the birth of their first child.

According to their Chinese custom, the mother and child remain in seclusion for one month after the birth of the child. At the end of the month, the joyous birth-party celebration replaces all the traditional American parties known as showers, brunches, and luncheons for mother and expected child. And what a replacement it is!

Over 150 of us crowded into the Canton Inn, the popular restaurant Yim and his family operate. In the midst of our "oohing" and "ahing," the new mother glowed with understandable joy over her sleeping baby, a bundle of black hair and pink blankets, wearing a jade pendant and a gold-coin pendant from Grandmother in Hong Kong. She slept blissfully unaware, first in her mother's arms, and then in her paternal grandmother's arms.

The restaurant tables, arranged in two long rows, were already set with cold roast duck and chunks of specially prepared pork with a crunchy crust. We nibbled. Soon to follow were bowls and bowls of Cantonese shrimp, jumbo shrimp dipped in a batter that when deep-fried came out fluffy and crisp. Traditional plum wine accompanied the appetizers.

For us Americans whose idea of Chinese appetizers is limited to egg rolls, these appetizers brought wide-eyed interest. We soon replaced our interest with wide-mouthed grins. Surprised by the chilled roast duck and infatuated by the contrast with the crunchy pork and the piping-hot shrimp, we devoured the appetizers—minus any sign of egg rolls—with relish and reckless abandon.

We shouldn't have. Before the dozens of ducks and bowls of pork and shrimp disappeared, a steady stream of main-course dishes filled and finally overfilled the tables. Surely far more dishes loaded the tables than there were people present. First a stir-fried chicken-and-almond dish with pea pods, bok choy, mushrooms, and water chestnuts tempted us. But fast-following dishes of stir-fried shrimp and sweet-and-sour pork distracted me from my usual favorite. The platter of squid and octopus prepared with onion and those black, almost filmy Chinese mushrooms wafted exotic past my nose, and I shoved the idea of squirmy squid to the back of my mind as I sampled the delicacy. It made the beef and broccoli dish taste mundane. We washed the exhorbitance down with pots and pots of aromatic hot tea.

Ah, but we weren't finished, yet. Each of us received a red egg. "Eat egg. Bring baby good luck," we were instructed.

Surely you jest, I thought to myself. Eat a hard-boiled egg after I've just glutted myself with this gourmet meal? I slipped mine, I hope unobtrusively, into my pocket. "I'll eat it later," I promised myself.

Then came dessert. No fortune cookies. Dessert. These dessert things looked rather like turnovers, pastry-covered somethings. "One has a meat filling; the other, a sweet filling," someone said who had just returned from the kitchen.

Meat for dessert? I opted for the sweet. Actually, I opted for half of a sweet and shared the other half with a new acquaintance to my left. What was the "sweet"? I have no idea. Maybe a combination of pureed fruit? With taste buds so overwhelmed by so many new flavors, they simply grew numb. A final cup of tea, thank you, and my stomach screamed, "No more!!"

And the baby slept through it all. What a joy, I thought to myself, that the Chinese feel the birth of a child merits a celebration of this degree. Ironically, at least to Americans, the only other Chinese celebration of equal magnitude is the celebration of their elders' birthdays.

Analysis of the Sample Narration

The sample narration above tells of the writer's attending a party. Certain characteristics make the sample particularly interesting:

- The narration appears in the first-person point of view.
- It tells a factual story of the writer's experiences.
- It employs elements of the short story. Dialogue appears occasionally. Good description, which tantalizes the senses, helps the reader identify with the writer's experiences.
- It follows a chronological order.
- The writer shows and does not tell about the festive activities. For instance, the reader is not told that the dishes were tasty but sees the dishes and can

imagine the taste. The writer does not tell the reader he is full, only that his stomach *screams*.

- The paragraphs change when the topics change or, in the case of dialogue, when the speakers change.
- The paragraphs do not include topic sentences, nor does the paper include a thesis sentence.
- A theme, however, does emerge, particularly in the final paragraph in which the writer shares his thoughts about the festive occasion.

By following the process, incorporating the characteristics, and comparing your narration with the sample and analysis above, you should be able to develop a satisfactory paper.

NEWS ARTICLE

News articles provide current information to newspaper and magazine readers. Most follow a specific plan which promotes brevity. [*Compare the news article with* FEATURE ARTICLE, *elsewhere in Part II. A news article reports straight "hard" news while a feature article focuses on human interest.*] Since most news-article writing appears in daily or weekly newspapers, we will focus on newspaper, rather than magazine, articles.

Most of us who have occasion to write a news article do so because of a responsibility as a publicity person for a club or organization or perhaps because we work in a public relations department for a business. In either case, unlike journalists who earn their livings writing news articles full time, we need to-the-purpose guidelines by which to prepare the article. This section should provide you that information.

Characteristics

News articles follow an *inverted-pyramid* plan. They are written to "rest" on an opening statement the way a pyramid, turned upside down, rests on its point. Sentences coming after the first statement (or *lead*) expand and broaden the topic, but the points made in them are ever less important. This structure is used because editors will often shorten articles to fit the space available. A news story written as an inverted pyramid can have its end cut without losing shape or meaning.

In general, then, the news article should

- report news, not advertise [*see* AD-VERTISING *earlier in Part II*],
- begin with the essentials: *who, what, why, when, where,* and *how,*

- add details in order of importance, most important first,
- include relevant details which may help answer anticipated questions [*see* DETAIL *in the Glossary*],
- avoid the sensational just for the sake of sensation,
- maintain the integrity of the writer and the publication,
- report information objectively, free from all opinion, judgment, and assumption,
- limit details to the facts, thus maintaining brevity,
- follow the standard rules of grammar, mechanics, and usage,
- begin a new paragraph for each new idea, often using paragraphs of only a sentence or two,
- be typewritten or printed on a letter-quality printer, double-spaced,
- be directed to a specific person at the newspaper, a person whose

name the receptionist will usually give you.

Compare these characteristics with those for an announcement [*see* ANNOUNCEMENT, *earlier in Part II*]. The news article extends and elaborates the idea presented in an announcement.

If you are not an employee of the publication, you should include certain additional information in a cover letter or on a separate sheet of paper:

- your name and title or the name and title of someone else who, as a company or organization representative, can verify the information,

- your mailing address,

- the telephone number at which you can be reached during the day.

This information is critical to an editor who, working under deadline, must contact you to clarify or to verify the facts. Without it, your article may go unpublished or be published too late. If you do not want your address and phone number published, be sure to write *Do Not Publish* alongside that information.

Process

In order to develop a satisfactory news article, follow these steps.

PREWRITING

STEP 1. GATHERING THE BASIC INFORMATION

On separate lines, list the basic questions: *who, what, why, when, where,* and *how.* Then answer each in as few words as possible. These responses provide the basic information which appears first in the inverted-pyramid construction.

STEP 2. ADDING DETAILS

Next, decide what additional information to include. Think in terms of reader interest. What impact will the news have on the community? Does the impact need further explanation? What additional information will the reader need to understand the importance of the news? In other words, what makes your article noteworthy?

As you answer these questions, make notes of additional and directly related facts which can be included. Remember: Omit judgment, opinion, and assumption.

List the details your article should include.

STEP 3. PLANNING THE INVERTED PYRAMID

Next, arrange the details listed in Step 2 above in order of importance. Note that the order of importance may not be the same as the order of interest. And it may not be the same for you as for the reader. Follow the order of importance from the point of view of the reader. Remember, the editor may need to shorten the article; he will cut from the end without revising. You must be objective. And you must be sure the reader gets the most important information first.

Arrange your list of details in the order of their importance.

WRITING

STEP 4. DEVELOPING THE FIRST DRAFT

Begin with a single sentence that includes as many of the answers to the basic-information questions as possible. If you need a second sentence to include all—the *who, what, why, when, where,* and *how*—use it. But use no more than two.

Next, add the information from Step 2, following the inverted-pyramid plan developed in Step 3. Continue adding information until you have included all the absolutely vital facts. Avoid rambling. Omit unnecessary details. Omit irrelevant information.

REVISING

STEP 5. POLISHING THE CONTENT

When you have finished the first draft, check for completeness. Ask yourself these questions:

- Have I included *who, what, why, when, where,* and *how*?

- Have I included explanations where necessary?

- Will the reader have questions I have not addressed? Can I anticipate and reply?

Next, check for good writing techniques:

- Are my sentences short and simple?

- Have I used a clear, nontechnical vocabulary?

- Have I begun a new paragraph for each new idea, recognizing that a newspaper paragraph is very unlike an expository paragraph?

- Do I follow the inverted-pyramid organization? Or will the reader lose vital information if the editor cuts the end of the article?

The answers to these questions will help you focus on areas in need of revision. Make whatever corrections and improvements you find necessary.

PROOFREADING

STEP 6. TAKING A CRITICAL LOOK

Check for accuracy. Consider the basic questions:

- Are dates accurate?

- Are times accurate, indicating Central Standard Time, Eastern Daylight Time, Pacific Time, etc.?

- Are places clearly identified, including street addresses and business locations?

- Are names included where necessary and are these people identified by title or position?

- Are other details accurate?

In addition, check for grammar, mechanics, and usage details. [*The*

Glossary provides rules, explanations, and examples.]

Finally, check spelling and word choice. Refer to *Webster's New World Dictionary* for an up-to-date spelling reference. Check *Webster's New World Thesaurus* for precise word choice.

After you have studied the characteristics and process for developing a news article, read the following sample news article and its accompanying analysis. Together, they should help you develop your own article.

Sample News Article

The public relations director of a local company submitted the following news article to the newspaper. Compare it with the announcement on the same subject released by the chairman of the board of the same company [*see* ANNOUNCEMENT *earlier in Part II*].

News Release

On June 10, Karson Manufacturing will break ground for a $6 million addition at its present location according to Lamont Karson, chairman of the board. The expansion will allow the company to increase production of its current stamping operation to meet increased sales.

As a result of the expansion, Karson expects to employ an additional 230 workers by late next year.

The information, made public at today's stockholders' meeting, confirms local business analysts' expectations of significant company profit margins. As sales increase, said Karson, profits "will be returned to the company."

The Karson stamping operation currently provides sheet-metal parts to both the automotive industry and to the small-appliance industry. The new expansion will allow the company to meet the increasing demands in both industries.

In addition, the company expects to begin operations that will serve the lawn-care industry. With the recent expansion of Jayne Lawn Equipment Manufacturing in adjoining Perigo County, Karson expects to take advantage of that growing market.

Karson explained that recent plant closings of three small area stamping operations have resulted in increased sales for Karson Manufacturing.

Since current land holdings adjoining the present manufacturing site permit extensive expansion, no residential or business properties will be affected by the plans. Ample transportation systems currently serve the site.

Analysis of the Sample News Article

As a news article, the sample above includes the characteristics which make it a satisfactory representation. Note the following specific details:

- The first two sentences provide the basic information: *who, what, why, when, where,* and *how.*
- The most important details appear first, followed by less and less important information. The final paragraph could easily be omitted without serious damage to the article.
- The writer has anticipated the reader's questions and answered them: about additional employment, increased profits, future potential, and impact on nearby homes and businesses.
- The paragraphs, unlike those in traditional expository writing, include only a few sentences so that only a single idea appears in each.
- The relatively short, uncomplicated sentences read easily and clearly.
- The article follows the standard grammar, mechanics, and usage rules.
- The article maintains an objective point of view—although another writer might have interviewed a representative from the labor community, the construction business, the stockholders' list, a competitive company, or neighboring households and businesses.

When you are ready to submit your own article, follow these suggestions:

1. Provide your name, address, and phone number so the editor can, if necessary, reach you to discuss any questions or matters needing clarification.

2. Submit the article far enough in advance so that it can be handled on a "future" basis.   Then, a few days before you want the article printed,   call the editor. This call will provide an opportunity to clear up questions and put your item in the eyes of the editor who must decide whether or not to use it.

3. Understand that the chances are good that what you submit will be changed to conform to newspaper style. Do not be surprised. In fact, some newspa-

pers routinely refuse to print material until an employee significantly re-writes it. The better your work, the better your chances that the article will carry the message and emphasis you want.

Combining the information above—the explanation and step-by-step process for writing the news article, the sample article and its analysis—should enable you to develop a successful news article for virtually any purpose.

NOTES

Notes serve two purposes: first, they help you concentrate on what you hear or read. Secondly, they help you *remember* what you have heard or read. Taking effective notes, either for a class or in preparation for writing a paper, requires you to pick out main points and supporting details. Sometimes this task is complicated by a poorly organized speaker or writer who is hard to follow. In other cases, a writer will include headnotes to indicate what each chapter covers, headings and subheadings to locate specific main ideas, and chapter summaries to emphasize the relationships among the main ideas. These will help you pick out major points and thereby take effective notes. Similarly, a good speaker or lecturer will help you take notes by telling you in the beginning what he or she intends to talk about and by listing his or her main points.

In this section, we will discuss two kinds of note-taking: for a class and for a paper. Since the approaches differ for each, we will look at them separately.

FOR A CLASS

One kind of note-taking is in preparation for a class. You may be taking notes from materials assigned to be read or from materials presented orally in class, either during a lecture or in-class discussion.

Characteristics

Notes for a class fall into two categories: notes on reading and notes on oral material. General characteristics exist for either kind. Usually, good notes

- should be brief but thorough,

- appear in short- or notehand or in a self-styled abbreviated form,

- may appear in formal outline style [*see* OUTLINES, KINDS: AS A SUMMARY *in Part II*], as a list, or as a series of phrases, according to the writer's purpose,

- include the main points,

- provide enough supporting details to show the significance of the main points,

- provide a chance to review the contents of the course prior to testing,

- stimulate recall of additional details and relationships among ideas discussed in class.

Frequently, notes taken in class are written hurriedly and in such an abbreviated form as to become meaningless later. As a result, some notes, particularly those taken in class, should be reread as soon as possible. Explanatory words, phrases, and supporting details should be added so that the notes will later retain their meaning.

Process

The process for taking notes is primarily a mental one. Preparation for taking notes is, therefore, primarily mental. Attentiveness and concentration are the two qualities most important to taking effective notes. Let's look at the process step by step.

PREWRITING

STEP 1.   GETTING READY TO TAKE NOTES

If you are getting ready to take notes from reading materials, gather the essential tools—the reading matter, paper, and pen or pencil—and find a comfortable place to work. Look through the assigned reading. Is there a headnote which describes the topics to be discussed? Are there headings? Subheadings? Section summaries? Chapter summaries? If so, read them through. This kind of preparation, sometimes called *surveying*, lets you know what to expect and helps you concentrate on and watch for major points.

If you are preparing to take notes in class, again make sure that you are prepared. Preparation assumes not only that you have the necessary materials but also that you have

studied the assignment. As a result, notes you take on reading matter will prepare you for note-taking in class. Some students, in fact, like to take notes in a notebook using the left-hand side of the page for assigned reading notes and the right-hand side of the page for parallel in-class discussion notes.

WRITING

STEP 2.   PICKING OUT THE MAIN IDEAS

In order to take effective notes, you must be able to pick out main ideas. The main ideas in reading matter are easier to pinpoint than the ones in oral presentations. The reasons are simple: most written matter is more carefully organized and constructed than is an oral presentation. In addition, you can reread as many times as necessary to find the main ideas. Together, these two conditions simplify note-taking from printed material. Understanding any preceding assignment, however, should help you select main ideas from a discussion. Certainly any topic that was important in a reading assignment will be important to the in-class discussion.

So we will concentrate on picking out main ideas in written matter. You know from your own writing experience that paragraph structures revolve around main ideas. While professional writers sometimes do not include a topic sentence in every paragraph, a good reader should be able to pick out the main idea from a paragaraph and put it into a sentence. As you take notes from reading matter, then, select one idea from each paragraph to include in your notes.

Include the main ideas in the order in which they appear in the reading matter.

As you write, watch for specifics: names, dates, and statistics you know the instructor will stress. Be sure this kind of information is in your notes.

If the reading matter includes charts, diagrams, tables, figures, graphs, or maps, determine the significance of the information they contain. Include this information in your notes as well. These kinds of details will help you later, as you review for an in-class discussion or exam.

Remember that notes can take varied forms, from formal outlines, to word lists, to phrases, to whole sentences. Use whichever form best suits your purpose.

REVISING AND PROOFREADING

STEP 3. CHECKING LEGIBILITY

Since note-taking is highly personal, it need not follow a particular style or form. There is little responsibility for revising and proofreading. But there is one exception: Many times during an oral presentation, notes must be taken rapidly; the results may be less thorough than you would like. In such cases, words or phrases are jotted down to remind you of whole ideas. And while using words or brief phrases is the best way to take notes under such conditions, two days later (and almost certainly, two weeks later) the notes may make little sense. As a result, it is imperative to read over the notes as soon as possible. In the course of rereading, add new details to help you later review for a test or prepare for a discussion.

Sample Notes for a Class

The following reading was assigned for class. Below, you will find the notes taken on the reading. [*For an example of notes on the same reading matter, prepared in a formal outline style, see* OUTLINES, KINDS: AS A SUMMARY, *later in Part II.*]

Original Passage

The food habits of birds make them especially valuable to agriculture. Because birds have higher body temperatures, more rapid digestion, and greater energy than most other animals, they require more food. Nestling birds make extremely rapid growth, requiring huge amounts of food. They usually consume as much as or more than their own weight in soft-bodied insects every day.

Young robins have been observed to gain eight times their original weight in the first 8 days of their life.

Insect-eating birds must fill their stomachs five to six times daily because they digest their food so fast and because of the large amount of indigestible material in insects.

One young robin, weighing three ounces, consumed 165 cutworms weighing 5-1/2 ounces in one day. If a ten-pound baby ate at the same rate, he would eat 18-1/3 pounds of food in a day.

Of course, birds cannot control insects completely, but they are of great value. By using soil- and water-conserving practices farmers and ranchers could probably double the population of helpful birds. Field and farmstead windbreaks, living fences, shrub buffers, grass waterways, and farm ponds are only a few of the many land use practices useful in attracting and increasing beneficial forms of wildlife.

Notes

Birds help control insects:
—eat more than weight
—fill stomach 5-6 times/day
—much indigest. stuff in insects.

Comparison: 10-lb. baby would eat 18-1/3 lbs./day.

To increase bird population:
windbreaks
living fences
shrub buffers
grass waterways
farm ponds

Analysis of the Sample Notes for a Class

The brief notes above will help the note-taker remember the contents of the reading matter. A few characteristics bear mentioning:

• The form includes phrases and lists rather than whole sentences, yet the notes present information clearly and completely.

- Certain stylistic gimmicks appear: the use of dashes, the substitution of the / mark to mean *per*, and abbreviations for long words. Each helps the writer take notes more quickly without clouding the content.
- The notes include all the main ideas from the reading matter and several, but not all, illustrations to show the significance of the main ideas.

Someone else's notes on the same reading matter would likely vary in form and style. Still, as long as the essential details appeared, the notes would serve their purpose: to quickly remind the reader of important information.

FOR A PAPER

The second kind of note-taking is that used in preparation for developing a lengthy paper that requires research; such a paper is frequently called a *term, research,* or *library paper.* [*See* RESEARCH PAPER *in Part II.*]

Characteristics

The characteristics of note-taking for a paper differ considerably from that for class assignments or in-class lectures. Notes taken in preparation for writing a paper require a great deal of attention to two details:

- maintaining careful records for source documentation,
- exercising extreme caution to avoid plagiarism [*see* PLAGIARISM *in the Glossary*].

As a result, notes taken in preparation for writing a paper should

- appear on 3″ × 5″ or 4″ × 6″ note cards with one card for each idea,
- acknowledge the source from which the note is taken, including the author, the title, and the page number [*see* RESEARCH PAPER *in Part II for documentation forms*],
- include quotation marks around any words taken directly from the source,
- paraphrase any technical information [*see* PARAPHRASE *in the Glossary and in Part II*],
- include words, phrases, lists, or sentences which summarize main ideas [*see* PRECIS *in the Glossary and in Part II*],
- be concise,
- address the main ideas,
- treat examples, illustrations, or other supporting details only when these are particularly telling,
- include a *slug,* or title, that names the topic of the note, one that will help the writer arrange the note cards later according to an organizational plan. [*See* RESEARCH PAPER *in Part II.*]

Process

The process of taking notes for a paper is considerably more complicated than for other reading matter. Notes for a paper must be preceded by the development of a preliminary outline and some reading in the general subject area. [*See* RESEARCH PAPER *in Part II.*]

As a result, even though we are beginning with the prewriting step, you must understand that other tasks (namely, selecting, narrowing, and determining the direction of the topic; reading the preliminary sources; preparing a preliminary bibliography; developing the preliminary outline) have been completed prior to the onset of your prewriting activity.

Look now at the steps in the actual note-taking process.

PREWRITING

STEP 1.   GETTING READY

You will need a preliminary outline, the research material, 3" x 5" or 4" × 6" note cards, and an ink pen. Using ink helps keep your note cards legibile through the extensive handling required to organize your paper.

The preliminary outline includes the words and phrases which become the slugs for your note cards. A *slug* is a title or topic for a note card, and it appears on the top line of the card. Accurate, descriptive slugs will help you organize your cards later. Remember, however, that the outline will undergo constant revision. You will no doubt add topics and subtopics, and you may well decide to eliminate some. You may change the overall organization as you please.

As you prepare to take notes, check the table of contents and index of any books from which you are gathering materials, looking for areas that appear pertinent to your subject. Refer to these sections or chapters and read for details relevant to your topic.

Keep your numbered bibliography cards nearby. [See RESEARCH PAPER *in Part II.*] Use the numbers on the cards to code the source of your notes. For instance, if you are reading from page 56 in a magazine whose bibliography card you have numbered 8, then the code 8–56 would appear in the upper-right corner of your note card. If you omit this designation, you will be unable to accurately document the reference later. Most instructors react harshly to sloppy documentation.

WRITING

STEP 2.   SELECTING THE DETAILS

As you find information in your reading matter that will help you develop main points or subpoints in your outline, take notes. Begin by noting the source of the material. Use either a code number, as discussed above, or the author's last name and the page number. Put this information in the upper right corner of your note card.

Write only one idea on each card, even if that idea is only a few words. If you include more than one idea, the cards will be useless when you begin to arrange them for your paper.

Put your notes in your own words. You may use a list, paraphrase, or precis form. [*Follow the suggestions in* PARAPHRASE *and* PRECIS *elsewhere in Part II for writing accurate summaries.*]

Avoid copying words from the text as if they were your own. Put quotation marks around words taken directly from the source. In order to avoid plagiarism, you must be scrupulously careful with your note cards. Omitting quotation marks around an author's words at this point will obviously cause you to omit them later, when you transfer the information from the cards to your paper. The price of such carelessness may be higher than you are willing to pay: your instructor will fail papers that include plagiarism. Be careful.

PROOFREADING AND REVISING

STEP 3. CHECKING THE NOTE CARDS

Since taking notes for a longer paper is merely for your own information, the format and style are generally unimportant. As long as you include the necessary information, your note card will be satisfactory. To assure accuracy, proofread and revise each card before you turn it aside to begin another one. Ask yourself the following questions about each card:

- Does the card designate, either in code or completely, the source from which it is taken, including author, title, and page number?

- Does it carry a notation of its subject, preferably in the form of a slug, taken directly from the preliminary outline?

- Have I avoided plagiarism by placing quotation marks around any words not my own?

- Does my paraphrase or precis accurately express the point of view of the author from whom I took the note?

- Have I correctly spelled the names of people and places?

- Have I accurately recorded dates, statistics, or other numbers?

When you finish checking one note card, go on to the next. Failing to check before turning a card aside is begging for a long search later to find a forgotten page reference, the end of an incomplete quotation, or the accurate spelling of a name.

─────────── **Sample of Notes for a Paper** ───────────

The following notes taken from the original passage quoted above, in Sample of Notes for a Class, illustrate three general concepts:

- Notes for a paper take a form very different from those for a class.

- Notes for a paper frequently use a type of summary called a *precis*.

- A single note card includes only one idea.

[*Compare* PRECIS, SAMPLE FOR SCIENCE, *in Part II, with the notes below.*]

The following notes would be included in a paper discussing environmentally safe ways of controlling insects that are agricultural pests.

---

4 - 16

Control—birds

Because of their rapid metabolism, birds daily eat more than their own weight. Since insects are not fully digestible, birds eat nearly twice their weight.

---

4 - 17

Control—birds

will "fill their stomachs 5 to 6 times daily" so eat large amounts—much of insect not digestible.

---

4 - 17

Control—birds

Comparison: 10-lb. baby would eat 18 1/3 lb. per day

(Do own comparison with adult, same proportions.)

---

4 - 19

Control—birds—encourage more

Add "windbreaks, living fences, shrub buffers, grass waterways, and farm ponds" to encourage insect-eating birds to stay.

Analysis of the Sample Notes for a Paper

The note cards above, taken from the same passage as the notes for a class, emphasize the differences between the two kinds of notes. Consider these items:

- Each card begins with a slug, or title, to show where the note fits into the overall topic. Each card deals with *Control—birds*, but the last adds a subdivision to the slug to help the writer organize the cards later.

- Each includes a single idea: some sketched as mere words and phrases, some by complete sentences, some with direct quotation, some entirely in the note-taker's own words.

- Each includes a code number in the upper-right corner. The code tells the writer in which book and page the information was found. The number 4 refers to the bibliography card the writer has designated 4; thus the number becomes shorthand for both the name of the author and the title of the book. The second number, (e.g., 16) indicates the page number on which the specific information is to be found.

Using these general guidelines will enable you to take accurate and useful notes. They will help you avoid plagiarism and allow you to include a variety of information from many sources without confusion. These are the two big hurdles which the successful note-taker must overcome. By following these processes, you will easily overcome both.

OPINION

Because an opinion, by definition, cannot be proven, a writer who expresses one has an important responsibility. The writer must somehow show she or he has examined all the facts, angles, possibilities, and, as a result, has made a judgment or formed an opinion.

The opinion paper may serve many purposes. It may attempt nothing more than to share ideas and stimulate thinking. Or it may serve to explain the writer's reasons for certain actions or reactions, thus playing an important role in interpersonal relationships. Or it may prepare the reader to accept an argument and change his or her mind.

The opinion paper and the persuasion (or argumentative) paper bear some similarities. Both express the writer's judgment and offer details as support. The persuasion paper, however, goes a step farther: it tries to change the reader's mind. [*As you work through this section, compare it with* PERSUASION, *elsewhere in Part II. Compare specifically the* SAMPLE FOR SOCIAL SCIENCES *in* PERSUASION *with the sample included in this section. Since both deal with the same topic, the comparison should be especially helpful.*]

A specific kind of opinion paper can be found in the form of a letter to the editor. While some letters to the editor attempt to persuade readers, many merely express an opinion. [*For a comparison, see* LETTERS, KINDS: EDITORIAL, *earlier in Part II. Compare especially the sample there with the sample included in this section. Again, both deal with the same topic.*]

By making a three-way comparison of the opinion essay with the persuasive essay and with the letter to the editor, you will better understand the characteristics and purposes of the three forms of writing and, as a result, write a more effective opinion paper.

Characteristics

The opinion paper should include a number of specific kinds of details. Generally, the opinion essay should

- deal with a subject which cannot be proven,

- deal with a topic worthy of the writer's effort and the reader's time, i.e., express an opinion not widely held,

- express an opinion likely to cause opposition,

- indicate the writer's careful examination of the available facts,

- provide details, illustrations, statistics, examples, comparisons, contrasts, definitions, descriptions, causes, effects, and analogies to support the opinion [*see* DE-

TAIL, ILLUSTRATION, STATISTICS, *and* EXAMPLE *in the Glossary and* COMPARISON AND CONTRAST, DEFINITION, DESCRIPTION, CAUSE AND EFFECT, *and* ANALOGY *elsewhere in Part II*],

- avoid phrases like *I believe, I think,* or *in my opinion* since the paper's purpose is to express opinion,

- anticipate the reader's point of view and thereby include the most appropriate supporting material,

- stop short of simply telling the reader to accept the writer's opinion or take some action.

Process

Developing an opinion paper calls for an objective examination of all information available and a careful analysis of your opinion. The following process should help you plan and develop an effective opinion paper.

PREWRITING

STEP 1. THINKING ABOUT THE SUBJECT

Even though we all have opinions, most of them are probably not well founded. For instance, we may be quick to express the opinion that heating with wood offers few advantages to modern households. But what do we really know about heating with wood? Do we know how to regulate room temperature with wood heat? Do we know how a house feels that is heated with wood? Or do we have some preconceived notion that conjures up images of sitting around a potbellied stove, roasting one side while freezing the other? If so, we are expressing an unfounded opinion. We really do not know all the facts.

Thinking about your subject demands that you determine objectively what you know and what you do not. [*See* PREWRITING *in Part I for additional suggestions.*] Is research necessary? Will your reader have information that you do not? If you make obvious errors, including errors of omission, you may look ridiculous; your credibility will suffer.

So, do whatever reseach is necessary. Know what you are writing about.

STEP 2. STATING THE SUBJECT

After careful thought and thorough research, you should be able to express your opinion in a single sentence. Consider the following examples:

Florida is the worst possible winter vacation spot.

Cats understand what we say to them.

Football players make more money than they are worth.

POSSIBLE PITFALL: As you write your sentence, check that you have a topic really suitable for an opinion paper. Avoid any subject that can be proved or disproved with statistics, research, or experimentation. Consider these examples:

Poor example: The Freedom Festival attracts more visitors to Kingston than any other activity the city sponsors.
(We can prove or disprove that by counting visitors.)

Better example: The Freedom Festival is more enjoyable than any other activity sponsored by the City of Kingston.
(We cannot prove or disprove *more enjoyable*. That becomes a matter of opinion.)

Write a single sentence which states the opinion you will develop in your paper.

STEP 3.   THINKING ABOUT THE READERS

Thinking about your audience helps determine what you need to include. Do you expect a strongly antagonistic reader? Or is the reader apt simply to sit back and read without really reacting one way or the other? If you anticipate antagonism, you will approach the organizational plan differently than if you anticipate idle interest.

Likewise, think about the reader's personal interest in your subject. Does the subject affect the reader's pocketbook, eating habits, health, family, life style, job, ability to work, recreation, or hobbies? Capitalize on whatever personal involvement may develop. [*See Part I,* PREWRITING, *for additional suggestions.*]

STEP 4.   SELECTING DETAILS

Select details appropriate for your audience. Referring to Step 3, select details that matter. You do not want the reader to finish your paper and say, "So what?"

Make a list of possible supporting details. Consider the following:

Radio stations should be prevented from airing local sports events.

interferes with gate receipts

interferes with simultaneous out-of-town broadcasts

intensifies feelings of ill will when two local events occur simultaneously

causes added confusion in the announcers' booth

causes traffic congestion when radio truck must park near stadium

ties sports events to commercial sponsors

interferes unnecessarily with regular radio programming

antagonizes regular listeners who are not sports enthusiasts

Develop your own list of details now. List anything that will help you explain or support your opinion.

STEP 5. ORGANIZING THE DETAILS

You will decide that not all the details on your list merit equal attention. You may, in fact, choose to eliminate some of them. Details may be cut because they represent a change in point of view. For instance, in the list above, some details express the view of the sports fan (*interferes with gate receipts; interferes with simultaneous out-of-town-games*) while others represent the view of those uninterested in sports (*interferes unnecessarily with regular radio programming; antagonizes regular listeners*).

Limit your supporting details to the three or four most relevant.

Next, organize the list logically. Most opinion papers follow some order of importance. [*See* PREWRITING *in Part I and* ORDERS OF IMPORTANCE *in the Glossary.*] Again, keep the reader in mind. How can you most likely gain and retain his or her attention? Apply those thoughts to the order of importance. For instance, if you can support your opinion with details concerning tax dollars, environmental issues, and human rights, the reader is most personally and immediately affected by taxpayers' dollars—in the pocketbook. Only if you can show the reader a direct personal stake in environmental issues (for instance, that air pollutants will destroy the paint of an expensive new car) will he or she be actively inter-

ested. The same holds true for the vague term *human rights*; the reader must be shown how such a concept affects him or her in daily life. A reader will be attracted first and foremost by what seems immediate and personal: in this case, taxes.

Now, organize the list. You will probably use the following order of importance:

Detail one:	second most important
Detail two:	least important
Detail three:	third most important
Detail four:	most important

This organization allows you to begin with something important enough to catch the reader's attention but still save the whopper for last, when the reader will most likely accept it.

WRITING
STEP 6. FOLLOWING THE PLAN

As you write, follow the organizational plan you established above. Use the items listed in the Characteristics section. In addition, try to include the following writing techniques:

- Begin with an effective introduction, one that will attract the reader's attention to your topic. If you are writing a paragraph, your introduction will comprise a sentence or two; but if you are writing a longer paper, your introduction will be a full paragraph ending with a thesis sentence. [*See* PARAGRAPHS *and* THEME *elsewhere in Part II. See also* TOPIC SENTENCE *and* THESIS SENTENCE *in the Glossary.*]

- If your subject is highly controversial, your topic or thesis sentence may appear at the end of your paper. By withholding your precise statement of opinion, you can prepare the reader throughout the paper's development to more readily accept your opinion.

- As you follow the organizational plan, maintain a single idea in a single paragraph. [*See* UNITY *in the Glossary.*]

- Provide adequate supporting details for each main idea. You can use a wide variety of methods of development, perhaps even several simultaneously. [*See* DEVELOPMENT, METHODS OF *in the Glossary.*]

- Include transitions—words, phrases, or sentences—both within and between paragraphs to help the reader follow your thoughts and see the relationships among your ideas. [*See* TRANSITION *in the Glossary.*]

- Remember that you are explaining why you hold your opinion. You are not attempting to persuade the reader to think as you do.

- In order not to offend the reader, maintain a third-person point of view. You should not include such phrases as *I believe* or *in my opinion.* At the same time, to use the second-person point of view *you* is to risk putting the reader ill at ease.

- Conclude with a reference to the topic or thesis sentence. A summary of your main points may also serve effectively as a conclusion.

Write quickly to get your ideas on paper. Do not worry about sentence structure, mechanics, grammar, and other technical details. Think about content. Think about the best examples or details to explain your opinion. Just write. [*See also* WRITING *in Part I.*]

REVISING

STEP 7. IMPROVING THE CONTENT

Rereading the draft will help you see trouble spots that need revision. Certainly some problems will be obvious, and you can correct those relatively easily. However, you should think through your draft, asking yourself specific questions to help you spot other problem areas. Use the following questions as a guide:

- Have I introduced my subject in such a way as to attract the reader's attention?

- With a subject likely to create antagonism, have I begun with details least apt to turn away the reader?

- Have I organized the details in the most effective manner? Do I attract interest early, maintain it, and build to the most significant supportive details?

- Does the topic or thesis statement appear in the introduction or, in the case of a highly controversial subject, in the conclusion?

- Do the details support the opinion I am trying to express? Have I maintained unity? [*See* REVISING: SAMPLE REVISION FOR UNITY *in Part I.*]

- Have I included effective transitions both between and within paragraphs? [*See* REVISING: SAMPLE REVISION FOR TRANSITION *in Part I.*]

- Are the supporting details specific? Have I used specific words, clear examples, good illustrations, effective explanations? Can the reader identify with the supporting details? [*See* REVISING: SAMPLE REVISION FOR SPECIFIC DETAIL *in Part I.*]

- Are my sentences varied in length and structure? Have I maintained sound emphasis within the sentences, putting the main ideas in the main clauses? [*See* REVISING: SAMPLE REVISION FOR SENTENCE VARIETY *and* REVISING: SAMPLE REVISION FOR EMPHASIS *in Part I.*]

- Is the conclusion effective?

Using these questions as guidelines, make whatever revisions necessary in order to improve your opinion essay. Be sure you can answer "yes" to the questions above. Then compare your essay with the sample and its analysis below.

─────────────── **Sample Opinion Paper** ───────────────

The following opinion essay adheres to the characteristics set out above. [*As you examine the sample paper, compare it with the Sample for Social Sciences in* PERSUASION *and with* LETTERS, KINDS: EDITORIAL (*both in Part II*) *to better understand how the same subject is handled for different purposes. The comparison will help you identify the specific emphasis and organization of an opinion paper.*]

The Eighth-District Congressional Race

Two qualified candidates have conducted their equally active campaigns to influence the voters of the eighth district. Democrat Jerrald Kinsingtonne and Republican Rodney Brolliette represent their parties well and have conducted themselves as gentlemen in what historically has been a sometimes less than gentlemanly race. Both deserve commendations for that. One man, however, has offered voters in the eighth district at least three reasons to earn their support.

As a conservative, Brolliette has taken a tough stand against illegal drugs, demanding unannounced testing of all city, state, and federal employees. Kinsingtonne, while also opposing illegal drug use, believes the drug testing proposed by his opponent may well be illegal. His respect for individual rights and concern for innocent victims makes him wary of possibly illegal measures. He cites test cases in which nondrug users tested positive as a result of recent surgery or as a result of legal, doctor-prescribed medications. At the same time, known users tested negative because they bought "legal" urine and made a quick transfer of specimens. Instead of such testing, then, Kinsingtonne believes a crackdown on illegal drug dealers—more arrests and stiffer penalties—may better serve to halt the drain on the nation's economic resources. His alternative protects honest citizens from undue harrassment.

As a result of the recent controversy over a proposed hazardous-waste incinerator to be located in the heart of the eighth district, voters have had the opportunity to examine the environmental position of the two candidates. Kinsingtonne announced his opposition early, risking the ire of construction workers who would likely build that plant as well as the ire of the general public who looked forward to thirty additional jobs in the area. As local environmentalists explained to the public the inherent dangers of the incinerator and pointed out its proximity to a major earthquake fault and the water supply for over half of the district, citizens joined the opposition. Only then, when it seemed popular, did Brolliette take a position, ironically one mirroring the apparently successful Kinsingtonne stand. Perhaps only the more aggressive candidate will help successfully fight the proposed plant.

Finally, each candidate sees the depressed economy as a major issue in the eighth district. Brolliette proposes tax incentives to lure big businesses into the area. The Republican incumbent, in fact, voted for the huge tax incentive that brought two moderate-sized businesses to the area. Suddenly, however, area citizens have been hit with major increases in their personal property tax bills, some as much as double. Although the businesses offered over 1,200 jobs, almost all have gone to employees who accepted a transfer as a result of one business' plant closing in the Southwest. So irate local citizens are footing the tax bill for jobs not open to them. Brolliette continues to defend the position. Kinsingtonne, on the other hand, warned City Council and County Council members that citizens would resent the increase. He fought for citizen protection even before he announced his candidacy for office. Apparently he understands the common man's plight and the ramifications of big business on the little man's pocketbook.

Surely little doubt remains who will make the best representative for the eighth district. Kinsingtonne understands the impact of proposals on individual rights, on local environment, and on taxpayers pocketbooks. He identifies with the individual and risks unpopular positions to do what he knows is right. That's good.

Analysis of the Sample Opinion Paper

The sample paper above follows the general guidelines for a good opinion paper. In addition to effective organization and good theme structure, note the following specifics:

- The introduction compliments both candidates but concludes with the intentionally vague thesis sentence alluding to three reasons the writer prefers one candidate over the other.
- Each paragraph explains an issue or a situation in which Kinsingtonne has, in the writer's opinion, proposed a better plan or behaved in a better way than Brolliette.
- While the paper gives the reader some individual issues with which to identify, the personal involvement is not as direct as that in a persuasive paper or in a letter to the editor. [See PERSUASION, *especially the Sample for Social Sciences, and* LETTERS, KINDS: EDITORIAL *elsewhere in Part II.*]
- The comparison-contrast approach allows the writer to discuss first Brolliette's position or proposal and counter it with the "better" Kinsingtonne position or proposal. [See COMPARISON AND CONTRAST, *earlier in Part II, for a careful discussion of organizational patterns.*]
- The conclusion permits the writer to state his position without asking readers to vote for Kinsingtonne or agree.

Compare the sample opinion paper above with your own. Apply the techniques to improve your own work. Consult the cross-references indicated. As a result, you should be able to develop a successful opinion paper.

OUTLINES

Outlines serve several purposes, primarily as summaries for something we have read or are about to develop into a paper or speech. They are somewhat like skeletons: the bare bones on which to hang the muscle of a composition. Sometimes their formality intimidates writers, but in reality they are merely lists that show the arrangement of details. In this section, we will look at an outline as a summary of reading matter, in preparation for a paper, and in preparation for a speech. While all follow the general characteristics, each will take a slightly different approach to suit its purpose.

Characteristics

The outline includes certain characteristics. An outline

- includes a title,
- may begin with a thesis statement or, in the case of a speech, an introductory statement,
- includes topics or sentences, but not both,
- follows a parallel structure [*see* PARALLEL STRUCTURE *in the Glossary*],
- uses a combination of Roman numerals, upper- and lower-case letters, and Arabic numbers to show relationships,
- shows the logic of development, so that the summary of the parts of any one subdivision equals the topic of that division,
- will include topics which are mutually exclusive,
- will include at least two divisions at any level, so that an item designated *1* will be followed by *2* and an item designated *a* will be followed by *b*,
- guides the paragraph structure of a written paper, with each main idea or subheading representing a separate paragraph,
- uses periods and parentheses to set number and letter designations apart from the outline topics or sentences,
- follows a pattern of indentation to show the relationship of ideas,
- capitalizes only the first word of each topic in a topic outline,
- omits periods after topics in a topic outline,
- capitalizes the first word of the sentence in a sentence outline,
- includes a period at the end of each sentence in a sentence outline.

A fully developed outline which includes numerous details will follow the pattern shown below:

Title

I. _____
   A. _____
   B. _____
     1. _____
     2. _____
   C. _____
     1. _____
     2. _____

II. _____
   A. _____
     1. _____
       a. _____
       b. _____
     2. _____
   B. _____
     1. _____
     2. _____
       a. _____
         1) _____
         2) _____
           a) _____
           b) _____
         3) _____
       b. _____
     3. _____

III. _____
   A. _____
   B. _____

Note that the sample outline form above illustrates characteristics peculiar to the form:

- The Roman numerals have a ragged left margin so that the periods after them align vertically.

- The number-letter designation follows this pattern:

  ○ Roman numerals,
  ○ capital letters,
  ○ Arabic numbers,
  ○ lower-case letters,
  ○ Arabic numbers followed by parentheses,
  ○ lower-case letters followed by parentheses.

- Each number or letter is followed by a period or a parenthesis.

- Each level is represented by equal indentation. Thus, all items designated by a capital letter appear at the same left margin.

- The total of the subpoints equals the main point. Thus, in the section labeled with a Roman numeral *II,* item *B* equals the total of subpoints *1, 2,* and *3.* Likewise, item *2* equals the total of subpoints *a* and *b* and item *a* equals the total of subpoints *1), 2),* and *3).*

- Divisions should be mutually exclusive. For instance, if you divide *college students* into *male, female,* and *nontraditional,* then you have a problem with mutual exclusion. Nontraditional students, those older than most, are either male or female. The divisions overlap. To solve the problem, divide *college students* into *traditional* and *nontraditional.* Those two subdivisions could in turn be divided into *male* and *female.* Then each division is mutually exclusive.
- Since outlines follow a parallel structure, you should note that items within categories are parallel to each other. Thus items listed after Roman numerals must be parallel. In addition, items *A, B,* and *C* in *I* must be parallel, but they need not be parallel with *A* and *B* in either *II* or *III.*

These general characteristics should help you develop an outline to meet the most demanding needs. Follow every detail with exceeding care if you are submitting a formal outline as part of a paper. Pay less attention to details if you are merely taking notes for your eyes only.

Recognizing those acceptable differences, let's talk next about the specific purposes of outlines and how we usually develop outlines for each of those purposes.

AS A SUMMARY

Frequently, as we read or listen to an oral presentation, we need to take notes. While the approach to note-taking varies from individual to individual and situation to situation [*see also* NOTES *elsewhere in Part II*], one form of note-taking is outlining.

The outline, while rather formal in appearance, permits a writer to show relationships among ideas. By keeping track of those relationships as they develop, either in the reading or in the oral presentation, the note-taker can later recall how one idea relates to another or how an example explains a general concept.

Process

The process of taking notes by means of an outline is only slightly different from taking any other kind of notes. The biggest difference is form.

PREWRITING

STEP 1. GETTING AN OVERVIEW

If you are taking notes from reading matter, skim the chapter or section and determine its main points. Write them down, perhaps on separate sheets of paper, allowing ample space for supporting details.

If you are taking notes from an oral presentation, listen carefully for the speaker's clues. He or she may say something like, "This afternoon we will discuss three methods for approaching the potentially irate client." You know, then, to look for three main ideas. In addition, listen for clues like *first, second, one of the reasons, another,* and other similar transitional devices that signal main and supporting ideas.

Having a general overview will help you determine which supporting details belong with which main ideas.

WRITING

STEP 2.   SHOWING RELATIONSHIPS AMONG IDEAS

As you list your main headings, designate their order by Roman numerals. As you read or hear about details which support or explain those main ideas, list them as subheadings, designated by capital letters. If additional supporting exam-

ples or illustrations appear as support for the subheadings, then indent for another "layer" of details.

Remember that listing topics in their appropriate levels of relationship will help you better understand the material you are studying.

REVISING AND PROOFREADING:

STEP 3.   CHECKING FOR ACCURACY

As you reread your outline, think about the relationships of ideas as your outline expresses them. For instance, start with the supporting ideas in one section. Do the ideas listed as subpoints really explain the topic under which you have them listed? In other words, do subtopics *1, 2* and *3* under *B* really illustrate, explain, list the parts, or make up the whole of topic *B*?

If you find illogical levels of support, revise the outline until you are certain it accurately reflects what you have read or heard.

Sample Outline as a Summary

The following outline summarizes reading material. For comparison's sake we are showing the outline first in topic form and then in sentence form. Use whichever best serves your purpose.

For the text from which the following outline was made, see NOTES, the section Sample Notes for a Class, elsewhere in Part II. In addition, in that same section, you will want to compare the less formal notes appearing with the original text in NOTES and the more formal notes appearing as an outline below.

Topic Outline

Birds as Insect Controllers

I. How birds help
   A. Have high metabolism rate
   B. Eat nearly twice weight
      1. 3-ounce to 5 1/2-ounce ratio in birds
      2. 10-pound to 18 1/3-pound ratio in humans
II. How environment helps
   A. Vegetation
      1. Windbreaks
      2. Living fences
      3. Shrub buffers
   B. Water
      1. Farm ponds
      2. Grass waterways

Sentence Outline

Birds as Insect Controllers

I. Birds eat insects.
   A. The birds have a high metabolism rate.
   B. The birds eat almost twice their own weight.
      1. A 3-ounce baby bird will eat 5 1/2 ounces of insects.
      2. A 10-pound human baby would have to eat 18 1/3 pounds of food.
II. The environment attracts birds.
   A. Planting the right vegetation attracts birds.
      1. Windbreaks provide birds protection.
      2. Living fences provide birds nesting and roosting sites.
      3. Shrub buffers provide birds protection.
   B. Developing water sources attracts birds.
      1. Farm ponds provide birds with water and food.
      2. Grass waterways attract birds of different varieties.

Analysis of the Sample Outline as a Summary

The sample outline above, which appears in both topic and sentence form, should help you see the importance of an outline in showing relationships among ideas. If you compare this outline with the notes [*see* NOTES *in Part II*] on the same reading material, you can see how ideas take on a new meaning when grouped by relation. Notice these characteristics about the two forms of the outline above:

- Each of the main headings is supported by two subheadings. Although such perfectly even distribution is not essential, it does indicate that the note taker has not given undue attention to one main idea while neglecting the others.

- Each division includes at least two items, thus following the logic that nothing can be divided into less than two.

- The subtopics, taken together, explain, illustrate, or provide other supporting detail to fully develop their respective main topics.

- Both the topic and sentence outline follow a parallel structure. Note that the main headings are parallel and that the subheadings are structurally parallel with the other subheadings in that same division. [*See* PARALLEL STRUCTURE *in the Glossary.*]

- The outlines use proper punctuation and indentation.

- The number-letter combinations establish relationships between and among ideas.

- The topic outline uses capital letters for only the first word in each topic.

- The topic outline does not include periods after the topics.

- The sentence outline follows the rules of capitalization for any sentence, and of course, each sentence ends with a period.

FOR A PAPER

Writing an outline for a paper requires a different thought process than writing an outline as a summary. When you outline as a summary, you reduce someone else's ideas to a bare-bones skeleton; however, when you outline in preparation for a paper, you must generate the bare-bones skeleton and then add the muscle. The process demands your creativity.

Developing a formal outline may not be necessary for all papers, but you will almost always develop a kind of outline, even if it is nothing but a loose listing of ideas you want to include. You will notice throughout this book, in the course of the prewriting work, we develop lists. We do not call them outlines, but in fact they are scratch outlines. To make them into formal outlines requires adding only the formality: the proper number-letter combinations, indentation pattern, capitalization and punctuation necessities, and parallel structures.

So let us study now the process for turning a loose listing into a formal outline.

Process

Assume, for the sake of practicality, that you are about to write a paper that requires a formal outline. It might be a research paper, a technical paper, or a long paper of unusual formality. Follow these steps for developing the outline.

PREWRITING

STEP 1.   LOOKING AT THE LISTS

As you work through the prewriting stages of your paper, you will develop one or more lists. From these lists you will develop your outline. One list may include the main points you plan to make. You probably have put that list into some kind of order. [*See* ORGANIZATION *in the Glossary for an explanation of the main kinds of order.*] You may have another list of the supporting details you plan to use to explain your main ideas: illustrations, examples, and so forth. These lists, reorganized and rearranged, will make up the outline.

WRITING

STEP 2.   PUTTING THE LISTS INTO OUTLINE FORM

Begin by writing your thesis statement. [*See* THESIS STATEMENT *in the Glossary.*] The prewriting activities for the particular kind of paper will have helped you develop that statement.

Next, list your main ideas either on separate sheets of paper or on a single sheet with ample space beneath each main topic. Designate these main ideas with Roman numerals.

Now begin adding the items from your list of supporting details, the *A, B, C* part. Quite possibly, an outline for a five-paragraph paper will go no farther than the second level of division. If you do have supporting ideas listed that actually develop a second-level topic, like *1* and *2* to develop *A*, then of course you will want to add them.

POSSIBLE PITFALL: For a five-paragraph theme, you should have no more than three Roman numerals. For a longer paper, you should have a separate Roman numeral for each main idea you will develop, five, six, or even more. Two hints:

1. The introduction and conclusion generally do not appear on the outline.

2. The Roman numerals usually represent body paragraphs. Thus, three Roman numerals designate three body paragraphs in a five-paragraph theme. [*See* THEME *in Part II for a complete discussion.*]

Consider these possible problems:

- You may have designated something less than a main idea by a Roman numeral. If you cannot develop at least a full paragraph for each Roman numeral, you have divided illogically.

- Your topic may be too broad. As a result, your main topics may include far more material than you can support in a single paragraph. While subheadings can also designate independent paragraphs, they usually do not, except in particularly long papers.

Note: When subheadings designate independent paragraphs, the main headings under which they appear do not represent paragraphs. For instance:

    I. Traditional college students
       A. Male
       B. Female
   II. Nontraditional college students
       A. Male
       B. Female

If you develop one paragraph for traditional male students and another for traditional female students, then the two paragraphs together equal the topic represented in the Roman numeral designation I.

REVISING

STEP 3. POLISHING THE OUTLINE

When you have listed all the supporting ideas in logical order under their respective topics, you are ready to polish the outline. Ask yourself the following questions about logic and organization:

- Together, do the main headings provide adequate support for the thesis sentence?

- Are the divisions logical? Are the items within a division mutually exclusive?

- Is the outline a suitable skeleton on which to build a paper? If you develop paragraphs according to the main headings or subheadings in the outline, will you have satisfactory development of your paper?

PROOFREADING

STEP 4. CHECKING THE PECULIAR DETAILS

When the content is accurately and logically represented, you should attend to the peculiar characteristics of the outline form itself. Check these points:

- Does the outline follow a parallel structure?

- Are the number-letter combinations in correct sequence?

- Is each number or letter followed by a period and, in the case of fifth-level divisions or greater, by a parenthesis?

- Does each topic or sentence begin with a capital letter?

- Is the indentation accurate and consistent?

- Does each sentence in a sentence outline end with a period? (And, by the same token, are periods omitted after topics in a topic outline?)

- Are sentences in a sentence outline structured accurately and punctuated appropriately?

- Is spelling accurate throughout?

When you can answer "yes" to all these questions, you should have an accurate outline.

———————————— **Sample Outline for a Paper** ————————————

The following outline was used to develop the cause-and-effect sample paper for social studies. [*See* CAUSE AND EFFECT, *Sample for Social Sciences, earlier in Part II.*]

Isle Royale's Riches

Thesis: Only three natural resources have merited man's battle with Isle Royale's isolation and climate.

    I. Lumber

        A. Destroyed by flood
        B. Halted by fire

    II. Fish

        A. Commercial activity
        B. Individual activity

            1. Decline by unknown causes
            2. Decline by man-made causes

    III. Copper

        A. Indian miners
        B. White settlers

Analysis of the Sample Outline for a Paper

The sample above illustrates the general characterisitcs of an outline used to develop a paper, in this case a five-paragraph theme. [*See* THEME *elsewhere in Part II.*] Note these particular features:

- The thesis statement, which also appears as the last sentence in the introductory paragraph of the paper, serves as a guide to the writer. It sets a tone (*battle with isolation and climate*) and suggests the kinds of details needed.

- Introductory paragraph matter does not appear in the outline.

- The three main divisions, designated by the Roman numerals, suggest the body paragraphs of the paper. [*Compare the outline's divisions with the actual paper in* CAUSE AND EFFECT, *Sample for Social Sciences, earlier in Part II.*]

- The outline indicates the order of development: the first body paragraph will discuss the lumber industry; the second, the fishing industry; the third, the copper industry. The order is one of importance, the most important last.

- Each of the main divisions is structurally parallel, each being a noun.

- The first level of a division, designated by a capital letter, represents the subtopic sentence of each paragraph. The paper's first body paragraph will discuss the flood that ruined the first business attempt by the lumber industry; then it will discuss the fire that destroyed the second attempt.
- Each pair of subtopics is parallel, but the three pairs are not parallel to each other. They need not be. For instance, *A* and *B* in *II* are parallel to each other but not to *A* and *B* in *III*; however, *A* and *B* in *III* are parallel to each other.
- Each body paragraph includes two subtopics, *A* and *B*; one subtopic includes two subtopics of its own, *1* and *2*.
- The outline suggests that the three body paragraphs will include nearly equal amounts of detail. Thus, the writer assures a balanced development.
- Material in the conclusion does not appear in the outline.

FOR A SPEECH

Although the outline for a speech resembles—logically so—the outline for a paper, most speech instructors suggest a few additional details which help the speaker deliver a successful extemporaneous speech. Think through the following process.

Process

Although this handbook is not designed to help you prepare a speech, we can certainly help you write a suitable outline that in turn may at least start you in the right direction!

PREWRITING

STEP 1. PLANNING THE CONTENTS OF THE SPEECH

Probably you must prepare a specific kind of speech: introductory, demonstrative, informative, persuasive, etc. No doubt you have suggestions for possible topics, either from a textbook, from the instructor, or from the person who has asked you to make the speech.

Use the same kinds of prewriting activities as you would for writing a paper. [*See* PREWRITING *in Part I and refer to specific sections in Part II.*] When you have developed lists of main and supporting ideas, you are ready to begin your outline.

WRITING

STEP 2. DEVELOPING THE BODY OF THE SPEECH

As you prepare your outline, do not concern yourself with the introduction or conclusion. Think only about the main ideas of the speech.

List your main ideas on separate note cards. Arrange them in order, but for the present omit number or letter designations. On each card, under the main idea, list the supporting points you want to include. Use the indented form. When you have listed all the necessary supporting details, arrange them in order. Finally, when you feel satisfied with the content and organization, add number and letter designations.

STEP 3. FORMING THE INTRODUCTION AND CONCLUSION

Many speakers make an effort to memorize their opening and closing statements. They believe that by so doing they can get into the speech smoothly and so proceed extemporaneously. Likewise, rather than risk a rambling search for just the right concluding words, they memorize the final sentence, and so they present a smooth, concise end.

As a result, many speakers develop a special outline form that permits them to include the introduction and conclusion. Here's a sample format:

Title

Purpose: (A sentence here indicates the purpose of the speech, which may be, for instance, to persuade the audience to vote for a specific candidate for class office. Think of this sentence as a thesis sentence for a speech.)

I. Introduction: (The introductory sentences appear here, written out word for word.)
II. (First main point of the body appears here, followed by supporting details as necessary.)
   A.
   B.
III. (Second main point of the body appears here. Use as many main points and supporting points as necessary, adding divisions to the outline as necessary.)
   A.
   B.
   C.
IV. ....etc.
V. Conclusion: (The concluding remarks are written out here, word for word.)

As you compose your introduction, include it in the outline as suggested above. Treat the conclusion in the same way.

REVISING AND PROOFREADING
STEP 4. PUTTING THE OUTLINE ON NOTE CARDS

When you think the outline works well for your speech, transfer it to note cards. Most speakers put their introductory statements on a single card and each of the main ideas on a separate card, with the concluding remarks on a single card. Write or type the cards, perhaps using all capital letters or large type such as orator's type. Do whatever you can to make the cards easily legible from a lectern.

When you finish, reread the note cards carefully to check for misspelled words that may cause you confusion or for the omission of key words necessary to help you remember what you plan to talk about. Be sure to practice your speech using the outline in note form so that you will be comfortable during the actual presentation.

Sample Outline for a Speech

The following outline uses the special format many speakers prefer.

Planning Your Garden by Computer

Purpose: The audience will learn how computers help gardeners plan their space for best productivity.

I. Introduction: Early last spring on a warm, sunny day my father and I headed for our 10' by 10' garden. He carried a bag of fertilizer, the hoe, and a rake. I came along behind with the stakes, string, packages of seed . . . and a computer printout.

II. Source of printout

A. Questionnaire
B. Procedure
C. Result

III. Contents

A. Direction of rows
B. Spacing between rows
C. Arrangement of varieties
D. Spacing between plants

IV. Results

A. Fewer plants
B. Greater production
C. Second plantings

V. Conclusion: It seems a little strange to trudge to the garden with a computer-printed diagram of how to plant. As a result of last year's experience, however, we will continue to rely on the computer's brain to do what we've been doing for years. But now we get results!

Analysis of the Sample Outline for a Speech

While the outline includes most of the characteristics of that for a paper, note the three distinguishing features:

- The *Purpose* statement replaces the thesis sentence.
- The introduction not only appears in the outline but is written as a full sentence (or sentences) even though the outline is a topic outline.
- The conclusion likewise appears in the outline, written out as full sentences.

The information above should help you to develop a suitable outline for whatever purpose you face, whether it be to take notes on reading matter or from an oral presentation, to prepare a long paper, or to plan a speech. Consult cross-references for thorough understanding.

PARAGRAPHS

Paragraphs help writers group their thoughts and help the reader follow those groups of thoughts. While the paragraph can stand alone as a unit of writing, it is frequently part of a larger work. This section will describe the paragraph as it can appear in three situations: *as an independent unit, as part of a longer paper*, and *in dialogue*.

AS AN INDEPENDENT UNIT

The paragraph which exists as a single unit of writing is written somewhat differently than one which exists as part of a longer piece of writing. Certain characteristics almost always appear in the single-unit paragraph.

Characteristics

The following elements appear in a single-unit paragraph:

- a subject narrowed sufficiently to be treated as a single idea,

- a topic sentence which announces the subject of the paragraph (often appearing as the first sentence, though it may appear later),

- a specific and consistent attitude toward the subject [*see* MOOD *in the Glossary*],

- supporting details which explain or illustrate the topic sentence [*see* SPECIFIC DETAIL *in the Glossary*],

- transitions which bridge the details to each other and to the topic sentence [*see* TRANSITIONS *in the Glossary*],

- a concluding statement which shows that the writer has completed his thoughts.

Process

In developing a single paragraph, a writer must limit the subject and select the precise idea he or she wants to convey. Use the following process to develop your own single-unit paragraph.

PREWRITING

STEP 1. NARROWING THE SUBJECT

Most writers face their greatest difficulty in narrowing a subject sufficiently for full development within the confines of a paragraph. The following questions will help you limit your subject. [*See* PREWRITING *in Part I for suggested topic sources.*]

- How many divisions are part of this topic? Will any one division better serve as a topic for a full paragraph? For instance:

    Topic:
    the best popcorn

    Divisions:
    black—tiny kernels, hull-less
    yellow—large kernels, some
        hulls
    white—moderate kernels,
        buttery flavor

- What attitude toward this subject do I want to share with my reader? (If I have more than one attitude, I must write more than one paragraph.)

    Topic:
    the best popcorn

    Attitudes:
    best popping
    favorite eating
    best keeping
    easiest to raise
    most readily available

    Single attitude:
    favorite eating

- Can I narrow the subject by putting it in a specific time and place? (For instance, if I want to describe my father in one paragraph, I must limit the description to a single incident.)

When you have narrowed your topic, write it a sentence and compare it with the following:

Too Broad:
Guitar music offers a variety of sounds.

Improved:
The bass-guitar accompaniment in this composition offers real challenges, even for an accomplished guitarist.

Too Broad:
Some students enjoy participating in peer social groups.
Improved:
I enjoy participating in the annual sorority Spring Sports Fling.

Too Broad:
Senator Joe Glick deserves to be reelected.
Still Too Broad:
Because of his stand on environmental issues, Senator Joe Glick deserves the support of environmentally concerned voters.
Improved:
Senator Glick's stand on the issue of acid rain helps voters understand his general attitude toward environmental issues.

Make whatever improvements you can to your own topic. Your finished product will be the topic sentence of your paragraph. In many cases, this topic sentence will begin the paragraph. Sometimes, however, circumstances require it to appear elsewhere. Note these exceptions:

- If an introductory statement or statements are necessary, the topic sentence may follow the brief introduction.

- If dealing with a highly controversial subject, the topic sentence may appear at the conclusion to better prepare the reader to accept the statement.

- If the paragraph builds to a surprise, the topic sentence may appear at the end.

- The topic sentence may never appear but only be implied. Be cautious if you use this approach that the topic sentence is clearly implied; otherwise the reader will be left wondering.

STEP 2.   SELECTING SUBTOPICS

In order to develop a paragraph, you will need to have supporting details. Usually the support comes in the form of subtopics: reasons, causes, examples, illustrations, steps, comparisons, differences, or other explanations. No magic number of supporting details makes a perfect paragraph; the details, added together, must clarify the topic and leave the reader satisfied.

In order to think through the logical subdivisions of your topic, divide either the subject or the predicate of your topic sentence. [*See* SUBJECT *and* PREDICATE *in the Glossary.*] For instance, consider the following examples and notice from which part of the topic sentence the accompanying subtopics come.

Topic Sentence:
Utility bills seem to reflect household activities.

Subtopics:
- Bills rise when school is out for the summer.
- Bills rise when school is out for spring recess.

- Bills rise during the winter holiday season.

(The subtopics divide the parts of the predicate referring to household activities.)

Topic Sentence:
Getting away from it all makes primitive camping a preferred vacation for many.

Subtopics:
- getting away from news media
- getting away from telephones
- getting away from job responsibilities
- getting away from household responsibilities

(The subtopics divide the part of the subject referring *to getting away from it all*.)

Jot down what you think will be evidence or ideas to support your topic. Use words, phrases, or complete sentences in order to get your ideas on paper. Your list may look something like this:

Topic:
Pulling out of the water on skis requires complex muscular coordination.

Subtopics:
- squatting position, ski tips out of the water, rope between knees
- back muscles lean against boat's power
- leg muscles keep skis in position
- arm muscles provide balance against towrope as rising to standing position

These four subtopics, each listing some part of the muscular coordination and each explaining the attitude *complex*, will make up the main points of the paragraph.

Write your own list of supporting details before you go on to Step 3.

HINT: If you have difficulty dividing your topic, reexamine the topic sentence. It may be too narrow or too broad.

STEP 3. ARRANGING THE DETAILS

Next, arrange your list in some kind of logical order: chronological, spatial, or an order of importance. [*See entries for each in the Glossary.*] The details above are arranged chronologically, the order in which the skier must react.

Number the items on your list in the order in which you will write about them.

WRITING

STEP 4. DEVELOPING THE NOTES

Using the organized list of details from Step 3, you should be able to develop the paragraph quickly. Follow these steps:

- Begin with the topic sentence unless you have a specific reason for saving it until later. In that case, begin with an attention-getter.

- Use an effective transition to move from your topic sentence to the first subtopic or supporting detail. [*See* TRANSITION *in the Glossary.*]

- Use specific supporting details. Show the reader; do not tell him your message. [*See* DESCRIPTION *in Part II for a good explanation of specific details. Also see* REVISING: SAMPLE REVISION FOR SPECIFIC DETAIL *in Part I.*]

- Use effective transitions to move on to additional supporting details. [*See* REVISING: SAMPLE REVISION FOR TRANSITION *in Part I.*]

- Conclude with an effective clincher or ending statement. (Note that some paragraphs can end with a final statement that merely finishes the final subtopic rather than with a true clincher sentence. The reader, however, must have a sense of completion and not be left to feel that the writer simply quit.)

REVISING

STEP 5. POLISHING THE DRAFT

First, check that you have followed the techniques suggested in Step 4 above. Then check the following:

- Have I used good sentence structure and worked toward sentence variety and emphasis? Have I balanced long sentences with short, complicated with simple? [*See* REVISING: SAMPLE REVISION FOR SENTENCE VARIETY *and* REVISING: SAMPLE REVISION FOR EMPHASIS *in Part I.*]

- Is the word choice appropriate to the audience? Have I used precise words that enhance specific details? Or instead, have I used general words like *walk* when I could have used *amble* or *stomp*. [*See* RE-VISING: SAMPLE REVISION FOR SPE-CIFIC DETAIL *in Part I.*]

- Have I used the best arrangement of details? Would another arrangement have a greater impact?

- Have I maintained consistency, both in verb tense and point of view? [*See* POINT OF VIEW *and* TENSE *in the Glossary for explanations and examples, and see* REVISING: CHECKING CONSISTENCY *in Part I for additional details.*]

PROOFREADING

STEP 6. CHECKING THE GRAMMAR AND MECHANICS

When you are satisfied with the content, go back to check grammar, mechanics, and usage. [*See* PROOFREADING *in Part I for additional guidelines.*] Refer to *Webster's New World Dictionary* to check spelling and *Webster's New World Thesaurus* for word choice.

——————— Sample Independent Paragraph ———————

The following paragraph, written as an independent composition, serves as a sample for analysis for this chapter. [*You will find numerous examples of other independent paragraphs in virtually every section of Part II.*]

From Sitting to Standing

Pulling out of the water on skis requires complex muscular coordination. The simplest part of the coordinated effort occurs when the skier positions himself on his skies behind the towboat. He assumes a squatting position, toes of the skis just above the water's surface, and the towrope between his knees. As the towboat idles forward to keep the towrope taut, the skier uses both leg and body muscles to keep himself in a ready position, squarely behind the skis. All muscles work against the steady pull. Then, as the towboat accelerates, back muscles work together with leg muscles, and the skier leans against the boat's power. As the pull intensifies, muscles from the toes to the hips work to keep the skis parallel, pointed forward, tips above the surface. Finally, the towboat's full thrust tests the skier's arm muscles. With his skis climbing to a plane and his body rising above the water, the skier must flex his arms to provide a counter-balance against the lessening drag behind the towrope, thus pulling himself to a standing position. Once a skier experiences this complex muscular coordination, it is like that for riding a bicycle: It comes without thinking and never leaves.

Analysis of the Sample Independent Paragraph

The sample above represents a good independent paragraph. While paragraph structure can vary widely, the following typical characteristics appear:

- A topic sentence begins the paragraph.
- Three subtopics divide the topic sentence predicate and emphasize the attitude *complex*.
- Each subtopic provides specific details to help the non-skier understand the complexity of the muscular coordination.
- Sentences vary both in length (from seven words to thirty-eight words) and complexity (from simple to compound-complex).
- Transitions connect the subtopic sentences into a smoothly flowing paragraph.
- The concluding statement refers back to the topic sentence and suggests the longevity of the experience.

For additional examples, read other independent paragraphs and their accompanying analyses in other sections of Part II.

AS PART OF A LONGER PAPER

While a paragraph which stands alone and a paragraph which makes up part of a longer paper have many similarities, they also have some fundamental differences. An independent paragraph logically carries the greatest burden. A paragraph in a longer paper need only develop an idea from the thesis and provide some kind of transition. [*See* THEME *in Part II for complete details about writing a longer paper.*]

Characteristics

A paragraph which functions as part of a longer paper will usually include the following characteristics:

- an opening transition which connects it to the preceding paragraph,
- a topic sentence derived from the thesis sentence [*see* THESIS SENTENCE *in the Glossary for a quick re-*

view, and see THEME *in Part II for a thorough discussion*],

- supporting details, such as explanations, illustrations, examples or reasons, to clarify the topic sentence,

- internal transitions to carry the reader's thought from one supporting detail to another [*see* TRANSITIONS *in the Glossary*],

- a final statement, or conclusion, which may also act as a transition into the following paragraph.

Process

Developing a paragraph for a longer paper is really not much different from developing a single-unit paragraph. [*In addition to the process outlined below, consult* THEME *in Part II for an explanation of the longer paper. This will clarify the relationship of the given paragraph to the rest of the paper.*]

PREWRITING

STEP 1. DECIDING ON A METHOD OF DEVELOPMENT

Since the thesis sentence of the longer paper determines the topic of each of the theme's paragraphs, the writer need only decide how best to support the subject. [*See Steps 1 and 2 in* THEME *in Part II for the process of developing a thesis sentence.*]

Thesis:
Hovey Lake wildlife refuge attracts a wide variety of visitors during the hunting, fishing, and bird-watching seasons.

Topic sentence one:
The swamp attracts hunters in early winter.

Topic sentence two:
In spring, fishermen replace the hunters on Hovey Lake waters.

Topic sentence three:
The swamp attracts bird watchers twelve months a year.

How a paragraph can be developed is the subject of virtually all of Part II, so the writer has nearly a dozen choices: analogy, cause and effect, classification, comparison and contrast, description, definition, narration, opinion, persuasion, or a combination of these. [*See entries for each in the Glossary for quick reference, and see entries for each in Part II for a thorough discussion with examples.*]

Select the method or combination of methods by which to develop a particular topic. Consider the following example:

You are planning the third body paragraph of the example about Hovey Lake [*see above*]. You decide the best method for developing this paragraph is to describe the birds that attract so many bird watchers. You will use description to develop the paragraph.

Choose the method of development most suitable to your paragraph.

STEP 2. MAKING A PLAN

Next, jot down three or four supporting details. For instance, if you can best develop the paragraph above about bird watchers by describing birds, you may develop a list similar to the following:

water birds:
    blue herons
    white egrets
    eagles
    ospreys
    ducks
    geese

tree dwellers:
    woodpeckers
    owls
    swifts

flocks:
    cowbirds
    grackles
    purple martins

Next, organize the details in logical order. In the example above, for instance, you may choose to talk about water birds last as they are most important in the swamp. The arrangement thus follows an order of importance. [*See* ORDERS OF IMPORTANCE *in the Glossary.*] You may choose instead chronologcial or spatial order. [*See each entry in the Glossary.*]

If necessary, convert the list into a formal outline. [*See* OUTLINES, KINDS: FOR A PAPER *in Part II for details.*]

WRITING

STEP 3. DEVELOPING THE PLAN

Begin the paragraph with a transition to connect it to the preceding paragraph. The transition may be a few words at the start of the topic sentence, or an entire sentence. [*See* TRANSITIONS *in the Glossary, and see* REVISING: SAMPLE REVISION FOR TRANSITION *in Part I for additional help.*]

Include the topic sentence, although it may not be the first sentence of the paragraph. [*See the exceptions in Step 1 in* PARAGRAPHS: AS AN INDEPENDENT UNIT *above.*]

As you develop the supporting details, be sure to connect them with transitions. Use specifics rather than generalities; show, don't tell. [*See additional explanation in* DESCRIPTION, *in Part II, and in* REVISING: SAMPLE REVISION FOR SPECIFIC DETAIL *in Part I.*]

Conclude the paragraph with a clincher or final statement, either of which may also include a transitional word or phrase to connect with the preceding paragraph.

REVISING

STEP 4. POLISHING THE CONTENT

Once you have completed the first draft, go back over the list of characteristics and the guidelines above for writing the paragraph. Check that you have included the basic contents. Then polish as the following questions suggest:

- Have I varied the length of my sentences? [*See* SAMPLE REVISION FOR SENTENCE VARIETY *in Part I.*]

- Have I varied the structure of my sentences, using simple as well as compound-complex sentences? [*See* SIMPLE SENTENCES, COMPOUND SENTENCES, COMPLEX SENTENCES, *and* COMPOUND-COMPLEX SENTENCES *in the Glossary for explanations and examples.*]

- Have I used good specific words that make vivid the supporting details?

- Have I maintained a consistent verb tense and point of view? [*See* TENSE *and* POINT OF VIEW *in the Glossary and* REVISING: CHECKING CONSISTENCY *in Part I for explanations and examples.*]

PROOFREADING

STEP 5. CHECKING THE DETAILS

With the content polished, look next for the little details that can be exceedingly distracting to your readers. Have you followed the rules for grammar, mechanics, and usage? [*See* PROOFREADING *in Part I for additional guidelines.*]

Next check carefully for spelling. Refer to *Webster's New World Dictionary*. Then, using *Webster's New World Thesaurus*, check word choice. Can you select better, more specific words?

Finally, reread the paragraph for any omissions or careless errors.

———— Sample Paragraph as Part of a Longer Paper ————

The following paragraph [*part of the longer paper developed in* THEME *in Part II*] illustrates the general characteristics of this kind of paragraph. Of course, you will find dozens of other examples, throughout Part II, that illustrate specific kinds of development. Refer to these for comparison.

The most experienced hunters and fishermen at Hovey Lake, however, are not human. They are avian. Boasting a greater variety of bird life than almost any other spot in Indiana, the swamp attracts bird watchers twelve months a year from a dozen states. With powerful binoculars, they scan the bald cypress trees and standing dead timber, known to attract woodpeckers, including the pileated, redheaded, redbreasted, downy, and hairy. Other tree dwellers, from grumpy-looking owls to scurrying swifts, stake out territory in the swamp growth. During the warbler migration, the trees house whole orchestras, but the prothonotary warbler stays most of the summer, flashing yellow among the yew-like lower branches of the cypress. Flocks of martins, cowbirds, and grackles fly in and out seasonally. In the more inaccessible parts of the swamp, the great blue herons and great white egrets wade the shallows near one of the last stands of bamboo-like cane this far north or perch high in treetops from which they can see the Ohio River. In winter, the bald eagles and ospreys soar among the thousands of geese and ducks, surely a testimony to the value of this wildlife sanctuary.

Analysis of the Sample Paragraph as Part of a Longer Paper

The paragraph above, taken from a five-paragraph theme, illustrates the general characteristics of a body paragraph from a longer paper. Note the following details:

- The first two sentences provide a transition from the ideas in the preceding two paragraphs (the first about hunters and the second about fishermen).
- The third sentence is the topic sentence.
- The supporting details are arranged roughly in the chronological order of the seasonal appearance of the various bird species.
- The details include specific, concrete, visual images. [*See* CONCRETE, SPECIFIC DETAIL, *and* IMAGERY *in the Glossary.*]
- Internal transition comes with the use of pronouns, like *they* and transitional words, like *other*, *during* and *in winter*.
- The concluding sentence reiterates why bird watchers come to the swamp and leads into the final paragraph of the paper, one which refers to the *precious ecology system* of the swamp.

IN DIALOGUE

When writing dialogue [*see* DIALOGUE *earlier in Part II*], paragraph divisions have nothing to do with topic sentences, supporting details, transitional devices, or clincher. Instead, they show who is speaking.

Characteristics

The characteristics of dialogue paragraphs can be summarized in one simple rule: *Start a new paragraph with each change of speaker.*

Process

Prewriting, writing, revising, and proofreading dialogue are explained in DIALOGUE, earlier in Part II. Refer to that section for process.

——————— Sample Paragraphs in Dialogue ———————

The following sample dialogue includes two speakers, Marty and Arlene. Note that as the conversation progresses, the only indication of speaker is the change in paragraph.

The Onion Sandwich

"Are you really eating an onion sandwich?" Marty asked in disbelief. "I never heard of such a thing!"

Arlene touched her napkin to her lips, smiled sweetly and said, "Of course, my dear. Why not?" She leaned forward with a confidential air. "You see, Marty," she explained, "the butter on the bread mingles nicely with the savory onion and rye."

"You can't be serious!"

"Oh, but I am. In fact, if you'll join me for lunch, I'll share half of it with you." She smiled mischievously.

"I'm sure; I'm sure." He wrinkled his nose, backed out of the room, and hurried down the corridor.

She smiled, leaned back, and pitched the untouched sandwich in the trash.

Analysis of the Sample Paragraph in Dialogue

The six brief paragraphs above illustrate the general rule for dialogue. Each new paragraph signals a new speaker, and quotation marks separate the speakers' exact words from reactions, thoughts, or behavior. Note the following details:

• In the first paragraph, Marty speaks. Two separate sentences contain his words, but only the first is followed by his identity.

• The second paragraph begins with Arlene's physical reaction. Her direct words are interrupted by additional description of her behavior.

• The third paragraph, made up only of Marty's reply, does not include the speaker's name. The reader knows, however, since only two speakers have been introduced and Arlene just spoke, that the new paragraph indicates Marty's reply.

• Likewise, the fourth paragraph includes Arlene's response as well as a statement of behavior.

- Beginning the fifth paragraph are Marty's words. At no time does the reader see *he said*, or some similar identification. Rather, the reader knows who is speaking by the change in paragraph and the clue word *he*.
- Finally, the last paragraph, while including no direct quotation, describes Arlene's reaction. The new paragraph is necessary, however, to show a change in speaker, even if the speaker is only reacting.

Using the information here [*as well as that in the sections on* DIALOGUE] should solve any problems you may encounter in developing meaningful paragraphs in dialogue.

In addition, the explanations in this section about all three forms of paragraph development should help you deal successfully with paragraphing in virtually any writing situation. Be sure to consult cross-references.

PARAPHRASE

A paraphrase is a kind of summary. The obvious purpose of a summary is to provide a shortened version of a piece of writing. A less obvious purpose is to alter the language or style to make it more comprehensible. The first case, the true summary, is shorter than the original passage and is called a *precis* or *synopsis*. [*See* PRECIS *and* SYNOPSIS *in Part II for comparison.*] The second case may be as long as the original passage, but its vocabulary and sentences will be altered to ease the difficulty of reading. This kind of summary is called a *paraphrase.*

A paraphrase restates a passage in your own words. In one sense, it is a summary because you are "translating" technical or complicated material into your own vocabulary. In another, however, it is not a summary, because it is usually the same length, or nearly the same length, as the original.

You may be asked to paraphrase passages to show you have read and understood them. You may be asked to paraphrase scientific results as part of a research project. You may write paraphrases for your own benefit, to clarify complicated passages. Whatever the reason for writing them, paraphrases provide a means of simplifying complicated, technical passages.

Characteristics

A paraphrase usually

- reflects the paraphraser's own vocabulary,

- reduces the original only slightly, usually by less than one-fourth,

- displays careful reading of the original,

- represents the original idea accurately and completely, without reflecting personal bias,

- uses clear, effective sentences as well as good mechanics, usage, and grammar.

Process

To write a paraphrase, use the following procedure.

PREWRITING

STEP 1.   READING THE MATERIAL

Read the original passage several times to be sure you understand its meaning. Look up unfamiliar words in *Webster's New World Dictionary.*

Next, before you begin writing, jot down the main ideas in the order in which they appear. Use only the key words or phrases, not sentences.

WRITING

STEP 2. DRAFTING THE FIRST SUMMARY

Once you have the material clearly in mind, put aside the original passage. Refer only to your list of main ideas, and write the summary in your own words. It is important to do so in order to avoid lifting whole phrases and sentences from the original. The temptation to plagiarize is the result of lazy thinking; by picking up an author's phrases and sentences, the paraphraser need not struggle to put the ideas into his or her own words. [*See* PLAGIARISM *in the Glossary.*]

Beneath the obvious theft involved lies a deeper problem. Since the very purpose of the paraphrase is to simplify and reduce difficult passages, the ultimate futility of using the author's words should be self-evident.

REVISING

STEP 3. CHECKING FOR ACCURATE CONTENT

Once you have completed your paraphrase, reread the original and compare it with your version. Ask yourself these questions:

- Have I included all the important ideas? If I haven't, how can I best include them?
- Have I avoided all insignificant and unnecessary ideas?
- Have I accurately represented specifics and generalities? If not, what can I change to produce an objective paraphrase?

- Have I developed each idea the same relative length as in the original? If not, how can I best adjust the imbalance?
- Have I placed the same emphasis on each idea as in the original? If not, how can I resolve the difference?
- Have I used a simple, straightforward vocabulary?
- Have I used clear, effective sentence structure?
- Have I plagiarized? If so, how can I rephrase things?

Make any additions, deletions, or changes necessary to maintain accuracy.

Be absolutely certain that you do not take phrases or sentences directly from the original. Read through the original passage again, line by line, comparing it with your paraphrase.

PROOFREADING

STEP 4. CORRECTING THE MECHANICS

Once you have revised the content to accurately reflect the original, make sure that the spelling, punctuation, grammar, usage, and mechanics are accurate. Make sure, too, that you have used accurate vocabulary. Check *Webster's New World Dictionary* and *Webster's New World Thesaurus*.

Check the sentence structure. Have you used effective sentences? Have you varied their structure? Are they easy to read? Finally, check one more time that you have not committed any of the deadly sins of paraphrase writing. Be certain that you have not

- misrepresented or changed the emphasis of an idea from the original source, or
- relied too heavily on the wording of the original passage and allowed plagiarism to creep into your work.

Use the following sample paraphrase to test your understanding of the process and the expected result. An analysis of the sample follows.

Sample Paraphrase

Because paraphrases are generally alike, we will examine just one sample. The original uses technical language to discuss the way in which we learn. The paraphrase simplifies this technical language and sentence structure. Note evidence of the process steps above.

Original Passage

Recent research has determined that humans tend to fall into one of four quadrants according to their learning styles. Quadrant one learners tend to be divergent thinkers and need personal and emotional involvement in order for learning to take place. As idea people, they function through social integration and strive to bring unity to diversity. Quadrant two learners are assimilators, needing systematic learning via a logical and intellectual approach. As analytic learners, they reflect on ideas to create concepts and models. Quadrant three learners tend to be convergent thinkers who are practical, problem-oriented people. Pragmatic decision makers, they restrict judgment to concrete things. Quadrant four learners are accommodators needing random patterns of learning. They aim to bring action to concepts and exercise authority through common vision, hesitating to make decisions affecting others.

Paraphrase

As learners, we fall into four groups. The first kind of learner needs to be caught up in an idea physically and personally. His personal involvement and concern for others make him seek harmony. He's emotional. The second kind of learner absorbs all the information around him, categorizes it, and reasons out the results. He will seek the data gathered to develop an ideal. He's systematic. The third kind of learner is opposite the first kind. He tends to be less emotional, more utilitarian. His thorough analysis results in a valid decision. He's practical. The fourth kind of learner needs numerous approaches to learning something new. As an opposite to the second kind of learner, he relies more on instinct than on logic. When decisions must be made, he doesn't like to interfere with other's lives. He's an accommodator.

Analysis of the Sample Paraphrase

Note the following characteristics regarding the sample paraphrase:

- The paraphrase presents the same ideas as the original passage and is nearly the same length.

- Its vocabulary is quite different from that of the original. This change marks its most important function: to reduce technical or complicated writing to simpler, easier-to-understand prose. For instance, the technical term *quadrant* is omitted, as are words like *divergent, convergent, assimilators, analytic learners,* and *pragmatic.*

- Complicated ideas are presented in simple sentences to make them easier to understand. In the original passage, *quadrant one learner* is defined by means of a sentence with a compound predicate. In the paraphrase, *first kind of learner* is defined by a simple sentence.

- The paraphrase and the original are nearly the same length, though the original includes nine sentences to the paraphrase's fifteen. Why? The sentences in the paraphrase are much shorter than those in the original.

- Words are shorter in the paraphrase. While words tend to be three syllables in the original, those in the paraphrase tend to two syllables.

- The paraphrase shows careful reading and thorough understanding of the original. No plagiarism has crept in.

- Sentence structure, mechanics, usage, and grammar are accurate.

Following these step-by-step procedures and heeding the suggestions above should enable you to create an equally successful paraphrase.

PERSUASION

A persuasive or *argumentative* paper is used to convince. It may attempt to convince the reader to follow a certain course of action or accept a belief or position. Because it assumes the reader to be antagonistic, persuasive writing relies on reasoning and clear logic. It appears in virtually every facet of our lives: convincing a potential employer to hire us, a neighbor to keep his dog from ruining our shrubbery, the electric company that the house meter is faulty, the appliance store that we did pay the bill on time. Others use persuasion to convince us to vote for them, to buy or use their products, to invest in their schemes, to follow their religious beliefs, or to accept their points of view.

Other kinds of writing may include elements of persuasion: letters (especially letters to the editor), short stories, comparison-contrasts, even biographies. At the same time, different means of development can be used in a persuasive paper: definition, analogy, cause and effect, comparison and contrast, opinion, classification, and description. [*See entries for each in Part II for additional details.*] A competent writer finds persuasion to be one of the most versatile tools available.

Characteristics

The following characteristics will be evident in a persuasive paper. In general, a persuasive paper

- deals with an appropriately debatable subject,

- assumes the reader to be antagonistic,

- begins on some common ground so that reader and writer have a point of agreement,

- anticipates the reader's concerns and opposing point of view,

- refutes opposing arguments,

- presents supporting details, including statistics, examples, cause-effect relationships, etc.,

- places the topic or thesis sentence at the beginning or the end, depending on the intensity of the reader's antagonism,

- follows an organizational plan which anticipates objections by the reader,

- relies on logical reasoning,

- uses subtle emotional or psychological appeals,

- depends in large part on the writer's credibility for acceptance,

- avoids a second-person point of view so as to avoid antagonizing the reader,

- avoids a first-person point of view to help the reader focus on the subject, rather than on the writer,

- uses effective transitions to move the reader smoothly through the evidence,
- concludes with a logically reasonable statement of what the reader should do or think.

Process

Use the following steps to successfully plan, write, and revise a persuasive or argumentative paper.

PREWRITING

STEP 1. FOCUSING ON THE SUBJECT

The subject for a persuasive paper must be debatable. It makes little sense to write a paper to persuade a reader to pay taxes. There would be no point in reading it. Likewise, there is little debate that we should eat balanced meals, observe the law, or exercise regularly.

In most cases, you probably already know the general topic of your persuasive paper. You have a reason for writing. In order to focus on that subject, however, you should first write a sentence that indicates what you ultimately want the reader to do or think. Consider the following examples:

- Attend the Homecoming activities.
- Vote for Gerald Morrison for Eighth-District Representative.
- Volunteer for a local charity.
- Write to the governor and local representatives to fight the proposed coke-processing plant.
- Run for an office.
- Attend a meeting to show opposition to the rezoning proposal.
- Buy only U.S.-made products.
- Invest in the stock market.
- Use vitamin supplements with caution.

Now write a sentence that indicates what you want the reader to do or to think. This sentence will serve as the core for your topic or thesis sentence. [*See* TOPIC SENTENCE *and* THESIS SENTENCE *in the Glossary for quick reference, and see* PARAGRAPHS *and* THEME *in Part II for details and examples.*]

STEP 2. STUDYING THE READER'S POSITIONS

Since the persuasive or argumentative paper assumes an antagonistic reader, put yourself in your reader's place. Anticipate his or her needs by answering the following questions:

- What is the reader's current position?
- What information does the reader have or not have which is relevant to the issue?
- What objections does the reader have toward your position?
- How will the issue affect the reader personally? In the pocketbook? At the dinner table? On the job? In his or her children's future?

Jot down the answers to these questions before you go on.

STEP 3. THINKING THROUGH THE ARGUMENTS

With the reader's position clearly defined, you can begin to plan your arguments. Answer the following questions concerning your point of view:

- What information can I give the reader to make his or her current position uncomfortable? Will something happen to the reader—to his or her job, home, or children as a result of this current position?

- What facts, statistics, examples, or illustrations will help the reader see the importance of changing his or her position?

- What information can I include that will negate the reader's counter-arguments?

- What personal appeal will most likely cause the reader to take action?

Answers to these questions will help you select appropriate details. In general, the persuasive paper relies on reason and logic to make a point. But never underestimate the need for clever psychology to get the reader's attention and to deal with his or her emotions.

Based on your work in Steps 2 and 3, write the three or four main points you must deal with in your persuasive paper.

STEP 4. DOING THE RESEARCH

If your topic so requires, you must now be prepared to do any necessary research. Seek out facts and illustrations to support your argument.

Look for authorities who support your point of view. Take notes, not only on their identity, but on their reasoned arguments. Read opposing arguments as well; understand the opposition's point of view, the better to refute it. [*See* NOTES, KINDS: FOR A PAPER *in Part II for suggestions on effective note taking. See also* PRECIS *and* PARAPHRASE *in Part II for help with writing effective summaries.*] Take notes on ideas which support your cause. Also note specific arguments your paper must refute.

STEP 5. USING THE RIGHT APPEALS

The writer must somehow appeal to the reader in order to change his or her position or opinion. Logic is certainly one way. Emotional appeal is another. Credibility is a third. A combination of these three will most likely persuade the reader. Look at each appeal:

Logic

You can use a number of approaches to logic, many of which are specifically addressed in other sections of this manual. Consider the following:

- Analogy, in which a simple situation is compared with a complicated one to make clear the general concepts of the more difficult situation [*See* ANALOGY *in Part II, including the section describing its limitations.*]

- Cause-and-effect relationships, in which one event is proved to be the cause or effect of another [*See* CAUSE AND EFFECT *in Part II.*]

- Facts, examples, and illustrations, which support or explain a given situation or idea [*See* FACTS *and* EXAMPLE *in the Glossary.*]

- Judgments or opinions, which support ideas that cannot be proven statistically [*See* OPINION *in Part II.*]

Emotional Appeal

Persuasive writing must somehow help the reader become personally involved in the argument. If a situation or belief will not affect the reader's life in some way, he or she will have little reason to respond, positively or negatively. Consider these possible emotional appeals:

- Physiological needs such as food, drink, and shelter

- Psychological needs such as the need to be loved, or to feel attractive, accepted, successful

- Emotions, such as love, hate, guilt, fear, loyalty, pride, self-esteem

Credibility

An author's credibility in large part determines the reader's reaction. A credible writer is one who approaches the reader as an equal, avoids logical fallacies, uses only subtle emotional appeal, and shows clear understanding of his topic, either as a result of firsthand knowledge or objective research. Content which enhances writer credibility enhances persuasiveness.

Choose the appeals which are most suitable for your topic and your audience. List them.

STEP 6. ORGANIZING THE APPROACH

The organization of a persuasive paper will vary somewhat depending how adamant the reader's opposition will be. The firmer the objection, the more carefully you must present the argument. Consider these two possibilities:

For a persuasive paper that merely asks the reader, for instance, to write to his or her Congressman or to show support for an issue, the most adamant opposition may be nothing more than his ignoring you. In that case, the organization may follow a straightforward plan:

Plan One

- Begin with the topic sentence or, in the case of a longer paper, with the thesis statement. [*See separate entries in the Glossary if you need help with topic or thesis sentences.*] The topic or thesis sentence will state both the subject and your attitude.

- Present the two, three, or even four arguments supporting the topic or thesis statement. Arrange them in some order of importance, probably from second most to most important. Thus, you present your most powerful argument last, hoping the reader has begun accepting the lesser arguments earlier. [*See the Glossary entry for* ORDERS OF IMPORTANCE *for additional details.*]

- Conclude by requesting specific action.

On the other hand, a persuasive paper may elicit strong reaction and deal with a controversial subject. For instance, the argument may suggest a change that will enable employees to arrange vacation time with the rest of their families. The proposal is important to you but will meet with resistance from those with greater seniority. Presented the wrong way, the arguments may turn the reader against the proposal even before he or she finishes reading. In fact, he or she may refuse to finish reading. Thus, in those situations, use a different plan of organization:

Plan Two

- Begin with general statements about the topic without stating a particular position. The opening remarks should serve only to indicate the subject under examination.

- Acknowledge the strongest opposing point of view and present counterarguments. You may use phrases like *some people sincerely believe* to introduce opposing points of view. When switching to the counterarguments, use transitions like *on the other hand* or *under careful analysis, however.*

- Then, acknowledge the second strongest opposing argument and present your rebuttal. Use transitions similar to those suggested above.

- Follow the pattern until you have negated the opposition's positions.

- When your rebuttal is completed, continue with additional points of persuasion. Use whatever psychological techniques are appropriate. Organize these points in the order of their importance, concluding with the most convincing argument.

- Because of the sensitivity of the argument, your topic or thesis statement will probably appear in the last paragraph. In fact, the concluding statement which calls for the reader's action may be the topic or thesis statement, appearing here for the first time.

From the two suggestions above, select the more appropriate and develop a tentative outline. Use the lists you developed in Steps 3, 4, and 5. [*See also* OUTLINES, KINDS: FOR A PAPER *in Part II.*] You may decide to change the organization slightly as you write, but the outline will serve as a reminder of where you have been and where you must go with the arguments.

WRITING

STEP 7. GETTING THE ARGUMENTS ON PAPER

Use the prewriting notes and outline developed above to write your persuasive paragraph or paper. Strive to include logical and emotional appeals in proper balance and to maintain your own credibility.

REVISING

STEP 8.   ANALYZING THE CONTENT

As you think through your first draft, ask yourself questions to pinpoint possible weaknesses:

- Is my subject appropriately debatable and therefore suitable for a persuasive paper?

- Does the paper begin on some common ground so that the reader and I begin with a point of agreement?

- Have I included a clear topic or thesis statement, either at the beginning or at the end?

- Have I followed an appropriate plan determined by the reader's probable antagonism?

- Is the organization clear? In a multi-paragraph paper, have I developed a single argument in each paragraph? Does each paragraph have a topic sentence, supporting details, and a conclusion? Have I used suitable transitions both within and between paragraphs to move from one argument to another or from the opposing view to my own? [*See* REVISING: CHECKING STRUCTURE *and* REVISING: SAMPLE REVISION FOR TRANSITION *in Part I.*]

- Is the content easy to follow with clear, concise sentences? Are the sentences developed with the main ideas in the main clauses and the subordinating ideas in the subordinate clauses? [*See* REVISING: SAMPLE REVISION FOR EMPHASIS *and* REVISING: SAMPLE REVISION FOR SENTENCE VARIETY *in Part I.*]

- Are the supporting arguments logical? Have I included facts, statistics, examples, or other supporting details to develop the arguments? [*See* REVISING: SAMPLE REVISION FOR SPECIFIC DETAIL *in Part I.*]

- Have I refuted the major opposing arguments and responded with additional supporting arguments? Have I dealt with the major arguments and eliminated from my paper unimportant, even petty, ones?

- Is the tone appropriate to the subject? [*See* TONE *in the Glossary.*]

- Have I carefully balanced the logical appeals with the more subtle emotional appeals?

- Do I maintain my credibility by avoiding hasty generalizations, faulty logic, propaganda techniques, and heavy emotional appeals? Do I show a broad understanding of *both* points of view?

- Does the conclusion specifically call for action? Is the reader apt to take that action based on the arguments included in the paper?

As you answer these questions you may find some weaknesses you can eliminate. [*See also,* REVISING *in Part I for additional guidelines for general revision.*]

Finally, remember that in a persuasive paper the more supporting details you provide, the stronger your argument.

PROOFREADING

STEP 9. CHECKING THE DETAILS

When you have revised the content, check for mechanics, usage, and grammar details. [*Refer to the Glossary if you need a quick example or information. Also see* PROOFREADING *in Part I for additional guidelines.]* Then check your spelling in *Webster's New World Dictionary* and check for precise word choice by referring to *Webster's New World Thesaurus.*

A Note about the Samples: The following sample papers include formal and informal papers, paragraphs and longer papers, all developed to illustrate the general characteristics of persuasive papers. Although each paper focuses on an argument for leading a better life, other subtle emotional appeals will be evident. Watch to see how the emotional and logical appeals interact.

--- **Sample for English** ---

The following persuasive paper, developed as a single paragraph, illustrates the characteristics described above:

Why Get Involved?

The first commandment of contemporary society lays down the law: Don't get involved. Somehow, though, we ignore the axiom sure to follow: If you don't get involved, you never grow, personally or professionally. Sure, the usual arguments come roaring to the defense: "I don't have time to get involved," or "I have enough problems of my own." True, we're busy, and we all have problems, some far more serious than others. But look at what the experts say. Using the buzz word "networking" to refer to the activity of meeting and working with others, authorities believe an activity that allows us to reach out to others allows us to benefit from others' experiences. In other words, by reaching out to others, we may learn not only to solve our own problems more easily but also to put those problems in perspective. Working with others helps prevent self-centered tunnel vision. Thus, networking becomes time well spent. In addition, however, the experts maintain that the reaching out improves humanizing qualities buried by the don't-get-involved approach. For instance, meeting with our professional peers may help us locate new business contacts and discover that a company across town boasts a superior office manager for whom it is a pleasure to work. Working voluntarily with social agencies may allow us to enjoy opportunities for improving interpersonal relationships and to understand why a deaf child resents being labeled "handicapped." Serving on church, school, and civic committees may develop an understanding of contemporary problems and their consequences like the impact an alternate bus route has on the city budget. Simply meeting and working with more people from different walks of life may even help us recognize alternatives to business, social, and personal dilemmas—new ways to deal with a power-hungry boss, with a terminally ill parent, or with a puppy that refuses to be housebroken. Someone with whom we network can offer suggestions. We can grow. If these goals sound like platitudes, nevertheless the result is singular: Meet people, get involved with their situations and see their problems, and we become better persons because of it. So it's time to break the first commandment of contemporary society. Get smart. Get the benefits. Get involved.

Analysis of the Sample for English

The paragraph above follows the guidelines for a good persuasive paper. Especially note the following points:

- The paragraph begins on common ground. The reader can agree with, or at least recognize having heard, what seems to be a *common law* of contemporary society.

- The second sentence suggests the writer's point of view and implies the topic sentence. (The topic sentence actually appears at the end, the last three sentences combined.)

- Immediately the writer deals with the opposition's two major arguments and rebuts them in the next couple of sentences. The rebuttal also allows a smooth transition into the writer's basic argument for getting involved.

- The writer maintains an informal approach, using dialogue, contractions, first- and second-person points of view, and a didactic approach which emphasizes the informality.

- While the paragraph uses primarily a first-person plural (*we/our*) point of view, the use of the second person at the beginning and at the end permits a more personalized, didactic approach. The writer draws the reader into the subject with the first-person plural pronouns. Note, however, that a more formal paper will rely entirely on a third-person point of view. [*See the following Sample for Social Sciences for a formal third-person point of view approach.*]
- The emotional appeals suggest that personal success, personal growth, personal happiness, and other "humanizing" qualities can come as a result of getting involved. In the conclusion, the general term *benefits* appears.
- Specific details follow more general ones. For instance, the readers can *improve interpersonal relationships,* a generally positive sounding goal made more specific by *understanding why a deaf child resents being called "handicapped."* Even a *puppy which refuses to be housebroken* provides a somewhat amusing detail, one with which the reader can identify even if not by personal experience.
- The series of four illustrations helps the reader see why he should get involved. The illustrations, in their specificity, promote the reader's personal involvement.
- The organizational plan moves the reader from the second most important reason (*business contacts*) to the most important (*personal support*). While another writer may choose a different order of importance, the intent here appears to be to support individual growth.
- The conclusion, actually a series of three short sentences, demands specific action. Using the second-person point of view (with the implied *you* as the subject), the writer involves the reader in a personal command.

Sample for Social Sciences

The following persuasive paper aims to convince voters to cast ballots for a specific candidate. Compare this persuasive paper with the sample opinion paper [*see* OPINION *in Part II*] and with the sample letter to the editor [*see* LETTERS, KINDS: EDITORIAL *in Part II*], all with the same subject but developed to meet the unique characteristics of the specific writing form. In addition, compare this more formal paper with the preceding informal one, noting the characteristics which seem to suggest formality or a lack of it.

The Eighth-District Congressional Race

Two qualified candidates have conducted their equally active campaigns to influence the voters of the eighth district. Democrat Jerrald Kinsingtonne and Republican Rodney Brolliette represent their parties well and have conducted themselves as gentlemen in an historically sometimes less than gentlemanly race. Both deserve commendations for that. The voters, however, must select only one man to serve, preferably the better man.

While Brolliette is a conservative and Kinsingtonne a liberal, labels may offer little help for voters. Actions, however, illustrate the labels. As a conservative, Brolliette has taken a tough stand against illegal drugs, demanding unannounced testing of all city, state, and federal employees. Kinsingtonne, while also opposing illegal drug use, believes the drug testing proposed by his opponent may well be illegal. His respect for individual rights and concern for innocent victims makes him wary of possibly illegal measures. He cites test cases in which nondrug users—ordinary employees in area businesses—tested positive as a result of recent surgery or as a result of legal, doctor-prescribed medications. At the same time, known users, people having been arrested for possession, tested negative because they bought "legal" urine and made a quick transfer of specimens. Instead of such testing, then, he believes a crackdown on illegal drug dealers—more arrests and stiffer penalties—may better halt illegal practices and at the same time protect innocent employees from undue harassment. Do eighth-district voters want on-the-job harassment?

As a result of the recent controversy over a proposed hazardous-waste incinerator to be located in the heart of the eighth district, voters have had the opportunity to examine the environmental position of the two candidates. Kinsingtonne announced his opposition early, risking the ire of local construction workers who would likely build the plant as well as the ire of the general public who looked forward to thirty additional jobs in the area. As local environmentalists explained to the public the inherent dangers of the incinerator and pointed out its proximity to a major earthquake fault and the water supply for over half of the district, citizens joined the opposition. Only then did Brolliette take a position, ironically one mirroring the apparently successful Kinsingtonne stand. A bandwagon approach to issues of such magnitude reflects poorly on a Congressional candidate. Do eighth-district voters want a "yes" man representing them in Congress?

Finally, each candidate sees the depressed economy as a major issue in the eighth district. Brolliette proposes tax incentives to lure big businesses into the area. The Republican incumbent, in fact, voted for the huge tax incentive that brought two moderately sized businesses to the area. Suddenly, however, area citizens have been hit with major increases in their personal property tax bills, some as much as double. Although the businesses offered over 1,200 jobs, almost all have gone to employees who accepted a transfer as a result of one business closing a plant in the Southwest. So irate local citizens are footing the tax bill for jobs not even open to them. Brolliette continues to defend the position. Kinsingtonne, on the other hand, warned City Council and County Council members that citizens would suffer the consequences and predicted the now-realized increase. He fought for citizen protection even before he announced his candidacy for office, again taking an initially unpopular position because he recognized the long-term burden in the plan. The common man's plight facing the ramifications of big business caused Kinsingtonne to fight for the common man's pocketbook. Do eighth-district voters want to continue paying increased taxes to provide outsiders with employment?

Little doubt remains, then, who will make the best representative for the eighth district. Kinsingtonne has shown his concern for individual rights and will be aggressive enough to take a stand that may initially appear to be unpopular. He has an uncanny understanding, however, of what is best for the most, and he is willing to take risks to fight for the most. So the issues boil down to three simple questions: Do you want on-the-job harassment? Do you want a "yes" man in Congress? Do you want increased personal property taxes? If your answer is a resounding "no" to those questions, you will vote a resounding "yes" for Kinsingtonne next Tuesday. Vote for a better life for all of us in the eighth district.

Analysis of the Sample for Social Sciences

The five-paragraph theme above illustrates most of the characteristics of a good persuasive paper. Note these specifics:

- The general title omits any reference to the writer's point of view, thus enticing proponents of both sides to read on.

- Beginning on common ground, the writer makes positive comments about both candidates. The objective approach in the opening paragraph does not antagonize the reader. On the other hand, most political battles are just that—battles. So the writer correctly assumes antagonism from at least half of the audience.

- The thesis sentence, the last in the introductory paragraph, makes a purposely vague reference to *one man,*thus avoiding the potential of turning off the reader before the writer has an opportunity to persuade.

- The organization, following an order of importance, begins with the opposition's strongest argument, the strong stance against illegal drugs. After refuting that argument, the following points move to the strongest argument for Kinsingtonne. [*See* ORDERS OF IMPORTANCE *in the Glossary.*]

- Using a comparison-contrast approach [*see* COMPARISON AND CONTRAST, *earlier in Part II*], the writer uses only positive comments, never slandering or name-calling. She merely establishes the relative strengths of Kinsingtonne.

- By the time she reaches her final argument, the writer has appealed to the voter's sense of self-worth, pocketbook, sense of justice, sense of morality, and fear of the future.

- A number of words suggest underlying issues: *air and water pollution, increased taxes, civil rights, unemployment, economic depression.*

- A topic sentence may be either implied or held until the end of a paragraph. Both techniques allow the writer subtlety in approaching an antagonistic reader.

- A real thesis sentence never appears, but we can write one: *Kinsingtonne deserves your vote because of his approach to the illegal-drug dilemma, his active concern in environmental issues, and his understanding of the plight of the common man in issues of big business.*

- The conclusion comes close to stating a thesis sentence and specifically asks for reader action. Only at this point does the writer rely on the second-person point of view in order to draw her reader personally into the argument.

- As a result, the paper assumes primarily a formal tone, using a third-person point of view until the final few sentences. Sentence structure supports the formal tone as does organization and word choice.

——————————— **Sample for Science** ———————————

The following persuasive essay opposes a coke-processing plant and illustrates the potential strength of a persuasive paper.

A Coke-Processing Plant: What Results?

Fir River Resources, Inc., has preliminary approval to build a coke-processing plant just three-and-a-half miles southwest of our town. There may be something you don't know about the proposed plant, some things that may cause concern.

If the proposed coke-processing plant is built, Posey County, as well as the neighboring counties, is likely to see an increased rate of death by lung cancer as a result of the plant's pollutants. In two independent studies carried out in the U.S., coke-oven workers exhibited a rate of lung cancer 2-1/2 to 10 times greater than that in other workers. In another study made in southern Ohio, scientists found that people living near coke-processing plants had significantly higher death rates from lung cancer than persons in other areas. Several counties also showed high death rates from cancer of the large intestine, liver, and bladder. In the same study, surrounding counties showed increased death rates from lung cancer. In yet another study, scientists discovered that by exposing mice to coke-processing plant emissions for a period of 50 weeks, 93% developed at least one cancerous tumor. Scientists believe that two kinds of chemical compounds, initiators and promoters, work together to cause cancer. The coking plant will emit benzo(a)prene, an initiator. The phenol plant, located near the proposed coke-processing plant, emits phenolics, which are promoters. The combination may lead to a significant increase in the possibility of cancer among local residents and phenol plant workers. Finally, particulate emissions from coke plants have been found to be 500 times more cancer causing than are the particulates in cigarette smoke.

If the coke-processing plant is built, we might expect other kinds of effects. For instance, we might expect to see a rise in mutations in babies. Some of course could die because of serious malformations; others will live, maybe a worse fate. The scientific data is so clear that it appears in college textbooks. The emissions from coking plants interfere with the development of DNA, that biological compound that makes us all different. Interference in that development causes mutations. In addition, we might expect to see some crop damage. Fir River says the proposed plant will cause no damage to crops. On the other hand, the plant's nine smokestacks, each only 50 feet tall, will emit 30,000 pounds of sulfur dioxide per day. Annually, the plant will emit 5,700 tons of sulfur dioxide, 1,181 tons of particulates, and 199 tons of nitrogen oxide. Finally, studies of other potential problems have not yet been completed. Scientists do know, however, that other kinds of pollution will occur; but they cannot, with the statistics Fir River has supplied, determine total impact. For instance, water pollution will occur from the quenching operation. Coal-pile run-off produces pollutants which will flow into the Ohio River. Increased truck and rail traffic will have a significant impact on the community. The proposed plant will ship in 750,000 tons of coal annually and will ship out 540,000 tons of coke annually. This leaves over one million pounds of waste per day in Posey County.

Finally, the pollutants could cause Posey County to become economically stagnant. While the proposed plant will provide 70 more jobs, the plant will consume 87% of the county's pollution increment for sulfur dioxide. Because it may lead to a violation of the National Ambient Air Stardard for Particulates, it could severely hamper further industrial expansion. As a result, present companies like General Electric will be unable to expand. Mead Johnson, which recently announced plans for a major new warehouse complex north of the highway in anticipation of a major manufacturing expansion, could be prevented from further industrial expansion. SIGECO, responsible for providing the tri-state area with power, may be unable to pursue plans to expand. Additional industries may not be allowed to locate in Posey County. In the future, then, as our county's population increases, one of two things will happen: Either unemployment will increase, or residents will be forced to leave the county to seek employment.

Whether your concern is for your personal health, your children's future, the economic future of the community, or the future of the world's environment, you cannot afford to ignore this proposed coke-processing plant. Your influence will help. Attend the hearing next Thursday, 7:00 PM in the high-school auditorium to show mass concern. We must fight politics in the political way—with the force of the multitudes.

Analysis of the Sample for Science

The five-paragraph theme above relies on scientific evidence to support the arguments. Hard evidence makes the persuasive paper all the more convincing. Note, too, these details:

- The introduction appeals to the reader's concern, suggesting that, armed with the facts, he or she may feel a need to fight the proposed facility.

- While the paper does not acknowledge any major arguments from the opposition and so does not appear to be building rebuttals, in fact the paper is a rebuttal to the entire process which has allowed the plant to gain preliminary approval.

- The rebuttals focus on three major points, each developed in a separate paragraph and organized in order of importance. [*See* ORDERS OF IMPORTANCE *in the Glossary.*]

- Supporting details establish the author's credibility and emphasize facts, statistics, studies, and authorities.

- Emotional appeals are subtle until the concluding paragraph in which the writer specifies the reader's possible concerns.

- Note the use of "guarded" words that enhance the writer's credibility but at the same time protect him against any potential liability: *is likely to see, believe, might expect, could, may.* Such vocabulary is essential in the scientific community where stronger words could be questioned on the basis of scientific evidence.

- The conclusion switches to the second-person point of view to involve the reader and ask for specific support by attending a meeting.

- The final sentence includes a first-person point of view so that the writer can include himself, not set himself apart with a didactic *you.*

- Remaining sections of the paper maintain a third-person point of view and suggest a rather formal approach.

- The vocabulary reflects the technical nature of a science paper.

──────────────── **Sample for Business** ────────────────

The following paragraph, supported by explanations of business principles, illustrates most of the characteristics of a persuasive paper. Since the writer does not assume the reader to be antagonistic, no rebuttal appears in the early part of the paragraph. The points are organized merely to explain why the investment seems wise.

Investing in Utility Stocks

Investing in the stock market is a matter of judgment and risk. Certainly, however, good judgment can minimize risk. Most investors who shy away from serious risk prefer to invest in relatively safe stocks. Many of those investors turn to utility stocks. Here's why. First, utility companies are stable. Essentially monopolies, they can raise rates as costs go up leaving the consumer no choice but to pay the increased rates. The rate increases can virtually guarantee a profitable company, so utility companies stand as stalwart businesses. Second, although the consumer has little or no recourse but to pay increased rates, from the investor's point of view the utility company thus guarantees steady profit. Then, as a result of the steady company profit, utility stocks offer high dividends and slow but steady growth. Although an increase in interest rates usually results in a decline in virtually all stock prices, utility stock remains as one of the safest, most stable stocks on the market. Investing in them at the right time can offer a significant financial advantage.

Analysis of the Sample for Business

The single paragraph above, short and to the point, offers two reasons for investing in utility stock, both showing dollars-and-cents logic. Consider, too, the following characteristics peculiar to a persuasive paper:

- The introductory sentence acknowledges what most people fear about the stock market. By acknowledging but without dwelling on that fear, the writer progresses directly to his point. Note that each sentence connects with the previous sentence and moves smoothly to the next idea.

- The cause-effect relationships are closely knit and clearly presented.

- Organization is emphasized by transitions like *first* and *second* as well as by the many transitions used to show relationships: *thus, as a result, then, although*. The paragraph moves chronologically to follow the cause and effect relationship.

- To maintain his credibility, the writer admits that stock prices usually drop when interest rates decline and that *buying at the right time* still determines stock growth potential.

- Appeals to logic and to the emotional desire for success mesh so well that they seem as one.

- The conclusion offers a guarded recommendation, guarded to avoid any potential liability. Good business practice suggests such approaches.

Sample for Vocational Education

The following persuasive paragraph, less formal than the one above, offers a reasonable comparison with preceding models.

When Should You Change Oil in Your Car?

Most automobile owner's manuals suggest an oil change every 7,500 miles. Many mechanics suggest your engine will last longer, however, if you change the oil at least every 3,000 miles. I know what you're thinking: the mechanics just want more business so they can rake in more dollars from the unsuspecting car owner. Well, certainly mechanics don't mind additional business or extra dollars, but the only thing unsuspecting about the car owner is his blind faith that engine oil changed every 7,500 miles will effectively lubricate his engine. In fact, as you drive, the lubricating oil picks up tiny particles from engine wear, particles so fine you can barely feel the grittiness when you rub it between your fingers. The tiniest piece of grit, forced between the piston and engine wall, creates more wear, more particles. Added to the particles, chemical contamination of the oil further increases engine wear. Moisture droplets, excess fuel from occasional incomplete combustion, and acid from the combustion itself all dissolve in the oil. Obviously the longer you drive without an oil change, the more particles and the more chemical contamination the oil contains. You are merely forcing the residues through the engine, creating abrasion, in effect running oily sandpaper through the valves and pistons. As the heavy particles react with engine heat, they create a buildup, commonly known as sludge. Engines hampered by sludge deposits perform poorly and ultimately must be rebuilt or discarded. So maybe it costs a few dollars extra to change oil more frequently, but in the long run you'll save dollars by extending the life of your engine.

Analysis of the Sample for Vocational Education

The single paragraph above illustrates a slightly different kind of persuasive paper than we have studied so far. Note these characteristics:

- The paragraph begins on common ground, immediately indicates the writer's position, and admits the first argument. The remainder of the paragraph rebuts the argument
- Facts, comparisons, and illustrations offer supporting details for the argument
- Organization follows order of importance while suggesting cause-and-effect relationships as well
- The informal style, especially the use of *I* and *you* and the use of contractions, appropriately matches the subject matter
- The conclusion refers again to the opposition's primary argument and extends the emotional fear of unjust cost to the emotional fear of greater cost
- Emotional appeals accompany logical appeals, but the logic far outweighs the fear or subtle threats in convincing the reader of the importance of more frequent oil changes

The characteristics, process, and models with analyses above should enable you to develop a successful persuasive paper. Whether your paper will be a paragraph or a full-length composition, whether it will be formal or informal, you have representative models from which to choose. Compare your own writing with the models and their respective analyses above.

POETRY

Poetry can satisfy a writer's most creative urges. Poetry appears in numerous forms—indeed sometimes apparently without form—and employs special kinds of language devices. Consequently, describing how to write poetry is somewhat like describing how to make snowflakes. No two poems are quite alike, and even poets cannot succinctly define poetry or explain how they write it. The following section, then, merely introduces the main ideas of poetry and offers suggestions for general poetic techniques.

Characteristics

Admittedly, poetry varies from two liners to book-length epics. Likewise the forms vary from carefully metered and elaborately rhymed verse to seemingly unstructured and unrhymed poems that look very much like prose. [See POEM *in the Glossary for a list of different kinds of poems.*] To list the characteristics of poetry is to deal in generalities and to acknowledge variety. Nevertheless, the following list may prove helpful to aspiring poets. Generally, a poem

- expresses the writer's feelings about a subject,

- relies on imagery [*see* IMAGERY *in the Glossary*] to stimulate the reader's thoughts, thus conveying a larger message,

- relies on figurative language [*see* FIGURES OF SPEECH *in the Glossary*], especially metaphor and simile [*see* METAPHOR *and* SIMILE *in the Glossary*] to tease the ear and mind,

- builds language in multiple layers of meaning, thus making every word count more than once,

- may include a rhyme pattern [*see* RHYME *in the Glossary*],

- may follow a specific rhythmic pattern called *meter* [*see* RHYTHM *in the Glossary*],

- uses nontraditional punctuation to clarify meaning and show relationships among ideas,

- may include lines grouped together to form stanzas.

Process

Since it is virtually impossible to tell someone how to write a poem, we will simply examine the process by which a poem can be developed.

PREWRITING

STEP 1. FINDING IDEAS

Ideas for poetry, like ideas for any other writing, come from observation and experience. Immediate surroundings and the intimate details of life's daily struggle are the stuff of poetry. To help focus on ideas which later become poetry, most poets keep journals. Usually they make entries daily—even several times daily—recording thoughts, observations, reactions, or images to be used at a later date. Writing daily helps one become more observant, more thoughtful, more aware. [*See also* PREWRITING *in Part I for additional suggestions.*]

After you have kept a journal for some time, you should be able to find suitable ideas with which to work.

STEP 2.   SELECTING IMAGES

Probably you will select an idea about which you have something to say and which expresses your pleasure, joy, fear, disgust, or perhaps irony, surprise, or awe. You should select images which best convey your primary message. For example, if you find the typical suburban American home distasteful, your poem need not *say* that it is distasteful. Instead, you can develop images that suggest distaste. *Show* plastic flowers and bleach-bottle ornaments, and let the reader decide for him or herself.

Your next step, then, is to list possible images. Perhaps the ideas in your journal will stimulate your thinking. Perhaps mere concentration on your subject and your reaction to it will stimulate thinking. You may need several days to think of just the right images.

WRITING
STEP 3.   WORKING ON THE POEM

Few poets sit down to write a poem saying, "Now I'm going to write a four-stanza poem with iambic pentameter and a rhyme scheme of abba/cddc/effe/ghhg." Rather, they allow the subject to determine the poem's form. Forcing yourself to write in a particular form is a superb discipline and often the basis for a class assignment. But in reality, creative poets do not tend to follow this practice.

Developing the poem, then, becomes a trial-and-error process. The struggle to write a poem, far more tedious than the struggle to write a long paper, grows frustrating only when a writer fails to "let go," to write ideas, images, figures of speech, even series of descriptive words without fighting for rhyme, rhythm, or form. Get the ideas on paper. Save the frustration for later!

REVISING
STEP 4.   FIGHTING FOR FORM

Once the ideas are on paper, then and only then should you worry about form, rhyme, and rhythm. Most of all, however, worry about content. Review the list of characteristics above. Remember the importance of layers of meaning in a poem? Remember the emphasis on imagery and figurative language to stimulate the reader's senses and imagination? These come only by conscious effort on the part of the writer. Using the additional explanations in the Glossary [*see* IMAGERY *and* FIGURES OF SPEECH], strive to include them in your own poem. For instance, if you can personify [*see* PERSONIFICATION *in the Glossary*] a computer program that is giving you nightmares, the reader can identify with that ''person'' who chases you using its power cord as a whip!

Select the images and figures of speech which will best enhance the message.

Next, struggle to improve rhythm. Even unrhymed poems usually have a rhythm that heightens their message. If your poem rhymes, check its pattern for consistency. Then see if you can improve the form, perhaps by altering stanzas or rearranging them for better flow and improved clarity.

Finally, check every single word in the poem. Is each necessary? Does each carry an important, or at least worthwhile, meaning? Can you eliminate any without affecting meaning? Use *Webster's New World Thesaurus* to find better, stronger words. Remember that strong nouns and verbs eliminate the necessity for weak, generally wordy, modifiers. This is as true of poetry as it is of prose, perhaps more so.

PROOFREADING

STEP 5. CHECKING THE FINAL DETAILS

Obviously, you will want your poem's presentation to be accurate. Therefore check your spelling carefully. A misspelled word suggests a lack of attention to detail, and poetry is synonymous with detail.

Next check punctuation. Remember that punctuation in a poem probably does not follow the general rules; rather it often serves to separate and show relationships between ideas. Make the punctuation work for you.

Once you have checked the final details, read the poem through for accuracy. Add a title and sign your name!

Sample Poems

The following poems represent two very different kinds of verse. One is freeform; the other, highly structured. Compare the two poems and their analyses with your own work. Perhaps some of the ideas—either in the poems or the analyses—will serve as springboards for improving your own work.

Ode to a Tupperware Container

Through a plastic-flower grotto
Mary offers peace and tanquility.
Clorox-bottle topiary trees welcome silver-balled
stands,

Snow White, Bambi, and bird baths.
No resemblance of nature left.
Plush-green-carpet-lawn, astroturf.

The tinker-toy community, all the originality
of tonka-toy blocks,
Bedecked in aluminum siding, adorned with
Precious carriages.
Precise. Exact. Car-ported. These monuments to man

Reveal more than they hide.

Afternoon Tea

The women sit and sip their tea
And gossip about some absentee,
Cite some authors in plebeian slur:
Whitman, Rousseau, and Joyce Kilmer.

"Wouldn't it be swell to get
Heston to read the great Hamlet
And selections from the poems of Edgar Guest?"

("I finally passed my driver's test—
I wore a knit dress!"

                    "Her daughter's sick."

"Betty's failed arithmetic!")

"I wish we could get Ogden free
Of charge to read his poetry."

"He's the greatest since Guthrie!"

The pseudos sit and sip their tea.

Analysis of the Sample Poems

The poems above show, at least in brief, the vast range of possibilities open to poets—vast subject matter, varied form, different approaches. Look closer at them:

- "Ode to a Tupperware Container" does not rhyme and includes two stanzas, the second broken by a separated line to enhance its meaning.

- "Afternoon Tea," on the other hand, follows a rhyme pattern of aabb/ccdd/eeaa/aa and includes four stanzas, the last three broken by the spacing in order to show changes in speaker.

- "Ode" expresses the writer's attitude toward modern suburban houses and what they say of their occupants.

- "Tea" expresses the writer's attitude toward groups of women who feign literary interest when, in fact, they spend more time gossiping.

- "Ode" contrasts words like *grotto* and *topiary trees* with *plastic flower* and *Clorox bottle*. These contrasts startle the reader into recognizing the poem's message.

- "Tea" uses phrases like *plebeian slur,* and references to passing a driver's test, to set the tone of the "pseudos" sitting and sipping their tea.

- "Ode" alludes to common trappings: *Snow White* and *Bambi* to ceramic yard decorations; *tonka-toy blocks* to houses set tightly together in suburban neighborhoods; *precious carriages* to the decorative pieces which appear on the sides of houses or above garage doors.

- "Tea" alludes to literature: the names *Whitman* (the American poet), *Rousseau* (a French philosopher and social reformer), and *Joyce Kilmer* (another American poet) point to a wide variety and quality of work. *Ogden* refers to the poet Ogden Nash, *Guthrie,* to an author of Wild West stories. Knowing these authors' works helps the reader understand the "pseudos."

- "Ode" is punctuated for emphasis, especially in the next-to-the-last line. Note how the periods force the reader to focus on each word.

- "Tea" uses punctuation and new lines to show change in speaker. The series of unrelated bits of gossip helps the writer to show the wide variety of topics discussed at this literary tea. Enclosing these quotations in parentheses separates them from the literary references in the rest of the poem.

The two poems illustrate diversity. As you begin writing verse, study poetry—all kinds of poetry, by all kinds of authors. The more you read, the more creative your writing will become. Use this section of your handbook as a guide to begin your first poetic efforts. Then read, study, and write more!

PRECIS

A precis (pronounced *pray-see*) is a kind of summary. [*Compare the precis with two other kinds of summaries, the paraphrase and the synopsis. See those entries elsewhere in Part II.*] The purpose of a precis is to provide a shortened version of a piece of writing. You may be asked to write precis (plural, pronounced *pray-sees*) to show that you have read and understood chapters or passages. You may be asked to write precis to present concisely the results of your research in a special project. You may write precis for your own benefit, as a kind of note-taking.

A precis, then, is a short restatement of the main points of a piece of writing. A precis of one page may well summarize the points presented in twenty-five pages of carefully supported detail. Similarly a precis of a hundred words may restate what an author explains in three pages. Finally, a precis of a single sentence may summarize a paragraph or two.

Characteristics

A precis usually

- omits details, illustrations, and subordinate ideas, presenting instead the major ideas,

- reduces the original passage by at least two-thirds,

- indicates careful reading of the original passage,

- portrays the original author's concept accurately, without adding personal bias,

- follows the guidelines of standard grammar, usage, and mechanics—using strong, effective sentence structure.

Process

To write an effective precis, follow these steps.

PREWRITING

STEP 1. READING THE MATERIAL

Read the passage quickly to grasp the general idea and purpose. Look up any unfamiliar words or references.

Read the passage again, more slowly, to detect details as they relate to the main points.

Jot down the main ideas in your own words.

Reread the original passage, comparing your skeleton outline with the text. Revise as necessary to maintain accuracy or correct omissions.

WRITING

STEP 2. PREPARING THE PRECIS

Without referring to the original, write the summary in your own words, following the skeleton outline developed in Step 1 above.

Use the following guidelines as you write:

- Organize your precis the same way as the original passage.

- Include only the bare essentials. If the original passage is well-organized, you should be able to select a single main idea from each paragraph.

- Be sure, however, to include all the main points from the original passage, perhaps even using the passage's key words. The expression *key words* refers to terms or expressions unique to the subject. Take pains to avoid plagiarism. [*See* PLAGIARISM *in the Glossary.*]

REVISING

STEP 3. CHECKING THE CONTENT

Once you have completed your precis, ask yourself the following questions:

- Have I reduced the content by at least two-thirds?

- In the process of reducing volume, have I presented the main ideas, all the essentials?

- Have I omitted nonessential details and information?

- Does the precis honestly reflect the original passage, or have my own biases crept in?

- Have I avoided plagiarism?

- Have I written simply and clearly, with unadorned vocabulary?

- When the reader finishes the precis, will he or she understand the intent of the original work?

If you answer ''no'' to any of the above questions, revise the precis to solve the problems suggested.

PROOFREADING

STEP 4. CHECKING FOR ACCURACY

Once you have completed the revisions, check the final copy for misspellings, punctuation and grammar errors, usage problems, and mechanical inaccuracies. Consult *Webster's New World Dictionary* to insure accurate spelling, and see *Webster's New World Thesaurus* to check for the accurate connotative as well as denotative meanings of synonyms.

A Note about the Samples: The following samples offer models for an examination of the results of the above process. Each sample includes the original passage from which the precis was written, and is followed by an analysis.

——————————— **Sample for English** ———————————

A student writing a research paper for an English class has chosen to write about automobile-induced air pollution. She has found a passage in "Autos and Air Pollution," a brochure published by the United States Environmental Protection Agency. This passage appears below, followed by her precis. Once you have studied both, read the analysis which follows.

Original passage

The use of leaded gasoline in vehicles designed for unleaded can increase tailpipe emissions 200 to 800 percent, EPA has determined. More than one million tons of hydrocarbons and 12 million tons of carbon monoxide were spewed from the tailpipes of cars with defective emission control systems during Fiscal Year 1983.

Studies show that most people who engage in fuel switching do so to save money—about 7 cents a gallon. However, these people are victims of faulty economics, according to Joe Cannon, EPA's assistant administrator for Air and Radiation. "In the long run, the use of leaded gas in the car will more quickly foul the spark plugs, wear out the exhaust system, degrade the oil, and foul the oxygen sensor in new cars, in addition to ruining the catalytic converter," he said.

Cannon estimates that people who substitute leaded for unleaded gasoline will end up paying 12 cents a gallon in extra maintenance and repairs.

Precis

Using leaded instead of unleaded gasoline contributes to a 200 to 800 percent increase in air-polluting emissions. According to Joe Cannon, EPA assistant administrator for Air and Radiation, while consumers save about seven cents a gallon at the pumps, they ultimately pay twelve cents a gallon more to repair the resulting damage to the car's ignition, exhaust, and lubricating systems.

Analysis of the Sample for English

The precis above follows the general guidelines for content, organization, and structure. Note the following specifics:

- The precis reduces the original passage of approximately 120 words to less than 60 words.

- Six sentences in the original passage become two in the precis.

- The choice of material included in the precis is determined by the general purpose of the research paper in which it is to be included. For instance, the information about the amount of pollutants emitted into the atmosphere as a result of defective emission-control systems is omitted, because the writer plans to deal only with problems resulting from the use of leaded gasoline.
- The choice of vocabulary is consistent with the original, especially as the original lacks technical terms needing simplification.
- The main ideas appear in the same order as in the original.
- EPA administrator Cannon is included to enhance the authenticity of the seven-cent/twelve-cent comparison; however, the writer chooses not to use his exact words. The summary of his comments is accurate and makes the same point more concisely.

Thus, a precis achieves its purpose and reduces a significant passage to a manageable size for use in a paper.

Sample for Social Sciences

To explain government regulations and their effect on business, one social sciences student needed a concise definition of the Clean Air Act. He found such an explanation in a brochure published by the United States Environmental Protection Agency and decided to summarize it in his paper. The original passage, its precis, and an analysis of the precis appear below:

Original passage

The Clean Air Act of 1970, amended in 1977 and 1981, is one of the basic laws under which EPA operates. Its purpose is "to protect and enhance the quality of the Nation's air resources so as to promote the public health and welfare and the productive capacity of its population."

In order to do that, Congress authorized a national research and development program to prevent and control air pollution. The act also provided for EPA to assist State and local governments in the development and execution of their air quality programs.

The Clear Air Act required EPA to set national primary and secondary ambient air quality standards for certain air pollutants. The law also required emission standards for mobile sources of air pollution (vehicles), and for new stationary sources such as smokestacks. In addition, the act called for regulation of hazardous air pollutants for which no ambient air quality standard is applicable.

Another section of the law was designed to protect air quality in national parks, wilderness areas, monuments, seashores, and other areas of special national or regional natural, recreational, scenic, or historic value, and to prevent significant deterioration of air quality in those areas.

Precis

The Clean Air Act, designed to protect air quality, provides a means for studying and building a program to solve air-pollution problems. The program decides when pollutants become problems by establishing and applying standard levels permissible for various emissions, from moving and stationary sources The act also addresses clean air standards in protected natural areas like wildernesses and seashores.

Analysis of the Sample for Social Sciences

The precis achieves the goals set for a good summary. Note these specific characteristics:

- An original of over 150 words is reduced to about 60 in the precis.
- Eight sentences in the original are reduced to three.
- Every major idea is included.
- The precis maintains the same organization as the original.
- Sentence structure and vocabulary are appropriate for the audience.

—————— Sample for Science ——————

In a class on ecology, one student did research on insect control, seeking a means of controlling insect damage without upsetting nature's balance. She found useful information in the booklet, "Teaching Soil and Water Conservation," published by the United States Department of Agriculture. Her precis and an analysis of it follow. [*For further comparison, see* NOTES *in Part II and* OUTLINES, KINDS: FOR A CLASS *also in Part II for sample notes taken from the following passage. Compare the notes with the precis below.*]

Original Passage

The food habits of birds make them especially valuable to agriculture. Because birds have higher body temperatures, more rapid digestion, and greater energy than most other animals, they require more food. Nestling birds make extremely rapid growth, requiring huge amounts of food.

They usually consume as much or more than their own weight in soft-bodied insects every day.

Young robins have been observed to gain 8 times their original weight the first 8 days of their life.

Insect-eating birds must fill their stomachs 5 to 6 times daily because they digest their food so fast and because of the large amount of indigestible material in insects.

One young robin, weighing 3 ounces, consumed 165 cutworms weighing 5-1/2 ounces in 1 day. If a 10-pound baby ate at the same rate he would eat 18-1/3 pounds of food in a day.

Of course, birds cannot control insects completely, but they are of great value. By using soil- and water-conserving practices farmers and ranchers could probably double the population of helpful birds. Field and farmstead windbreaks, living fences, shrub buffers, grass waterways, and farm ponds are only a few of the many land use practices useful in attracting and increasing beneficial forms of wildlife.

Precis

Because of their rapid metabolism, birds daily eat more than their own weight. Because insects are not fully digestible, insect-eating birds may eat nearly twice their weight in these pests. Residents can double the numbers of insect-eaters by providing coniferous trees, dense and thorny shrubs, and ponds to attract them to an area.

Analysis of the Sample for Science

The precis achieves the purpose of a summary. By condensing the long original passage to a manageable paragraph, the writer prepares to incorporate the information directly into her report. Note these specifics:

- The original passage is reduced from over 200 words to 55 words.
- Eleven sentences are reduced to three.
- The supporting details of the original, explaining specifics about nestlings and young robins, do not appear. While the details are interesting they are unnecessary to convey main ideas.
- Scientific references not mentioned in the original appear in the precis. For instance, *windbreaks* becomes *coniferous trees*; and *living fences and shrub buffers* become *dense and thorny shrubs*. The Ecology student recognized windbreaks and living fences as such.
- The precis is developed with the ultimate goal of supporting the main idea in the Ecology paper. This kind of goal helps determine which ideas go into a

precis, and thus reflects editorial judgment. The materials still mirror the content and emphasis of the original. Nothing is distorted, or taken out of context, to meet the goals of the proposed paper.

Sample for Business

Students in a business class were asked to consider the businesses which use a single resource. One student chose to look at wood. In researching, he discovered a passage on its many uses. This passage, from a Department of Agriculture booklet, appears below. Afterward appears the student's precis and its analysis.

Original passage

Wood is a universal material and no one has ever been able to make a satisfactory count of its many uses. The Forest Products Laboratory, a research institution of the United States Forest Service, at Madison, Wis., once undertook to make an official count of wood uses. When last announced, the number was more than 5,000 and the argument had only started over how general or how specific a use had to be to get on the list.

Just one well-known wood-cellulose plastic, including its conversion products, claims 25,000 uses—among them such different items as dolls' eyes and advertising signs. The use of wood fiber as the basis for such products is increasing every day.

Another important use of wood is paper for printing our books, magazines, and newspapers. A high point in our culture came less than a century ago with the discovery that wood fiber could take the place of cotton or linen in paper manufacture. Today we use more than 73 million tons of paper and board each year. Of this amount each person's annual share of all kinds of paper and board is about 660 pounds. When paper was made chiefly of rags, each person's annual share was less than 10 pounds.

Container board accounts for about a fourth of our paper and board use. Newsprint accounts for an additional 17 percent of paper use. The rest is used in a myriad of forms—writing paper, sanitary cartons for prunes, cereals, butter, ice cream; paper cups, plates, disposable napkins, towels, handkerchiefs; wrapping paper for groceries, meats, dry goods.

Precis

The Forest Products Laboratory, a research institution of the United States Forest Service, suggests over 5,000 uses for wood, but admittedly no one knows how to set the limits of specificity for the list. For instance, some wood fiber products alone can boast over 25,000 uses, including dolls' eyes and billboards. In another example, wood supplies annually over 73 million tons of paper and board, used for everything from containers to newsprint, amounting to over 40% of paper use.

Analysis of the Sample for Business

The precis achieves the usual goals of a summary and does some additional things as well. Notice these characteristics:

- It reduces the original by about two-thirds.
- While it includes several specific examples (*dolls' eyes, billboards, containers to newsprint*), it mostly confines itself to main ideas.
- Statistics and sources are considered *key words* and thus appear in the precis just as they did in the original.
- The writer has achieved some organizational patterns not evident in the original and used transitions to clarify relationships. Note particularly *for instance* and *in another example,* which alert the reader that these two show how hard it is to quantify the uses of wood. Should the industry list *paper products* as a single use or list each product as a separate use? Thus, the precis-writer achieves what the author of the original passage did not: helps the reader reach a conclusion about the various facts and figures.

—————— Sample for Vocational Education ——————

A student studying food preservation chose to investigate the history of canning. She remembered her great-grandmother's tales of working over a woodstove all day, only to have the food spoil three days later. The student wondered what went wrong. The following material is summarized in a precis below:

Original Passage

Not until the nineteenth century did canning become a part of food preservation. Until then, foods were dried, salted, or smoked. In 1795, during the Napoleonic Wars, the French government offered a reward to the first person who could preserve food satisfactory for military use. In 1809, M. Nicholas Appert won the 12,000 francs and earned recognition as the father of canning. Although he used glass bottles, sealed with cork and processed in a hot-water bath, he did not know why his process worked.

Ultimately, Louis Pasteur determined why improperly processed foods spoil. Microorganisms found in the air, and on all objects, cause spoilage as soon as they come in contact with food. Only proper sterilization, found Pasteur, could kill these microorganisms.

Prior to 1850, the only sterilization method known to farm women called for canning—first in tin cans and later in glass jars, both of which had a groove around the top, into which a tin lid fit. Hot food, placed in hot cans or jars and topped with a hot lid, was sealed with hot sealing wax—a hard red wax, quite unlike today's paraffin. When dry, the brittle wax seal was broken only by pelting the wax with a blunt object, usually a knife handle.

In 1858, John L. Mason invented a glass jar that could receive a screw-on zinc lid sealed by a rubber gasket. For the first time, home canning became easy, economical, and popular. By 1903, Alexander H. Kerr perfected the two-piece lid, a snap lid and a ring, still in use nearly ninety years later. Home canning literally snapped forth a new option for homemakers.

Precis

M. Nicholas Appert first canned food in 1809 in cork-sealed glass bottles processed in a hot-water bath. Pasteur's discovery that sterilization killed microorganisms and kept food from spoiling explained Appert's success. As a result, women learned to can successfully in tin and glass, using a hard wax to seal the hot food. Then, in 1858, John L. Mason sealed glass jars with a screw-on lid and rubber gasket. Finally, in 1903, Alexander Kerr developed the two-piece lid still in use.

Analysis of the Sample for Vocational Education

The passage above exhibits the general characteristics of a good precis:

- The original has been reduced by two-thirds.
- Virtually no supportive details are included.
- Transitions show relationships between ideas: *as a result, then, finally.*
- Every major idea, represented by a paragraph in the original passage, is included.
- Key words like *processed, hot-water bath, sterilization, microorganism, hard wax, screw-on lid, rubber gasket,* and *two-piece lid* are included accurately.
- The writer conceals any personal prejudice.
- The writing is concise, bare of supportive or illustrative material.

- The writer avoids plagiarism.
- Sentences read well, and the paragraph flows well as the result of internal transition.

Using similar techniques will enable you to develop successful precis for your own work.

PROCESS ANALYSIS

A process analysis paper explains how something is or was done. The difference, of course, is in time. In the first case, a paper may explain how to build a bird feeder, taking readers step by step through the process they will follow as they make their own feeders. The time is the present. On the other hand, a process paper may explain how a bird feeder was built, again taking readers step by step through the already completed process. The time is the past.

The process paper may serve one of two purposes: to instruct, so that readers can complete a similar process, or to inform, so that they can develop a deeper understanding or appreciation of some process. For instance, a process analysis may tell readers how to fill out tax forms, how to dry wall a new room, how to refinish furniture, how to drive safely in heavy traffic, how to set up a double-entry bookkeeping system, how to use a spread sheet, or even how to antagonize a younger sister. In each case, by following the instructions, readers may complete the process on their own. Similarly a process analysis may explain how a military coup was accomplished, how a spacecraft provides oxygen during an extended flight, how a fuel-injection system works, how gold leaf is made, how a cancer patient coped with his terminal illness, or how the perfect crime was committed. In these cases, readers need not plan to complete the process personally. The paper broadens understanding for the process and, in some situations, appreciation for the people involved. In some instances, process analysis becomes the basis for a television program or best seller!

So the process paper serves a multitude of functions, from providing technical directions, to suggesting philosophical self-help, to creating best-seller books.

Characteristics

A process analysis paper takes many forms and numerous directions but in general

- demonstrates the writer's familiarity with the subject,

- gives step-by-step directions or explanations,

- clarifies cause-and-effect relationships [see also CAUSE AND EFFECT, elsewhere in Part II],

- follows a chronological order [see CHRONOLOGICAL ORDER in the Glossary],

- includes illustrations, examples, and other specific details [see SPECIFIC DETAIL in the Glossary],

- includes ample transitions to allow the reader to follow the logical steps [*see* TRANSITIONS *in the Glossary*],

- uses terminology appropriate for the audience, but avoids overly technical words.

Process

The following steps will help you develop a suitable process paper.

PREWRITING

STEP 1. FOCUSING ON THE SUBJECT

A satisfactory process analysis deals with a subject narrow enough to permit a thorough discussion within the length planned. For instance, to effectively analyze the process of building a house, a writer must plan for a nearly book-length manuscript. On the other hand, a writer can effectively analyze the process of constructing adequate footings for a house in a few pages.

To focus on your own subject, complete the following sentence:

My paper will explain how

_____.

Now look at your sentence. Are you planning a paragraph or a book? Is your subject appropriate to the length? If not, adjust it to be narrow enough, or broad enough, to suit your purpose. [*For additional suggestions for sources of topics, see* PREWRITING *in Part I.*]

STEP 2. DETERMINING ESSENTIAL DETAILS

Once you have selected a focus for your paper, begin jotting down the steps involved in the process. In addition to the specific steps, must the reader anticipate other problems? Consider these ideas:

If the reader may actually complete the process,

- Are certain materials or equipment required to complete the job? Protective clothing or goggles? Tools? Special materials? Perhaps you can prepare a shopping list for the reader.
- Must certain conditions prevail, either for satisfactory results or for safety reasons? For instance, must the temperature lie between 50 and 75 degrees? Is humidity detrimental? Should the work space be well-ventilated?
- How long will the process take? A few minutes? Several hours? A week? Offer guideline so that the reader can better decide how, or if, to follow the process.
- Does he or she need additional terminology? Should you supply definitions or technical explanations? [*See* DEFINITION *earlier in Part II.*]
- Which parts of the process will be most difficult to understand? Can you provide clarifying examples, illustrations, and comparisons? [*See* ANALOGY, CLASSIFICATION, *and* COMPARISON AND CONTRAST *in Part II for additional help.*]

As you jot down steps, place notes beside them listing whatever additional information the reader may need to understand the process.

Complete the list of steps before you go on to Step 3.

STEP 3. ORGANIZING THE DETAILS

Using the list of details from Step 2 above, group the details into three, four, or maybe even five divisions. By forcing yourself to put related ideas together into no more than five steps (and preferably fewer), you will present an easy-to-follow process. Imagine the frustration of trying to remember fifteen steps for anything!

Once the items are grouped logically, organize them chronologically. Rarely in process analysis will any other form make sense. Be sure, of course, to include supporting details in your chronological plan. [*See* CHRONOLOGICAL ORDER *in the Glossary.*]

STEP 4. CREATING THE TOPIC OR THESIS SENTENCE

Having completed Steps 1, 2, and 3, you have all the necessary information listed and are organized to write your topic or thesis sentence. [*See* TOPIC SENTENCE *and* THESIS SENTENCE *in the Glossary for quick reference. See* PARAGRAPHS *and* THEME *in Part II for details and examples.*]

As your write your topic or thesis sentence, include some clue to the reader regarding the complexity of your topic. Use the following examples as guides:

> Onscreen instructions permit even first-time users to work successfully with the library's computer catalog.

> Building a doghouse requires materials, common tools, and three general steps in construction.

> Making sure a diesel engine will start in cold weather requires certain precautionary steps.

Now, based on your work in the first three steps, write your own topic or thesis sentence.

Next, list the details which will support your sentence. If necessary, convert the list into an outline. [*See* OUTLINES, KINDS: FOR A PAPER *in Part II.*]

WRITING

STEP 5. GETTING THE PROCESS ON PAPER

With the prewriting steps completed, you should have little trouble with the actual writing. Use the following guidelines to help:

- Begin each paragraph with a topic sentence.

- Begin a longer paper with an introductory paragraph and thesis sentence. [*See the Glossary entries* TOPIC SENTENCE *and* THESIS SENTENCE. *For additional help, see also* PARAGRAPHS *and* THEME *in Part II.*]

- Follow the chronological order established in Step 3, above.

- Use the outline or list, from Step 4, to determine subtopics (for paragraphs) or paragraphs (for full-length papers).

- Include ample transitions to help the reader follow the explanation. Common transitions used in process include the following: *next, then, once, afterward, until, when, later, first, second, furthermore, now, simultaneously, at this time, following this, similarly.* [*See the Glossary entry* TRANSITIONS *and* REVISING: SAMPLE REVISION FOR TRANSITION *in Part I for additional help.*]

- Indicate the importance of the process in the concluding sentence or paragraph, but avoid merely reiterating the steps.

REVISING

STEP 6. POLISHING THE WRITING

Once you have finished the first draft, use the following guidelines as you look for areas for improvement:

- Does my introduction establish the importance of the process? If not, will it be self-evident?

- Are the topics grouped into three or four (but no more than five) divisions, so the reader can easily remember the main points?

- Does each division of the subject correspond to a structural division in my paper? [*See* REVISING: CHECKING STRUCTURE *in Part I.*]

- Have I organized my paper chronologically, so the reader can follow it logically?

- Have I included adequate transitions to help the reader follow the organization? [*See* REVISING: SAMPLE REVISION FOR TRANSITION *in Part I.*]

- Is my vocabulary appropriate for the intended audience? Have I defined any unfamilar technical words? Do my definitions include meaningful examples or illustrations? [*See* DEFINITION *in Part II.*]

- Are adequate details provided? Have I used comparisons, analogies and illustrations to clarify the parts of the process? [*See* REVISING: SAMPLE REVISION FOR SPECIFIC DETAIL *in Part I, and see* COMPARISON AND CONTRAST *and* ANALOGY *in Part II.*]

- Have I maintained unity by omitting irrelevant material? [*See* REVISING: SAMPLE REVISION FOR UNITY *in Part I.*]

- Have I used good sentence variety and emphasis? [*See* REVISING: SAMPLE REVISION FOR SENTENCE VARIETY *and* REVISING: SAMPLE REVISION FOR EMPHASIS *in Part I.*]

- Does the conclusion offer a sense of completeness to the paper?

Use the answers to these questions as a guide for your revisions. [*In addition, see* REVISING *in Part I for questions to guide general revision.*]

PROOFREADING

STEP 7. CHECKING THE DETAILS

As you check your final copy, look for grammar, mechanics, and usage problems. [*See* PROOFREADING *in Part*

I for additional guidelines.] Consult *Webster's New World Dictionary* to check spelling and *Webster's New* *World Thesaurus* for accurate word choice.

A Note about the Samples: The following analyses, all focusing on photography, illustrate various approaches a process paper can take. Note that while some subjects can be developed in a single paragraph, others require longer papers. Note also that some subjects are more technical than others—but that all are aimed at a similar audience.

--- **Sample for English** ---

The following paragraph illustrates process analysis appropriate for a journalism class. The discussion focuses on editorial photography, i.e., photography that causes a newspaper reader to think or react emotionally. The narrowed subject, suitable for a single paragraph, deals only with how to frame an editorial photograph. The term *frame* is a photographer's word for selecting and arranging the subject matter in the camera's viewfinder. Thus, this paper is aimed at the aspiring editorial photographer. Watch for the typical characteristics of a process paper.

How to Frame Editorial Photographs

Thought-provoking photographs grab reader attention. Anything that grabs reader attention necessarily helps sell newspapers, and that grabs editors' attention. So the aspiring photojournalist will do well to move beyond news photographs and work toward editorial photographs, those photos which evoke emotional response or rouse the typical reader from his stupor. Probably the most important concern in editorial photography is framing. Three steps aid a technically accurate photographer in the process of capturing that all-important meaning on film. First, he frames for details. Requiring close-up photographs, such framing probably calls for something other than the normal 50 mm lens. For instance, by using a normal lens, the photographer snaps a photo showing a political candidate from the waist up, waving to the crowd. The picture has no real meaning, no message, only the typical politician-and-crowd photo. On the other hand, by using a 105 mm lens, the photographer gets a head shot which captures a puzzled frown or a satisfied smirk. Then, when he has framed for details, he next seeks a meaningful point of view. Too much photography is from shoulder height eight feet away. Instead, he moves down to shoot up, or he climbs up to shoot down. Maybe he walks all the way around the subject to find the most meaningful approach. While he avoids dramatic angles for the mere drama, he will depend on unusual point-of-view framing to heighten meaning. Photographing from the shoulder a block-long stretch of a potholed street hardly heightens the driver's plight, but a photo from street level showing the sharp edges gouging an automobile tire evokes reader reaction. Finally, third, he frames to omit extraneous matter. Every detail in the photograph must have purpose, meaning. Even though the subject should rarely be centered in the viewfinder, neither will the careful photographer allow irrelevant details to creep into focus around the corners and edges. Thus, the photojournalist frames to create editorial comment rather than click-click name-place-date pictures.

Analysis of the Sample for English

The paper above describes the process a photographer may use to frame a specific kind of photograph. Note these characteristics:

- The introduction sets the scene, beginning broadly and then narrowing to the specific topic.
- The thesis sentence, the fifth in the paragraph, states the specific focus.
- Chronological order helps the reader follow the organization, with single-word transitions such as *first, second, third, finally, then* and *thus,* transitional phrases such as *such framing,* and *on the other hand,* and transitional clauses such as *when he has framed for details* and *while he avoids dramatic angles for the mere drama.*
- Each of the main points is supported by details. The first two include specific illustrations with which the reader can identify.
- The writer maintains a third-person point of view, referring to *the photographer* and using the masculine pronoun *he,* thus avoiding *you.*
- The conclusion, a single sentence, is tight and to the point; it emphasizes the importance of the process by which a photographer may avoid mundane photographs.

———————— Sample for Social Sciences ————————

The following paragraph includes characteristics similar to those found above. But notice here the changes brought by a different point of view. The writer uses the first- and an implied second-person to talk directly to the reader.

Analyzing Historical Photographs

Confronting historical photographs in books and magazines sometimes leaves readers with little or no reaction. Worse, the reaction is one of "Why put that silly picture in here? What's the point?" By contrast, however, we can learn a great deal about history by merely studying photographs of the period. The photographer will have had a general purpose for taking a picture, and an editor will have had a specific reason for including a picture in the text. Almost always, the people in the picture, their clothing and accessories, will date the picture and locate its historical perspective. Beyond that, however, we can often glean other interesting bits of historical perspective if we know how to study the background in the photograph. Using an old photograph taken outdoors, try this process. First, look for indications of the state of technology. Are there utility poles visible? What about streetlights? Are there gaslights? What kind of transportation is evident? Are there hitching posts and water troughs for horses? Can you see evidence of automobiles or trains? Are there trolley tracks or overhead wires? Is the road or street surfaced? Next, study any printed matter which shows in the photograph, perhaps using a magnifying glass to enhance the letters. Look for signs above doorways or on windows that name or advertise businesses. Look for phone numbers. If they appear, count how many digits they have. What does all this tell you about the period? Next look for packaging materials. Are commodities stored in barrels, cloth bags, wooden crates, cardboard boxes, or paper sacks? Remember that cardboard boxes and paper sacks are relatively recent additions to the retail market; and the more substantial storage methods better withstood the rigors of rough shipment. Finally, look at the materials with which buildings are constructed. Are they mostly wood? Is stone or brick readily available in the area? Is there evidence of concrete? Can you spot aluminum or plastic? Does glass seem to be readily available? Of course, these guidelines limit application to outdoor photographs, but at the same time they suggest the broader process of evaluating any photograph for its historical clues.

Analysis of the Sample for Social Sciences

The paragraph employs most of the characteristics of a good process paper. The following items are particularly worthy of note:

- The introduction establishes the importance of the topic.
- The topic sentence, the seventh in the paragraph, narrows the focus to a single topic.
- The structure of the paragraph is an example of the rather unusual situation in which chronology is *not* the primary means of organization. While the paragraph suggests a chronology by which the reader should apply the process, the process may in fact be completed in any order: thus, an order of importance makes most sense.
- The use of the second-person, especially the implied *you* [*see* POINT OF VIEW *in the Glossary*], allows the writer to address the reader directly. While formal writing generally requires use of the third-person this process analysis lends itself naturally to a less formal approach.
- The ample use of transitions moves the reader smoothly through the material.
- The use of questions helps focus the reader's attention on details.
- The conclusion restates the importance of the process and broadens its applicability.

Sample for Science

The following paragraph continues the informal approach we just saw. Here, however, we find a precise chronological order.

Photographing Microscopic Specimens

Photographing microscopic specimens permits simultaneous large-group study of a single slide, a situation otherwise impossible. The photography process requires basic equipment: a prepared slide, a microscope, a single-lens reflex camera, and a microscope attachment which accepts the camera body. This attachment, available through most scientific supply companies, comes with either a screw mount or a bayonette mount; and the choice, of course, depends on the type of lens mount on the camera.

The following steps should lead to a successful photograph:

1) Remove the camera lens from the camera.
2) Fasten the microscope attachment to the camera.
3) Remove the eyepiece from the microsope.
4) Slip the camera's microscope attachment into the microscope.
5) Place the slide under the microscope.
6) Focus the microscope for a clear image through the camera viewfinder.
7) Adjust the light coming through the microscope so that a clear image appears through the camera's viewfinder.
8) Adjust camera speed based on light-meter readings, and bracket shots to assure success. (The use of an automatic camera will eliminate the need for light-meter readings and camera-speed adjustments.)

These steps should result in crisp, clear photographs which can be enlarged or projected as slides.

Analysis of the Sample for Science

The paper gives specific directions in numerical order. The steps are clear. This approach represents one way to give precise, uncluttered instructions. Note these details:

- The paper begins by explaining why the procedure is important and what results it can yield.
- The second sentence, almost in lab-experiment style, lists the necessary equipment.
- The third sentence offers additional information about the microscope attachment.
- The body of the paper appears as a list. Each item is an imperative sentence that begins with a verb. [See IMPERATIVE SENTENCE *in the Glossary.*] The use of such lists is especially appropriate in a scientific writing.
- The steps are arranged chronologically.

- The brief conclusion emphasizes the results of the procedure without taking a persuasive approach.

---------------------- **Sample for Business** ----------------------

The following full-length paper illustrates a process analysis that covers too much material to limit itself to a single paragraph. Note that the introductory paragraph outlines the steps of the process and explains why their particular order is the only sensible one.

Building the Photographer's Advertising Plan

The portrait photographer's business does not just happen. He builds his business as carefully as a contractor builds an office complex. The advertising plan to promote that business develops in exactly the same way. The photographer starts with an evaluation of his needs, then lays a solid foundation, builds the basic structure, and then adds the amenities. Any step without the preceding ones makes the advertising plan—and maybe the business—sure to topple.

Initially, the portrait studio has two basic advertising needs in order to survive. The cliche "hanging out the shingle" probably best summarizes the first advertising step, displaying a sign that announces the business location. The sign may be nothing more than a placard on the door or a name painted on the window, but customers must feel they are entering a place of business, not just a temporary setup in an empty room. The second basic advertising need is a listing under "photographers" in the yellow pages of the telephone directory. The listing need not be elaborate; the basic name-address-phone gives an official ring to the business.

Once the essentials are met, a successful portrait photographer must build the foundation for his advertising plan. A solid foundation comes from quality work. Going the proverbial extra mile to create fine work, above and beyond what competitors offer, will allow a portrait photographer's work to serve as the most powerful advertising campaign of all. Portraits must more than satisfy; they must delight the customer. Wedding albums must more than record; they must re-create the high emotion of the moment. Certainly masterful technique plays a large part in that kind of quality, but personal touch helps create quality as well. Courtesy, friendliness, and cooperation, even in the face of thoughtless, grouchy customers, help establish a quality advertising image.

Atop the foundation of quality, three basic structures of outside-the-studio advertising can be put in place. First, as an extension of the studio itself, attractive window displays foster public awareness. The window display is just as much a part of advertising as anything else the portrait photographer does. A potential customer walks or drives past every few minutes. Since people usually look without stopping, the overall impression of the display creates a business image. If it is neat, colorful, and tasteful, it creates a very different image from the one created by a cluttered and sloppy display. In addition, window displays which carry a monthly theme can entice new business. For instance, if March is Pet Month, maybe some customers will decide they want their member-of-the-family pet photographed. Without the suggestion from the window display, however, the thought may never have occurred to them! A second basic advertising medium can reach the potential customer via the mail. In the advertising business, a good direct mailing will bring in 2% of the recipients, but carefully selected mailing lists will assure profits. For instance, lists of graduates from the local high schools and universities will provide an excellent mailing list for commencement portraits and employment application photographs. Then a third basic advertising approach contacts the potential customer amid other businesses aimed at weddings. Bridal shows give the portrait photographer an opportunity to display his work, to provide competitive price sheets, and to introduce himself personally to brides-to-be. Sometimes only two or three bookings will more than pay for the show's exhibit fee.

Finally, when the basic advertising structure stands firm, the portrait photographer can add the amenities in advertising. Maybe it is time to consider radio or television spots, newspaper advertising, or a big splash in the yellow pages of the telephone directory. Maybe a billboard during strategic times of the year could attract anniversary and family portraits. These kinds of advertising, however, cost dearly. Probably only the most successful studios can afford the fees; and in view of the success, perhaps then the amenities are unnecessary.

So the advertising program for a successful portrait photographer's studio should build with the business and build in a logical, economical process. Beginning with a few essentials and then building a solid foundation allows the photographer to begin with a solid structure and then—only then—add the amenities of advertising.

Analysis of the Sample for Business

This six-paragraph composition clearly sets out the process of planning an advertising campaign for a portrait studio. Because it is more detailed than the single-paragraph and three-paragraph samples, you should note its specific characteristics:

- The introductory paragraph attracts attention with an analogy [*see* ANALOGY *earlier in Part II*]. The writer carries this analogy through to the conclusion.

- The thesis sentence alludes to the four parts of the analogy: *essential needs, foundation, structure,* and *amenities.*

- Separate paragraphs develop the parts, with several subtopics in each. The continuing analogy helps the reader remember the four parts and see the importance of the chronology.

- Transitions help clarify the order and show relationships.

- Specific illustrations clarify the steps of the process.

- The conclusion emphasizes the importance of the process and completes the analogy.

- The use of the third-person point of view maintains throughout a more formal tone than a second-person point of view, as represented by the social-sciences and science samples.

This analysis should help you determine which ideas will work best for your own process paper.

—————— **Sample for Vocational Education** ——————

Although the next sample is a single paragraph, it illustrates some fresh points about process papers. Watch for the differences between this and the earlier single-paragraph process samples.

How to Use Aperture Settings

Using the aperture settings effectively on a 35 mm camera requires only three basic steps. The aperture setting, otherwise called "f-stops," determines how much light the lens lets into the camera when the shutter trips. How wide the lens opens determines how much light hits the film. Too much light overexposes and washes out the photograph while too little light underexposes and leaves the photograph dark. So the first step in choosing the aperture setting is to determine available light. Many cameras have a built-in light meter which, as it registers the intensity of the light, will give an aperture setting to correspond with a particular shutter speed. Using that or some similar meter will suggest a reasonable aperture setting. A light meter, however, can misread the real situation. For instance, a light reading will vary wildly from reflected light (from snow, water, or fog or heavy bright/dark contrasts on a brilliantly sunny day) and will gauge light only where the sensory "eye" is aimed. As a result, a careful photographer must move the light meter or camera lens left and right, up and down to see if the meter fluctuates. If so, she takes an average reading. After determining a reasonable reading, the photographer must next translate that reading into an aperture setting. To create a light picture, she will use a lower f-stop number, say 8 instead of 16. If she wants the picture darker, perhaps to compensate for glare, she will use a higher f-stop number, say 8 instead of 4. While the numbers move in the reverse of what seems logical, the rule is that the higher the f-stop number, the smaller the hole in the lens through which the light can travel. Finally, the third step in the effective use of aperture settings applies the readings to a series of shots, a practice called "bracketing." Bracketing calls for using at least a half stop, perhaps as much as one and a half stops, on either side of the suggested reading. Thus, the photographer shoots at least three shots of every subject—one shot at the suggested reading as well as one shot a half stop above and one shot a half stop below. She may even choose to shoot two additional exposures: one a full stop below and one a full stop above the suggested reading. Effective use of the aperture settings determines photographic success.

Analysis of the Sample for Vocational Education

The paragraph includes significant techniques for developing effective process analysis papers:

- The introduction is brief and to the point and offers no enticement beyond the reader's need for information.

- The topic sentence, the second in this paragraph, focuses on the subject and helps the reader think in terms of *three*.

- The terminology assumes that the audience is at least roughly familiar with modern 35 MM cameras.

- Chronological order, essential to the organization of the paragraph, allows the reader to follow, step by step, to completion.

- The transitions move the reader smoothly through the organization.

- The conclusion provides a sufficient ending to the single paragraph and at the same time suggests the importance of the process described.

Sample for Mathematics

A photographer has a poster-size print 20″ high and 30″ wide, but she wants to reduce it to 15″ high. Assuming she will maintain the same proportions for her new print, she must know how to figure the width of the reduced print. Students were asked to explain to the photographer how to figure the width of the new print. Here is one student's how-to explanation:

Figuring Proportions

In order to figure the height of the new print, the photographer must set up a proportion and solve it. The relationship between the width and the height of a print is a ratio. A proportion, which compares two ratios, sets up the relationship of the width and height of the original print to the width and height of the new print. The proportion would read this way: the unknown value is to 30 inches as 15 inches is to 20 inches. The photographer wants to find the unknown value. Mathematically, the proportion looks like this:

$$X : 30 \text{ in.} = 15 \text{ in.} : 20 \text{ in.}$$

To solve the proportion, she would follow these steps:

Set up the proportion.

$$\frac{X}{30} = \frac{15}{20} \text{ , where } X = \text{height in inches}$$

Then cross multiply to solve the proportion.

$$20X = (15)(30)$$

Next, solve the proportion for X.

$$X = \frac{(15)(30)}{20} \qquad \text{So, } X = 22.5$$

Therefore, to maintain the same proportions as the old print, the width of the new print will be 22 1/2 inches.

Analysis of the Sample for Mathematics

The math sample includes typical techniques for creating effective process analysis papers:

- The first three sentences give background and define terms. The writer assumes readers are familiar with the photographer's problem.
- The next three sentences set up the problem. The writer assumes an audience is generally familiar with setting up and solving simple equations and uses terminology accordingly.
- The remaining sentences and illustrations explain, in step-by-step order, how to solve the problem and reach the solution. Transitions like *then* and *next* clarify the chronological order.

With the information from this section in mind, you should be able to write effective process analyses. Use the models and their analyses as a standard for your own paper, and revise as necessary to improve the comparison. Do not neglect to consult the cross-references in other parts of this book for help with specific problems.

RESEARCH PAPER

A research paper, sometimes called a *term* or *library* paper, reports research findings. Most often, the research is a literal *searching again* through what others have written on a subject. In some cases, when the paper reports entirely on primary research [*see* PRIMARY RESEARCH *in the Glossary*], the writer may find a laboratory or technical report more suitable than a research paper. [*See* LAB REPORT *and* TECHNICAL REPORT *elsewhere in Part II.*]

Research papers may either report research or evaluate research information. If the paper reports on research, tell only what you have read; this reading may be from a single source or from many sources. If the paper evaluates research information, it considers questions of *why* or *how*; frequently it is either a comparison-contrast or cause-effect paper. [*See* CAUSE AND EFFECT *and* COMPARISON AND CONTRAST *in Part II.*] An evaluative paper requires numerous sources, and it assumes a writer's ability to show originality and imagination. We will discuss below one type of evaluative paper.

Characteristics

An effective research paper

- indicates careful, comprehensive reading and understanding of the topic,

- establishes, in its introduction, a thesis to be developed during the course of the paper [*see* THESIS STATEMENT *in the Glossary and* THEME *in Part II*],

- follows a clear organization [*see* ORGANIZATION, CHRONOLOGICAL ORDER, SPATIAL ORDER, *and* ORDERS OF IMPORTANCE *in the Glossary*],

- employs the principles of good composition [*see* WRITING, REVISING, *and* PROOFREADING *in Part I*],

- includes direct quotations, paraphrases, or precis which support

the thesis [*see* PARAPHRASE *and* PRECIS *in Part II*],

- includes endnotes, footnotes, or parenthetical notes,

- includes a list of works cited,

- exhibits careful, thorough documentation of sources of ideas,

- includes direct quotations in support of its thesis,

- follows a carefully prescribed format [*see* FORMAT *in the Glossary*],

- is almost always typed or, if prepared on a computer, printed with a letter-quality printer.

Process

The step-by-step development of a research paper, as spelled out below, seems rather direct. Be aware, however, that the research process always requires a kind of yo-yo approach: rather than completing one step and moving neatly to the next, you will find that you confront problems that either cause you to go back to a previous step or to think ahead to the next. Just when you think you have completed the research, you may discover that you need new information to fill a gap or add support. And just when you think you have completed a sensible outline, you may find that the paper does not flow smoothly, given its method of organization. So you must go back—rethink, reread, rewrite. The yo-yo process continues until you have typed your final draft.

The following steps will show how to develop an effective research paper. The process works well, especially if you understand—and accept as a fact of the research life—the yo-yo approach.

PREWRITING

STEP 1. SELECTING A SUITABLE SUBJECT

In some cases, you may be assigned a broad research topic; in other cases, you may be free to select whatever topic you wish. Selecting the right topic often determines the success of the paper.

You will probably begin with an idea of general, broad topics that interest you. [*See* PREWRITING *in Part I for suggestions for sources of topics.*] In order to select one topic, narrow it, and wed it to the paper's purpose, you should do exploratory reading in the general area. Browse through en-

cyclopedias, magazines, and reference books for thought-provoking ideas. Read quickly, letting your mind work freely. Put your general subject in the form of a question. Answers to this question will suggest narrowed topics, some of them possibly suitable for your research paper.

General topic:
What influenced us as children to become the kinds of young adults we are?

Narrowed topics:
television, parents, neighborhood, siblings, games, toys, books, food, friends, relatives

Perhaps, after reading exploratively in the area of child psychology, you discover a comment by one author that attracts your attention. He writes that parents exert a significant influence on a child by what they read to him or her. You decide to pursue this subject.

Further exploratory reading convinces you that the topic is still too broad. You list all the kinds of books you can think of that parents read to their children:

fairy tales	classical stories
jingles	rhymes, poetry
fantasy	picture books
number books	nonfiction books
alphabet books	animal stories

Doing still more exploratory reading, you find a reference to the impact Mother Goose rhymes have on children. Now *that's* what you'd like to research! Finally, you have a suitably narrowed subject:

The Impact of Mother Goose Rhymes on Children

Use a similar process to narrow your own broad subject to something manageable.

POSSIBLE PITFALLS: Selecting a suitable subject is so vital that a few warnings are in order. Be critical enough to evaluate your proposed subject according to these possible pitfalls:

- The subject may be too broad. Even though you have been asked to write a 1500-word paper, keep in mind that most five-paragraph themes may run well over 700 words. Magazine articles often run no more than 3000 words. So do not try to cope with a book-length subject in half the length of a magazine article.

- The subject may be too limited for research. Although you may have a special interest in a subject, if little or no research is available, you cannot write a successful research paper.

- The subject may be too technical. Unless you already have a good background in computer technology, for instance, you should not attempt to write a paper explaining how a computer works. Unless a paper is part of an assigment for a technical class, avoid subjects which rely heavily on technical terms.

- The subject may be too ordinary. Research should provide new information. To try to do research on the effects of sun lotion on skin exposed to ultraviolet rays will probably prove tiresome and dull unless, of course, you have just invented a revolutionary lotion.

- The subject may be too controversial. A highly contested issue may prove more than a single, carefully organized research paper can describe or evaluate. If volumes have already been written, chances are you have not chosen well.

Avoiding these pitfalls will help you select a workable, satisfactory subject.

STEP 2.   LISTING THE POSSIBLE PARTS

Once you have narrowed the subject, apply your logic and imagination to determine what to include. Make a list of possible topics to cover.

To help you think through the list, put yourself in the reader's seat. What do you want to know about this subject? What questions need answers? For example:

Suitable subject:
Impact of Mother Goose Rhymes on Children

Possible subtopics:
author of rhymes
publication of book
distinguishing fact from fiction
educational value
musical quality
teaching rhythm
promoting memorization
any negative aspects
characterizations
lulling to sleep
introduction to literature
classical allusion
stimulating imagination
translations

By developing a list of topics at the start, you can prevent a significant waste of time later and avoid reading unrelated material. Of course, a preliminary list is just that—preliminary. It will change as you do your research.

So, develop a list of possible subtopics to guide your early research.

STEP 3.   WRITING THE THESIS STATEMENT

Once you have narrowed the topic and developed the list for Step 2 above, you are ready to write a thesis statement. [*See* THESIS SENTENCE *in the Glossary*.] Like the list, the thesis statement may change somewhat, but it will serve throughout your research. So write one now:

The Mother Goose nursery rhymes have a positive influence on children.

STEP 4.   DEVELOPING A PRELIMINARY BIBLIOGRAPHY

The bibliography is a list of the sources used in developing a research paper. Now that you have a thesis and a list of possible topics to explore within the confines of your narrowed subject, you will need to select books, magazines, pamphlets, and other pertinent sources. Go to the library and consult the card catalog [*see* CARD CATALOG *in the Glossary*], the *Reader's Guide to Periodical Literature* [*see* READER'S GUIDE TO PERIODICAL LITERATURE *in the Glossary*], the vertical file [*see* VERTICAL FILE *in the Glossary*], and the various reference books available.

As you find seemingly useful materials, prepare bibliography cards for them. Prepare a separate 3″ × 5″ card for each source. Using this approach, you can throw away cards for sources which later prove useless. Similarly, you can alphabetize those which prove helpful. Follow these general instructions for making bibliography cards:

For books:

- List the call number in the upper left corner.

- List the author, last name first.

  ○ If there is an editor, list his or her name, followed by *ed.*
  ○ If there are two authors, list the name of the first author in reverse order but list the name of the second author in natural order.
  ○ If there are more than two authors, list the name of the first

author in reverse order and follow it with *and others*.

- Write the title and underline it.
- Give the publication information: city of publication, publisher, and year of publication.
- Add any notes from the card catalog which may be helpful to your later search (bibliography, illustrations, number of pages, etc.).
- If you use more than one library, note the library in which you found this source on the bottom line of the card.

- Number the card in the upper right corner. Begin with 1, and continue sequentially. Later, the numbers will help to quickly identify your sources.

[*See Step 11, later, for a comprehensive list of sample bibliography entries.*]

For a book, then, a bibliography card may look something like this:

808.46   1
Hu

Huck, Charlotte S., and Doris Young Kuhn. <u>Children's Literature in the Elementary School.</u> Chicago: Holt, Rinehart, and Winston, Inc., 1968.

       has good bibliography
       includes excerpts from rhymes

Willard Library

For an article:

- List the author, if there is one, last name first.

- List the title and enclose it in quotation marks.

- List and underline the name of the magazine, newspaper, or encyclopedia in which the article appears.

- Include, for magazines, volume number, page numbers, and date.
- Include, for newspapers, the section and page numbers and date.
- Include, for encyclopedias, the volume number, the page numbers, place of publication, publisher, and year of publication.
- Add any notes that may be helpful in locating or using the source.

- Number the card in the upper right corner.

A sample bibliography card for a magazine will look like this:

```
                                                        2

Likens, Rebecca. "In Defense of Mother Goose." PTA Magazine
June 1973: 21-23.

Roseville Library
```

As you work with the preliminary bibliography, you can begin to decide which books will be of value and which will not. Before you cart home stacks of books and periodicals, check quickly for their usefulness. In books look at tables of contents, indexes, and any bibliographies. If nothing suggests information related to your topic, leave those books at the library. On the other hand, since you will be working primarily with nonfiction books, which are arranged on the library shelf by subject, look through books located near the ones you have selected from the card catalog. Perhaps one of them will be helpful.

Likewise, as you search through the *Reader's Guide* and other periodical indexes, think of alternate headings under which to find sources. Sometimes the headings which appear in the guide are not the ones you might think of first. And do not hesitate to ask the reference librarian for suggested *Reader's Guide* headings suitable for your topic.

Finally, for particularly obscure topics, you may wish to do a computer search. A computer search will say what information is available in computer-linked libraries all over the United States. This information is available through interlibrary loan. Check with your librarian for details.

STEP 5. SHAPING THE PRELIMINARY OUTLINE

The immediate purpose here is to develop an outline from the list you wrote in Step 2 above. By now, as a result of your work with the preliminary bibliography, you have done additional skimming. You may be ready to think through the organization of ideas. If not, read a couple of general articles about your subject. If an encyclopedia includes an article about your subject, begin there. Then, once you have done some general reading and skimming, develop an outline.

[*For a thorough discussion of the process of outlining, see* OUTLINES, KINDS: FOR A PAPER *elsewhere in Part II.*]

While your first reaction may be to skip the preliminary outline, do not. Your argument may be the typical one: How can I develop an outline when I have not read all the materials available? The answer comes in the form of another question: How do you know which materials to read if you have not determined what your paper ought to do? In other words, developing a preliminary outline now guides your reading in the future, saving hours of reading and avoiding stacks of useless notes.

So, do the outline now.

Using a list like the example in Step 2 above, you could develop a preliminary outline that looks as follows:

I. Origins

    A. Author
    B. Publisher

II. Educational value

III. Literary introduction

    A. Fact or opinion
    B. Fun
    C. Rhythm

IV. Imagination

Remember, your final outline may be quite different from your preliminary one. You will no doubt choose to make changes, not only in content but also, perhaps, in organization. That is part of the yo-yo approach. [*By way of example, compare this preliminary outline with the final outline that appears on page i of the sample research paper.*]

STEP 6. TAKING NOTES

Now that you have a preliminary bibliography and outline, you are ready to begin reading seriously and taking notes. Remember, your reading will be guided by your outline, while your outline can be changed as you proceed.

Because you used 3″ × 5″ cards for your bibliography, you may wish to use 4″ × 6″ cards for your notes. The larger cards hold more and allow for easier reading, but above all, they cannot be accidentally mixed with the bibliography cards.

Regardless of the size, you will put only one idea from one source on a card. Why? Because once you are ready to write your paper, you will arrange the cards in the order in which you will use their respective bits of information. If more than one idea appears on a card, it will be useless in helping you arrange your ideas. If a card reflects more than one source, you will be unable to document its contents accurately.

Use the following guidelines for taking notes [*see also* NOTES, KINDS: FOR A PAPER *in Part I*]:

- Write the number of the bibliography card in the upper right corner of the note card. You will need this information later, in documenting your paper. Remember that poor documentation is a serious shortcoming. Early and ongoing precautions significantly decrease the potential for error. So be sure to list the source number on *every* note card.

- List the page numbers from which you are about to take notes alongside the bibliography card number. This information will also be essential to your documentation. Take the time to be accurate and complete with your note cards; it will reduce the potential for error in your paper.

- Write the topic (called the *slug*) on the top line of the card. The slug may be taken from your outline, or it may later become an outline topic. Do not use the Roman numerals and letters from your outline, however, as they may well change, confusing your references. By using a slug, you can later reorganize your cards by stacking all the cards with identical slugs together.

- Use a separate card for each idea from each source. Then, when you organize your note cards, each card will support only one topic.

- Take notes in your own words. You may use phrases, lists, key words, sentences, or paragraphs. [*See* PARAPHRASE, PRECIS, *and* NOTES, KINDS: FOR A PAPER *elsewhere in Part II for further, more specific help with note-taking.*]

- When you find a particularly poignant passage, a phrase, perhaps, or a sentence or two, copy it onto your note card *exactly* as it appears: comma for comma, letter for letter. Enclose the passage in quotation marks. If you omit words, or choose not to quote the complete sentence, show the omission by using ellipsis points. Use three points for the omission of a word or phrase; use a fourth point to represent a period at the end of a sentence.

> **WARNING**: If you carelessly omit the quotation marks around words not your own, you are in essence stealing. The act is called *plagiarism*, and it is such a serious error that some instructors will automatically fail a paper which neglects to acknowledge sources accurately. So, quote and document accurately.

- As you take notes, revise your preliminary outline as often as necessary. You will no doubt add subpoints, maybe even main points. Perhaps you will want to change the organization or to rethink relationships between topics.

- You may need to find additional sources if gaps appear or you have no note cards for certain sections of the outline.

The following sample note cards illustrate some of the principles listed above:

Origins   3-2

M.G. rhymes famous in France, America
First published in England, 1765
Author listed as Mistress Elizabeth Goose

Intro to Lit   6-287

When child grows up with M.G., he's "apt to be a child who learns rapidly, who discovers early in life the commingling pleasures that words and pictures award to those who read books."

Note that the first card, from page 2 bibliography source 3 consists of fragments, including author, place, and date of origin. The slug, *Origins*, comes from the preliminary outline. [*See Step 5 above.*] The second card, from page 287 of bibliography source 6, includes a direct quotation. Note the use of quotation marks. Again, the slug comes from the preliminary outline.

POSSIBLE PITFALLS: As you take notes, try to avoid these potential trouble spots:

- Do not rely too heavily on any one source. In general, you should have about an equal number of note cards from each source. While it is not uncommon to find one source meeting most of your needs, your paper will be seriously weak from lack of broad research if you limit the variety of sources.

- If your subject permits, try to use book and periodical references equally. To rely too heavily on books will date your paper. To rely too heavily on periodicals may result in cursory research, especially for a topic more thoroughly discussed in book-length sources. Of course, the topic determines the appropriate sources. Nonprint media can also provide additional perspectives. Television documentaries, public-radio talk shows, films, lectures—all are legitimate sources. [*See also Step 7 below,* CONDUCTING PRIMARY RESEARCH.]

- If your subject is controversial, consult equally the sources supporting each side. If your paper is persuasive, you must answer the "other" side. If your paper is comparison-contrast, you must present both sides.

- Do not overuse direct quotations. You can usually summarize ideas in fewer words. Probably less than one-fourth of your cards should quote directly.

- Make absolutely certain that you have put quotation marks around any words not your own.

- Make absolutely certain that you have listed the bibliography card number and the page number(s) on *each* card.

- Be sure to include a single idea from a single source on each card.

STEP 7.   CONDUCTING PRIMARY RESEARCH

Not every topic lends itself to primary research. [*See* PRIMARY RESEARCH *and* SECONDARY RESEARCH *in the Glossary.*] Some topics, however, will benefit significantly from first-hand information: interviews, experiments, personal data gathering, audience experience.

If, for instance, your subject deals with air pollution, excerpts from an interview with an EPA official or with an official from a power plant will add perspective. Books, magazines, and periodicals are never as immediate as firsthand experience. Similarly, if your subject deals with the psychological problems of nursing-home residents, interviews will give credibility to your paper.

Finally, if your subject deals with the best methods for storing fresh vegetables, a tabulation of the results of your own experiments will add an important dimension to your paper.

Use primary research whenever the subject suggests.

STEP 8.   CREATING THE FINAL OUTLINE

Use the slugs to sort your cards into piles, each representing a topic in your revised outline. Next sort through each pile, thinking about order. Will chronological order be best? Spatial order? An order of importance? Will a comparison-contrast method of development determine order? [*See* COMPARISON AND CONTRAST *in Part II.*] Will a cause-effect method determine it? [*See* CAUSE AND EFFECT *in Part II.*] Put the cards in order. Expand or alter the outline as suggested by your cards. If you have not already done so, add subtopics to your outline as suggested by the slugs.

At this point, the final outline should nearly write itself. After referring to OUTLINES, KINDS: FOR A PAPER, elsewhere in Part II, complete the final outline for your paper.

POSSIBLE PITFALLS: As you develop your outline, keep these points in mind:

- A full-length research paper probably should have no more than five or six main points. This means you should have no more than five or six Roman numerals in your outline. Too many main headings indicate fuzzy thinking.
- The outline divisions correspond to paragraph divisions or to subtopics within the paragraphs. To determine if the organization is logical, think through your outline in terms of paragraphs.
- The outline divisions, added together, must equal your thesis sentence. If they do not, make whatever adjustments are necessary.

WRITING

STEP 9.   DEVELOPING THE FIRST DRAFT

With your revised outline and organized note cards in front of you, you are ready to write the first draft. A research paper, like a good theme, begins with an introductory paragraph. This states the subject and leads to the thesis sentence. The body of the paper follows the organization established in the outline, the divisions corresponding directly to the paragraphs. The conclusion wraps up the main ideas in a neat package. [*See* THEME, *elsewhere in Part II, for more specifics on effective introductions, body organization, transitional devices—words, phrases, sentences, and paragraphs—and conclusions.*]

Beyond the typical content and organization of a good theme, the first draft of a research paper also includes one feature peculiar to the form. Material from your note cards must be acknowledged by source, whether you put the idea in your own words or quote it directly. As a result, each time you refer to a note card in your first draft, add in parentheses the coded reference from the top right of your card (the bibliography source and page number). For example:

The Mother Goose rhymes have survived because of their ageless quality of rhythm, rhyme, and motion. (4–3)

The idea is summarized in the writer's own words, but the information came from page 3 of bibliography source 4. This information will later go into the documentation. By using a code, you can move rapidly through the first draft without the burden of developing an exact form of documentation.

Complete the first draft as quickly as you can, working to get the ideas on paper. You need not necessarily write fine sentences or model paragraphs. Follow the outline, using the yo-yo approach, revising the outline, altering the methods of organization, and adding supporting details.

REVISING
STEP 10. POLISHING THE CONTENT

Once you have completed the first draft, polish its content. [*Refer to separate sections in this handbook for additional information as you need it.*]

- Using the same techniques as you did for a theme, make sure the introduction gives a general statement about your subject and brings the reader from the general to the specific.

- Check the thesis statement for completeness and accuracy.

- Be sure the paper follows the organization established in the thesis sentence. [*See* REVISING: CHECKING ORGANIZATION *in Part I.*]

- Check for good paragraph development, with clear topic and concluding sentences and supporting details. [*See* REVISING: SAMPLE REVISION FOR SPECIFIC DETAIL *and* REVISING: CHECKING STRUCTURE *in Part I.*]

- Make certain you have included a sufficient number of transitions within and between paragraphs. [*See* REVISING: SAMPLE REVISION FOR TRANSITION *in Part I.*]

- Reread for good sentence structure and variety. [*See* REVISING: SAMPLE REVISION FOR SENTENCE VARIETY *and* REVISING: CHECKING STRUCTURE: SENTENCES *in Part I.*]

- Assure yourself that your subject is fully and carefully explained, and is supported by adequate research.

- Be sure the conclusion reiterates the thesis and adds a an appropriate clincher.

[*See also the general guidelines for revising any composition in* REVISING, *in Part I. Use the questions there to help you spot areas in need of possible revision.*]

Once you have improved the contents of your paper, you are ready to tackle the details of preparing the final draft.

STEP 11. PREPARING THE DOCUMENTATION

The forms of documentation will vary with the style manual preferred by the teacher or school. Most style manuals have changed recently, primarily as a result of word processors. [*See* WRITING WITH A WORD PROCESSOR *in Part I.*] The most important principle, however, is to use a consistent style throughout a paper.

Preparing Notes

In this chapter, you will find five common research paper styles. Parts of the sample research paper are repeated to illustrate the five forms. These are

1. MLA (Modern Language Association) parenthetical style: documentation notes appear parenthetically, within the text.

2. MLA endnote style: documentation notes appear at the end of the paper, just before the list of works cited.

3. MLA footnote style: documentation notes appear at the bottoms of the pages.

4. MLA numbered bibliography style: documentation notes appear in numerical form, parenthetically, within the text.

5. APA (American Psychological Association) style: documentation notes appear parenthetically, within the text.

Use whichever form of notation your instructor requires; or, if none is required, use the form easiest for you. In any case, be consistent throughout the paper. [*For additional comparison, note also that the sample papers for English and business in the* BIOGRAPHY *section, and the sample paper in the* LAB REPORT *section, use parenthetical notes.*]

End- and footnotes follow the same form. Note these peculiarities:

- End- and footnotes are numbered consecutively.

- The numbers, both in the text and in the notes themselves, are raised, written as superscript.

- The notes are indented like paragraphs.

- They are followed by periods, as if they were complete sentences.

- Footnotes are typed single-spaced, with a double-space between notes.

- Endnotes are typed double-spaced.

Sample note forms are listed below, along with their corresponding bibliography entry forms.

PREPARING A BIBLIOGRAPHY

A bibliography is always part of a research paper. It may be one of two kinds: a list of those works cited in the paper, or a list of all works consulted, some of which may not have been cited. The advantage of the former is its brevity; the advantage of the latter is its demonstration of thorough research. Use whichever form your instructor prefers.

Note, too, the following peculiarities of the bibliography in general.

- The bibliography begins on a new page at the end of the paper. The entries are arranged alphabetically by authors' last names.

- If two cited works are written by the same author, they should be alphabetized by title. The author's name is not listed in front of the second citation; instead, substitute three hyphens followed by a period.

- The bibliography uses hanging indentation: all lines but the first are indented. This format allows for ease in finding listings.

- Items in the bibliography are followed by a period, as if each were a sentence.

- Each note has a corresponding bibliography entry.

- Bibliography entries are typed double-spaced (though less common style uses single-spacing with two spaces between entries).

- If two cited works are written by the same author, they should be alphabetized by title. The author's name is not listed in front of the

second citation; instead, a long dash (the equivalent of three hyphens) should appear.

Additional details of format are noted in the illustrations below.

Note and Bibliography Forms for Books

In general, a note or bibliography entry for a book will include the author's name, the book title italicized (underlined), and publication information (city of publication, publisher, and date). The note will also include a page reference. The samples below list bibliographic forms, endnote forms, and parenthetical-note forms. Footnotes appear in the same form as endnotes but are single-spaced, with a double-space between entries.

A book by one author:

Parenthetical note:
(Lannon 139)

Endnote:
1 John M. Lannon, Technical Writing (Boston: Little, Brown and Company, 1982) 139.

Bibliography:
Lannon, John M. Technical Writing. Boston: Little, Brown and Company, 1982.

A book by two authors:

Parenthetical note:
(Gibaldi and Achtert 140)

Endnote:
    2 Joseph Gibaldi and Walter S. Achtert, <u>MLA Handbook for Writers of Research Papers.</u> 3rd ed. (New York: The Modern Language Association of America, 1988) 140.

Bibliography:
Gibaldi, Joseph, and Walter S. Achtert. <u>MLA Handbook for Writers of Research Papers</u>. 3rd ed. New York: The Modern Language Association of America, 1988.

Note that the above entries refer to the third edition of a book. The publisher is an organization.

A book by three or more authors:

Parenthetical note:
(Frew and others 111-112)

Endnote:
    3 Robert Frew and others, <u>Survival: A Sequential Program for College Writing</u> (Palo Alto, California: Peek Publications, 1978) 111-112.

Bibliography:
Frew, Robert and others. <u>Survival: A Sequential Program for College Writing</u>. Palo Alto, California: Peek Publications, 1978.

A book with an editor:

Parenthetical note:
(Williams 925)

Endnote:
    4 Becky Hall Williams, ed., <u>1991 Writer's Market: Where to Sell What You Write</u> (Cincinnati: Writer's Digest Books, 1991) 925.

Bibliography:
Williams, Becky Hall, ed. <u>1991 Writer's Market: Where to Sell What You Write</u>. Cincinnati: Writer's Digest Books, 1991.

A signed encyclopedia article:

Parenthetical note:
(von Brandt)

Endnote:
    5 Andres R. F. T. von Brandt, "Fishing, Commercial," <u>Encyclopaedia Britannica: Macropaedia</u>, 1983 ed.

Bibliography:
von Brandt, Andres R. F. T. "Fishing, Commercial." <u>Encyclopaedia Britannica: Macropaedia</u>. 1983 ed.

An unsigned encyclopedia article:

Parenthetical note:
("Crowley")

Endnote:
    6 "Crowley, Robert," <u>Encyclopedia Americana,</u> 1984 ed.

Bibliography:
"Crowley, Robert." <u>Encyclopedia Americana</u>. 1984 ed.

A selection in an anthology:

Parenthetical note:
(Winters 59-60)

Endnote:
    7 Yvor Winters, "Robert Frost: Or the Spiritual Drifter as Poet," in <u>Robert Frost: A Collection of Critical Essays,</u> ed. James M. Cox (Englewood Cliffs: Prentice-Hall, Inc., 1962) 59-60.

Bibliography:
Winters, Yvor. "Robert Frost: Or the Spiritual Drifter as Poet." <u>Robert Frost: A Collection of Critical Essays</u>. Ed. James M. Cox. Englewood Cliffs: Prentice-Hall, Inc., 1962.

A translation:

Parenthetical note:
(Vergilius 48)

Endnote:
    8 Publius Vergilius Maro, <u>Virgil</u> trans. H. Rushton Fairclough, rev. ed. (Cambridge: Harvard University Press, 1935) 48.

Bibliography:
Vergilius Maro, Publius. <u>Virgil</u>. Trans. H. Rushton Fairclough. Rev. ed. Cambridge: Harvard University Press, 1935.

A signed magazine article:

Parenthetical note:
(Rupp 67)

Endnote:
    9 Becky Rupp, "Home Schooling," <u>Country Journal</u> December 1986: 67.

Bibliography:
Rupp, Becky. "Home Schooling." <u>Country Journal</u> December 1986: 67-74.

An unsigned magazine article:

Parenthetical note:
("S.A.D. Truth" 123)

Endnote:
    10 "The S.A.D. Truth about Sunlight," <u>Harrowsmith</u> November/December 1986: 123.

Bibliography:
"The S.A.D. Truth about Sunlight." <u>Harrowsmith</u> November/December 1986: 123.

An article from a newspaper:

Parenthetical note:
(Reibstein 23)

Endnote:
    11 Larry Reibstein, "A Finger on the Pulse: Companies Expand Use of Employee Surveys," <u>The Wall Street Journal</u> 27 October 1986, midwest ed.: 23.

Bibliography:
Reibstein, Larry. "A Finger on the Pulse: Companies Expand Use of Employee Surveys." <u>The Wall Street Journal</u> 27 October 1986, midwest ed.: 23.

A pamphlet:

Parenthetical note:
(<u>*Geologic Story*</u> 2)

Endnote:

12 <u>Geologic Story of Tur-</u>
<u>key Run State Park</u>, (Bloom-
ington, Indiana: State of Indiana Department of Natural
Resources Geological Survey,
1977) 2.

Bibliography:

<u>Geologic Story of Turkey Run</u>
<u>State Park</u>. Bloomington,
Indiana: State of Indiana
Department of Natural
Resources Geological
Survey, 1977.

A government publication:

Parenthetical note:
(U.S. Dept. of Commerce 8-9)

Endnote:

13 United States Depart-
ment of Commerce, Bureau of
the Census, <u>Neighborhood</u>
<u>Statistics from the 1980 Cen-</u>
<u>sus</u> (N.p.: n.p., n.d.) 8-9.

Bibliography:

United States. Department of
Commerce. Bureau of the
Census. <u>Neighborhood</u>
<u>Statistics from the 1980</u>
<u>Census</u>. N.p., n.p.: n.d.

For a second note from the same source:

In the course of writing a paper,
you will probably cite some sources
more than once. The primary note
forms, illustrated above, are simplified considerably for secondary
notes.

First note:

14 David Powell, <u>What</u>
<u>Can I Write About? 7000 Top-</u>
<u>ics for High School Students</u>,

(Urbana, Illinois: National
Council of Teachers of English, 1981) 26.

Subsequent note:

15 Powell 38.

REVISING
STEP 12.   MAKING THE FINAL DRAFT

The final draft, which should be
typed or printed with a letter-quality
printer, demands careful attention to
format details. Use these general
guidelines for typing your paper:

1. The entire paper, including quotations, notes, and bibliography,
is double-spaced.

2. Except for page numbers, use
one-inch margins on all four
sides of each page.

3. Use a running head to number
all pages consecutively, including the bibliography page(s). To
create a running head, type your
last name and the page number a
half inch from the top of each
page and flush with the right
margin.

4. All text begins a double space below the running head.

5. On the first page of text, include
the heading and title. At the left
margin, type your name one
inch from the top. On three subsequent double-spaced lines,
type your instructor's name, the
course title, and the date, using
day-month-year order. Center
the title a double space below the
last line of the heading and capitalize only the first letter of appropriate words. Do not use
quotation marks or underscores

with the title. (If your instructor requires a title page, eliminate this step and see item 11 below.)

6. Begin the text a double space below the title. Indent five spaces for each new paragraph.

7. Insert parenthetical notes as necessary to credit sources of facts, ideas, statistics, and exact words. Parenthetical notes refer readers to the bibliography and include only the author's last name and page number(s). Use no punctuation between the name and number. If the author's name appears in the text, a page number is sufficient.

8. If you use a quotation that requires more than four typed lines, set off the entire passage by indenting it ten spaces from the left margin. Type it double-spaced, without quotation marks. Another style for designating a long quotation is to indent it ten spaces from both left and right margins and type it single-spaced, without quotation marks. [*See* LITERARY ANALYSES, KINDS: FOR LITERARY ELEMENTS, *the "Sample for a Symbol," for an illustration of this second style.*] Use whichever style your instructor prefers.

9. The bibliography page should have the title *Works Cited* (most common), *References*, or *Bibliography* (least common), centered. Double-space and begin the entries. Use hanging indentation, and double-space all entries.

10. If you use endnotes, type the title, *Notes*, centered, one inch from the top of a new page. Begin the notes two spaces below the title. Indent each note five

spaces, type the note number slightly above the line, skip a space, and begin the note. Any additional lines for a note appear at the left margin. Double-space all.

11. If you use footnotes at the bottom of the page, begin two double spaces below the text. Arrange as for endnotes (see item 10 above), but single-space footnotes with a double-space between. On the last page, if the text does not fill the page, space the footnotes near the bottom.

12. If your instructor requires it, prepare a title page. (Do NOT use a title page along with the heading described in item 5 above.) Center from top to bottom and left to right the following five items: title of the paper, your name, the name of the course, the instructor's name, and the date. If you use a title page, repeat the title, centered, on the first page of the text, skip four spaces, and begin the text. Do not number the first page of the text.

13. If your instructor requires it, type your final outline, in standard indented form, on a separate page. [*See* OUTLINES *elsewhere in Part II.*] Include the thesis statement at the head of your outline. If your instructor prefers, this outline may be rearranged to appear as a table of contents. [*See* LAB REPORT *for an example.*] Number the outline page(s) with lower-case Roman numerals, centered, at the bottom of the page.

PROOFREADING

STEP 13. CHECKING THE DETAILS

In addition ot the usual checks for spelling, mechanics, grammar, and usage, you will want to check documentation forms carefully, period for period and comma for comma. Check for underscoring and quotation marks. Read carefully for typing errors. [*See also* PROOFREADING *in Part I for additional guidelines.*]

The most important proofreading you will do for a research paper, however, is quite different from that for any other paper. *Be sure to check the use of quotation marks for any quoted materila you have included.* Remember, if you use another author's words as if they were your own—even accidentally—you can suffer severe penalties. Plagiarism is a serious error, almost a crime. You should check your original sources against the ideas included in your paper just to be certain you have not simply forgotten a set of quotation marks or neglected to copy the quotation marks from your note cards onto your paper.

A Note about the Samples: Five research-paper samples follow. The first, which is a complete paper, illustrates one widely accepted form of documentation, the MLA (Modern Language Association, 1988) parenthetical style. Rapidly becoming singularly popular, parenthetical documentation omits all superscript numbers, thus permitting the use of even the most basic word-processing software and printers.

[*For additional examples of a title page, table-of-contents page, parenthetical documentation, and an appendix, see the sample paper in* LAB REPORT. *Also see the sample papers for English and business in* BIOGRAPHY *for slightly different parenthetical documentation.*]

The second sample, an excerpt from the first, illustrates the MLA endnote style, a common alternative to the MLA parenthetical style.

The third sample is also an excerpt from the first and shows the MLA footnote style. The sample also illustrates a title page, an outline page, and footnote documentation.

The fourth sample, another excerpt, illustrates the APA (American Psychological Association) style. Parenthetical documentation and mode of bibliography entries distinguish this style.

The fifth sample illustrates, in a brief paragraph, the MLA numbered bibliography style.

Certain style manuals will suggest combining these basic formats. For instance, you may be asked to include a title page and a table of contents in a paper documented with endnotes. Thus the five samples offer sound guidelines, no matter which format you are asked to follow.

If your instructor permits you to choose your own style, choose the easiest to prepare.

Combined, the five models flesh out the principles we have discussed. The subsequent analyses point out details peculiar to the research process. Note particularly the combination of primary and secondary research going into this paper.

────── Sample MLA Parenthetical Style Paper ──────

The following sample illustrates the MLA (1988) parenthetical style. The paper illustrates a widely accepted style, often preferred by those who use word processors. Parenthetical style omits the use of superscript numbers as required in endnote and footnote styles.

Ann Commens

Instructor A. Kamp

Senior English II

18 January 1991

Mother Goose: A Devoted Teacher

Mother Goose has survived generations of critics. Perhaps the most trying test of all for Mother Goose has been through the honest and often unrestrained criticism of children (Grover 1). These rhymes have survived because of their ageless quality of rhythm, rhyme, and motion (Arbuthnot 3). They have been passed from parent to child for generations (Parker 46), becoming such a part of the English-speaking world that it is a handicap for a child not to know them (Becker 11). The nursery rhymes of Mother Goose, loved and recited by generations of children, help introduce children to good literature, create fantasy friends, provide contentment, stimulate imagination, and promote learning.

According to legend, Mistress Elizabeth Goose, known widely as Mother Goose, lived in Boston two hundred years ago. She is supposed to have recited her varied rhymes to her numerous grandchildren. Her son-in-law, Thomas Fleet, is said to have published her nursery rhymes in order to make some well-deserved money (Grover 2). Tourists and children still visit the site in Boston where Dame Goose is believed to be buried (Huck and Kuhn 62). Contrary to the Mother Goose legend, most authorities agree that Mother Goose appeared in 1697 as the title of a book of fairy tales by Charles Perrault. The original Mother Goose contained such popular tales as "Cinderella," "Red Riding Hood," and "Sleeping Beauty" (Huck and Kuhn 61). Mother Goose's fame spread from France to America and to England, where the first collection of rhymes was published under her name in 1765 (Grover 2). Many of the traditional nursery rhymes contained in this publication and those succeeding it were recited and sung long before they were ever written down. Most of the rhymes popular today have existed for so long that their actual author is unknown (Becker 13). The famous Mother Goose rhymes have been passed from parent to child, and both enjoy these rhymes together, the child for the first time and the adult once again in remembrance of his childhood (Parker 46).

In remembering their own exposure to the nursery rhymes, parents approve of Mother Goose, for she has proved to be a good influence upon a child. She serves as a child's first introduction to literature (Huck and Kuhn 104). Children of all backgrounds are exposed to the rhymes before they can read (Parker 46), and it is the literature a child grows up with which greatly influences the type of an adult he will become (LaRouche 114). A child who grows up with Mother Goose is "apt to be a child who learns rapidly, who discovers early in life the commingling pleasures that words and pictures award to those who read books" (Huck and Kuhn 387). Although Mother Goose is not actually poetry, her rhymes provide a background for the child to accept and understand real poetry (Grover 2). The child who is exposed to Mother Goose will progress to other classics, such as Shakespeare, more easily because Mother Goose encourages a child to read good literature (Likens 22).

A child who grows up with Mother Goose not only learns the pleasures of reading, but he discovers that the Mother Goose characters can become his friends (Huck and Kuhn 99). Many of the Mother Goose characters are reminiscent of real people, such as Mother Hubbard and her concern for her dog, Mary with her pet lamb, the Old Woman in the Shoe with her housing problem, and Little Bo Beep with her lost sheep. When the child reads about Jack and Jill and Peter, he is reminded of everyday people (de Angeli 8).

Not only do the rhymes provide a child with friends, they provide a child with contentment and satisfaction. The rhymes remind the child of the happiness and family harmony in his life

(Huck and Kuhn 99). One of the most appealing qualities of Mother
Goose is the humor the rhymes contain (Likens 23), which helps
the child laugh and be happy (Mitchell 67). Even the nonsense in
Mother Goose cultivates a child's mind, because a child must be able
to recognize the nonsense in "the cow jumped over the moon"
(Huck and Kuhn 100) in order to think it funny. Mother Goose also
provides many amusing rhymes and riddles for a child to enjoy,
such as "There was a girl in our towne, / Silk an' satin were her
gowne, / Silk an' satin, gold an' velvet, / Guess her name, three times
I've told it" (Baring-Gould 271). The answer, of course, is "Ann." A
child always enjoys telling the old joke, "Adam and Eve and Pinch
me/ Went down to a river to bathe./ Adam and Eve got drownded,/
Which one of the three was saved?" (Baring-Gould 261). The
innocent listener pipes in, "Pinch me," and indeed gets just that
(Baring-Gould 261)!

    The value of Mother Goose, however, is not only that the child
learns to laugh; he learns to build his imagination by changing and
adding to the familiar old Mother Goose rhymes (Rackham 2). The
development of the imagination is a very necessary factor in a
child's life (Huck and Kuhn 331).

> Pretending, playing, making up stories about life, are some of
> the richest talents a person can develop when she or he is
> very small. Fantasy is at the root of all invention, both
> mechanical and social. No one would have developed airplanes
> if someone hadn't pretended that people could fly. No one
> would have formed the American Constitution if someone
> hadn't imagined that people could govern themselves (Rogers
> 39).

When a child grows up with Mother Goose, "he is a child who's apt
to grow up with a mind wide open to new ideas" (Likens 23).

    Growing up with a mind wide open to new ideas provides
opportunities for children to learn about poetry, to identify

universal problems, to learn satisfaction, and certainly to exercise their imaginative expression. Together, these kinds of mind-opening opportunities permit authorities to name one more advantage to exposing children to Mother Goose: to promote learning.

Most authorities agree that Mother Goose stimulates a child's learning process. It has become evident that "the excitement of learning, the excitement of performing, can still begin with something so simple as the rhymes of Mother Goose" (Likens 22). Teachers use the child's knowledge of Mother Goose rhymes to help him want to learn to read, to participate, and to respond (Parker 46). Through the rhymes, a teacher can help the child memorize the day of the week without drills or boredom (Likens 23). Every child who knows "Solomon Grundy, / Born on Monday, / Christened on Tuesday, / Married on Wednesday . . ."(Addams 22) will be able to remember the days of the week. A child is introduced to his first lesson in numbers when he recites "One, two, three, four, five, / Once I caught a fish alive;/ Six, seven, eight, nine, ten, / Then I let it go again" (Mitchell 115) and "1, 2, Buckle my shoe, / 3, 4, Knock at the door, / 5, 6, Pick up sticks . . ." (Baring-Gould 244). A child remembers his Roman numerals through the rhyme "X shall stand for playmates Ten;/ V for Five stout stalwart men;/ I for one . . ." (Baring-Gould 244). A child easily learns his alphabet with "A, B, C, and D, / Pray, playmates agree. / E, F, and G, / Well so it shall be . . ." (Baring-Gould 241) and "A was an apple pie, / B bit it, / C cut it . . ." (Baring-Gould 241). Mother Goose also helps a child develop his language through tongue twisters and riddle rhymes because between the ages of two and six is when the greatest part of a child's language is developed (Huck and Kuhn 98). Mother Goose aids a child in learning the numbers, in learning the alphabet, and in developing his language.

The values of Mother Goose are many: as an introduction to literature, as a child's companion, as a source of happiness and contentment, as a stimulant to his imagination, and as a catalyst in the child's learning process.

> Mother and teacher agree that the best of these verses have an even more potent influence. . . . The healthy moral, so subtly suggested in many of the rhymes, is unconsciously absorbed by the child's receptive mind, helping him to make his own distinction between right and wrong, bravery and cowardice, generosity and selfishness (Grover 1).

Surely, then, it is no wonder the Mother Goose rhymes have survived generations of critics. In fact, without the Mother Goose rhymes as part of his childhood, a youngster may suffer a social if not an educational handicap.

Works Cited

Addams, Charles. The Chas Addams Mother Goose. New York:
        Windmill Books, 1967.

Arbuthnot, May Hill. The Real Mother Goose. Chicago: Rand McNally
        and Co., 1944.

Baring-Gould, William S., and Ceil Baring-Gould. The Annotated
        Mother Goose. New York: C. N. Potter, 1962.

Becker, May Lamberton, ed. The Rainbow Mother Goose. Cleveland:
        The World Publishing Company, 1974.

de Angeli, Marguerite. Book of Nursery and Mother Goose Rhymes.
        Garden City, New York: Doubleday and Company, Inc., 1954.

Grover, Eulalie Osgood, ed. Mother Goose. Chicago: M. A. Donahue
        and Company, 1915

Huck, Charlotte S., and Doris Young Kuhn. Children's Literature in
        the Elementary School. 2nd ed. Chicago: Holt, Rinehart, and
        Winston, Inc., 1968.

LaRoche, Nancy E. "Save the Children," Harper's December 1973:
        114-115.

Likens, Rebecca. "In Defense of Mother Goose," PTA Magazine June
        1973: 21-23.

Mitchell, Donald, ed. Every Child's Book of Nursery Songs. New
        York: Bonanza Books, 1967.

Parker, Patricia. "What Comes after Mother Goose?" The Education
        Digest October 1969: 46-49.

Rackham, Arthur. Mother Goose Nursery Rhymes. New York:
        Franklin Watts, Inc., 1969.

Rogers, Fred. "Three Classic Nursery Tales," Redbook December
        1973: 39-44.

Analysis of the MLA Parenthetical Style Sample

The paper illustrates many of the important principles which should be evident in a research paper. While you can make many observations on your own about the approach the sample paper takes, note these specifics:

- The topic is interesting and narrowed appropriately for the length of the paper.

- The paper employs both primary and secondary research. Many of the comments are drawn directly from the rhymes themselves, rather someone's criticism of them. The two types of research enhance the quality of the paper and fulfill the requirement to write an evaluative paper.

- Quotations, especially those from the rhymes, support the writer's ideas. The few long quotations included offer insight into other critics' interpretations. Notice how the passages blend smoothly into the text, in some cases finishing sentences begun by the writer.

- Far more paraphrases appear than quotations. The writer avoids a paper that is little more than a string of quotations. Because of her paraphrasing, the paper reads evenly and reflects a thoughtful analysis of relationships among ideas.

- The paragraphs follow a clear organization. [*See the third model to compare the paper with the writer's actual outline.*] The paper includes a two-paragraph introduction (not part of the outline), and each of the remaining paragraphs corresponds to a main or subheading the outline.

- The paper exhibits good sentence variety and sophisticated writing technique.

- Transitional words, phrases, and sentences move the reader smoothly from idea to idea, paragraph to paragraph. The seventh paragraph is transitional; it summarizes the main points covered so far and introduces the final point.

- The format, which includes accurate parenthetical notes and a list of works cited, follows the guidelines for good typing technique. Long quotations are set apart from the rest of the text. The bibliography page is accurate and complete, citing only those sources used in the text.

By following carefully all the steps in the research process, you will be able to develop a satisfactory research paper. Remember that the precise form may well be determined by your teacher, department, or school policy.

Sample MLA Endnote Style Paper

This excerpt illustrates another widely accepted style. The documentation appears in the text as raised numbers which refer to a list of notes at the end of the paper.

Commens 1

Ann Commens

Instructor A. Kamp

Senior English II

15 January 1991

Mother Goose: A Devoted Teacher

Mother Goose has survived generations of critics. Perhaps the most trying test of all for Mother Goose has been through the honest and often unrestrained criticism of children.[1] These rhymes have survived because of their ageless quality of rhythm, rhyme, and motion.[2] They have been passed from parent to child for generations,[3] becoming such a part of the English-speaking world that it is a handicap for a child not to know them.[4] The nursery rhymes of Mother Goose, loved and recited by generations of children, help introduce children to good literature, create fantasy friends, provide contentment, stimulate imagination, and promote learning.

Notes

[1] Eulalie Osgood Grover, ed., Mother Goose (Chicago: M. A. Donahue and Company, 1915) 1.

[2] May Hill Arbuthnot, The Real Mother Goose (Chicago: Rand McNally and Co., 1944) 3.

[3] Patricia Parker, "What Comes after Mother Goose?" The Education Digest October 1969: 46.

[4] May Lamberton Becker, ed., The Rainbow Mother Goose (Cleveland: The World Publishing Company, 1974) 11.

Analysis of the MLA Endnote Style Sample

The excerpt above illustrates endnote documentation. The bibliography page will appear with the same form with endnote documentation as it did with parenthetical documentation.

───────── **Sample MLA Footnote Style Paper** ─────────

The footnote style which follows is still preferred by some. Although exceedingly difficult to develop on most word processors, this format was originally set forth by MLA as most suitable for general purposes. It is no longer so highly favored, because of its incompatibility with modern technology, but still has its advocates.

MOTHER GOOSE: A DEVOTED TEACHER

By

Ann Commens

Senior English II

Ms. Aurelia Kamp

January 15, 1991

Statement of Purpose:

The nursery rhymes of Mother Goose, loved and recited by generations of children, introduce children to literature, serve as fantasy companions, provide forms of contentment, stimulate imagination, and promote learning.

Outline:

I.   Introduce literature
   A.   Listening skills
   B.   Poetry appreciation

II.   Offer friends
   A.   Mother Hubbard
   B.   Mary
   C.   Old Woman
   D.   Little Bo Peep
   E.   Jack and Jill
   F.   Peter, Peter

III.   Provide contentment
   A.   Happiness
   B.   Humor
   C.   Riddles

IV.   Stimulate imagination
   A.   Alteration
   B.   Fantasy

V.   Promote learning
   A.   Days
   B.   Numbers
   C.   Roman numerals
   D.   Alphabet
   E.   Language

Mother Goose: A Devoted Teacher

Mother Goose has survived generations of critics. Perhaps the most trying test of all for Mother Goose has been through the honest and often unrestrained criticism of children.[1] These rhymes have survived because of their ageless quality of rhythm, rhyme, and motion.[2] They have been passed from parent to child for generations,[3] becoming such a part of the English-speaking world that it is a handicap for a child not to know the rhymes.[4] The nursery rhymes of Mother Goose, loved and recited by generations of children, help introduce children to good literature, create fantasy friends, provide contentment, stimulate imagination, and promote learning.

According to legend, Mistress Elizabeth Goose, known widely as Mother Goose, lived in Boston two hundred years ago. She is supposed to have recited her varied rhymes to her numerous grandchildren. Her son-in-law, Thomas Fleet, is said to have published her nursery rhymes in order to make some well-deserved money.[5]

---

[1] Eulalie Osgood Grover, ed., <u>Mother Goose</u> (Chicago: M. A. Donahue and Company, 1915) 1.

[2] May Hill Arbuthnot, <u>The Real Mother Goose</u> (Chicago: Rand McNally and Co., 1944) 3.

[3] Patricia Parker, "What Comes after Mother Goose?" <u>The Education Digest</u> October 1969: 46.

[4] May Lamberton Becker, ed., <u>The Rainbow Mother Goose</u> (Cleveland: The World Publishing Company, 1974) 11.

[5] Grover 2.

Analysis of the MLA Footnote Style Sample

The excerpt illustrates a title page, an outline page (which could be altered to appear as a table of contents), and footnotes. Notice that the footnotes appear at the bottom of each page, separated from the text by two double spaces. The footnotes are single-spaced with spaces between items. The bibliography form will be the same as that for endnotes, except single-spaced, with two spaces between items, to follow the pattern established in the footnotes.

Sample APA Style Paper

The *Publication Manual of the American Psychological Association* establishes a specific style for psychology papers. Referred to as the APA style, it calls for a distinctive form. Note especially:

- The title page includes the title, the author's name, and the author's school affiliation, double-spaced, centered left to right and top to bottom. A title requiring more than one line is also double-spaced. A running head, which is a shortened version of the title followed by the page number (1), appears at the top right margin.

- An abstract follows, summarizing the paper. The abstract page includes a shortened form of the title and a running head in the upper right corner. The title, *Abstract*, appears centered one inch from the top. The abstract is a single paragraph written in block form (i.e., without indentation) beginning a double space below the title. The abstract should be seventy-five to one hundred words for theoretical articles or reviews and one hundred to one hundred fifty words for empirical papers.

- The first page of the paper repeats the title, centered, one inch from the top. Text begins a double space below the title.

- The parts of the paper are labeled (*Method, Results, Discussion, References*) in a manner similar to other technical reports. [*See* TECHNICAL REPORT *elsewhere in Part II.*] Headings of the same level are typed in the same format.

- All pages include a running head and are double-spaced.

- The notes are parenthetical and include the author's last name followed by a comma and the date of publication. When the author's name appears in the text, only the date appears in parentheses. If reference is made to a specific page or chapter, or if a quotation is included, the parenthetical note must also include a page or chapter number. Use the abbreviation *p.* or *pp.* preceding page numbers: (Smith, 1992, pp. 78-81).

- Instead of a bibliography, the APA style calls for a reference list. This list must include every citation in the text. Note, too, that the form for entries differs considerably from the MLA style. The use of surnames with only initials, the use of parentheses around the date of publication, the omission of capital letters in all but the first word and proper names of periodical titles, the omission of quotation marks around periodical titles, and the under-scoring of volume numbers of periodicals are some obvious differences. Note, too, that the entries are double-spaced with hanging indentation, the second line and following lines being indented only three spaces, rather than five as in the MLA style.

Mother Goose Rhymes: Their Influence on Children's
Literary Introduction, Imagination, and Reading Readiness
Ann Commens
St. Philips College

Abstract

Mother Goose rhymes have been determined to be useful aids in developing educational readiness in preschool children. First, the rhymes introduce children to literature by helping them learn to appreciate sound and imagery in poetry. Second, as part of that introduction, children also learn to recognize the difference between real and imaginary friends. Third, the rhymes help children create their own contentment. Fourth, the combination of these elements stimulates imagination. The ultimate result, of course, is the promotion of learning by stimulating reading readiness in preschool children.

Mother Goose has survived generations of critics. Some authorities (Grover, 1915, p. 1) profess that the most trying test of all for Mother Goose has been through the honest and often unrestrained criticism of children. These rhymes have survived because of their ageless quality of rhythm, rhyme, and motion (Arbuthnot, 1944, p. 3), and they have been passed from parent to child for generations (Parker, 1969, p. 46), becoming such a part of the English-speaking world that some believe (Becker, 1974, p. 11) it is a handicap for a child not to know the rhymes. The nursery rhymes of Mother Goose, loved and recited by generations of children, help introduce children to good literature, create fantasy friends, provide contentment, stimulate imagination, and promote learning.

According to legend, Mistress Elizabeth Goose, known widely as Mother Goose, lived in Boston two hundred years ago. She is supposed to have recited her varied rhymes to her numerous grandchildren. According to Grover (1915, p. 2), Thomas Fleet, son-in-law to Dame Goose, published her nursery rhymes in order to make some well-deserved money. Today, tourists and children still visit the site in Boston where Dame Goose is believed to be buried (Huck & Kuhn, 1968, p. 62). Contrary to the Mother Goose legend, most authorities (Huck & Kuhn) agree that Mother Goose appeared in 1697 as the title of a book of fairy tales by Charles Perrault.

References

Addams, C. (1967). The Chas Addams Mother Goose. New York:
    Windmill Books.

Arbuthnot, M. H. (1944). The Real Mother Goose. Chicago: Rand
    McNally and Co.

Baring-Gould, W. S., and Baring-Gould, C. (1962). The Annotated
    Mother Goose. New York: C. N. Potter.

Becker, M. L. (Ed.). (1974). The Rainbow Mother Goose. Cleveland:
    The World Publishing Company.

De Angeli, M. (1954). Book of Nursery and Mother Goose Rhymes.
    Garden City: Doubleday and Company, Inc.

Grover, E. O. (Ed.). (1915). Mother Goose. Chicago: M. A. Donahue
    and Company.

Huck, C. S., and Kuhn, D. Y. (1968). Children's Literature in the
    Elementary School (2nd ed.). Chicago: Holt, Rinehart, and
    Winston, Inc.

LaRoche, N. E. (1973, December). Save the children. Harper's, pp.
    114-115.

Likens, R. (1973, June). In defense of Mother Goose. PTA Magazine,
    pp. 21-23.

Mitchell, D. (Ed.). (1967). Every Child's Book of Nursery Songs. New
    York: Bonanza Books.

Parker, P. (1969, October). What comes after Mother Goose? The
    Education Digest, pp. 46-49.

Analysis of the APA Style Sample Paper

The APA style serves its purpose well, which is to provide logical, convenient documentation for psychological research. More complicated papers will take on the specific divisions (*Method, Results, Discussion*) after an initial introduction like that given above. In this respect, the paper looks more like a technical report than it does a research paper. Be sure to compare the format of a technical report [*in* TECHNICAL REPORT *elsewhere in Part II*] with what you see here.

——— Sample Numbered Bibliography Style Paper ———

Numbered bibliography style simplifies documentation. Some readers object to this style because they must flip to the bibliography to determine each source as it appears in the text. Other readers, especially those who place less emphasis on sources, prefer its uncluttered format. Writers generally like it because it eases documentation. Here's how numbered bibliography style works:

- Before writing the final draft of the paper, prepare an alphabetical listing of sources used in the paper. Number the list consecutively, beginning with 1. (Note that other arrangements are also possible. For instance, scientific papers often list the sources in order in which they are first cited in the text. Use whichever arrangement works best for your purposes.)

- When you document a source in your text, refer parenthetically to the work by number. Follow the number with a comma and a space, and then add the page number. A numbered parenthetical note looks like this: (8, 32) In this case, *8* refers to the eighth source listed in the numbered bibliography and *32* refers to the page number within the source. A multiple-page reference looks like this: (12, 114–23).

The following excerpt illustrates numbered bibliography style:

Mother Goose: A Devoted Teacher

Mother Goose has survived generations of critics. Perhaps the most trying test of all for Mother Goose has been through the honest and often unrestrained criticism of children (6, 2). These rhymes have survived because of their ageless quality of rhythm, rhyme, and motion (2, 3). They have been passed from parent to child for generations (11, 46), becoming such a part of the English-speaking world that it is a handicap for a child not to know the rhymes (4, 11). The nursery rhymes of Mother Goose, loved and recited by generations of children, can have a combination of good and bad effects upon the children.

Works Cited

1. Addams, Charles. The Chas Addams Mother Goose. New York: Windmill Books, 1967.

2. Arbuthnot, May Hill. The Read Mother Goose. Chicago: Rand McNally and Co., 1944.

3. Baring-Gould, William S., and Ceil Baring-Gould. The Annotated Mother Goose. New York: C. N. Potter, 1962.

Analysis of the Numbered Bibliography Style Sample

Note that the format for the numbered bibliography is the same as for earlier MLA samples. The addition of numbers marks the only difference.

A Final Note: Reexamine the five forms. Note their differences and similarities, then follow the format which works best for you. In spite of the emphasis here on format, keep in mind that your instructor is more interested in content. Be sure that you use superior writing technique and that your paper reflects thorough research. Accurate form will not substitute for careful research or polished writing.

RESUME

A resume (pronounced *reh-zoo-may*) is a summary of your qualifications for a job. It usually includes your educational background, work experience, and references.

Submitted with a cover letter [*see* LETTERS, KINDS: BUSINESS: TO ACCOMPANY A RESUME *in Part II*], delivered either personally or by mail, the resume may be your only opportunity to make a good impression. While formats vary considerably, all take one of three approaches:

- Chronological organization: experiences are listed beginning with the earliest. The most recent experiences appear last.

- Reverse chronological organization: the most recent experiences appear first.

- Experiences grouped in relation to the job currently sought: little effort is made to show time relationships, but dates are included.

In seeking employment early in one's life, a reverse chronological pattern is usually most appropriate. We will follow this form in our discussion here.

Characteristics

No matter its format, a resume will include these common characteristics:

- your name, address, and phone number (including area code),
- the position for which you are applying,
- your experience, including places, dates of employment and responsibilities or duties held,
- your education and special training,
- references.

In many cases, the resume is the only picture the personnel manager sees of you, so you must make the best impression you can without being dishonest or misleading.

Process

The following process will help you develop a complete, accurate, and impressive resume.

PREWRITING

STEP 1. ANALYZING THE EMPLOYMENT REQUIREMENTS

Before you develop a resume, name the specific position you are seeking. Then make a list of the skills, duties, responsibilities, and education you think the job requires. If possible, ask for a job description and tailor your list from that.

The implications for doing this analysis are twofold:

- First, you will design a resume to best show your qualifications for the specific job.

- Second, you will design different resumes for different kinds of job.

Redesigning a resume to suit different positions may sound dishonest; in fact it is not. You simply emphasize the experiences appropriate to the position. For instance, if you were applying for a job as an attendant at a horticulture nursery, you would want to emphasize your experience with plants and your understanding of gardening—how to plant various seedlings and what yield to expect from different varieties. On the other hand, if you were applying for a position as an appliance salesperson where nobody cared what you know about gardening, you would emphasize your sales experience (even if the experience was in selling plants) and your ability to relate well to other people.

So, yes, it is important to name the specific position and precisely determine its responsibilities so that your resume can be geared toward that goal.

STEP 2. ANALYZING YOUR EXPERIENCE

Next, list your work experience. Jot down dates and employers. If you are young and lack job experience, do not hesitate to include volunteer work and major committee assignments. After all, it *was* work, even if you were not paid for it. It required responsibility and commitment; it shows willingness to work and achieve goals.

Once you have listed all the experiences you can, or all that seem appropriate, arrange them in reverse chronological order (i.e., the most recent first).

STEP 3. MEETING THE JOB REQUIREMENTS

As you review each of the items on the list you developed in Step 2, write beside each experience the kinds of responsibilities you held or the duties you performed. List responsibilities and duties especially appropriate for the position you currently seek. If none seem especially appropriate, list those which show the greatest responsibility or skill.

If, for instance, you apply for the nursery job, the employer will be interested in knowing that you worked every spring preparing your neighbor's garden: fertilizing, planting, and mulching. On the other hand, the same job listed in a resume for the appliance salesperson might refer only to *seasonal yard work*, with duties listed merely as *responsible for developing necessary routine to maintain health and attractiveness of garden*. Thus, you show self-discipline and responsibility for a product, both important aspects of a sales job.

With these general examples in mind, complete your own list.

STEP 4. MEETING THE EDUCATIONAL REQUIREMENTS

Gather information about your education and training in a manner similar to that used in Step 3. Remember to emphasize those aspects which bear particularly on the position sought. Mention specific majors or minors or even specific courses related to the position. In addition, list any private lessons, seminars, workshops, and other noncredit classes you may have taken that add to your experience.

STEP 5. SEEKING REFERENCES

Most job applications request references. By including these on your resume, you will be better prepared to complete any application form the potential employer may request.

List two or three people, not relatives, who can vouch for your ability, especially as it relates to the position sought. Remember that the more responsible and credible your references, the more helpful their recommendations. Choose wisely, but make sure you choose someone who can honestly speak well for you. If a reference begins by saying to your potential employer, "I really don't know the applicant well, but, . . ." you have done yourself no favors.

Never include as a reference the name of someone who has not given you permission to do so. Your presumption may be just enough to earn a poor recommendation. After all, by neglecting to ask first, you have demonstrated a lack of responsibility.

Once you have selected the best references and gained their permission, write down their names, titles or positions, and addresses. In some cases, you will also include a home and/or business phone number.

STEP 6. FOLLOWING A FORMAT

As you begin to arrange your information into a resume, you should choose a logical format. While many exist, most center the applicant's name, address, and phone number at the top. The remainder of the resume is set in columns, the left listing the general headings, and the right giving the details:

Your Name
Your Street Address
Your City and State and Zip Code
Your Phone Number, Including Area Code

Position Sought:	Position named
Experience:	Places, dates, and details of duties and responsibilities listed. Type single-spaced, but double-space between specific jobs. List the second job experience here.
Education:	List education and any specific honors or leadership experiences appropriate for the position sought.
References:	Gives names, positions or titles, addresses and phone numbers. Skip a line between individual references.

If possible, limit your resume to a single page. Only when you are more experienced can you afford the risk of a multipaged resume.

REVISING

STEP 7. EVALUATING YOUR RESUME

Examine your resume as if you were a personnel manager. How does it read?

Next, look for ways to enhance your image. Ask these questions:

- Have I listed my most impressive duties or responsibilities, relating them to this position?
- Have I overlooked experience or abilities that would make me a better candidate? If so, how can I include them?

- Are the details accurate? Dates, places, names?
- Have I described my experience accurately? (Remember, the potential employer may check these details even though you do not list references connected with every position.)
- Can I make any revisions to improve my image without being misleading or dishonest?

PROOFREADING

Step 8. Making a Sharp Impression

After you have typed the resume, look at the details. Is everything spelled correctly? Punctuated accurately? Is the grammar correct? Have you maintained standard usage and mechanics?

Now back off and take a critical look at the appearance. Remember, this is your only chance for a first impression. The resume must be immaculate. Ask yourself:

- Is it neat?
- Is the format crisp and clean?
- Is the type crisp?
- Have I used good-quality paper?
- If I used a word processor, did I use a letter-quality printer?
- In other words, did I do everything possible to provide for a slick, professional looking resume?

Remember, this is your image to a potential employer.

——— Sample Resume ———

The following resume complies with the suggestions above:

Kevin L. McDermitt
12806 South Pike Road
Mt. Simon, Lousiana 23306-4441
(712) 877-5602

Position Sought:	Consumer Computer Trainer
Experience:	Community College, Computer Education Lab, Sept. 1987 to present. Supervisor: Dr. Clarence K. Elliott. Duties include tutoring students in word processing and spread-sheet work, using over 40 different pieces of software with five major computer brands. Twenty-eight hours per week.
	Computer Land, Dixon, Georgia, part-time sales, summers, 1985, 1986, and 1987. Supervisor: Jeannette Shovers. Duties included working with customers seeking software to meet specific needs and altering software to solve user problems and maintain compatibility with hardware.
Education:	Community College, Mount Simon, Louisiana. Associate Degree in Business with minor in computer education, 1987. Special award for extensive volunteer tutoring in area secondary school computer labs.
	Rushing High School, Dixon, Georgia. Graduated with honors, 1984. Served as President of Senior Class and Treasurer of Junior Achievement business group, 1983.
References:	Dr. Clarence K. Elliott, Instructor, Community College, 100 North Judson, Mount Simon, Lousiana 23307-8211
	Dr. Jeannette Shovers, Manager, Computer Land, 817 East Elm, Dixon, Georgia 27711
	Mr. Rodney Tresseur, Junior Achievement Sponsor, Rushing National Bank, 1200 Bloom Street, Dixon, Georgia 27711-7003

Analysis of the Sample

The sample includes all the characteristics suggested in the process. Note particularly these matters:

- The overall format is neat, clean, and crisp.
- The resume is limited to a single page.
- The spacing helps group the subject matter.
- The labels are clear.
- The content is clearly aimed at the position sought and extraneous material is omitted. For instance, there is no mention of athletic activities in high school or work backstage for dramatic productions at Community College.
- Honors and specific duties are included in the appropriate areas.
- References are related to the computer business or to the applicant's abilities.

Studying the process, sample, and analysis should help you develop a strong resume. [*Turn now to* LETTERS, KINDS: BUSINESS: TO ACCOMPANY A RESUME *in Part II so you can develop an effective cover letter.*]

Best wishes for a good interview!

REVIEW

Reviews of novels, films, concerts, scientific work, art exhibits, or plays often serve as an audience's introduction. The reader decides to buy a literary work on the basis of an interesting review; the moviegoer decides to take in a Sunday afternoon matinee on the basis of a good review; the music lover decides not to risk the price of admission on the basis of a poor review. But there is really very little we can say that will hold true for all reviews. They are free-form and highly personal, reflecting the opinions and experiences of the reviewer. As a result, then, in order to write good reviews, you must have broad experience in your chosen field. And you must have sound criteria with which to judge the work.

In spite of the minimal formal direction we can provide here, we will look at the general characteristics of reviews, examine the process by which they are written, and analyse a sample review.

Characteristics

As you might guess, reviews have few strict characteristics, but good reviews almost always include certain elements and use certain techniques for development. A good review

- begins with an explanation that gives the work a frame of reference—including information about the author, background, genre, or general issues pertinent to the work,

- explains a work by indicating generally what it is about,

- includes material pertinent to the reader, aimed toward his or her interests,

- selects the most interesting, important, or thought-provoking ideas for discussion or examination,

- generates interest in the work, either positive or negative,

- describes strengths and weaknesses,

- concludes with an evaluation based on the points discussed,

- uses good style, sound sentence structure, and other techniques of excellent writing.

The remainder of this section will focus on the most common kind of review, that for a literary work, particularly a novel. While reviews of literary works are not the same as literary analyses, reviews share certain techniques with them. Keep in mind, however, that reviews do not follow the typically thorough and technical nature of literary analyses.

[*Refer to* LITERARY ANALYSES *elsewhere in Part II for comparison.*]

Process

No matter what approach you intend to take, the following steps will help you develop a satisfactory review.

PREWRITING

STEP 1. SELECTING THE FOCUS

In writing a literary review, you must select ideas both interesting and capable of being developed in the allotted space. In order to help you think about points worth discussing, ask yourself the following questions:

- What is the purpose of the work? What is its theme? What message does the author convey? [*See* THEME *in the Glossary.*]

- Who are its major characters? What are they like? Can the reader identify with them?

- What problems do the characters face? Does the reader see the characters grow as a result of struggle? Is the main character a hero or an antihero?

- What is the setting? Is it important to the plot, the theme, or the characters' struggle?

- Are other literary elements (imagery, symbolism, personification, etc.) important in the work? If so, how are they used? [*See* IMAGERY, SYMBOL, *and* FIGURES OF SPEECH *in the Glossary.*]

- What is your reaction to the work? Do you like it, find it fascinating?

Or would you prefer never to think about it again? Why?

Once you have answered these questions, pick out the few questions which, in your opinion, either touch upon the most important aspects of the book or are likely to generate interest in the reader. That these two options should be the same is irrelevant. It may not be the case!

STEP 2. PLANNING THE REVIEW

Once you have selected the questions that serve as guidelines in Step 1 above, use them to generate a list of ideas you want to include. Try these steps:

First, determine your attitude toward the work. Do not allow yourself to be noncommittal; the reader may think you cannot make up your mind. Granted, you may be positive about some aspects and negative about others, but determine your opinion either way.

Next, use the responses developed in Step 1 to support your opinion. If you have both positive and negative reactions, then form two lists: one with items you liked and the other with items you disliked. If your reaction is consistent, then you need only one list. In either case, select those items which best explain why you feel as you do.

Third, state your ideas in a single sentence. This is a tall order, and you may need to group items on the lists, but you must get a handle on where you are going. Consider the following example:

Positives	Negatives
peculiar setting	unbelievable re-
scientific research	lationships with animals
learn about prehistory	too coincidental
speculation of discovery of new techniques	
heroic female character	
alien culture	
spiritual rituals	
daily lives and relationships in society	
living habits	

The positive list includes many items which overlap. By grouping these together, the writer came up with a single sentence:

> The novel's prehistoric setting, made believable by the author's thorough research, allows an heroic female character to overpower the plot's unlikely coincidental events to give the reader a fascinating epic-like book.

The writer has sharpened his focus and can now see exactly what he wants to discuss:

1. prehistoric setting couched in thorough research
2. heroic female character
3. coincidental events

The overall attitude will be favorable (two positives and one negative).

Now, formulate your own single sentence. [*See also* THESIS SENTENCE *in the Glossary, and* THEME *in Part II for additional details.*]

STEP 3.   ORGANIZING THE PLAN

Even though we said that reviews are free-form, they still must follow some kind of organization plan, for the sake of both writer and reader. Frequently this organization follows the most-to-least-important pattern [*see* ORDERS OF IMPORTANCE *in the Glossary*]. But it may take almost any other pattern, such as cause and effect or comparison-contrast. [*See entries for each in Part II.*] Other kinds of reviews, particularly for performances, tend to follow a chronological order.

Determine the best means of organizing your review. Look at the list and sentence you completed in Step 2. By putting them together, you should be able to decide which items should appear first, second, and so on. Put the list in order.

WRITING

STEP 4.   FOLLOWING THE PLAN

Use the list at the beginning of this chapter as a general guide to writing your review. Begin with an introductory paragraph that places the work in perspective. Include any information about the author, like other works or follow-up plans. Identify the specific genre of the work. [*See* GENRE *in the Glossary.*] And entice the reader. Somewhere in the introductory paragraph, you will want to include the thesis sentence. In fact, you may choose to revise the sentence you wrote in Step 2 to this end.

Use proper writing techniques to develop the body of the review. Support your opinions with examples drawn from the work, much as you would in an opinion paper or literary analysis. [*See* LITERARY ANALYSES *and* OPINION *elsewhere in Part II.*] Hold to your plan so the reader can follow your logic. Smooth the way with transitions. [SEE TRANSITIONS *in the Glossary.*]

The conclusion should include an evaluation of the work and either recommend or reject it, based on the main ideas developed in the body of the review.

REVISING

STEP 5. IMPROVING THE CONTENT

As you revise, ask yourself the following questions:

- Have I introduced the work effectively? Will my reader understand the general idea of the work, its purpose, its message?
- Have I avoided giving away the plot? Or will the reader hate me for destroying the pleasure of discovering the outcome?
- Do the body paragraphs clearly support my opinion? Or have I muddled the supporting details with extraneous materials? [*See* REVISING: SAMPLE REVISION FOR SPECIFIC DETAIL *in Part I.*]
- Have I been consistent or varied in my attitude toward different seg-

ments? Do my transitions reflect these consistencies or changes? [*See* REVISING: SAMPLE REVISION FOR TRANSITION *in Part I.*]
- Recognizing that a review is a matter of opinion, have I been fair in my reactions? Have I been too hasty to applaud or criticize? Do I have a basis on which to commend or condemn the work?
- Have I maintained a good writing style, neither too flowery nor too blunt, showing things rather than merely telling about them? Are my sentences varied in length and structure? [*See* REVISING: SAMPLE REVISION FOR SENTENCE VARIETY *and* REVISING: SAMPLE REVISION FOR EMPHASIS *in Part I.*]

Make whatever revisions your answers suggest. In addition, recheck the list of Characteristics, above. Does your review include those general qualities? If not, revise to improve your work.

Finally, refer to REVISING, in Part I. Allow the questions there to guide further possible revisions.

PROOFREADING
STEP 6. CHECKING TECHNICAL DETAILS

A review, like any other piece of writing, must follow the standards of grammar, usage, and mechanics. Once you have completed your revisions, reread your paper for technical errors. [*Refer to the Glossary for brief examples to help you apply effective writing techniques.*]

Finally check specific spelling and word choice. Refer to *Webster's New*

World Dictionary for spelling and *Webster's New World Thesaurus* for word choice.

The process above will help you write a successful review. Reading magazine and newspaper reviews will show you the techniques used by professionals. Because reviews are free-form, and because they rely so heavily on personal opinion, they vary as much as their writers. For the sake of discussion, however, we have included below a review of a novel. Study it before completing your own review. Maybe you will find ideas worth considering.

Sample Review

The following review is included for several reasons. It shows what a review can do. It enables you to compare a book review with a book report. And it lets you compare a book review with a literary analysis of a novel. How? The same book serves as the topic for the sample book reports [*in* BOOK REPORT, *earlier in Part II*] and the sample analysis of a novel [*in* LITERARY ANALYSES, *also earlier in Part II*]. A comparison of all three will help you develop a more effective review.

When Neanderthal-Reared Meets Cro-Magnon:

A Review of <u>The Valley of the Horses</u>

Whisked back 25,000 years to the last Ice Age, readers of Jean Auel's <u>The Valley of the Horses</u> land in prehistoric civilization peopled by cave-dwelling Neanderthals and tribes of Cro-Magnons. The second book in the Earth Children series, <u>Valley</u> alternately follows its two main characters until they ultimately meet. Ayla, the beautiful, willowy orphaned Cro-Magnon girl raised by a Neanderthal tribe, has been exiled and separated from her son because she dared to dispute the word of the leader. Turned out alone with no provisions to wander the Eurasian steppes, she uses her ill-gotten hunting skills and knowledge of medicinal plants to survive the loneliness and unrelenting environment for five years. She raises a foundling colt after she kills the mare for food. As a kind of surrogate mother to the colt, she develops a fond relationship with the animal which, when mature, provides transportation and labor for the young woman. A similar relationship develops with an injured lion cub. Together the three of them form a kind of family. Eventually, Ayla meets Jondalar, an exceptionally handsome Cro-Magnon man astounded by Ayla's family, her beauty, her refined skills. He is the first non-Neanderthal man Ayla has ever seen. The remainder of the plot revolves around their efforts to learn to understand one another and to communicate. Ayla knows only the nonverbal communication skills of the Neanderthals; Jondalar never masters the subtle variations of her "primitive" language. Their biggest obstacle is Jondalar's unwillingness to accept Ayla's only filial attachment, the Neanderthals, as anything other than subhuman, animal-like flatheads.

Even without the fascinating characters who struggle with their social and cultural differences, the book provides superb reading. The scientific research evident in the book gives curious readers an insight into a world they would never take the time to study in biology, botany, anthropology, and archaeology books. Woven into a highly readable novel, however, the medicinal plants, woolly mammoths, cave lions, wild horses, glaciers, flint qualities, food preparation, hunting techniques, clothing construction, even sanitation habits of prehistoric tribes make for startling new perspectives on human evolution. While the fictionalized portions blend harmoniously with the obviously thorough scientific investigation, the result is pleasantly mind-stretching.

With a beautiful heroine and a strikingly handsome hero set in the midst of an unspoiled environment, Auel could have lapsed into a Garden of Eden paradise. But all does not go well; difficulties inherent in the uncivilized, lonely arena of <u>Valley</u> provide gripping episodes, a few tears, and satisfying joy. Only a few unlikely coincidences mar the otherwise delightful novel. That a young woman can stop a lion's attack in midair, even if she "knows" the lion, seems less than believable. That a young woman who happened to ride farther than usual also happened to arrive just as the lion was about to attack also seems preposterous. Since these incidents make up a major pivotal point in the plot, they present a significant weakness. With the remainder of the epic-like novel so carefully plotted and so logical in its possibilities, these incidents seem all the more unlikely.

For its insight into a world that preceded modern man, <u>The Valley of the Horses</u> offers an imaginative approach to how man—or, in this case, woman—came to think about riding a horse, how she may have learned to make fire with stones, how she may have learned to make medicine, how she may have learned to hunt animals that were too large or too fast to kill with a sling or a spear. That strange animals roamed the earth 25,000 years ago is no secret, but to see them roaming the grasslands, to watch their habits, to learn how prehistoric people relied on them for both food and protection—that is an eye-opener. Thanks to Auel, readers now have a delightful opportunity to learn about another world through the eyes of two arresting Cro-Magnon characters.

Analysis of the Sample Review

The review lets the writer express his opinion, supported by details. Note these specific characteristics:

- The opening paragraph places the book into perspective, establishing it as part of a series and summarizing its plot without giving too much away. In introducing the main characters, the author gives a brief description of their difficulties but rightfully omits any reference to the outcome of their struggles.

- The second paragraph elaborates on the best attributes of the novel. Detailed references to scientific research support the reviewer's opinion.

- The third paragraph, which begins positively, permits the reviewer to offer his only disparaging comments about the book. While admitting that one incident should not discredit an entire work, he indicates the pivotal importance of the incident. At the same time, he shows how other aspects of the book work so favorably that the criticism must be taken in their light.

- The final paragraph concludes favorably. Without directly saying so, the reviewer implies we should dash out, pick up a copy, and immediately read it.

- Because this is a review, we know that a different reviewer might easily present a very different opinion.

Review writing is an art. The more you read reviews, and the works treated by them, the broader your own ideas will become as to what constitutes good practice. The guidelines above should get you off to a good start.

SCRIPTS

Scripts are used for all kinds of audio productions: plays, television dramas, radio shows, commercials, documentaries, pageants, ceremonies, etc. Most scripts consist of two parts: a *narration* or *dialogue* (the spoken portion) and a set of *directions* for visual or sound effects (to enrich the spoken portion). The script for a play will include the lines for the actors and the stage directions to describe the setting, lighting, movement of characters, and so fourth. The script for a television play will include everything found in the stage play, and add camera directions and editing cuts.

Scripts are often used in other kinds of media productions as well. Slide programs, for instance, may have either prerecorded narratives or printed scripts. Museum tours, similarly, may have prerecorded audio presentations or written scripts for the guides. The more traditional forms are also used for subjects other than drama. Radio uses more scripts for commercials than for any other purpose. Television employs scripts in documentaries, news broadcasts, variety shows, comedy routines, and commercials.

Scripts vary less in how they present dialogue than in their format and technical vocabulary. As television or film script includes camera directions, it appears in two columns: *audio* and *video*. The drama script needs no camera cues; it appears in full-page format with italicized stage directions. The television script will refer to *pan* or *dissolve*, the drama script to *upstage* or *fast curtain*. By such differences are the various types set apart.

Even though scripts are used in many media, we will limit our discussion here to few representative examples: for drama, radio, and television.

DRAMA SCRIPTS

We are most familiar with drama scripts. We have all read plays in literature textbooks and are accustomed to the elements they include. Drama is one of the oldest forms of human expression, and drama scripts, as a form, find their roots in equally remote times. Though the technical aspects of staging a play have altered somewhat over the centuries, the basic components and process of developing a play have not. Actors still speak lines, and the plot moves forward by showing, rather than telling. The more modern forms we will examine later, those for radio and television, take the drama script as a starting point, altering elements as needed to fit the peculiar characteristics of their media.

481

Characteristics

In a drama script we expect to see

- a cast of characters, sometimes merely named, sometimes also identified by relationships,
- a setting in time and place,
- a description of the stage setting,
- a division of the play into acts and scenes,
- speeches, identified by character name,
- stage directions, to suggest characters' movements and changes in scenery and/or location.

In addition to these, we also expect the script to contain the essential dramatic elements. [*See* LITERARY ANALYSES, *especially the section* FOR LITERARY WORKS: DRAMA, *and* SHORT STORY, *both in Part II, for a discussion of character, plot, setting, theme, and conflict.*]

The following elements appear in good dramatic productions:

- characters who in the course of their dialogue and interaction tell the audience everything it needs to know,
- clearly developed characters, including at least one protagonist and antagonist [*see* PROTAGONIST *and* ANTAGONIST *in the Glossary*],
- believable behavior and dialogue,
- motivation to account for behavior and attitudes,
- believable conflict [*see* CONFLICT *in the Glossary*],
- ample action,
- good plot or story line,
- rising action, crisis, climax, and falling action [*see each of these entries in the Glossary*],
- a theme [*see* THEME *in the Glossary*].

Process

To develop a drama script, you must bring together a number of writing skills. In one respect, you are writing a kind of short story, one filled with action but lacking the story's narration. In another respect, you are mapping people's actions within the confines of the stage. In still another, you are writing dialogue [*see* DIALOGUE *elsewhere in Part II*] and following the techniques of that creative art form. Along with these go concise descriptions of setting, staging, and direction. This combination requires care and skill. The following process can help you develop the total script.

PREWRITING

STEP 1.   DETERMINING THE MESSAGE

Before you can write a drama script, you must decide what message, or theme, you hope to convey. [*See* THEME, *as it relates to literature, in the Glossary*.] Think about what matters to you. If this is your first attempt at writing a drama, avoid dealing with world-impact messages. Instead, deal with something closer to home. Put your message in a single sentence.

Consider the following examples of one-sentence statements:

Showing responsibility develops trust.

Punctuality suggests responsibility.

We learn about people by watching how they treat animals.

Dishonesty usually ruins a friendship.

Each states a message on which a satisfactory drama could be based. Write your own message now.

STEP 2. PLANNING THE PLOT

Once you have selected the message, think about the kind of action that will help the viewer understand it. For instance, if you wish to show that dishonesty ruins a friendship, your plot should revolve around a friendship destroyed by the lying of one or both of friends. Certain necessary situations become immediately apparent:

- the established friendship
- the occurrence of the dishonesty
- the discovery of the dishonesty
- the deterioration of the friendship
- the inability of the characters to mend the friendship as a result of lack of trust

Thus, five listed items become an outline of a drama. The problem, of course, is how best to show these occurrences. How can friendship be shown? What kind of dishonesty occurs? How does it occur? How is it discovered? What is the result of its discovery? Hurt feelings? Or something more serious, like physical injury? Does one friend try to mend the friendship? Who? How? What happens?

Asking these kinds of questions will help outline the plot. Develop your own outline now.

STEP 3. BUILDING THE CHARACTERS

As you outline the plot, you must simultaneously create characters. Some writers claim they develop characters before they begin plotting. In reality, characters and plot are so interdependent that the processes for developing them cannot be separated easily. For instance, if you decide the dishonesty occurs when one friend feigns illness to avoid going fishing with the other, then your character must pretend to enjoy fishing while actually preferring something else. How you develop a character determines the believability of his or her actions and, ultimately, that of the plot.

In order to create believable characters, write a list of their traits. As you develop the plot, you can add or delete traits to clarify the characters in your own mind. Only when you see each character clearly will you be able to make him or her real for the audience. Consider the following:

First Female Character	Second Female Character
naïve	self-assured
honest to a fault	tells white lies
slightly paranoid	assertive
follows others	assumes leadership role
is introspective	is introspective
concerned for others	self-centered

Develop a list of traits for each character in your play.

STEP 4.   SELECTING THE SETTING

Where does the action take place? Picture it in your mind's eye. Can a producer build a set of the place within reasonable financial limits? Alter your vision as necessary. Once you are certain the setting is suitable, not only for the needs of the plot but also for the limits of scenery design, develop a complete description of it. Include details that bear on the plot. For instance, if the characters discuss what they see out a window, include a description of the window's location. If a character makes a surprise entrance from an adjoining room, describe where the room is in relationship to the rest of the setting, as well as the door's location.

If acts and scenes take place in more than one setting, develop similar descriptions of each.

WRITING

STEP 5.   PUTTING THE PLOT INTO SCRIPT

As you write, keep in mind that the audience knows only what the characters say or do. Without being blunt, you must have your characters clue the audience as to time, place, and situation. Dialogue tells all.

Follow the traditional form of scriptwriting. Note these techniques in particular:

- The name of the character speaking is listed first, followed by a colon. Then comes the line as the character would speak it.

- Quotation marks are omitted around a speaker's words. The identification of speaker by name eliminates the need for them.

- Stage directions appear in parentheses, printed in italics (underlined). Stage directions serve as general guidelines for blocking the play, the finer nuances being left open to the director.

As you write, make every effort to include the items listed in the Characteristics section, above. Picture the action as you want the audience to see it.

Include sufficient directions to achieve that reality. Also keep in mind that stage directions should be written from the actor's point of view: hence, *stage left* is to the audience's right. Use the following chart to locate your characters onstage.

STAGE DIRECTIONS

Upstage Right	Upstage Center	Upstage Left
Right	Center	Left
Downstage Right	Downstage Center	Downstage Left

Audience

REVISING

STEP 6. POLISHING THE CONTENT

As you complete your script, you will, of course, improve plot and dialogue. Consider the following questions to suggest potential changes:

- Have I developed believable characters?

- Are their words consistent with their characters?

- Does the dialogue help the audience make deductions?

- Do the characters behave according to clearly defined motives?

- Does the plot develop smoothly, from rising action, through crisis and climax, to falling action? [*See entries for each in the Glossary.*]

- Is the plot believable, avoiding frequent coincidences and shaky cause-effect situations?

- Have I used good techniques to portray my characters, allowing the audience to see and hear them as well as hear what other characters have to say about them?

- Do I show rather than tell?

- Is my message clear by the end of the play?

In addition to content, you will need to make some final revisions with the script format. Note these specific details:

- Add a title to your script.

- Precede the script with a list of characters, perhaps stating their relationships to one another. Keep the identifications brief.

- Follow the cast of characters with a description of the setting: time, place, scene. Describe it clearly enough for a producer to stage your play. [*Use the information developed in Step 4, above*]

- Identify each speaker as he or she speaks.

- Offset the stage directions with parentheses, and print them in italics. [*See* ITALIC *in the Glossary.*]

Revise whatever you can to improve your script. Then go on to the sections below to make final adjustments.

PROOFREADING

Step 7. Checking the Mechanical Details

As you proofread the final script, look for the usual kinds of errors: grammar, usage, mechanics, spelling, and word choice. In addition, look for certain details unique to scriptwriting:

- Have I used different print for the stage directions than for dialogue?
- Have I identified each speaker with a name followed by a colon?
- As the format identifies each speaker, have I omitted quotation marks?
- Do grammar and usage accurately reflect the character? [*See* Dialogue *elsewhere in Part II for a discussion of nonstandard grammar and usage to build character.*]

Finally, consult *Webster's New World Dictionary* and *Webster's New World Thesaurus* to check spelling and word choice. Remember, no matter the character's words you, as a writer, must spell accurately. And remember, too, the right word choice can help develop character insight. Careful use of your thesaurus will strengthen your work.

Sample Drama Script

The example below illustrates the format for a drama script. Compare it with radio and television scripts that follow.

THE LIE

CHARACTERS

Renee

Julianne

Mrs. Westbrook, Renee's mother

Mrs. Hollis, Julianne's mother

Walter, Westbrook's neighbor

Kathaleen

Janna

TIME: <u>The present.</u>

PLACE: <u>Middle-class suburban community.</u>

<u>The Westbrook living room suggests nothing outstanding</u>
<u>except an active teen-ager. The furnishings, generally</u>
<u>traditional and colorless in beiges and greys, are</u>
<u>decorated by Renee's school jacket, her cheerleader's</u>
<u>uniform, a stack of books on the end table and another</u>
<u>on the floor by the sofa. Assorted shoes, sweaters,</u>
<u>scarves, book bags, and tennis rackets litter the chairs</u>
<u>and floor. The kitchen, offstage left, connects to the</u>
<u>living room by a door center left. The upstairs</u>
<u>bedrooms connect with the living room upstage center</u>
<u>where the stairway enters. The only sense of quality is</u>
<u>in the painting stage right of the stairway, a Flemish</u>
<u>oil of obviously fine quality.</u>

ACT I

Scene 1: <u>Saturday morning.</u>

<u>As curtain opens, Renee, dressed in an oversized shirt</u>
<u>and floppy house shoes, enters from the kitchen munching</u>
<u>a sweet roll. Her hair uncombed, she has obviously just</u>
<u>awakened. Still eating, dropping crumbs across the</u>
<u>floor, she flops on the only empty chair in the room, at</u>
<u>downstage right.</u>

Mrs. Westbrook: (<u>From the kitchen.</u>) Renee, are you
     eating in the living room again?

Renee: (<u>With obvious disdain.</u>) No, Mother. (<u>Licks</u>
     <u>her fingers and adds quietly to herself.</u>) Not any
     more. (<u>She gets up, crosses to the sofa where she</u>
     <u>picks up her tennis racket and takes a few practice</u>
     <u>swings.</u>)

Mrs. Westbrook: (<u>Entering from the kitchen, wiping her</u>
     <u>hands on a towel.</u>) Is Julianne making her usual
     trek by here today, dear?

Renee: (<u>Continuing her practice swings.</u>) I suppose.
     I haven't talked to her today. (<u>She flops back in</u>
     <u>the chair downstage right, one leg draped over the</u>
     <u>arm.</u>) She hasn't called, and I'm not calling her.

Mrs. Westbrook: (<u>Looking carefully at her daughter.</u>)
     Oh? (<u>Renee does not respond. Mrs. W. shrugs</u>)
     Well, whatever. At any rate, I want this living
     room straightened up. Pick up this mess and put it
     away. Looks like pigs live here. (<u>Mrs. W. exits</u>

upstage center toward bedrooms and then calls
down.) Oh, by the way, your father called about
an hour ago. (*Mrs. W. reappears in the doorway.*)
He said if you'd meet him at Weston's at noon, you
could put in your two cents' worth on your new car.

Renee: (*With an explosion of excitement.*) Mom,
really? Are you just kidding me? Is he really
going to get me a car—a *new* one? (*Mrs. W.*
beams at her daughter.) Mom, really? (*Renee*
dances around the furniture, over stacks of books,
doing a ballet with the tennis racket.)
Whooppeeeee!

Mrs. Westbrook: Only if you get the living room
straightened before you go. It's 10:30 now. (*She*
exits upstairs, then calls back.) And don't
forget to change the sheets on your bed this
morning.

(*Renee begins furious activity. Stacking books, piling*
clothes and jackets in her arms, dropping some
as she goes, she heads for the upstairs bedroom. In her
scurry, she fails to hear the telephone ringing.)

Analysis of the Sample Drama Script

The excerpt illustrates the form and style of this kind of writing. As you study it, note particularly these details:

- The cast list includes the relationships of three characters. The others need no such detail.

- The time, place, and setting are described, printed in italics (underlined) to prevent their confusion with dialogue.

- As the first scene opens, the description of Renee's activities is printed in italics, again to prevent its confusion with dialogue.

- Characters' names, followed by a colon, precede their lines or any description of their actions.

- The stage directions appear in parentheses.

- The stage directions begin with a capital letter and end with a period, even when they are not complete sentences.

- Hanging indentation (all lines indented except the first) offsets the speakers' names, thus enabling players to find their lines easily.

These techniques, peculiar to drama scripts, serve a purpose: they help the producer, director, and players work effectively together. Granted the techniques are gimmicks, but such gimmicks separate dialogue from instructions and clarify the sets of stage directions.

Use the sample and analysis to refine your own drama script.

RADIO SCRIPTS

The most frequent use of radio scripts is to provide *continuity* (materials which introduce and conclude programs, and provide transitions within them), commercial advertising, public-service announcements, and other spots. Because radio scripts differ significantly from drama scripts, we must first examine their general characteristics.

Characteristics

Radio scripts rely of the sense of sound. Since the only means radio has to attract the listener's attention is auditory, the *sound* of words and phrases bears a greater importance than how they look on paper. Radio scripts, whether for commercials, continuity, or dramas include certain characteristics. In general they

- use short, concise sentences or phrases,
- rely on the listener's sense of sound,
- employ sensory images which affect the ear: repetition, alliteration, assonance, or onomatopoeia [*see entries for each in the Glossary*],
- frequently take a conversational tone,
- often use an imperative mood [*see* IMPERATIVE MOOD *in the Glossary*],
- are precisely timed to fill, for instance, a 60-second or 30-second spot.

In addition, the format of radio scripts follows certain specific characteristics. In general they

- appear typed, double-spaced, on a *continuity form* (a special form used by radio stations),
- follow one of two formats: either material to be read typed in upper-case letters, or material *not* to be read typed in upper-case letters (the format is determined by the station or advertising agency),
- include all references to sound effects,
- rely heavily on nontraditional punctuation—dashes, exclamation points, and underlining—to indicate pauses and points of emphasis,
- use ellipses in a nontraditional way to indicate a pause or *topping line* (which interrupts, coming just a word or two prior to the end of the other speaker's words),
- spell difficult words phonetically.

Because the radio industry uses a vocabulary unfamiliar to the general public, you should learn the following terms:

across the board   advertisements or programs aired throughout the week at the same time every day

availability list   a list of the amount of air time that can be sold

cart   the shortened form of *cartridge*; a tape loop containing an advertiser's message which automatically returns to the start after playing

co-op copy   advertising copy in which both the sales store and the manufacturer's name are mentioned and for which both usually pay a portion of the advertising fee

donut   a commercial which begins with a jingle, has a hole for a spoken segment, and ends with a jingle

double spotting   using two commercials back-to-back with no commentary or music in between

down and under   to lower music to a background level so that the spoken voice becomes audible

fade in   to bring music gradually from zero volume to within acceptable balance

fade out   to bring music gradually from full level to zero sound

station ID   the identification of a radio station by its call letters and channel

open-end transcription   a national program aired by a local station which allows room at the beginning and at the end for local advertising

outcue   the final words of a commercial spot, (often the same words for the same advertiser) that cue an on-the-air person to be ready for whatever is scheduled next

plug   an advertisement, often free, in the form of a Public Service Announcement (PSA), to promote an activity or a business

prestige copy   advertising that promotes a positive image rather than a specific product

program log   a list required by the Federal Communications Commission, summarizing the announcements, commercials, and other broadcast materials aired by a given radio station, with reference to type of program or announcement, source of material (recorded, live, or other point of origin), and classification (record, tape)

promo   promotional announcements advertising another program on the station

Public Service Announcement (PSA)   an announcement (or sometimes a longer broadcast) made without charge, in keeping with the Federal Communications Commission ruling that stations serve the public

punch   special emphasis placed on the delivery of certain words or even on an entire commercial (as opposed to a conversational tone)

ROS or **run of schedule**   an advertisement that is scheduled by the station (rather than by the sponsor); often computer scheduled

signature a piece of music played to introduce or conclude a program; sometimes called a *theme song*

sound effects (SFX) sounds to enhance a broadcast, either recorded live or made by substituting other sounds (e.g., crinkling paper to sound like cracking fire)

spec a speculation commercial used to try to attract a new advertiser

sponsor an advertiser who pays for a program in return for advertising during that program

spot a radio commercial

stand by copy used as a backup

sting to bring music in at proper level

stinger the process of bringing music in at proper level (as opposed to *fade in*)

tag information added by the announcer to the end of a commercial: the name, address, and perhaps business hours of the advertiser

up and out to increase the volume gradually to full and then fade it out

up full to raise the volume to maximum

These terms will appear in work with radio programming. If you write scripts for radio, you may find yourself dealing with them.

Process

Radio scripts require three essentials on the part of the writer: a good ear, a keen sense of brevity, and a well-developed technique for quickly gaining the listener's attention. Gaining attention amid daily distractions is no small challenge, especially as most radio listeners do not really listen: They merely want some background noise.

Try the following process to hone these three skills as we discuss the development of a typical radio script for a commercial:

PREWRITING

STEP 1. SHARPENING THE FOCUS

In planning your script, you must first decide which features to emphasize. For a 30-second spot of co-op copy, you must know what the sponsor hopes the commercial to accomplish. [*See* ADVERTISING *in Part II.*] As a writer, you are responsible for finding this out, either from the station's sales person or by your own inquiries. Does the sponsor want to advertise an upcoming sale on a particular brand of furniture? Does he pride himself on service and special orders? Free home delivery? Easy financing? Will the sale be on special-purchase inventory, overstock, or slightly damaged merchandise? Will the sale run three days or three weeks?

Focus on the commercial in two stages. First, determine its purpose. Second, list the main ideas the sponsor wants to emphasize. Consider the following example:

Purpose of commercial:

to encourage people to attend a new appliance store's open house

Main ideas to be included:
The open house will feature:
 5 door prizes valued at
  $100 each
 a grand prize valued at
  $500
 a gift for everyone who
  attends
 tours of the facility
 refreshments

Now write your own focus.

STEP 2.   PLANNING THE APPROACH

Consider the purpose of the message and how best to get the listener's ear. Since sound is your only tool, think of sounds that are attractive. Consider some of the following questions:

- Do I want a conversational tone?
- Will dramatic dialogue better serve the purpose?
- Could a dramatic or comic situation work well?
- Will background music suggest a tone or attitude that better conveys the message?
- Would other sound effects be better than music? Should the two be used together?
- Should I use a donut to capitalize on an already-familiar jingle?
- What other technique can I use to catch attention?

Try a test approach. Because success largely depends on creativity, you may need to try several before you finally decide upon one.

WRITING

STEP 3.   DEVELOPING THE SPOT

Now write the spot. Do not think about form, format, or the special techniques of scriptwriting. Just think about your message and the best means of conveying it. As you write, try some of these techniques:

- Read aloud what you have written. Let your ear tell you whether or not it works.
- Read at the pace best for the commercial, timing yourself. A normal pace is approximately 150 words a minute. If the ad calls for punch, the announcer can read at 170–180 words in a minute. Quiet conversation can be as slow as 100 words a minute. If you exceed the time limit, start cutting. [*See* REVISING: SAMPLE REVISION FOR WORDINESS, *in Part I for a sample revision which cuts excess words and ideas.*]
- Use your imagination to enhance the audio message.

REVISING

STEP 4.   POLISHING THE SPOT

Radio commercials must grab attention and convey their message in a precise time. No matter how effective the spot may be, if it is too short or too long, it is unsatisfactory. So, the first step in the revising process is to check the timing. Read the spot aloud at the desired pace and time yourself. The announcer and the director assume the final responsibility for getting the time right, but the script must set reasonable limits. Make any revisions necessary to adjust the timing

Second, since the radio commercial relies entirely on audio to convey its message, listen carefully to how the spot sounds. Ask yourself these questions:

• Is the spot appropriate to the product? That is, will the tone [*see* TONE *in the Glossary*] attract the right listener?

• Have I used good word choice? Or can I convey more precisely by replacing weak adjectives and adverbs with strong nouns and verbs?

• Are my sentences varied? Or do they sound dull and monotonous? [*See* SENTENCE STRUCTURE *in the Glossary, and see* REVISING: SAMPLE REVISION FOR SENTENCE VARIETY *in Part I.*]

• Do my sentences convey a proper emphasis? [*See* EMPHASIS, IN SENTENCES *in the Glossary, and see* REVISING: SAMPLE REVISION FOR EMPHASIS *in Part I.*]

• As commercials employ nonsentence word groups, have I used such groups effectively?

• Have I maintained accuracy? Or have I been distracted by technique?

Finally, as you work on the revision, reread your spot. Check the timing and listen with a critical ear for anything needing improvement. Radio commercials are brief: every word must be perfect. Revise carefully.

[*For more general guidelines, see* REVISING *in Part I.*]

PROOFREADING
STEP 5.   ATTENDING TO DETAILS

Once you have revised your script, you must attend to one last detail. Unlike other kinds of writing which follow traditional rules, radio scripts encourage nonstandard practices. Consider the following:

• If difficult-to-pronounce names appear, spell them phonetically so the announcer does not misread them.

• Certain words may need emphasis. Underline those words.

• Similarly, certain parts may need the emphasis lent by a pause. Indicate such pauses with a dash or series of periods. Neither mark is used traditionally, but both are suitable in scriptwriting.

• Commas may also show pauses, even where traditional rules do not call for any punctuation.

Next, read the copy for anything misleading. Be sure you spell accurately (except in the phonetic spellings indicated above) to avoid confusing the announcer. And be sure your punctuation, including the nontraditional, enhances the copy.

Finally, prepare the typed copy. Use either of the formats illustrated below, and be consistent in style. Include references to any sound effects, but do not use sound effects just to be using them. Read the copy one last time to make sure everything is accurate and that you have omitted nothing.

─────── Sample Radio Script ───────

The following script is for a 30-second, ROS commercial. The script appears in both formats to highlight differences. Compare the radio script with the drama script, above, and the television script, below. You will find significant differences. Finally, compare it with your own radio script.

Format One

(Music down and under)

Announcer: ANIMAL LOVERS LOVE "THE ANIMAL STORE." WHETHER IT'S A POODLE PUPPY—A CUDDLY KITTY—OR EVEN A FEISTY FERRET YOU WANT, "THE ANIMAL STORE" HAS IT. AND TO PUT A SONG IN YOUR LIFE, STOP BY TO HEAR THE MELODIES OF CANARIES, FINCHES, PARAKEETS, AND COCKATOOS—ALL AT "THE ANIMAL STORE"... WHILE YOU'RE THERE, STOP BY TO SAY "HELLO" TO BARNEY ... HELLO, BARNEY!

Parrot
voice: AWK, HELLO. HELLO THERE.

Announcer: NO, HE DOESN'T WANT A CRACKER—HE JUST WANTS SOMEBODY TO TAKE HIM HOME! ... "THE ANIMAL STORE"— WHERE <u>EVERY</u> ANIMAL LOVER FINDS SOMETHING TO TAKE HOME.

(Music up and out.)

Format Two

(MUSIC DOWN AND UNDER)

ANNOUNCER: Animal lovers love "The Animal Store." Whether it's a poodle puppy—a cuddly kitty—or even a feisty ferret you want, "The Animal Store" has it. And to put a song in your life, stop by to hear the melodies of canaries, finches, parakeets, and cockatoos—all at "The Animal Store". ... While you're there, stop by to say "hello" to Barney. ... Hello, Barney!

```
PARROT
VOICE:          Awk, hello. Hello there.

ANNOUNCER:      No, he doesn't want a cracker—he just wants somebody to
                take him home! ... "The Animal Store"—where every animal
                lover finds something to take home.
```

(MUSIC UP AND OUT)

Analysis of the Sample Radio Script

This commercial illustrates many typical techniques of radio scriptwriting. Note specifically the following:

- The technical terms, like *down and under* and *up and out,* tell the announcer, director, or engineer how to handle the sound effects. Note that in reality, a spot will either name a specific piece of music or else be accompanied by prerecorded music that neither violates copyright nor necessitates royalties.
- The audio directions appear in parentheses.
- The announcer's lines appear as upper-case letters in the first format and lower-case letters in the second. Both are acceptable.
- The unusual punctuation indicates pauses (three periods and dashes) or emphasizes specific words (underlining).
- The use of *Barney the Parrot* appeals personally to animal lovers. The next spot could use *Pepper the Poodle* or *Doxie the Dalmatian* to appeal to dog lovers. Advertisers use such ongoing gimmicks to identify their product or store.

The writer gives general directions; the director (or, occasionally, the announcer) adds further interpretation. The printed word is like a blueprint; the rest is artistic approach. A good radio announcer will read the above spot with significant vocal variety. While another voice may do the parrot, the announcer will assume a very personal approach as he or she asks listeners to stop by to say "hello" to Barney, a change in voice suggested by the three periods. The point is that the writer's responsibility ends with the preparation of the copy.

Now, check your own radio script against the information presented here. Make whatever revisions you find necessary to create a satisfactory product.

TELEVISION SCRIPTS

Because they must deal with both audio and video elements, television scripts have one part for each. The two-column format appears in virtually every television script, whether it be for a commercial, news broadcast, drama, or variety show.

Characteristics

Television scripts vary significantly from those for radio or for drama, even when for television drama. In general, a television script

- appears in two-column format, the video directions in the left-hand column (one-third the width of the page) and the audio script in the right-hand column (two-thirds the width of the page),
- accounts for the limitations and abilities of the television camera,
- accounts for studio limitations,
- follows a careful time structure in accordance with FCC regulations regarding the number of commercial breaks per broadcast hour,
- includes technical terms appropriate to camera work [*see those terms, listed and defined below*],
- takes a format similar to that of a radio-script [*see the* SAMPLE RADIO SCRIPT, *above*].

The following technical terms are essential for accurate video directions. Study them until they become comfortable. Without them, no television script can succeed.

angle: the position of the camera; to *angle on* a character is to position the camera so that the character is emphasized

beat: a one-second pause in a character's speech or action

clip: a short piece of film or tape integrated into the program

close shot: a camera shot that eliminates everything except the person or item on which the close shot is made

close-up or **CU:**   a camera angle that shows a person's head or head and shoulders; an extreme close-up (XCU) may show only the eyes or mouth

cut to or **cut:**   an editing direction which requires the abrupt shift from one scene to another, as opposed to *fade* or *dissolve*

dissolve or **dissolve to:**   an editing direction which has one scene fading into another so that for a very brief moment the two scenes appear simultaneously

dolly in/out: to move the camera and mount to establish a closer or more distant shot

establishing shot: a broad shot of a large area, used to help set the scene

fade in: an editing direction which requires the picture to start from black (or some other color) and gradually become a full picture

fade out: an editing direction which calls for the picture to slowly go to black

full shot: a camera angle that shows all of a person or a scene, like a yard, room, or football field

hold: to maintain a camera shot on an individual to emphasize his or her reaction or attitude

off-screen: a sound heard but whose source is not seen by the viewers

pan: to swing the camera from side to side without moving the base in order to show a broad scene; hence *pan right, pan left,* and *whip* (meaning to *pan quickly*),

super: to superimpose, placing titles, credits, or images over the picture so that both are simultaneously visible

two shot: a camera shot of two characters; thus, a *three shot* is of three characters, etc.

voice over: a voice that is heard though the speaker is not seen, especially used in newscasts and documentaries

wide angle: a camera shot made from a distance or with a wide-angle lens in order to show panoramic view

zoom in/out: to mechanically establish a closer or more distant shot by adjusting the lense of the camera.

Knowing and understanding these terms will help you direct the camera crew and make the most of their capabilities.

Process

Because television drama scripts resemble stage scripts, and television commercials resemble radio commercials, we will assume in this section

we are planning a short documentary. [*If you are preparing to write a television drama script, see also the* DRAMA SCRIPT, PREWRITING, *above. If you are preparing to write a television commercial, see the* RADIO SCRIPT, PREWRITING *above. Also refer to* ADVERTISING *in Part II.*]

Scripts for television documentaries require significant research. The short documentary we are writing here shows the basic process and peculiar techniques of the form.

PREWRITING

STEP 1. DOING THE PRELIMINARY RESEARCH

Assume you are preparing a ten-minute documentary on an aspect of your school or college, a video program to be presented to incoming freshmen. Because you are active in the forensics program, you will deal with that subject. Begin by asking the kinds of questions your viewer will be likely to ask. These questions serve as a stable guide for developing this—and most any other—documentary:

- Why is this subject important?

- If the subject is not obviously important, how can I make it interesting and appealing?

- What kinds of things would a viewer want to know about the subject? Its beginnings? Its present situation? Its future?

- How can I personalize the subject?

- Who can best explain the subject? Are certain people a must for interviews?

Do whatever reading or interviewing is necessary to develop a list of ideas to be included in your documentary. A list for the school forensics documentary might look something like this:

provides good training, no matter career choice

after-school activity

extra-curricular events good for experience

good coach/friend

general activities for a school year

specific activities of one team member

kinds of events

rewards: personal growth, friendships, scholarships, contacts in other schools

Certainly, this list is too long for a ten-minute documentary; still, too many ideas are better than too few. Stop now and make your own list. [*See also* PREWRITING *in Part I, for additional suggestions.*]

STEP 2. PLANNING THE VIDEO

Once you have completed your preliminary research, begin thinking about what kind of video elements will enhance your subject. You may ask questions like the following:

• What images will best show the aspects of the subject I hope to emphasize?

• What objects or which people should appear?

• Will I need still-life photographs to illustrate past events? If so, how can I make them look less static and more like film?

• How can I get the best action shots? Should I stage mock situations or shoot live on location?

Begin developing your list of video elements. Consider the following example for some general ideas, and then apply your creativity to your own list:

interview with speech coach

interview with award-winning debate-team members

interview with award-winning speech-team members

segments from a debate meet

segments from a dramatic interpretation event

footage from the all-school awards assembly

shots of trophies and plaques

interview with debate or speech-meet judge

interview with graduate participant

interview with novice speech-team member

segments from practice/coaching sessions

shot of team member working with coach

Obviously, this list is too long for a ten-minute documentary. However, an extensive list allows you later to choose the most suitable and successful ideas.

So, complete your list now.

As you think about the video, you may also think of new things to add to the list you wrote in Step 1. The two steps should complement each other. Revise the list you developed in Step 1.

WRITING

STEP 3. DEVELOPING THE AUDIO SCRIPT

Once you have clarified on paper what you hope to accomplish, begin to write the audio script. The following suggestions can help you get started:

- Begin with an attention-getting device. For instance, in the forensics documentary, you could show the excitement of winning a divisional speech tournament, make a startling statement about the impact of program on individual students (scholarships, friendships, career opportunities), or provide something else to gain interest. Generally, television programs must catch a viewer's attention within twenty seconds.

- Allow yourself the freedom of interviews. Although you cannot script an interview, you should write out the questions in advance. Then, once the interview has been taped, edit it to include the most useful segments. These segments, called *clips*, become part of the final script.

- Always think from the point of view of your audience. What does it want or need to know about

your subject? How can you best convey this information?

- Work for variety. If you include segments without visible action, intersperse them with activity. Obviously don't add unrelated action for its own sake. Remember, too, altering camera angles suggests action and thus creates variety.

- Conclude satisfactorily, perhaps with something dramatic, fulfilling, or futuristic. Documentaries may point to an upcoming event or end with a summary. Sometimes a statement of impact or potential works best.

- Time your script carefully, to the second. Additional editing may be required to keep the program within the limit. Live programming, which cannot be edited, requires not only careful scriptwriting but also superb on-the-air talent who can adjust their performance on the spot. Because of these demands, very little television programming is live.

STEP 4. ADDING THE VIDEO

Once you have completed the audio script, turn to the video. Plan camera shots to best illustrate your topic. Rely on your creativity to develop video which really tells the story. (Watching televised programs similar to your own will give you additional ideas.) Specify the kind of camera work you want, using the right terminology.

REVISING

STEP 5.   CHECKING THE SCRIPT

Once your own program is fully planned, put the script in proper format. Use this simple guide:

- Draw a line, vertically, down the middle of a standard 8–1/2″ × 11″ sheet of paper; leave one-third of the space on the left and two-thirds on the right.

- Label the left hand column *Video* and the right *Audio*.

- Enter the talent identification (*narrator, interviewee,* etc.) and the narration or dialogue in the right-hand column.

- Include sound effects in the audio column.

- Give appropriate camera directions in the video column alongside their corresponding narration or dialogue. Note: *Where* you place the camera directions in the video column determines *when* the directions will be executed. As a rule of thumb, camera shots should change every twenty or thirty seconds. But creativity means that rules may be broken, for a purpose. Keep your purpose in mind.

PROOFREADING

STEP 6.   CHECKING THE DETAILS

Once the script is complete, reread it for accuracy. Ask yourself the following questions:

- Have I made typing errors which will confuse the technical director or on-the-air talent?

- Are words spelled accurately? Consult *Webster's New World Dictionary* to check.

- Have I included phonetic spellings for difficult words?

- Is the script free from grammatical and usage errors?

- Finally, is it easy to read, both for the on-the-air the talent and the technical director who must oversee the camera work? *Hint*: Never continue a sentence from one page to the next. It can cause the on-the-air talent to misread the script.

Polish your script using these questions.

Sample Television Script

The following sample represents a portion of a full-length script. It shows most of the significant characteristics of the genre.

Speech: Another Shawnee Team

Video	Audio
OPEN WITH FILM CLIP OF TEAM RECEIVING TROPHY AT AWARDS ASSEMBLY	NARRATOR (VOICE OVER): And the team with the most points, for first place in the divisional speech tournament ... Shawnee Senior High School!
CLOSE SHOT OF STUDENT WITH TROPHY	(APPLAUSE; CHEERS; 6 SECONDS)
CUT TO CLOSE SHOT OF TEAM PRESIDENT ZOOM IN TO CLOSE-UP	STUDENT TEAM MEMBER: Hi! Welcome to Shawnee. I'm Robin Oaks, president of the Shawnee Senior High Forensics Team. We love winning, but more than that, we love the challenge, the preparation, and the stimulation of good competition!
CUT TO MALE AND FEMALE WALKING HAND-IN-HAND DISSOLVE TO BOY LEANING AGAINST DOOR, BACK TO CAMERA	Every one of us has gained new friends in area schools and some of the friends have become ... really good ones! Sure, we work hard, practice a lot, and (SLOWLY) sometimes we even loose. But doesn't everyone, at least sometimes?
CUT TO NARRATOR	NARRATOR: You've heard the adage that it's not whether you win or lose, but how you play the game that counts. Maybe that's the best way to describe the Shawnee
CUT TO GROUP SHOT OF TEAM	forensics team. The kids on this team specialize in their best areas, some in dramatic interpretation ...

CUT TO CLOSE-UP OF STUDENT TWO AND MOVE TO TIGHT CLOSE-UP	STUDENT TWO (PRESENTING A DRAMATIC INTERPRETATION): ... Don't make me lie to you. Just don't ask questions, please. You've got to trust me, have faith that I'll make the right decision. Please ...
SLOW DISSOLVE TO FOUR DEBATE TEAM MEMBERS	NARRATOR (VOICE OVER): ... And other students excel in debate, pitting their logic, research, and wit against one another.
ZOOM IN SLOWLY TO CLOSE-UP OF STUDENT THREE	STUDENT THREE: ... And so my worthy opponents have left us little choice but to question the feasibility of such a radical, untried plan. Certainly, you must agree with the negative that the status quo will be financially more reasonable than the economically disastrous plan we've heard here today.
CUT TO ESTABLISH-ING SHOT OF NARRATOR AND COACH	NARRATOR: Dramatic interpretation, debate, and what else? Just what is forensics, Miss Calloway? You've coached the team to victory for the past three years. Tell us about this whole idea of forensics.
ZOOM IN TO CLOSE SHOT OF COACH	COACH: Forensics refers to debate or argumentation, but as we define it for national competition, it includes about a dozen kinds of speech activities—radio announcing, debate, comedy, original oratory, extemporaneous speaking—you name it and we probably do it.

CUT TO CLOSE SHOT OF NARRATOR	NARRATOR: How do students get involved in forensics?
DOLLY BACK TO TWO SHOT OF COACH AND NARRATOR	COACH: During a sign-up period early in the school year, we accept any student willing to work. We select areas most suitable to individual students and then begin gathering materials. We do
CUT TO FILM CLIP OF STUDENT WORKING WITH COACH	individual work with my working closely with the students until they are ready for the first team practice ...

Analysis of the Sample Television Script

The sample illustrates the characteristics which make television scripts so different from dramatic or radio scripts. Note, in particular, these details:

- The script includes two distinct portions, a *Video* portion on the left and an *Audio* portion on the right.

- The Video column gives specific directions in accurate technical terms printed upper-case.

- The Audio column, as in a radio script, includes narration and dialogue— here in lower-case letters, with speaker identification and directions in upper-case.

- The camera shots provide variety for the viewer and, at the same time, enhance the content and message of the audio portion.

Television probably offers the largest outlet for creative scriptwriting today. The rudiments included here will establish a general direction for your work. But serious students of television production recognize the extensive work— practice and analysis—needed to learn scriptwriting. As cameras and technical equipment become more sophisticated, the writer's options increase proportionately. The guidelines above should help you begin to explore scriptwriting.

SHORT ANSWERS

Short-answer responses are often required on tests and job, scholarship, and college aplications. Sometimes we are asked for a *brief response, short definition,* or *list*. All are short answers. All require careful thought. A writer who jots down whatever comes to mind first may omit important, even critical, ideas. Thus, short-answers, whether to tests or requests-for-information, take planning and care, perhaps even more than do longer essays.

Although you may face the need for a variety of short-answer responses, most begin with phrases like *briefly explain, summarize the main points, list the general characteristics, define the main issues, state in a single paragraph, outline the principles,* or *give a brief review*. In most cases, you are expected to provide a brief response, definition, or list. We will examine each of these three in turn.

BRIEF RESPONSES

Brief responses can rely on virtually any method of development: analogy, cause and effect, classification, comparison and contrast, definition, narration, opinion, or process analysis. [*See entries for each elsewhere in Part II.*] They differ from more typical pieces of expository writing, however, in purpose. The reader wants highlights, not details.

Characteristics

Brief responses generally

- run no longer than a short paragraph,
- limit themselves to main ideas, avoiding supporting details,
- follow a logical organization to clarify the relationship of main ideas,
- rely on strong nouns and verbs, avoiding weak and generally wordy modifiers,

- demand specificity [*see* SPECIFIC DETAIL *in the Glossary*],
- focus on the requested information, omitting unrelated matters.

Process

Developing a brief response takes careful planning, concise writing, and critical revision. Frequently in test situations these steps must occur within strict time limits, so planning becomes essential.

PREWRITING

STEP 1.   ANALYZING THE QUESTION

Before you begin writing, be sure you understand what to include. Look for clue words in the question or statement. The following are typical clue words:

> **summarize** (give the main ideas)
>
> **outline** (give the main ideas and show their relationships)
>
> **explain briefly** (make clear)
>
> **give reasons** (show why)
>
> **complete the sentence** (finish the idea)
>
> **when** (give date, historical period, or other time relationship)
>
> **why** (give reasons)
>
> **how** (explain the steps or stages)
>
> **where** (give place)
>
> **who** (identify person by name or position)
>
> **what** (name the items)

STEP 2.   PLANNING YOUR ANSWER

Brief responses of a word, phrase, or sentence need little planning; brief responses of several sentences take more.

In responding to a test question, use this quick line of questioning:

- What are the key ideas? Write them in a list.

- In what order should they be presented? Place them in order.

- Is anything essential omitted? If so, what?

In completing an application, use the guiding questions above as well as the following ones:

- Why is this question on the application? What is the reader trying to learn about me?

- Are my ideas important to the reader or just to me?

- As I respond, how can I show myself in the most favorable light?

As you develop your short-answer response for an application, you may have difficulty being objective about yourself, being either too modest or too complimentary. Take every opportunity to discuss your list with someone you trust. Your friend may have an insight into a qualification or characteristic you have overlooked.

WRITING

STEP 3.   COMPLETING THE BRIEF RESPONSE

As you list your answers to the questions above and turn them into a written response, keep in mind these suggestions:

- Reread the question or request for information to make sure you have not strayed from your purpose. [*See* REVISING: SAMPLE REVISION FOR UNITY *in Part I.*]

- The amount of space provided for for your response may be misleading. Use the space you need to give an accurate response, no more and no less.

- Be concise. Avoid wordy, rambling explanations. [*See* REVISING: SAMPLE REVISION FOR WORDINESS *in Part I.*]

- Use complete sentences unless otherwise directed.

- In a test situation, allot yourself a specific amount of time to complete the response. Then stick to the schedule. [*See also* ESSAY-QUESTION RESPONSES: TEST QUESTIONS *in Part II for an illustration of planning time allotments.*]

REVISING

STEP 4.   CHECKING THE FOCUS

In tests the only revision you can afford is to check for focus. Reread the question or statement, thinking in terms of your response. Did you respond directly to the question or statement? Did you respond to every part of it?

On an application you have time for careful revision; indeed, the reader expects polished work. Write your first draft on scratch paper, revise it, and enter the final draft on the application form.

The revision process for an application should deal with these possible weaknesses:

- Have I responded directly to the question or statement?

- Have I put myself in the most positive light without being inaccurate?

- Does my sentence structure reflect my personal maturity? [*See* SENTENCE STRUCTURE *in the Glossary, and see* REVISING: SAMPLE REVISION FOR SENTENCE VARIETY *in Part I.*]

- Does my writing reflect my skill with the language? [*See* REVISING: SAMPLE REVISION FOR EMPHASIS *in Part I.*]

- Is the vocabulary appropriate to my purpose?

- Have I focused on the aspects most important to the reader?

PROOFREADING

STEP 5.   CHECKING FOR MECHANICS

Before you hand in a test paper, reread it for spelling, grammar, usage, and mechanics. If you are permitted, use your dictionary to check questionable items.

On an application, take extreme care with your proofreading, perhaps even asking a friend to check your work, too. Use *Webster's New World Dictionary* to confirm accurate spelling and *Webster's New World Thesaurus* to verify accurate word choice. [*The Glossary will also help you with the technical aspects of writing.*]

Sample Brief Response

The following sample typifies the sort of brief responses called for by scholarship and college applications.

Question

Why do you want to attend Middletown College?

Response

Because Middletown College offers a nationally recognized equestrian program, I look forward to completing my associate degree there. Our family business involves breeding, training, and showing horses as well as retailing trappings. As a result, my already deep personal involvement in my career has prepared me for the rigors of the curriculum.

Analysis of the Sample Brief Response

The sample illustrates ways the writer can say things without really saying them. Consider these techniques:

- The writer compliments the college by acknowledging it is *nationally recognized*.

- He indicates a two-year stay at the college, to complete *my associate degree.* At the same time, he emphasizes his intent to fulfill requirements.

- He refers to a family business to stress his personal involvement in what the school offers.

- He clarifies that the curriculum requires hard work and emphasizes he is prepared to complete that work.

As a result of this writer's brief response, the college personnel will see certain characteristics they like. They want a student who plans to finish a degree, who comes to work not to play, who is motivated, and who shows maturity and a sense of direction. This writer's brief response shows all those characteristics.

DEFINITIONS

You will find an entire section on definition papers earlier in Part II [*see* DEFINITION]. Short-answer definitions contain certain specific characteristics that are quite unlike those of a full-length essay.

Characteristics

Short-answer definitions usually

- identify the term to be defined,
- identify the class to which this term belongs,
- contrast the term with all others in its class,
- give this information in one sentence.

Process

In order to develop a definition, use the following process.

PREWRITING

STEP 1.   IDENTIFYING THE CLASS AND THE DIFFERENCES

If asked to define a given term, you must first decide to what larger group, or class, the term belongs. Next you must show how the term differs from others in its class. Consider the following:

Term to be defined:
simile

Class:
figure of speech

Difference:

compares one thing to another, using *like* or *as*

In other words, the term *simile* belongs to the larger class called *figures of speech*. It is different from other figures of speech in that it *compares one thing to another using "like" or "as."*

WRITING

STEP 2.   PUTTING THE DEFINITION INTO A SINGLE SENTENCE

Once you have established the class and difference, the rest is simple. Combine the ideas in a sentence, in this order:

1. term to be defined
2. class to which it belongs
3. difference between the term and others in the class

Example:

A simile (*term*) is a figure of speech (*class*) which compares one thing to another using *like* or *as* (*difference*).

REVISING AND PROOFREADING

STEP 3.   CHECKING MECHANICAL DETAILS

Once you have completed your definition, make sure you have included all three parts, in order, and that you have used accurate spelling, grammar, mechanics, and usage.

——————— **Samples of Short Answer Definitions** ———————

The following definitions can serve as examples for your own work.

A lien is a claim on the property of another as security for the payment of a debt.

An armadillo is a burrowing mammal of Texas and Central and South America that has an armorlike covering of bony plates over its body.

A bulkhead is an upright partition dividing a ship or airplane into compartments to protect against the spread of fire or water in case of an accident.

Analysis of the Sample Definitions

The definitions above follow the pattern suggested. Each begins with a term and continues by giving the class identification. The remainder of the sentence contrasts the term with others in its class. Note the precision used:

Term	Class	Difference
lien	claim on property	as security for the payment of a debt
armadillo	burrowing mammal	has an armorlike covering of bony plates
bulkhead	upright partition	dividing a ship or airplane into compartments to protect against the spread of fire or water in case of an accident

This format guarantees precise and accurate definitions of virtually any term. [*If you need more than a short-answer definition, see* DEFINITION *earlier in Part II.*]

LISTS

While lists may seem easy to develop, too many students write them as mere groups of items. Lists which serve as short answers on tests and applications should reflect thought and show some sense of organization.

Characteristics

While lists may be either a series of words or of phrases, carefully composed lists

- maintain parallel structure [*see* PARALLEL STRUCTURE *in the Glossary*],

- show evidence of logical order [*see* CHRONOLOGICAL ORDER, SPATIAL ORDER, *or* ORDERS OF IMPORTANCE *in the Glossary*],

- omit unrelated, extraneous items.

Process

In order to develop a list, use these simple steps.

PREWRITING

STEP 1.   ANALYZING THE REQUEST FOR INFORMATION

What does the question or statement really require from you? Look for clue words. Are you asked to list *the most important facts, the most significant events,* or *the most influential activities?* Or are you asked to list *the activites,* meaning, virtually *all* the activities? Be sure you know what is expected.

WRITING

STEP 2.   DEVELOPING THE LIST

As you write, think about these questions:

For a Test

- Is the instructor looking for key words or phrases?
- What is the most logical order in which to list the key items? Chronological? Spatial? An order of importance?

For an Application

- What is the reader hoping to learn about me? Am I including items which best reflect my personal characteristics and abilities?
- Have I arranged items in a logical order (e.g., in an order of importance, with the most important first)?

For Both

- Is my list complete?

REVISING AND PROOFREADING

STEP 3.   CHECKING THE LIST

Certainly a list leaves little room for grammar, usage, and mechanical problems. You will still want to check spelling and word choice. See

Webster's New World Dictionary and *Webster's New World Thesaurus* for help in these areas.

Punctuation usually causes some problems in lists written horizontally. Use commas to separate items, unless the items require internal commas. In that case, use semicolons.

In addition, check your list for logical arrangement. Remember, on an application you should list the most important items first, unless instructed otherwise. For other short-answer responses, use the organization most appropriate.

Sample List

The following request for information resulted in the list below:

Request Item

List your extracurricular activities. Indicate the number of years in which you participated in each.

Response List

Student Council, president 2 years; Mayor's Youth Council, 1 year; National Forensics League, debate team and individual categories, 3 years; Computer Club, 1 year; library assistant, 2 years; office assistant, 2 years; usher for auditorium events, 2 years.

Analysis of the Sample List

The list includes several details worthy of special attention:

- The writer shows his attitude toward his various activities. He sees his two-year stint as president of the Student Council as more important than his year with the Mayor's Youth Council. Likewise, he seems to think his library assistantship more important than his work in the office.
- Items are separated by semicolons because commas appear within most of them.
- The period denotes not the end of a sentence but the completion of the list.

Using the guidelines, model, and analysis above, you should be able to develop lists which not only show your knowledge, characteristics, or abilities, but also your recognition of their relative importance. Taking care with lists shows far more responsibility and maturity than providing hodgepodges arranged in the order in which items were remembered.

Whether it be a brief response, a definition, or a list, effective short answers can improve your standing with your instructor, potential employer or school.

SHORT STORY

Whole books have been written to explain how to write short stories. As an imaginative literary form, the short story varies as much as its authors.

In the most simplified description, a short story has a beginning, middle, and end. The characters meet and somehow resolve a conflict, thereby permitting the author to convey a message (otherwise called a *theme*). Learning to develop the art form includes two steps, one simple, the other a lifelong effort. First, the potential short-story writer must learn the elements of the form. That is the easy part. Then, he must practice combining those elements until his skills are as finely honed as those of E. A. Poe or O. Henry. That is the lifelong part.

Characteristics

The short story has certain general characteristics. Although the approach to and interaction with these characteristics is the stuff by which short stories vary, certain elementary techniques will help a beginning writer develop a story. A short story, in general, should

- follow a consistent point of view [*see* POINT OF VIEW *in the Glossary*],
- develop believable characters with whom the reader can identify and whose motives the reader can understand,
- be placed in a setting consistent with the characters' personalities,
- develop a plot that includes conflict, rising action, climax, and resolution [*see* CONFLICT, RISING ACTION, CLIMAX, *and* RESOLUTION *in the Glossary*],
- contain a theme, or message, for the reader [*see* THEME *in the Glossary*],

- show, rather than tell, about characters, themes, and conflicts [*see* NARRATION *in Part II*],
- present concise, specific description [*see* DESCRIPTION *in Part II and* SPECIFIC DETAIL *in the Glossary*],
- include appropriate imaginative language and imagery [*see* FIGURES OF SPEECH *and* IMAGERY *in the Glossary*],
- employ other literary devices as appropriate: flashbacks, symbolism, foreshadowing [*see* FLASHBACK, SYMBOL, *and* FORESHADOWING *in the Glossary*],
- use dialogue appropriate for the characters [*see* DIALOGUE *earlier in Part II*],
- maintain a consistent tone and mood [*see* TONE *and* MOOD *in the Glossary*],
- be of appropriate length, from 200 to 10,000 words, but most likely 1,500 to 3,500,
- have each character, action, and word lead to a single end.

Process

Developing the short story takes careful thought and planning. Not every writer works the same way. Some begin with plot and create characters to fill it. Others start by inventing characters and letting them interact; the plot grows from this interaction. Most writers, however, follow a kind of yo-yo process, changing characters as plot develops and altering scenes to improve characterization. No matter which process serves you best, you must reach a certain point in the prewriting stage before you begin to put words on paper. At that point, you should be able to put the specifics in this sentence:

My fully developed characters will interact in these ways in order to achieve this resolution so that the reader will get this message.

In order to arrive at that point, you must thoroughly prepare. Try the following steps.

PREWRITING

STEP 1.   DETERMINING THE THEME

Before you can plan specific incidents in the story line, you must know what message you hope to convey. By setting characters against each other, what do you hope to tell the reader? Too early to know, you say? No! If you have no message, you have no story. You cannot reach your destination without a sense of direction. So stop now and write a sentence which expresses the message you hope to leave with the reader. Consider the following:

Living by one's principles requires sacrifice.

A winning attitude helps people climb the business ladder.

Winning isn't important; it's how you play the game.

Treat the land with respect and you will reap the rewards.

STEP 2.   OUTLINING THE PLOT

Once you have a clear message, decide what conflict your characters will face to illustrate it.

Notice that you will not *state* the message in the story; your characters and plot must *reveal* the message. Begin by making a list:

- What events lead to the conflict?
- What initial conflict do they encounter?
- What are its results?
- How do the results build to additional, more complicated conflicts? In other words, what is the rising action? [*See* RISING ACTION *in the Glossary.*]
- What brings events to a crisis? [*See* CRISIS *in the Glossary.*]
- What is the crisis?
- What happens as a result of the crisis? In other words, what is the climax? [*See* CLIMAX *in the Glossary.*]
- What is the end result? Do the characters change? If so, what makes them change? Personal re-

alization? The influence of other characters? In other words, what is the resolution? [*See* RESOLUTION *in the Glossary.*]

By answering these questions, you will outline the plot of your story.

STEP 3. DEVELOPING THE CHARACTERS

Believable, motivated characters make or break a story. If the reader cannot understand or accept them, nothing else you do matters.

Before you begin writing, then, sketch each of your characters. [*See* CHARACTER SKETCH *and* NARRATION *elsewhere in Part II.*] Use the following guidelines:

• What does the character look like?

• What is the character's background? Family? Education? Business experience? Home life?

• What kind of surrounding does he or she like? Plush furniture? Luxury apartment? Bare walls? Rustic cabin? Disheveled office? Open water? Northern forest?

• What does the character think about? How does he or she react emotionally to frustrating situations? What does he or she value in life?

• How does he or she behave, move, respond?

• What does he or she sound like in speaking? What kind of vocabulary does he or she use?

• How do others react to the character? Do they all see the character in the same way? Does the character

see himself or herself the way others do?

Now do one last thing. Look critically at your answers. Do your characters portray consistent, realistic behavior? Are their reactions a natural outgrowth of their backgrounds? Do their surroundings support their values? If not, do you have logical motives for uncharacteristic behavior? Will the reader accept those motives? Or do you need to alter the characters?

Few of your responses to these questions will actually appear in your story, since they are not related to your message directly. But by answering them you will force yourself to examine each character in turn, the only way to develop consistent, believable characters.

STEP 4. ESTABLISHING THE SETTING

By now you probably have a fairly good idea of where the story should take place. Jot down a brief description of the setting, mere notes to yourself. Picture it in your mind's eye listing as many details as you can. Imagine how it feels, smells, and sounds, not just how it looks. [*See* DESCRIPTION *and* NARRATION *earlier in Part II.*]

STEP 5. SELECTING POINT OF VIEW

The reader identifies with the point of view from which the story is told, so how you tell things determines message. The cliche, ''There are two sides to every story,'' is accurate only so far as it goes: there are as many sides as there are people involved. Even someone outside the conflict will have a perspective from which to relate the tale, though one which necessarily omits the personal reactions of the participants, which he or she has no way of knowing.

The story writer may select among three points of view. Consider each before choosing one for your own story.

Omniscient Point of View: The all-knowing, all-seeing point of view almost always represents the author as such. Only the author knows, sees, and understands all. Only he or she can tell what every character thinks and feels. For example:

> Jerod and Krista stood contemplating the stack of sales records to be compiled before they could call it quits for the day. Neither wanted to work late; that was understandable. But Jerod liked to ease back and let Krista assume the real burden. He hoped she'd make quick work of it tonight. Little did he know that Krista resented his mere presence.
>
> "Lazy rat," she thought. "He doesn't even know how to enter the basic data." Her stomach growled.

First Person Point of View: This uses *I, me, my,* and *our.* The first-person permits the author to tell the story from the point of view of a character, major or minor. Only those feelings, observations, and reactions which the character experi-

ences appear in the story. For example:

> I stood there contemplating the stack of sales records to be compiled before we could call it quits for the day. I just wanted to go home, be with the kids, watch the ball game.
>
> I hesitated. "Well, Krista," I began, hoping she wouldn't be her usual grouchy self, "What do you want me to do first?"
>
> She frowned. "Why don't you sort the reports by department code?"
>
> She sounded cross. I thought I heard her stomach growl. I guessed she must be hungry.

Third Person Point of View: The third person uses *he, she, they, them,* and *their,* as well as people's names. The author tells the story, but he or she is more removed from the story than in the omniscient point of view. In fact, the story is told from only one character's point of view, describing only what that character can observe. For example:

> She stood there, contemplating the stack of sales records they had to compile before they could call it quits for the day. She just wanted to go home, have a quiet dinner with Tom, and curl up with a good book. She looked at Jerod.
>
> "Lazy rat," she thought, "he doesn't even know how to enter the basic data."
>
> "So what do you want me to do first," he asked. Krista thought he sounded almost willing to

help. She hesitated, looked at him again, frowning, unsure why he seemed so helpful.

"Why don't you sort the reports by department code?" she suggested. Silently she added, "And we'll see if you have any idea what you're doing."

Select the point of view which will best allow you to tell your story, reveal your characters, and convey your message. Maintain a consistent point of view throughout.

WRITING

STEP 6.   PUTTING THE STORY TOGETHER

Now you have a plot line and characters. You have placed them in a setting. You have selected a point of view. You are ready to write. As you begin, you may want to think about some of the following techniques:

- Dialogue adds life to characters. Allowing the reader to eavesdrop grants insight into your characters' thoughts, reactions, observations, and emotions.

- Showing, rather than telling, makes for a superior story. Allow the reader to discover your characters and their conflicts. [*See* DESCRIPTION *and* NARRATION *in Part II.*]

- Paragraphing in short stories bears no similarities to paragraphing in expository writing. [*See* PARAGRAPHS, KINDS: IN DIALOGUE *in Part II for additional explanation.*]

- Sentence structure should vary with character and action. [*See* EMPHASIS *in the Glossary for additional explanation. See also* REVISING: SAMPLE REVISION FOR SENTENCE VARIETY *and* REVISING: SAMPLE REVISION FOR EMPHASIS *in Part I.*]

- Description should be specific and concrete. [*See* DESCRIPTION *in Part II for additional help. Also see* SPECIFIC DETAIL *in the Glossary.*]

Writing is the tough part. Keep at it until you are done. Remember, you will be making revisions later, so aim now only for completion.

REVISING

STEP 7.   POLISHING THE STORY

Once you have completed your story, you can begin to look for weaknesses. Try these questions:

- Have I avoided simply telling my reader about characters, motives, reactions? Instead, did I show these?

- Are my characters believable? Are their actions apt? Are their motives clear?

- Is the setting suitable?

- Does the conflict seem likely or contrived?

- Did I select the most appropriate point of view?

- Have I maintained a consistent point of view?

- Does the resolution grow naturally out of the conflict?

- Have I used effective sentence structure?

- Are my paragraphs appropriate to a short story?

- Are my descriptions specific rather than flowery?

- Have I included any of the finer points of literature: figurative language, imagery, foreshadowing, flashback, symbolism, etc?

- Is my message clear? Have I avoided merely stating the message, making it, instead, evident through the action and resolution of the story?

- Have I selected an appropriate title that suggests some important element of the story?

Revise your story as many times as necessary to make it smooth, readable, and believable.

PROOFREADING

STEP 8. POLISHING THE FINAL DRAFT

No matter how "creative" you think your story may be, do not be creative with the standards of language. Characters may speak incorrectly to illustrate their lack of education, but your own writing must be accurate. [*See also* REVISING *and* PROOFREADING *in Part I for guidelines.*]

Next check word choice. Can you improve a description or enhance a character with a better word? Check *Webster's New World Thesaurus* and *Webster's New World Dictionary* for the most precise word for your purpose. Finally, check the spelling.

The process above should give you a running start in the development of your own short story. Before you complete your work, however, study the following model and its analysis.

Sample Short Story

The following story serves as a model in which we can see many of the ideas listed above.

Spud

Emile looked up at the clock. Almost two. He was going to be late. After creeping down the broken stairs, he ducked into the kitchen, sneaked a potato from the burlap bag beneath the sink, and slipped out the side door into the alley. He ran between the crumbling buildings to an abandoned lot where the neighbor boys, lined up with their backs to the wind, were building a fire. They yelled at him across the field to hurry and to pick up some broken lumber for the fire along the way.

"Got your spud?" asked Melby.

"Yeah!"

"Throw 'er in."

They all tried their best to sneak away on Saturday afternoons with a potato or two. Then they sat around the hissing flames for an hour, discussing the cusses Mrs. Yakov had yelled down at her husband from their apartment window, or where Felix had been while he hookied, or who they thought Mrs. Brubaker was going to flunk in spelling, until the potatoes were thoroughly baked beneath the embers.

"Dibs on ya!" Emile yelled, as Melby accidentally uncovered his potato with his poking stick.

"No more dibs!" Melby yelled back, lest anyone else lay claim to a portion of his spud.

Every boy prepared to remove his potato as slyly as possible, scraping around in the coals to find them. Emile had this game all worked out. Instead of scraping the embers, he gently poked them, lowering the risk of accidentally exposing his spud as Melby had. Feeling the tip strike the spud's charred shell, he sidled it underneath and violently flipped the potato out of the fire with an accompanying rain of cinder and smoke that made his companion's eyes water.

"No dibs, no hunks!" he shouted while the potato was still in midair. Then he sat down to his meal.

In school, Mrs. Brubaker wrote long lists of words on the board while the class stared at the clock and yawned. Emile doodled in his spelling book. When Mrs. Brubaker turned around, the rest of the class straightened up, pretending to be awake, but Emile kept on doodling.

"Emile Gallois!"

He jerked upright. "Yes, Ma'am!" and fixed his gaze on the reflections in her spectacles. All at once, her face shifted and buckled, falling into a mosaic of angles and distortion. He averted his eyes.

"Look at me when I'm talking to you!"

Thankfully, the image had disappeared. "Yes, Ma'am."

"Spell 'attentive.' "

"A-t-t-e-n-t-i-v-e."

"Very good. Now be attentive."

She turned back to the board and Emile turned back to his doodles. He drew her face as it had seemed, slipping her nose across the side of her cheek; skewing her eyes one way, her wire-rimmed spectacles the other; rolling her scalp forward and her right ear around until all sides of her head appeared superimposed on the flat surface of the page. He drew back to examine the drawing and slapped the book shut.

That weekend, he sneaked a potato as usual, but he didn't go to the field. He tiptoed back up to his room and flipped to the doodled page of his spelling book. With his rusty pocket knife, he began carving Mrs. Brubaker's head. He remembered the reflections in her eye-glasses and expanded them, projecting the ceiling beams into her brow, the ceiling panels onto her forehead, mixing the foliage of the window plants with the curl of hair about her ear, until her whole face was filled with foreign objects. Then he drizzled water color not too carefully onto her various parts—red on her brow, blue on her forehead, green on her lips—but left the majority of her surface to the yellow pallor of drying potato flesh. In the corner of his bottom drawer he nestled it—the first.

In homeroom Monday morning, Melby approached.

"Where were you?"

"Huh?"

"Saturday?"

"I didn't feel well."

"What?"

"I was sick."

"SO. What'd you do, draw all day? You should have come."

"My mom wouldn't let me."

"Well, are you gonna play ball after school, or what?"

"Yeah, I'll be there."

"Good. Four o'clock."

At lunchtime, Emile picked at the peanut butter sandwich his mother had packed for him, and he ended up throwing it all in the trash. His stomach bothered him throughout the rest of the afternoon, and several times he was reprimanded for inattentiveness. His mind tossed about, settling momentarily on the shadowy image of a rugby ball, or Melby's ruddy face, or Mrs. Brubaker's carved head. He tried to concentrate, but succeeded only in sending a pile of half-formed images recoiling through the grey.

On the way to his last class, Emile stopped to heave up yellow stomach bile into the bathroom sink, then proceeded straight to his classroom desk where he laid his head. Did he want to go home? No. Or lie down in the cloak room? No. He didn't stir until the bell rang the close of school. Then he lifted himself up and began the walk home.

On the edge of a run-down park, a rotten limb had fallen, and Emile stopped to examine its shattered length. He pulled free a short, fat segment near the base and chipped at its surface with his thumbnail. It was soft, but not yet rotting. Just then, Melby accosted him from the other side of the street.

"You're coming, right?"

"Yeah." He tucked the chunk of wood beneath his arm and continued on, parallel to Melby, but never glancing over or saying a word. At the end of the street, they turned in opposite directions, each proceeding down his own alley.

Emile walked through the empty house up to his bedroom and stuck the chunk of wood in his drawer. After changing into a dirty sweater, he returned downstairs, nibbled at a piece of biscuit, and started for the lot. Several others were already there, including Melby.

"Hurry up, Emile!" he shouted. "You and me are gonna be captains!"

After a half dozen more neighborhood kids had straggled in, the boys chose up sides and started the game.

It was a friendly game—tackle of course, but not too hard, especially since the lot was strewn with gravel and wood debris. Emile, however, felt Melby was getting a little overzealous.

"Cool it," he told him.

The next play, Emile was passed the ball, and darting a glance to his left, he saw Melby fast approaching. Emile dished off the ball, but Melby didn't stop running, smothering Emile in his sweater as they rolled onto the ground. Emile didn't say a word, but the next play, he went straight for Melby, put his fist into his chest, grabbed his arm, and flung him to the ground. Melby skidded across the gravel on his stomach and then lay still, moaning. Everybody stopped where they stood and gaped. The ball wobbled unnoticed into the street. Emile smiled and pretended like he had done it in sport, but when he saw Melby's nose bleeding, he backed up a few steps, turned, and ran home.

He mounted the steps to his room and, curling into a ball, buried his head beneath his pillow. The images returned—the rugby ball, Melby, Mrs. Brubaker. He remembered the chunk of wood he had in his drawer, and pulling out his pocket knife, his hands went to work on it. He knew what he was carving, but he didn't let himself think about it, concentrating instead on the minuteness of the wood grain. The features began to pronounce themselves—a high, square forehead, a pair of dimpled cheeks, a broad flaring chin—and slowly, the hard lines melted into a point between the eyes . . . where his blade came to a knot. He sawed at it with the blade's edge, bored at it with the tip, but the knot was like steel. In desperation, he gouged his blade beneath its edge in an effort to pry it out, but its roots ran deep, and the whole left side of the face splintered away. Underneath, invisible fungi were slowly eating their way outward, rendering the wood useless. A single saline drop splashed onto the rotten vein of wood as he walked to the window. Leaning over the window ledge, he let the half-carved head drop from his hands onto the cobblestones below. One by one, the stars awoke to a quiet street, where a young boy stared down at the scattered pieces of a chunk of wood.

Analysis of the Sample Short Story

This story includes all the essentials of the form. Note these details:

- The title suggests the significance of the potato, not only to the circle of boys who roast them but to Emile, who applies his artistic talents to it.

- The writer never says where the story takes place. The multi-ethnic names (*Yakov, Gallois,* and *Brubaker*) suggest a large city. References to an alley, crumbling buildings, and an abandoned lot suggest a poor neighborhood. The boys' first names (*Melby* and *Felix*) suggest the 1930's or 1940's.

- The only developed character is Emile. Melby, the antagonist, represents the boys in general, boys who cannot understand Emile's interest in art.

- The reader is not told about characters; the reader sees them in action—hears them, watches them interact.

- The result is consistent, believable characters.

- The dialogue is realistic. It includes grammatical errors and sentence fragments. Brevity, candor, and idioms all add to character development.

- The writer consistently uses a third-person point of view (in this case, Emile's).

- Two conflicts emerge from the story, the first within Emile, the second, between Emile and Melby. The inner conflict is undoubtedly the greater. Emile, whose artistic nature differentiates him from his schoolmates, must choose either to remain "one of the guys" or to develop his talent. Developing his talent brings ridicule, but remaining one of the guys results in internal frustration, even illness. Emile's attempt to integrate the two, by carving a realistic sculpture of Melby, fails. His is a talent requiring external and internal abstraction. He realizes his failure. The story concludes with Emile facing a choice between the two ways of life.

- The Picasso-like faces that emerge from his spelling book and the potato contrast with the realistic wooden carving he attempts.

- The story plot can be outlined as follows:

- ○ Emile realizes he is different, draws Mrs. Brubaker in his spelling book.
- ○ He experiments with the art, shirks his friends to carve the potato.
- ○ He tries to go back to his old way of life, plays football. The effort brings frustration.
- ○ He tries to integrate the two lives, carves the realistic wooden head. His effort fails.
- ○ He realizes his failure, drops the carving out the window.
- ○ He contemplates the choice, stares down at the scattered wood.

- The crisis occurs when Emile bloodies Melby's nose. The physical battle parallels Emile's inner conflict.

- Once the carving splinters (as a result of the fungus, which signifies, too, the rotting friendship between Emile and Melby), the climax leads quickly to the resolution. Emile realizes (as shown by his crying and his dropping of the carving) that he must choose between his friends and the life of an artist.

- By the end of the story, the potato has become symbolic. It carries Emile from childhood to the pain of self-discovery, from the roasting fire to the secret carving; from physical to spiritual value, from food to art. The potato now symbolizes Emile's growth.

- A message develops from Emile's actions: Often, those who deal with creative processes must choose between their buddies and their art. The choice is never painless.

- Thus, the imagery and figurative language are assets to the story.

- The plain sentence structure shows good variety and adds emphasis.

- The punctuation is accurate.

- The paragraphing is appropriate for dialogue.

- The description is concise, the narrative effective. Specific details show, rather than tell about, Emile's daily life.

- The tone and mood remain consistent throughout.

- The conclusion leaves the reader without a decision. But the world goes on; the stars come out. The reader is wisked from Emile's room to the street and to the larger world, where people face similar problems, perhaps without any more satisfactory solutions but with a recognition that life demands choices.

Certainly you will make other observations about the sample to arouse your interest and give you ideas for your own story.

The list of general characteristics, explanation of process, and ideas gleaned from the sample should help you write a successful story.

SUMMARIES

Because summaries vary according to their purposes, this book deals with three kinds: *paraphrase, precis*, and *synopsis*. A paraphrase is nearly the same length as the original passage but reworded in simpler language. A precis reduces the original by about two-thirds while retaining its main ideas and general tone. A synopsis reduces a long work, like a book or play, into a short summary of a few paragraphs or pages.

[*See* PARAPHRASE, PRECIS, *and* SYNOPSIS, *elsewhere in Part II, for a complete description and analysis.*]

SYNOPSIS

A synopsis is a summary. [*See* PARAPHRASE *and* PRECIS, *elsewhere in Part II.*] The purpose of a summary is to provide a shortened version of a given piece of writing. Most frequently a synopsis is a multi-paragraph summary of a chapter, book, article, or drama. It makes no effort to address every idea. The reader understands that a synopsis is necessarily subjective because the writer must select the items to be included. Thus, the synopsis reflects editorial bias.

Characteristics

A synopsis generally

- selects main ideas which, in the writer's opinion, best represent the original piece,

- reflects the style of the current writer, as opposed to the author of the original,

- gives sufficient details to clarify the main ideas,

- is sufficiently informative to aid further investigation,

- has a reporter's objectivity.

Process

Use the following process to develop a synopsis.

PREWRITING

STEP 1. READING THE MATERIAL

Quickly read the original passage without taking notes. Look for re-peated themes and the general treatment of ideas. If unfamiliar names are difficult for you, you may want to list them for later reference, noting the correct spelling.

Once you've finished reading, jot down the three or four most important ideas. The will serve as the skeletal outline of your synopsis.

Remember, you will not cover all the ideas in a synopsis.

WRITING

STEP 2. PREPARING THE SYNOPSIS

Begin the synopsis by identifying in a single sentence the main idea of the original. Weave the title and author into an early (though not necessarily the first) sentence. Follow with a brief description of the main ideas.

Follow the organization of the original.

Keep in mind that a synopsis will be short, maybe only a paragraph in length. Deal only with essentials.

REVISING

STEP 3. IMPROVING THE CONTENT

Your synopsis will almost invariably be too long. Begin cutting. Omit needless details. Shorten sentences. Use strong nouns and verbs in order to omit modifiers. Keep cutting. [*See* REVISING: SAMPLE REVISION FOR WORDINESS *in Part I for an illustration.*]

Try this challenge: If you had to summarize the original in a single sentence, what would you say? If you could add one more sentence, what would you say? Follow this progression until you have stated all the important ideas.

[*Finally, see* REVISING, *in Part I, for guidelines for improving organization,* sentence structure, unity, emphasis, and transition.]

PROOFREADING

STEP 4. CHECKING THE DETAILS

Once you have completed the revision, check for spelling, punctuation, grammar, mechanics, and usage. [*Refer to the Glossary.*] Refer also to *Webster's New World Dictionary* and *Webster's New World Thesaurus* for spelling and vocabulary problems.

The steps above should enable you to develop a synopsis. Compare your own with the example below, and study the analysis which follows.

--- **Sample Synopsis** ---

The following synopsis summarizes a novel of nearly 550 pages.

Ice-Age Novel

The second book of a trilogy, The Valley of the Horses fictionalizes the beginning of civilization in the Asian area north of the Beran Sea. Like Jean M. Auel's other two books, The Clan of the Cave Bear and The Mammoth Hunters, this one gets its foundation from archaeological research supporting the evolution of man. In this unusual historical novel, the reader follows Ayla, a child of the Others who has been reared by the Clan of the Cave Bear only to be ejected from the Clan when she violates customs she cannot understand or accept. In exile in the valley of the horses, she survives five years alone until she meets Jondalar, a man of the Others.

Ayla faces a lonely struggle for survival after her death curse by the Clan. To solve basic survival problems, she must use logic: alone, how can she kill, butcher and process an animal large enough to feed her through the severe winter; alone, how can she provide clothing, cooking utensils, sleeping skins, and shelter for protection; alone, how can she protect herself from the dangers around her? Her training as a medicine woman and her knowledge of hunting coupled with the large brain characteristic of the Others allow her to succeed. Also as a result of her background she saves Jondalar's life after a lion mauls him and kills his traveling-companion brother. Jondalar is the first of the Others that Ayla has seen. After Ayla's medicinal powers help Jondalar regain his health, the two of them suffer from their inability to understand each other's customs. Jondalar finally teaches her to speak, however, and they are able to establish a strong bond, sharing their creative ideas to find solutions for both the physical and mental problems they face as a team.

Analysis of the Sample Synopsis

The sample (which appears earlier in this handbook as part of the formal book report) illustrates most of the characteristics of a good synopsis:

- In two paragraphs, it summarizes a book of nearly 550 pages.
- The introduction includes the name of the work and the author's name, both woven naturally into the single-statement summary.
- The second sentence places the novel in its historical perspective, without adding details about the archaeological research, evolution, or the setting.
- The third sentence introduces the main character and explains why she is in the valley of the horses. We are given no details about the Clan or the Others, but the labels are sufficiently suggestive for the purpose of a synopsis.
- The second paragraph summarizes the plot and lists the problems facing Ayla. By using the colon and a list, the author condenses chapter after chapter into a simple series.
- Without explaining *tempestuous,* the writer alludes to problems facing Ayla and the male character, Jondalar.

- Simple phrases like *when Ayla interferes* and *after he regains his health* summarize whole chapters.

Thus, the synopsis condenses the contents of a major work. The responsibility to select the most significant ideas weighs heavily on the writer.

Compare your own synopsis with the one above. Think through the analysis. You should now be able to analyze your own synopsis as effectively.

TECHNICAL REPORT

Technical reports are used to present facts, clearly and objectively. Their purpose may be to inform or to persuade. In either case, they can help the reader solve a problem or make a decision. The audience is usually specified.

A technical report differs from nontechnical writing in two respects: First, its writing is objective and factual, reporting information without reflecting personal opinion. (Nontechnical writing, on the other hand, may be subjective, reflective, or emotional.) Second, it uses headings and visual aids as a matter of course. Nontechnical writing generally avoids such reminders of content and organization.

Virtually all professionals write technical reports. A foreman must explain a new procedure to his workers. A scientist must show the results of a recent study. [See also LAB REPORT in Part II for a specific kind of technical report.] A computer programmer must explain the operation of a new piece of software. A sales manager must report progress and problems in the market place. A chief executive officer must convince the board of directors of the importance of company expansion. All rely on technical writing to achieve their goals.

Characteristics

In general, a technical report

- uses comparison, contrast, description, cause, effect, classification, definition, etc., [see entries for each elsewhere in Part II],
- follows a chronological order, spatial order, or order of importance [see entries for each in the Glossary],
- uses clear, concise language,
- uses clear sentence structure,
- takes an objective, impersonal tone,
- uses a third-person point of view,
- uses denotative rather than connotative language [see DENOTATION and CONNOTATION in the Glossary],
- omits figurative language and other subtleties [see FIGURES OF SPEECH in the Glossary],
- directs the reader's attention with headings,
- includes charts, graphs, tables, and illustrations,
- includes a table of contents and of charts, graphs, and illustrations,
- may include an appendix containing statistics or other supportive material too cumbersome or complex to include in the text,
- may include documentation.

Process

The following steps outline the process of writing a technical report. [*Compare with* LAB REPORT, *earlier in Part II. Because the lab report is a special kind of technical report, similarities and differences between the two will clarify each.*]

PREWRITING

STEP 1.   DETERMINING THE PURPOSE

Begin by pinpointing the purpose of your report. Do you need to convince someone to take a certain course of action? For instance, should your company consider developing a new product? Should the sales staff try a new approach to selling? Should the operator's manual be rewritten to avoid confusion? On the other hand, you may have a different purpose. Are you merely giving information? Will the information help others solve a problem? Will the information be used in certain decisions? Will it determine whether or not you earn a pay raise or a promotion? Is it likely to affect your working conditions?

State the purpose of the report in a sentence or short paragraph. Try to avoid saying *the purpose of this report is;* instead say *this report provides . . .* or *this report presents . . .* or *this report summarizes . . .* or something similar.

STEP 2.   ANALYZING THE AUDIENCE

You must also identify your audience. For instance, as a salesman preparing a report on field work, if you do not know your readership, you may include irrelevant information and omit important details. The sales manager and engineering staff may want to know different things. So determine your audience and decide what it needs.

List the general ideas you think your audience wants or needs.

STEP 3.   GATHERING MATERIALS

Obviously, technical reports *report* something, and you must collect that information or data. Reports usually omit secondary research, unless for background purposes. [*See* SECONDARY RESEARCH *and* PRIMARY RESEARCH *in the Glossary. See* LAB REPORT *for an example of background research, and see* RESEARCH PAPER *for detailed information on documenting secondary research.*] Rather, they report the results of personal experience or primary investigation conducted by the writer alone or as a member of a team.

For instance, the quality control personnel on an assembly line will prepare a report for the plant manager. It will be based on their observation and evaluation of the robots on the line. Ultimately the report will help management determine how many robots to use.

In another instance, an aerobics instructor will prepare a report for the health center's manager. The report, which could lead to a different class structure, will be based on the instructor's experience with complaints about schedules.

As you gather your own materials, consider your audience. What background information does it need? Is it familiar with your subject? If so, leave out unnecessary details. If it needs basic background information, be sure to include this without "talking down."

List the ideas you must include. Let your knowledge of the audience guide your selection. Do the ideas listed here support the list developed in Step 2 above?

Step 4. Planning the Development and Organization

Technical reports set the introduction and conclusion apart from the main section. Other aspects of organization are like those for similar nontechnical writing. [*See* Prewriting *in Part I. For additional guidelines, see the prewriting suggestions for specific kinds of reports. For instance, if your report analyzes how something works or is done, see* Process Analysis *earlier in Part II. For other means of development and organization, see* Comparison and Contrast, Cause and Effect, Classification, Description, Definition, Precis, *and* Lab Report, *in Part II. For quick definitions, see the entries for each term in the Glossary.*]

Choose a method of development that suits your purpose.

Step 5. Selecting the Headings

Once you have determined your method of organization, decide on appropriate headings. Make a list of the three major divisions of your paper: the *introduction, exposition,* and *conclusion.*

The introduction must

- state your purpose in terms of audience [*from Step 2 above*],
- define any unfamiliar terms,
- state your purpose in terms of subject [*from Step 1 above*],
- summarize your findings.

The exposition, like the body of a theme, carries out the statement of purpose.

The conclusion summarizes and clarifies the report's contents.

The divisions permit a busy reader to read only what he finds most important.

Now make your own list. Consider the example below. A report which compares electrical printed circuits and wire-wrapped circuits may include the following divisions:

Introduction
    Purpose
    Definitions
    Comparisons
    Preference
Comparisons
    Cost
        Printed
        Wire-wrapped
    Construction
        Printed

Wire-wrapped

Reliability

Printed

Wire-wrapped

Conclusion

The list serves not only as an outline but with some revision can provide the headings and subheadings for the final report.

WRITING

STEP 6. PREPARING THE FIRST DRAFT

Using the list prepared in Step 5, write a brief statement to support each of the headings. Be as concise and as objective as possible.

Plan visual aids (tables, charts, graphs, and illustrations) to replace narrative description as necessary. Use visual aids for the following purposes:

- to increase interest

- to emphasize certain data

- to condense information

- to show relationships among data

Sketch these visual aids where they should appear in the final draft. Remember to refer to them in the text, pointing out their significance or summarizing their contents in a sentence or two.

As you work with the content of your report, feel free to revise the list/outline as often as necessary, so that as you follow it, and develop its headings and subheadings, the ideas flow smoothly.

REVISING

STEP 7. POLISHING THE CONTENT

Reread your rough draft, asking yourself the following questions:

- Does the introduction clarify my report's audience, purpose, content, and findings? Will a reader, finishing the introduction, know all the main ideas in my report?

- Does the body deal with each topic separately under a separate subheading?

- Does the conclusion state my results clearly and concisely?

- Have I used appropriate vocabulary?

- Are my sentences simple and clear?

- Are my headings and subheadings logical and parallel? [*See* PARALLEL STRUCTURE *in the Glossary for a quick reference.*]

- Have I used visual aids effectively?

- Does my text treat the visual aids adequately, without repeating everything the reader will find in them?

[*For guidelines on improving writing techniques (structure, consistency, sentence variety, emphasis, transition, unity, and specific detail) see* REVISING, *with its series of samples, in Part I.*]

STEP 8. DEVELOPING THE VISUAL AIDS

Once the first draft has been revised, you should know which charts, graphs, tables, and illustrations to use. Prepare the visual aids neatly and professionally on separate sheets of paper. Once your final draft is ready, trim and cement them into place. Rubber cement works best.

Use the following guidelines for tables:

- Number the tables consecutively.
- Give each table a title.
- Give each table column a heading.
- Leave ample space around each table to offset it from the text.
- Refer to each table in the text and show its relation to the discussion.
- Place each table as near to the discussion as possible.
- Tables which give additional information, not directly related to the discussion, should be placed in the appendix.

Anything that is not a table is called a *figure*. For figures:

- Number the figures in the order of their appearance.
- Give each figure a descriptive title.
- Label both the horizontal and vertical axes of a graph.
- Place all labels horizontally on charts and diagrams.
- Include a legend, if necessary, to identify multiple lines, multiple-bar patterns, or pie-chart patterns.
- Keep the figures simple. Show no more than three ideas per graph, and keep other figures as uncluttered as possible.
- Leave ample space around each figure to offset it from the text.

- Refer to each figure in the text, and show its relation to the discussion.
- Place each figure as near to the discussion as possible.
- Figures which give additional information, not directly related to the discussion, should be placed in the appendix.

STEP 9. DEALING WITH FORMAT

The final draft of the technical report must include certain unique features. Follow these suggestions:

- Begin the first page with the word INTRODUCTION, centered, in capitals. Additional main headings will also be centered, in capitals.
- Place the subheadings, typed with initial capital letters and underlined, flush with the left margin.
- Indent the paragraphs five spaces.
- Leave space for tables and figures at the appropriate places in the text.
- Place each table or figure close to the relevant text pages.
- Number the text pages in the upper right corner.
- Begin the appendix at the top of a new page. Center and type the word APPENDIX in capitals. Follow these specific suggestions for items in the appendix:
  ○ Place each table, figure, or other piece of information on a separate page, labeled as referred to in the text.
  ○ Place each piece of information in a separate appendix, headed *Appendix A*, *Appendix B*, etc.

○ Do not include information in the Appendix to which there is no reference in the text.

• If you include parenthetical documentation notes, add a bibliography after the appendix. If you include endnotes and a bibliography, place both after the appendix. [*See* RESEARCH PAPER *for proper parenthetical, endnote, and bibliography forms.*]

• Prepare a title page. Center the information, horizonatally and vertically. Include a title for the report, your name, any specific meeting or occasion for which the report was prepared, and the date.

• Make a table of contents. Center the words TABLE OF CONTENTS. Then follow these suggestions:
  ○ Type in capitals any text heading which appears so in the text.
  ○ Indent and type in initial capital letters the text subheadings.
  ○ Double-space between main headings.
  ○ Use dots to help the reader find page numbers.
  ○ Use lower case Roman numerals (*i, ii, iii*), centered, at the bottom of the page, to number the table of contents page(s).

• Prepare a list of tables and figures in a manner similar to that for the table of contents. Number the page(s) at the bottom, with lower case Roman numerals, following sequentially after the table of contents page(s).

• Prepare an abstract. This may be a sentence or paragraph, but no more than a single page no matter how long the report. [*See Step 2 above.*] Center and type the word ABSTRACT in capitals. Number the page at the bottom with a lower case Roman numeral, following sequentially after the list of tables and figures.

• Rubber cement the charts and figures in place. If you have the facilities, you may wish to make a high-quality photo copy of the pages which include charts and figures so the reader does not see the paste-up copy.

• Assemble the pages in the following order:
  title page
  table of contents
  list of tables and figures
  abstract
  body of the report
    introduction
    exposition
    conclusion
  appendix(es) [optiona]
  endnotes [optional]
  bibliography [optional]

Place the pages in a binder or staple them together, whichever best suits the occasion.

PROOFREADING

STEP 10. MAKING A FINAL CHECK OF DETAILS

Once the final draft is complete, proofread it carefully. Check for errors of grammar, mechanics, and usage. [*The Glossary will provide quick references and give cross-references for more detailed information.*]

Use *Webster's New World Dictionary* and *Webster's New World Thesaurus* to check vocabulary and precise word choice.

Finally, check and recheck your statistics. Have you miscopied any figures or made mistakes typing the visual aids? Does the information in the text agree with the latter?

As you make a last check, try to read the report as if you were its intended audience. Make any final revisions you think necessary.

Sample Technical Report

The following report is a comparison and contrast paper that exhibits the characteristics and follows the guidelines given above. Use it as a model. [*In addition, compare the sample paper in the section* LAB REPORT, *in Part II, for a slightly different kind of technical report. The comparison will help you understand the meaning of "technical" writing. For other format styles, see the samples in* RESEARCH PAPER, *also in Part II.*]

PRINTED CIRCUITS VERSUS WIRE WRAPPING

Comparisons and Contrasts

Prepared

by

Timothy L. Rife

for

Composition 216E

Scientific and Laboratory Report Writing

March 19, 1988

TABLE OF CONTENTS

LIST OF TABLES AND FIGURES

ABSTRACT

This report provides a guide for the beginning electronics hobbyist debating the use of printed circuits and wire wrapping.

INTRODUCTION

Purpose

Any beginning electronics hobbyist about to undertake construction of an electronic circuit must evaluate the comparisons between printed-circuit construction and wire-wrapping construction. This report will help the hobbyist make a good decision.

Definition

There are two major methods of electrical circuit construction: printed-circuit construction and wire-wrapping construction.

Printed-circuit construction uses a nonconducting board material with copper covering one or both sides. The interconnections between electronic components are made by removing copper to leave a metal foil pattern. This pattern forms the wiring for the circuit (Figure 1). Components are installed on the board and soldered directly to the copper foil pattern.

Wire-wrapping construction uses thirty-gauge wires wrapped around the component leads to form the electrical connections (Figure 2). Wire wrapping is similar to point-to-point wiring; however, instead of using solder to form the connections, wire wrapping uses tightly wrapped wires to form the electrical connections.

FIGURE 1   A Printed-Circuit Board

FIGURE 2   Wire-Wrapping Construction

Comparisons

The printed-circuit and wire-wrapping techniques will be discussed and evaluated on three main points. Cost, construction, and reliability are among the most important considerations when building electronic projects.

Preference

The printed-circuit construction seems preferable to wire-wrapping construction. Compared to wire-wrapping construction, printed-circuit construction is much more rigid and permanent; and it is less susceptible to electrical noise from the surrounding environment. In addition, it appears far less cluttered than does wire wrapping.

COMPARISONS

Cost

Part of the cost consideration involves tools. Three tools essential to either construction method are as follows: needle-nosed pliers, diagonal cutters, and wire strippers. Their cost is about nine dollars.

In addition, printed-circuit construction requires several specialized tools (Table 1). Although some of the equipment can be reused, solder and circuit boards are not reusable items.

TABLE 1:

Printed-Circuit Construction Materials

Material	Cost
Printed-circuit kit	$ 9.00
Soldering iron	3.50
Solder	1.00
Circuit board (6″ × 6″)	3.00
Total	$16.50

The printed-circuit kit includes all materials needed for making the foil patterns. Circuit boards are sometimes included with the kit; however, additional boards may be purchased at any electronic-parts supplier.

The materials necessary for wire-wrapping construction are listed in Table 2. The wire-wrapping tool can be used repeatedly; other materials are consumable.

TABLE 2:

Wire-Wrapping Construction Materials

Material	Cost
Wire-wrapping tool	$ 6.00
Wire (30 gauge/50 feet)	2.50
Circuit boards (not copper clad)	2.50
Total	$11.00

The wire-wrapping tool priced in Table 2 is one of the least expensive. More expensive motorized tools make wire wrapping easier.

Materials used for both methods are inexpensive, and some may be used repeatedly. The cost difference, therefore, is negligible.

Construction

Printed-circuit construction involves the fabrication of a board with a metal foil pattern forming the wiring. The fabrication process is the most difficult part of constructing the printed-circuit method. When the circuit board is completed, assembly of the circuit goes quickly. The electronic components are installed on the board and soldered directly to the foil pattern. The leads are cut at the top of the solder joint, and the process is completed. Circuit board fabrication is the most time-consuming aspect of the printed-circuit method. The end benefit, however, is that with this method, complex circuits can be constructed easily and neatly with a minimum of trouble-shooting.

Wire-wrapping construction avoids the process of making the circuit board; however, wires must be wrapped around the component leads to make the electrical connection. This procedure will become tedious and time-consuming as the circuits become more and more complex.

<u>Reliability</u>

The printed-circuit method affords high reliability. Components are rigidly attached to the board; vibrations and sudden shocks do not affect the printed circuit. A circuit constructed by this method can be used for years without maintenance to tighten loose connections.

Wire wrapping, on the other hand, is highly sensitive to vibration and shock, either of which can jar loose the electrical connections. In a complex circuit, countless hours could be spent in trouble-shooting and looking for loose connections.

Any electronic equipment currently on the market uses the printed-circuit technique. Manufacturers realize that the durability and reliability of this method are far superior to those of the wire-wrapping method.

CONCLUSION

The cost and construction involved in the printed-circuit and wire-wrapping construction techniques are nearly equal. Reliability, then, is the deciding factor. When durable and permanent circuitry is desired, the printed-circuit method has clear advantages.

In short, the printed-circuit technique is far more reliable than the wire-wrapping method. Printed-circuit electrical contacts are durable and long lasting, and the circuitry is neatly organized, thus providing a pleasing appearance.

Analysis of the Sample

Compare this report with the sample in LAB REPORT, earlier in Part II. In addition, note the following items:

- The title page, table of contents, list of tables and figures, and abstract serve as the front material for the actual report.
- The report includes three main sections, the titles of which appear centered, in capitals.
- Subheadings appear flush with the left margin, typed in initial capitals, and underlined.
- The introduction gives an overview of what follows. In fact, anyone who reads the introduction will know generally what the report says.
- The tables and figures enhance the content and permit the writer to condense otherwise unwieldy material.
- The writer compares and contrasts throughout, discussing printed-circuit then wire-wrapped construction.
- The conclusion clarifies the preference stated in the introduction.
- The language is clear, concise, and objective.
- The use of passive voice and linking verbs is typical of technical reporting.
- Sentence variety adds interest and emphasizes the main ideas.

By studying the characteristics and process above, and by comparing your own product with the model and analysis, you should be able to write a satisfactory technical report. Be sure, however, to consult the cross-references for additional help.

THEME

Themes are multi-paragraph papers that use any method of development suitable to the topic. [*See* DEVELOPMENT, METHODS OF *in the Glossary.*] They usually contain an introductory paragraph, a concluding paragraph, and separate body paragraphs for each main idea of the thesis. Because they follow a rather formal structure, themes typify expository writing.

When we are asked to write a theme, we frequently think in terms of a five-paragraph paper; yet themes may contain as few as three and as many as several dozen paragraphs. Because the five-paragraph theme readily illustrates the concept, this section will treat it as the model. [*Models, throughout Part II, illustrate themes of varying lengths.*]

Characteristics

The five-paragraph theme represents a common denominator among the various kinds of expository writing. In general, a theme

- contains an introductory paragraph, three body paragraphs, and a concluding paragraph,

- begins with an introductory paragraph which includes any one of a number of devices to attract reader attention [*see* ATTENTION-GETTER *in the Glossary*],

- concludes the introductory paragraph with a thesis sentence that states or implies the topics to be developed in each of the body paragraphs,

- shows in the thesis sentence the order in which the body paragraphs will be developed,

- includes a separate body paragraph for each main idea,

- includes in each body paragraph a topic sentence derived directly from the thesis sentence,

- relies on careful use of transitional words and phrases to connect ideas within and between paragraphs,

- employs, on occasion, transitional sentences to connect ideas between paragraphs,

- follows a logical plan, using any one of the orders of development [*see* ORDER, IN PARAGRAPH DEVELOPMENT *in the Glossary*],

- concludes with a paragraph that summarizes, emphasizes, or otherwise brings the paper to a satisfying end,

- includes the characteristics peculiar to the chosen method of development [*see various sections in Part II such as* ANALOGY, CAUSE AND EFFECT, CLASSIFICATION, COMPARISON AND CONTRAST, DEFINITION, DESCRIPTION, NARRATION, OPIN-

ION, PERSUASION, *and* PROCESS ANALYSIS].

Shorter or longer themes include many of the same characteristics, but they follow somewhat different patterns. Listed below are characteristics peculiar to themes of different lengths.

The Two-Paragraph Theme

The two-paragraph theme includes a brief introduction, thesis sentence, and supporting details for the first main idea in its first paragraph. The second paragraph includes supporting details for the second main idea and a concluding sentence. [*See Sample for Social Sciences in* DEFINITION *in Part II for an example.*]

The Three-Paragraph Theme

The three-paragraph theme begins with a paragraph containing a brief introduction, a thesis sentence, and supporting details for the first main idea. The second paragraph develops the second main idea. The third paragraph develops the third main idea and adds a concluding statement. [*See Sample for English in* CLASSIFICATION, *Sample for English in* PROCESS ANALYSIS, *and Sample for a Poem in* LITERARY ANALYSES, *all in Part II, for examples.*]

The Four-Paragraph Theme

The four-paragraph theme usually contains two main ideas. It follows the same pattern as the five-para-graph theme but develops only two body paragraphs. The introductory paragraph concludes with the thesis sentence; each of the two body paragraphs develops a main idea; the concluding paragraph summarizes or reiterates the main ideas and refers back to the original thesis. [*See Sample for Science in* CLASSIFICATION *and Sample for Business in* COMPARISON AND CONTRAST, *both in Part II, for examples.*]

The Six-Paragraph Theme

The six-paragraph theme also follows the basic pattern of the five-paragraph theme, but develops four body paragraphs. [*See Sample for Social Sciences in* CLASSIFICATION *and Sample for Business in* PROCESS ANALYSIS, *both in Part II, for examples.*]

The Longer Paper

A paper with more than six paragraphs follows the basic pattern of the five-paragraph theme but develops more complicated main ideas. Even when a paper has only three main ideas, more paragraphs may be required for support purposes. In addition, a longer paper may also include paragraphs which serve only as transitions (i.e., which summarize the ideas presented thus far and so lead into the next idea). [*For examples and more thorough discussions of longer papers, see Sample for a Symbol in* LITERARY ANALYSES, *the sample paper in* RESEARCH PAPER, *and the sample paper in* LAB REPORT, *all of which appear in Part II.*]

Process

To develop a satisfactory five-paragraph theme, follow the steps below. Adjust as indicated above for longer or shorter themes.

PREWRITING

STEP 1.   CHOOSING THE FOCUS

You must decide what you want to say about your topic. For instance, if you write about your favorite hobby, building model gliders, you must decide what to emphasize. Do you want to focus on the skill making gliders requires? How you became involved with them? Why you build them? Their aereodynamics? How to paint them? Flying them? Narrowing your subject in this way will help give you a manageable topic.

Depending on what you must write, you may want to consult the corresponding section of this handbook for suggestions. [*For example, if you are writing a comparison paper, consult* COMPARISON AND CONTRAST *in Part II for specific suggestions.*]

Once you have selected a narrow topic, like *how to paint model gliders,* you must decide how to explain things to the reader. In other words, how do you want to treat your subject? Do you want to describe the process of painting gliders? [*See* PROCESS ANALYSIS *in Part II.*] Do you want to describe common designs and patterns? [*See* DESCRIPTION *in Part II.*] Do you want to compare painting methods? [*See* COMPARISON AND CONTRAST *in Part II.*] Can you best support your topic by analogy? [*See* ANALOGY *in Part II.*] Will the reader understand your topic better if you classify the various kinds of painting? [*See* CLASSIFICATION *in Part II.*]

Most writers decide by making lists of approaches, ideas, examples, or illustrations.

So, select your focus and make a list of the points you want to make. Your list may look something like this:

Narrowed topic:
How to paint model gliders
Ideas:
Use startling over/under
   patterns
Use humorous color
   combinations
Use simple two-tone
   combinations

Complete your list before going on to Step 2.

STEP 2.   WRITING THE THESIS SENTENCE

The thesis sentence determines every aspect of a theme's structure and organization. You must take care to write an effective one. Thesis sentences have two characteristics:

1. They state or suggest the topics of each of the body paragraphs. Hence a five-paragraph theme will have a thesis sentence suggesting three ideas.

2. They state or imply the order in which the ideas will appear. In other words, the subtopic appearing first in the thesis sentence ap-

pears in the first body paragraph. You determine the theme's organization by the arrangement of its thesis statement. [*See* ORDER, IN PARAGRAPH DEVELOPMENT *in the Glossary.*]

Develop the list from Step 1 into a thesis sentence. Then compare with the following examples:

A model-glider builder may paint a simple two-tone combination, but a more creative builder will develop a startling over-under pattern or even a humorous color combination.

Three points:
1. two-tone combination
2. over-under pattern
3. humorous combination

Working with pets requires tedious daily routines, occasionally heartbreaking responsibilities, and frequent loving attention.

Three points:
1. tedious daily routines
2. occasionally heartbreaking responsibilities
3. frequent loving attention

A diamond broker must have expertise in color, clarity, and cut.

Three points:
1. color
2. clarity
3. cut

Note that each example includes three points. Each point will become the subject of a body paragraph. Re-

vise your thesis sentence as suggested by reading these models.

STEP 3. CHOOSING THE ORDER

In organizing paragraphs and themes, writers use one of three orders: spatial, chronological, or order of importance.

Spatial order presents topics as they appear in space: left to right, top to bottom, front to back. [*See* SPATIAL ORDER *in the Glossary.*] Useful transitional phrases in a left-to-right spatial order would include:

At the far left…
Next to that…
Near the center…
Just right of center…
At the far right…

Chronological order presents topics as they appear in time. [*See* CHRONOLOGICAL ORDER *in the Glossary.*] Useful transitions include:

Yesterday…
Late last evening…
This morning…
An hour ago…
Now…

Orders of importance present topics in one of three ways:

• from most to least important
• from least to most important
• from second most, through least, to most important

[*See* ORDERS OF IMPORTANCE IN THE GLOSSARY.] Useful transitional phrases include:

One important idea…

Less important but equally interesting...

Another important factor...

Most importantly...

Select the order you think best. If necessary, rearrange your thesis sentence to reflect this order.

STEP 4.   WRITING THE TOPIC SENTENCES

Once you have developed the thesis sentence, you can easily write a topic sentence for each body paragraph. Study the following:

Thesis sentence:
Caring for pets requires tedious daily chores, sometimes heartbreaking tasks, and loving attention.

Topic sentence for first body paragraph:
Tedious chores are necessary for a pet's good health and demand daily routines.

Topic sentence for second body paragraph:
Caring for a sick or injured pet can be heartbreaking and demands even more time than the normal routines.

Topic sentence for third body paragraph:
 The joy of pet care lies in the constant loving attention owner and pet heap upon each other.

Using this as a guide, develop topic sentences for each of your body paragraphs. With their completion, your theme will be well under way.

STEP 5.   SELECTING THE METHOD OF DEVELOPMENT

A theme can be developed in at least a dozen ways. Choose any of the methods included in this handbook [*see* DEVELOPMENT, METHODS OF *in the Glossary*] or any combination of methods. Each body paragraph may follow a different method. Use the one most appropriate to the subject and purpose.

Make a tentative list of the method(s) you will use in each body paragraph.

For the example above, the list might appear as follows:

First body paragraph

Method of development:
description (daily chores)
Organization:
chronological order

Second body paragraph

Method of development:
cause and effect (pet's illness or injury and resulting care)
Organization:
order of importance

Third body paragraph

Method of development:
comparison (pet's point of view and owner's point of view)
Organization:
order of importance

WRITING

STEP 6. DRAFTING THE FIRST ATTEMPT:

THE INTRODUCTION

Some writers prefer to begin writing with the introductory paragraph. Others prefer to begin with the body paragraphs. Use whichever method suits you.

No matter when you write it, your introduction must attract the reader's attention and set the tone for the paper. You may choose to use one of the following approaches:

- Say something startling, either by making a statement or by giving statistics. For example:

  To form one cubic inch of stalactite, that stone icicle found hanging from cave ceilings, nature requires about one hundred years.
  (This statistic startles the reader who has seen stalactites the diameter of a human body dropping twenty or more feet from a cave ceiling.)

- Describe a compelling scene or situation:

  One week before St. Patrick's Day, the plane touched down at London's Heathrow International Airport. A train would take the tour group to Devonshire, the land of rolling hills and centuries-old stone fences. Settled into their coaches, the group relaxed and let busy London glide past them, as they slipped into something more comfortable—the rural, pastoral English spring.

  (The scene helps the reader identify with the mood and perhaps arouses some curiosity. What happens to the tour group?)

- Refer to an event, either historical or current, perhaps in the form of a story or conversation:

  A year ago today, Jerrod Hunt graduated from high school. He and his friends celebrated even before the formal ceremony, but the real celebration came afterward. Today, Jerrod is trying desperately to learn to walk again.
  (The reader anticipates what has happened to Jerrod.)

- Show a controversy, contradiction, or unusual opinion.

  Despite computerized technology and presorted, zip-coded mail, most of us open an envelope with a handwritten address first.
  (A contradiction is posed between technology and the personal touch.)

- Ask a question:

  What keeps woodpeckers from destroying their brains when they pound relentlessly on wood?
  (A thought-provoking question is asked about a common occurrence.)

- Use a quotation, adage, or proverb:

  It's not what you know but who you know.
  (The reader wonders whether the writer will agree or disagree with this adage.)

Other methods to will serve as well. These offer a place to start.

Finally, conclude your introductory paragraph with the thesis sentence.

STEP 7.   DRAFTING THE FIRST ATTEMPT:

THE BODY

In Step 4 you wrote topic sentences for the three body paragraphs of the theme. Now write a transition that will move readers from the thesis sentence of the introduction to the topic sentence of the first body paragraph. [*See* REVISION *in Part I for a discussion of types of transitional devices.*] The topic sentence may be the first sentence of the paragraph and include the transitional device, or it may appear later in the paragraph. In either case, develop the first paragraph using the method of development that seems most appropriate. Conclude the first paragraph with a reference to the topic sentence or with a clincher statement.

Next develop the second body paragraph. Again, begin with a transition. Develop the topic with adequate supporting details. Add a conclusion.

Develop the third body paragraph in the same manner.

STEP 8.   DRAFTING THE FIRST ATTEMPT:

THE CONCLUSION

A transitional device must connect the final body paragraph with the conclusion. The conclusion itself should summarize or reemphasize the main idea; it will probably also refer to the thesis sentence. But most importantly it should refer to the attention-getter used in the introductory paragraph. This approach gives the best sense of completeness, a feeling of having seen the full picture.

REVISING

STEP 9.   POLISHING THE FIRST ATTEMPT

Once you have finished the first draft, begin polishing. For a full-length theme, you may choose to tackle the revision one step at a time.

First, look at the introductory paragraph and ask yourself:

- Have I used an effective attention-getting device?
- Does the introductory material lead smoothly into the thesis sentence?
- Is the thesis sentence the final sentence?
- Does it state or imply the topic of each of the body paragraphs?
- Does it indicate the order in which the body paragraphs will appear?

You should be able to answer "yes" to each question. If not, revise as necessary.

Next ask yourself the following about each of the three body paragraphs:

- Is the paragraph connected to the ones before and after by transitional devices? [*See* REVISING: SAMPLE REVISION FOR TRANSITION *in Part I for help with transitions.*]
- Does it include a topic sentence derived from the thesis sentence?

- Does it support the topic sentence with adequate details? [*See* REVISING: SAMPLE REVISION FOR SPECIFIC DETAIL *in Part I.*]

- Are the details specific and concrete or general and abstract? [*See* SPECIFIC DETAILS, CONCRETE, *and* ABSTRACT *in the Glossary.*]

- Do I omit unrelated ideas and thus maintain unity throughout the paragraph and theme? [*See* REVISING: SAMPLE REVISION FOR UNITY *in Part I.*]

- Have I provided adequate internal transitions to show the relationship among ideas within the paragraph?

Make whatever revisions these questions suggest.

Next consider the conclusion:

- While not a traditional, fully developed paragraph, does it tie together the main ideas of the theme?

- Does it refer to the thesis sentence without repeating it?

- Does it refer to the attention-getting device used in the introduction?

- Will it give the reader a sense of completeness?

Make any revisions suggested by your answers.

Finally, ask yourself the following about the entire theme:

- Have I used good sentence structure?

- Are my sentences varied? [*See* REVISING: SAMPLE REVISION FOR SENTENCE VARIETY *in Part I.*]

- Do the sentences carry the proper emphasis? [*See* REVISING: SAMPLE REVISION FOR EMPHASIS *in Part I.*]

- Do I use parallel structures effectively? [*See* PARALLEL STRUCTURE *in the Glossary.*]

- Have I used a variety of modification structures? [*See* ABSOLUTE, APPOSITIVE, PREPOSITIONAL PHRASE, GERUND, INFINITIVE, *and* PARTICIPLE *in the Glossary.*]

- Is my vocabulary appropriate to the topic?

- Have I used specific, concrete words? Refer to *Webster's New World Thesaurus* to make the most accurate word choice.

- Does my paper sound smooth when read aloud?

Make whatever revisions your answers suggest. Remember, you should be able to answer "yes" to all questions.

[*Finally, review* REVISING *in Part I for additional guidelines on revision.*]

PROOFREADING

STEP 10. CHECKING THE FINAL DETAILS

As you reread your final revision, check it for grammar, usage, and mechanics. [*See* PROOFREADING *in Part I for general guidelines. A quick check in the Glossary will give definitions and brief examples.*]

For a better understanding of the characteristics and process explained above, study the sample theme and analysis below.

———————— **Sample Five-Paragraph Theme** ————————

The following five-paragraph theme includes the traditional introductory paragraph, three body paragraphs, and a concluding paragraph. Once you have finished your own theme, compare its structure with the one below.

Land of the Free and the Wild

A great horned owl hoots across the quiet water and then glides through the stand of bald cypress along the eastern side of the swamp. Whip-poor-wills call; bullfrogs croak; mosquitoes hum. Darkness creeps across the swamp. Hovey Lake, Indiana's cypress swamp, protected as a wildlife refuge, greets visitors with night sounds common to the uncommon 1,400-acre environment. Offering a different set of treats every season, the refuge attracts a wide variety of visitors during the hunting season, during the fishing season, and during the bird-watching season.

Because the swamp is situated along the Mississippi flyway, it offers refuge to 40,000 to 50,000 waterfowl each winter. Canada geese far outnumber other waterfowl, but snow geese, blue geese, and occasionally white-fronted geese winter there, too. Nearly every variety of duck, diver and puddle, reside in the quiet, smaller sloughs. As a result, the swamp attracts hunters in early winter, goose hunters to the pits and duck hunters to the blinds. The hunters' closely regulated success is the result of hundreds of acres of corn left standing by Posey County farmers, who rent the rich bottom land between the lake and the river by sealed bid. The farmers' contracts require them to leave twenty-five percent of the harvest as food for the thousands of waterfowl, encouraging them to stay. The encouragement works, much to the hunters' delight.

In spring, however, the fishermen replace the hunters on Hovey Lake waters. Attracted by the spring crappie run, fishermen haul in hefty stringers of slabs and return to fish for bluegill. Evening campfires turn skillets full of fresh fillets into plates full of succulent morsels. Then sunrise sends the bass fishermen scurrying to secret waters, some to return with empty bags. One fisherman, however, boats three, one weighing in at eight pounds two ounces. Later in the day, a few trotlines yield spoonbill catfish, those prehistoric monsters weighing thirty pounds or more, as long as a man is tall. In late afternoon or early evening, a jug fisherman occasionally bags perch, catfish, or even a wily gar, long, slender, and sharp-toothed. Spring moves into summer, and summer moves into autumn. Only then, when the lake is closed for waterfowl migration, do the fishermen leave.

The most experienced hunters and fishermen at Hovey Lake, however, are not human. They are avian. Boasting a greater variety of bird life than almost any other spot in Indiana, the swamp attracts bird watchers twelve months a year from a dozen states. With powerful binoculars, they scan the bald cypress trees and standing dead timber, known to attract woodpeckers, including the pileated, redheaded, redbreasted, downy, and hairy. Other tree dwellers, from grumpy-looking owls to scurrying swifts, stake out territory in the swamp growth. During the warbler migration, the trees house whole orchestras, but the prothonotary warbler stays most of the summer, flashing yellow among the yew-like lower branches of the cypress. Flocks of martins, cowbirds, and grackles fly in and out seasonally. In the more inaccessible parts of the swamp, the great blue herons and great white egrets wade the shallows near one of the last stands of bamboo-like cane this far north or perch high in treetops from which they can see the Ohio River. In winter, the bald eagles and ospreys soar among the thousands of geese and ducks, surely a testimony to the value of this wildlife sanctuary.

Boasting none of the amenities of modern campgrounds, Hovey Lake nevertheless attracts 90,000 visitors a year, visitors who hunt and fish and watch the birds. They come to appreciate the swamp for what it is, a precious ecological system struggling to survive man's intrusion. They hear the owls, the whip-poor-wills, the frogs, even the mosquitoes, and know that in the chain of this uncommon swamp life, every link must stay intact.

Analysis of Sample Theme

The sample illustrates the basic characteristics of the five-paragraph theme. Note these specifics:

In the first paragraph:

- The introduction uses the attention-getter to set the scene. The reader will readily identify with the lure of the swamp.
- The thesis sentence appears as the last sentence, to which the paragraph has led smoothly.
- The thesis sentence names the topics of the three body paragraphs in the order in which they will be discussed.

In the second paragraph:

- A long introduction and series of transitional devices precede the fourth, topic sentence.
- Supporting details explain why the hunters come and are successful.
- The concluding sentence refers back to the topic sentence and ties together the ideas in the paragraph.

In the third paragraph:

- The first sentence serves as both a transition and a topic sentence.
- The supporting details show the kinds of fishing and the kinds of fish without giving the reader the feeling of reading a list.
- The concluding sentence shows the fishermen in three seasons.

In the fourth paragraph:

- Two sentences of transition tie the description of hunters and fishermen to that of the birds.
- The third sentence serves as the topic sentence.
- Supporting details are piled one after another to emphasize the variety of bird life. The writer finds no need to repeat the information given about waterfowl in the first body paragraph.
- The concluding sentence in the last body paragraph ties together not only the paragraph but the general idea as well.

In the fifth paragraph:

- The reference to the thesis sentence does not simply repeat the thesis.

- Reference is also made to the scenic description of the introductory paragraph, concluding with an analogy between the uncommon environment and a chain.

Note, too, some characteristics about the writing style:

- The method of organization emphasies the writer's message. The writer clearly thinks wildlife preservation to be more important than hunting and fishing; thus, his last body paragraph deals with bird watching, and his conclusion carries an ecological message.
- Organization within the paper is roughly seasonal, moving from winter (*hunting*) to spring (*fishing*) summer (*fishing*) and autumn (*fishing*); references to all-season bird watching round out the structure.
- Within the paragraph on fishing, the organization is chronological from evening to evening.
- In the bird-watching paragraph, the writer follows the birds from spring to winter, (though perhaps only someone familiar with migratory birds would recognize the organization).
- The writer employs specific, concrete language, including strong verbs.
- Good sentence variety is evident throughout, from three-word sentences to lengthy, complicated sentences with multiple appositives and subordinate clauses.
- Figures of speech enhance the quality of the writing. [*See* FIGURES OF SPEECH *in the Glossary.*]
- The paper maintains unity throughout, offering only details directly related to the topic.
- The paper includes dozens of descriptive and factual details to help the reader "see" the writer's point of view. [*See* IMAGERY *in the Glossary.*]

The characteristics and process described in the beginning of this section, and the model and analysis above, should help you write a dynamic theme. In addition you will want to refer to the sections describing specific kinds of themes in order to take advantage of the various methods of development illustrated. [*Examples of multi-paragraph papers are to be found throughout Part II.*]

Glossary

A

abbreviation a shortened form of a word. A period after the shortened form indicates the abbreviation. **Example:** *Sat.* is the abbreviation for *Saturday*; *Ave.* for *Avenue*. **Note:** Many writers avoid abbreviations in formal writing.

absolute a phrase made up of a noun and a participle, which begins and modifies an entire sentence. **Example:** *The wind chill factor being well below zero*, we bundled up to protect ourselves.

abstract 1. nouns which name things which cannot be observed by the senses: hope, memory, belief. **2.** writing which lacks specific detail. **Example:** The weather was too cold for us to wait outside. (abstract) **Revised:** With the temperature at fifteen degrees below zero and the wind howling at forty miles an hour, we could not safely wait outside thirty minutes for the bus. (specific) [*See also* SPECIFIC DETAIL *in the Glossary and* DESCRIPTION *in Part II.*] **3.** A short summary, no more than a page long, that precedes a technical report. [*See also* TECHNICAL REPORT *in Part II.*]

action verb shows the action of the subject. **Example:** We *wrote* letters. (action) Letters from good friends *are* fun to receive. (linking) Most experienced writers prefer action verbs to linking verbs. [*See also* VERBS.]

active voice refers to the verb whose subject is doing the acting. **Example:** Sheila ate an apple with her lunch. (*Ate* is in active voice; the subject *Sheila* is acting.) [*See also* PASSIVE VOICE *in the Glossary.*] **Note:** Because active-voice verbs make stronger sentences than do passive-voice verbs, most experienced writers prefer active voice. Exceptions are noted in Part II under respective types of writing which often utilize the passive voice.

address a three-line indication of where one receives mail. It includes the person's name, street name and number, and the city, state, and zip code. **Example:** Dr. Chung Wong; 4274 Longshore Avenue; Lake Charlene, Arkansas 33061. **Note:** for businesses, the address is sometimes four or more lines, the additional lines adding the person's title and company name. [*See also* LETTERS *in Part II.*]

adjective 1. a word that modifies nouns or pronouns. **2.** a group of words functioning as an adjective, notably a prepositional, participial, or infinitive phrase, an adjective clause. **Example:** Students *who work hard* succeed. (The adjective clause *who work hard* functions as an adjective to modify the noun *students*.) [*See also* PHRASE, PREPOSITION, PARTICIPLE, INFINITIVE, VERBAL PHRASE *and* CLAUSE, SUBORDINATE.]

adverb **1.** a word that modifies a verb, adjective, or adverb. **2.** a group of words functioning as an adverb, notably a prepositional, participial, or infinitive phrase, or an adverb clause. **Example:** *After our team won the game,* we celebrated. (The adverb clause modifies the verb *celebrated.*) [*See also* PHRASE, PREPOSITION, PARTICIPLE, INFINITIVE, VERBAL PHRASE *and* CLAUSE, SUBORDINATE.]

agenda a chronological list of topics to be discussed at a meeting. An agenda serves several purposes: to give advance notice of topics so that the membership and/or the public can be prepared to speak, to keep the meeting organized, and to limit discussion.

agreement the correct grammatical use of words of like number and gender. Two kinds of agreement problems exist in everyday language. **1.** Pronoun-antecedent agreement requires a pronoun to agree in number and gender with its antecedent. [*See* ANTECEDENT *in the Glossary.*] **2.** Subject-verb agreement requires a subject and its verb to agree in number. [*See* SUBJECT-VERB AGREEMENT.]

alliteration repetition of a beginning sound, usually of a consonant, in two or more words of a phrase, line of poetry, etc. **Example:** *full fathom five thy father lies.*

allusion a casual or indirect reference. **Example:** By the end of the day, the apprentice was a virtual mad hatter. (The allusion, *mad hatter,* suggests, to the informed reader, the character from *Alice in Wonderland.*) **Note:** While the effectiveness of an allusion depends on an informed reader, its use adds considerable vitality and enrichment to written works.

ambiguity the quality or state of being unclear or uncertain in meaning. Ambiguity may result from **1.** unclear pronoun references, **2.** vague or abstract words and phrases [*See* ABSTRACT *in the Glossary*]. **Example:** Maggie asked Stacey to move her car. (The sentence is ambiguous since the reader doesn't understand whose car is to be moved.) **Revision:** Maggie, who does not own or drive a car, asked Stacey to move hers.

analogy a comparison in which two objects are compared with the more complex explained in terms of the simpler. **Example:** The instructor complained that manuals were not compatible with the computer. "It's like have a sewing machine manual to explain how to play a pipe organ." [*See also* ANALOGY *in Part II for complete explanation and a series of examples.*]

analysis a careful examination of a cause, effect, process, or product. Sometimes referred to as *cause-effect, process, critical analysis,* the term suggests precise thought and logic. [*See* CAUSE AND EFFECT, LITERARY ANALYSES, *and* PROCESS ANALYSIS *in Part II for examples.*]

anecdote   a short, entertaining story of some happening, usually personal or biographical, useful in introductions, both oral and written, as well as in supporting examples in less formal situations.

announcement   a written, printed, or oral notice. [*See* ANNOUNCEMENT *in Part II.*]

antagonist   a person who opposes or fights with the protagonist. [*See also* PROTAGONIST *in the Glossary.*]

antecedent   the word, phrase, or clause to which a pronoun refers. **Example:** *Sue* likes frills, and she often trims her sleeves with lace. (The pronouns *she* and *her* refer to *Sue*, the antecedent.)

apostrophe   a punctuation mark (') used to show **1.** omitted letters in a word, or **2.** the possessive case.

appositive   a word, phrase, or clause which functions as a noun and explains another noun. **Example:** Mr. Jetson, *the mechanic*, is a wizard at repairing cars. (*The mechanic* explains the noun *Mr. Jetson* and is an appositive.)

arabic numerals   the figures *1, 2, 3, 4, 5, 6, 7, 8, 9,* and *0.*

articles   the words *a, an,* and *the. The* is a definite article; *a* and *an* are indefinite articles.

assonance   **1.** likeness of sound, especially of vowels, as in a series of words or syllables **2.** a partial rhyme in which the stressed vowel sounds are alike but the consonant sounds are not, as in *late* and *make.*

attention-getter   an introductory device that gains the reader's or listener's attention. Common devices include **1.** asking a question or questions **2.** making an unusual statement **3.** describing a scene **4.** presenting a conversation **5.** telling a brief story **6.** presenting surprising or alarming statistics **7.** referring to an event, either historical or current **8.** showing a controversy or contradiction **9.** using a quotation, adage, or proverb **10.** stating an unusual opinion.

autobiography   the story of one's own life. [*See* AUTOBIOGRAPHY *in Part II.*]

auxiliary verb   a verb that helps form the tense, mood, or voice of another verb: *have, be, may, can, do, shall,* etc. **Example:** She *must* work harder. (*Must* is an auxiliary verb accompanying the main verb *work.*) [*See* VERBS *in The Glossary.*]

B

bias   a mental leaning for or against someone or something; partiality; prejudice; bent.

bibliography   a list of books, articles, etc. referred to by an author. The list follows one of several formats. [*See* RESEARCH PAPER *for form.*]

bibliograhy cards   cards, usually 3 × 5 inches, on which bibliographic information is recorded prior to the preparation of a bibliography. [*See*

RESEARCH PAPER *for a full explanation of preparing the cards.*]

biography the account of a person's life. [*See* BIOGRAPHY *in Part II for an explanation and examples.*]

body the main part of a paragraph or paper, in which ideas are developed and supported.

book report an essay which gives a brief summary of a book and a reaction to it. [*See* BOOK REPORT *in Part II for the process of developing a book report and samples.*]

brackets punctuation marks [ ] used to enclose words, figures, etc., such as those used for explanation.

C

capitalization the use of upper-case letters.

card catalog a file, either on cards or on computer, which lists books in a library by title, author, and subject. The cards or computer display describe the book and give publication information.

case the inflected form taken by a noun, pronoun, or adjective to show its relationship to other words. **Example:** That is *his* watch. (*His* is a pronoun in the possessive case.) [*See* PRONOUN *in the Glossary.*]

catharsis a relieving of the emotions, especially by art, as by watching a tragic play.

cause and effect a method of developing a paper showing **1.** what produced an effect or result; the reason for some action, feeling, etc., or **2.** anything brought about by a cause; result; or **3.** both the producer and the result. [*For an explanation and examples, see* CAUSE AND EFFECT *in Part II.*]

characterization the act of describing or showing a person's particular qualities or traits. **Example:** Tennyson characterized King Arthur as *wise and brave.*

chronological order an arrangement in the order in which things occur. Chronological order may move from past to present or, in reverse chronological order, from present to past.

classification a method of development in which objects are arranged according to class. [*For an explanation and examples, see* CLASSIFICATION *in Part II.*]

classified advertising advertising, as in newspaper columns, under such listings as *help wanted, for sale,* etc. [*See* CLASSIFIED AD *in Part II for an explanation and examples.*]

clause, main a group of words, containing a subject and verb, which can stand alone; also called an *independent clause,* or *sentence.* **Example:** After the celebration was over, *we had a big cleanup job.* (The main clause is *we had a big cleanup job.*)

clause, subordinate a group of words containing a subject and verb which depend on a main clause for meaning; also called a *dependent clause.* Three kinds of subordinate clauses function as modifiers and nouns: *adverb, adjec-*

tive, and *noun clauses*. [*See* ADVERB, ADJECTIVE, *and* NOUN *in the Glossary*.] **Example:** *After the celebration was over*, we had a big cleanup job. (The subordinate clause, *after the celebration was over*, functions as an adverb.) [*See also* CLAUSE, SUBORDINATE.]

cliche an expression that has become stale from too much use. **Example:** *as old as the hills.*

climax the decisive turning point of the action, as in a drama.

clincher the decisive point or argument; often used as a conclusion for paragraphs, speeches, and short papers.

coherence the quality of being logically consistent and intelligible, and of having all parts connected in a way that makes sense. Coherence is achieved by the effective use of transition. [*See* TRANSITION *in the Glossary*.]

collective noun a noun which is singular in form but is the name for a collection of individuals (e.g., *army, crowd*). It is treated as singular when the collection is thought of as a whole and as plural when the individual members are thought of as acting separately. **Example:** The *crowd is* restless. (singular) The *jury were* arguing over one piece of evidence. (plural) [*See* AGREEMENT, SUBJECT-VERB.]

colloquial expression words, phrases, and idioms found in everyday speech but avoided in formal writing; labeled in the dictionary as *Colloq.* **Example:** *John is on the beam* is a colloquial way of saying *John is alert and keen.*

colon a mark of punctuation (:) used **1.** before a long quotation, explanation, examples, series, etc. **2.** after the salutation of a formal letter.

comma a mark of punctuation (,) used to show a pause that is shorter than the pause at the end of a sentence, as for nonrestrictive or parenthetical elements, quotations, items in a series, etc.

comma fault the error of joining two main clauses by a comma instead of a semicolon or comma and coordinating conjunction. Sometimes called a *comma splice.*

common noun a noun that names a thing in general; as opposed to a *proper noun.* **Example:** Students in college take a wide range of courses. (common nouns: *students, college, range, courses*) Students at the University of Colorado take Humanities. (proper nouns: *University of Colorado, Humanities*)

comparative a form of adjective or adverb showing a greater, but not the greatest, degree in meaning. The comparative degree is usually indicated by the suffix *-er* (*harder*) or by the use of *more* (*more beautiful, more beautifully*). [*See* ADJECTIVE *and* ADVERB.]

comparison a method of development by which two subjects, seemingly different, are shown to be similar. [*See* COMPARISON AND CONTRAST *in Part II for the organization and general techniques used to de-*

velop a comparison paragraph or paper.]

complement a word that completes the meaning of the predicate. It may be a direct or indirect object, or a predicate word. **Example:** We paid *him.* (direct object) John gave *Beth* a present. (indirect object) Karen is *tall.* (predicate word) **Note:** The object of a gerund, participle, or infinitive is also considered a direct object and is, therefore, a complement. **Example:** Watering her flower *garden* daily keeps Minnie busy. (object of the gerund *watering*) [*See also* DIRECT OBJECT, INDIRECT OBJECT *and* PREDICATE.]

complex sentence a sentence with one main clause and one or more subordinate clauses. The subordinate clause(s) may be noun, adjective, or adverb. **Example:** The child who performed the intricate ballet showed great promise. (one main clause, *the child showed great promise,* and one noun clause, *who performed the intricate ballet*) Compare with other kinds of sentences. [*See* SIMPLE SENTENCE, COMPOUND SENTENCE *and* COMPOUND-COMPLEX SENTENCE *in the Glossary. See also* CLAUSE, MAIN *and* CLAUSE, SUBORDINATE.]

compound-complex sentence a sentence with two or more main clauses and one or more subordinate clauses. The subordinate clause(s) may be noun, adjective, or adverb. **Example:** The child who performed the ballet showed great promise, so the choreographer gave her special atten-

tion. (two main clauses, *the child showed great promise* and *the choreographer gave her special attention;* one subordinate clause, *who performed the ballet*) Compare with other kinds of sentences. [*See* SIMPLE SENTENCE, COMPOUND SENTENCE, COMPLEX SENTENCE, CLAUSE, MAIN *and* CLAUSES, SUBORDINATE *in the Glossary.*]

compound object two or more direct or indirect objects following a verb or verb form. **Example:** They ate *meat* and *vegetables.* (compound direct objects of the verb *ate*) Mother bought *Betty* and *me* class jackets. (compound indirect objects of the verb *bought*)

compound predicate two or more complete verbs. **Example:** The canoe *rolled on its side* and *dumped us in the water.* [*Compare with* COMPOUND VERB *below. See also* VERBS *and* COMPOUND SENTENCE.]

compound sentence a sentence with two main clauses. **Example:** Tom made a touchdown and the crowd cheered. (two main clauses: *Tom made a touchdown* and *the crowd cheered*) [*Compare with entries for* SIMPLE, COMPLEX, *and* COMPOUND-COMPLEX.]

compound subject two or more subjects. **Example:** Casting *rods* and spinning *reels* are useless together. (two subjects: *rods* and *reels*) [*See also* SUBJECTS.]

compound verb two or more simple predicates. **Example:** The canoe *rolled* on its side and *dumped* us in the water. [*Compare with* COM-

POUND PREDICATE *above. See also* VERBS.]

compound word   a word made from joining two or more words: sister-in-law, household.

computer search   a research tool which permits access to multiple data bases throughout the national computer network to locate research data.

conclusion   a last statement, which either summarizes or ties together the main points of a composition. May include a restatement of the topic or thesis sentence; may also include a clincher.

concrete   designating a thing or class of things that are real or exist in material form; not abstract. *Tree* is a concrete noun.

conflict   the fight, struggle, disagreement, or opposition on which a plot is based.

conjunction, coordinating   a word used to show relationships between or among ideas of equal rank. The coordinating conjunctions include *and, but, or, nor, for,* and sometimes *yet* and *so.* Used to join .compound sentences and compound parts. [*See* COMPOUND SENTENCES.]

conjunction, correlative   a pair of words used to express mutual relation: *neither . . . nor, either . . . or, both . . . and, not only . . . but also, whether . . . or.*

conjunctive adverb   an adverb functioning as a conjunction that introduces an adverb clause: *accordingly, again, also, besides, conse-*

quently, finally, for example, furthermore, however, in addition, indeed, moreover, nevertheless, on the other hand, otherwise, then, therefore, thus. [*See also* ADVERB *and* CLAUSE, SUBORDINATE.]

connotation   any idea suggested by or associated with a word, phrase, etc. in addition to its basic or literal meaning, or denotation.

consistency   agreement, following the same format or form.

consonant   any letter of the alphabet not a vowel.

contraction   a shortened word: *shouldn't, couldn't, can't, won't, weren't wasn't,* and so forth. **Note:** Formal writing usually does not include contractions. [*See also* APOSTROPHE.]

contrast   a method of development which shows how seemingly similar subjects are, in fact, different. [*See* COMPARISON AND CONTRAST *in Part II for an explanation and examples.*]

coordinate   of equal order, rank, or importance, such as the *coordinate* main clauses in a compound sentence.

correlative   expressing mutual relation; used in pairs, like *neither . . . nor,* correlative conjunctions.

crisis   the turning point of a conflict, when it becomes clear how the conflict will be resolved.

critical writing   aesthetic judgment based on analysis, most often applied to paragraphs or papers written about a piece of literature.

D

dangling modifier a modifier with no clear reference. **Example:** His heart beating fast, the car sped away. (The participial phrase *his heart beating fast* seems to modify *car* but logically cannot. Thus, it is a dangling modifier.)

dash a mark of punctuation (—) used to indicate a sudden break in thought, as for something added or left out. Most experienced writers avoid dashes in formal writing.

declarative sentence a sentence which makes a statement, as opposed to *interrogative, imperative,* and *exclamatory* sentences. [*See also those Glossary entries.*] **Example:** Dogwood and redbud blossoms give the first hint of spring.

definition a method for developing an expository paragraph or paper in which a term or idea is defined. [*See* DEFINITION *in Part II for an explanation and examples.*]

demonstrative pronoun one of four pronouns which point: *this, that, these,* and *those.* [*See also* PRONOUN.]

denotation the basic or literal meaning; opposite of *connotation.*

dependent clause a clause which cannot stand alone, but depends on an independent or main clause for its meaning; also called *subordinate clause.* [*See* CLAUSE, SUBORDINATE.]

description a method of developing an expository paragraph or paper by picturing something in words. [*See* DESCRIPTION *in Part II for an explanation and examples.*]

detail a small part, item, or particular used to support a main idea. [*See* REVISION *in Part I for examples of writing with and without detail.*]

development, methods of means by which a subject can be supported or explained. Methods of development include *analogy, cause and effect, classification, comparison and contrast, definition, description, narration, opinion, persuasion,* and *process analysis.* [*See each of these headings in the Glossary for quick reference and in Part II for detailed explanation and examples.*]

dialogue **1.** a written work in the form of conversation **2.** the actors' lines in a play, story, etc. [*See* DIALOGUE *in Part II for detailed explanations for writing dialogue as well as for examples and analyses.*]

diction **1.** the choice and arrangement of words. **Example:** The *diction* of everyday speech is different from that of a formal essay. **2.** manner of speaking or pronouncing words; enunciation. **Example:** An actor must have good, clear *diction.*

direct address a form of noun which names a specific person. **Example:** How are you, Mary? (*Mary* is a noun of direct address.)

direct object a noun that tells who or what receives the action of a transitive verb. **Example:** Paul flew the *plane.* (The noun *plane* receives the action of the verb *flew.*) [*For comparison, see also* INDIRECT OBJECT *in the Glossary.*]

direct question   the exact words of another's question; as opposed to *indirect* question. **Example:** Mark asked, ''Did you see many snakes?'' (The words inside the quotation marks are Mark's exact words, a direct question.) [*For comparison, see* INDIRECT QUESTION *in the Glossary.* [*See also* QUOTATION MARKS.]

direct quotation   someone's exact words, either written or spoken. **Example:** Samantha explained, ''These overcooked vegetables lack the vitamins of properly steamed vegetables.'' [*For comparison, see* INDIRECT QUOTATION *and* QUOTATION MARKS *in the Glossary.*]

documentation   the supplying of supporting references by notation (*foot-, end-,* or *in-text notes*) and use of a bibliography. [*See* RESEARCH PAPER *in Part II for a discussion and examples of each of the kinds of documentation.*]

E

editorial   a statement of opinion in a newspaper, etc. or on radio or TV that gives the views of the owner, publisher, etc. [*See also* EDITORIAL *in Part II.*]

ellipsis   **1.**   the omission of a word or words necessary for complete grammatical construction but understood in the context. **Example:** *If possible* is understood to mean *if it is possible.* **2.**   a mark of punctuation (...) indicating an intentional omission of words or letters, a lapse of time, etc.

elliptical clause   a clause in which grammatically necessary elements are omitted but implied by context. **Example:** Kelly is taller than she. (implied: than she *is*)

emphasis, in sentences   special attention given to a sentence part so as to make it stand out; importance, stress. **Example:** He contributed fifty dollars to the volunteer fire department. (emphasis on *fire department*) To the fire department, he contributed fifty dollars. (emphasis on *fifty dollars*) [*For discussion and examples of various methods of emphasis, see* REVISION *in Part I.*]

emphatic form   a present or past tense in which a form of the verb *to do* is used as an auxiliary, for emphasis. **Example:** I *do* care.

endnote   a reference or comment appearing at the end of a paper. A note with similar information appearing elsewhere in the paper is called a *foot-* or *in-text note.* [*See also those references in the Glossary. For detailed information on format, see* RESEARCH PAPER *in Part II.*]

essay question   a question, as on a test or application, which requires an organized, logical, well developed answer. [*See* ESSAY-QUESTION RESPONSES *in Part II for a thorough discussion and examples.*]

essential modifier   a word, phrase, or clause essential to the identification of the word it modifies. **Example:** The man *who ran the stop sign* hit the pedestrian. Compare with *nonessential modifier.* **Note:** Do not use commas to set off essential elements.

evidence   something that makes another thing easy to see or perceive; makes it clear, obvious, plain. In written work, evidence may take the form of an illustration, example, analogy, etc.

example   a thing selected to show the nature or character of the rest; a sample. In written work, an example gives support and detail to a main idea.

exclamation point   a mark of punctuation (!) used to express surprise, a strong feeling, etc.

exclamatory sentence   a sentence showing or using excitement or strong emotion. **Example:** Stop that thief! Compare also with *declarative, interrogative,* and *imperative* sentences. [*See separate Glossary entries.*]

explanation   something that clarifies or interprets. In writing, an explanation may take the form of a definition, example, specific detail, etc.

exposition   writing that sets forth facts, ideas, and detailed explanations; as opposed to purely creative writing such as short stories and poetry.

F

facts   things that are actual. In writing, facts serve as evidence to explain or support a main idea.

falling action   the part of the plot following the climax, when the conflict is resolved.

feature acticle   a special story, article, etc. in a newspaper or magazine; shows human-interest side rather than straight news. [*See also* FEATURE ARTICLE *in Part II.*]

figure of speech   an expression with an unusual or fanciful meaning used to add vividness, etc., to what is said. Figures of speech include *hyperbole, metaphor, personification, simile,* and *symbol.* [*See also these separate entries in the Glossary.*]

final draft   a complete, carefully revised and proofread copy.

finite verb   a verb having limits of person, number, and tense.

five-paragraph theme   a paper following a formal organization in which the first paragraph serves as an introduction and includes the thesis statement; the second, third, and fourth paragraphs develop a single topic from the thesis; and the fifth paragraph serves as a conclusion. [*See* THEME *in Part II for a complete discussion and an example.*]

flashback   the introduction into the events of a story, etc., of an episode that took place earlier.

focus   in writing, a narrowed topic suitable for development into a paragraph or paper.

footnote   a comment or reference placed at the bottom of a page. Similar information appearing elsewhere may be called an *end-* or *in-text note.* [*See also those entries in the Glossary. For detailed format for footnotes, see* RESEARCH PAPER *in Part II.*]

foreshadowing   a sign of something to come, a device used especially in short stories, plays, and novels.

formal language English usage which employs traditional rules of grammar and vocabulary; as distinguished from *colloquial language.*

formal style a characteristic manner of writing which incorporates formal language and avoids colloquialisms. [*See* REVISION *in Part I for examples of formal and informal styles.*]

format 1. the physical layout of a paper **2.** a general arrangement, as of a television program.

fragment an incomplete sentence used improperly, as if it were complete. **Example:** Running repeatedly around the track.

function the manner in which a part of speech behaves in a given sentence. **Example:** The girl is *tall.* (*Tall,* as an adjective, *functions* as a predicate adjective after the linking verb *is.*) **Note:** A word may function one way in one sentence and differently in another.

fused sentence two sentences joined improperly into a single sentence. **Example:** Glacial ice acted like a giant bulldozer it leveled hills and ridges as it moved south. (two sentences fused into one) Sometimes called a *run-on sentence.* [*See* RUN-ON SENTENCE *and* COMMA FAULT.]

future perfect tense a form of verb which shows action in the future, prior to the completion of some other future action. **Example:** By the the time I finish waxing the car, I *will have used* every good polishing rag we have. [*See also* VERBS.]

future tense a form of verb which shows action beyond the present, signaled by the auxiliaries *will* or *shall.* **Example:** He *will park* the car.

G

gender the classifying of nouns, pronouns, adjectives, etc., into groups regarded as masculine, feminine, or neuter; in English only some nouns (such as *actor* and *actress*) and all pronouns in the third person singular (as *he, she,* and *it*) are classified into these groups. [*For additional information, see* PRONOUNS *and* AGREEMENT, PRONOUN-ANTECEDENT.]

generalization a statement which refers to a genus, kind, class, or order. Generalizations should be avoided unless well supported with specific details. [*See* REVISIONS *in Part I for a discussion of specific details.*]

genre a kind, or type. Literary genres include *short story, poetry, nonfiction, novel,* and *drama.*

gerund a verbal noun ending in *-ing* used like a noun but capable of taking an object or an adverbial modifier. **Example:** *Playing* golf is his only exercise.

grammar a body of rules for speaking and writing a given language.

H

hyperbole exaggeration used for effect, not meant literally. **Example:** He's *as strong as an ox.*

hyphen a mark of punctuation (-) used between the part of a compound word (as *court-martial*) or the syllables of a divided word, as at the end of a line.

I

imagery 1. mental images, as produced by memory or imagination **2.** descriptions and figures of speech, as in the *imagery* of a poem. In writing, usually referring specifically to sensory images, i.e., those created through the five senses.

imperative mood the mood of a verb that expresses a command or strong request. **Example:** *Open* that window now.

imperative sentence a sentence expressing a command or strong request. **Example:** *Open that window now.* Compare with *declarative* and *interrogative* sentences. [*See those entries in the Glossary.*]

incomplete constructions [*See* ELLIPTICAL CLAUSE *above.*]

indefinite pronoun a pronoun that does not specify, like *any*, *someone*, *everyone*, and *each*.

independent clause a clause which can stand alone, a sentence; also called a *main clause*. [*See* CLAUSE, MAIN.]

indicative mood designates that mood of a verb used to express an actual fact, state, etc., or asks a question of fact. Compare with *imperative* and *subjunctive* moods. [*See entries in the Glossary.*]

indirect object the word or words identifying the person or thing that something (the *direct object*) is given to or done for. **Example:** Sid gave *him* the ball.

indirect question states a question but not the exact words. **Example:** He asked *if we were tired.* [*Compare with* DIRECT QUESTION *earlier in the Glossary.*] **Note:** Do not use quotation marks or a question mark with indirect questions.

indirect quotation reports the speaker's or writer's meaning without using his or her exact words. **Example:** Professor Clough said *that American literature merits careful study.* [*Compare with* DIRECT QUOTATION *earlier in the Glossary.*] **Note:** Do not use quotation marks with an indirect quotation.

infinitive a form of verb which expresses existence or action without reference to person, number, or tense; usually following the marker *to*. **Example:** He likes *to work.*

inflection a change of form by which words show number, case, gender, tense, comparison, etc. For instance, the inflection of a noun can be singular (*car*), plural (*cars*), or possessive (*car's*).

informal language colloquial language, used on a daily basis for conversation and other informal communication.

informal style a manner of writing which relies on colloquial language and pays only casual regard to precise grammar. Informal writing, which is not to be confused with poor writing, permits the use of contractions, conversational language, and a first- or second-person point of view.

intensive pronoun pronoun ending in *-self* or *-selves* which emphasizes, or intensifies, the antecedent. **Example:** I'll take care of the work *myself*. [*Compare with* REFLEXIVE PRONOUN *later in the Glossary*.]

interjection an exclamatory word or phrase, such as *ah!* or *good grief!* **Note:** Interjections are followed by exclamation marks.

interrogative pronoun a pronoun used to ask a question. **Example:** *What* did you say?

interrogative sentence a sentence which asks a question. **Example:** When did you arrive? Compare with *imperative, exclamatory,* and *declarative* sentences. [*See separate Glossary entries.*]

interview a meeting in which a person is asked about his opinions, activities, etc., as by a reporter.

in-text note a comment or reference inserted parenthetically into the text of a paper, as opposed to a *foot-* or *endnote*; sometimes referred to as *parenthetical documentation*. [*See* FOOTNOTE *and* ENDNOTE *entries in the Glossary. For specific details for form of in-text notes, see* RESEARCH PAPER *in Part II*.]

introduction the first part of a paragraph or paper, which attracts the reader's attention and announces the subject. The introduction sets the tone and mood and, except in certain situations, tells the reader what ideas to expect in the composition. [*See also* PARAGRAPHS *and* THEME *in Part II for examples of introductions. In addition, see each kind of writing for sample introductions appropriate for that kind of writing*.]

intransitive verb a verb that does not require a direct object to complete its meaning. **Example:** He *shouted* with joy. Opposite of *transitive*. [*See* TRANSITIVE VERB.]

inverted pyramid organization a means of organizing a paper or news article, which puts important information first and follows with increasingly less important details.

irony **1.** a method of humorous or sarcastic expression in which the meaning given to the words is the opposite of their usual sense. **Example:** She used *irony* when she said the stupid plan was clever. **2.** an event or result opposite to what might be expected. **Example:** That the fire station burned down was an *irony*.

irregular verb verb which does not follow the regular *-ed* ending for past and past participle. **Example:** *see, saw, have seen* (irregular verb) *walk, walked, have walked* (regular verb)

italic a printing type in which the characters slant upward to the right, used especially to call attention to words. **Example:** *This is italic type*. **Note:** In type- or hand-written work, use an underscore to indicate italics.

L

laboratory report A summary of scientific findings; commonly called a *lab report*. [*For an explana-*

tion of format, content, and organization, see LAB REPORT *in Part II.*]

letter **1.** a written or printed message, usually sent by mail. [*See* LETTERS *in Part II.*] **2.** a character of the alphabet.

likenesses-differences pattern of organization a means of organizing a comparison-contrast paper in which all similarities are discussed in one part and all differences discussed in another. [*See* COMPARISON AND CONTRAST *in Part II.*]

linking verb a verb that functions chiefly as a connection between a subject and its predicate complement. **Example:** He *seems* tired.

loose sentence a sentence which follows the usual subject-verb order so that the essential part of the sentence comes first, followed by additional details; probably the most common kind of sentence. **Example:** He drove the car home after the ball game. **Note:** A loose sentence can be simple, compound, complex, or compound-complex. Compare with *periodic sentence.* [*See* REVISION *in Part I for a discussion of sentence variety.*]

lower case small letters, as opposed to *upper-case* or *capital* letters.

M

main clause a clause which can stand alone; a sentence; sometimes called an *independent* clause. [*Compare with* DEPENDENT CLAUSE *or* SUBORDINATE CLAUSE.]

mechanics the technical aspects of writing, including punctuation, capitalization, etc.

metaphor a figure of speech that suggest likeness by speaking of one thing as if it were another. **Example:** Her moods are *the endless myriads of a kaleidoscope.* [*Compare with* SIMILE.]

meter rhythm in verse; regular arrangement of accented and unaccented syllables in each line.

minutes an official record of what was said and done at a meeting. [*See* MINUTES OF A MEETING *in Part II for a detailed explanation of how to write minutes.*]

misplaced modifier a phrase or clause placed away from the word it refers to, resulting in unclear meaning. **Example:** They made an announcement about the closing of school during the news report. (sounds as if school is closed during the news report)

modifier a word, phrase, or clause that limits the meaning of another word or phrase. [*See* ADJECTIVE, ADVERB, INFINITIVE, PARTICIPLE, PHRASE, *and* CLAUSE, SUBORDINATE *in the Glossary.*]

mood **1.** the aspect of a verb which shows whether it is regarded as expressing a fact (*indicative mood*), a wish, desire, or possibility (*subjunctive mood*), or a command (*imperative mood*) **2.** the prevailing spirit or feeling in a piece of writing.

monologue **1.** a long speech, especially one that keeps anyone else from talking **2.** a poem, story, or scene in which one character speaks alone or tells a story.

N

narration   a method of developing a paper or paragraph by means of telling a story. [*See* NARRATION *in Part II for details and examples.*]

news article   an account of an event or situation written for the print media. [*See* NEWS ARTICLE *in Part II for the process of writing a news article and for a sample news article and analysis.*]

nominative case   the case of the subject of a verb and the words (*appositive, predicate adjectives,* etc.) that agree with it. *She, he,* and *who* are in the nominative case. Compare with *objective* and *possessive case.*

nonessential modifier   a modifier not necessary to the identification of the word modified; sometimes called a *nonrestrictive modifer.* **Example:** Mrs. Heeger, *who is my neighbor,* is a superb seamstress. **Note:** Use commas to set off nonrestrictive modifiers. Compare with *essential modifier.*

notes   brief, written statements of facts, etc., as an aid to memory; a comment or explanation. [*See* RESEARCH PAPER *in Part II for information on taking notes for a paper. See* NOTES *in Part II for information on taking notes both for class and for a paper.*]

noun   any of a class of words naming or denoting a person, thing, action, quality, etc.

number   the change in form used to show whether one or more than one is meant; singular and plural forms show *number.* [*See* SUBJECT-VERB AGREEMENT.]

O

objective case   the case taken by an object. *Me, her, him,* and *whom* are examples of pronouns in the objective case. Compare with *nominative* and *possessive case.*

objective complement   word, phrase, or clause that completes the object. **Example:** The group named John its *representative.*

omniscient point of view   the point of view of an all-knowing, all-seeing speaker.

onomatopoeia   the formation of a word (as *chickadee* or *tinkle*) by imitating the sound associated with the object or action.

opinion   a method of developing a paragraph or paper by which the writer expresses personal belief. [*See* OPINION *in Part II for complete details related to developing an opinion paper and for a sample paper and analysis.*]

order, in paragraph development   the method of organizing a paragraph or paper. The orders include *chronological, spatial,* and *orders of importance.* [*See those entries in the Glossary.*]

order of business   the usual order in which business is conducted during a meeting. [*See* MINUTES OF A MEETING *in Part II for a list of that usual order.*]

order of importance a method of organizing a paragraph or paper according to the relative significance of the subtopics. One standard arrangement is from most to least important; another is from least to most. A frequently used variation begins with the second most important idea, followed by the remaining details, listed from least to most important.

organization the way in which the parts of a paragraph or paper are put together, with all parts properly connected. General plans of organization vary with the kind of paragraph or paper being written. [*See individual listings in Part II.*]

outline a plan for a paragraph or paper, generally using letters and numerals to designate the relationships among and between topics. [*See* OUTLINES *in Part II for a discussion of various kinds of outlines and methods for developing them.*]

P

paragraph a separate section of a paper, letter, etc., dealing with a particular point and made up of one or more sentences. A paragraph begins on a new line and is usually indented. [*See* PARAGRAPHS *in Part II for a discussion of different kinds of paragraphs and the process for writing them.*]

paragraph development the means by which the main point of a paragraph is explained, supported, or detailed. [*See* DEVELOPMENT, METHODS OF *in the Glossary*, PARAGRAPHS *in Part II, and* REVI-SION *in Part I for additional information about paragraphs and the difference between poorly developed and well-developed paragraphs.*]

parallel structure like grammatical structures used for ideas of equal rank. **Example:** *Using computers* and *accessing data bases* are almost like second nature to him. (Two gerund phrases form parallel structures, here the compound subjects of the sentence.)

paraphrase to put something spoken or written into different words having the same meaning. Used frequently in writing research and technical papers. [*See* PARAPHRASE *in Part II for an explanation and examples.*]

parentheses punctuation marks, always used in pairs, ( ) used to set off a word, clause, remark, etc., added as an explanation or comment within a complete sentence. **Example:** The television special tomorrow night (Channel 9, 8:00 PM) will discuss laser surgery. **Note:** Parentheses rarely appear in formal writing.

parenthetical element a word, phrase, or clause added as an aside or additional comment within a complete sentence. **Example:** He is, *I'm convinced*, an honest person. **Note:** The parenthetical element is set off from the rest of the sentence with commas.

part-by-part organization a means of organization, particularly in a comparison or contrast paper, in which the the similarities (or differences) of one point of both topics are discussed followed by the similarities (or differences) of another point. Compare with *whole-by-whole organization*. [*See* COMPARISON AND CONTRAST *in Part II for a more complete discussion.*]

participial phrase a word group made up of a participle and its object(s) and any modifier(s). **Example:** The boy *wearing a baseball cap* must learn to take it off when entering a building. (The participle *wearing* includes an object, *cap*, and a modifier, *baseball*.) [*See* PARTICIPLE *and* VERBAL PHRASE.]

participle a verbal form having the qualities of both a verb and an adjective. Participles are used as adjectives, either present (a *raving* beauty) or past (the *beaten* path). As a verb part, participles take auxiliaries to form a verb phrase, either present (was *walking*) or past (had *walked*).

parts of speech the eight terms given words according to their function: *noun, verb, adjective, adverb, preposition, conjunction, article, interjection.* [*See separate entries in the Glossary.*]

passive voice the voice or form of a verb whose subject is the receiver (object) of the action of the verb. Example: I *was hit* by the ball. Compare with *active voice.*

past participle a participle used
1. with helping verbs to show completed action or a time or state gone by. **Example:** He has *started.*
2. as an adjective. **Example:** He is a *grown* man. [*See* PARTICIPLE *and* VERBAL PHRASE.]

past perfect tense a verb tense used to show an action completed in the past prior to some other past action. **Example:** He *had gone* before we arrived.

past tense a verb tense used to show an action completed before the present, including the simple past tense, present perfect tense, and past perfect tense.

perfect tenses the three verb tenses used to show relationships between actions, including present perfect tense (*have gone*), past perfect tense (*had gone*), and future perfect tense (*will have gone*). [*See separate entries in the Glossary.*]

persuasion a method of development in which the writer attempts to convince the reader to agree with a certain position or to take a certain action. [*See* PERSUASION *in Part II for the process for developing a persuasion paragraph or paper and for a sample and analysis.*]

period a mark of punctuation (.) used at the end of a declarative sentence or to indicate an abbreviation.

periodical a publication appearing at regular intervals.

periodical sentence a sentence so written that the full meaning cannot be understood until the end. **Example:** Under the porch, out of the sun, hidden from the prying eyes of mischievous little children, the old dog slept. Compare with *loose sentence.* [*See also* REVISION *in Part I for a discussion of sentence variety.*]

personal pronoun any one of a group of pronouns divided into three sets: first person (*I, my*), second person (*you, your*), and third person (*he, her, their, it*).

personification a figure of speech in which a thing or idea is represented as a person. **Example:** The sunshine *brushed my face with a warm hand.*

phrase a group of words conveying a single thought or forming a distinct part of a sentence but not containing a subject and predicate, including prepositional, gerund, infinitive, participial, absolute, appositive, and verb phrases.

plagiarism the act of stealing ideas or words from another and passing them off as one's own. To avoid plagiarism, a writer uses careful documentation. [*See* RESEARCH PAPER *in Part II for an explanation of the documentation process.*]

plot the plan of action of a play, novel, short story, etc.

plural of or including more than one. Because plural forms vary, consult *Webster's New World Dictionary* for irregular plural forms.

poem an arrangement of words having rhythm and, often, rhyme; usually set in imaginative or emotional language. Some poems are in meter, some in free verse. Common poetic forms include *ballad, blank verse, epic, dramatic monologue, elegy, epigram, free verse, haiku, light verse, limerick, ode, sonnet,* and *villanelle.*

point of view the place from which, or way in which, something is viewed; standpoint. [*See* SHORT STORY, STEP 4, PREWRITING: SELECTING POINT OF VIEW, *in Part II for a detailed explanation and examples.*]

possessive a case, form, or construction expressing ownership. **Example:** *Duane's* book is different from *mine*. [*See also* APOSTROPHE.]

precis a concise summary. [*See* PRECIS *in Part II to learn how to develop an accurate precis.*]

predicate the verb or verbal phrase that says something about the subject of a sentence or clause. A predicate may be a verb (the wind *blows*), a verb and an adverb (the wind *blows hard*), a verb and its object (the wind *blows the leaves down*), or a linking verb and its complement (he *is the happiest man I know*).

predicate adjective an adjective which follows a linking verb and describes the subject. **Example:** He is *handsome*.

predicate noun a noun which follows a linking verb and identifies the subject. **Example:** Marcia is my *friend*.

preposition a relation word, as *in, by, for, with, to,* etc., that connects a noun or pronoun, or a noun phrase, to another noun (the sound *of* rain), to a verb (he went *to* the store), or to an adjective (late *for* the tea party).

prepositional phrase a word group formed by a preposition and its object(s) and any modifier(s); functions as an adjective or as an adverb. **Example:** She supervised children *on the playground*. (functions as an adjective modifying the noun *children*) [*See also* PREPOSITION.]

present perfect tense a verb tense indicating an action or state as completed at the time of speaking but not at any definite time in the past. **Example:** He *has gone*. [*See* VERBS.]

present tense the verb tense which indicates current action or state of being. **Example:** He *walks*. [*See* VERBS.]

prewriting an activity used to prepare for writing, including reading, research, discussion, interviewing, brainstorming, journal writing, note-taking, list-making, outlining, etc. [*See also* PREWRITING *in Part I and the specific prewriting activities included in the sections on each kind of writing.*]

primary research research conducted by the writer himself, including laboratory work, interviews, statistical analysis, surveys, etc. Compare with *secondary research*. [*See also* RESEARCH PAPER *in Part II the research process.*]

process a particular method of doing something, in this case writing, in which there are a series of steps. [*See Part I for an overview of the writing process, and then see specific process steps included in the sections on each kind of writing.*]

progressive form a verb form showing continuing action. **Example:** I *am working*. [*See* VERB.]

pronoun a word used to refer to or in place of a noun, including personal, reflexive, intensive, demonstrative, relative, indefinite, and interrogative pronouns.

pronoun agreement the agreement in number and gender of pronouns with their antecedents. [*See* AGREEMENT, PRONOUN-ANTECEDENT.]

pronoun reference the word to which a pronoun refers; antecedent.

proper noun a noun that names a specific individual, place, etc., is not used with an article, and is normally capitalized, as *Donald* and *Boston*. Compare with *common noun*. [*See* NOUNS *and* CAPITALIZATION.]

protagonist the main character in a drama, novel, or story, around whom the action centers. Compare with *antagonist*.

punctuation the use of standardized marks in writing and printing to separate sentences or parts of a sentence or to make meaning clearer. [*See* COMMA, COLON, DASH, ELLIPSIS, HYPHEN, ITALICS, QUOTATION MARKS, *and* SEMICOLON.]

purpose, statement of a sentence which states the topic and intended direction of a paper; thesis sentence. [*See* THEME *in Part II for additional explanation.*]

Q

question mark a mark of punctuation (?) used to end interrogative sentences.

quotation the words or passage cited as an example or authority, as from a book or author. Enclosed in quotation marks. [*See* QUOTATION MARKS *below. See also* RESEARCH PAPER *in Part II for a discussion of the proper use of quotations as supporting details.*]

quotation marks marks of punctuation (" ") used in pairs to enclose a direct quotation. Single quotation marks (' ') are used to enclose a quotation within a quotation.

R

Reader's Guide to Periodical Literature an annual reference book, which catalogs periodical articles by subject and by author. Found in the reference section of libraries.

redundancy the use of more words than are needed; wordiness. [*See* REVISION *in Part I for a discussion of how to eliminate wordiness.*]

reference, for research paper any book, periodical, or other source used as secondary research for the development of a research paper. [*See* RESEARCH PAPER *in Part II.*]

reflexive pronoun a pronoun ending in *-self* or *-selves* which refers back to the antecedent. **Example:** I bought the book for *myself*. Compare with *intensive pronoun*. [*See also* PRONOUN.]

relative clause a subordinate clause introduced by a relative pronoun, *who, whose, whom, which,* and *that.* **Example:** I wore the hat *which you bought.* [*See also* PRONOUN.]

relative pronoun a pronoun used to introduce relative clauses: *who,*

whose, whom, which, and *that.* [*See also* PRONOUN.]

research systematic study or investigation in a field of knowledge, to discover or establish facts or principles, including both *primary* and *secondary* methods or research. [*See separate entries in the Glossary.*]

research paper a paper which reports research, both primary and secondary, and includes documentation presented according to a specified form. [*See* RESEARCH PAPER *in Part II for a detailed explanation, examples, and analysis.*]

resolution the part of a novel, play, etc., in which the plot is explained or made clear.

resume a statement of a job applicant's previous employment experience, and education. [*See* RESUME *in Part II for details and examples.*]

review a report, as in a newspaper, telling about a recent book, play, concert, etc., and giving one's opinion of it. [*See* REVIEW *in Part II for additional details and examples.*]

revision the act of correcting, improving, or bringing up to date as necessary. [*See* REVISION *in Part I for a thorough discussion.*]

rhyme likeness of sound at the ends of words or lines of verse.

rhythm **1.** the flow or movement having a regularly repeated pattern of accents, beats, etc. **2.** the form or pattern of the regularly repeated stressed and unstressed or long and short syllables.

rising action   in a play, novel, short story, etc., the building action which occurs from the beginning until the climax.

Roman numeral   the Roman system of letters used as numerals: I = 1, V = 5, X = 10, L = 50, C = 100, D = 500, and M = 1,000.

rough draft   an early version of a paragraph or paper prior to revision and proofreading.

run-on sentence   two main clauses improperly joined. **Example:** We ate too much we got sick. (run-on sentence) We ate too much, so we got sick. (corrected)

S

script   the text of a play, movie, etc. [*See* SCRIPTS *in Part II for a discussion of drama, radio, and television script writing.*]

secondary research   research examining previously published findings. Compare with *primary research.* [*See* RESEARCH PAPER *in Part II for a discussion of implementing research into a formal paper.*]

semicolon   a mark of punctuation (;) showing more separation than a comma and less than a period; usually used between certain closely related independent clauses. **Example:** The door slammed shut; she was locked out.

sentence   a word or group of words which states, asks, commands, or exclaims something, usually has a subject and predicate and which, in writing, begins with a capital letter and ends with a period, question mark, or exclamation point. [*See* SIMPLE SENTENCE, COMPOUND, SENTENCE, COMPLEX SENTENCE, *and* COMPOUND-COMPLEX SENTENCE.]

' **sentence outline**   an outline which states topics and subtopics in complete sentences. [*See* OUTLINES *in Part II for additional information. Compare with* TOPIC OUTLINE.] **Note:** Sentence outlines should maintain parallel structure.

sentence structure   the relation of phrases, clauses, and sentence parts within a sentence. [*See* REVISION *in Part I for a discussion of sentence variety.*]

series   a number of similar grammatical structures appearing consecutively.

setting   the time, place, and environment of an event, story, play, etc.

shifts, confusing   an unwarranted change of tense or viewpoint within a given segment of writing.

short answer   a brief response to a test question, job application question, or college and scholarship application requests. [*See* SHORT ANSWERS *in Part II for additional information about how to develop successful short answer responses.*]

short story   a short work of fiction developing a single theme and of limited scope and number of characters. [*See* SHORT STORY *in Part II for additional details.*]

simile   a figure of speech in which one thing is compared to another, using the word *like* or *as.* **Example:**

His muscles were *as loose as last year's slingshot.* [*See* METAPHOR.]

simple sentence a single main clause without any subordinate clauses. **Example:** The boy in the red shirt won the race without difficulty.

singular referring to only one. [*See* PLURAL.]

slang coarse or highly informal language, avoided in formal speech and writing; it consists of new words and existing words given new meanings, and is usually fresh, colorful, or humorous for only a short time.

slant to write or speak so as to appeal to a particular point of view or to express a particular bias.

software programs for a computer.

spatial order an arrangement according to space, from left to right, right to left, etc.

specific detail supporting information that is concrete and nongeneral in nature. [*See* REVISION *in Part I for examples of writing with and without specific detail.*]

split infinitive the separation of the marker *to* from the verbal form of the infinitive by inserting modifiers, as in *to boldly go* instead of *to go boldly.* Generally, experienced writers avoid split infinitives. [*See also* INFINITIVES.]

squinting modifier a modifier which could indifferently affect two or more references. **Example:** He ran down the hall with poor light. (*With poor light* could modify

either hall or *ran.*) [*See* MISPLACED MODIFIER.]

statistics numeric data arranged so as to show certain information.

subject 1. in a sentence, a noun, noun phrase, or noun clause about which something is said. **Example:** The *building* was vacant. **2.** in a paragraph or paper, the main topic.

subject complement [*See* PREDICATE ADJECTIVE *and* PREDICATE NOUN.]

subject-verb agreement agreement in number of a subject and verb. [*See also* AGREEMENT, SUBJECT-VERB.]

subjunctive mood the mood of a verb used to express supposition, desire, possibility, etc., as opposed to actual fact. **Example:** If I *were* you, I'd go home.

subordinate clause a clause which cannot stand alone and depends on a main clause for its meaning; also called *dependent* clause. **Example:** The man *who came to dinner* is Dad's boss.

summary a brief report covering the main points. [*See* SYNOPSIS *and* PRECIS *in Part II for further details.*]

superlative degree a form of adjective or adverb that shows the greatest degree in meaning; the superlative degree is usually shown by the suffix *-est* (*hardest*) or by the use of *most* (*most beautiful*). Compare with *comparative form.* [*See also* ADJECTIVE *and* ADVERB.]

syllabify to form or divide into syllables, as in *syl-lab-i-fy.*

symbol a thing that stands for another thing; especially, an object that stands for an idea, quality, etc.

synopsis a short outline or review of the main points, as of a story; summary. [*See* SYNOPSIS *in Part II for a thorough discussion, example, and analysis.*]

T

tense a form or set of forms of a verb that show the time. [*See also* VERB.]

theme 1. a topic or subject, as of a lecture, essay, etc. 2 an idea or subject that is repeated or presented in a number of ways in a work of art, literature, etc., to unify it. 3. a short essay, especially one written as a school assignment. [*See also* THEME *in Part II for a detailed explanation.*]

thesis statement or sentence the sentence which states the subject of a theme and states or implies the division of that subject into subtopics as they will be developed. [*See* THEME *in Part II for additional information and examples.*]

thesaurus a book containing synonyms and antonyms.

tone a way of wording or expressing things that shows a certain attitude.

topic the subject of a writing, speech, discussion, etc.

topic outline an outline which uses parallel words or word groups for the topics and subtopics. Compare with *sentence outline*. **Note:** Do not use both sentences and topics in the same outline. [*For additional information, see* OUTLINES *in Part II.*]

topic sentence a sentence which states the subject of a paragraph and may state or imply the attitude, time, and place of the subject. [*See* PARAGRAPHS *in Part II for additional information and examples.*]

transitions words, phrases, or sentences which connect one idea with another either within or between paragraphs. [*See* REVISION *in Part I for discussion and examples.*]

transitive verb a verb that requires a direct object to complete its meaning. **Example:** He *softened* the blow. Compare with *intransitive*. [*See* INTRANSITIVE VERB.]

trite a word or expression worn out by constant use; no longer fresh or original; stale. **Example:** It came like *a bolt out of the blue.*

U

understatement putting things more weakly than is warranted by truth, accuracy, or importance. **Example:** (after a heavy rain) Things are *a little damp.*

unity in a work of art or literature, an arrangement of parts so as to produce a single effect. [*See* REVISION *in Part I for how to maintain unity in a composition.*]

upper case capital letters, as opposed to *lower case*.

usage the way in which a word, phrase, etc., is used in speaking or writing.

V

vagueness not clearly or exactly expressed or stated; not sharp. **Example:** We waited *a long time.* (*vague*) We waited *thirty-two minutes.* (*specific*) Compare with *specific detail* and *concrete.* [*See also* REVISION *in Part I for examples of writing with and without specific details.*]

verb a word expressing action, a state of being, or a happening, and forming the main part of a predicate.

verbal phrase a group of words made up of a main verb and its auxiliaries. **Example:** He *had been working* before lunch.

verse 1. poetry in general, sometimes more specifically poetry of a light or amusing nature **2.** a stanza or short subdivision of a poem.

vertical file in a library, a file which contains bulletins, pamphlets, and other miscellaneous publications, usually located in the reference section.

voice a verb form showing the connection between the subject and the verb, either as performing (*active voice*) or receiving (*passive voice*) the action. [*See* ACTIVE VOICE, PASSIVE VOICE *and* VERB *in the Glossary.*]

W

whole-by-whole organization in a comparison or contrast paragraph or paper, a method of organization which treats all subpoints of one topic before moving on to treat all subpoints of the second topic. Compare with *part-by-part organization.* [*See* COMPARISON AND CONTRAST *in Part II for a detailed explanation and examples.*]

wordiness the excessive use of words. [*See* REVISION *in Part I for an example of wordiness and an explanation of methods for eliminating it.*]

word processor a system by which letters, papers, etc., are prepared, edited, stored, and reproduced, as by using an electronic typewriter or personal computer.

INDEX